Munich Studies on Innovation and Competition

Volume 9

Series Editors
Josef Drexl, Germany
Reto M. Hilty, Germany

More information about this series at http://www.springer.com/series/13275

Julia Molestina

Regional Competition Law Enforcement in Developing Countries

Springer

Julia Molestina
München, Germany

ISSN 2199-7462 ISSN 2199-7470 (electronic)
Munich Studies on Innovation and Competition
ISBN 978-3-662-58524-5 ISBN 978-3-662-58525-2 (eBook)
https://doi.org/10.1007/978-3-662-58525-2

Library of Congress Control Number: 2018965468

This Springer imprint is published by the registered company Springer-Verlag GmbH, DE part of Springer Nature.
The registered company address is: Heidelberger Platz 3, 14197 Berlin, Germany

Acknowledgements

This thesis was written at the Max Planck Institute for Innovation and Competition and the Faculty of Law of the Ludwig-Maximilians-University of Munich. A large part of the research was done through field research in the Andean Community and the Caribbean Community in 2012/2013.

The work contributes to the research on effective competition law in developing countries and places special emphasis on the institutional framework of competition law enforcement.

A number of people have contributed to the realization of this thesis, to whom I am very grateful. I would like to thank, first of all, my supervisor Prof. Dr. Josef Drexl, LL.M. (Berkeley), Director of the Max Planck Institute for Innovation and Competition, for the possibility to investigate on the issue of competition law in developing countries, his support and above all his valuable advice. Moreover, I would like to thank Prof. Dr. Matthias Leistner, LL.M. for his interest in the particular topic of competition law enforcement in developing countries and for reviewing the thesis as second referee.

I would also like to thank Dr. Mor Bakhoum, my academic advisor, for not only providing me with insider information on competition law enforcement in West Africa but also for encouraging me to research further in this particular field of law. The same goes for Dr. Tania Zúñiga-Fernández, who with her exceptional enthusiasm and legal knowledge has been a great inspiration along the way.

I cannot thank enough the people who accompanied me along the long and oftentimes burdensome process: Philipp Schautschick and Lisa Fey, you have become trusted and dear friends. Christian, Dora and Alois Aichner, thank you for providing me a substitute family in Munich.

Finally, and above all, I want to thank my family for not only their emotional support but also for challenging me to rethink my ideas occasionally and putting this research in a broader perspective. Renate, Pablo and Luis, you are my greatest inspiration.

Munich, Germany
November 2018

Julia Molestina

Contents

List of Abbreviations

ACF	African Competition Forum
Adpostal	Administradora Postal Nacional
Afr.	African/Africain(e)
ALADI	Asociación Latinoamericana de Integración
ALALC	Asociacíon Latinoamericana de Libre Comercio
AndeanC	Andean Community
ANDI	Asociación Nacional de Empresarios de Colombia
Antitrust L.J.	Antitrust Law Journal
Antitrust Rev. Americas	Antitrust Review of the Americas
Brook. J. Int'l. Law	Brooklyn Journal of International Law
CAIPIR	Centro Andino para la Implementación de Políticas de Integración Regional
CAN	Comunidad Andina
CARICOM	Caribbean Community
CARIFTA	Caribbean Free Trade Association
CELAC	Comunidad de Estados Latinoamericanos y Caribeños
CEMAC	Central African Economic and Monetary Community
Chi.-Kent L. Rev.	Chicago-Kent Law Review
COMESA	Common Market for Eastern and Southern Africa
Comp.	Competition/Competencia
COMPAL	Competencia y Protección del Consumidor en America Latina—Competition and Consumer Protection for Latin America
Conc.	Concurrences
COTED	Council for Trade and Economic Development
CSME	CARICOM Single Market and Economy

ECCAS	Economic Community of Central African States
ECOWAS	Economic Community of West African States
Eds.	Editors
EPA	Economic Partnership Agreement
Et seqq.	Et sequentia
EU	European Union
EUR	Euro
Eur. Comp. J.	European Competition Journal
FARC	Fuerzas Armadas Revolucionarias de Colombia
Fordham Int'l. L.J.	Fordham International Law Journal
FTAA	Free Trade Area of the Americas
GAR	Global Antitrust Review
GDP	Gross domestic product
GRUR Int	Gewerblicher Rechtsschutz und Urheberrecht Internationaler Teil
Harv. L. Rev.	Harvard Law Review
ICC	Incentives for the Colombian Currency
INDECOPI	Instituto Nacional de Defensa de la Competencia y de la Propriedad Intelectual
ISF	Sanitary Incentive for Flowers
Iss.	Issue
J. Comp. L. Policy	Journal of Competition Law and Policy
Jur.	Jurídica
J. W. Trade	Journal of World Trade
LORCPM	Organic Law of Regulation and Control of Market Power
Loy. U. Chi. L.J.	Loyola University of Chicago Law Review
MNE	Multinational enterprise
No.	Number
Nw. J. Int'l. L. Bus.	Northwestern Journal of International Law and Business
N.Y.U.	New York University
OECS	Organisation of Eastern Caribbean States
OHADA	Organisation pour l'harmonisation en Afrique du droit des affaires
OSIPTEL	Oficina Supervisora de la Inversión Privada de las Telecomunicaciones
Rev. Afr. de l'Intégration	Revue Africaine de l'Intégration
Rev. Comp. Propriedad Intelectual	Revista de la Competencia y la Propiedad Intelectual
Rev. Jur. Univ. Católica	Revista Jurídica Universidad Católica de Santiago de Guayaquil
R.I.D.E.	Revue Internationale de Droit Économique

RJLSC	Regional Judicial and Legal Services Commission
RTA	Regional Trade Agreement
RTC	Revised Treaty of Chaguaramas
SADC	Southern African Development Community
S. Cal. L. Rev.	Southern California Law Review
SIC	Superintendence of Industry and Trade
SIEC	Significant impediment to effective competition
SIRESE	Sistema de Regulación Sectorial
Sw. J.L. Trade Americas	Southwestern Journal of Law and Trade in the Americas
UNCTAD	United Nations Conference on Trade and Development
USD	United States Dollar
Vol.	Volume
WAEMU	West African Economic and Monetary Union
WAMU	West African Monetary Union
W. Comp.	World Competition
Wis. L. Rev.	Wisconsin Law Review
W.I.L.J.	West Indian Law Journal

Part I
Challenges of Competition Law in Developing Countries and the WAEMU, the AndeanC and the CARICOM

The fight against global poverty is the overall goal that drives development initiatives worldwide. The United Nations emphasizes the importance of reducing poverty and hunger in its Millennium Development Goals[1] and later in its Agenda of Sustainable Development (2015).[2] The fact that the UN "Agenda for Sustainable Development" should include the reduction of poverty as well as the enhancement of growth reveals the close entwinement between these two goals.

In a market economy, the private sector is the most important agent in the achievement of economic growth. It should be capable to sustain itself, independently of a central government. This calls for effective competition policy and enforcement structures. Competition law and policy reduce possible exploitations and enhance fair distribution of innovations that are made through economic growth. They protect the population, in particular the poor without economic or political power, from inflated prices of consumer goods and reduce barriers to market entry.[3] Competition law enforcement thus constitutes a crucial 'development driver'. It is essential for markets to work. This especially applies to developing countries, in which markets are prone to corruption and tend to display high levels of concentration.

As a positive development, the number of developing countries that have implemented national competition laws is constantly increasing and the topic has received considerable attention in the last decades. Yet consistent and thorough enforcement has remained scarce for various reasons.[4] At the same time, developing countries started to engage more in South-South agreements creating regional integration groups with their own common markets in order to gain independence from the traditional North-South trade alliances. These regional integration regimes also

---

[1] <http://www.un.org/millenniumgoals/> accessed 11 November 2018.

[2] <http://www.un.org/sustainabledevelopment/development-agenda/> accessed 11 November 2018.

[3] *Gal/Fox*, Drafting competition law for developing jurisdictions: learning from experience, 4 N.Y.U. L. Econ. Working Papers 2 (2014).

[4] Typical enforcement difficulties will be dealt with below in Sect. 2.2.

include competition laws and appear to offer an efficient instrument to overcome typical enforcement difficulties in developing countries.[5] Typical advantages brought forward in this context are: regional competition law has the potential to reduce the lack of resources by pooling them on the regional level, to create a credible threat in particular regarding international anticompetitive practices and to strengthen a common market by increasing legal certainty and by avoiding distortions of it.[6] Furthermore, a regional competition authority is structurally less prone to political interest and pressure groups.

Nevertheless, the actual enforcement success of the regional integration groups remained limited.[7] *Gal* identified inefficient institutional design as one of the major problems that plague regional competition law enforcement.[8] In fact, the allocation of competition law enforcement competences is a particularly sensitive and important issue, when competition culture is genuinely weak and a competition law system has to create incentives for the enforcers to actually apply the law.

In this regard, the AndeanC, the WAEMU and the CARICOM have not only adopted different approaches towards the allocation of competences, but actually display different extremes of the range of such allocation possibilities. Although they all relied on the European competition law system as a raw model, the enforcement systems differ in essential aspects. In the WAEMU the regional level is vested with far-reaching competences and thus constitutes a highly centralized system. The CARICOM's competition law's main characteristic is the lack of direct effect. Thereby enforcement mostly remains national and decentralized. The AndeanC has adopted an intermediate approach, in which member states without a proper national law were allowed to "download" the Andean competition law.

The aim of this research is to evaluate the potential of regional competition law systems as an enforcement mechanism in developing countries. Furthermore, it formulates recommendations regarding the optimal institutional design under given circumstances. The underlying research question is: under which conditions should a regional competition law system in developing countries be decentralized, when should it be centralized and to what extent.

---

[5] Generally on the benefits and dangers of regional agreements of developing jurisdictions, see *Gal/Faibish Wassmer,* in: *Drexl/Bakhoum/Fox/Gal/Gerber,* Competition Policy and Regional Integration in Developing Countries, 2012, pp. 291, 291ff.

[6] *Gal/Faibish Wassmer,* in: *Drexl/Bakhoum/Fox/Gal/Gerber,* Competition Policy and Regional Integration in Developing Countries, 2012, pp. 291, 293ff.

[7] The competition law enforcement systems in the WAEMU, the AndeanC and the CARICOM will be analysed in Part II of this research.

[8] *Gal/Faibish Wassmer,* in: *Drexl/Bakhoum/Fox/Gal/Gerber,* Competition Policy and Regional Integration in Developing Countries, 2012, p. 291, 311.

Chapter 1
Overview of the WAEMU, the AndeanC and the CARICOM

1.1 General History of Integration in the WAEMU, AndeanC and CARICOM

The institutional design of regional integration varies from bilateral cooperation agreements to custom unions.[1] The degree of centralization or decentralization usually correlates to the depth of integration.[2] Generally, South-South agreements tend to aim at deeper integration than North-South agreements. This finding is supported by the design of the WAEMU, the AndeanC and the CARICOM. They all constitute economic unions that aim at the creation of a common market.

1.1.1 WAEMU

The integration movement in the WAEMU can be traced back to 1973 when eight States created the WAMU (West African Monetary Union), which aimed at the creation of a currency union. On 10 January 1994 seven member states (Guinea-Bissau only joined in 1997) signed the Treaty of Dakar, which further deepened integration by creating a customs and economic union, namely in form of a common market.[3]

---

[1] *Cernat,* in: *Brusick/Alvarez/Cernat,* Competition Provisions in Regional Trade Agreements, 2005, pp. 1, 2. On a taxonomy of RTAs that contain competition related provisions, see *Cernat,* in: *Brusick/Alvarez/Cernat,* Competition Provisions in Regional Trade Agreements, 2005, pp. 1, 8ff.

[2] *Behrens*, Integrationstheorie, Internationale wirtschaftliche Integration als Gegenstand politologischer, ökonomischer und juristischer Forschung, RabelsZ 8, 40 (1981).

[3] Treaty of Dakar, see <http://www.uemoa.int/Documents/TraitReviseUEMOA.pdf> accessed 11 November 2018.

J. Molestina, *Regional Competition Law Enforcement in Developing Countries*,
Munich Studies on Innovation and Competition 9,
https://doi.org/10.1007/978-3-662-58525-2_1

In Sub-Saharan Africa, colonialism has been the shaping influence on political and economic development.[4] It created a strong economic dependency of African States and a fragility of economies based on exports, which can still be felt today.[5] The abolishment of colonialism did not abolish the lack of political institutions and political culture.[6] Frequent state intervention on national markets and high economic concentration levels persisted. Generally, Africa is among the least-integrated regions in world economy.[7]

Regional integration in Sub-Saharan Africa did not only respond to spreading globalization, but also internal African incentives to integrate led to a high number of regional integration groupings in Africa.[8] However, not only have most integration groupings not lived up to their expectations, but the large number of the organizations has also created a situation of multiple memberships. In the context of the WAEMU, all WAEMU member states are also members of the ECOWAS and OHADA.[9]

Regional integration in Sub-Saharan Africa is closely entwined with the idea of economic growth and development.[10] The common market constitutes a priority that is supposed to create economic opportunities for member states while allowing for an efficient allocation of resources.[11] In this context, the formulated objectives of the WAEMU include the strengthening of the economic and financial competitiveness of member states, the achievement of convergence of economic policies and actions, the installation of coordination of national sectorial policies and harmonization of national legislations.[12]

In contrast to other integration movements, the WAEMU was able to rely on stable communitarian structures. Moreover, member states share a common cultural

---

[4] *Gerber,* Global Competition, 2010, p. 249.

[5] *Gerber,* Global Competition, 2010, p. 252.

[6] *Gerber,* Global Competition, 2010, p. 249.

[7] *UNCTAD,* Voluntary Peer Review on Competition Policies of WAEMU, Benin and Senegal, 2008, p. 1.

[8] For example: COMESA (Common Market for Eastern and Southern Africa), OHADA (Harmonization for the Business Law in Africa), ECCAS (Economic Community of Central African States), ECOWAS (Economic Community of West African States), EAC (East African Community), CEMAC (Central African Economic Monetary Community), SADC (Southern African Development Community).

[9] OHADA has not implemented a regional competition law policy so far. Therefore, conflicts of jurisdictions are still of theoretical nature. For more information on the competition law developments in the OHADA, see *Drexl,* Perspectives européennes sur la politique de la concurrence dans l'espace OHADA, XXV R.I.D.E. 281 (2011).

[10] *UNCTAD,* Voluntary Peer Review on Competition Policies of WAEMU, Benin and Senegal, 2008, p. 1.

[11] *UNCTAD,* Voluntary Peer Review on Competition Policies of WAEMU, Benin and Senegal, 2008, pp. 3f.

[12] See Article 4 of the Treaty of Dakar; See also Webpage of the WAEMU, "Historique de l'UEMOA" <http://www.uemoa.int/Pages/UEMOA/L_UEMOA/Historique.aspx> accessed 11 November 2018.

heritage and language.[13] Yet the integration movement suffers from several deficiencies. Member states still lack economic competitiveness and are highly concentrated and marked by state intervention. In a similar vein, inter-state trade is relatively weak within the common market. This is, not solely, but to a large extent attributed to the lack of diversification of production of the WAEMU's member states. In addition, tariff barriers persist.[14] Member states display different levels of economic development—Senegal constituting the economically strongest member state. Finally and among the most severe deficiencies for the West African integration movement and Sub-Saharan Africa overall remains political instability and internal political turmoil, which are capable of immobilizing an entire country and its administration.[15]

1.1.2 AndeanC

The integration process in the Andean countries started in 1969 with the signing of the *Acuerdo de Cartagena*[16] between Bolivia, Chile, Ecuador, Colombia and Peru. Venezuela joined later in 1973, however left the integration group in 2006 for political reasons. Chile also left the group in 1976, however regained a "partner status" in 2006.[17] The *Acuerdo de Cartagena* created a subgroup to the free trade zone ALALC (Asociacíon Latinoamericana de Libre Comercio),[18] in which the mentioned countries did not feel sufficiently represented. It moreover introduced a new focus on development-oriented policies instead of mere industrial policies. Among the most important institutional changes was the introduction of direct effect and the applicability of community law in 1979.[19] It was only in 1986 that the Andean Pact became an independent treaty and was separated from the ALALC. The signature of the

[13] With the exception of Guinea-Bissau, where Portuguese is the official language.

[14] *UNCTAD,* Voluntary Peer Review on Competition Policies of WAEMU, Benin and Senegal, 2008, p. 3.

[15] For an overview of Sub-Saharan economic and political contexts, see *Gerber,* Global Competition, 2010, pp. 249ff.

[16] Acuerdo de integracion subregional andino (Acuerdo de Cartagena) <http://intranet.comunidadandina.org/IDocumentos/c_Newdocs.asp?GruDoc=14> accessed 11 November 2018.

[17] Decree No. 645, 20 September 2006. Further South American associated countries today are: Argentina, Brazil, Paraguay and Uruguay.

[18] Free trade zone in South America, which was established in 1960 with the signature of the Treaty of Montevideo. In 1980 it was replaced by the ALADI (*Asociación Latinoamericana de Integración*).

[19] Article 3 of the Treaty on the Creation of the Tribunal of Justice of the Andean Community (*Tratado de Creación del Tribunal de Justicia de la Comunidad Andina*) <http://www.tribunalandino.org.ec/sitetjca/TCREACION.pdf> accessed 11 November 2018.

Trujillo-Protocol[20] and the Cochabamba-Protocol[21] in 1996 led to a change of the institutional design of the Andean Pact, including the new title: the Andean Community (Comunidad Andina). In 1993, the principle of free circulation of goods was installed.[22] The Sucre-Protocol of 1997[23] implemented further reforming changes concerning a common external tariff and free movement of goods.

"Import-substitution Industrialization", whose aim was to lessen the Latin American "dependency" on international capital centres, characterized the economic policy in the post-war period in Latin America and in the Caribbean.[24] This led to strong state intervention, central planning by the government or other related measures such as "price controls, detailed government regulation, stringent foreign investment rules, nationalization of broad sectors of the economy, and discretionary selection of winners".[25] As a result, the Andean Pact did not only lack competitive markets, but also faced a general economic and political crisis.

While the Andean Pact had emerged rapidly at the beginning, its later development is marked by crises of economic, financial, trade and political natures.[26] Already in the 1970s and 1980s the evolution of the AndeanC stagnated and from 1983 inter-state trade declined drastically.[27] One of the major incidents was the oil crisis in 1973 and 1979/80, when the Andean Pact almost fell apart.[28] Moreover, in 1977 Peru and Ecuador gradually failed to comply with community laws because of unresolved political and territorial conflicts.[29] It was only starting from the 1990s when political and economic changes supported increasing liberalization in the member states.[30] The AndeanC also promoted cooperation with other trading blocs, most predominantly in 2002 with the European Union.[31]

---

[20] *Acta de Trujillo Protocolo Modificatorio del Acuerdo de Integracion Subregional Andino*, 10 March 1996 <http://www.comunidadandina.org/normativa/tratprot/trujillo.htm> accessed 11 November 2018.

[21] *Protocolo Modificatorio del Tratado de Creacion del Tribunal de Justicia del Acuerdo de Cartagena* included changes to the organization of the Andean Court of Justice, 26 May 1996 <http://www.comunidadandina.org/normativa/tratprot/cochabamba.htm> accessed 11 November 2018.

[22] From 1992 to 1995 Peru was excluded from the Andean Pact and only held an observer status. This was due to the self-inflicted coup ("*autogolpe*") of the Peruvian president Fujimori.

[23] *Protocolo de Sucre*, 25 June 1997 <http://www.comunidadandina.org/normativa/tratprot/sucre.htm> accessed 11 November 2018.

[24] *De León*, An Institutional Assessment of Antitrust Policy, 2009, pp. 22ff.

[25] *De León*, An Institutional Assessment of Antitrust Policy, 2009, pp. 24f.

[26] *Zúñiga-Feranández,* Fusionskontrolle in einer "small market economy" in Lateinamerika, 2009, p. 130.

[27] *Mancero-Bucheli*, Competition Law of Latin America and the European Union, 2001, p. 11.

[28] *O'Keefe,* Latin American and Caribbean Trade Agreements, 2009, p. 9.

[29] *Ibid.*

[30] *Mancero-Bucheli*, Competition Law of Latin America and the European Union, 2001, p. 12.

[31] See for example the "EU-CAN Association Agreement", *European Commission,* Andean Community Regional Strategy Paper 2007–2013, 2007 <http://www.eeas.europa.eu/andean/rsp/07_13_en.pdf> accessed 11 November 2018.

The main goals of the AndeanC are the creation and encouragement of balanced and harmonic development, the acceleration of economic growth, and enhanced regional integration in order to gradually form of a common Latin American market. A common market is supposed to diminish economic vulnerability of member states in view of international trade, to strengthen sub-regional solidarity and to improve living standards of citizens in the member states.[32] The AndeanC adopted a system of "open regionalism",[33] in which regional integration is conceived as an intermediate step towards global integration.[34] Yet the AndeanC is still struggling with the achievement of these goals. As free circulation of goods and people is still limping, inter-state trade similarly remains low. Moreover, national political turmoil remains an obstacle to integration. In this context, national security and defence conflicts arose between Ecuador, Bolivia and Colombia based on the hideout of the Colombian guerrilla group "FARC" (Fuerzas Armadas Revolucionarias de Colombia).[35] Moreover, the lack of legal convergence hampers the integration process. It also reflects a general lack of the member states' political will to support and further Andean integration.[36]

1.1.3 CARICOM

Caribbean integration is an old process that goes back to 1958 when the West Indies Federation was created.[37] Originating from British colonialism, the West Indies Federation reflected the conception of its members that a move towards independence would be easier to achieve in conjunction within a political union.[38] Yet, it was not sustainable. The Federation was marked by the dominance of Jamaica and Trinidad and Tobago.[39] Jamaica withdrew from the Federation in 1961 and in 1962 the West Indies Federation finally collapsed. Nevertheless, integration movement in the region did not cease. Shortly after the collapse, in 1965, Antigua and Barbuda,

---

32 Webpage of the Andean Community, "Somos Comunidad Andina" <http://www.comunidadandina.org/Quienes.aspx> accessed 11 November 2018.

33 Actually, there does not exist a common definition of the term "open regionalism". This research refers to the term in the sense of "open membership", according to which member states may enter other trading blocs as long as they fulfil the criteria of the RTA, of which they are already a member.

34 For more information on the relevance of the creation of a common market among developing countries, see below Part III, Sect. 11.3.1.

35 *Zúñiga-Feranández,* Fusionskontrolle in einer "small market economy" in Lateinamerika, 2009, p. 130.

36 *Böttcher*, Kartell- und Lauterkeitsrecht in den Ländern der Andengemeinschaft, 2004, p. 36.

37 For more information on the West Indies Federation, see the webpage of the CARICOM <http://www.caricom.org/jsp/community/west_indies_federation.jsp?menu=community> accessed 11 November 2018.

38 *O'Keefe,* Latin American and Caribbean Trade Agreements, 2009, p. 10.

39 *Ibid.*

Barbados, Guyana and Trinidad and Tobago signed the Caribbean Free Trade Association (CARIFTA).[40] Three years later other countries joined the CARIFTA as well. The main objectives of the CARIFTA included trade and development goals, in particular the promotion of industrial development and the rationalization of agricultural production.[41]

In 1973, Barbados, Guyana, Jamaica and Trinidad and Tobago signed the Treaty of Chaguaramas in order to transform the CARIFTA into a common market. The other eight member states followed. The Bahamas and Haiti became a member of the CARICOM, but not of the common market. This demonstrates the hybrid situation between the common market and the CARICOM, according to which states can become members to the community without participating in the common market.[42] Moreover, an additional organization, the CARIFORUM, was created, which encompasses not only the Caribbean member states, but also the Dominican Republic. It was created in order to represent the Caribbean States during negotiations concerning an economic partnership agreement with the EU.[43]

The CARICOM had, similar to the AndeanC, relied on an import-substitution approach.[44] Although the economic focus of the member states remained on exportation, there was an initial increase of intra-community trade through the creation of group.[45] Yet, with the global recession in the 1980s, also intra-Caribbean trade was struggling. As a consequence, the member states started to re-introduce import quotas and unilateral restrictions.[46] The implementation of a Common External Tariff by 1981 failed.[47] It was only in the 1990s when political and economic changes supported a recuperation of the CARICOM. In the late 1980s, initiatives regarding the establishment of a single market and economy re-emerged.[48] The Revised Treaty

---

[40] For more information on the CARIFTA, see webpage of the CARICOM <http://www.caricom.org/jsp/community/carifta.jsp?menu=community> accessed 11 November 2018.

[41] *O'Keefe,* Latin American and Caribbean Trade Agreements, 2009, p. 11.

[42] Haiti and the Bahamas, which are members of the CARICOM, do not constitute signatories to the CARICOM Single Market and Economy (CSME). While Haiti was so far unable to comply with certain requirements of the CSME, the Bahamas opted out *inter alia* for national considerations related to the free movement of peoples and bigger trade interests with the North. Difficulties that stem from this hybrid situation will not be dealt with in this study. Likewise, the Bahamas and Haiti are not part of this study. For more general information see webpage of the CARICOM, "History of the Caribbean Community (CARICOM)" <http://www.caricom.org/jsp/community/history.jsp?menu=community> accessed 11 November 2018.

[43] For more information see <http://www.caricom.org/jsp/community_organs/cariforum/cariforum_main_page.jsp?menu=cob> accessed 11 November 2018. More information on the CARIFORUM-EC Economic Partnership see below Part II, Dimension I: Section "The CARIFORUM-EC Economic Partnership Agreement".

[44] *O'Keefe,* Latin American and Caribbean Trade Agreements, 2009, p. 11.

[45] *Ibid.*

[46] *O'Keefe,* Latin American and Caribbean Trade Agreements, 2009, p. 12.

[47] *Ibid.*

[48] While the provisions of the original Treaty of Chaguaramas of 1973 also already addressed essential freedoms of a common market, they did not constitute obligations for the Member States

of Chaguaramas was signed in 2001.[49] It included the CARICOM Single Market and Economy (hereafter CSME), which arose as a distinct concept to the establishment of a common economic and political union.[50] Whereas the establishment of the latter entails the adoption of a common monetary and fiscal policy and the ceding of political power by the member states, the CSME covers those freedoms and harmonisations that are relevant for the installation of a common market.[51] Thus the CSME in theory includes the freedom of goods, services, labour, capital and persons, the right to establishment and a common trade policy.[52] Yet not only the principle of free movement of people, but also the right of establishment remains limited.[53] Moreover, CARICOM's member states differ in their level of economic development. Trinidad and Tobago constitutes the most dominant player *inter alia* due to its petroleum resources. In accordance, dominant enterprises in the common market originate mostly from Trinidad and Tobago. As a possible solution, the Revised Treaty of Chaguaramas entails several provisions on differential treatment for less-developed member states. While such provisions might be necessary tools in order to guarantee that all member states profit from the CARICOM and the common market, they also create loopholes for solely national considerations and increase legal uncertainty.[54] Slow and imperfect privatization has allowed member states to exercise influence on national markets.[55] Other impeding factors are the preponderance of foreign-owned economic activities, low entrepreneurship and

for the lack of credible sanctions in case of non-compliance. Accompanied by unclear wordings, the integration process lacked the necessary political commitment, thus causing that "competent decision-makers were caught up in semantic, theory and concepts rather than the identification of practical measures to make regional integration a reality". See *Pollard,* The CCJ and the CSME, 24 May 2006, St. John's Antigua, pp. 4f.; *O'Keefe,* Latin American and Caribbean Trade Agreements, 2009, p. 12.

[49] Revised Treaty of Chaguaramas establishing the Caribbean Community including the CARICOM Single Market and Economy, see <http://www.caricom.org/jsp/community/revised_treaty-text.pdf>. For more information see <http://www.caricom.org> both accessed 11 November 2018. The CARIFORUM-EU EPA also includes a chapter on competition policy, however the provisions of the EPA are quite "soft". For further information on the EPA, see below and see *Stewart,* in: *Drexl/Bakhoum/Fox/Gal/Gerber,* Competition Policy and Regional Integration in Developing Countries, 2012, pp. 161, 181ff.

[50] In fact, it arose in the context of the Grande Anse Declaration and Work Programme for the Advancement of the Integration Movement in July 1989. For more information on the CSME see <http://www.caricom.org/jsp/single_market/single_market_index.jsp?menu=csme> accessed 11 November 2018.

[51] The separation between the creation of a political and an economic union is *inter alia* explicable by the failure of the Federation of the West Indies.

[52] <http://www.caricom.org/jsp/single_market/single_market_index.jsp?menu=csme> accessed 11 November 2018.

[53] On the state of progress of the common market in the CARICOM, see below, Part II, Dimension I: Section "State of Progress of the Common Market".

[54] For an analysis of the provisions on preferential treatment of less developed member states or regions in the CARICOM, see Part II, Dimension I: Sect. 5.3.2.3.

[55] *Smith-Hillman,* The Prospect of a Caribbean Competition Policy, 40 J. W. Trade 405, 416 (2006).

generally low inter-state trade.[56] Moreover, the CARICOM is shaken by internal socio-political difficulties. Despite common culture and language,[57] the CARICOM suffers from a strong distrust of member states against each other.[58] Finally, social implications from drug trade and accompanying violence, as well as a predisposition for natural disasters have hindered fast economic growth.[59]

1.2 Development of Regional Competition Policy in the WAEMU, AndeanC and CARICOM and Main Enforcement Difficulties

1.2.1 WAEMU

The core competition law provisions in West Africa are codified in the Articles 88, 89 and 90 of the Treaty of Dakar, which was enacted in its actual version in 1994.[60] Further secondary legislation, Directives and Regulations, specify the competition law regime in the WAEMU.[61] WAEMU's competition law framework is strongly influenced by the European Union's legislation and jurisdiction. The Court of Justice of WAEMU in its opinion no. 003/2000[62] analysed the West African competition law provisions by comparing them to the European competition provisions as set out in the former articles 85 and 86 in the Treaty of Rome.[63] It thereby applied a

[56] *Stewart*, in: *Drexl/Bakhoum/Fox/Gal/Gerber*, Competition Policy and Regional Integration in Developing Countries, 2012, pp. 161, 169f.

[57] With the exception of Suriname and Haiti.

[58] *Stewart*, in: *Drexl/Bakhoum/Fox/Gal/Gerber*, Competition Policy and Regional Integration in Developing Countries, 2012, pp. 161, 162ff.

[59] *Stewart*, in: *Drexl/Bakhoum/Fox/Gal/Gerber*, Competition Policy and Regional Integration in Developing Countries, 2012, pp. 161, 170.

[60] 10 January 1994 signing of the treaty of Dakar, it entered into force on 1 August 1994, <http://www.uemoa.int/actes/2003/TraitReviseUEMOA.pdf>. The treaty was revised 2003; however, the changes did not concern the competition law provisions.

[61] Réglement No. 2/2002/CM/UEMOA"relatif aux pratiques anticoncurrentielles à l'intérieur de l'Union Economique et Monétaire Ouest Africaine; Réglement No. 3/2002/CM/UEMOA "relatif aux procédures applicables aux ententes et abus de position dominante à l'intérieur de l'Union Economique et Monétaire Ouest Africaine; Réglement No. 4/2002/CM/UEMOA "relatif aux aides d'Etat à l'intérieur de l'Union Economique et Monétaire Ouest Africaine et aux modalités d'application de l'article 88 (C) du traité; Directive No. 2/2002/CM/UEMOA "relative à la coopération entre Commission et les structures nationales de concurrence des Etats Membres pour l'application des articles 88, 89 et 90 du traité de l'UEMOA; Directive No. 1/2002/CM/UEMOA "relative à la transparence des relations financières entre d'une part les Etats Membres et les entreprises publiques, et d'autre part entre les Etats Membres et les organisations internationales ou étrangères; <http://www.uemoa.int> accessed 11 November 2018.

[62] *Avis n° 003/2000/CJ/UEMOA* of 27 June 2000, pp. 119ff. <http://www.parcesmotifs.net/IMG/pdf/Recueil1996_2001.pdf>.

[63] Since 2009 the European competition provisions are comprised in the Articles 101, 102 of the Treaty of the Functioning of the European Union (TFEU).

very literal interpretation of the Articles 88 lit. a) and lit. b) of the Treaty of Dakar, which vested the Commission of WAEMU with the exclusive competence to legislate on issues of agreement, abuse of dominance and state aids.[64] It moreover determined that regional competition law would apply to all allegedly anticompetitive practices within the WAEMU, irrespective a cross-border effect.[65]

The decision of the Court of Justice of the WAEMU caused several enforcement issues.[66] First, the regional competition authority is not vested with sufficient resources to adequately deal with the large number of practices that theoretically fall under the scope of community competition law. Second, national competition authorities are unwilling to efficiently cooperate with the WAEMU Commission in the enforcement of regional rules. In a similar vein, member states are still struggling to establish a competition culture. Third, the centralized system displays unresolved hierarchical problems with regard to national competition-related laws. Nevertheless, the WAEMU Commission was able to deal with a number of legal competition cases. It is noteworthy that the majority of these legal precedents involve state-related measures.

1.2.2 AndeanC

The AndeanC reformed its competition law provisions in 2005. In order to provide the regional competition authority with concrete sanctioning and investigatory powers, Decision 608[67] replaced the former Decision 285.[68] Decision 608 is the product of a "harmonization project of competition rules" (PROYECTO COMPETENCIA)[69] between the EU and the AndeanC, in which the former supported the reform of the

---

[64] In more detail see Part II, Dimension I: Sect. 5.1.5.1.

[65] *Avis n° 003/2000/CJ/UEMOA* of 27 June 2000, pp. 119ff.

[66] The following section only constitutes an overview of enforcement difficulties. The particular problems will be discussed in the respective section of the following analysis.

[67] *Comisión (CAN), Decisión 608, Nórmas para la protección y promoción de la libre competencia en la Comunidad Andina*, approved on 29 March 2004, published in the Gaceta Oficial del Acuerdo de Cartagena n° 1180 of 4 April 2005 <http://www.sice.oas.org/trade/junac/Decisiones/DEC608s.asp> accessed 11 November 2018.

[68] Comisión (CAN), Decisión 285, Normas para prevenir o corregir las distorsiones en la competencia generadas por prácticas restrictivas de la libre competencia, of 22 March 1991. <http://www.comunidadandina.org/normativa/dec/d285.htm> accessed 11 November 2018. On one of the main deficiencies of the former Decision 285, see Part II, Dimension I: Sect. 5.1.5.2.

[69] *"Proyecto Armonización de las Reglas de Competencia en la Región Andina" - Convenio de Financiamiento* (ASR/B7-3110/IB/98/0099), 2003, 2004, 2005; *European Commission,* Andean Community Regional Strategy Paper 2007–2013, 2007, p. 12 <http://www.eeas.europa.eu/andean/rsp/07_13_en.pdf> accessed 11 November 2018; *Gallardo/Domínguez,* 20 Boletín Latinoamericano de Competencia 36, 36ff. (2005) <http://ec.europa.eu/competition/publications/blc/boletin_20_1_es.pdf> accessed 11 November 2018.

regional Andean competition norm by offering financial and technical support.[70] On the one hand, a supranational norm was considered to harmonize the objectives of competition in the sub-region in the medium terms and thus to increase the efficacy of the application of national laws.[71] On the other hand, the European Union specifically aimed at strengthening the common market of the AndeanC.[72] Additionally, from the European perspective, the implementation of an efficient competition law system was considered a necessary condition for the long-term goal of the creation of a free-trading zone.[73] Although the representatives of the European Union in the legislation process of Decision 608 underlined that the intention of the European Union was not to impose the European competition law system on the AndeanC,[74] the involvement of experts from the EU explains the large convergence between the Andean law and the European competition law provisions.[75]

---

[70] Competition-law-related cooperation already began on 23 April 1993 with the signing of the “Acuerdo de Cooperación” in Copenhagen between the European Community (now: European Union) and the Acuerdo de Cartagena (now: Andean Community) and its member states, whose priority is the support and strengthening of the institutions of the AndeanC.

[71] *Secretaría General de la Comunidad Andina,* Informe de la Primera Reunión de Expertos Gubernamentales en Materia de Libre Competencia, 29 October 1998, Lima (SG/REG.LC/I/Informe/Rev.1), p. 2 (available from the author).

[72] See Speech of the *Ambassador Mendel Goldstein,* Chief of the Delegation of the European Union of Peru, during the Reunion on the installation of the Competition Project between the AndeanC and the European Union, Lima, 3 March 2003: “Resultado de esta política [cooperation between the EU and the CAN and the institutional strengthening] es el convenio suscrito entre la Comisión Europea y la Secretaría General de la Comunidad Andina, que busca contribuir a consolidar el mercado común andino en el 2005, mediante el apoyo en material de libre competencia a las autoridades nacionales e instituciones comunitarias, dotándolas de instrumentos normativos y administrativos modernos y eficientes.”

[73] See citation of *Mendel Goldstein,* Chief of the Delegation of the European Union of Peru, in: *El Peruano,* 4 March 2003, “La UE buscará facilitar el comercio con andinos”.

[74] See Speech of the *Ambassador Mendel Goldstein,* Chief of the Delegation of the European Union of Peru, during the Reunion on the installation of the Competition Project between the AndeanC and the European Union, Lima, 3 March 2003: “No se pretende exporter el modelo europeo como está, a la Comunidad Andina (…) Realmente no tenemos ninguna intención de copier, ni difundir nuestro concepto en la materia.”

[75] The “Proyecto Competencia” is also considered an important step towards the enactment of the “EU-CAN Association Agreement”. More information on the “EU-CAN Association Agreement” see *European Commission,* Andean Community Regional Strategy Paper 2007–2013, 2007, p. 15 <http://www.eeas.europa.eu/andean/rsp/07_13_en.pdf> accessed 11 November 2018. A general cooperation between the EU and the AndeanC already started in 1983 with the “Agreement of the second generation”, which focused on trade relations between the two blocks. The “Agreement of the third generation” installed a legal framework for the cooperation between the two regional groups in 1992. In 2003, the “Political Dialogue & Cooperation Agreement” replaced the first declaration. In 2002 a EU-CAN summit took place in Madrid and in 2004 another one took place in Guadalajara. Both meetings inter alia aimed at the creation of the “EU-CAN Association Agreement”. The agreement’s main objectives are the intensification of political cooperation and trade. For more information on the cooperation between the EU and the AndeanC see <http://eeas.europa.eu/andean/index_en.htm> accessed 11 November 2018 <http://eeas.europa.eu/la/docs/lima_en.pdf> accessed 11 November 2018. See *Decisión 667 “Marco general para las negociaciones del Acuerdo de*

Decision 616 contains specific regulations on the competition law system in Ecuador.[76] Decision 456, 457 and Decision 283 deal with the competition-related matters, subsidies and rules on anti-dumping.[77] Procedural and administrative provisions are contained in further Decisions and Treaties.[78] A particularity of the Andean competition law is the "Downloading Option", which allowed member states without a domestic competition law to directly apply the regional provisions as national law within their jurisdiction.[79]

Despite innovative elements and improvements to the former regional competition law, Decision 608 has not lived up to its expectations. First and above all, Decision 608 has remained unapplied and is actually ignored by national competition authorities. Second, although all member states have by 2011 enacted national competition law provisions (at least in their sectorial control) and have installed national competition authorities, a harmonization of national laws with Decision 608 has not been achieved. Rather the domestic laws reflect differing underlying economic market conceptions in Bolivia and Ecuador on the one hand, and Colombia and Peru on the other hand. Third, vertical and horizontal cooperation between competition authorities remains very low. This is also attributed to the fact that

Asociación entre la Comunidad Andina y la Unión Europea", 8 June 2007 <http://www.comunidadandina.org/normativa/dec/D667.htm> accessed 11 November 2018 and *Decisión 669 "Política Arancelaria de la Comunidad Andina"*, 13 July 2007 <http://www.comunidadandina.org/normativa/dec/D669.htm> accessed 11 November 2018.

[76] *Comisión (CAN), Decisión 616, Entrada en vigencia de la Decisión 608 para la República del Ecuador,* approved on 15 July 2005, published in the Gaceta Oficial del Acuerdo de Cartagena n° 1221, 25 July 2005 <http://www.sice.oas.org/trade/junac/Decisiones/DEC616s.asp> accessed 11 November 2018.

[77] Comisión (CAN), Decision 456, Normas para prevenir o corregir las distorsiones en la competencia generadas por prácticas de dumping en importaciones de productos originarios de Países Miembros de la Comunidad Andina, approved on 4 May 1999, published in the Gaceta Oficial de Acuerdo de Cartagena n° 436 of 7 May 1999; Comisión (CAN), Decisión 457, Nórmas para prevenir o corregir las distorsiones en la competencia generadas por prácticas de subvenciones en importaciones de productos originarios de Países Miembros de la Comunidad Andina, approved on 4 May 1999, published in the Gaceta Oficial del Acuerdo de Cartagena n° 436 of 7 May 1999; Comisión (CAN), Decisión 283, Nórmas para prevenir o corregir las distorsiones en la competencia generadas por prácticas de dumping o subsidies, approved on 21–22 March 1991, published in the Gaceta Oficial del Acuerdo de Cartagena n° 80 of 4 April 1991 <www.comunidadandina.org>.

[78] Consejo Andino de Ministros de Relaciones Exteriores (CAN), Decisión 623, Reglamento de la Fase Prejudicial de la Acción de Incumplimiento, approved on 16 July 2005, published in the Gaceta Oficial del Acuerdo de Cartagena n° 1221, 25 July 2005; Consejo Andino de Ministros de Relaciones Exteriores (CAN), Decisión 425, Reglamento de Procedimientos Administrativos de la Secretaría General de la Comunidad Andina, approved on 14 December 1997, published in the Gaceta Oficial del Acuerdo de Cartagena n° 314, 18 December 1997; Governments of Bolivia, Colombia, Ecuador, Peru and Venezuela, Tratado de Creación del Tribunal de Justicia de la Comunidad Andina, approved on 10 March 1996.

[79] Generally on the "downloading option", see *Marcos,* in *Fox/Sokol,* Competition Law and Policy in Latin America, 2009, pp. 453–468. For more details on the "downloading option" see Part II, Dimension II: Sect. 6.3.2.

national authorities have been seeking more and more assistance and cooperation with competition authorities outside the AndeanC.

1.2.3 CARICOM

Chapter VIII of the Revised Treaty of Chaguaramas covers provisions on competition and consumer protection. The wording of the actual prohibition of anticompetitive practices, namely agreements and abuse of dominance, mirrors the European prohibitions in Articles 101 and 102 TFEU. The main competition law agency's, the CARICOM Competition Commission's, start-up funding was provided by the EU in the framework of the Ninth European Development Fund.[80]

The enforcement of the Caribbean competition policy is characterised by two elements: the objective to harmonize national legislations and a flexible enforcement approach by applying special and differential treatment for less-developed states.[81] Nevertheless, actual application of competition law within CARICOM has remained limited. First, the implementation process of national competition laws and structures is slow. In the same vein, competition culture is rare. Only two member states, Jamaica and Barbados, possessed domestic competition laws before the enactment of regional competition law. Yet even in these more experienced competition law jurisdictions, constitutional issues have led to a stagnation of competition law enforcement.[82] Second, for the lack of direct effect in the CARICOM, regional competition law enforcement requires the implementation of regional law into national law. This does not only affect individuals' rights protection, but also hampers a potential cooperation between regional and national competition authorities. However despite the slow national implementation and ratification processes, one should positively acknowledge that the CARICOM Competition Commission was capable of dealing with an important competition law case.[83] Third, the high degree of decentralization and p large impact of member states within the CARICOM system is capable of hollowing out the scope of application of regional law.[84] Generally, there remain unresolved hierarchical issues and the lack of direct effect and application create considerable legal uncertainty with regard to regional competition law that might hamper convergent application.

---

[80] On the European Development Fund, see <http://europa.eu/legislation_summaries/development/overseas_countries_territories/r12102_en.htm> accessed 11 November 2018.

[81] *Beckford,* in: *Drexl/Bakhoum/Fox/Gal/Gerber,* Competition Policy and Regional Integration in Developing Countries, 2012, pp. 185, 187.

[82] This is the case in Jamaica, see below Part II, Dimension I: Sect. 5.2.3.1.

[83] In fact, the CARICOM Competition Commission initiated investigations against a large and dominant firm from Trinidad and Tobago, the Trinidad Cement Limited. See below Part II, Dimension IV: Sect. 8.1.1.1.

[84] This in particular concerns the influential role of the COTED (Council of Trade and Economic Development).

Chapter 2
Competition Law in Developing Countries

2.1 Competition Policy and Development

The question of whether competition law implementation and enforcement[1] constitutes a relevant concern for developing countries is certainly legitimate.[2] In fact, it was a common view that the implementation of competition laws in developing countries in the first place was not a sovereign decision of these countries, but one that was obtruded by the pressure of foreign international institutions.[3] In the absence of liberalized markets in developing countries, there was little incentive to support the introduction and development of competition laws.[4] Rather, the enactment of competition laws was in some instances made a precondition by the developed world for economic cooperation and trade with developing countries.[5] This perceived imposition, occurring in the context of local markets marked by strong state intervention, constituted and still constitutes a hurdle to effective competition law enforcement in developing countries.

An even more drastic view denies the necessity of introducing competition law and policy in developing countries in the first place. Developing countries lacked the basic institutional structures to apply it and wasted resources, which were

[1] The particular competition law enforcement difficulties of developing countries will be dealt with below in Sect. 2.2.

[2] *Marcos* also raises this question, see *Marcos,* Do developing countries need Competition Laws and Policy?, 21–23 September 2006, Madrid, pp. 4ff.

[3] *Stewart/Clarke/Joekes,* Competition Law in Action, 2007, p. 1. With regard to the competition law experiences in Africa, see *Gerber,* Global Competition, 2010, p. 250.

[4] With regard to Latin America and Sub-Saharan Africa, see *Gerber,* Global Competition, 2010, pp. 240ff., 252ff.

[5] *Dabbah*, 33/3 W. Comp. 457, 459f. (2010); *Gerber,* Global Competition, 2010, p. 250.

J. Molestina, *Regional Competition Law Enforcement in Developing Countries*,
Munich Studies on Innovation and Competition 9,
https://doi.org/10.1007/978-3-662-58525-2_2

needed elsewhere.[6] However, such a conception of competition law and policy—as a merely externally imposed mechanism—ignores that the implementation of competition laws and policy in developing countries often contributes to a liberalization process of national markets and improves economy overall. There is evidence indicating that the absence of rules on competition matters "negates whatever effects that may have been gained from liberalization and privatization."[7]

The crux for developing countries remains the attainment of economic growth. Struggling with a population suffering from poverty, low education levels, malnutrition and high unemployment rates,[8] it is held that economic "growth is the key for the poverty alleviation."[9] In particular with regard to the long-term sustainability of development, an economic system has to provide for economic opportunities for their citizens to participate and to make a living. These opportunities allow for the establishment of an "economic democracy",[10] in which no market participants are excluded from the economy and from "making a living".

In this context, the implementation of competition law and policy plays an integral role, as they set the rules of the economic game.[11] In developing countries, the "invisible hand" of the market is weaker than in developed and industrialized countries. Merely relying on market forces is hence not a feasible solution, because developing countries are extremely prone to exclusionary and exploitative anticompetitive practices from dominant firms.[12] Competition law and policy might in particular tackle anticompetitive practices originating from state-imputed behaviour, remnants of closed import-substitution based economies and remaining results of limping liberalization. Similarly, illicit agreements, such as price-fixing in the retail sector or in consumer goods sectors, directly affect the poorest parts of civil society by raising prices.[13] Moreover, in developing countries consumers' 'sovereignty' requires additional supporting measures, because consumers lack sufficient information and the

---

[6] *Godek*, One U.S. Export Eastern Europe Does Not Need, 15 Regulation 20, 21 (1992) <http://object.cato.org/sites/cato.org/files/serials/files/regulation/1992/1/v15n1-2.pdf#page=11> accessed 11 November 2018. In this context *Godek* states: "Worrying about antitrust issues shows an unhealthy anxiety about the imagined ills of capitalism. Exporting antitrust to Eastern Europe is like giving a silk tie to a starving man. It is superfluous; a starving man has much more immediate needs. And if the tie is knotted too tightly; he will not be able to eat what little there is available to him.", *Godek: Ibid.*, p. 21.

[7] *UNCTAD*, The relationship between competition, competitiveness and development, 2002, p. 1.

[8] *Fox*, in: *Drexl/Bakhoum/Fox/Gal/Gerber*, Competition Policy and Regional Integration in Developing Countries, 2012, pp. 273, 274.

[9] *Alvarez/Evenett/Wilse-Samson*, in: *Alvarez/Wilse-Samson*, Implementing Competition-Related Provisions in Regional Trade Agreements, 2007, pp. 59, 61.

[10] *Stewart/Clarke/Joekes*, Competition Law in Action, 2007, p. 13.

[11] *Mateus*, Competition and Development: What Competition Law Regime?, 2010, p. 276 <http://ssrn.com/abstract=1699643> accessed 11 November 2018.

[12] *Brusick/Evenett*, Should Developing Countries Worry about Abuse of Dominant Power?, 2 Wis. L. Rev. 269, 292ff. (2008); *Jenny*, Cartels and Collusion in Developing Countries, 29/1 W. Comp. 109, 133 (2006).

[13] *Jenny*, Cartels and Collusion in Developing Countries, 29/1 W. Comp. 109, 134 (2006).

attainment of information requires high transaction costs and a certain level of education.[14]

Clearly, competition law and policy should not be regarded as the sole cure for the malfunctions of developing countries' economies.[15] Whereas it is difficult to quantify the specific effectiveness of competition law implementation and enforcement, competition law and policy create a framework for firms that strengthens dynamic and innovative processes in an economy.[16] In this regard, evidence and research has confirmed the positive effect of competition policy on growth.[17]

Competition policy does not solely constitute an economic safeguard, but also has a social dimension and can thus be placed in the framework of the attainment of the Millennium Development Goals.[18] Sufficient economic opportunities constitute a precondition for political participation in civil society and should thus be weighted as one of the fundamental intermediate steps towards overall growth and sustainable development. The preponderance of weak administration and governance as well as high levels of corruption make developing countries prone to a biased distribution of potential benefits of liberalization and economic growth. Implementing competition laws can reduce powers of government officials, for example when issuing licences or subsidies, thereby reducing loopholes for corruption.[19] Nevertheless, a reduction of corruption levels depends on the degree of independence of the competition authority. This leads us to the underlying premise of this research: benefits of competition law and policy can only arise through its effective enforcement.[20]

---

[14] *Lachmann,* The Development Dimension of Competition Law and Policy, 1999, p. 5 <http://unctad.org/en/Docs/poitcdclpm9.en.pdf> accessed 11 November 2018.

[15] *Waked,* Competition Law in the developing world, GAR 69, 73 (2008).

[16] On the problematic issue of measuring efficiency of competition law enforcement, see below Sect. 3.3. *Mateus*, Competition and Development: What Competition Law Regime?, 2010, pp. 276f.

[17] *Dutz/Hayri,* Does More Intense Competition Lead to Higher Growth?, 2000, pp. 1–25 <http://elibrary.worldbank.org/doi/pdf/10.1596/1813-9450-2320> accessed 11 November 2018. For an overview of the research on the positive effect of competition policy on economic growth, see *Mateus*, Competition and Development: What Competition Law Regime?, 2010, p. 279 <http://ssrn.com/abstract=1699643> accessed 11 November 2018.

[18] *Alvarez/Evenett/Wilse-Samson,* in: *Alvarez/Wilse-Samson,* Implementing Competition-Related Provisions in Regional Trade Agreements, 2007, pp. 59–95; *Fox,* in: *Drexl/Bakhoum/Fox/Gal/Gerber,* Competition Policy and Regional Integration in Developing Countries, 2012, pp. 273, 274.

[19] *Kovacic*, Institutional Foundations for Economic Legal Reform in Transition Economies, 77 Chi.-Kent L. Rev. 265, 296 (2001).

[20] In the same vein, *Waked,* Competition Law in the developing world, GAR 69, 75 (2008).

2.2 Taxonomy of Competition Law Enforcement Difficulties in Developing Countries

Although many laws are drafted after the model of developed countries (mostly after the US and EU competition law enforcement system), the actual enforcement level in developing countries remains weak.[21] The relation between substantive laws in "the books" and their enforcement is reciprocal and the application of these laws does not take place in a legal vacuum.[22] While limping enforcement might render a 'well drafted' law obsolete, the value of a substantive law depends on its appropriateness with regard to prevailing conditions in a country.[23] The next section therefore highlights the prevailing conditions in developing countries.[24] The conditions and factors are not mutually exclusive, but are interrelated and sometimes overlapping.[25] Moreover, the intensity, the weight and number of enforcement difficulties might vary between developing countries. Finally, enforcement difficulties as described below might not solely be exclusive difficulties of developing countries, but can also occur in competition law enforcement in developed countries.

2.2.1 *Economy Related Enforcement Difficulties*

The economic enforcement difficulties can be broken down to three aspects, which are interrelated: First, economic enforcement issues arise out of the particularities of the typical market structures in developing countries. Second, enforcement issues arise from the economic actors and the prevalent kind of anticompetitive practices on the market. Third, economic enforcement difficulties arise also from the internal economics of a competition authority, namely its financial and human resources at hand. These internal aspects relate to the institutional efficacy of a competition authority. The interaction of these elements leads to competition law enforcement difficulties that are characteristic of developing countries' jurisdictions.

---

[21] *Gal*, The effects of market size on optimal competition policy, 74 S. Cal. L. Rev. 1437, 1438 (2001).

[22] *Gal*, Institutional Solutions when Antitrust Enforcement Resources are Scarce, 41 Loy. U. Chi. L.J. 417, 417 (2010); *Trebilcock/Iacobucci*, Designing Competition Law Institutions, 41 Loy. U. Chi. L.J. 455, 455 (2010).

[23] *Kovacic*, Creating New Competition Policy Institutions in Transition Economies, 23 Brook. J. Int'l. Law 403, 404 (1997).

[24] For more information on the range and types of developing countries, see *Tybout*, Manufacturing Firms in Developing Countries, 38 J. Econ. Lit. 11, 13 (2000).

[25] Enforcement difficulties related to deficits in the drafting of a law are deliberately left out. Although the drafting of substantive competition law provisions of developing countries is a problematic issue, it would exceed the scope of this study. For more information on the substantive law of competition law in developing countries, see *UNCTAD*, Model Law on Competition, 2004; *Bakhoum*, A Dual Language in Modern Competition Law?, 34/3 W. Comp. 495–520 (2011).

2.2.1.1 Market Particularities

Several market particularities are repeatedly observed in developing economies. They are interrelated and can be easily exploited to the disadvantage of the development of the country and to the detriment of the "Millennium Development Goals".[26]

Small Market Economy

Gal defines a small economy as "an independent sovereign economy that can support only a small number of competitors in most of its industries."[27] However, there is no numerical threshold that defines the distinction to a large or normal economy. The capacity of a market is determined by the population size, population dispersion, and openness to trade.[28] The impact of geographical or political state borders has decreased in the process of globalization and the internalization of trade. Generally, all aspects, economic, geographical, technological, legal or political that have an impact on the creation of boundaries, influence a market's economic size.[29] Thus, the mere classification as a developing country does not automatically lead to the classification as small market economy. Similarly, developed countries can constitute small markets and vice versa.[30]

Small market economies suffer mainly from the disability to achieve efficient scales of production. The smaller the demand, the fewer the enterprises are that can operate profitably in the market.[31] This handicap affects not only the choice of technology and a low level of specialization of a firm, but more importantly leads to high economic concentration levels, fragmentation of the market or even a situation of a "natural monopoly".[32] High concentration by itself does not automatically lead to higher prices, but small economies are particularly susceptible to them. Although low barriers to entry might theoretically discipline a monopoly's price-setting

---

[26] Generally on the interaction between competition law enforcement and the attainment of the Millennium Development Goals, see *Alvarez/Evenett/Wilse-Samson,* in: *Alvarez/Wilse-Samson,* Implementing Competition-Related Provisions in Regional Trade Agreements, 2007, pp. 59, 59ff.

[27] *Gal*, Competition Policy for Small Market Economies, 2003, p. 1; *Gal*, The effects of market size on optimal competition policy, 74 S. Cal. L. Rev. 1437, 1439 (2001).

[28] *Gal*, Competition Policy for Small Market Economies, 2003, p. 1.

[29] *Gal*, The effects of market size on optimal competition policy, 74 S. Cal. L. Rev. 1437, 1439 (2001).

[30] For example India: Although considered a developing country, it is not a small market economy. Israel on the other hand, considered part of the developed world, only constitutes a small market economy. All the examined Member States of the three Regional Trade Agreements can be classified as small market economies.

[31] *Gal*, Competition Policy for Small Market Economies, 2003, p. 15.

[32] A situation in which the market can only support one efficiently sized firm. *Gal*, The effects of market size on optimal competition policy, 74 S. Cal. L. Rev. 1437, 1446 (2001); *Brusick/Evenett*, Should Developing Countries Worry about Abuse of Dominant Power?, 2 Wis. L. Rev. 269, 274ff. (2008).

strategy through the general possibility of other market entrants, this 'disciplining' threat by other potential entrants remains theoretical if the market can only support one firm. Furthermore, high concentration levels increase the interdependence between firms and thereby create incentives to engage in anticompetitive behaviour.[33] *Gal* to the point describes that small market size as resembling a "magnifying glass" in which "special market phenomena are highly significant as extremes become the rule."[34]

Moreover, developing countries typically suffer from low levels of infrastructure. Roads are often impassable for commerce-carrying trucks and seasonally blocked.[35] This increases undertakings' production costs even more and makes market access more difficult and costly. Neither the state itself, nor the few firms that (sometimes barely) produce efficiently are capable of investing in the country's infrastructure.

Several factors can influence the creation of entry barriers or their intensity. In order to achieve minimum efficient scales of operation, firms need to produce at levels that supply a large portion of the entire demand.[36] This leads to high sunk costs for other enterprises trying to enter the market. Further factors that increase entry barriers to a market are supply constraints on factors of production, limited production resources or vertically integrated markets.[37] The combination of high concentration levels and high entry barriers bears the risk of high prices. In Peru, the domestic live poultry market was excluded from foreign trade and concentrated through entry barriers in the form of local industry associations.[38] Until 2005, this had led to a long-running cartel, in which the local producers gained unfairly high profits.[39] Additionally, poultry products are among products with highest demand by the low- and middle-income population.[40] One the other hand, entry barriers have been justified by governments in order to protect the domestic industry. In Belize, which is almost self-sufficient in its agricultural sector, the local industry complained that it would not be capable of coping with subsidized agricultural products

[33] *Cernat,* in: *Brusick/Alvarez/Cernat,* Competition Provisions in Regional Trade Agreements, 2005, pp. 1, 6; Stewart/*Clarke/Joekes,* Competition Law in Action, 2007, p. 15.

[34] *Gal,* The effects of market size on optimal competition policy, 74 S. Cal. L. Rev. 1437, 1441 (2001); *OECD,* Small Economies and Competition Policy: A Background Paper, 2003, pp. 4ff. <http://vi.unctad.org/windiesst09/docs/presentations/wednesday13/oecdsmalleconomybackground.pdf> accessed 11 November 2018.

[35] *Brusick/Evenett,* Should Developing Countries Worry about Abuse of Dominant Power?, 2 Wis. L. Rev. 269, 276 (2008).

[36] *Gal,* Competition Policy for Small Market Economies, 2003, p. 22; *Gal,* The effects of market size on optimal competition policy, 74 S. Cal. L. Rev. 1437, 1447 (2001).

[37] *Gal,* The effects of market size on optimal competition policy, 74 S. Cal. L. Rev. 1437, 1447f. (2001).

[38] *Boza,* Tailor-Made Competition Policy in a Standardizing World, 2005, pp. 48ff.

[39] *Ibid*; *Stewart/Clarke/Joekes,* Competition Law in Action, 2007, p. 19.

[40] *Boza,* Tailor-Made Competition Policy in a Standardizing World, 2005, p. 49.

from the EU or the US.[41] While in theory the export of tradable goods to foreign markets can increase the range of a firm and enable it to meet economies of scale,[42] it is doubtful whether this also occurs in developing economies.

Dependence on Foreign Direct Investment and Vulnerability to International Anticompetitive Conduct

The typical problems of small market economies are accompanied by weak capital markets. In developing countries, national capital is usually only of reduced availability.[43] This hinders national undertakings to compete with bigger multinational firms, non-speaking of competing on a larger global or multi-national scale.

Whereas, an interaction of local and foreign firms can benefit developing countries "in terms of increasing the contestability of host markets, improving the performance of local industry and lowering prices", the foreign direct investment cannot substitute for the domestic strive for competition.[44] First, foreign investments are usually limited in time and technical spill-over may remain weak due to the discrepancy between the technical level of the local firms and that of the foreign large firm.[45] Second, profits do not necessarily contribute to the economic growth of a country, but are typically extracted by the foreign firm.[46] Third, local firms are usually incapable of facing competition of larger international firms and are easily usurped by them. Yet, this does not signify that international firms are thus more efficient than local undertakings.[47] In fact, local economies in the process of liberalization need a competition law framework that prevents "government owned inefficient monstrosity [from] becoming a privately owned inefficient monstrosity resulting in even more abuses of the company's monopolistic powers."[48] As frequently mergers and acquisitions contribute to the share of foreign direct investment, a competition law might provide for a merger control that also includes certain protection measures in favour of local companies.[49]

---

[41] *Stewart*, An Empirical Examination of Competition Issues in Selected Caricom Countries, 2004, pp. 149f.; *Stewart/Clarke/Joekes*, Competition Law in Action, 2007, p. 20.

[42] *Gal*, Competition Policy for Small Market Economies, 2003, p. 36.

[43] *Krakowski*, Competition Policy Works, 2005, p. 1 <http://papers.ssrn.com/sol3/papers.cfm?abstract_id=854908> accessed 11 November 2018.

[44] *UNCTAD*, The relationship between competition, competitiveness and development, 2002, p. 13.

[45] *Ibid.*: In general, the evidence indicates that in countries that are technologically weak, the extent of technology transfer by transnational corporations is correspondingly weak.

[46] In the CARICOM, the tourism sector, the leading economic sector in the Caribbean, is largely owned by foreign-based firms; *Stewart*, An Empirical Examination of Competition Issues in Selected Caricom Countries, 2004, p. 114f.

[47] *Boza*, Tailor-Made Competition Policy in a Standardizing World, 2005, p. 10.

[48] *Ibid.*

[49] *UNCTAD*, The relationship between competition, competitiveness and development, 2002, p. 14.

Dependence on Imports

At the same time, markets of developing countries are dependent on imports.[50] This is particularly the case, if the market can only rely on limited resources and if access to them is hindered by strong vertical integration of the market. This interrelated dependence on external trade, imports and foreign direct investment induces vulnerability to international anticompetitive behaviour, in particular international (export) cartels. Surprisingly, despite their negative impact on developing countries, they are hardly prosecuted by the affected countries.[51] *Levenstein* and *Suslow* estimated that in 1997 developing countries had imported about USD51, 1 billion in goods that were affected by cartel activity.[52]

2.2.1.2 Economic Actors

Developing countries' markets often consist of a large informal sector.[53] In the WAEMU, it measures up to 80% of the employment.[54] In Latin America 63.3% of the non-agricultural sector are held to belong to informal economy.[55] In the CARICOM, despite the lack of specific estimations regarding the size of the informal market, one can presume that it is similarly large, because even in Jamaica, one of the largest countries of the CARICOM, about 40% of its GDP are generated by informal economic activities.[56] More problematic, the informal sector in the CARICOM even started to tend towards a criminal structure.[57] Moreover, the

[50] *Stewart/Clarke/Joekes*, Competition Law in Action, 2007, p. 22; *UNCTAD*, The relationship between competition, competitiveness and development, 2002, p. 7.

[51] Specifically regarding the impact on Latin America, see *Connor*, in: *Fox/Sokol*, Competition Law and Policy in Latin America, 2009, pp. 291, 291ff.

[52] *Levenstein/Suslow*, Contemporary International Cartels and Developing Countries, 71 Antitrust L.J. 801, 804 (2004); *UNCTAD*, The relationship between competition, competitiveness and development, 2002, pp. 7ff. The vulnerability of developing countries towards international anticompetitive practices prevails irrespective the finding that the duration of international cartels has declined, see *Connor*, in: *Fox/Sokol*, Competition Law and Policy in Latin America, 2009, pp. 291, 310.

[53] Unlike the formal economy, the informal sector refers to a part of an economy, which is not taxed, not supervised by the government and not included in the evaluation of the GDP of a country. Due to its nature the informal sector is difficult to measure in statistical numbers.

[54] *Tchapga*, La politique de la concurrence dans la CEMAC et l'UEMOA, 1 Conc. 237, 239 (2013); *Bakhoum*, in: *Zimmer*, The Goals of Competition Law, 2012, pp. 408, 426.

[55] *Tokman*, Informality in Latin America, 2008, p. 2 <http://wiego.org/sites/wiego.org/files/publications/files/Tokman-Informality_in_Latin_America_2008.pdf> accessed 11 November 2018.

[56] *Stewart*, An Empirical Examination of Competition Issues in Selected Caricom Countries, 2004, p. 152.

[57] *Stewart*, An Empirical Examination of Competition Issues in Selected Caricom Countries, 2004, pp. 150ff.

informal sector lacks "innovative features"[58] thereby contributing to the lack of competitiveness of the market and increasing entry barriers and social disparities.

Yet due to high investment costs and highly concentrated markets, the engagement in the informal sector remains the form of economic activity accessible to large parts of the population.[59] Instead of attempting to abolish the informal sector overall, competition law enforcement reduces market entry barriers and might in the long run allow companies to move from the informal market to the official one and thereby attribute to local growth.

Developing countries furthermore encounter a pervasiveness of small and medium-sized local enterprises.[60] The small size implies that the firms are only active on a geographically limited area, which is in line with the fragmentation of markets of developing countries. Irrespective of their ability to produce at scale efficiencies, they face competition in form of multinational or transnational firms, which are at least relatively more efficient and have deeper pockets.[61]

Generally, the process of liberalization in developing countries is burdensome. Firstly, it is prone to opportunistic political influences and a negative public perception. Secondly, privatization of economic sectors creates technical difficulties, as the state has to find the appropriate legal form to implement privatization. In Latin America privatization was conducted through concession contracts in order to avoid constitutional issues. However, the contracts were often renegotiated and induced political intervention. As a consequence in Bolivia, for example water concessions were cancelled in 2005.[62] In Jamaica, the privatization of the telecommunications sector ran more positively. In this case, privatization was achieved through long-term contracts that limited regulatory discretion.[63] Yet such long-term contracts might require renegotiation, in particular if they create a monopoly based on an exclusive licence.[64] Such renegotiation might be difficult for small states of the developing world, which might face structural disadvantages compared to large multinational firms.[65]

---

[58] *Bakhoum*, in: *Zimmer*, The Goals of Competition Law, 2012, pp. 408, 434.

[59] *Stewart*, An Empirical Examination of Competition Issues in Selected Caricom Countries, 2004, p. 150. *Stewart* even describes the informal sector as "safety net" for the disadvantaged parts of society.

[60] *Tybout*, Manufacturing Firms in Developing Countries, 38 J. Econ. Lit. 11, 13ff. (2000): The conclusions on the scale effectiveness of small firms vary, "(…) some finding that small enterprises are at least as efficient as others, and others finding their efficiency relatively low" (p. 18).

[61] *Baetge*, Globalisierung des Wettbewerbsrechts, 2009, pp. 44ff.; *Bakhoum*, A Dual Language in Modern Competition Law?, 34/3 W. Comp. 495, 509 (2011); *UNCTAD*, The relationship between competition, competitiveness and development, 2002, p. 5; *Alvarez/Horna*, Implementing competition law and policy in Latin America: The role of Technical Assistance, 83 Chi.-Kent L. Rev. 91, 107 (2008).

[62] *Mehta/Agarwal/Singh*, Politics Trumps Economics, 2007, p. 16.

[63] *Ibid.*

[64] *Ibid.*

[65] *Ibid.*

Hence despite ongoing liberalization and privatization, markets in developing countries are generally still immature. This results in a pervasiveness of state-owned facilities or a high number of enterprises that enjoy a preferential treatment by the state.[66] The pervasiveness of state-imputed enterprises is also based on a frequent perception by the civil society that the state guarantees essential facilities and basic infrastructure for the country, better than a private entity could.[67]

2.2.1.3 Institutional Incapacities

Usually competition authorities in developing countries are coping with a lack of resources (human, material or financial) in order to enforce the competition law effectively.[68] Legal and economic expertise in matters of competition law are rare in countries where the academic structure is only accessible for a small elite.[69] Additionally, the private sector is usually capable of offering more attractive work conditions, thereby skimming the few well-trained persons from the public sector.[70] The fluctuation of personnel also hampers the creation of an "institutional memory".[71]

The lack of expertise is even accentuated by the immaturity of the agency. Although the learning curve of a young authority might be very steep and often technical assistance is provided to the developing agency, achieving efficient mechanisms is a matter of time. Errors are particularly problematic regarding the civil support, because they can reduce the credibility of the agency. Even more so, during the initial phase of building up a competition authority, choosing the right cases is a highly sensible matter.[72]

Finally, the issue of data shortcomings and lack of experience concerns all market participants, including professional associations, but also the judiciary.[73] Therefore,

---

[66] In this regard see *Smith-Hillman*: "Incomplete privatization enables the State to maintain a dominant position in several industries, potentially laying the basis for the abuse of a dominant position funded through access to public funds.", *Smith-Hillman,* The Prospect of a Caribbean Competition Policy, 40 J. W. Trade 405, 416 (2006).

[67] This argument is also applied in the developed world, for example in the context of a preferential treatment of the telecommunication or electronic sector.

[68] *Trebilcock/Iacobucci*, Designing Competition Law Institutions, 41 Loy. U. Chi. L.J. 455, 467 (2010); *Gal,* Institutional Solutions when Antitrust Enforcement Resources are Scarce, 41 Loy. U. Chi. L.J. 417, 468 (2010); *Dabbah,* Competition Law and Policy in Developing Countries, 33/3 W. Comp. 457, 468 (2010).

[69] Even in relatively developed competition law regimes such as Jamaica (since 1994), there are only few competition law experts, see *Stewart,* An Empirical Examination of Competition Issues in Selected Caricom Countries, 2004, p. 18.

[70] *Dabbah,* Competition Law and Policy in Developing Countries, 33/3 W. Comp. 457, 468 (2010).

[71] *Kovacic,* Creating New Competition Policy Institutions in Transition Economies, 23 Brook. J. Int'l. Law 403, 437 (1997).

[72] *Stewart/Clarke/Joekes,* Competition Law in Action, 2007, p. 29.

[73] *Kovacic,* Institutional Foundations for Economic Legal Reform in Transition Economies, 77 Chi.-Kent L. Rev. 265, 308 (2001); *Bakhoum,* A Dual Language in Modern Competition Law?, 34/3 W. Comp. 495, 509 (2011).

competition law enforcement by the competition authority cannot be compensated by trade associations' initiatives or by an efficient judicial control of competition-law-related matters. Even well-educated judges regularly lack the necessary competition law specific legal and economic expertise.[74]

2.2.1.4 Difficulties in Dealing with International Anticompetitive Practices

International anticompetitive practices can consist of an international export cartel, cross-border economic activity or the involvement of multinational enterprises. Developing countries can only to a limited extent threaten a foreign firm or a large multinational enterprise in case of a competition law infringement.[75] Limited gains from the presence of the foreign firm on the affected market might be an incentive for the firm to exit the market, instead of abstaining from the anticompetitive conduct. The "exit"-option might even be a threat that the firm uses in order to pressure the competition law agency. Even if the developing country is only trying to address the subsidiary of a large multinational enterprise, the same difficulties arise.

Political interferences from the home jurisdiction of the multinational enterprise may also impede the effective enforcement of competition law. Based on the assumption that a country's economic size is positively correlated with its political power, it may be difficult to keep up with the resistance of larger and more developed countries, in which the conduct of the firm might have positive effects.[76] Necessary cooperation with more developed jurisdictions might therefore be difficult, in particular concerning the gathering of necessary information.[77] In the view of globalization, developing countries are often trying to adopt their national legislation to the needs of the foreign investor at the expense of domestic interests and needs.[78]

Finally, effective competition law enforcement against large international firms also depends on the general administrative structure and public institutions. Large firms might try to avoid sanctions by interrupting an investigation through judicial appeals. Given the "deep pockets" of international companies and also bearing in mind the frequently slow judiciary in developing countries, the actual adoption and

---

[74] *Dabbah*, Competition Law and Policy in Developing Countries, 33/3 W. Comp. 457, 469 (2010).

[75] *Gal*, The Unique Enforcement Challenges Faced by Small Economies, 33 Fordham Int'l. L.J. 1, 20 (2009).

[76] *Gal*, The Unique Enforcement Challenges Faced by Small Economies, 33 Fordham Int'l. L.J. 1, 23 (2009).

[77] For developing countries it is in particular difficult to enter into cooperation agreements with developed jurisdictions. For more details on this problematic issue see below in Sect. 2.2.4.

[78] *Salah, M. M.* notes that codes of investments have more and more become canvassers: "On note ainsi que les codes des investissements se font de plus en plus racoleurs!". See *Salah M.M,* La Mise en Concurrence des Systèmes juridiques nationaux, XV R.I.D.E. 251, 281 (2001).

enforcement of a competition decision might be delayed considerably and drives up the authority's costs.

2.2.2 *Politically Related Enforcement Difficulties*

Competition law enforcement moreover relates to the industrial and trade policy of a country.[79] Irrespective of the form of enforcement—administrative, through private or criminal law[80]—it constitutes an act that is influenced by public policy and thus also relies on the prevailing political opinion.[81] The impact of political influences on competition law enforcement is however often underemphasized.[82]

2.2.2.1 Competition Authorities' Lack of Independence

The lack of operative, personal or financial independence is a prominent feature of developing countries' administrative and public institutions.[83] One has to differentiate between operational and structural independence.[84] The former refers to the institutional position of the agency, while the latter refers to the actual or effective decision-making power of the agency.

The influence from interest groups is very strong. This is *inter alia* due to the small market size and strong concentration, where the economic influence is distributed among few market participants. They are also able to exercise pressure on the political sector. The problem is even aggravated in micro-economies, such as the islands in the Caribbean. Elites are generally very prevalent in developing countries

[79] On the interdependencies of economic development, poverty and competition law and policy, see *Fox,* Economic Development, Poverty, and Antitrust: The Other Path, 13 Sw. J.L. Trade Americas 101 (2007); *Fox,* in: *Drexl/Bakhoum/Fox/Gal/Gerber,* Competition Policy and Regional Integration in Developing Countries, 2012, p. 273 *Gerber,* in: *Drexl/Bakhoum/Fox/Gal/Gerber,* Competition Policy and Regional Integration in Developing Countries, 2012, p. 253.

[80] On different forms of antitrust enforcement, see *Borrell,* Choosing among American, European, or no antitrust at all, 2005 <http://ssrn.com/abstract=669282> accessed 11 November 2018.

[81] This research relies on a broad definition of the term "political". "Political" thus refers to any action of an individual or institution that is based on the creation, exercise or maintenance of political authority.

[82] *Gerber,* in: *Drexl/Bakhoum/Fox/Gal/Gerber,* Competition Policy and Regional Integration in Developing Countries, 2012, pp. 253, 253.

[83] Public-choice-theory-related considerations are deliberately left out, because they are not a distinct feature of developing countries' institutions, but may also apply to institutions of developed jurisdictions. See *Dabbah,* Competition Law and Policy in Developing Countries, 33/3 W. Comp. 457, 466 (2010).

[84] *Clark,* Competition Advocacy: Challenges for Developing Countries, 6/4 OECD J. Comp. L. Policy 69, 70 (2005).

and therefore determine the staff of influential positions in politics and economics.[85] From a practical point of view incentives to enforce the law consequently are low if the competition law infringer in the private sector is a friend of or even related to the competition authority's staff.[86]

Changes of governments in developing countries are very frequent and politicians underlie a high fluctuation. Staff is not only lost due to better offers from the private sector, but also through replacements initiated by new governments.[87] In the same vein, a functioning competition authority can be dismantled by the creation of other governmental bodies or by the erosion of the private sector and market through far-reaching state intervention.[88] Therefore, instead of being able to rely on a constant body of staff and knowledge, competition authorities in developing countries are usually highly dependent on the individuals' effort and expertise.

2.2.2.2 Lack of Political Incentive to Effectively Enforce Competition Law

The preponderance of strong interest groups and state-owned enterprises leads to a conflict of interest during the enforcement of competition law. This is especially true if the notion of competition is new and the business sector is unaware of its benefits.[89] Even if competition laws exist in the books, there might be a lacking political will to enforce it. In Latin America, the lacking incentive to enforce competition law partly resulted from the enforcers' and practitioners' perception of it, as being conceived in a different legal tradition, namely, in the US legal tradition.[90] In addition, corruption and cronyism attribute to reluctant enforcement.[91]

---

[85] *OECD,* Small Economies and Competition Policy: A Background Paper, 2003, p. 8 <http://vi.unctad.org/windiesst09/docs/presentations/wednesday13/oecdsmalleconomybackground.pdf> accessed 11 November 2018.

[86] *Stewart* describes the Caribbean societies as "extremely stratified, with a strong correlation between race, class, unequal distribution of wealth and income that creates a 'caste' system and generates social tension and instability." See *Stewart,* in: *Drexl/Bakhoum/Fox/Gal/Gerber,* Competition Policy and Regional Integration in Developing Countries, 2012, pp. 161, 163f.

[87] Regarding "The phenomenon of short-lived governments", see *Dabbah*, Competition Law and Policy in Developing Countries, 33/3 W. Comp. 457, 465 (2010).

[88] This was the case in Venezuela, in which the private sector has been expropriated in the context of creating a socialist market system. In October 2013, the High Authority for the People's Defence Economy, the highest supervisory body for private production, was created. For more information see *Curiel Leidenz,* in: *Drexl/Bagnoli,* State-Initiated Restraints of Competition, 2015, pp. 213–238.

[89] *Gerber,* in: *Drexl/Bakhoum/Fox/Gal/Gerber,* Competition Policy and Regional Integration in Developing Countries, 2012, pp. 253, 260. For more information see below in Sect. 2.2.3.2.

[90] *Alvarez/Horna*, Implementing competition law and policy in Latin America: The role of Technical Assistance, 83 Chi.-Kent L. Rev. 91, 104 (2008).

[91] *Baetge*, Globalisierung des Wettbewerbsrechts, 2009, pp. 48ff.

2.2.3 *Socio-Cultural Enforcement Difficulties in Developing Countries*

The more a legal rule corresponds to the prevailing social values in a society, the more effective it will be.[92] In this context, some authors even argue that the social dimension or reputation of a competition law system should be given priority, thereby arguing that developing countries should focus on competition advocacy more than on enforcement in its narrow sense.[93] Competition law is not merely sanctioning law, but also entails rights and protection, such as the protection of consumers and of enterprises that are harmed by anticompetitive behaviour.

2.2.3.1 Systematic Poverty

In many developing countries, systematic poverty causes distribution problems. Small elites are dominant in the private business and political influential positions and try to distribute profits among themselves, thereby excluding the large portion of poor citizens. This clearly contradicts the notion of an "economic democracy."[94] A competition law authority therefore has to put a special emphasis on the passing-on of benefits to the consumers, in order for them to profit from competition law enforcement, for example through the reduction of prices. Moreover, sectors that concern the basic needs and provide for a number of employment opportunities, such as food and agriculture, should be given special attention.[95] The success of enforcing a competition law in developing economies will therefore depend upon "how the gains are distributed, rather than on growth per se."[96]

---

[92] *Alvarez/Horna*, Implementing competition law and policy in Latin America: The role of Technical Assistance, 83 Chi.-Kent L. Rev. 91, 95 (2008).

[93] On the general role of competition advocacy, see *Evenett*, Competition Advocacy, 26 Nw. J. Int'l. L. Bus. 495, 495ff. (2006).

[94] *Fox*, Economic Development, Poverty, and Antitrust, 13 Sw. J.L. Trade Americas 101, 105ff. (2007).

[95] *Jenny* inter alia highlights concentrations in trade or price-fixing as prominent anticompetitive practices in developing countries. From empirical evidence he sees that the following sectors are mostly affected by anticompetitive practices: bread, chicken, beer, retail distribution, cement, aluminium, steel, telecommunications, railways, bus services, freight, professional services. See *Jenny*, Cartels and Collusion in Developing Countries, 29/1 W. Comp. 109, 113ff., 132ff. (2006).

[96] *Mehta/Agarwal/Singh*, Politics Trumps Economics, 2007, p. 23.

2.2.3.2 Lack of Competition Culture

Experiences from a sample of hundred countries show that the intensity of application of competition legislation and overall government effectiveness explain a substantial part of the perception of the effectiveness of competition policy.[97] Competition culture is an important element of competition law, because awareness of a right by its right holders, such as consumers, is a necessary precondition for its enforcement. However, due to frail academic infrastructure, weak professional associations and/or consumer groups, competition culture remains limited in developing countries. Even worse, general awareness of the notion of competition; of the benefits of a market economy in general; of its benefits to consumers in particular; and also to the private business sector are often underdeveloped.[98] If the private sector does not acknowledge that competition law offers economic freedom instead of merely restricting economic decisions of firms, it will be extremely difficult to achieve deterrence of competition law.

2.2.3.3 The Need to Protect Minorities or Disadvantaged Population Groups in Developing Countries

A further aspect of socio-cultural particularities in developing countries may be the necessity to protect minorities.[99] Notwithstanding the fact that racial discrimination is also an issue in developed nations, elites tend to originate from the same cultural and ethnic backgrounds in developing countries in particular, where political and economic elites are very small.[100] While one has to abstain from over-generalizing the link between economic or political power and ethnical background of citizens, there is evidence that indicates that civil society in developing countries tends to be very attentive of racial differences.[101] Thus one can note that the informal sector is

---

[97] *Krakowski*, Competition Policy Works, 2005, p. 14 <http://papers.ssrn.com/sol3/papers.cfm?abstract_id=854908> accessed 11 November 2018.

[98] In this vein, in the WAEMU, national governments are often called upon by consumers to provide for prices and quality products, for example via price-fixing; see *Bakhoum,* A Developing-Country Perspective on "Global Competition", 28 October 2011, Chicago, p. 14.

[99] Apart from the discussion on the necessity to provide special rules for minorities, there is also a general ongoing debate on the appropriate goals of competition law in developing countries, see this regard *Bakhoum,* in: *Zimmer,* The Goals of Competition Law, 2012, pp. 408–440.

[100] This is particularly the case in the Caribbean. *Stewart* states in this regard: "The role of colour is still very much a factor in social mobility. The race factor impinges natively on access to finances and other support systems, and stifles entrepreneurship.", see *Stewart,* in: *Drexl/Bakhoum/Fox/Gal/Gerber,* Competition Policy and Regional Integration in Developing Countries, 2012, pp. 161, 164.

[101] In this context, the case of the Peruvian competition authority, INDECOPI, on a case of alleged racial discrimination in 1998 offers interesting insights on the Peruvian society. A Peruvian newspaper published a letter of the editor *Lenkiza Valcárcel*, in which she complained of an alleged racial discrimination against her darker skinned friend by an upscale club bouncer in Lima. Despite the lack of an unambiguous competence provision of the INDECOPI, the latter decided to proceed based on economic and market considerations, instead of strictly human rights issues. For more

often composed by parts of the population with similar ethnic or cultural backgrounds.[102] In highly concentrated societies, where elites exercise a lot of influence in many sectors, competition law should also protect the indigenous and disenfranchised groups.[103]

In the CARICOM region, the taxi drivers in St. Lucia offer an interesting example. Most of them are black and come from parts of the population with lower income.[104] On the other hand, companies owned by white families aim at increasing their market power on the tourism management market and on the transportation sector generally. Although the expansion of these companies could arguably render the taxi drivers' market more competitive (at least in the short run), it would lead to the displacement of the ancient taxi drivers and cause severe racial tensions in the region.[105] This argument is in line with the protection of SMEs and requires the application of exemption provisions and very careful examination before enforcing competition law vigorously.

Another related aspect is the special treatment of disadvantaged regions or sectors. Weak infrastructures, but also natural disasters, affect the productivity and efficacy of different regions or sectors. Furthermore, aspects such as the creation or maintenance of employment possibilities is a factor that is usually not incorporated in classical competition law enforcement, but which might be relevant for developing countries.

2.2.4 Lack of Formal Cooperation Mechanisms on the International Level

Despite growing participation of developing countries in international competition platforms, such as the International Competition Network (ICN),[106] actual cooperation or information-sharing on international issues remains scarce.[107] Accordingly,

---

information on the case see *Boza*, Tailor-Made Competition Policy in a Standardizing World, 2005, pp. 62ff.

[102] This is the case in the Caribbean. According to *Stewart* "(…) the majority of the black population [is left] in poverty and [is] engaging in informal economic activities to survive.", see *Stewart,* in: *Drexl/Bakhoum/Fox/Gal/Gerber,* Competition Policy and Regional Integration in Developing Countries, 2012, pp. 161, 170.

[103] *Stewart/Clarke/Joekes,* Competition Law in Action, 2007, p. 23. South Africa is a very prominent example for this. Its competition law includes special public policy considerations that aim at the alleviation of (often historically created) economic inequalities. For more information on the new South African competition law, see *Lewis,* Enforcing Competition Rules in South Africa, 2013, pp. 5ff.

[104] *Stewart/Clarke/Joekes,* Competition Law in Action, 2007, p. 23.

[105] *Stewart,* in: *Drexl/Bakhoum/Fox/Gal/Gerber,* Competition Policy and Regional Integration in Developing Countries, 2012, pp. 161, 164; *Stewart*, An Empirical Examination of Competition Issues in Selected Caricom Countries, 2004, p. 121; *Stewart/Clarke/Joekes,* Competition Law in Action, 2007, p. 23.

[106] <http://www.internationalcompetitionnetwork.org/> accessed 11 November 2018.

[107] *UNCTAD*, The relationship between competition, competitiveness and development, 2002, p. 8.

an extraterritorial application of national competition law is extremely dependent on the bilateral cooperation of the jurisdiction in which the allegedly anticompetitive practice took place. However, political incentives for cooperation between developed and developing countries are lower than between two developed countries. On the one hand, this is due to a lack of economic interest of the developed country in the developing country's economy. In a similar vein, the allegedly anticompetitive practice might originate from a good tax-paying company that is located in the developed country. In the absence of political or economic importance of the developing country, the incentives for the respective developed country to sanction the anticompetitive behaviour of the (possibly domestic) enterprise in another country are thus low. On the other hand, limping administrative and judicial structures in developing countries, as well as the vulnerability towards corruption might refrain developed countries from sharing or disclosing information.

Chapter 3
Terms and Premises of Regional Competition Law Enforcement

3.1 Taxonomy of Institutional Design in Regional Competition Law Enforcement

Clearly, the institutional design of a RTA does not constitute the only factor that determines the success of regional competition law enforcement. General enforcement difficulties related to economical, socio-cultural or political parameters have an essential impact. Yet the correlation between these prevailing circumstances and a certain institutional design cannot be neglected, as institutions do not constitute abstract and isolated constructs. Rather, institutions can be defined as a set of rules that set a standard of behaviour for the members of a society.[1] On the other hand, organizations are groups of individuals that follow a common purpose in order to reach a common goal.[2] Organizations, such as public agencies, are created in order to render these institutions effective and to enforce the set of rules. The interplay of both determines the framework of rules for members in a society.[3] Institutions and their particular design are thus entwined with a society and its members: on the one hand they are defined by the society's purpose and on the other hand they set the rules for the society.

In the context of a discussion on the structural design of a RTA, a broad institutional approach on integration offers interesting insights.[4] It offers insights on the

[1] "Institutions are the rules of the game in a society or, more formally, are the humanly devised constraints that shape human interaction." *North,* Institutions, institutional change and economic performance, 1992, p. 3.

[2] "[Organizations] (...) are groups of individuals bound by some common purpose to achieve objectives." *North,* Institutions, institutional change and economic performance, 1992, p. 5.

[3] *North,* Institutions, institutional change and economic performance, 1992, p. 7.

[4] There exists no explicit legal integration theory. Political integration theory is more oriented towards the assessment of the integration process itself and economic integration theory focuses more on external trade and industrial policies and different integration forms. See *Behrens,*

J. Molestina, *Regional Competition Law Enforcement in Developing Countries*,
Munich Studies on Innovation and Competition 9,
https://doi.org/10.1007/978-3-662-58525-2_3

role of social arrangements on the enforcement of competition laws and raises issues of law and economics.[5]

Translated into a competition law regime, formal institutions comprise the substantial codified competition laws, usually containing the core provisions such as abuse of dominance, and the prohibition of cartels. On the other hand, competition culture is the most relevant informal uncodified competition-law-related institution, which is defined by the legal and economic history of a jurisdiction. Enforcement agencies constitute organizations that have the common goal of rendering substantive competition law effective. Procedural rules are the codification of this enforcement process. Competition policy enforcement is hence influenced by a combination of different institutional factors.[6]

A regional integration group also has to demarcate competences between the national and regional level: the vertical delimitation of competences. The concrete enforcement measures that are adopted thus additionally depend on the internal vertical centralization or decentralization of decision-making power.[7] This also includes controlling mechanisms, for example through judicial reviews. Finally, underlying legal principles of regional law application will influence the allocation of competences in the first hand or might solve disputes of conflicting competences or legislations.

Hence, the design of a regional competition law enforcement regime does not rely on a single criterion of competence allocation. Rather, it is a composition of competences of regional and national institutions and the relation of regional and national competition laws, which are described as "dimensions" of regional competition law enforcement in the following sections. The design of a regional competition law regime covers the following questions: Which entity enforces what? Which law is applicable when? Which entity can legislate what? What happens in case of conflicting laws or enforcement measures? In this sense decentralized and centralized competition law enforcement are not opposing and exclusionary designs, but define the endpoints of the spectrum of different enforcement degrees.

Integrationstheorie, Internationale wirtschaftliche Integration als Gegenstand politologischer, ökonomischer und juristischer Forschung, RabelsZ 8, 8ff. (1981). Therefore, this study adopts a broad institutional approach towards integration, which is capable of combining political, economical, socio-cultural and legal aspects.

[5] *De León,* Institutional Analysis of Competition Policy in Transition and Developing Countries, 3 Wash. U. Global Stud. L. Rev. 405, 405 (2004).

[6] *De León,* Institutional Analysis of Competition Policy in Transition and Developing Countries, 3 Wash. U. Global Stud. L. Rev. 405, 406 (2004). *De León* organizes the institutional factors at three levels: the organizational, the ideological and cultural level. This study focuses on the organizational level by comparing the organizational arrangements of regional trade agreements.

[7] *Behrens*, Integrationstheorie, Internationale wirtschaftliche Integration als Gegenstand politologischer, ökonomischer und juristischer Forschung, RabelsZ 8, 12 (1981).

3.2 The Multi-Layered Notion of 'Enforcement' in Competition Law

Similar to the notion of institutional design, the notion of enforcement entails several tasks that have to be fulfilled by a competition law authority. Typically enforcement measures in the narrow sense are the investigatory and sanctioning functions of a competition agency. Furthermore, one could also add the supervision of the market and its actors. In systems, in which competition laws are applied by sectorial agencies on specific sectors, the agency is also vested with a regulatory function.

The advocacy role of competition agencies has also become widely acknowledged.[8] According to the ICN[9] "(c)ompetition advocacy refers to those activities conducted by the competition authority related to the promotion of a competitive environment for economic activities by means of non-enforcement mechanisms, mainly through its relationships with other governmental entities and by increasing public awareness of the benefits of competition" (advocacy as follow-up).[10] *De León*, regarding Latin America but certainly paradigmatic for other regions in the stage of development as well, points out that "the reluctance of businesses to compete is by-product of prior interventionist policies that have influenced the Latin American business culture."[11] Accordingly, competition advocacy, in particular educating businesses and consumers, constitutes an integral step towards the achievement of effective competition law enforcement and in the long run greater competitiveness.

Kovacic also includes research and studies to the forms of competition policy.[12] Although research and studies of markets are not part of enforcement in the narrow sense, the collection of data helps an agency to understand the prevailing conditions of a jurisdiction, which facilitates the appropriate and efficient use of enforcement tools.

Having highlighted the different layers of enforcement, this does not imply that an agency has to fulfil them all at the same time. Different enforcement measures have to be applied at a different time or are only applicable by a mature agency.[13]

---

[8] *Evenett*, Competition Advocacy, 26 Nw. J. Int'l. L. Bus. 495, 495ff. (2006); *Clark*, Competition Advocacy: Challenges for Developing Countries, 6/4 OECD J. Comp. L. Policy 69, 69ff. (2005).

[9] <http://www.internationalcompetitionnetwork.org/> accessed 11 November 2018.

[10] *Advocacy and Competition Policy*, Advocacy and Competition Policy, 22–23 September 2002, Naples, p. 2 <http://www.internationalcompetitionnetwork.org/uploads/library/doc358.pdf> accessed 11 November 2018. While the ICN's definition seems to exclude the advocacy role from the enforcement mechanisms of an agency, this study counts advocacy to the enforcement in the wider sense.

[11] *De León*, An Institutional Assessment of Antitrust Policy, 2009, p. 381.

[12] *Kovacic*, Institutional Foundations for Economic Legal Reform in Transition Economies, 77 Chi.-Kent L. Rev. 265, 283 (2001).

[13] This study does not differentiate between the sequencing of different enforcement measures.

Yet, all enforcement measures have in common that they have as their objective that "the real enforcement of rules results in the absence of violation."[14]

3.3 Measuring the Efficiency of Regional Competition Law Enforcement in RTAs Among Developing Countries

Generally, the competition law enforcement's efficiency is difficult to measure, because the benefits might not become instantly visible (e.g. through changes of consumer prices), but might lead to a general change of market structures or long-term deterrence. In the same vein, the frequency of detected anticompetitive practices can only be evaluated in relation to the number of anticompetitive practices within a territory. Yet, this presumes that anticompetitive practices are revealed in the first place. In addition the measurement of competition law enforcement's efficiency entails several points of reference and is not solely outcome based. *Smith-Hillman* aptly summarizes that "[t]he effective implementation of competition policy can be measured through three critical indicators: law enforcement, competition advocacy and institutional effectiveness."[15] In any case, measuring efficiency of competition law enforcement requires large sets of data that cover the market situation before and after competition law enforcement and that give sufficiently detailed information in order to establish causalities.

Measuring the successes and the failures of regional competition law enforcement in developing countries is an even more difficult task. This is on the one hand attributed to the several layers of regional competition law enforcement. Regional integration implies two points of reference, namely national markets and the common market. In this context, enforcement measures might create benefits for one market, while negatively affecting another.

As regional competition authorities are genuinely young and have only dealt with a limited number of cases, it is generally difficult to draw conclusions regarding their efficiency.[16] Moreover, given the preponderance of small market economies in RTAs among developing countries, the optimum of competition law enforcement might differ from a RTA among developed countries.[17] In fact, often-present high levels of market concentration are not a result of inefficient competition

---

[14] *Frison-Roche,* in: *Drexl/Idot/Monéger,* Economic Theory and Competition Law 2009, pp. 211, 212.

[15] *Smith-Hillman,* The Prospect of a Caribbean Competition Policy, 40 J. W. Trade 405, 418 (2006).

[16] The mere number of cases that a competition authority has dealt with does not constitute a useful indicator for its efficiency. *Kovacic/Hollman/Grant* state: "To be busy is not the same thing as to be productive.", see *Kovacic/Hollman/Grant,* How does your competition agency measure up?, 7 Eur. Comp. J. 25, 28 (2011).

[17] In this context, *De León* argues that "(…) the failure to measure antitrust effectiveness lies (…) in the lack of an unanimously accepted normative yardstick to measure the success of the policy.", see *De León,* Latin American Competition Policy, 83 Chi.-Kent L. Rev. 39, 40 (2008).

law enforcement, but are based on the small size of markets or lacking productivity or entrepreneurship. In addition, the vulnerability to corruption, political instability and partially also natural disasters affects the market processes' transparency and impairs the establishment of clear causal links between competition law enforcement and market outcomes.

For the measurement difficulties mentioned above, this study adopts a selective method of evaluation, according to which it analyses how specific elements of an institutional design cope with specific prevailing conditions. Such a "punctual" approach is incapable to draw a general solution, according to which decentralized or centralized regional competition law enforcement is favourable, but it offers assistance for developing jurisdictions to better understand processes within their regional competition law system. It thereby offers guidance regarding a potential re-allocation of competences. To sum up, this work aims at identifying possible incentives or disincentives for competition law enforcement in developing countries that arise out of a certain institutional design.

Chapter 4
Structure of the Study

Irrespective of the strong influence of the European competition law system, the WAEMU, the AndeanC and the CARICOM have adopted different institutional designs, ranging from a decentralized system, in which member states and national competition law authorities are vested with most competition law enforcement competences (e.g. CARICOM) to a centralized system, in which the main focus of competition law enforcement remains regional (e.g. WAEMU).

An institutional design is not detached from economical, political, socio-cultural or legal circumstances. Rather, it has to fit in a RTA's general background conditions that have an impact on competition law enforcement in the member countries of a RTA. These conditions have been titled "competition constraints".[1] Hence, the premise underlying this study is that the interplay between "competition constraints" and an institutional design is an important factor that determines the efficacy of regional competition law enforcement. The study identifies the impact of these "competition constraints" on the degree of decentralization or centralization and delimits the optimal degree in respect to the given "competition constraints" within a RTA with special regard to the particular conditions in developing countries.[2]

Part II contains a description of the institutional design of the WAEMU, the AndeanC and the CARICOM regional competition law system. Particular focus is placed on the institutional elements and allocation of competences that shape the degree of centralized or decentralized competition law enforcement. Instead of merely describing the institutional design of the WAEMU, the AndeanC and the

[1] *Bakhoum/Molestina,* in: *Drexl/Bakhoum/Fox/Gal/Gerber,* Competition Policy and Regional Integration in Developing Countries, 2012, pp. 89, 103ff. See also below regarding the competition constraints' impact on an institutional design, Part III Chap. 12.

[2] Although this study places special emphasis on the particular conditions in developing countries, this does not exclude the identification of elements that generally influence regional competition law enforcement—also in developed countries.

J. Molestina, *Regional Competition Law Enforcement in Developing Countries*,
Munich Studies on Innovation and Competition 9,
https://doi.org/10.1007/978-3-662-58525-2_4

CARICOM, the section discerns efficiencies and inefficiencies that stem from a certain institutional design. Moreover, the comparison of the experiences of the three RTAs leads to certain conclusions on specific institutional elements. Some general consistencies in regional competition law enforcement depending on a specific institutional design can already be outlined at this point.

The section follows the above outlined taxonomy of institutional design of regional competition law enforcement. In this context, the section is divided into five dimensions: (1) the substantive regional competition law provisions, (2) the competence to legislate on competition law matters, (3) the organization of the competition law enforcing authorities, (4) the enforcement procedures of regional competition law in the narrow sense and (5) the underlying legal principles that govern the allocation of competences and resolve potential disputes between laws, authorities or enforcement measures. Similar to the teeth of gearwheels, the dimensions mesh together and should thus not be understood as alternative but interlocked parts of a regional competition law system.

Part III constitutes the theoretical part of the work. It constitutes a general evaluation of the experiences of the WAEMU, the AndeanC and the CARICOM and draws general conclusions on regional competition law enforcement in developing countries based on the typical prevailing enforcement difficulties. These conclusions set the stage and define the general conditions that should be taken into account in designing the institutional structure of a regional competition law enforcement regime.

In a second step, the study takes the perspective of a regional legislator who designs a regional enforcement system. Shaping the elements of regional competition law enforcement cannot remain a one-dimensional analysis. Rather, it is necessary to take into account the interdependencies between several institutional elements. Instead of pointing out the single effects of the design of a specific element, the work discerns possible cumulative effects. The results of the previous analysis are then applied to the systems in the WAEMU, the AndeanC and the CARICOM. The work formulates careful propositions regarding a possible reallocation of competences in order to improve the competition law enforcement efficiency in the respective system.

The final section covers the relation between "competition constraints" and the institutional design of a regional competition law enforcement system. It formulates guidelines, according to which under a given "competition constraint" certain institutional elements should be designed rather centralized or decentralized.

Part II
The Institutional Design of Regional Competition Law Enforcement in the WAEMU, AndeanC and CARICOM

Chapter 5
Dimension I: The Content of Substantive Law

5.1 Core Substantive Competition Law Provisions

5.1.1 Anticompetitive Agreements and Abuse of Dominant Position

All of the three regional trade agreements entail provisions that prohibit agreements between undertakings that have the object or effect to restrict competition: Article 88 lit. a) Treaty of Dakar; Articles 4, 7 of Decision 608; Article 177(1) lit. a), Article 177(2) of the Revised Treaty of Chaguaramas.

The abuse of dominance is also prohibited in all three jurisdictions: Article 88 lit. b) of Treaty of Dakar[1]; Articles 4, 8 of Decision 608; Article 177 lit. b), Article 178 and Article 179 of the Revised Treaty of Chaguaramas.

5.1.2 Subjective Scope of Application

While the WAEMU's[2] and the CARICOM's[3] competition provisions refer to "enterprises", the AndeanC prohibits and sanctions conducts exercised by "economic agents" according to Article 4 of Decision 608. Article 1 of Decision 608 defines the notion of an "economic agent" as all natural or judicial persons, of public or private

[1] Regulation no. 02/2002/CM/WAEMU specifies the general prohibition in Art. 88 of Treaty of Dakar. Article 3 of the Regulation includes *per se* prohibitions regarding anti-competitive agreements, Article 4 defines an abuse of dominance and prohibits certain conducts such as the imposition of inequitable sale or purchase terms or prices.

[2] Article 88(1) and (2) Treaty of Dakar.

[3] Article 174(1) Revised Treaty of Chaguaramas.

J. Molestina, *Regional Competition Law Enforcement in Developing Countries*, Munich Studies on Innovation and Competition 9,
https://doi.org/10.1007/978-3-662-58525-2_5

law, with or without profit that offer or demand material or immaterial goods, or services in the market, as well as unions or associations of such persons.[4]

The WAEMU also follows an equal broad approach as the European definition. Annex 1 of Regulation no. 03/2002/CM/UEMOA, defines the notion of an undertaking as a "unified organisation of personal, material and immaterial elements, which exercises an economic activity, with profit making aim, of durable way, irrespective its legal status, private or public, or its mode of financing, and which can take decisions autonomously".[5]

According to Article 1 of the Revised Treaty of Chaguaramas the notion of enterprise "means any person or type of organisation, other than a non-profit organisation, involved in the production of or the trade in goods, or the provision of services".[6] The exclusion of non-profit organisations from the definition creates a loophole, because it is difficult to draw a clear-cut line between completely altruistic non-profit companies and commercially active companies. This issue can eventually only be resolved by the Caribbean Court of Justice, which holds the exclusive and compulsory jurisdiction on the interpretation of the treaty.[7]

While the three RTAs have adopted a broad definition of enterprise, the AndeanC's definition leads to the broadest subjective scope of application of the three regional competition laws. Interestingly, the WAEMU has excluded non-profit organizations in contrast to the European notion of an undertaking.

5.1.3 Dealing with State-Related Behaviour and Public Undertakings

State-related behaviour with a potential effect of distorting competition can encompass a broad range of practices: direct state aids in form of subsidies or indirect advantages, for example granted in the form of tax aid schemes or tariffs, the establishment of public undertakings with particular rights or other state measures. According to European competition law, state aid is defined as an advantage in any form whatsoever conferred on a selective basis to undertakings by national public

[4] Article 1 of Decision 608: "toda persona natural o jurídica, de derecho público o privado, con o sin fines de lucro, que oferta o demanda bienes materiales o inmateriales, o servicios en el mercado, así como los gremios o asociaciones que los agrupen".

[5] Definition of an undertaking: "Dans l'application de la législation communautaire de la concurrence, la notion d'entreprise se définit comme une organisation unitaire d'éléments personnels, matériels, et immatériels, exerçant une activité économique, à titre onéreux, de manière durable, indépendamment de son statut juridique, public ou privé, et de son mode de financement, et jouissant d'une autonomie de décision. (…)".

[6] On the possible definitions of the concept of "non-profit organisation", see *Kaczorowska-Ireland*, Competition Law in the CARICOM Single Market and Economy, 2015, pp. 71ff. She argues in favour of a narrow interpretation.

[7] Article 211 of the Revised Treaty of Chaguaramas

authorities.[8] The underlying aim is to prevent governments from distorting competition. This is especially necessary in young and recently privatized and deregulated markets, in which the notion of the state as market player and provider of economic goods is still present. Closely linked to the notion of state aids, is the establishment of public undertakings, which in many cases hold a monopolistic position in a sector and profit from being financed by the government.

The issue of distorting state behaviour is further discussed under the theme of "competitive neutrality",[9] which "implies that no business entity is advantaged (or disadvantaged) solely because of its ownership."[10] The notion of "competitive neutrality" is broader than merely sanctioning anticompetitive behaviour conducted by the state, because it entails the installation of a general framework and mechanisms that generally encourage the identification and elimination of unjustified competitive advantages through the state.[11] One should thus generally analyse whether legislations enhance "competitive neutrality".

The treatment of state-related behaviour in the context of a competition policy is a highly sensible matter, because it touches core issues of a member state's sovereignty. In most cases states grant exclusive rights to undertakings or create public undertakings to guarantee the provision of public services. Regional competition law enforcement has to make sure that competition on the common market is not distorted by such exclusive treatments. Therefore, state aids constitute an area of possible conflicts between national and regional objectives and require careful balancing between national interests and the objective of the creation of a common market.

The WAEMU, the AndeanC and the CARICOM have acknowledged that a RTA's success largely depends on the commitment of the member states towards the obligations arising out of the regional rules and legal framework. In this vein, all three RTAs have adopted "loyalty clauses" similar to the European loyalty clause[12] that oblige member states to support the objectives of the regional agreement and to refrain from measures that could impede these objectives, in particular with regard

---

[8] Article 107 of the Treaty on the Functioning of the European Union (TFEU).

[9] *Healey,* Competitive Neutrality Project, 7 July 2013 <http://unctad.org/meetings/en/Presentation/RPP2013_Healey_en.pdf> accessed 11 November 2018.

[10] *Capobianco/Christiansen,* Competitive Neutrality and State-Owned Enterprises, 2011, p. 3, <http://www.oecd-ilibrary.org/docserver/download/5kg9xfgjdhg6.pdf?expires=1385377786&id=id&accname=guest&checksum=5544908D37FAB684ADDD3EADCFDF4438> accessed 11 November 2018.

[11] *Ibid.* According to *Capobianco/Christiansen* examples for government-created competitive advantages that distort competition are: outright subsidisation, concessionary financing and guarantees, other preferential treatment by government, monopolies and advantages of incumbency, captive equity, exemptions from bankruptcy rules and information advantages. *Ibid.,* pp. 6f. Moreover, also public procurement policies might hinder "competitive neutrality"; see in this regard *CUTS CCIER,* A Time for Action, 2010, p. 9.

[12] The loyalty clause used to be expressly included in European Law in the former Art. 10 TEC. Although, the TFEU does not entail an explicit provision of it, the principle still exists and is expressed indirectly, for example in the Art. 2(3) TFEU.

to the implementation of a common market. In the WAEMU, Article 7 of the Treaty of Dakar comprises a general loyalty clause, ensuring that member states adopt all necessary measures to realize the objectives of the Treaty of Dakar and refrain from impeding the latter. In the AndeanC, the Articles 36 and 37 of Decision 608 provide for the obligation of member states to respect the common market during the adoption and application of regulatory policies, to support regional instruments and to foster national enforcement authorities, mainly through the exchange of information and experiences with regard to competition.[13] In the CARICOM, Articles 170(1) lit. b) and 170(2) of the Revised Treaty of Chaguaramas instruct the member states to take necessary legislative and institutional steps to ensure consistency and compliance with the rules of competition. They are in accordance with Article 9 of the Revised Treaty, which generally governs that "Member States should take all appropriate measures (…) to ensure the carrying out of the obligations arising out of this Treaty or resulting from decision taken by the Organs and Bodies of the Community. (…) They shall abstain from any measure which could jeopardise the attainment of the objectives of the Treaty".[14]

The WAEMU competition law regime adopted a "dualist approach" to state-related anticompetitive behaviour. On the one hand, it adopted the prohibition of state aids that are capable of distorting competition in Article 88 lit. c) of the Treaty of Dakar, thereby following the European system. The application of Article 88 lit. c) is specified in the Regulation no. 04/2002/CM/UEMOA, which provides for an *ex ante* and a permanent control of state aids by the Commission.[15] Certain state aids are considered compatible with the common market, according to the non-exhaustive list in Article 3 of Regulation no. 04/2002/CM/UEMOA. Other state aids can only be granted after the consultation of the Advisory Committee of Competition,[16] according to Article 3(2) of the same Regulation. On the other hand, the WAEMU legislator included general provisions regarding anticompetitive practices related to

[13] There does not exist a definition of "regulatory measures" in Article 36 of Decision 608. In the Dictamen N° 01-2007 of the Secretariat General, the latter rejected a complaint of Colombian flower companies based on Article 36 of Decision 608 for the lack of a cross-border effect. It did not deal with the question whether the concerned state programs actually constituted regulatory measures in the sense of Article 36 of Decision 608 and if the implementation of these programs by the Colombian State actually fell under the subjective scope of application of Decision 608. In fact, the Colombian state had argued during the procedure that the programs did not fall under the scope of application of Decision 608, because Colombia was thereby not acting as an economic agent in the market, but only in its public function in the economy; see *Secretaría General de la Comunidad Andina,* Dictamen N° 01-2007, p. 9.

[14] For more information on the "loyalty clauses" with regard to the principle of effectiveness, see below Part II, Dimension V: Sect. 9.3.

[15] Réglement n° 04/2002/CM/UEMOA, relatif aux aides d'Etat à l'intérieur de l'Union Économique et Monétaire Ouest Africaine et aux modalités d'application de l'article 88(c) du traité, entered into force on 1 January 2003.

[16] The Advisory Committee of Competition constitutes an advisory entity in WAEMU competition law enforcement. For more information see below Dimension IV: Sect. 8.2.1.1.

a state in the Articles 5 and 6 of Regulation no. 02/2002/CM/UEMOA.[17] According to Article 6(1) of the Regulation, any measures contrary to the principles set out in Article 88 lit. a) and lit. b) of the Treaty of Dakar are prohibited, in particular through the creation of public undertakings or through the attribution with special powers for undertakings. In Article 6(2) of Regulation no. 02/2002/CM/UEMOA in accordance with Article 89 of the Treaty of Dakar, the WAEMU legislator provides for exemptions for such state-related anticompetitive practices, however emphasizes that even undertakings, charged with services of general economic interest or representing a fiscal monopoly, still remain within the scope of application of the Treaty of Dakar.[18] Directive no. 01/2002/CM/UEMOA *inter alia* sets out transparency obligations regarding the financial relation between member states and public undertakings.[19]

In the AndeanC, the definition of an economic agent is very broad and also includes public undertakings that exercise governmental or administrative tasks.[20] Thus, Article 7 of Decision 608, the provision on anticompetitive agreements, could partly cover the results from state intervention or actions by public undertakings without tackling state aids directly.[21] The broad definition of an economic agent was a clear result from the deficient former competition law provision, Decision 285, which did not cover governmental actions. This incompleteness was abused by member states, which engaged in market intervention without having to worry about principles of free competition.[22]

Due to the broad wording, state aids and the granting of exclusive rights to undertakings by the state, which have a distorting effect on the subregional market, could be subsumed under the scope of the Articles 36 and 37 of the Decision 608. However, Articles 36 and 37 of Decision 608 are mainly characterized as a promotion of competition and explicitly recognize the freedom of member states to enact market regulatory policies and measures.[23] The drafters of the regional competition

---

[17] Réglement n° 02/2002/CM/UEMOA, relatif aux pratiques anticoncurrentielles à l'intérieur de l'UEMOA, entered into force on 1 January 2003.

[18] Article 6(2) of Regulation no. 02/2002/CM/UEMOA.

[19] Directive n° 01/2002/CM/UEMOA relative à la transparence des relations financières d'une part entre les états membres et les entreprises publiques et d'autre part entre les états membres et les organisation internationales ou étrangères.

[20] *Secretaría General de la Comunidad Andina,* Guía Práctica para la aplicación de la Decisión 608 "Normas para la protección y promoción de la libre competencia en la Comunidad Andina", 2007, p. 7 <http://intranet.comunidadandina.org/Documentos/DTrabajo/SGdt396.doc> accessed 11 November 2018.

[21] Informe Técnico elaborado por *José María García Alvarez-Coque*, en el marco del Proyecto COMPETENCIA, Instrumentos de Apoyo al Sector Agropecuario y Competencia en la Comunidad Andina, SG/di 775, 9 December 2005, p. 56 (available from the author).

[22] *Falla/Quintana*, in: Pontificia Universidad Católica del Peru, Derecho Comunitario Andino, 2003, p. 143, 168.

[23] *Secretaría General de la Comunidad Andina,* Guía Práctica para la aplicación de la Decisión 608 "Normas para la protección y promoción de la libre competencia en la Comunidad Andina", 2007, p. 42 <http://intranet.comunidadandina.org/Documentos/DTrabajo/SGdt396.doc> accessed 11 November 2018.

law framework in the AndeanC refrained from adopting a principle of general incompatibility of state aids with free competition in the common market.[24] Article 36 of Decision 608 only provides for a specific procedure before the Andean Committee on the Defence of Free Competition[25] in case a regulatory measure of a member states distorts competition in the subregional market.

The exclusion of state aids from Decision 608 results from an explicit decision in the 3rd Reunion of Governmental Experts on 24 and 25 October 2001 during the drafting process of Decision 608.[26] The governmental experts were incapable to find a consensus on this matter.[27] Other regional rules that could be applicable to state aids are the rules on subsidies and antidumping, namely Decision 283,[28] Decision 456[29] and 457.[30] Although the Agreement of Cartagena, in Article 105, does not differentiate between provisions that prohibit the distortion of competition and measures related to trade such as dumping, the Andean legislator dealt with the regulation of subsidies and dumping and competition law matters separately.[31]

A possible explanation for the exclusion of state aids from the regional competition law provisions is the diverse national experiences as regards the regulation of state aids. While Bolivia and Ecuador had no national competition policy at all during the implementation of Decision 608, the Peruvian competition and intellectual property agency, the INDECOPI, was one of the first competition agencies that was vested with powers to control state actions that affect the market.[32] In the famous

[24] Informe Técnico elaborado por *José María García Alvarez-Coque*, en el marco del Proyecto COMPETENCIA, Instrumentos de Apoyo al Sector Agropecuario y Competencia en la Comunidad Andina, SG/di 775, 9 December 2005, p. 56 (available from the author).

[25] The Andean Committee on the Defence of Free Competition is an advising entity in Andean competition law enforcement, for more information see below Dimension IV: Sect. 8.2.1.2.

[26] Informe de la Tercera Reunion de Expertos Gubernamentales en Materia de Libre Competencia, 24 and 25 October 2001, p. 2 (available from the author).

[27] *Falla/Quintana*, in: Pontificia Universidad Católica del Peru, Derecho Comunitario Andino, 2003, p. 143, 173.

[28] Decisión 283, Normas para prevenir o corregir las distorsiones en la competencia generadas por prácticas de dumping o subsidios, 21 March 1991.

[29] Decisión 456, Normas para prevenir o corregir las distorsiones en la competencia generadas por prácticas de dumping en importaciones de productos originarios de Países Miembros de la Comunidad Andina, 4 May 1999.

[30] Decisión 457, Normas para prevenir o corregir las distorsiones en la competencia generadas por prácticas de subvenciones en importaciones de productos originarios de Países Miembros de la Comunidad Andina, 4 May 1999.

[31] Regional competition laws and subsidies and antidumping provisions both contribute to the protection of the common market in the long run. However, they are different legal instruments with distinct objectives. Rules on subsidies and antidumping aim at the protection of national industries and intend to counteract the economic exploitation of national markets by stronger foreign trading partners. On the other hand, a regional competition law framework aims at the protection of the common market, thereby incorporating a different perspective; *Falla/Quintana,* in: *Pontificia Universidad Católica del Peru,* Derecho Comunitario Andino, 2003, p. 143, 151.

[32] *Boza*, Tailor-Made Competition Policy in a Standardizing World, 2005, p. 86.

"Taxi Services case",[33] the INDECOPI had to deal with bureaucratic barriers imposed by the municipal government of Trujillo on taxicabs. Although the case was very controversial, the INDECOPI managed to diminish the imposition of bureaucratic barriers by the government on the basis that they were illicit and irrational.[34] The Tribunal of the INDECOPI in particular found that the administrative action hindered economic activity by reducing consumer's choices and limiting competition.[35] Similarly, in Colombia a state aid in the form of a granted monopoly to *Adpostal* (*Administradora Postal Nacional*) was abolished in 1994, which led to the liberalization and competitiveness of the postal service sector in Colombia.[36] It was held that the state aid was not in accordance with the Articles 333 and 334 of the Colombian Constitution[37] and the national competition legislation,[38] because it attributed *Adpostal* with an unjustified right that distorted competition within the postal sector.[39] On the other hand, Bolivia and Ecuador introduced national

---

[33] *Boza*, Tailor-Made Competition Policy in a Standardizing World, 2005, p. 86; Resolución 03-CAM-96-Indecopi/Exp.-036, 20 February 1997; Resolución 0182-1997/TDC-Indecopi, 16 July 1997.

[34] Resolución 03-CAM-96-Indecopi/Exp.-036, 20 February 1997; Resolución 0182-1997/TDC-Indecopi, 16 July 1997.

[35] *Boza*, Tailor-Made Competition Policy in a Standardizing World, 2005, p. 83. Other cases involving anticompetitive government measures are the Colombian case *Gasocaña Ltda., Norgas S.A.* (1997) or the Peruvian *Miraflores taxation* case (1996). For more information see *De León*, An Institutional Assessment of Antitrust Policy, 2009, pp. 399ff.; *Boza*, Tailor-Made Competition Policy in a Standardizing World, 2005 (only Peruvian cases).

[36] *Flórez*, La Empresa Colombiana, 45 Rev. de Derecho Privado 1, 16ff. (2011).

[37] Artículo 333: La actividad económica y la iniciativa privada son libres, dentro de los límites del bien común. Para su ejercicio, nadie podrá exigir permisos previos ni requisitos, sin autorización de la ley.

La libre competencia económica es un derecho de todos que supone responsabilidades.

La empresa, como base del desarrollo, tiene una función social que implica obligaciones. El Estado fortalecerá las organizaciones solidarias y estimulará el desarrollo empresarial.

El Estado, por mandato de la ley, impedirá que se obstruya o se restrinja la libertad económica y evitará o controlará cualquier abuso que personas o empresas hagan de su posición dominante en el mercado nacional.

La ley delimitará el alcance de la libertad económica cuando así lo exijan el interés social, el ambiente y el patrimonio cultural de la Nación.

Artículo 334: La dirección general de la economía estará a cargo del Estado. Este intervendrá, por mandato de la ley, en la explotación de los recursos naturales, en el uso del suelo, en la producción, distribución, utilización y consumo de los bienes, y en los servicios públicos y privados, para racionalizar la economía con el fin de conseguir el mejoramiento de la calidad de vida de los habitantes, la distribución equitativa de las oportunidades y los beneficios del desarrollo y la preservación de un ambiente sano.

El Estado, de manera especial, intervendrá para dar pleno empleo a los recursos humanos y asegurar que todas las personas, en particular las de menores ingresos, tengan acceso efectivo a los bienes y servicios básicos. También para promover la productividad y la competitividad y el desarrollo armónico de las regiones.

[38] For more information on the competition law in Colombia and Peru, see below Part II, Dimension I: Sect. 5.2.2.1.

[39] For general information on state aids and competition law in Colombia, see *Flórez*, La Empresa Colombiana, 45 Rev. de Derecho Privado 1–36 (2011).

competition policies only recently, previously relying on a state regulation system.[40] In fact, the Bolivian system is still drawn by a preponderance of sector regulation and Article 314 of the constitution of Bolivia[41] only refers to private monopolies and oligopolies and agreements by natural or judicial private persons.[42]

In the CARICOM, there is no provision on state aids in Chapter VIII of the Revised Treaty of Chaguaramas. In fact, the coverage of state aids in the scope of regional competition law was not discussed during its drafting process. This may be due to very limited direct state aid in the Caribbean region.[43] Legal monopolies and state-owned undertakings are still present throughout the region.[44]

While there have not been any legal precedents on the interpretation of the notion of an "enterprise", Article 1 of the Revised Treaty defines that it means any person or type of organization, other than a non-profit organization, involved in the production of or the trade of goods, or the provision of services. Public monopolies are explicitly included in Article 31 lit. a) of the Revised Treaty. It states that government monopolies are subject to "the agreed rules of competition established for Community economic enterprises". Likewise, the Revised Treaty of Chaguaramas entails specific provisions regarding public undertakings outside of Chapter VIII. Generally, member states shall ensure the elimination of practices of public undertakings that are based on quantitative restrictions, government assistance or trade discrimination, according to Article 94 of the Revised Treaty.[45] The provision aims at the protection of the benefits of the creation of a common market. Furthermore, it provides for consultation mechanisms between the involved member states and the Council for Trade and Economic Development (hereafter COTED). In the same vein, Article 152 of the Revised Treaty of Chaguaramas entails exceptional measures with respect to public undertakings for disadvantaged countries. Precondition however is prior approval of COTED. Moreover, Article 165 of the Revised Treaty of Chaguaramas sets out that Article 94(1) of the Revised Treaty, which deals with the general elimination of discriminatory restrictions to trade based on territorial considerations in the practices of public undertakings, does not apply to less developed countries.

---

[40] For more information on the competition law in Bolivia and Ecuador, see below Part II, Dimension I: Sect. 5.2.2.2.

[41] Artículo 314: Se prohíbe el monopolio y el oligopolio privado, así como cualquier otra forma de asociación o acuerdo de personas naturales o jurídicas privadas, bolivianas o extranjeras, que pretendan el control y la exclusividad en la producción y comercialización de bienes y servicios.

[42] *Mostajo*, Prácticas Anticompetitivas y Derecho de la Competencia en Bolivia, 32 Boletín Latinoamericano de Comp. 1, 11ff. (2012).

[43] *Stewart*, An Empirical Examination of Competition Issues in Selected Caricom Countries, 2004, pp. 8, 73. According to *Stewart*'s study the only countries that offer direct state aids are Belize, offering price support for rice farmers, and Trinidad and Tobago, granting state aids to its sugar industry.

[44] *Stewart*, An Empirical Examination of Competition Issues in Selected Caricom Countries, 2004, pp. 74f.

[45] Article 94(1) of the Revised Treaty of Chaguaramas.

The wording of Article 31 lit. a) RTC seems to imply a narrow interpretation of the notion of "enterprises". It refers to the competition rules established for "economic enterprises", but only refers to private organisations for the production of goods or services.[46] Moreover, there are systematic arguments, which support a narrow interpretation. Article 31 lit. a), Article 94 and Article 152 of the Revised Treaty of Chaguaramas would be obsolete, if public monopolies and undertakings would automatically fall under the scope of Chapter VIII.[47] A deliberate exclusion of state-related practices from regional competition law provisions in Chapter VIII reemphasizes the decentralized design of CARICOM, constituting a "community of sovereign states".[48]

It seems that in particular in the WAEMU the law acknowledged the high potential of distortion of the common market by state-imputed behaviour and the necessity to encourage "competitive neutrality".[49] In fact, the WAEMU Commission's competition-related precedents support this conclusion. Most of the regional cases brought to the Commission concern state aids or other state-imputed behaviour.[50] This does not only support the hypothesis of the prevailing presence of states as market actors despite ongoing privatization, it also shows that member states are willing to use regional competition law in conflicts with other member states.[51] One could go even further and argue that member states have acknowledged the efficiency gains of having a centralized system with regard to state-related anticompetitive practices. Furthermore, far-reaching regulation of state-related anticompetitive practices reflects a strong commitment towards the common market, especially if one recalls that state aids constitute an issue that is closely linked to aspects of national sovereignty. This does not signify that the objective of the creation of a

[46] Article 32(5) lit. a) and lit. b) of the Revised Treaty of Chaguaramas.

[47] Subsidies are also dealt with apart from Chapter VIII in the Articles 96ff. of the Revised Treaty of Chaguaramas.

[48] *Grenade,* in: *Hall/Chuck-A-Sang,* The Caribbean Community in Transition, 2008, p. 114, 119.

[49] The WAEMU also adopted regional rules on public procurement and public services, see Directive no. 04/2005/CM/UEMOA and Directive no. 05/2005/CM/UEMOA, Directive n° 04/2005/CM/UEMOA portant procedures de passation, d'exécution et de réglement des marchés publics et des délegations de service public dans l'Union économique et monétaire ouest africaine; Directive n° 05/2005/CM/UEMOA portant contrôle et régulation des marchés publics et des délegations de service public dans l'Union Économique et Monétaire Ouest Africaine, both of 9 December 2005, which govern that public procurement has to be governed by the principles of efficiency, free access to public procurement, equality of treatment and transparency; for more information see *CUTS CCIER,* A Time for Action, 2010, p. 10.

[50] For example: SOCOCIM v Ciment du Sahel (state aids in the cement industry); Total/Mobil (negative clearing for a stock purchase between private oil companies and state-sponsored oil multinational joint venture); West African Commodities (subsidies for oil mills by the Senegalese state); RUFSAC/Sengalese State (concerning the granting exonerations for kraft paper); Farine au Mali (concerning import restrictions on flour originating from Senegal by Mali); CAMEG (Distortions in market of pharmaceutical products caused by preferential treatment of Burkina Faso).

[51] *Bakhoum,* L'articulation du droit communautaire et des droits nationaux de la concurrence dans l'Union Economique et Monétaire Ouest Africaine, 2007, p. 133.

common market always prevails national objectives, but it clearly demonstrates that WAEMU's competition law system has acknowledged the need to balance these partly opposing positions.

By contrast, what does the non-inclusion of state aid provisions in the context of competition rules in the AndeanC and the CARICOM signify? The AndeanC by including public undertakings in the subjective scope of application of the regional competition law has acknowledged that the common market can also be distorted by state-imputed practices. The CARICOM enacted non-competition rules for public undertakings and subsidies that vest the COTED with decision-making powers and provide for consultation mechanisms among member states. Although both RTAs are aware of the potential distorting effects of state aids, they are considered as original competences of a state, which require special treatment.

The inclusion of "loyalty clauses" does not substitute special competition law rules on state aids and public undertakings. Rather, the experiences in the AndeanC and the CARICOM show that state aids were deliberately not included in the competition law rules. It would also contradict the taxonomy of their legal framework if state aids were governed by a general rule. The different approaches to state-related behaviour are in line with the institutional systems. While the WAEMU has adopted a centralized system, the AndeanC and the CARICOM constitute regional competition law systems, in which the member states have kept more sovereignty. Nevertheless, the inclusion of "loyalty clauses" in all three RTAs demonstrates a will to integrate and to create convergence, which entails a certain limitation to the legislative sovereignty of the member states.[52]

5.1.4 *Regional Merger Regulation*

None of the three regional competition law provisions comprise separate and explicit merger regulations. This might be surprising, because the competition law systems of the WAEMU, the AndeanC and the CARICOM mirror the European competition law system, which since 1990 provides for a system of regional merger control.[53] While the recommendability of a merger policy in small market economies has been contested on several occasions,[54] a merger policy on the regional level

---

[52] Even in the case of the European "soft harmonization"- approach, in which the EU refrained from obliging member states to harmonize their national competition laws, member states have to refrain from taking legislative or other measures that are capable of counteracting the Articles 101 and 102 TFEU.

[53] The actual main merger control provisions are contained in Council Regulation (EC) No 139/2004 of 20 January 2004 on the control of concentrations between undertakings (the EC Merger Regulation), OJ L 24/1, 29 January 2004.

[54] There is an ongoing debate whether the implementation of a merger regulation is advisable in small market economies. One of the main counterarguments refers to limited possibilities to reach economies of scale within a small market economy. However, in the context of regional merger control, the creation of a larger common market intends to abolish or to diminish these inefficiencies.

can be more efficient than on the national level. In view of the creation of a common market, a "merger policy is best centred in a jurisdiction that encompasses the entire relevant geographic market or markets for a particular transaction, rather than in each of several smaller jurisdictions within that market."[55]

However, the lack of an explicit merger regulation does not have to create a legal loophole. The abuse of dominance and agreement provisions, which all three RTAs have, offer the possibility of an *ex post* regulation of a firm's behaviour and of an *ex post* control of concentrations.[56]

The WAEMU legislator has adopted an *ex post* regulatory mechanism regarding mergers in Article 4 of Regulation no. 03/2002/CM/UEMOA and Articles 4(1) and 4(3) of Regulation no. 02/2002/CM/UEMOA.[57] The notion of an abuse of dominant position comprises the creation or strengthening of concentrations that significantly hinder an effective competition in the common market. Article 4(3) lit. c) of Regulation no. 02/2002/CM/UEMOA further specifies that a concentration also encompasses a merger between two undertakings, through which a joint undertaking is created. While these rules actually refer to an *ex post* regime regarding mergers, via the possibility of negative clearing rulings or the granting of an individual exemption of the Commission, a merger may even be indirectly controlled *ex ante*.[58]

Moreover, the application of the SIEC-test ("significant impediment to effective competition") (as in the European merger regime) instead of a mere "dominance"-based test appears as a feasible instrument for merger control regulation to adapt to the particular conditions of a small market economy. For more information on merger control in small market economies see: *Zúñiga-Feranández,* Fusionskontrolle in einer "small market economy" in Lateinamerika, 2009; *Gal,* Competition Policy for Small Market Economies, 2003, pp. 194ff.

[55] *Owen,* Competition Policy in Latin America, 13–15 November 2003, Stanford, p. 11 <http://papers.ssrn.com/paper.taf?abstract_id=456441> accessed 11 November 2018.

[56] *Monti,* EC Competition Law, 2007, p. 246; *Beckford* argues for a flexible interpretation of the abuse of dominant position provision in CARICOM regarding the obligation of Member States to implement a domestic merger control; *Beckford,* Enforcement of competition law in CARICOM: Perspectives on challenges to meeting regional and multilateral obligations, 20–21 April 2009, Caracas, p. 1. Under European Law before the enactment of Regulation no. 4064/89 in 1989, mergers fell under the scope of application of the provisions governing abuse of dominant position and agreements, see: Case 6/72 *Europemballage and Continental Can v. Commission* [1973] ECR 215; Cases 142 and 156/84 *BAT and Reynolds* [1987] ECR 4487.

[57] Art. 4 of Regulation no. 03/2002/CM/UEMOA refers to the regulation n° 02/2002/CM/UEMOA. Art. 4(1)(2) of Regulation no. 02/2002/CM/UEMOA states "(…) Constituent une pratique assimilable à un abus de position dominante les opérations de concentration qui créent ou renforce une position dominante, détenue par une ou plusieurs entreprises, ayant come conséquences d'entraver de manière significative une concurrence effective à l'intérieur du Marché Commun." Art. 4(3) Regulation no. 02/2002/CM/UEMOA specifies that the notion of "concentration" in Art. 4(1)(2) of the same regulation can also mean the merger of two enterprises.

[58] Décision n° 09/2008/COM/UEMOA portant attestation negative à l'egard du Projet de Concentration entre les Sociétés UNILEVER-CI, SIFCA, COSMIVOIRE, PALMCI, NAUVU, PHCI, SHCI et, SANIA, 22 October 2008, p. 4: "Dans le dispositif de l'UEMOA, le contrôle à priori des opérations de concentration se fait indirectement, suivant les dispositions de l'article 89 b) du Traité qui interdit les pratiques assimilables à l'abus de position dominante." Further cases that were based on a negative attestation under Article 3 of Regulation no. 03/2002/CM/UEMOA,

In the AndeanC merger regulation was deliberately excluded from the regional competition law during the drafting process of Decision 608, because the national representatives were unable to find a consensus.[59] Nevertheless, in the 1st "Reunion of Governmental Experts on Free Competition", the participants highlighted that although mergers should "in principle" be excluded from the objectives of the regional norm, there should be cooperation mechanisms between national agencies regarding the exchange of information.[60] The participants recognized that even national merger control could involve cross-border issues and that certain cooperation and coordination among national agencies would increase its efficacy.[61] Although the notion of "in principle" leaves room for discussion regarding the application of the regional provisions of Decision 608 on merger cases, the intention was to emphasize enforcement of merger control on the national level.

The exclusion of a regional merger control regime can be traced back to the diversity of national merger policies at the time of implementation of Decision 608, ranging from enforced merger control regimes such as in Venezuela,[62] to deficient national merger control regimes such as in Colombia or a complete absence of merger control such as under Peruvian competition law.[63] Although the national competition law systems including merger control have been reformed—Colombia initiated reforms and now comprises a rigorously enforced national competition law and merger control system,[64] in Peru a draft merger law is currently discussed in

---

or request for an individual exemption, Article 7 of Regulation no. 02/2002/CM/UEMOA and Article 7 of Regulation no. 03/2002/CM/UEMOA, comprise Decision no. 06/2004/COM/UEMOA and Decision no. 02/2005/COM/UEMOA regarding the project GAZODUC for the exploitation of natural gas in West Africa. While the former concerned an abuse of dominant position, the latter dealt with state aid provisions; see Décision n° 06/2004/COM/UEMOA portant Decision de ne pas soulever d'objections à l'égard des lois portant diverses dispositions relatives au regime juridique et fiscal unique et harmonise applicable dans la République du Bénin et dans la République Togolaise dans le cadre de la réalisation du projet GAZODUC de l'Afrique de l'Ouest, 23 December 2004 and Décision n° 02/2005/COM/UEMOA portant attestation negative à l'égard des accords créant des entreprises communes dans le cadre de la réalisation, de l'exploitation du GAZODUC de l'Afrique de l'Ouest et de la vente du gaz naturel sur les marchés du Bénin et du Togo, 21 January 2005.

[59] Informe de la Tercera Reunion de Expertos Gubernamentales en Materia de Libre Competencia, 24 and 25 October 2001, p. 2 (available from the author); *Falla/Quintana,* in: *Pontificia Universidad Católica del Peru,* Derecho Comunitario Andino, 2003, p. 143, 173.

[60] Informe de la Primera Reunion de Expertos Gubernamentales en Materia de Libre Competencia, SG/REG.LC/I/Informe/Rev.1, 29 October 1998 (available from the author).

[61] Mechanisms for cooperation are included in Article 37 of Decision 608.

[62] Venezuela withdrew from the AndeanC in 2006.

[63] Concerning the differing merger control systems in the Andean Countries, see *Jatar/Tineo,* Competition Policy in the Andean Countries: A Policy in Search of its Place, 1997, p. 3 <http://www.sice.oas.org/compol/articles/cpandea.asp> accessed 11 November 2018.

[64] Ley 155 de 1959 and Ley 1340 de 2009.

congress,[65] Ecuador has included merger control in its national competition law[66]—the implementation of a regional merger control still remains unrealistic. National initiatives actually mirror the ongoing distancing from regional competition law towards national enforcement. For the same reason the application of Article 7 of Decision 608 on merger cases, as happened in European merger control, seems unrealistic and contrary to the drafters' intention.[67]

Chapter VIII of the Revised Treaty of Chaguaramas currently does not include any merger control. However, there are initiatives to develop a regional policy on merger control.[68] More specifically, CARICOM member states initiated a consultancy that issued a Draft Analytical Report including a recommendation with regard to the merger and acquisition policy in the CSME.[69] This process also renders the discussion on a flexible *ex post* application of the regional provision Article 177 on illicit agreements on mergers obsolete.[70]

The urgency to adopt a regional merger control in the Caribbean region had been expressed on several occasions.[71] Regarding the regional airline sector, the merger between *Air Jamaica* and *Caribbean Airlines* was cited as anecdotal evidence.[72] In

---

[65] *La República,* "Mañana empieza en el Congreso foro por una ley antimonopolio", 4 December 2016, available at <http://larepublica.pe/impresa/economia/827590-manana-empieza-en-el-congreso-foro-por-una-ley-antimonopolio> last accessed 5 September 2017; *La República,* "Proyecto de ley que regula fusions listo en marzo del 2017", 6 December 2016, available at <http://larepublica.pe/impresa/economia/828126-proyecto-de-ley-que-regula-fusiones-listo-en-marzo-del-2017> last accessed 5 September 2017. Regarding older draft merger laws, see Congreso de la República, Proyecto de Ley n° 972/2011-CR, Ley de promoción de la libre competencia y la eficiencia en los mercados para la protección de los consumidores, 28 March 2012.

[66] Sección IV, de la concentración económica, Ley Orgánica de Regulación y Control del Poder de Mercado.

[67] A different prediction gives *Cortázar*, see *Cortázar,* Curso de Derecho de la Competencia, 2011, pp. 180ff.

[68] *CARICOM Secretariat,* Competition Policy and Law in the CSME, 2010, p. 7.

[69] The final draft of the consultancy was originally expected to be finalized by 11 November 2010.

[70] See for example *Beckford,* Enforcement of competition law in CARICOM: Perspectives on challenges to meeting regional and multilateral obligations, 20–21 April 2009, Caracas, p. 2.

[71] *Stewart,* An Empirical Examination of Competition Issues in Selected Caricom Countries, 2004; with respect to the banking sector also *Stewart,* in: *Drexl/Bakhoum/Fox/Gal/Gerber,* Competition Policy and Regional Integration in Developing Countries, 2012, p. 161, 179.

[72] The two biggest companies on the Caribbean airline market are Caribbean Airlines and Liat. The airline market displays a high level of concentration. Interestingly, in 2009, before the acquisition of *Air Jamaica,* there was no overlap regarding international services and minimal overlap regarding the East and South CARICOM sub-regions between LIAT and Caribbean Airlines. LIAT is owned by the Governments of Antigua and Barbuda, Barbados and St. Vincent and the Grenadines. According to the "Concept Paper Strategic Plan for Air Transport Services in CARICOM" of 11 January 2009 issued by the CARICOM Community <http://www.caricom.org/jsp/single_market/services_regime/concept_paper_air_transport.pdf> all of the airlines are public sector controlled and all are unprofitable. According to the concept paper, Caribbean airlines is the only airline that is capitalised. Depending on the notion of an "enterprise" the application of Chapter VIII could thus be problematic. Further criticism arose in the context of the subsidised fuel in Trinidad and Tobago that was held to create an unfair competitive advantage for Caribbean Airlines in view of

the banking sector mergers take place frequently.[73] Regional merger control is particularly needed in this sector, because it is exempted from the national competition law of Trinidad and Tobago. Concentrations and interlocking directorates are a persistent difficulty in the creation of efficient markets.[74] The general argument made against regional merger control relies on the small size of the Caribbean economies. It is argued that the economies of the member states are in need of mergers in order to reach economies of scale in order to compete in the globalized international economic environment. Moreover, merger control enforcement is often held as too resource-consuming. Article 51(2) lit. b) of the Revised Treaty of Chaguaramas even explicitly calls for the creation of linkages among economic sectors and enterprises within and among the member states of the CSME in order to attain the objectives of the "Community Industrial Policy". The reasoning that underlies this argumentation is based on the misconception that merger control generally prohibits any kind of mergers. On the contrary, a regional merger regime can constitute an efficient tool to prevent larger enterprises from "squeezing out" smaller vulnerable firms. The functioning merger regulation in Barbados supports this finding. Likewise, Trinidad and Tobago has incorporated a national merger control system and Guyana has prepared a draft merger control law.

There were rumours upholding the view that especially Trinidad and Tobago was trying to avoid the implementation of a regional merger regime, because it was trying to protect national businesses that were planning to enter other Caribbean member states through mergers. However, there is no written evidence supporting this position of Trinidad and Tobago during the drafting process of Chapter VIII and the inclusion of a merger control in Trinidad and Tobago's domestic competition law also rebuts this view.[75] It is yet another demonstration of Caribbean member states' distrust against each other and in particular in view of economic preponderance of Trinidad and Tobago.

Although the WAEMU, the AndeanC and the CARICOM generally agree with the potentially anticompetitive dimension of mergers, only the WAEMU has incorporated regional provisions that allow for a control of regional mergers, apart from an *ex post* control under abuse of dominant position. The lack of a regional merger control cannot be explained by a general absence of regional mergers. Rather, mergers and acquisitions are a common way of penetrating markets and small political

---

LIAT; Caribbean News Now!, 4 February 2011, "St Vincent Prime Minister accuses Caribbean Airlines of creating unfair competition for LIAT"; Caribbean News Now!, 11 March 2011, "Commentary: CARICOM chairman should act to end airlines standoff".

[73] *Stewart*, in: *Drexl/Bakhoum/Fox/Gal/Gerber*, Competition Policy and Regional Integration in Developing Countries, 2012, p. 161, 179.

[74] *Stewart*, An Empirical Examination of Competition Issues in Selected Caricom Countries, 2004, p. 148.

[75] Part III of the Fair Trading Act 2006. Regarding Trinidad and Tobago's position on regional merger control, see also the Communication from Trinidad and Tobago for the World Trade Organization Working Group on the Interaction between Trade and Competition Policy, WT/WGTCP/W/143 of 12 June 2000, in which Trinidad and Tobago recommends to introduce a merger control regulation in the CARICOM.

and economic elites favour interlocking directorships.[76] Moreover, firms engaging in anticompetitive mergers within an RTA were often found to be active in several member states.[77] Consequently, a regional merger control regime could constitute an efficient instrument to render a common market more competitive. It appears that the implementation of a regional merger control constitutes a highly sensitive matter. This is not only based on theoretical misconceptions regarding the scope of application or the economical benefits of a regional merger regulation, but mainly relates to political opposition. In the AndeanC and the CARICOM, discussions surrounding the implementation of a regional merger regime actually referred to national industry protectionist considerations. This ignores that a regional merger control is structurally more capable of protecting industries of the region from anticompetitive practices originating from large international enterprises.[78]

5.1.5 *Territorial Scope of Application*

Among the substantive provisions of a regional competition law, the territorial scope of application has the furthest reaching impact on the delimitation of competences between the regional and national level. It determines which cases will be dealt with by the regional authority. In developing countries, a frequent argument brought in favour of regional competition laws is the ability to deal with international anticompetitive practices, namely export cartels and conduct by multinational enterprises (MNEs). The scaling of the territorial scope of application also touches on political sovereignty issues, because it reflects, but also affects the will of member states to cede political power to the regional level.

Building on the European "effect-doctrine",[79] the three RTAs rely on the effect of an anticompetitive behaviour on a relevant market.[80] The European development of the "effect-doctrine" however shows that the notion of effect is a manifold and

---

[76] This mode of entry is often used by financial institutions from Trinidad and Tobago in CARICOM, see *Stewart,* in: *Drexl/Bakhoum/Fox/Gal/Gerber,* Competition Policy and Regional Integration in Developing Countries, 2012, p. 161, 179.

[77] *Jenny,* Cartels and Collusion in Developing Countries, 29/1 W. Comp. 109, 134 (2006).

[78] See below Part III, Sect. 11.3.

[79] See *Budzinski,* The Governance of Global Competition, 2008, pp. 153f.; *Terhechte,* International Competition Enforcement Law, 2009, pp. 42ff.

[80] The "effect-doctrine" allows for extraterritorial application of domestic competition law because the application criteria solely relies on the effect on the domestic market and does not require that the action has been performed in the domestic market. However, extraterritorial application of domestic competition law by its nature does not constitute a substitute for regional competition law enforcement. Extraterritorial competition law enforcement fights anticompetitive practices with effects on the domestic markets, leaving aside possible objectives of regional integration. Also from a global perspective, extraterritorial application of competition law—mainly by the active competition law agencies of developed jurisdictions—cannot sufficiently take into account the interests and needs of developing jurisdictions.

complex term. It was only in 2004 after numerous cases before the Court of Justice of the European Union that the European Commission published guidelines on the definition of the "effect-on-trade concept".[81] In order to analyse the terms used in the WAEMU, the AndeanC and the CARICOM, it may thus be helpful to briefly look at the European interpretation and utilization of the term.

Article 101 and 102 of the Treaty of the Functioning of the European Union apply to practices of undertakings that "may affect the trade between Member States". The European law applies a broad definition of "trade", covering not only goods and services, but also economic activity in general.[82] The notion of "may affect" is more difficult to interpret, because it requires the definition of the nature of the impact on trade between Member States.[83] In this context the European Court of Justice developed the "standard test", which indicates that "it must be possible to foresee with a sufficient degree of probability on the basis of a set of objective factors of law or fact that the agreement or practice may have an influence, direct or indirect, actual or potential, on the pattern of trade between Member States."[84] In order to avoid too remote links between a practice and the effect on the pattern of trade, the claimant has to show the likelihood of the particular relation including an appreciable effect on trade between member states.[85] The appreciability then again depends on the specific circumstances of the individual case, such as the type of agreement, products and market position of the undertaking in question.[86]

5.1.5.1 Literal Interpretation of Articles 88, 89 and 90 of the Treaty of Dakar in the WAEMU by the Court of Justice

In the WAEMU, the applicability of the regional competition law only requires an effect of the respective anticompetitive practice on the common market, Article 88 lit. a), b) of the Treaty of Dakar.[87] However, the Court of Justice in its Advisory Opinion no. 003/2000 on 27 June 2000 defined the notion very broadly, subsuming any practice under the scope of regional law that affects or has the objective to affect

---

[81] Commission Notice (EU) of 27 April 2004, Guidelines on the effect on trade concept contained in the Articles 81 and 82 of the Treaty, [2004] OJ C 101/07.

[82] Commission Notice (EU) of 27 April 2004, Guidelines on the effect on trade concept contained in the Articles 81 and 82 of the Treaty, [2004] OJ C 101/07, para. 19.

[83] Commission Notice (EU) of 27 April 2004, Guidelines on the effect on trade concept contained in the Articles 81 and 82 of the Treaty, [2004] OJ C 101/07, para. 23.

[84] ECJ, Decision of 30 of June 1966, Case 56/65, *Société Technique Minière v. Maschinenbau Ulm GmbH* [1966], para. 249; Commission Notice (EU) of 27 April 2004, Guidelines on the effect on trade concept contained in the Articles 81 and 82 of the Treaty, [2004] OJ C 101/07, para. 23.

[85] Commission Notice (EU) of 27 April 2004, Guidelines on the effect on trade concept contained in the Articles 81 and 82 of the Treaty, [2004] OJ C 101/07, para. 43.

[86] Commission Notice (EU) of 27 April 2004, Guidelines on the effect on trade concept contained in the Articles 81 and 82 of the Treaty, [2004] OJ C 101/07, para. 44ff.

[87] Art. 88 lit. a), b) Treaty of Dakar: "à l'intérieur de l'Union"/"sur le marché commun".

the territory of the common market, irrespective of an effect on trade between member states.[88]

During the drafting of competition law related directives and regulations in 2000, questions between experts of the member states and the Commission arose regarding the allocation of competences between the national level and the Union in the WAEMU and regarding the interpretation of the Articles 88, 89 and 90 of the Treaty.[89] The Commission supported the view that the Union should have exclusive competence to deal with cartels, abuse of dominance and state aids. This exclusivity of community law in its opinion, not only signified a primacy of regional law over national law, but also covered the right to legislate on competition law-related matters. For the member states' experts on the other hand, the Treaty of Dakar entailed a shared and concurrent competence for antitrust matters between national and regional entities. Similar to the European system, the Treaty of Dakar only included the principle of primacy of community law over national law. The Commission referred the question to the Court of Justice of the West African Economic and Monetary Union.

In accordance with the Additional Protocol no. 1 regarding the organs of control of WAEMU, the Additional Act no. 10/96 regarding the status of the Court of Justice of WAEMU, Regulation no. 01/96/CM regarding the rules of procedure of the Court of Justice of WAEMU and Regulation no. 01/2000/CDJ, the Court of Justice of WAEMU decided in favour of the Commission's opinion.

The Court of Justice compared the European competition law provisions with the Articles 88, 89 and 90 of the Treaty of Dakar. Following a literal interpretation, it assumed that since the West African provision did not include the requirement of an "effect on trade between member states" an effect on the "common market" would be sufficient in order to fall under the regional scope of application.[90] The Court also cited Article 87 of the European Community Treaty (now Article 107 TFEU). While the latter refers to an effect on trade between member states, the according West African provision, Article 88 lit. c) of the Treaty of Dakar only mentions state aid capable of causing distortion of competition.[91] The Court interpreted that the absence of the latter requirement showed that the West African legislator deliberately refrained from defining the relationship between national legislation and

[88] Advisory Opinion no. 003/2000/CJ/WAEMU of 27 June 2000, "Demande d'avis de la Commission de l'UEMOA relative à l'interprétation des articles 88, 89 et 90 du Traité relatifs aux règles de concurrences dans l'Union", p. 8.

[89] Advisory Opinion no. 003/2000/CJ/WAEMU of 27 June 2000, "Demande d'avis de la Commission de l'UEMOA relative à l'interprétation des articles 88, 89 et 90 du Traité relatifs aux règles de concurrences dans l'Union", p. 1.

[90] Advisory Opinion no. 003/2000/CJ/WAEMU of 27 June 2000, "Demande d'avis de la Commission de l'UEMOA relative à l'interprétation des articles 88, 89 et 90 du Traité relatifs aux règles de concurrences dans l'Union".

[91] Advisory Opinion no. 003/2000/CJ/WAEMU of 27 June 2000, "Demande d'avis de la Commission de l'UEMOA relative à l'interprétation des articles 88, 89 et 90 du Traité relatifs aux règles de concurrences dans l'Union".

community laws because this was not necessary under the system of the Union's exclusive competence on competition law matters.[92]

The Court of Justice in its Advisory Opinion went even further than merely interpreting the Articles 88, 89 and 90 of the Treaty of Dakar, but generally expressed its view on the allocation of competition law competences. Thereby the Court of Justice of WAEMU did not only rely on the literal reasoning but also based the exclusive competence of the Union on an analysis of the general institutional design of WAEMU. Although the Court analysed that the Treaty of Dakar included legal mechanisms, such as the attribution of competences to the regional level, which limited the legislative competence of the Union, it inconsistently used this institutional design as argument in favour of the Union's exclusive competence on competition law matters. Based on the broad interpretation, the Court argued that the Articles 89 and 90 of the Treaty of Dakar contained an explicit attribution of competences to the Union. Doing that, the Court actually confused the notions of attribution of competences and exclusivity. As the European competition law systems shows, the European Commission has the competence to deal with practices that may affect trade between member states, but member states are still allowed to legislate on anticompetitive practices that only affect the national scope of application. In the WAEMU, member states are only left with the legislative competence on criminal sanctions of anticompetitive practices, infringements of provisions regarding the transparency of the market and the organization of competition.[93]

Finally the Court of Justice of WAEMU also explained the legislator's intention based on possible disadvantages of the principle of double barrier, as followed in the European Union. In its view, the parallel application caused inefficiencies and conflicts of jurisdictions, while the unification of competition legislation guaranteed for a convergent application of competition laws in the territory of a regional trade agreement.[94]

The Advisory Opinion no. 003/2000 has been highly criticised for the creation of a very centralized competition law system. Sixteen years after the Advisory Opinion, the system has showed its flaws and revealed severe inefficiencies regarding competition law enforcement and implementation in the West African region.[95]

---

[92] Advisory Opinion no. 003/2000/CJ/WAEMU of 27 June 2000, "Demande d'avis de la Commission de l'UEMOA relative à l'interprétation des articles 88, 89 et 90 du Traité relatifs aux règles de concurrences dans l'Union".

[93] Advisory Opinion no. 003/2000/CJ/WAEMU of 27 June 2000, "Demande d'avis de la Commission de l'UEMOA relative à l'interprétation des articles 88, 89 et 90 du Traité relatifs aux règles de concurrences dans l'Union".

[94] Advisory Opinion no. 003/2000/CJ/WAEMU of 27 June 2000, "Demande d'avis de la Commission de l'UEMOA relative à l'interprétation des articles 88, 89 et 90 du Traité relatifs aux règles de concurrences dans l'Union".

[95] The specific inefficiencies of the centralized system are dealt with separately in each respective Chapter. To give a few examples, the centralized system suffers from resource constraints on the regional level, conflicts of competences are not resolved because of remaining sectorial or competition law related national provisions. The centralization has led to a decline of national competition law enforcement and cooperation between the regional and national level remains weak. The

Consequently, the WAEMU legislator envisages to reform the system. Currently, there are ongoing revisions and studies of the centralized system that call for a "controlled decentralization"[96] of WAEMU's competition law system.[97]

5.1.5.2 Article 5 of Decision 608 in the AndeanC

The AndeanC's Decision 608 entails a detailed list of the requirements for the territorial scope of application. According to Article 5 of Decision 608, Andean competition law is applicable in three constellations: (1) The practice originates from one member state and has an effect on at least one other member state, (2) The practice originates from at least two member states and has an effect on at least one other member state, (3) The practice originates from outside the Andean Community and has an effect on at least two member states.[98]

It is interesting to note, that the former Decision 285 did not apply to practices originating from abroad even if they had an effect on the subregion (now covered under category no. 3). Art. 2(2) of Decision 285 relied on the "territoriality principle" by additionally to the effect on the subregion[99] requiring that the "origin" of the concerned practices was within the community's region or that the relevant undertaking was active in at least one member state.[100] The widening of the scope of

---

Advisory Opinion no. 003/2000 also neglected possible conflicts with competition law provisions of other regional trade agreements in the region, such as ECOWAS.

[96] *Bakhoum,* L'articulation du droit communautaire et des droits nationaux de la concurrence dans l'Union Economique et Monétaire Ouest Africaine, 2007, pp. 286ff.

[97] More details on the Advisory Opinion no. 003/2000/CJ/WAEMU of 27 June 2000, "Demande d'avis de la Commission de l'UEMOA relative à l'interprétation des articles 88, 89 et 90 du Traité relatifs aux règles de concurrences dans l'Union". See *Bakhoum,* L'articulation du droit communautaire et droits nationaux de la concurrence dans l'Union Economique et Monétaire Ouest Africaine, 2007, pp. 57ff.; *Bakhoum,* Delimitation and Exercise of Competence between the West African Economic and Monetary Union (WAEMU) and its Member States in Competition Policy, 29/4 W. Comp. 653–681 (2006); *UNCTAD,* Voluntary Peer Review on Competition Policies of WAEMU, Benin and Senegal, 2008, pp. 18ff.

[98] See Art. 5 of Decision 608; *Secretaría General de la Comunidad Andina,* Guía Práctica para la aplicación de la Decisión 608 "Normas para la protección y promoción de la libre competencia en la Comunidad Andina", 2007, p. 8 <http://intranet.comunidadandina.org/Documentos/DTrabajo/SGdt396.doc> accessed 11 November 2018.

[99] The requirement of an effect on the subregion had already been established under the regime of Decision 285, Sentence of the *Tribunal de la Justicia de la Comunidad Andina* of 13 November 2002. Proceso 87–IP-2002. Interpretación prejudicial de los artículos 1, 2, 4 literal a) y 5 literales a) y d) de la Decisión n° 285; artículos 1, 2, 17 y 18 de la Decisión n° 439; 28, 29 y 34 de la Decisión n° 462 de la Comisión de la Comunidad Andina, así como los artículos 4, 5 y 6 de la Resolución n° 432 expedida por la Secretaría General de la misma Comunidad, solicitada por la Sala Plena de la Honorable Corte Sorprema de Justicia de la República de Bolivia. Expediente Interno n° 160/2001, contencioso Administrativo. Telefonia Celular de Bolivia S.A.—Telecel contra Superintendente General del Sistema de Regulación Sectoral, SIRESE.

[100] Article 2 of Decision 285. See *Prada,* Wettbewerbspolitik und Wirtschaftsintegration in den Amerikas, 2001, p. 59; *Gallardo/Domínguez,* 20 Boletín Latinoamericano de Comp. 36, 47 (2005)

regional competition law was an important step towards facilitating enforcement against international anticompetitive practices.

In the drafting process of Decision 608, Peru advocated restricting the territorial application of the regional competition clause by excluding conducts that have an effect in a single member state and originate from another.[101] The Peruvian representatives were in favour of a narrow regional geographical scope of application, limited to conducts that have an effect on at least two member states. The Peruvian opposition demonstrates that, already during the drafting process of Decision 608, issues regarding the restriction of national sovereignty arose. The opposition remained even 7 years after the enactment of Decision 608. Peru, which already at the time of the implementation of Decision 608 had established a national competition policy, is predominantly concerned with the protection of its protagonist role in the field of competition law in entire South America[102] and does not participate actively in the fostering of the regional competition law system.[103]

Despite the reference to specific examples regarding the territorial scope of application of Andean competition law, Article 5 of Decision 608 still bears ambiguities. The notion of "effect" is neither defined in the Decision, nor in other legal documents, nor does there exist case law that deals with the matter.

The Guidelines of the AndeanC on Decision 608[104] do not directly address the problematic issue of the concept of "effect" and do not specify whether also the mere capacity of a practice or agreement to affect the subregional market would be sufficient. The notion of appreciability, if applicable at all, is also unclear. Article 5 lit. a) and lit. b) of Decision 608 only refer to "real effects", thereby hinting at a narrow interpretation that would exclude potential effects. However, the Guidelines mention an opinion of the General Secretary from 2007[105] (hereafter opinion no. 01-2007), which touched upon the interpretation and application of the concept.

<http://ec.europa.eu/competition/publications/blc/boletin_20_1_es.pdf> accessed 11 November 2018; *Böttcher*, Kartell- und Lauterkeitsrecht in den Ländern der Andengemeinschaft, 2004, p. 50; *Mancero-Bucheli*, Competition Law of Latin America and the European Union, 2001, p. 79. For more information on reform proposals of Decision 285 see *Böttcher*, Harmonisierungsbemühungen der Andengemeinschaft im Bereich des Kartellrechts, GRUR Int 217–223 (2003).

[101] Informe de la Segunda Reunion de Expertos Gubernamentales en Materia de Libre Competencia, 16 and 17 February 2000, pp. 2, 9 (available from the author); Informe de la Tercera Reunion de Expertos Gubernamentales en Materia de Libre Competencia, 24 and 25 October 2001, pp. 4, 12 (available from the author).

[102] There have been other national competition law regimes that have gained increasing reputation, in particular the Chilean and Brazilian system.

[103] Interview with representatives from the INDECOPI conducted by the author on 19 January 2012 in Lima.

[104] *Secretaría General de la Comunidad Andina,* Guía Práctica para la aplicación de la Decisión 608 "Normas para la protección y promoción de la libre competencia en la Comunidad Andina", 2007 <http://intranet.comunidadandina.org/Documentos/DTrabajo/SGdt396.doc> accessed 11 November 2018.

[105] *Dictamen N° 01-2007,* Secretaría General de la Comunidad Andina

On 27 June 2006, three Colombian flower companies addressed the Secretariat General during the prejudicial phase of an action for non-compliance in accordance with the procedures of Decision 623[106] and Articles 23 to 31 of the Treaty regarding the Creation for the Tribunal of Justice of the AndeanC.[107] They argued that the Republic of Colombia had infringed Article 36 of Decision 608 and Article 4 of the Treaty of the Creation of the Tribunal of Justice of the AndeanC.[108] The Republic of Colombia was accused of eliminating and distorting competition in the market of flower production aimed at the exportation by applying the programs "Incentives for the Colombian Currency" (ICC)[109] and "Sanitary Incentive for Flowers" (ISF).[110] The ICC program was perceived to benefit agricultural product exporters, which had adopted currency-hedging mechanisms.[111] The ISF aimed at the creation of an incentive for the exportation of flowers.[112] The claimants accused the Colombian State to apply these programs in a discriminatory and arbitrary way, thereby infringing Article 36 of Decision 608 and Article 4 of the Treaty regarding the Creation of the Tribunal of Justice of the AndeanC. Article 36 of Decision 608 entails the obligation of member states to refrain from adopting regulatory market-relevant measures that impede, endanger or distort competition in the subregional market and Article 4 of the Treaty regarding the Creation of the Tribunal of Justice of the AndeanC promulgates that member states have to adopt all necessary measures to secure the compliance with the legal framework of the AndeanC and that they have to refrain from adopting measures that hinder its application.

The Secretariat General's reasoning in the opinion no. 01-2007 regarding Article 5 of Decision 608 resulted in the rejection of the complaint. The Secretariat General firstly established that Article 36 was only applicable if there was a cross-border effect in accordance with Article 5 of Decision 608.[113] Accordingly, the General Secretary firstly had to decide whether the Colombian programs had an effect on one (other than Colombia itself) or more member states in the vein of Article 5 of Decision 608.[114] With regard to Article 5 of Decision 608, explicitly referring to European jurisprudence, the claimants argued *inter alia* that the conduct of the Colombian government would not only affect the domestic market, but also the subregional market, since Colombia is part of the latter.[115] Colombia replied that the membership of Colombia to the AndeanC by itself could not constitute an effect of

[106] Decisión 623 Reglamento de la Fase Prejudicial de la Acción de Incumplimiento, 16 July 2005.

[107] Regarding the action of non-compliance see below Part II, Dimension IV: Sect. 8.3.2.5.

[108] Tratado de la Creación del Tribunal de Justicia de la Comunidad Andina.

[109] Incentivo de la Cobertura Cambiaria (ICC).

[110] Incentivo Sanitario para Flores (ISF).

[111] *Dictamen N° 01-2007,* Secretaría General de la Comunidad Andina, p. 4.

[112] *Dictamen N° 01-2007,* Secretaría General de la Comunidad Andina, p. 6.

[113] *Dictamen N° 01-2007,* Secretaría General de la Comunidad Andina, p. 13.

[114] Contrary to the European Guidelines on the "effect on trade"-concept contained in the Articles 81 and 82 of the Treaty, the Secretariat General did not have to define the notion of "trade", because Article 5 of Decision 608 only refers to an effect on member states.

[115] *Dictamen N° 01-2007,* Secretaría General de la Comunidad Andina, p. 8.

the subregional market. It held that the case at hand only had domestic effects, which would also be supported by the fact that one of the flower companies, Rosas de Sopó S.A., had submitted a complaint before the Colombian Administrative Tribunal.[116]

The Secretariat General rejected the complaint on the basis that the claimants had not been able to show sufficient proof for the fulfilment of Article 5 of Decision 608. It firstly established that Article 36 was not automatically applicable to all policies adopted by member states.[117] On the contrary, it had to be proven by facts and in an objective way that the national policy actually produced cross-border effects.[118] The Secretariat General further illuminated that Article 5 of Decision 608 required the production of "real effects".

In line with the European approach regarding the effect on inter-state trade, the Andean Secretariat General evaluated the case separately based on the specific circumstances.[119] In the footnotes of the decision, the Secretariat General also explicitly referred to the application methods of the European competition law. However, some differences have to be pointed out.

The Secretariat General did not mention the European "standard test". It did not make references to effects on the pattern of trade between the member states either. While this might indicate a narrow interpretation of the "effect on inter-state trade", one also has to highlight that the claimants did not argue on the basis of a change of the pattern of trade.

The Secretariat General's emphasis of the support by "elements of facts" on an "objective basis" and the demonstration of "real effects" clearly demonstrate formal requirements.[120] The Secretariat General thereby defined the degree of evidence that is necessary to support a case. At the same time, the reference to "real effects" and the European jurisprudence in the footnotes is an indicator that it wanted to include the requirement for a "degree of sufficient probability" or in other words "appreciability". The underlying logic seems to be that a practice that does not demonstrate any "real effects" cannot be appreciable. Unfortunately, since the claimants' arguments were not well elaborated, the Secretariat General did not have to decide whether the Colombian policy actually caused sufficiently appreciable anticompetitive effect.

---

[116] *Dictamen N° 01-2007,* Secretaría General de la Comunidad Andina, p. 10.

[117] *Dictamen N° 01-2007,* Secretaría General de la Comunidad Andina, p. 13.

[118] *Dictamen N° 01-2007,* Secretaría General de la Comunidad Andina, p. 13: "(…) merced a lo dispuesto por el artículo 5 de la Decision 608, la aplicabilidad del artículo 36 de esa Decisión y, por tanto, la competencia de los órganos comunitarios para pronunciarse sobre el grado de cumplimiento de las obligaciones en él contenidas, debe encontrarse sustentada por elementos de hecho (en particular los aspectos económicos de la supuesta práctica discriminatoria) y de derecho de los que se desprenda, de manera objetiva, que la política nacional investigada produce efectos (…)".

[119] Commission Notice (EU) of 27 April 2004, Guidelines on the effect on trade concept contained in the Articles 81 and 82 of the Treaty, [2004] OJ C 101/07, para. 12.

[120] *Dictamen N° 01-2007,* Secretaría General de la Comunidad Andina, p. 13.

5.1.5.3 Articles 173(1) lit. a) and 174(1) of the Revised Treaty of Chaguaramas in the CARICOM

Chapter VIII of the Revised Treaty of Chaguaramas does not draw a clear distinction between the territorial scope of application of the regional law and the jurisdiction and competences of the CARICOM Competition Commission. Article 173 of the Revised Treaty of Chaguaramas comprises the general obligation of the Commission to apply the competition rules "in respect of anti-competitive cross-border business conduct" and Article 174(1) of the Revised Treaty of Chaguaramas accordingly sets out that the CARICOM Competition Commission can take actions against enterprises "in respect of cross-border transactions or transactions with cross-border effect".[121] Section 54 of the CARICOM Model Law on Competition determines that a national competition authority shall refer a matter to the CARICOM Competition Commission where it "seeks to determine whether conduct by an enterprise in another member states prejudices trade and prevents, restricts or distorts competition" in the home country. Yet this wording does not specify whether the "conduct by an enterprise" has to actually cross a border or whether the effect or even potential effect of such a conduct of an enterprise in another member state is sufficient for a referral to the CARICOM Competition Commission.[122]

The Revised Treaty of Chaguaramas does not define the notion of "cross-border transactions", "transactions with cross-border effect" or "cross-border business conduct". Article 174(1) of the Revised Treaty of Chaguaramas specifies that the CARICOM Competition Commission may take actions against an enterprise whose business conduct prejudices trade or prevents, restricts or distorts competition within the CSME. Nevertheless, neither the broad definition of "trade" set out in Article 1 of the Revised Treaty, covering any "business, industry, profession or occupation relating to the supply or acquisition of goods or services", nor the notion of "competition within the CSME", which is not defined at all in the Revised Treaty, clarifies the required elements for a "cross-border effect". The delimitation between domestic and regional conduct becomes particularly vague with respect to allegedly anticompetitive practices that solely take place in one member state, but which may create entry barriers for other companies of other member states.[123]

Article 175(2) of the Revised Treaty of Chaguaramas clearly distinguishes between actual and likely effects. While this provision mainly sets out the requirements for COTED to initiate an investigation of the CARICOM Competition

---

[121] "Subject to Articles 175 and 176, the Commission may, in respect of cross-border transactions or transactions with cross-border effects, monitor, investigate, detect, make determinations or take action to inhibit and penalise enterprises whose business conduct prejudices trade or prevents restricts or distorts competition within the CSME."

[122] Arguing in favour of a broad definition of cross-border effect, see *Kaczorowska-Ireland*, Competition Law in the CARICOM Single Market and Economy, 2015, pp. 106ff.

[123] *Beckford*, Enforcement of Competition Law in CARICOM, 35/2 W.I.L.J. 109, 131f. (2010); *Beckford*, Enforcement of competition law in CARICOM: Perspectives on challenges to meeting regional and multilateral obligations, 20–21 April 2009, Caracas, p. 5.

Commission, it also reflects that the Caribbean legislator was aware of the inclusion of potential anticompetitive effects. When applying the concept of potential anticompetitive effects, one can thus not only include potential domestic competitors, but also has to consider potential competition originating from other member states in the analysis of a "cross-border anticompetitive effect".[124]

In the CARICOM, regional competition policy is emphasized as a protection tool for the creation and maintenance of the CSME.[125] As a consequence, an emphasis of the internal market-objective is likely to favour a broad "cross-border" definition, which would guarantee a frequent and convergent application of competition law in the entire Caribbean market. On the other hand, the Revised Treaty of Chaguaramas also limits territorial application of the regional competition law. The Revised Treaty excludes business conduct with only minimal impact on competition and trade within the CSME, Article 181 of the Revised Treaty. However, contrary to the European *de minimis*-rule, Article 181 of the Revised Treaty of Chaguaramas constitutes an exemption that the CARICOM Competition Commission has to decide upon. Thus business conduct with minimal conduct can still fall within the scope of application of regional competition law.

The other Articles of Chapter VIII also do not offer further insights on the definition of "cross-border trade". Article 175(1), Article 175(2) and Article 176(1) of the Revised Treaty of Chaguaramas specify the jurisdiction of the Commission. Interestingly, the wordings referring to the "cross-border effect" of the examined business conduct differ based on the party that initiates the investigation. In case of a member state's request, according to Article 175(1), the alleged enterprise has to be located in another member state and its conduct has to affect competition within the territory of the requesting member state, thereby requiring the actual "crossing" of borders by the alleged anticompetitive practice. A request from COTED based on Article 175(2) on the other hand only requires the prejudice of trade and competition within the CSME with actual or likely cross-border effect. Article 176(1), which entails the *ex officio* power of the CARICOM Competition Commission to request a national competition authority to undertake a preliminary examination,[126] mirrors the wording of a request from COTED; with the exception that it does not include business conduct with only "likely" effects. Nevertheless, the diverging use of terms does not constitute a systematic argument for a certain interpretation of the notion of "cross-border effects" in Article 173(1) and 174(1) of the Revised Treaty.

---

[124] *Beckford,* Enforcement of Competition Law in CARICOM, 35/2 W.I.L.J. 109, 132 (2010).

[125] See Article 169(1) of the Revised Treaty of Chaguaramas: "The goal of the Community Competition Policy shall be to ensure that the benefits expected from the establishment of the CSME are not frustrated by anti-competitive business conduct".

[126] The CARICOM Competition Commission generally has an *ex officio* right to start an investigation. However, it's competence is limited in the sense that the Commission has to ask a national competition authority to undertake a preliminary examination before it can actually start investigating, Article 176(1) of the Revised Treaty of Chaguaramas. See below, Part II, Dimension IV: Sect. 8.1.2.

Rather, they postulate different requirements for a request before the CARICOM Competition Commission depending on the requesting party.[127]

Apparently, the drafters of Chapter VIII had foreseen possible conflicts between national and the regional competition agency, especially in the case of the *ex officio* competence of the Commission as set out in Article 176(1) of the Revised Treaty. According to Article 176(5) of the Revised Treaty "differences of opinion between the Commission and the member state regarding the nature and effect or jurisdiction of the investigating authority" shall be resolved by the COTED.[128] In the same vein, Article 176(4) of the Revised Treaty determines that the member states and the CARICOM Competition Commission hold consultations with regard to the competence to exercise an investigation when the preliminary examination revealed an allegedly anticompetitive practice. In the CARICOM, such conflicts regarding the competent jurisdiction can arise from an ambiguous scope of application of regional competition law, because Chapter VIII does not draw a clear-cut distinction between the territorial scope of application and the enforcement competences of the regional competition authority. The consultation mechanisms clearly emanate from the intention to avoid protracted disputes before the Caribbean Court of Justice.[129] Yet, the provisions also reflect the awareness that the term of "cross-border effect" is open to interpretation. The first stage of discussions takes place vertically between national and regional authority and the final decision lies within the COTED, respectively horizontally among the member states. Yet, according to Article 176(6) of the Revised Treaty of Chaguaramas, member states can still challenge COTED's decision before the regional Court of Justice.[130]

The unresolved meaning of "cross-border effects" creates a risk of diverging referral activities of the national competition authorities to the CARICOM Competition Commission. This may even lead to a situation, in which referrals always originate from the same member state(s), thereby mostly taking into account considerations of this(these) member state(s). This could result in a one-sided and non-representative enforcement of community competition law with regards to issues of the entire region, which in the long run could also challenge the overall

[127] See below, Part II, Dimension IV: Sect. 8.1.2.

[128] Actually the wording of Article 176(5) only refers to the situation, in which the CARICOM Competition Commission has initiated an investigation based on its ex officio competence (after having asked the national authority to conduct a preliminary examination) and the member state does not agree with the opinion of the Commission. However, by its wording, Article 176(5) does not cover the situation, in which a national authority conducts an investigation and the CARICOM Competition Commission disagrees with the national agency's competence.

[129] *Beckford,* Enforcement of Competition Law in CARICOM, 35/2 W.I.L.J. 109, 132 (2010).

[130] *Lee,* Caricom Competition Commission: Enhancing Competition Enforcement in the Caribbean Community, 3–5 June 2009, Zurich, p. 4. However, *Beckford* points out that the procedure regarding the jurisdictional dispute contained in Article 176 of the Revised Treaty of Chaguaramas is not unambiguous. It is unclear whether the Commission must conduct the investigation until the Caribbean Court of Justice resolves the matter or whether the investigation has to be halted. See *Beckford,* The Appropriate Design and Enforcement of Competition Law and Policy in Countries at Different Stages of Market Development, 26–28 May 2010, Brasilia, p. 7.

competitiveness of the CSME. Unfortunately, the CARICOM already finds itself in a similar situation for the lack of national competition agencies. Only Jamaica and Barbados currently possess the sufficient institutional framework to efficiently assist the CARICOM Competition Commission or to request investigations from it.[131]

In all regional competition law frameworks, the territorial scope of application of the regional law and the interpretation of a "cross-border effect" are of crucial importance. In the WAEMU, the definition of the notion of "cross-border effect" has determined the centralized design. In the AndeanC, although Decision 608 was intended to widen the scope of application in contrast to the former Decision 285, this goal was not achieved. The territorial scope of application of the Andean competition law is constructed relatively formal by relying on specific constellations. Moreover, the case law—the little there is—indicates that the Secretariat General itself will apply Article 5 of Decision 608 in a restrictive way. In the CARICOM, the Revised Treaty of Chaguaramas gives no reference to the interpretation of "cross-border effects". However, there is a clearly perceived link between regional competition policy and the common market. The practical application and actual definition will thus also reflect the implementation progress of the CSME. In fact, the CARICOM provides a good example for the finding that the definition of a "cross-border effect" in a regional integration movement has to be different than in a non-regional integration system. In the AndeanC, the decreasing interest of member states in the common Andean market has attributed to the reluctance to apply or promote the application of Decision 608.

5.1.6 Exemptions

National and regional competition law objectives may conflict in the field of block and individual exemptions. From a national perspective, it may appear necessary to exempt sectors from the application of competition law that are conceived as sensitive and important for the national economy and sustainable development such as basic utilities or the agricultural sector. Regional competition policy has to serve the establishment and protection of the common market and might also function as a harmonizing tool, furthering general integration.

In the WAEMU, Article 89(3) of the Treaty of Dakar provides for the possibility to enact exemptions. According to Article 7 of Regulation no. 02/2002/CM/UEMOA the Commission can grant individual or block exemptions for agreements. Article 6 of Regulation no. 03/2002/CM/UEMOA[132] specifies the content and requirements for such block exemptions, while Article 7 of the same Regulation includes the

[131] Despite a lacking national competition authority, representatives from Trinidad and Tobago also participated during the drafting process of Chapter VIII.

[132] Règlement n° 03/2002/CM/UEMOA relatif aux procédures applicables aux ententes et abus de position dominante a l'intérieur de l'Union Économique et Monétaire Ouest Africaine.

requirements and procedure regarding individual exceptions. Article 6(2) of Regulation no. 02/2002/CM/UEMOA provides that the Commission can exempt undertakings that are charged with a service of general economic interest of the application of Article 88 lit. a) and lit. b) of the Treaty of Dakar. Since this provision is aimed at anticompetitive practices related to states, it sets out that the involved parties and/or member states notify the Commission via the Council of Ministers. In Regulation no. 03/2002/CM/UEMOA, Article 3 provides for the possibility of a negative clearance ruling, which can be requested by any undertaking from the Commission. In this procedure the Advisory Committee of Competition has to be consulted prior to the publication of the Commission's decision regarding the potential block exemption according to Article 6(7) of Regulation no. 03/2002/CM/UEMOA. The prior consultation is, however, no requirement in the context of an individual exception, Article 7 of Regulation no. 03/2002/CM/UEMOA.

In the AndeanC according to Article 6 of Decision 608 member states can request the Commission to grant an individual or block exemption for an economic activity that is necessary to achieve the fundamental objectives of the policies of a member state.[133] The exemption has to bring significant benefits to the development of the subregion.[134] Further requirements are set out in Article 6 lit. a) and lit. d) of Decision 608. The specific requirements for the granting of an exemption limit the discretion of the Commission as well as the requests by member states regarding exemptions. Article 6 of Decision 608 enables member states to theoretically exclude economic activities based on reasons of national interest, if they unanimously agree.[135] Whereas the differences of economic policy will already make such unanimous consensus-finding difficult, the guidelines on the application of Decision 608 also clarify that Article 6 of Decision 608 ought to be applied in the community interest.[136] Article 6 of Decision 608 thus provides for a sensitive balancing of national and regional competition-related objectives. It demonstrates that the Andean legislator was aware of the impact that exemption provisions can have on the scope of application of the regional competition law and of the potential of conflicts between national and regional objectives. On the other hand, it seems that the Andean legislator also acknowledged a certain weekness of Article 6 of Decision 608. Accordingly, in order to prevent member states from impeding regional competition

[133] *Secretaría General de la Comunidad Andina,* Guía Práctica para la aplicación de la Decisión 608 "Normas para la protección y promoción de la libre competencia en la Comunidad Andina", 2007, p. 21 <http://intranet.comunidadandina.org/Documentos/DTrabajo/SGdt396.doc> accessed 11 November 2018.

[134] *Ibid.*

[135] *Botta,* The Role of Competition Policy in the Latin American Regional Integration: A Comparative Analysis of Caricom, Andean Community and Mercosur, 21–22 October 2011, St. Gallen, p. 20.

[136] *Secretaría General de la Comunidad Andina,* Guía Práctica para la aplicación de la Decisión 608 "Normas para la protección y promoción de la libre competencia en la Comunidad Andina", 2007, p. 21 <http://intranet.comunidadandina.org/Documentos/DTrabajo/SGdt396.doc> accessed 11 November 2018.

law investigations, exemptions or exceptions cannot be requested for economic activities that are the object of an investigation.[137]

According to Article 6 of Decision, exceptions or exemptions have to be approved or modified by a Decision and need to be previously recommended by the Andean Committee of Defence of Free Competition. The Andean Committee of Defence of Free Competition has 30 day to approve of the request.[138] In this process, member states are also obliged to provide the Committee with all necessary information.[139] Nevertheless, despite the obligation to take into consideration the opinion of the Committee, it remains a mere recommendation for the Commission. On the other hand, the Andean Committee of Defence of Free Competition is in charge of the periodical supervision and revision of the granted exclusion or exemption. The Andean regional competition law underlines that exceptions or exemptions to Decision 608 only comprise a transitory character and should therefore be limited in their duration.[140]

Decision 608 is supposed to distinguish between absolute and relative prohibitions.[141] Yet Article 7 and Article 8 of Decision 608 only provide for a list of practices that are presumed to constitute a restriction to free competition or an abuse of dominant position. Although the listed practices in Article 7 lit. a)–e) and Article 8 lit. a)–g) of Decision 608 are commonly considered as absolute prohibitions, which are *per se* illegal, the listing in form of legal presumptions leaves room for the application of the *rule of reason*.[142] One can thus hope that the Secretariat General in the actual enforcement of Decision 608 will develop an internal prioritization scheme regarding the application of the *rule of reason*. In this context, the criteria set out in Article 6 lit. a)–d) of Decision 608 provide for a good starting point. As Decision 608 also refers to consumer welfare in its objectives, the efficiency criteria should be complemented with the requirement that consumers are allowed a fair share of

---

[137] Article 6 of Decision 608.

[138] *Secretaría General de la Comunidad Andina,* Guía Práctica para la aplicación de la Decisión 608 "Normas para la protección y promoción de la libre competencia en la Comunidad Andina", 2007, p. 22 <http://intranet.comunidadandina.org/Documentos/DTrabajo/SGdt396.doc> accessed 11 November 2018.

[139] *Ibid.*

[140] *Ibid.*

[141] The governmental experts that participated in the legislative process of Decision 608 agreed on the differentiation between absolute and relative prohibitions. Informe de la Segunda Reunion de Expertos Gubernamentales en Materia de Libre Competencia, SG/REG.LC/I/Informe/Rev.2, 16 and 17 February 2000, p. 2 (available from the author). With regard to the drafting process of Decision 608, see *Böttcher*, Harmonisierungsbemühungen der Andengemeinschaft im Bereich des Kartellrechts, GRUR Int 217, 220ff. (2003).

[142] *Secretaría General de la Comunidad Andina,* Guía Práctica para la aplicación de la Decisión 608 "Normas para la protección y promoción de la libre competencia en la Comunidad Andina", 2007, p. 11; Informe de la Primera Reunion de Expertos Gubernamentales en Materia de Libre Competencia, SG/REG.LC/I/Informe/Rev.1, 29 October 1998, p. 2 (available from the author); Informe de la Segunda Reunion de Expertos Gubernamentales en Materia de Libre Competencia, SG/REG.LC/I/Informe/Rev.2, 16 and 17 February 2000, p. 2 (available from the author).

the resulted benefit.[143] Interestingly, in one of the first draft versions of Decision 608 an according provision and the explicit differentiation between relative and absolute prohibitions were still incorporated.[144] Moreover, first drafts did not phrase the list of anticompetitive practices as legal presumptions.[145]

The CARICOM has adopted a method similar to the European legal exception principle. Article 177(4) of the Revised Treaty of Chaguaramas generally exempts business conduct that for example contributes to the improvement of production or distribution of goods and services while allowing the consumers a fair share of the resulting benefit.[146] Article 179(3) of the Revised Treaty specifically refers to exemptions to abuses of dominant position. In contrast to the European system, Article 180 includes the right of a member state to request a negative clearance ruling regarding the applicability of Article 177(1) of the Revised Treaty of Chaguaramas.

Another interesting feature of the Caribbean system is Article 183(2) of the Revised Treaty of Chaguaramas. This article provides the COTED with the right to suspend or exclude the application of Article 177 of the Revised Treaty to certain

[143] See in the EU: Commission Notice (EU) of 27 April 2004, Guidelines on the application of 81(3) of the Treaty, [2004] OJ C 101/08.

[144] Informe de la Segunda Reunion de Expertos Gubernamentales en Materia de Libre Competencia, SG/REG.LC/I/Informe/Rev.2, 16 and 17 February 2000, pp. 18f.: "Artículo 6.- Constituyen conductas restrictivas a la libre competencia sujetas a prohibición absoluta, los acuerdos entre competidores o las recomendaciones a competidores, que tengan como objeto o efecto: (…) Artículo 7- Constituyen conductas restrictivas a la libre competencia sujetas a prohibición relativa: (…) Artículo 8.- (…) Sin embargo, las conductas a que se refiere el Artículo anterior serán objeto de medidas si el presunto responsable no demuestra que los costos derivados de la reducción de la rivalidad en el mercado están justificadas por razones de eficiencia, inversión o innovación."

In the third reunion of governmental experts the Member States disagreed on the wording of Article 7 and 8 of Decision; Informe de la Tercera Reunion de Expertos Gubernamentales en Materia de Libre Competencia, SG/REG.LC/I/Informe/Rev.3, 24 and 25 October 2001, pp. 5f.: "[Alternativa A: Colombia, Ecuador, Perú y Venezuela: Artículo 8- Constituyen conductas de abuso de posición de dominio en el mercado: (…) Estas conductas podrán ser justificadas por razones de eficiencia, inversión o innovación, entre otras.] [Alternativa B: Boliva (en consulta): Artículo 8- Constituyen conductas restrictivas de la libre competencia sujetas a prohibición relativa (…) Se entenderá por conducta sujeta a prohibición relativa, acquella que admita prueba de la inexistencia de efectos restrictivos o, en caso contrario, prueba que dichos efectos restrictivos se encuentran justificados conforme al segundo párrafo del articulo siguente. Artículo 8a.- (…) Sin embargo, dichas conductas no serán objeto de medidas si los presuntos responsables demuestran que los costos derivados de la reducción de la rivalidad en el mercado están justificados por razones de eficiencia, inversión o innovación.]".

[145] Informe de la Cuarta Reunion de Expertos Gubernamentales en Materia de Libre Competencia, SG/REG.LC/I/Informe/Rev.4, 1 August 2003, p. 11: "Artículo 7.- Constituyen conductas restrictivas a la libre competencia, sujetas a prohibición absoluta, los acuerdos que tengan como objeto: (…). Artículo 8- Constituyen conductas de abuso de posición de dominio en el mercado: (…)."

[146] Article 178(4) lit. a)(i) of the Revised Treaty of Chaguaramas. Arguing against a literal interpretation of Article 177(4) of the Revised Treaty of Chaguaramas, see *Kaczorowska-Ireland*, Competition Law in the CARICOM Single Market and Economy, 2015, pp. 161ff.

sectors or enterprises "in the public interest".[147] COTED may either do this on its own initiative or pursuant to a request by a member state.[148] Article 183(2) of the Revised Treaty of Chaguaramas vests the COTED with far-reaching powers to limit the territorial scope of application of the community competition policy. It can even do this without any involvement of the CARICOM Competition Commission. One also has to recall that COTED is composed by representatives from national ministries.[149] The practical relevance of the Article 183(2) of the Revised Treaty of Chaguaramas is questionable. First, the other member states would have to decide upon an exemption based on a qualified majority vote or based on a two-thirds majority vote of the member states, depending on the critical importance of the matter.[150] It will be difficult to reconcile all fifteen national interests and reach an agreement regarding a necessary exemption "in the public interest". Such an agreement only seems probable in a situation, in which neither the internal market nor other national interests are touched by the exemption. Second, Article 176(6) of the Revised Treaty of Chaguaramas guarantees the right of member states to challenge COTED's decision before the Caribbean Court of Justice with regard to conflicts of competences between the CARICOM Competition Commission. The provision reformulates the general possibility to initiate court proceedings on the basis "that an organ or body of the Community has acted *ultra vires*" or "that the purpose or object of the Treaty is being frustrated or prejudiced", Article 187 lit. c) and lit. d) of the Revised Treaty of Chaguaramas. Member states can thus still initiate a procedure against a decision of the COTED.

It is not clear whether the CARICOM Competition Commission would be similarly entitled to initiate the same procedure against COTED's decision. Article 211 of the Revised Treaty of Chaguaramas, which shapes the Court's jurisdiction in contentious proceedings, does not refer to disputes between two community organs. Generally, although the COTED is composed by national ministers, it is still considered as a community organ in the Revised Treaty.[151] The CARICOM Competition Commission's judicial personality was explicitly emphasized in the Caribbean Court of Justice case *Trinidad Cement Limited v The Competition Commission.*[152] Yet, it would be an important instrument to strengthen the influence of the CARICOM Competition Commission, if it could also formulate a claim on the basis that COTED acted *ultra vires*, based on the argument that also competition law enforcement is in the public interest and outweighs the particular exemption. If such

[147] Slightly different is the right of the COTED set out in Articles 182 and 183(1), according to which the COTED can enact special rules to certain sectors or enterprises and then suspend them from the "general" Article 177.

[148] Art. 183(2) of the Revised Treaty of Chaguaramas.

[149] Article 15 of the Revised Treaty of Chaguaramas.

[150] Article 29 of the Revised Treaty of Chaguaramas.

[151] Article 10(2) lit. b) of the Revised Treaty of Chaguaramas.

[152] *Trinidad Cement Limited v The Competition Commission,* Caribbean Court of Justice Application No. OA 1 of 2012, CCJ 4 (OJ). For more information on the judgement see below Part II, Dimension IV: Sect. 8.1.1.1.

proceeding was admissible, the regional competition commission could participate in the exemption process of Article 183(2) indirectly, by invoking a judicial control before the CCJ after the exemption has been pronounced by the COTED.

In conclusion, the three RTAs have included the possibility of exceptions or exemptions to their competition law provisions. While only the CARICOM follows the European system of legal exception, the WAEMU and the AndeanC provide procedures of request to their competition commissions.[153] One the other hand, the CARICOM attributes a particular role to the COTED, which is vested with the competence to enact sectorial exceptions. Given that the competence to implement exceptions or exemptions has a crucial impact on the competition law enforcement, the COTED, which is an inter-governmental institution composed of national ministers, plays a decisive role in the Caribbean regime of competition law enforcement. In the WAEMU and the AndeanC, besides the competition authorities themselves, only advisory organs participate in the exemption process in the form of prior consultations, which are however non-binding.

5.1.7 Summary of Substantive Regional Competition Law Provisions

Unsurprisingly, the substantive law's content has an impact on the enforcement of competition law. There are manifold points of reference to determine the scope of application of regional competition law—via a limited territorial scope of application, a restrictive definition of terms, such as "cross-border effect" or in a second step through the exemptions. Evidently, the content of the substantive law, such as merger control or state aids, also impacts the addressees of the law. All three competition regimes also cover international anticompetitive practices that have an effect on the common market.[154] WAEMU's substantive competition law constitutes the most centralized regional competition law enforcement regime. The AndeanC and the CARICOM both rely on a broad territorial scope of application, while providing for (possibly) far-reaching exemption possibilities.

Although, the core competition law provisions of the WAEMU, the AndeanC and the CARICOM are derived from the European competition law rules, they were not completely "cut and pasted".[155] Without going into the details of the discussion

---

[153] In the EU the notification system was abolished with the entry into force of Council Regulation 1/2003 of 16 December 2002 on the implementation of the rules on competition laid down in Articles 81 and 82 of the Treaty.

[154] Respectively, they cover those international anticompetitive practices that have a cross-border effect.

[155] On the discussion regarding legal transplantation, see *Berkowitz/Pistor/Richard,* Economic development, legality, and the transplant effect, 47 Eur. Econ. Rev. 165–195 (2003); *Edwards,* Legal Transplants and Economics, 9 Eur. J. Law Reform 243–283 (2007); *Gal,* The 'Cut and Paste' of Article 82 of the EC Treaty in Israel, 9 Eur. J. Law Reform 467–484 (2007); *Gal/Padilla,*

regarding the pros and cons of legal transplantation, one should underline the consequences that the transfer of the European concepts had in the WAEMU, the AndeanC and the CARICOM.

First, in the absence of proper competition law experiences, judicial interpretation partly has to take place against the backdrop of foreign jurisdictions. In fact, in all three RTAs, the interpretation of the territorial scope of application has caused difficulties. The WAEMU's literal interpretation demonstrates that although the European provisions and competition law system might function as guidelines, the concrete application and transformation in developing countries should be adapted to domestic requirements and to the constitutional framework. This is particularly complex in an RTA, in which national and regional interests have to be reconciled. Legal transplants into RTAs not only have to adapt to horizontal conditions, but also have to be vertically adapted. This two-tiered requirement is especially difficult in RTAs among developing countries, because the common market and economic interdependencies between member states are much weaker (horizontal) and divergences with regard to competition law experience, economic development and commitment to regional integration often vary between member states (vertical).

5.2 Current Framework of National Competition Law Regimes

Prevailing national competition laws play a decisive role. Not only does the existence of a competition culture in the member states influence the competition law's application, but also a high degree of congruence between national and supranational substantive competition law provisions decreases possible conflicts and inconsistencies regarding the competition law enforcement in the entire region of the RTA. This is in particular the case under a decentralized system such as under the European Regulation 1/2003, as well as in a system, in which regional law does not have direct effect as in the CARICOM.

Implications for the Design of Monopolization Rules in a Global Economy, 76 Antitrust L.J. 899–927 (2010); *Glaeser/Shleifer,* Legal Origins, 117 Q. J. Econ. 1193–1229 (2002); *Lee,* Legal traditions and competition policy, 45 Q. Rev. Econ. & Fin. 236–257 (2005); *Mattei,* Taxonomy and Change in the World's Legal Systems, 45 Am. J. Comp. L. 5–45 (1997); *Rodriguez,* Does Legal Tradition Affect Competition Policy Performance?, 21 Int'l. Trade J. 417–454 (2007); *Spector,* Constitutional Transplants and the Mutation Effect, 83 Chi.-Kent L. Rev. 129–145 (2008).

5.2.1 Taxonomy of National Competition Law Regimes in the WAEMU

By 2007, all member states, except Guinea-Bissau,[156] have enacted national competition laws or laws that comprise competition related provisions. Member states' legislations include provisions prohibiting illicit agreements and abuse of dominant position. Hence, generally, the national competition law systems conform to the regional substantive law and its core competition law rules. Similar to the WAEMU rules, most member states do not possess a national merger regulation.[157] Another feature of national legislation is the preponderance of competition-related rules in sectorial regulation.[158] Despite the exclusive competence of the WAEMU competition authority, national sector regulators still retain competition-related competences.

5.2.1.1 Advanced National Competition Law Systems in Senegal, Burkina Faso, Ivory Coast and Mali

Senegal's national competition law is the most elaborate competition law regime within WAEMU. The relevant competition Law no. 94/63/SN had already been enacted in 1994 and the competent authority, the National Commission of Competition is operative and has dealt with a number of competition law cases.[159] The Minister of Commerce, more specifically the Directorate of Internal Trade, is in charge of domestic economic legislation.[160] The Directorate is entitled to conduct competition investigations on its own or to assist the National Commission of Competition.[161] Despite resource constraints,[162] the Commission issued consistent

---

[156] There exists a draft law regarding the facilitation of formalities to engage in commercial activities in Guinea Bissau, the Decreto-Lei n° 3/2005. Community competition law constitutes the only legal competition framework, however, regional law is not well known and the language constitutes a further hurdle for efficient national enforcement and perception. Additionally, there exists national sector regulation.

[157] For example, the national provisions in Ivory Coast covering concentrations are very similar to the WAEMU's provision. Article 34 of Loi n° 91-999 du 27 decembre 1991 relatif à la concurrence states that concentrations, which significantly attribute to a reenforcement of a dominant position may be subject to a national competition commission's opinion.

[158] *CUTS CCIER,* A Time for Action, 2010, pp. 32ff.

[159] See below Affaire CIBA contre Fédération Sénegalaise des Sociétés d'Assurances (FSSA), Décision n° 01-D-01 of 16 October 2007. For a summary see *Weick,* Competition Law and Policy in Senegal, 33/3 W. Comp. 521, 530 (2010); Affaire Syndicat des Agences de Voyage et de Tourisme du Sénégal contra Air France, Décision n° 02-D-02 du 27.12.2002. For a summary see *Weick,* Competition Law and Policy in Senegal, 33/3 W. Comp. 521, 531 (2010).

[160] *UNCTAD,* Voluntary Peer Review on Competition Policies of WAEMU, Benin and Senegal, 2008, p. 95.

[161] *UNCTAD,* Voluntary Peer Review on Competition Policies of WAEMU, Benin and Senegal, 2008, p. 101.

[162] Commission Nationale de la Concurrence du Sénégal, Rapport Public 2002–2003, 2004, pp. 19f.

decisions on anticompetitive practices. Among the most prominent cases *Central Insurance Broker Agency*[163] and *Air France*,[164] both decided in 2002, demonstrate the Senegalese Commission's ability to deal even with multinational enterprises.

The national competition law of Senegal[165] differentiates between individual and collective abuse of dominant position. Moreover the concept of abuse of dominance includes the abuse of economic dependency,[166] which is not included in the WAEMU legislation.

Burkina Faso passed its first national competition law in 1994 and the enforcement decree in 1996.[167] In 2001, the law was amended by Law no. 33-2001, which enlarged the investigations and inquiry powers of the national authority.[168] The National Commission of Competition and Consumption[169] is in charge of the enforcement of competition law. However is particularly struggling with a lack of human and skilled resources and a high concentration of the domestic markets.[170]

Finally, Mali's and Ivory Coast's national competition law systems can be traced back to the 1990s. Mali's national competition law[171] is administered by the National Competition Council, which only holds consultative functions and the National Directorate of Commerce and Competition, which actually does not constitute an independent authority but belongs to the Ministry of Trade.[172] Moreover, the authorities share competition law competences with sector regulators.[173] Mali's economy remains concentrated and competition mostly takes place between the formal and

[163] Affaire CIBA contre Fédération Sénegalaise des Sociétés d'Assurances (FSSA), Décision n° 01-D-01 of 16 October 2007. For a summary see *Weick*, Competition Law and Policy in Senegal, 33/3 W. Comp. 521, 530 (2010).

[164] Affaire Syndicat des Agences de Voyage et de Tourisme du Sénégal contra Air France, Décision n° 02-D-02 of 27 December 2002; for a summary see *Weick*, Competition Law and Policy in Senegal, 33/3 W. Comp. 521, 531 (2010).

[165] For more information on the Senegalese competition law, see *Weick*, Competition Law and Policy in Senegal, 33/3 W. Comp. 521 (2010).

[166] Senegalese abuse of dominant position case including the concept of abuse of economic dependence: *Syndicat des Agences de Voyages et de Tourisme du Sénégal (SAVTS) CF/la Compagnie Air France*, Decision no. 02-D-02 of the National Competition Commission of the Republic of Senegal, 16 January 2003.

[167] Loi n° 15/94 du 15 Mai 1994 *relative à la concurrence*; Décret n° 96/62/PRES/PM/MCIA du 14 Mars 1996 fixant les modalités d'application de la Loi n° 15/94 du 5 Mai 1994.

[168] *CUTS CCIER*, A Time for Action, 2010, p. 20.

[169] Commission Nationale de la Concurrence et de la Consommation (CNCC); Decret n° 2002-605/ PRES/PM/MCPEA portant composition attributions et fonctionnement de la Commission Nationale de la Concurrence et de la Consommation.

[170] *CUTS*, Document préliminaire Burkina Faso sur les scénarios de concurrence, 2008 <http://www.cuts-ccier.org/7up4/pdf/PCP-Burkina_Faso.pdf> accessed 11 November 2018; *CUTS CCIER*, A Time for Action, 2010, p. 20.

[171] L'Ordonnance n° 07-025 du 18 juillet 2007 portant organisation de la concurrence.

[172] *CUTS CCIER*, A Time for Action, 2010, p. 21. More information on Mali's competition system, see *UNCTAD*, Voluntary Peer Review on Competition Policies of WAEMU, Benin and Senegal, 2008, pp. 42f.

[173] *CUTS CCIER*, A Time for Action, 2010, p. 21.

informal sector.[174] Although Mali initiated reforms that enhanced economic participation of the private sector,[175] competition culture and awareness remains limited in civil society.[176] For similar reasons competition policy enforcement is often superseded by other policies, such as industrial or employment policy.[177]

In Ivory Coast, while there exists a specific competition commission, the Ministry of Trade is vested with the decision-making power regarding competition law enforcement.[178] The core substantive competition law provisions correspond to the WAEMU legislation.[179]

5.2.1.2 Young or Non-existing Competition Law Regimes in Niger, Togo, Guinea-Bissau and Benin

Niger, Togo, Guinea-Bissau and Benin are the member states of WAEMU with limited or no competition law experience. These states particularly feature systems that allow a price control by the state. The level of development regarding competition varies.

Guinea-Bissau is the least developed national jurisdiction, lacking not only a national competition law, but also a specialized authority. The General Directorate on Trade and Competition monitors prices of basic goods.[180] Sectorial provisions include competition related matters; however in fact they remain regulated by the state.

In Togo, although there is a national law, the Law no. 99-011,[181] Decree no. 2001-207/PR[182] regulating the application of the foregoing Law no. 99-011 and the Decree no. 2001-208/PR[183] on the composition and functioning of the National Competition and Consumer Commission,[184] the National Competition and Consumer Commission's enforcement is hampered by the lack of human and finan-

---

[174] *CUTS,* Document Préliminaire du Mali sur les Scénarios de Concurrence, 2009, p. 42 <http://www.cuts-ccier.org/7up4/pdf/PCP-Mali.pdf> accessed 11 November 2018.

[175] According to *CUTS,* participation of private national and foreign enterprises rose from 5% in 1991 up to 85% in 2005. *Ibid.,* p. 17.

[176] *Ibid.,* p. 13.

[177] *Ibid.,* p. 27.

[178] More information on Ivory Coast's competition system, see *UNCTAD,* Voluntary Peer Review on Competition Policies of WAEMU, Benin and Senegal, 2008, pp. 43f.

[179] L'Ordonnance n° 2013-662 du 20 septembre 2013 relative à la concurrence.

[180] *UNCTAD,* Voluntary Peer Review on Competition Policies of WAEMU, Benin and Senegal, 2008, p. 41.

[181] Loi n° 99-011 du 28 décembre 1999 portant organisation de la concurrence au Togo.

[182] Décret n° 2001-207/PR fixant les modalités d'application de la loi de 1999 sur la concurrence.

[183] Décret n° 2001-208/PR portant composition et fonctionnement de la commission nationale de la concurrence et de la consommation.

[184] Commission Nationale de la Concurrence et de la Consommation.

cial resources.[185] In any event, the competition authority only holds consultative powers.[186] Similarly to Guinea-Bissau, sectorial provisions are meant to foster competitive markets. Nevertheless, market access is hampered by high entry barriers.

In Niger, despite the implemented Ordonnance no. 92-025,[187] which among others includes provisions on anticompetitive practices, the jurisdiction is still characterized by a strong price regulation by the state and national markets display a high level of economic concentration.

Finally, Benin only enacted a national competition law in 2016. Before, Ordonnance no. 20/PR/MFAEP[188] governed the regulation of prices. They were generally free, but may be subject to the regulation of the state. Competition enforcement does not take place via an independent administrative authority, but through a technical directorate of the Ministry of Commerce, the Directorate for Competition and the Fight against Fraud. In addition, sectorial authorities regulate competition.[189]

5.2.2 Taxonomy of National Competition Law Regimes in the AndeanC

In the AndeanC, by 2011 all member states had enacted national competition law provisions. However, they vary in their content and systematic approach. One can distinguish between the experienced competition law regimes in Colombia and Peru and the young jurisdictions Bolivia and Ecuador, which are still in the implementation process. In the AndeanC the development of competition legislation correlates to the level of liberalization in the domestic markets. While Colombia and Peru have installed open economies, Bolivia and Ecuador are still characterized by a strong state intervention and the prevalence of state-owned or state-supported businesses.

5.2.2.1 Advanced Competition Law Regimes in Colombia and Peru

Colombia's competition law tradition can be traced back to the year 1959, in which the Law 155 on restrictive commercial practices was enacted.[190] In 2009, the Law 1340[191] reformed the existing system by *inter alia* determining the Superintendence

---

[185] *Présidence de la République de Togo,* Stratégie de Gestion de la Concurrence au Togo, final report, 2015, p. viii.

[186] Article 9 of Loi n° 99-011.

[187] Ordonnance n° 92-025 du 7 juillet 1992 portant réglementation des prix et de la concurrence.

[188] Ordonnance n° 20/PR/MFAEP du 5 juillet 1967 portant réglementation des prix et des stocks.

[189] See also Autorité de Régulation des Marchés Publics, <http://www.armp.bj/>.

[190] Ley 155 de 1959 (Diciembre 24), Diario Oficial No. 30.138 del 22 de enero de 1960, "Disposiciones sobre prácticas comerciales restrictivas".

[191] Ley 1340 de 2009 (Julio 24), Diario Oficial No. 47.420 del 24 de julio de 2009, "Normas en materia de protección de la competencia".

of Industry and Trade[192] (hereafter SIC) as the central competent antitrust authority,[193] by redefining the calculation basis for sanctions and by introducing a leniency program.[194] The leniency regime was amended again in 2015 through Decree 1523, which set up clearer rules for leniency proceedings. Leniency applications in particular in sensitive sectors have become an essential pillar of competition law enforcement in Colombia.[195] Likewise, the government has been working on a new bill since 2015 that will allow the SIC to impose higher fines. In fact, the fines imposed by the Colombian competition authority have increased constantly, amounting up to a total of 89 billion pesos in 2014.[196] Decree 019 of 2012[197] introduced changes to administrative procedures regarding restrictions of competition and merger cases. It also imposed publication obligations on the Superintendence of Industry and Trade, thereby increasing the authority's transparency. Other relevant competition regulations are contained in Legislative Decree 2153 of 1992,[198] later modified by Decree 3523 of 2009 and Decree 1687 of 2010, which *inter alia* deal with the institutional structure of the Superintendence of Industry and Trade.

Peruvian competition legislation initiatives began in 1979.[199] In 2008 the Legislative Decree no. 1034[200] changed the former competition laws contained in the Legislative Decree no. 701.[201] The Legislative Decree no. 1034 clarified aspects of the former provisions such as the distinction between *per se* and *rule of reason*

---

[192] Superintendencia de Industria y Comercio (SIC), see <www.sic.gov.co>.

[193] Since the legislative reform in 2009 the SIC is the sole authority to enforce competition laws in all sectors. Two specific sector regulators have competition powers with regards to merger control, namely the civil aeronautic authority (aerocivil) and the superintendence of finance (SFC).

[194] In interviews with the author representatives from the private sector and from the SIC considered these three aspects of the reform as the most important changes. For more information on the competition law reform see *Uribe Pedrahita,* Reforma al Régimen de Libre Competencia en Colombia, 2009; *Miranda Londoño,* Developments and Perspectives in Colombian Competition Law, 21 Boletín Latinoamericano de Comp. 17 (2006); *Cortázar,* Hacia un Nuevo Derecho de la Competencia en Colombia, 2003.

[195] *Serrano Pinilla,* Colombia: Superintendence of Industry and Commerce, Antitrust Rev. Americas 112, 112 (2016).

[196] The highest fine so far was imposed on a Colombian water utility company in 2014 and reached approximately US$32 million.

[197] Decreto 019 de 2012, (Enero 10), "Por el cual se dictan normas para suprimir o reformar regulaciones, procedimientos y trámites innecesarios existentes en la Administración Pública".

[198] Decreto 2153 de 1992 (Diciembre 30), Diario Oficial No. 40.704 del 31 de diciembre de 1992, "Decreto por el cual se reestructura la Superintendencia de Industria y Comercio y se dictan otras disposiciones".

[199] *Zúñiga-Feranández,* Fusionskontrolle in einer "small market economy" in Lateinamerika, 2009, p. 68ff.

[200] Decreto Legislativo N° 1034, "Decreto Legislativo que aprueba la Ley de Represión de Conductas Anticompetitivas" of 24 June 2008, published on 25 June 2008, enacted on 24 August 2008.

[201] Decreto Legislativo N° 701, "Eliman las prácticas monopólicas, controlistas y restrictivas de la libre competencia" of 5 November 1991, published on 7 November 1991.

prohibitions by introducing absolute and relative prohibitions.[202] Further changes regarding the administrative competition law procedures were introduced in 2015 through the Legislative Decree no. 1205.[203] Likewise, Peruvian competition law has already comprised leniency rules since 1996. Although the first leniency application was only submitted in 2012, it has now become a frequent enforcement mechanism.[204]

The content of the developed national competition law regimes in general corresponds to the Andean competition law provisions. The Colombian Law 1340 and the Peruvian Legislative Decree no. 1034 both include the prohibition of illicit agreements and abuse of dominant position. Interestingly, the Peruvian competition law follows a more liberal and free market[205]-based approach by focusing on "exclusionary abuses".[206] Under Colombian competition law, in addition, "exploitative" prices can be subsumed under Article 1 of the Law 155 of 1959, which is still applicable according to Article 4 of Law 1340 of 2009.[207] A novelty introduced by the Peruvian competition law is the absence of the notion of collective dominance or tacit collusion.[208] Yet, both notions are included in Decision 608.[209] On the other hand, Article 48 of the Colombian Legislative Decree 2153 of 1992 prohibits certain conducts without the prevalence of a dominant position.[210] The Colombian competition law has therefore a partly larger scope of application than Decision 608. Similar

---

[202] Article 8 and 9 of Decreto Legislativo N° 1034.

[203] Decreto Legislativo N° 1205 of 23 September 2015.

[204] In 2015 and 2014, four leniency applications were submitted covering five markets, *Espinoza Lozada*, Peru: National Institute for the Defence of Competition and the Protection of Intellectual Property, Antitrust Rev. Americas 138, 138 (2016).

[205] *Boza*, Tailor-Made Competition Policy in a Standardizing World, 2005, p. 102.

[206] There had been some controversy whether excessive pricing was prohibited by the Peruvian competition law norms due to a decision of the INDECOPI Tribunal. The explicit referring to abuses of dominant position with an "efecto exclusorio" in Article 10(2) of the Legislative Decree no. 1034 supports the deliberate exclusion of exploitative abuses of dominant position such as "excessive pricing". This assessment was also supported by representatives of the INDECOPI in interviews with the author, 19 January 2012. On the controversy on "excessive pricing", see *OECD*, Competition Peer Review Report of Peru, 11/1 OECD J. Comp. L. Policy 177, 191ff. (2009).

[207] Article 1 of the Law 155 of 1959: "Quedan prohibidos los acuerdos o convenios (…) y en general, toda clase de prácticas, procedimientos o sistemas tendientes a limitar la libre competencia y a mantener o determinar precios inequitativos".

[208] *Zúñiga-Feranández*, Fusionskontrolle in einer "small market economy" in Lateinamerika, 2009, pp. 74,75.

[209] *Secretaria General de la Comunidad Andina*, Guía Práctica para la aplicación de la Decisión 608 "Normas para la protección y promoción de la libre competencia en la Comunidad Andina", 2007, p. 10.

[210] Superintendencia de Industria y Comercio, Radicación No. 01061192 del 8 de Julio of 2002: competition law case, in which the SIC imposed a fine on the Association of Retail Distributors of Fuels and Petroleum Derivatives (ADICONAR) based on Article 48 of Decree 2153 of 1992; *OECD*, Peer Review on Competition Law and Policy in Colombia, 2009, p. 25.

to Decision 608, the Colombian and Peruvian competition laws also apply to public entities.[211]

Regarding the exemption system, Colombia explicitly includes exceptions in Article 49 of Decree 2153 of 1992 that are based on efficiency considerations or the introduction of new technologies. Another important exception in the Colombian system is contained in Art. 1 of Law 155 of 1959, according to which "[t]he government may authorise agreements or understandings, that despite limiting free competition, are intended to defend the stability of basic sectors producing goods or services of interest for the general economy".[212] Although this provision allows state intervention and is therefore prone to potential abuse by interventionist governments, it remained unchanged by the legal reform in 2009. In fact, it was only applied once in 2003.[213]

Despite the reform and the general application of the national competition law, further uncertainty is caused by Article 5 of Law 1340 of 2009 and the Decree 3280 of 2005 in Colombia. In order to authorise or terminate an agreement that intends to stabilise the agricultural sector, the Superintendence of Industry and Commerce must seek the non-binding opinion of the Ministries of Agriculture and Rural Development and of Commerce, Industry and Tourism.[214] Whereas this provision expresses high importance attributed to the agricultural sector, it also creates a potential loophole for abusive state intervention. In the same vein, in the Peruvian competition law system, there exists a special agency for telecommunication[215] and special provisions on the electricity sector[216] in addition to the INDECOPI and general competition law.

---

[211] Colombia: Article 4 of Law 1340 of 2009: "La Ley 155 de 1959, el Decreto 2153 de 1992, la presente ley y las demás disposiciones (…) constituyen el regimen general de protección de la competencia, aplicables a todos los sectores y todas las actividades económicas."; SIC Concepto Número 04254 of 1 December 1993; SIC Resolución Número 15661 of the 10 August 1999. Peru: Article 2(1) of the Legislative Decree N° 1034: "La presente Ley se aplica a las personas naturales o jurídicas, sociedades irregulars, patrimonios autónomos u otras entidades de derecho public o privado, estatales o no, con o sin fines de lucro, que en el Mercado oferten o demanden bienes o servicios (…).". See also 014-93-INDECOPI/CLC of 23 December 1993 regarding the state as economic actor and subject to the competition law.

[212] Article 1 of Law 155 of 1959: "El Gobierno, sin embargo, podrá autorizar la celebración de acuerdos o convenios que no obstante limitar la libre competencia, tengan por fin defender la estabilidad de un sector básico de la producción de bienes o servicios de interés para la economía general".

[213] SIC, Resolución Número 04332, 25 February 2003.

[214] Article 1 of Decreto 3280, 19 September 2005, "Reglamiento del parágrafo del artículo 1° de la Ley 155 de 1959 para el sector agropecuario", published in the Diario Oficial No. 46.037, 20 September 2005.

[215] "Oficina Supervisora de la Inversión Privada de las Telecomunicaiones" (OSIPTEL).

[216] Decreto Ley N° 25844 of 19 November 1993, published 25 November 1993 in the Diario Oficial El Peruano; Decreto Supremo N° 27-95-ITINCI of 18 October 1995, published 19 October 1995 in the Diario Oficial El Peruano.

In contrast to Peru and the AndeanC, Colombia possesses a merger regulation, which is based on mandatory *ex ante* notifications.[217] Peru has specialized sectorial merger regulation for the electricity market. Moreover, there are current initiatives in Peru to enact a general merger regulation. Especially the INDECOPI, the competent antitrust authority, is in favour of such a regulation.[218] Currently, a legislative proposal is discussed in congress.[219]

Similar to Decision 608, both the Colombian and Peruvian competition law system include explicit provisions on competition advocacy.[220] In particular the possibility to issue opinions on legislative initiatives is worth mentioning in this regard.[221]

The Colombian and Peruvian competition law systems have gained considerable competition law experience and have increased their competition law enforcement activities in the last years.[222] Both systems have also already introduced reforms to their existing laws. The SIC has defined its leniency rules, while the INDECOPI has scheduled to issue guidelines on mergers and the leniency rules as well. Fines imposed on undertakings are also increasing in both jurisdictions. Finally, both authorities are conducting thorough and regular market studies in order to identify

---

[217] Article 4 of Law 155 of 1959, modified by Article 9 of Law 1340 of 2009; *Cortázar,* Curso de Derecho de la Competencia, 2011, pp. 165ff.

[218] See for example Congreso de la República, Proyecto de Ley n° 972/2011-CR, Ley de promoción de la libre competencia y la eficiencia en los mercados para la protección de los consumidores, 28 March 2012. With regard to prior legislative initiatives regarding the introduction of a merger control see *Zúñiga-Feranández,* Fusionskontrolle in einer "small market economy" in Lateinamerika, 2009, pp. 169ff. In 2004 and 2008 draft laws on a general merger regulation were unsuccessfully proposed to the Congress in Peru. In cooperation with the Fordham University employees of the INDECOPI received further education on merger regulation in a one-week seminar in 2011. Also in 2005 the INDECOPI proposed a draft legislation that inter alia included a merger regulation. The proposal was sent to the Cabinet of Ministers and to the Congress for discussion, but was rejected. See *OECD,* A Follow-Up on Peer Reviews of Competition Law and Policy in Latin America, 2007, p. 25.

[219] *La República,* "Mañana empieza en el Congreso foro por una ley antimonopolio", 4 December 2016, available at <http://larepublica.pe/impresa/economia/827590-manana-empieza-en-el-congreso-foro-por-una-ley-antimonopolio> last accessed 5 September 2017; *La República,* "Proyecto de ley que regula fusions listo en marzo del 2017", 6 December 2016, available at <http://larepublica.pe/impresa/economia/828126-proyecto-de-ley-que-regula-fusiones-listo-en-marzo-del-2017> last accessed 5 September 2017.

[220] *Uribe Pedrahita,* Reforma al Régimen de Libre Competencia en Colombia, 2009, pp. 60ff. and pp. 117ff.

[221] Colombia: Article 7 of Law 1340 of 2009. For more information on the competition advocacy function of the SIC, see *Cortázar,* Curso de Derecho de la Competencia, 2011, pp. 220ff.; Peru: Article 14(2) lit. e) of Legislative Decree N° 1034.

[222] In Peru, the INDECOPI carried out 15 dawn raids to 76 undertakings between 2013 and 2014. Between 2011 and 2012 dawn raids were directed against 12 companies. In 2014, INDECOPI decided 8 cases on antitrust infringements. For more information see *Espinoza Lozada*, Peru: National Institute for the Defence of Competition and the Protection of Intellectual Property, Antitrust Rev. Americas 138–140 (2016). In Colombia, the SIC has also increased the number of dawn raids. The authority is also entitled to impose fines on undertakings that do not cooperate. For more information see *Pardo Cuéllar*, Colombia: Overview, Antitrust Rev. Americas 114, 114 (2016).

sensitive sectors with regard to the basic needs of the population, such as petroleum gas, health, cement or transportation, which might be particularly vulnerable to anti-competitive practices.[223]

5.2.2.2 Young Competition Law Regimes in Bolivia and Ecuador

On 16 April 2008, Bolivia enacted the Supreme Decree no. 29519[224] and as completion to it on 29 May 2009 the Ministerial Resolution 190/2009,[225] which terminated the former system based on the sectorial SIRESE-law.[226] However, Bolivia still lacks a general competition law, which is currently in the legislation process.[227] The most important issue that still has to be agreed upon concerns the identification of the competent agency.[228] Currently, the Authority for Finances and Social Control of Enterprises[229] deals with competition law issues.[230]

The scope of application of the new competition law and Supreme Decree no. 29519 is and will be very limited due to continuation of a regulative system in strategic sectors, such as water, electricity, transportation and telecommunication. Generally, the Bolivian economy under the new paradigm of a "Plural Economy" and the new Constitution of 2009 feature a high degree of state intervention.[231]

---

[223] *Espinoza Lozada*, Peru: National Institute for the Defence of Competition and the Protection of Intellectual Property, Antitrust Rev. Americas 138, 138 (2016).

[224] Decreto Supremo N° 29519 of 16 April 2008, "Reglamento de Regulación de la Competencia y Defensa del Consumidor", published in the Gaceta Oficial de Bolivia N° 3082.

[225] Resolución Ministerial 190/2009, "Reglamento de Regulación de la Competencia en el Marco del Decreto Supremo N° 29519", 29 May 2009.

[226] Ley del Sistema de Regulación Sectorial (SIRESE), Ley N° 1600 of 28 October 1994; *Otero*, El Derecho de la Competencia en Bolivia, 2/2 Rev. Derecho Comp. 15–31 (2006); *Ochoa Urioste*, Régimen General del Derecho de la Competencia en Bolivia, 26 Boletín Latinoamericano de Comp. 8, 9 (2009); *Lozano*, La Decisión 608 de la CAN y sus Implicaciones en Bolivia, 21 Boletín Latinoamericano de Comp. 43, 44ff. (2006).

[227] There have already been concrete competition law projects in 2003. However due to changes in the government and social conflicts, the project has never been introduced in the Parliament. See *Urquieta Arias*, in: *CUTS International*, Competition Regimes in the World, 2006, p. 546, 547.

[228] Several unpublished documents of different entities express their opinions regarding the current competition law project. The Vice Minister of Internal Trade and Exportations is in favour of the creation of a new, mixed (dealing with competition law and consumer rights protection such as the Peruvian INDECOPI) competition authority, which would institutionally be part of and organically dependent on the Ministry. On the other hand, the current competent authority, the Autoridad de Fiscalización y Control Social de Empresas (AEMP) wants to keep its competence to deal with general competition law issues independently.

[229] Autoridad de Fiscalización y Control Social de Empresas (AEMP).

[230] According to Article 44 of Decree no. 0071 of 9 April 2009.

[231] "Economía Plural": This new economic model comprises 4 different forms of economic organization: communitarian, state, private and socio-cooperative. Furthermore, the new concept promulgates a strong state intervention, leaving aside the former system of a free market. See also: *Ministerio de Desarrollo Productivo de Bolivia,* Política Marco Antimonopolio, 2011, p. 1: "la

Bolivia's Supreme Decree no. 29519 distinguishes between absolute and relative prohibitions. The system follows the Mexican competition model.[232] Interestingly, the absolute prohibitions exclude unilateral behaviour and the Supreme Decree no. 29519 does not mention nor define a dominant position. The Decree also contains provisions with regard to a leniency program in Article 13. Article 16(10) of the Decree refers to the function of the Superintendence of Enterprises[233] to take a stand on subsidies and state aids. However, the latter are not explicitly regulated in the Decree. Merger regulations are contained in the specific sectorial regulations.

Ecuador passed its competition law, the "Ley Orgánica de Regulación y Control del Poder de Mercado", on 29 September 2011. It entered into force on 13 October 2011. The domestic competition law also created the Superintendence for the Control of Market Power.[234] However, the Superintendence for the Control of Market Power only became operative starting from the 31 July 2012 with the appointment of its first Superintendent.[235] In the meantime, the Subsecretariat of Competition,[236] which had been created by the Decree 1614,[237] was in charge of investigating potential competition law breaches. At the end of 2012, the Superintendence for the Control of Market Power then conducted its first actions, *inter alia* a control of the telecommunications, airline, alimentation, pharmaceutical and textile sectors.[238] In fact, in one of its first resolutions the competition authority fined the telecommunication operator *CONECEL*,[239] an Ecuadorian subsidiary of América Móvil, US$138 million for having abused its dominant position. The National Corporation of Telecommunications had submitted a complaint, arguing that the exclusivity arrangements exercised by CONECEL with landowners with regard to where telecommunications masts had to be situated excluded other operators from the

---

CPE (Nueva Constitución Política del Estado) relanza la nueva faceta de intervención estatal en la economía, dejando de lado ese estado residual heredado por el anterior sistema de libre mercado, y posicionando un estado fuerte que regula la economía, (...) que interviene en la producción de bienes y servicios y que planifica el desarrollo económico." According to the Ministry of Economy and Public Finances in 2011, the New Economic Model is to set the base for a transition to a socialist production.

[232] *Ochoa Urioste,* Régimen General del Derecho de la Competencia en Bolivia, 26 Boletín Latinoamericano de Comp. 8, 10 (2009).

[233] Superintendencia de Empresas. Nevertheless, the AEMP still exercises all functions with regard to competition law enforcement.

[234] Superintendencia de Control del Poder de Mercado. For more information see <http://scpm.gob.ec/>.

[235] The deadline for appointment of the Superintendent set out in the law was actually 13 April 2012.

[236] The Subsecretariat of Competition organisationally belonged to the to the Ministry of Industries and Productivity.

[237] Decreta n° 1614, Normas para la aplicación de la Decisión 608 de la CAN, 14 March 2009.

[238] El Comercio, 10 December 2012, "Ecuador busca en China propuestas para su nueva agencia antimonopolio" <http://www.elcomercio.com/negocios/Pekin-China-Pedro_Paez-Superintendencia_de_Control_del_Poder_de_Mercado_0_826117390.html> accessed 11 November 2018.

[239] Consorcio Ecuatoriano de Telecomunicaciones S.A. CONECEL.

market.[240] The fine amounted to 10% of CONECEL's total annual revenues. In compliance with the law, the payment of the fine was not suspended despite a pending appeal against the decision by CONECEL.[241]

The new law explicitly refers to the control of market power. Although prohibitions cover illicit agreements (Art. 11) and abuse of dominance (Art. 9) and even provide for a merger control regime (Art. 14ff.), the risk of creating loopholes as regards state intervention is inherent to the law. In a conference on the new competition law in Ecuador, representatives criticised the lack of certainty regarding Article 10 LORCPM, which sanctions the abuse of economic dependency.[242] The concept of abuse of an economic dependency could lead to an intervention or regulation of private entrepreneurial activity.[243] Furthermore, the Articles 28ff. LORCPM allow direct state intervention. According to the provisions, competition can be restricted in any sector of the Ecuadorian economy through a Resolution of the "Junta de Regulación"[244] for reasons of public interest. The broad notion of "public interest" vests public authorities with large discretion to limit the scope of application of the new Ecuadorian competition law. In the same vein, one of the objectives of the Ecuadorian competition law is to achieve "just commerce" and the establishment of a "social and sustainable economic system".[245]

Although Bolivia and Ecuador include ambitious competition law provisions, such as merger control or leniency programs, the inclusion of non-technical, competition law terms that still have to be defined aggravate the risk of state intervention

---

[240] Superintendencia de Control del Poder de Mercado, Expediente No. 002-SCPM-CRPI-2013, 30 April 2013.

[241] Superintendencia de Control del Poder de Mercado, Expediente No. SCPM-CRPI-2014-024, 30 April 2013.

[242] *Dávila,* La vision empresarial sobre la Ley, speech at international conference on the competition law in Ecuador, Quito, 16 February 2012 (not published).

[243] *Dávila,* La vision empresarial sobre la Ley, speech at international conference on the competition law in Ecuador, Quito, 16 February 2012 (not published).

[244] The "Junta de Regulación" is an executive body composed of the highest state authorities, or their delegates, in charge of Production, Economic Policy, Strategic Sectors and of Social Development, whose main function is (inter alia) to issue binding rules (e.g. Exemptions according to Art. 28 LORCPM) without altering the existing provisions in the law, Article 35 LORCPM.

[245] In Ecuador Article 1 LORCPM sets out: "El objeto de la presente Ley es evitar, prevenir, corregir, eliminar y sancionar el abuse de operadores económicos con poder de mercado; la prevención, prohibición y sanción de acuerdos colusorios y otras prácticas restrictivas; el control y regulación de las operaciones de concentración económica; (…), buscando la eficiencia en los mercados, el comercio justo y el bienestar general y de los consumidores y usuarios, para el establecimiento de un sistema económico social, solidario y sostenible." In Bolivia the notion of "just competition" is not included directly in the law. However, the notion of "just competition" is one of the objectives of the new Plural Economy and antitrust policy, *Ministerio de Desarrollo Productivo de Bolivia,* Política Marco Antimonopolio, 2011, p. 3: "Política antimonopolio y de Regulación y Ordenamiento de la Economía Plural: Conjunto de medidas gubernamentales, estrategias y programas conducentes a (…) establecer (…) las condiciones para que los mercados del país operen en un ambiente de libre y justa competencia (…)".

and finally the risk of undermining the content of the law and its scope of application.

5.2.3 *Taxonomy of National Competition Law Regimes in the CARICOM*

Since 1990, a paradigm shift from public state ownership toward market economies and private ownership has supported the creation of competition laws and institutions in the CARICOM.[246] Additionally, utility regulation has also been introduced at an early stage.[247] Although some states have abolished sectorial regulators and installed single agencies[248] dealing with competition law matters, competition law enforcement through utility sector regulation is still a frequent feature in the CARICOM.[249]

In the CARICOM, one can distinguish between three different blocs of implementation stages of domestic competition law and policy. The Jamaican and Barbados' competition laws were applied prior to the entering into force of the Revised Treaty of Chaguaramas and prior to the inauguration of the CARICOM Competition Commission. Trinidad and Tobago and Guyana have enacted a national competition law and installed a national competition authority recently. Belize and Suriname are currently in the implementation process, either already installing the domestic authority or drafting the law. The third bloc comprises the member states that form the Organisation of Eastern Caribbean States (hereafter OECS). They have adopted a different approach, by planning to adopt individual domestic competition laws, but a shared authority. This process is still ongoing.

5.2.3.1 Advanced Competition Law Regimes in Jamaica and Barbados

The Jamaican competition law is the oldest competition law in the Caribbean region. The Fair Competition Act was passed on 9 March 1993 and took effect on 9 September of the same year. The national competition law agency, the Fair Trading Commission, opened its doors on 8 November 1993. Coming from an interventionist and state-regulated economy, Jamaica had started in the early 1980s to embark towards a liberalized new economic policy. However, it was struggling with this process as also consumers were accustomed to protectionism and price control and the private sector had attuned to rely on government protection as financial and

[246] *Sampson/Sampson,* in: *Mehta/Evenett,* Politics Triumphs Economics?, 2009, pp. 327, 327f.

[247] *Sampson/Sampson,* in: *Mehta/Evenett,* Politics Triumphs Economics?, 2009, p. 327, 331.

[248] See for example Barbados.

[249] *Sampson/Sampson,* in: *Mehta/Evenett,* Politics Triumphs Economics?, 2009, p. 327, 355.

economical support.[250] While the draft Bill was presented in Parliament in 1991, it took 2 more years until the Fair Competition Act was finally enacted.

In Barbados, the Fair Trading Commission began its operations on 2 January 2001 and replaced its predecessor, the Public Utility Board, which was responsible for regulating public utilities, such as electricity or telecommunication. The Commission is a mixed authority, dealing also with utility regulation and consumer protection.[251] The Commission is staffed with eleven Commissioners from different sectors. The competition legislation in Barbados, the Fair Competition Act,[252] was enacted on 3 January 2003. The general powers of the Fair Trading Commission reflect the proactive standing of the Barbados legislator towards liberalization. Main incentives also originated from the World Trade Organization, but also the private sector. In particular, the telecommunication sector constituted an active supporter of the liberalization process.[253]

The Jamaica Fair Competition Act prohibits abuses of dominant position and agreements that have anticompetitive effects in Part III of the Act. The Act also provides for and the explicit prohibition of resale price maintenance.

The Jamaica Fair Competition Act has general application. However, a judgement of the Court of Appeal created ambiguity by finding that certain sector-specific legislation took precedence over the general competition law.[254] Presently exempted from the application of competition law are the General Legal Council[255] and the Jamaica Stock Exchange. The Jamaica Fair Competition Act is for several reasons currently undergoing a reforming process.[256]

In Barbados, the Fair Competition Act does not only comprise provisions with regard to agreements and abuse of dominant position, but also includes a merger control regime. The number of merger cases before the Fair Trading Commission is

---

[250] *Malahoo,* Competition Law in Emerging Economies: The Jamaican Experience, 2000, p. 5.

[251] Chapter 326B Fair Trading Commission Act: "An Act to provide for the establishment of a Fair Trading Commission to safeguard the interests of consumers, to regulate utility services supplied by service providers, to monitor and investigate the conduct of service providers and business enterprises, to promote and maintain effective competition in the economy, and for related matters."

[252] Chapter 326C Fair Competition Act: "An Act (a) to promote and maintain and encourage competition; (b) to prohibit the prevention, restriction or distortion of competition and the abuse of dominant positions in trade in Barbados and within the Caricom Single Market and Economy; (c) to ensure that all enterprises, irrespective of size, have the opportunity to participate equitably in the market place; and (d) for connected matters."

[253] Statements made by representatives of the Fair Trading Commission during an interview with the author, 23 October 2012 in Bridgetown.

[254] *Jamaica Stock Exchange v Fair Trading Commission,* Supreme Court Civil Appeal No. 92/97 of 2001; *UNCTAD,* Voluntary Peer Review on Competition Policy: Jamaica, 2005, p. 33.

[255] The Council is responsible for the organisation of legal education and to safeguard standards of professional conduct of lawyers in Jamaica. For more information see <http://www.generallegalcouncil.org/> last accessed 30 August 2017.

[256] The FTC's institution was held to be in breach of natural justice. For more information see below in this Chapter.

still relatively small. As in the Jamaican legislation, the Barbados Fair Competition Act also includes an explicit provision on resale price maintenance.[257] The law has general application, but the telecommunication and electricity sector fall under special regulation. However, the Fair Competition Act remains applicable to these sectors if a competition matter arises.[258]

The Jamaica Fair Competition Act stipulates the "maintenance and encouragement of competition in the conduct of trade and business in Jamaica with the view to providing consumers with competitive prices and product choices".[259] Apart from addressing mere anticompetitive practices, the long title demonstrates that the Jamaican competition law places a special emphasis on consumer protection in a broad sense. This has created problems, as resources had been concentrated on the consumer-related issues in the first years of the Fair Trading Commission.[260] While this is clearly attributed to the large number of complaints that concern consumer protection, one might hope that the Fair Trading Commission will invest resources to further consumers' awareness with regard to competition law and policy.[261] Since 2005 there exists a Consumer Protection Act, which is applied by the Consumer Affairs Commission.[262] In case of overlaps, the Fair Trading Commission and the Consumer Affairs Commission cooperate and refer the matter to the competent authority.

The Jamaica Fair Competition Act has been criticised for its confusing wording, duplication and partial contradiction of requirements. Horizontal agreements for example underlie several provisions, which complicate a decision regarding the applicable rule.

Further competition law enforcement difficulties arose in the context of the merger between Digicel and Claro. On 11 March 2011, Digicel, the participant with the largest market share announced its intention to acquire Claro, the telecommunications competitor with the third largest market share.[263] The Fair Trading Commission challenged the merger on the grounds of Section 17 of the Fair Competition Act, according to which the acquisition would lead to a substantial lessening of competition. The merger was however approved by the Prime Minister

---

[257] Part IV of the Barbados Fair Competition Act.

[258] Section 3(2) of the Fair Competition Act.

[259] Long title of the Fair Competition Act.

[260] *Stephenson,* Role, Function and Development of Jamaica's Competition Law and Policy, 12–13 October 1999, Port-of-Spain, p. 12; *Malahoo,* Competition Law in Emerging Economies: The Jamaican Experience, 2000, p. 23; *UNCTAD,* Voluntary Peer Review on Competition Policy: Jamaica, 2005, p. 47.

[261] *Stephenson,* Role, Function and Development of Jamaica's Competition Law and Policy, 12–13 October 1999, Port-of-Spain, p. 11.

[262] In this sense in May 2005, the Minister of Commerce, Science and Technology, the Honorable Phillip Paulwell, directed the Fair Trading Commission to "take steps to divest itself from matters in relation to consumer issues and concentrate on competition issues".

[263] There is only one more competitor in the telecommunications market besides Digicel and Claro, namely Lime.

Bruce Golding in 2011 and took effect in 2012. The Fair Trading Commission then brought the matter before the Jamaican Supreme Court in 2012 and finally before the Court of Appeal in 2014, which delivered its judgement on 19 December 2014.[264] Although, the Fair Trading Commission was generally held to have jurisdiction over telecommunication matters, it negated an infringement of Section 17 of the Fair Competition Act for the lack of collusion in the agreement between Digicel and Claro. Moreover, the Court held that the Fair Trading Commission did not have the competence to review an agreement that was the result of a ministerial approval with regard to a transfer of a licence under the Telecommunications Act. Interestingly, the Court of Appeal explicitly imported considerations regarding Article 101 TFEU because of the similarities with Section 17 of the Fair Competition Act. In 2015 the Court of Appeal then granted the Fair Trading Commission conditional and final leave to appeal the judgement before the Privy Council[265] in the United Kingdom in order to seek clarification on several aspects of judicial interpretation. The Privy Council issued its decision on 24 August 2017. Relying on European precedence, in particular on the development of European merger control, the Privy Council held that (1) Jamaican competition law was of general application and special sector regulation did not overrule it. (2) Section 17 of the Fair Competition Act also applied to mergers. Parallel to the European interpretation, the Privy Council held that anti-competitive agreements do not only encompass commercial cooperations that lessen competition, but also any agreement that creates a structure likely to be used for such cooperation. Finally, (3) also approvals by the Minister did not impair the general applicability of Jamaican competition law, as the Minister would not conduct a competition law assessment.[266]

Despite the lack of a merger control regime, the Fair Trading Commission had tried to impose conditions on the merger. At the end of its recommendation,[267] the Fair Trading Commission argued for the possibility to make "co-location agreements mandatory and [to regulate] the rates, terms and conditions pursuant to such agreements" in order to guarantee island-wide telecommunication coverage.[268] Ironically, the proposed competition law draft bill in 1991 included a merger control.[269] However, due to public opposition, which relied on the small-scale economy

---

[264] *Digicel Jamaica Limited v Fair Trading Commission,* Supreme Court Civil Appeal No. 75/2012 of 2014.

[265] The Privy Council is a relict from colonial times. It is a court based in Great Britain, but also serves as appellate court for some member states of the CARICOM. For more information see Part II, Dimension IV: Sect. 8.3.2.1.

[266] Fair Trading Commission v Digicel Jamaica Limited, Privy Council Appeal No. 0059 of 2016.

[267] The Fair Trading Commission cannot make any decisions and enforce them. It can only make recommendations, which it then has to enforce before the courts.

[268] Investigation into the acquisition of Oceanic Digital (Jamaica) Limited by Digicel Jamaica Limited, Pursuant to Section 17 of the Fair Competition Act Staff Report December 8, 2011, Case no. 6997-11, p. 42.

[269] *Malahoo,* Competition Law in Emerging Economies: The Jamaican Experience, 2000, p. 7; *UNCTAD,* Voluntary Peer Review on Competition Policy: Jamaica, 2005, p. 36.

argument and criticized a limitation of concentration in the newly opened Jamaican economy, the government eventually excluded the merger provisions.[270] In the context of a reformation process of the Fair Competition Act, the Commission also made representations with regard to the inclusion of a merger control system to the parliament. Whereas the process regarding a proper merger control regime is still at an early stage, the Privy Council has denied the application of the current competition laws and has underlined the exclusivity of sectorial regulation.

Moreover, the constitutionality of the status of the Fair Trading Commission was successfully challenged before the Court of Appeal in the *Jamaica Stock Exchange v Fair Trading Commission* case in 2001.[271] This decision rendered the Commission to a large extent inoperative and many core provisions of the Act unenforceable.[272] The Court of Appeal held that the institutional design of the Fair Trading Commission constituted a breach of natural justice. In 1994, the Fair Trading Commission initiated an investigation against the *Jamaica Stock Exchange*, alleging that it had infringed the provisions dealing with agreements and abuse of dominance. The *Jamaica Stock Exchange* appealed successfully based on procedural grounds. The Court of Appeal *inter alia* held in 2001 that the combination of the function as "complainant and adjudicator" of the agency constituted a breach of natural justice. Subsequent to the decision, the Fair Trading Commission refrained from enforcing the core competition provisions.[273] Since then, it conducts investigations, but the agency can only seek voluntary compliance, especially in the case of *per se* breaches, or it can bring a case to the courts.[274]

The *Jamaica Stock Exchange v Fair Trading Commission* case not only displays the institutional struggle of the Commission and the weaknesses in the law itself, it also demonstrates the large judicial discretion in the review of Fair Trading Commission's decision. Yet national courts are not necessarily vested with competition law experts, which may lead to "misunderstandings of competition law".[275] In the above-mentioned case, the Court of Appeal for example held that an entity offering a service, cannot be said to be restraining competition "when there is no evidence of the appellant being in competition with anyone else. (…)The question of competition can only arise if there is another entity, real, or potential, that can offer

---

[270] *Malahoo,* Competition Law in Emerging Economies: The Jamaican Experience, 2000, p. 8; *UNCTAD,* Voluntary Peer Review on Competition Policy: Jamaica, 2005, p. 36.

[271] *Jamaica Stock Exchange v Fair Trading Commission,* Supreme Court Civil Appeal No. 92/97 of 2001.

[272] *UNCTAD,* Voluntary Peer Review on Competition Policy: Jamaica, 2005, p. 26.

[273] Different solutions for the constitutional and institutional struggle of the FCA are the creation of a competition tribunal, the installation of an internal "firewall" in the FCA, the utilisation of existing courts or tribunals. For more information see: *UNCTAD,* Voluntary Peer Review on Competition Policy: Jamaica, 2005, pp. 28ff.

[274] For more information on the decision, see *UNCTAD,* Voluntary Peer Review on Competition Policy: Jamaica, 2005, p. 27.

[275] *Beckford,* Enforcement of competition law in CARICOM: Perspectives on challenges to meeting regional and multilateral obligations, 20–21 April 2009, Caracas, p. 7.

competition."[276] The lack of competition law expertise among national courts may also be problematic with regard to preliminary reference rulings before the Caribbean Court of Justice according to Section 7(1) of the CCJ Act of 2005.[277] National judges might be inclined to refrain from approaching the regional level and might only consider national aspects of a matter, because they might just not be aware that the matter actually concerns Chapter VIII of the Revised Treaty of Chaguaramas.

One can conclude by saying that the Jamaican Fair Trading Commission is coping relatively well with the enforcement of competition law despite the present issues at stake. One should also point out that the drafters of the Jamaica Fair Competition Act already in its legislation process emphasized the importance of harmonization requirements with CARICOM law, thereby expressing a political will to participate in the CSME and in the according regional competition law framework.[278]

In contrast to the Jamaica Fair Trading Commission, the Fair Competition Act and the Fair Trading Commission Act in Barbados have never provided for an adjudicative function in competition law matters. The Fair Trading Commission publishes findings, which however are not legally binding. In case an enterprise does not comply, the Fair Trading Commission has to address the courts, which then issue an enforceable decision. Interesting to highlight is that the Court in competition law matters hears the entire substantive case, instead of being limited to breaches of law. The finding of the Commission serves as a recommendation. In order to avoid problems with regard to the limited competition law expertise of the judges, the Fair Trading Commission provides for regular training sessions and workshops for judges. Moreover, the problem is attenuated, because undertakings usually respect the findings of the Commission. So far, there has only been one case that needed to be resolved before the court.[279]

The Barbados Fair Competition Act also makes explicit reference to the regional structure. According to the title of Chapter 326C, the Fair Competition Act, the national law is envisaged "to prohibit the prevention, restriction or distortion of competition and the abuse of dominant positions in trade in Barbados and within the Caricom Single Market and Economy". While this reflects the economic consider-

---

[276] *Jamaica Stock Exchange v Fair Trading Commission,* Supreme Court Civil Appeal No. 92/97 of 2001, p. 66.

[277] "Where a court or tribunal is seized of an issue whose resolution involves a question concerning the interpretation or application of the Treaty, the Court or tribunal concerned may, before delivery of its judgement in the matter in writing request the designated authority to refer the question to the Court for an advisory opinion to be given."

[278] *Malahoo,* Competition Law in Emerging Economies: The Jamaican Experience, 2000, p. 7. Unfortunately, regarding Jamaica's compliance with Chapter VIII, it is still lagging behind with the obligatory amendments to its national competition legislation, see below Part II, Dimension II: Sect. 6.2.2.

[279] *Barbados National Oil Company Limited v Fair Trading Commission,* Supreme Court Suit No. 1811 of 2009.

ation to safeguard economic benefits of liberalization, it also displays a national commitment towards the regional framework.

5.2.3.2 Young Competition Law Regimes in Guyana, Trinidad and Tobago, Suriname and Belize

Most member states of CARICOM are currently in the implementation process of a domestic competition law and authority. However, the progress among these member states varies.

Although Guyana enacted its domestic competition law in 2006[280] and created its competition authority, the Competition and Consumer Affairs Commission, in September 2011, it has so far mostly engaged in advocacy activities. According to the Commission, in particular the recruitment process of the staff, five Commissioners including one director, and human resource training constituted the main challenges to the functioning of the authority.[281] As in Barbados, the Guyana competition authority enforces both competition and consumer protection. Accordingly, the Competition and Fair Trading Act does not only incorporate core competition law provisions, but also consumer protection rules. The Guyana Competition and Fair Trading Act also complies with the obligations set out in the Revised Treaty of Chaguaramas. In Sections 53, 54 and 55 the national Act refers to the Community Competition Commission and its decisions. The Act sets out enforcement mechanisms for regional decisions and common investigation procedures. Section 55 constitutes the bindingness and enforceability of Community Competition Commission's decisions. Guyana has also prepared a draft merger control and review act in 2013 as separate piece of legislation in addition to the national competition law.[282]

Trinidad and Tobago constitutes the largest and most diversified economy within CARICOM.[283] This is partly due to its large resources of Petroleum. Already in 1997/1998, the Ministry of Trade and Industry of Trinidad and Tobago published a proposal for a Fair Trading Act (Green Paper)[284] and a Legislative Brief for Proposed Fair Trading Bill (White Paper),[285] whose implementation process however only started in 2006 and is still ongoing.[286] Several disagreements between the Ministry

---

[280] Guyana Act. No. 11 of 2006, Competition and Fair Trading Act 2006.

[281] *Rambaran,* Competition and Consumer Affairs Commission of Guyana, 11 July 2012, Geneva.

[282] *OECD,* Merger Control in Latin America and the Caribbean, 2017, p. 2.

[283] For information on economic landscape within the CARICOM, see *Stewart*, An Empirical Examination of Competition Issues in Selected Caricom Countries, 2004.

[284] Ministry of Trade and Industry, *A Competition Law for Trinidad and Tobago, A Proposal for a Fair Trading Act,* Green Paper, 1997 (available from the author).

[285] Ministry of Trade and Industry, *A Competition Law for Trinidad and Tobago, Legislative Brief for Proposed Fair Trading Bill,* prepared for The Government of Trinidad and Tobago by Maxwell Stamp PLC., 1998 (available from the author).

[286] The Fair Trading Act has not been fully proclaimed yet. Some parts' proclamation is still pending.

and other shareholders from the private and public sector, in particular regarding the relevant threshold in a merger regulation,[287] contributed to the lengthy process. The Fair Trading Commission was only established in 2014. Moreover, full proclamation of the Fair Trading Act is still pending.[288]

Although the Trinidad and Tobago competition law relies on the experience of long-established competition law jurisdictions and in particular adopted similar provisions to the Jamaica Fair Competition Act, the national legislator emphasizes that the law "is shaped by the distinctive features of our own economy".[289] Consequently, the Fair Trading Act pays particular attention to the small size of the Trinidad and Tobago economy and small size of businesses.[290] Consumers are also acknowledged as protected group under the Act. Trinidad and Tobago competition law covers not only abuse of monopoly power[291] and anticompetitive agreements, but also merger regulation. The necessity to include a national merger control emerged from experiences in Trinidad and Tobago, in which two beer companies, *Carib* and *Stag*, were engaging in a price war, the so called "beer war".[292] While consumers benefited from competitive prices for a short period of time, the prices increased after *Carib* acquired its competitor *Stag*.[293] The Ministry of Trade and Industry was aware of this, but did not have the legal tools to intervene or discipline the companies.[294] Further interesting points of the content of the Fair Trading Act in Trinidad and Tobago are the exemption of banks and non-bank financial institutions, Section 3(1) lit. h) and exemptions of companies, which fall under the scope of the Telecommunications Authority Act, Section 3(1) lit. g).

Apart from the Fair Trading Commission, a Fair Trading Tribunal is supposed to be established. In order to avoid breaches of natural justice,[295] only the Fair Trading Tribunal will be vested with adjudicative functions, while the Commission conducts the investigations. Also related to competition law enforcement, is the Regulated Industries Commission's competence, which overrides the enforcement compe-

---

[287] In this context, *Gal* notes that "the size of the economy is negatively correlated with the height of the legal threshold it employs.", *Gal*, Competition Policy for Small Market Economies, 2003, p. 231. The Trinidad and Tobago Fair Trading Act does only challenge mergers of enterprises that exceed fifty million dollars, Section 14.1 lit. b)(i) of the Fair Trading Act.

[288] See website of the Trinidad and Tobago Fair Trading Commission, <http://tandtftc.org/>.

[289] Ministry of Trade and Industry, A Competition Law for Trinidad and Tobago, A Proposal for a Fair Trading Act, Green Paper, 1997, p. 3.

[290] See for example special provisions on interlocking directorship, the merger threshold or the definition of monopoly power. Yet, in relation to other Caribbean states, Trinidad and Tobago would not be classified as small market economy.

[291] The Trinidad and Tobago Fair Trading Act does not speak of "dominant position", but "monopoly power".

[292] *Maharaj*, The Trinidad and Tobago Government proposes a Competition Law, 2000, p. 16.

[293] *Ibid.*

[294] Statements made by representatives from the Ministry of Trade and Industry of Trinidad and Tobago during an interview with the author in Port-of-Spain, 30 October 2012.

[295] The *Jamaica Fair Trading Commission* was held to be in breach of natural justice, see *Jamaica Stock Exchange v Fair Trading Commission*, Supreme Court Civil Appeal No. 92/97 of 2001.

tence of the Fair Trading Commission in case of regulated industries, Section 3.2. However, the Act also acknowledges the sensible interplay between regulation and competition, by incorporating the obligation for the Regulated Industries Commission to consult the Fair Trading Commission in case of a merger or anticompetitive agreement of a service provider, Section 3(3). Nevertheless, the review of monopolies of service providers and a possible abuse is thus not under the competence of the Fair Trading Commission. Similarly, financial institutions are exempted from the Fair Trading Act and fall within the supervision of the Financial Regulatory Body.[296]

Yet, the Fair Trading Commission has *ex officio* powers to initiate general competition law investigations. It may also advise the Minister on matters related to the operation of the Act.[297]

The Fair Trading Commission consists of three to five Commissioners, including a Chairman of the Commission.[298] The Commissioners are appointed and may be withdrawn by the President, Section 26(1) and 28(1) of the Act. The President's discretion might constitute a weak point to the Commission's political independence. In the same vein, the Commission's budget is mainly determined by the Parliament or by the Ministry of Trade. The Parliament decides on the appropriate amounts of funds and resources and the Minister may grant resources for special purposes. In addition, the Fair Trading Commission relies on fines imposed on undertakings and other payments made to it.[299] Evidently, at its initiation phase, those amounts will make out the smaller share of its budget.

Finally, the Fair Trading Act of Trinidad and Tobago complies with its regional obligations in Section 48, 49 and 50 of the Fair Trading Act by shaping the enforcement procedures of regional cases and constituting the bindingness of decisions of the CARICOM Competition Commission.

Belize relied on the *CARICOM Model Law on Competition* to issue its national competition law draft.[300] The draft contains provisions on anticompetitive practices with national effects, provisions regarding the enforcement cooperation with the CARICOM Competition Commission in case of practices with cross-border effect

[296] *Stewart*, in: *Drexl/Bakhoum/Fox/Gal/Gerber*, Competition Policy and Regional Integration in Developing Countries, 2012, p. 161, 179. While the exemption might not cause difficulties on the national level, because the Financial Regulatory Body can also control possible anticompetitive practices on that sector, the exemption of the particular sectors from national competition law is probable to create problems with regard to the cross-border monitoring and enforcement of regional competition law in case of cross-border anticompetitive effects. See for a general analysis of the aspects of exemptions in regional competition law systems, Part III, Dimension I: Sect. 12.1.4.

[297] Section 5(1) lit. a) and lit. b) of the Fair Trading Act.

[298] Section 26(1) of the Trinidad and Tobago Fair Trading Act, 2006.

[299] Section 48 of the Trinidad and Tobago Fair Trading Act, 2006.

[300] See on the competition law initiatives in Belize, "Belize Competition Project", available at <http://www.bcc.org.bz/> last accessed 5 September 2017.

and the inclusion of a national merger control is also probable.[301] However, a national competition authority still does not exist and its institutional structure remains unclear. While its independence from political interference is emphasized, it has not been resolved whether Belize will install a joint competition and consumer protection authority.[302] The incentives to implement a national competition law structure in Belize are manifold. They do not only originate from the obligations arising out of Chapter VIII of the Revised Treaty of Chaguaramas and active support through the CARICOM Competition Commission. Belize intends to participate actively in the CSME and is very aware of its obligations arising out of other bilateral and multilateral treaties with foreign jurisdictions, in particular obligations arising out of the Economic Partnership Agreement with the European Union. Moreover, in order to integrate itself fully in the CSME, Belize has been granted financing by the Regional 10th European Development Fund. However, this funding incorporates a clear-cut deadline: the funds had to be utilized until 27 March 2015.[303]

Suriname is still awaiting the enactment of its draft competition law by its parliament. A national competition agency does not exist either. Representatives from the Suriname Ministry of Trade and Industry named the common law system in the CARICOM as one of the major difficulties that have been slowing down the implementation process in Suriname. In this regard, they did not only struggle to implement the specific formulations in a common law system, but also mentioned general translation difficulties into the Dutch language.[304] Furthermore, according to the representatives, the common law system relied on criminal sanctions, which would have to be translated into administrative sanctions in a civil law jurisdiction.[305] In Suriname, the ultimate enforcement of the national competition law might prove particularly difficult. Suriname's economy is not only signed by a high degree of concentration, but also the government has been an active economic participant by fixing prices or maximum prices for a large range of products.[306]

---

[301] Synopsis of Submitted Competition Legislation, October 2012. The paper is not published, but was prepared for the highest level of government in Belize. Statements made by John Rivero, Directorate for Foreign Trade (available from the author).

[302] *Ibid.*

[303] *Ibid.*

[304] Statements made by Jenny Karmin, representative from the Ministry of Trade and Industry in Suriname, in an Email to the author in December 2012.

[305] Statements made by Jenny Karmin, representative from the Ministry of Trade and Industry in Suriname, in an Email to the author in December 2012.

[306] *WTO,* Trade Policies and Practices by Measure, 2004, pp. 30, 49ff.

5.2.3.3 Young Competition Law Regime in the OECS

The member state's composition in CARICOM features a special characteristic as seven member states[307] form a distinct sub-regional organization, the Organisation of Eastern Caribbean States (OECS).[308] The OECS was created in 1981 with the signing of the Treaty of Basseterre and provides for sub-regional institutions, namely a Secretariat, the Director General and the Eastern Caribbean Supreme Court. The OECS was originally conceived as a cooperation mechanism in external affairs representation after the member states had gained independence.[309] However, with increased cooperation the objectives of the OECS shifted towards economic integration, finding its codification with the Revised Treaty of Basseterre, which established the Organisation of Eastern Caribbean States Economic Union in 2011.[310]

With regard to a competition law regime, the OECS has a draft competition bill, but has not installed a competition authority. The CARICOM Competition Commission is actively supporting the establishment process by offering technical assistance. While the OECS' member states agreed on the inclusion of the core anti-trust provisions and the inclusion of a merger control smoothly, the institutional design of the common authority caused disagreements. In order to comply with the obligation to establish and maintain a national competition authority as set out in Article 170(2) of the Revised Treaty of Chaguaramas, two options were discussed: the creation of small national competition authorities in each member state or the creation of a common OECS competition authority to coordinate all alleged anticompetitive practices in the OECS region.[311] While the CARICOM representatives pleaded for the second option, member states of the OECS were reluctant to cede sovereignty and thus tended towards the creation of several small national agencies.[312]

The dispute has been finally resolved with the Agreement establishing the Eastern Caribbean Competition Commission in favour of the creation of a common regional authority, the Eastern Caribbean Competition Commission. The Agreement states in its preamble that the Eastern Caribbean Competition Commission will be an independent and autonomous regional body, which will operate as national authority for each member state of the OECS.[313] The Agreement in its preamble also demarcates the sub-

[307] Antigua and Barbuda, Dominica, Grenada, Montserrat, Saint Kitts and Nevis, Saint Lucia, Saint Vincent and the Grenadines.

[308] The OECS has two additional associated member states, namely Anguilla, British Virgin Islands.

[309] *Huntley,* The Treaty of Basseterre & OECS Economic Union, 2003, pp. 1ff.

[310] For more information see <http://www.oecs.org/> accessed 11 November 2018.

[311] *OECS,* Competition Bill – Explanatory Memorandum, 24–25 March 2009, Saint Lucia, p. ii.

[312] *Ibid.*

[313] "CONSCIOUS of the need for a national competition authority to be established and empowered to investigate allegations of anti-competitive business conduct within an OECS Member State and monitor compliance with the national competition law of that OECS Member State:

CONSCIOUS also of the need to establish a sub-regional competition authority with competence over matters arising within an OECS Member State, and not over matters that involve more

regional authority's competence from the CARICOM Competition Commission's competence. Matters that involve more than one OECS member state do not fall within the scope of competence of the Eastern Caribbean Competition Commission, but within the competence of the CARICOM Competition Commission.[314]

Clearly, the decision for a shared sub-regional authority derives from considerations regarding the scarcity of resources and limited economic activity in the OECS member states.[315] One the other hand, the drafters of the agreement were aware of the importance of accessibility for the appropriate functioning of a competition authority. Although, the principle office of the Eastern Caribbean Competition Commission will be located in one member state of the OECS, additional agencies and offices or single agents may be established and appointed in each OECS member state.[316] Furthermore, fixed addresses in each OECS member state shall facilitate the submission of documents.[317]

5.3 Regional Competition Law Objectives and Their Embeddedness

"To be effective, competition policy law reform strategies require careful pre-reform analysis of existing conditions in the host country and rigorous attention to how the host country will implement nominal competition policy commands."[318] Phrased differently, competition policy should be embedded in the existing conditions in order to be efficiently enforced. The notion of "embeddedness" in the context of regional competition policy entails two dimensions. On the one hand, regional competition policy has to be in accordance with the overall integration movement, responding in particular to the objectives of regional integration and regional industrial trade policies (horizontal embeddedness). On the other hand, there is a need to analyse the previous, existing national competition law landscape (vertical embeddedness).[319] In this context, one should also bear in mind the national liberalization progress and related industrial policies, because national measures that

than one OECS Member State, even if they are both OECS Member States;", Preamble of the Agreement Establishing the Eastern Caribbean Competition Commission.

314 Preamble of the Agreement Establishing the Eastern Caribbean Competition Commission.

315 "RECOGNISING that: (...) there is a scarcity of relevant resources and limited economic activity in the OECS Member States;", Preamble of the Agreement Establishing the Eastern Caribbean Competition Commission.

316 Article 8 of the Agreement Establishing the Eastern Caribbean Competition Commission.

317 Article 9 of the Agreement Establishing the Eastern Caribbean Competition Commission.

318 *Kovacic*, Institutional Foundations for Economic Legal Reform in Transition Economies, 77 Chi.-Kent L. Rev. 265, 301 (2001).

319 *Horna/Kayali*, in: *Alvarez/Wilse-Samson*, Implementing Competition-Related Provisions in Regional Trade Agreements, 2007, p. 21, 31.

foreclose domestic markets and obstruct liberalization might clash with regional goals of integration.

5.3.1 Regional Competition Law Objectives

The European competition law experiences demonstrate that shifts in economic theory and political ideology might also change competition policy, thereby redefining competition law enforcement and the relevant institutional structure.[320] Competition provisions and their enforcement respond to the underlying objectives, which shape the "choice of a perspective"[321] and form the "centre of gravity"[322] of the competition law regime and policy. Hence a theoretical analysis of competition law objectives and policy is crucial for understanding enforcement measures and institutions.

Competition law is conceived under the economic paradigm of increasing "the economic gains of the participating countries".[323] In developing countries, economic gains particularly encompass the attainment of sustainable development and eradication of poverty. Competition law is considered as instrument to achieve development gains, because it enables people to become "participatory and creative economic actors"[324] without being restrained by artificially created barriers in the form of anticompetitive practices.[325]

In an RTA, economic gains have an additional dimension. While there are different forms and stages of integration, economic integration can generally be understood as the abolition of all barriers to trade such as tariff barriers in order to increase trade between nations. Thus, according to this definition, the most advanced stage of economic integration constitutes the creation of a common market.[326] A common market usually imposes a common external tariff on imports from non-member states and thereby creates economic advantages for the participating states. The intensity of the common market relies on and reflects the political commitment of member states. Accordingly, its relevance for member states depends on the intensity of intra-community trade. In a regional integration movement among developing countries, the economic paradigm of competition law is thus embodied in the

---

[320] *Monti,* EC Competition Law, 2007, p. 20.

[321] *Fox,* in: *Drexl/Bakhoum/Fox/Gal/Gerber,* Competition Policy and Regional Integration in Developing Countries, 2012, p. 273, 276.

[322] *Ibid.*

[323] *Gerber,* in: *Drexl/Bakhoum/Fox/Gal/Gerber,* Competition Policy and Regional Integration in Developing Countries, 2012, p. 253, 253.

[324] *Fox,* in: *Drexl/Bakhoum/Fox/Gal/Gerber,* Competition Policy and Regional Integration in Developing Countries, 2012, p. 273, 275.

[325] In more detail, see above Part I, Chap. 2.

[326] In the European Union, the common market is based on the four basic freedoms, free circulation of goods, services, capital and labour.

installation and maintenance of a common market, yet placing special considerations on development objectives. Therefore, in order to delimitate the objective of a regional competition law, one also has to bear in mind the general founding treaties and the general objectives of an RTA.[327]

5.3.1.1 Competition Law Objectives in the WAEMU

One of WAEMU's main competition policy objectives according to the Treaty of Dakar is the creation of an open and competitive market.[328] In line with the principles of free movement of goods, persons, services and capital, the objectives set out in Article 4 of the Treaty of Dakar all support the creation of a common market.[329] Regional competition law is not conceived as an end in itself, but supports the creation of a common market by appearing as a "fundamental pillar" of it.[330] One has to clarify the latter finding.

The community competition law provisions in the WAEMU were introduced simultaneously with other common economic policies in the Treaty of Dakar in 1994. Even the relevant directives and regulations that were implemented later in 2003 did not enter a landscape of a void common economic space. In fact, the

---

[327] In the European Union the former treaty emphasized in Art. 3 lit. g) EC Treaty the creation and promotion of a common market. However, it is interesting to note that the EU's process of integration was not only based on economic considerations, but entailed political intentions as well. After World War II, the European States expressed their political will to guarantee peace and stability by creating common economic relations without questioning the sovereignty of the member states, especially regarding the regulation of sensitive domains. See *Govaere*, De l'état régulateur souverain aux organisations d'intégration régionale promotices, protectrices et intermédiaires, XVII R.I.D.E. 313, 317 (2003). However, since then the objective of economic integration and the creation and maintenance of the common market has been an important objective of European competition law. The underlying objectives of competition law *inter alia* determine the actual enforcement. In this vein, *per se* condemned behaviour, as for example absolute territorial protection, may be allowed for a certain period of time in order to promote product diversity. As regards the prohibition of absolute territorial protection, see ECJ, Decision of 13 of July 1966, Case 56 and 58/64, *Consten and Grundig* [1966]. Now, under the European guidelines on vertical restraints, restrictions of passive sales generally fall outside the scope of Article 101(1) if the restrictions are necessary in order to enter a new market, Commission Notice (EU) of 19 May 2010, Guidelines on Vertical Restraints, [2010] OJ C 130/07, para. 61.

[328] Article 4 of the Treaty of Dakar.

[329] Article 4 lit. c) of Treaty of Dakar: "(…) créer entre les Etats membres un marché commun (…)". See *Coulibaly,* Le Droit de la Concurrence de l'Union Économique et Monétaire Ouest Africaine, Rev. burkinnabé de droit 43 (2003). Other objectives set out in Article 4 of Treaty of Dakar are the assurance of convergence of performances and economic policies of the member states, the coordination of national sectorial policies, the harmonization of legislations of the member states as far as it is necessary to the functioning of the common market.

[330] *Bakhoum,* Delimitation and Exercise of Competence between the West African Economic and Monetary Union (WAEMU) and its Member States in Competition Policy, 29/4 W. Comp. 653, 655 (2006); *UNCTAD,* Voluntary Peer Review on Competition Policies of WAEMU, Benin and Senegal, 2008, p. xi.

WAEMU already possessed common monetary and economic policies.[331] Integration was thus already proceeding and a shared language and cultural heritage favoured the general and relatively fast integration process in the WAEMU. Hence, regional competition law provisions deepened economic integration.

Nevertheless, even more fundamental than its integrationist function, community competition law in the WAEMU supports open and competitive markets, abolishing the state's function as active economic player. While integration was forging ahead, liberalization of the West African markets was still lagging behind. Despite national liberalization and development policies,[332] national markets remained characterized by state intervention and regulation, mainly in the form of state-owned enterprises.[333] The introduction of the concept of open and liberalized markets was not a completely intrinsic decision of the West African states, but derived from incentives of international and multinational organizations, such as the World Trade Organization, the World Bank, the International Monetary Fund or the European Union.[334] Generally speaking, globalisation nourished the exponential development of international norms that infiltrate internal national laws, in particular national economic laws.[335] While this explains the similarities between the WAEMU community competition law objectives and other regional competition law objectives, in particular the objectives of the European Union, it is incapable of substituting limited political support of a liberalization process. Economic development between the EU and the WAEMU varies. In the European Union competition law objectives shifted from the core objectives of market integration and economic freedom to economic efficiency.[336] The lack of political support will most likely impede a similar development in the WAEMU, although Article 4 lit. c) of the Treaty of Dakar offers a similar starting point by emphasizing the creation of a common market as

[331] See for example the Convergence, Stability, Growth, and Solidarity Pact (1999), West African Accountancy System (1998), the WAEMU Banking Commission (1990) or other multilateral surveillance mechanisms. For more details see *UNCTAD,* Voluntary Peer Review on Competition Policies of WAEMU, Benin and Senegal, 2008, p. 9.

[332] By the end of 1990s, many West African countries engaged in poverty reduction and liberalization programs, which aimed at an acceleration of growth; with regards to the reforms in Burkina Faso, Senegal and Togo, see *CUTS CCIER,* A Time for Action, 2010, pp. 4f.

[333] *CUTS CCIER,* A Time for Action, 2010, pp. 17f.

[334] *Bakhoum,* L'articulation du droit communautaire et des droits nationaux de la concurrence dans l'Union Economique et Monétaire Ouest Africaine, 2007, p. 13; *Bakhoum,* A Developing-Country Perspective on "Global Competition", 28 October 2011, Chicago, p. 6; *Gerber,* Global Competition, 2010, p. 250; *UNCTAD,* Voluntary Peer Review on Competition Policies of WAEMU, Benin and Senegal, 2008, p. 4.

[335] *Salah M.M,* La Mise en Concurrence des Systèmes juridiques nationaux, XV R.I.D.E. 251, 259 (2001).

[336] *Monti,* EC Competition Law, 2007, p. 51. See generally on economic integration in the European Union, *Govaere,* De l'état régulateur souverain aux organisations d'intégration régionale promotices, protectrices et intermédiaires, XVII R.I.D.E. 313, 313 (2003).

core competition law objective. In addition, regional competition law objectives also include the optimal allocation of resources and economic efficiency.[337]

5.3.1.2 Competition Law Objectives in the AndeanC

Article 2 of Decision 608 sets out as regional competition policy's objective: "the protection and promotion of free competition in the space of the Andean Community, while striving for efficiency in the markets and for the wellbeing of consumers."[338] The guidelines to Decision 608 of the General Secretary clarify that the guarantee of market access through the abolition of trade barriers is supposed to increase competition between economic agents and to contribute to the diminution of transaction costs and of prices of goods and services.[339] They emphasize that competition law is a necessary tool to ensure that the benefits of a competitive market are passed on to the consumer.[340]

The underlying conception sees integration and commercial opening of markets as mechanisms to cope with globalization. Decision 608 is supposed to enhance and protect free competition in the Andean Community.[341] Hence, Decision 608 is conceived as an economic integrationist instrument.[342] The underlying objective of economic integration is further enunciated in comparison to the former Decision 285, which did not entail the protection of free competition as explicit objective of regional competition policy.[343] However, Decision 608 does not refer to the creation of a common regional market. Even Article 2 of Decision 608 only refers to the efficacy of "the markets", hence referring to the four national markets. One can conclude from this that the objective of market integration will play a less determining role than consumer welfare or economic efficiency considerations in the AndeanC than in other comparable regional competition laws. This finding is in accordance with other general tendencies in the AndeanC, in which member states

[337] Preamble of Regulation no. 02/2002/CM/UEMOA, Preamble of Regulation no. 03/2002/CM/UEMOA, Preamble of Regulation no. 04/2002/CM/UEMOA: "DESIREUX de renforcer l'efficacité et la compétitivité des activités économiques et financières des Etats membres dans le cadre d'un marché ouvert, concurrentiel et favorisant l'allocation optimale des ressources;".

[338] Article 2 of Decision 608: "La presente Decisión tiene como objectivo la protección y promoción de la libre competencia en el ámbito de la Comunidad Andina, buscando la eficiencia en los mercados y el bienestar de los consumidores".

[339] *Secretaria General de la Comunidad Andina,* Guía Práctica para la aplicación de la Decisión 608 "Normas para la protección y promoción de la libre competencia en la Comunidad Andina", 2007, p. 4.

[340] *Ibid.*

[341] Preamble of Decision 608.

[342] *Falla/Quintana,* in: *Pontificia Católica del Peru,* Derecho Comunitario Andino, 2003, p. 143, 145; *Cortázar,* in: *Drexl/Bakhoum/Fox/Gal/Gerber,* Competition Policy and Regional Integration in Developing Countries, 2012, p. 133, 135.

[343] *Gallardo/Domínguez,* 20 Boletín Latinoamericano de Comp. 36, 46 (2005) <http://ec.europa.eu/competition/publications/blc/boletin_20_1_es.pdf> accessed 11 November 2018.

instead of supporting and furthering Andean economic integration and intra-community trade, have shifted to enter in bilateral trade agreements with other external jurisdictions.[344] These bilateral trade agreements also incorporate provisions on competition policy.[345]

5.3.1.3 Competition Law Objectives in the CARICOM

Article 169 of the Revised Treaty of Chaguaramas sets out the specific objectives of the CARICOM's competition policy: "The goal of the Community Competition Policy shall be to ensure that the benefits expected from the establishment of the CSME are not frustrated by anti-competitive business conduct."[346] Article 169(2) of the RTC specifies that in fulfilment of these goals, the Community shall promote and maintain competition and efficiency, prohibit anti-competitive business conduct that hinders competition, and shall promote consumer welfare.[347]

Competition law is perceived as an instrument to proliferate economic efficiency and follows a consumer welfare approach. Chapter VIII does not only deal with competition policy, but also consumer protection. The CARICOM Competition Commission is competent for both areas of law and has to cooperate with national competition agencies as well as national consumer associations.

The regional competition law provisions also entail an integrationist dimension. Article 169(1) of the Revised Treaty of Chaguaramas demonstrates that the regional competition policy is conceived as insurance for the expected benefits of a common market. Accordingly, Article 177(1) lit. c) of the Revised Treaty of Chaguaramas, the prohibition of anti-competitive business conduct, is broadly formulated covering "any other like conduct by enterprises whose object or effect is to frustrate the benefits expected from the establishment of the CSME". The artificial division of markets is explicitly included as constituting an anticompetitive practice in Article 177(2) lit. c) of the Revised Treaty. However, one should not conclude that in the CARICOM the prevention of market disintegration would always be defended at the expense of economic efficiency or consumer welfare. The structure of Chapter VIII indicates that the three objectives are similarly important. In particular the inclusion of consumer protection policy in Chapter VIII implies that special consideration will be given to consumer welfare.[348]

---

[344] Among the most important to mention are the bilateral trade agreement between the United States and Peru and the bilateral trade agreement between the United States and Colombia.

[345] See for example Chapter 1 Articles 125 to130 of the *CARIFORUM-EC Economic Partnership Agreement*.

[346] Article 169(1) of the Revised Treaty of Chaguaramas.

[347] Article 169(1)lit. a) to (c) of the Revised Treaty of Chaguaramas.

[348] Kusha Haraksingh, the Chairman of the CARICOM Competition Commission, said at the 6th United Nations Conference to Review the UN Set on Competition Policy in Geneva, Switzerland, 9 November 2010: "Given the primacy attributed to the goal of sustainable development in

5.3.1.4 Summary of Regional Competition Law Objectives

The WAEMU, the AndeanC and the CARICOM follow similar competition law objectives. Similar to the European competition law, they adopt concepts of economic efficiency and consumer welfare, although the interface and the weight of each objective are still partly unclear. In contrast to their European counterpart, the examined RTAs refrained from adopting a purely technical or formal common market approach that solely aims at market integration. Clearly, for the lack of competition law expertise on the regional level and a large number of young or inexperienced competition law jurisdictions, especially at the initiation phase of a regional competition law, a consumer welfare and/or economic analysis might be more challenging to apply than a formal common market approach. Yet the inclusion of competition law objectives of consumer welfare and economic efficiency in addition to a formal common market approach provides for more flexibility to incorporate modern economic analysis in regional competition law enforcement. This might be in particular feasible in situations, in which the political support of member states for a common regional market is not as strong as it was in the European Union.

The decision to adopt a regional competition policy in all three RTAs did not constitute a purely internal decision. Often such incentives originated from developed jurisdictions and international organizations. Finally, the WAEMU, the AndeanC and the CARICOM experiences differ with regard to the sequencing of regional competition law. They have incorporated regional competition policies at different stages of the development of integration: the WAEMU being the furthest developed at the moment of the implementation of regional competition policy.

5.3.2 Horizontal Embeddedness: State of Implementation of the Common Market and Congruence with General Goals of Regional Integration

5.3.2.1 WAEMU

The WAEMU was clearly created in the light of a monetary and economic paradigm. Accordingly, the Treaty of Dakar is characterized by economic integration aspects.[349] The Treaty particularly points out the relevance of furthering harmoniza-

CARICOM, it is understandable that the litmus test of a successful competition policy would come to reside in the benefits delivered to the consumer".

[349] Article 2 of the Treaty of Dakar and its preamble accordingly reemphasize the promotion of economic integration as the objective of the WAEMU, in addition to the already proceeding monetary integration. See the Treaty of Dakar's preamble: "Convaincus de la nécessité d'étendre en conséquence au domaine économique la solidarité qui les lie déjà sur le plan monétaire,(…)". The objective of economic integration is further accentuated in Article 4 of the Treaty of Dakar, which names the reinforcement of the economic and financial activity of the member states in an open

tion of national legislation and convergence of economic and sectorial policies of the member states.[350] The implementation of a regional competition law fulfils an integral part in economic integration, as it protects potential benefits arising out of the common market and enhances its competitiveness. The underlying objectives of regional competition law[351] are in line with the general goals of regional integration in the WAEMU.

The provisions regarding state aids are a positive example of how the WAEMU deals with potential areas of conflict. Article 2(1) of Regulation no. 04/2002/CM/UEMOA points out that public aids that are capable of distorting competition by favouring a specific undertaking or production are void. However, according to Article 2(2) of the same regulation the economic and social development of the member states has to be taken into account, as long as inter-state trade and the community integration objectives are not jeopardized.[352] Having these balancing mechanisms in mind, the exclusive and centralized competence of competition law enforcement in favour of the Union did not emerge as an inevitable necessity of the objectives of harmonization and convergence set out in the Treaty of Dakar. Rather, the regional legislator could have also installed an equilibrated enforcement system, in which competences are distributed between the national and regional level. Moreover, although the centralized system theoretically leads to a convergent application of competition law within the region in theory, practically, member states

and competitive market as an objective of the Treaty of Dakar. See Article 4 of the Treaty of Dakar: "Sans préjudice des objectifs définis dans le Traité de l'UMOA, l'Union poursuit, dans les conditions établies par le présent Traité, la réalisation des objectifs ci-après:

a) renforcer la compétitivité des activités économiques et financières des Etats membres dans le cadre d'un marché ouvert et concurrentiel et d'un environnement juridique rationalisé et harmonisé;

b) assurer la convergence des performances et des politiques économiques des Etats membres par l'institution d'une procédure de surveillance multilatérale;

c) créer entre les Etats membres un marché commun basé sur la libre circulation des personnes, des biens, des services, des capitaux et le droit d'établissement des personnes exerçant une activité indépendante ou salariée, ainsi que sur un tarif extérieur commun et une politique commerciale commune;

d) instituer une coordination des politiques sectorielles nationales, par la mise en oeuvre d'actions communes et éventuellement de politiques communes notamment dans les domaines suivants: ressources humaines, aménagement du territoire, transports et télécommunications, environnement, agriculture, énergie, industrie et mines;

e) harmoniser, dans la mesure nécessaire au bon fonctionnement du marché commun, les législations des Etats membres et particulièrement le régime de la fiscalité."

[350] Preamble of the Treaty of Dakar: "Affirmant la nécessité de favoriser le développement économique et social des Etats membres, grâce à l'harmonisation de leurs législations, à l'unification de leurs marchés intérieurs et à la mise en oeuvre de politiques sectorielles communes dans les secteurs essentiels de leurs économies,(…)" and Article 4 of the Treaty of Dakar.

[351] For the regional competition law objectives in the WAEMU, see above Part II, Dimension I: Sect. 5.3.1.1.

[352] *UNCTAD*, Voluntary Peer Review on Competition Policies of WAEMU, Benin and Senegal, 2008, p. 30.

might still try to circumvent the centralized application by referring to non-unified, but competition law-related national legislation.

The advanced stage of integration in the WAEMU at the moment of implementation of regional competition policy in its current form justifies that its objectives are relatively sophisticated.[353] The gradual introduction of regional competition law can thus revert to the advanced integration, instead of having to establish or justify regional governance in the first place. Yet generally, a "late" introduction after the installation of the custom union bears the danger of conflict with existing common industrial and trade policies.[354] In an apparent effort to further convergence and coherence among the WAEMU member states and among different regional policies, conflicts have been avoided based on the principle of "fair and equal treatment of all investors".[355]

5.3.2.2 AndeanC

In the AndeanC, Article 1 of the Agreement of Cartagena declares that one of the objectives of the Agreement is the "equilibrated and harmonic development of the member states in terms of equality, through economic and social integration and cooperation; (…) keeping in mind the gradual formation of a common Latin-American market" thereby aiming at the ultimate goal to "procure a persistent improvement of the living standards of the inhabitants of the Subregion".[356] There are two aspects that are important to point out.

First, one has to clarify the notion of a "common Latin-American market". It does not necessarily refer to the creation of an Andean market limited to the Andean Community. Rather, based on the political circumstances of the signing of the Agreement of Cartagena, it refers to a larger concept of a common market that includes the entire Latin-American hemisphere. The signing of the Agreement of Cartagena in 1969 took place in the framework of the ALALC (Asociación Latinoamericana de Libre Comercio).[357] The signatory states of the Agreement of

---

353 The objectives encompass consumer welfare as well as efficiency considerations instead of a formal market integration, see above Part II, Dimension I: Sect. 5.3.1.1.

354 *UNCTAD,* Voluntary Peer Review on Competition Policies of WAEMU, Benin and Senegal, 2008, p. 15.

355 *UNCTAD,* Voluntary Peer Review on Competition Policies of WAEMU, Benin and Senegal, 2008, p. 15.

356 Article 1 of Acuerdo de Integración Subregional Andino, "Acuerdo de Cartagena".

357 ALALC was a regional organization in Latin America, which was created on 18 February 1960 with the Treaty of Montevideo. Participating member states were Argentina, Bolivia, Brazil, Chile, Colombia, Ecuador, México, Paraguay, Perú, Uruguay and Venezuela. In 1980 ALALC was replaced by the ALADI (Asociación Latinoamericana de Integración). For more information see <http://www.aladi.org/>. In February 2010 incentives for a new Latin American organization emerged with the creation of the CELAC (Comunidad de Estados Latinoamericanos y Caribeños) in Mexico. CELAC consists of 33 member states, not including Canada and the United States of America. For more information see: Süddeutsche Zeitung, 3 December 2011, "Lateinamerika

Cartagena did not feel sufficiently represented in the ALALC and believed to accelerate their development in a separate regional agreement.[358] The AndeanC member states remained members of the ALALC until 1986.[359]

While the integration movement of the AndeanC is conceived as an instrument to achieve a more influential negotiation position of the member states in the international context, it is also conceived as intermediate step towards larger South-American integration.[360] This conception can be explained by a deep-rooted understanding of America as divided continent, namely between the United States, Canada, to a certain extent Mexico, and the South-American states.[361] In the meetings concerning the reform of the former competition law, Decision 285, representatives of the member states explicitly placed the new Andean competition regime in the framework of the competition policies of ALALC and the anticompetitive practices covered by it.[362]

One also has to highlight that intra-community trade in the AndeanC at the moment of the signature of the Agreement of Cartagena was insignificant. In 1969 intraregional trade only constituted 0.7% of the entire trade of the member states and also 10 years later the share of intraregional trade only increased by 3.8%.[363] The Andean experience differs drastically from the European Union, in which intra-community trade was already very vivid from the start.[364] As a consequence, the creation of a common market can only have constituted a weak incentive for member states to further economic integration in the AndeanC.

Second, Article 1 of the Agreement of Cartagena refers to the improvement of the living standards of the population of the member states.[365] There is a strong

rückt zusammen" <http://www.sueddeutsche.de/politik/gruendungsgipfel-fuer-neuen-staatenbund-lateinamerika-rueckt-zusammen-1.1225684>.

358 *Salmón Gárate*, in: *Pontificia Católica del Peru*, Derecho Comunitario Andino, 2003, p. 21, 22; *Böttcher*, Kartell- und Lauterkeitsrecht in den Ländern der Andengemeinschaft, 2004, pp. 28, 29; *Baumann/Bustillo/Heirman/Macario/Máttar/Pérez*, Los procesos de integración de los países de América Latina y el Caribe 2000–2001, 2002, pp. 29, 30.

359 *Salazar Manrique*, El Derecho Comunitario Andino, 8 Rev. Jur. 247, 249 (1993).

360 *García-Belaunde*, El Sueño de Bolívar: De la Federación de los Andes a la Comunidad Andina, 2000 <http://www.comunidadandina.org/documentos/docIA/IA27-9-00.htm> accessed 11 November 2018.

361 *García-Belaunde*, El Sueño de Bolívar: De la Federación de los Andes a la Comunidad Andina, 2000 <http://www.comunidadandina.org/documentos/docIA/IA27-9-00.htm> accessed 11 November 2018.

362 Informe de la Segunda Reunion de Expertos Gubernamentales en Materia de Libre Competencia, SG/REG.LC/II/INFORME, 16 and 17 February 2000, p. 1 (available from the author).

363 *Francés/Palacios*, in: *San Martino de Dromi/Rubio/de Navarro*, Integración Eurolatinoamericana, 1998, p. 485, 494.

364 According to *Francés/Palacios* intraregional trade in the European Union amounted up to 35% of all exportations in the first years of integration. Ten years later intraregional trade even reached a 50% share according to *Francés/Palacios*; *Francés/Palacios*, in: *San Martino de Dromi/Rubio/de Navarro*, Integración Eurolatinoamericana, 1998, p. 485, 494.

365 *Marcos*, in *Fox/Sokol*, Competition Law and Policy in Latin America, 2009, p. 453, 454.

perceived link between social development and economic efficiency on the one hand and the creation of a larger market on the other hand.[366] In the same vein, Article 1 of the Agreement of Cartagena mentions the strengthening of extra-regional relationships, the diminution of international vulnerability of the member states. Article 2 of the Agreement of Cartagena expresses the objective of decreasing existing differences between the member states and to reach an equitable distribution of benefits. Economic integration is thus not a goal by itself, but the main objectives of the AndeanC as set out in the Agreement of Cartagena are of social and humanitarian nature.[367] The AndeanC is an integration movement that attributes equal weight to economic and political integration.

The objectives set out in Decision 608, which are the protection and promotion of free competition within the AndeanC, aim at the efficiency of markets and consumer welfare.[368] Yet neither the Agreement of Cartagena nor Decision 608 refers to the creation of an Andean common market.[369] Instead, the Andean competition law seems to emphasize a consumer welfare approach and economic efficiency. Generally, these objectives are in line with the general understanding of RTAs between developing countries as a tool to formalize economic reforms and to prevent intrusion by anticompetitive practices of economic actors.[370] However, due to the lack of use of Decision 608, the concrete application in the framework of a consumer welfare approach remains uncertain. For the lack of legal precedents in regional competition law it remains unclear how the use of economic integration as intermediate goal for other social and humanitarian goals in the AndeanC translates into competition law enforcement.

The AndeanC follows a so called "open regionalism"-approach.[371] Under this model, the member states can continue to enter into bilateral trade negotiations and agreements with third parties. Regional groups are not conceived as ends in themselves, but intermediate "paths" towards international or global economic integration.[372] The open regionalism in the AndeanC has *inter alia* led to the signing of

[366] *Francés/Palacios*, in: *San Martino de Dromi/Rubio/de Navarro*, Integración Eurolatinoamericana, 1998, p. 485, 488.

[367] *Sáchica*, Introducción al derecho comunitario andino, 1985, p. 51.

[368] Article 2 of Decision 608.

[369] In the same vein, the territorial scope of application in Article 5 of Decision 608 does not refer to general cross-border effects or effects on the common market, but lists specific scenarios, in which a conduct or its effect crosses national boundaries.

[370] *Alvarez/Clarke/Silva*, Negociación y Aplicación de Disposiciones de Competencia en Acuerdos Bilaterales y Regionales de Comercio: Pautas para la Reflexion, 2 Rev. de la Comp. Propriedad Intelectual 5, 12 (2006).

[371] *European Commission*, Andean Community Regional Strategy Paper 2007–2013, 2007, p. 8 <http://www.eeas.europa.eu/andean/rsp/07_13_en.pdf> accessed 11 November 2018.

[372] *Baumann/Bustillo/Heirman/Macario/Máttar/Pérez*, Los procesos de integración de los países de América Latina y el Caribe 2000–2001, 2002, pp. 34ff. <http://www.eclac.org/publicaciones/xml/5/11175/lcl1780e.pdf> accessed 11 November 2018; *Rodríguez*, in: *Inter-American Dialogue*, Integrating The Hemisphere, 1997, p. 10, 10.

bilateral preferential trade agreements between Peru and the United States[373] and Colombia and the United States.[374] Peru and Colombia also entered into a trade agreement with the European Union.[375] On the other hand, large shares of Bolivia's exports go to the MERCOSUR (Mercado Común del Sur).[376]

The bilateral trade agreements with the United States also entail obligations to implement competition policy and to establish competition authorities.[377] Moreover, the treaties make explicit reference to the Andean competition law and regional authority.[378] Title VIII of the trade agreement between the European Union and Colombia and Peru contains competition-law related obligations and refers to national as well as Andean competition legislation. Hence, for the congruence of competition law obligations under Andean law and the bilateral preferential trade agreements, the bilateral agreements provided an incentive for the implementation of national[379] and for the support of regional competition law structures apart from the AndeanC.

Nevertheless, one has to point out that the spread of bilateral trade agreements has superseded trade negotiations *en bloc* in the AndeanC. Despite a slight increase in intra-community trade, the spread of bilateral trade agreements demonstrates that trade flows mainly keep taking place between the North and the South, between developing and developed jurisdictions. Hence, the strong focus on bilateral trade relations in the AndeanC reduced the economic relevance of the common market. Dependent on the specific preferential provisions in such an agreement, it is also capable of jeopardizing convergence of trade policies within the region. Moreover, bilateral trade agreements without prior discussion *en bloc* might even hamper the overall integration process, as some member states have felt politically excluded or threatened by the bilateral agreement with a non-AndeanC country.[380] Although, the

---

[373] Signed on 12 April 2006 and entered into force on 1 February 2009. For more information see <http://www.sice.oas.org/ctyindex/PER/PERagreements_e.asp> accessed 11 November 2018.

[374] Signed on 22 November 2006 and entered into force on the 15 May 2012. For more information see <http://www.sice.oas.org/ctyindex/COL/COLagreements_e.asp> accessed 11 November 2018. Ecuador also negotiated with the United States with regard to a preferential trade agreement, but the parties did not reach an agreement.

[375] Signed on 21 December 2012 and entered into force on 1 March 2013 in Peru and on 1 August 2013 in Colombia; for more information see <http://www.fdcl.org/wp-content/uploads/2012/04/CELEX_22012A122101_EN_TXT.pdf>.

[376] *European Commission,* Andean Community Regional Strategy Paper 2007–2013, 2007, p. 8 <http://www.eeas.europa.eu/andean/rsp/07_13_en.pdf> accessed 11 November 2018.

[377] Article 13(2)(1) und (2) of the Preferential Trade Agreements between Peru–US and Colombia–US.

[378] Article 13(2)(4) of the Preferential Trade Agreements between Peru–US and Colombia–US.

[379] However, one has to recall that Colombia and Peru at the moment of the signing and entry into force of the bilateral trade agreements already possessed national competition law policy, laws and institutions.

[380] El Comercio Perú, 23 May 2010, "Evo Morales critica a Europa por "dividir" a la Comunidad Andina con TLC". According to the article, the President of Bolivia, Evo Morales, criticized the trade agreement between the European Union and Peru and between the European Union and Colombia.

obligations contained in the bilateral and regional trade agreements have so far not conflicted,[381] the underlying objectives of the regional and bilateral trade agreements' competition law chapters differ. While Decision 608 *inter alia* aims at the protection of free competition within the AndeanC,[382] bilateral trade agreements are generally signed to enhance trade between the countries involved.[383] In the case of the US-Peru trade agreement, the US sought to achieve greater market access to the Peruvian market and aimed at improving the legal framework for investors. The Peruvian interest in the inclusion of a competition law chapter in the bilateral trade agreement mainly resulted from its interest to protect its exports.[384] Moreover, as Peru possesses a functioning national competition law system, it will tend to refrain from enforcing the competition law chapter in the bilateral trade agreement regionally, but will rely on its national authority. Yet, considering that the US is the largest trading partner of Peru,[385] the investigated competition law cases will most probably not be of regional interest anyway, but rather be related to conduct that could affect the Peruvian exports to the US.

5.3.2.3 CARICOM

The Revised Treaty of Chaguaramas is focused on economic and trade matters and does not primarily aim at political integration.[386] In the CARICOM, the underlying objective of the creation of the *CARICOM Single Market and Economy* (CSME) is visible throughout the Revised Treaty of Chaguaramas and other regulatory documents of the CARICOM. Its overarching importance is already accentuated in the first paragraph of the preamble of the Revised Treaty of Chaguaramas, which refers to "the commitment to deepening regional economic integration through the establishment of the *CARICOM Single Market and Economy* (CSME) in order to achieve sustained economic development based on international competitiveness, co-ordinated economic and foreign policies, functional co-operation and enhanced trade and economic relations with third States". It goes on by stating that "(...) market-driven industrial development in the production of goods and services is essential for the economic and social development of the peoples in the

[381] See for example Article 13(2)(4) of the Preferential Trade Agreement between Peru–US, which explicitly refers to the AndeanC's regional competition law structure. See also Title VIII of the Preferential Trade Agreement between Peru and Colombia and the European Union.

[382] Article 2 of Decision 608.

[383] *Horna/Kayali,* in: *Alvarez/Wilse-Samson,* Implementing Competition-Related Provisions in Regional Trade Agreements, 2007, p. 21, 52.

[384] *Horna/Kayali,* in: *Alvarez/Wilse-Samson,* Implementing Competition-Related Provisions in Regional Trade Agreements, 2007, p. 21, 28.

[385] According to *Horna/Kayali* the United States accounts for 26% of Peru's exports and 19% of its overall imports. *Horna/Kayali,* in: *Alvarez/Wilse-Samson,* Implementing Competition-Related Provisions in Regional Trade Agreements, 2007, p. 21, 52.

[386] *Belle Antoine,* Commonwealth Caribbean, 2008, p. 215.

Community."[387] Hence, the Revised Treaty of Chaguaramas is committed to the creation of an open and competitive regional market, for which the promotion of competition policy is perceived as a "critical policy objective of the Revised Treaty of Chaguaramas".[388] Market integration is not considered an additional benefit of integration, but constitutes an imperative for the Caribbean community to enhance economic growth and most importantly to improve the standard of living for the Caribbean people.[389] The regional competition law in Chapter VIII is drafted in accordance with the creation of the CSME as it is conceived as an instrument to prevent market disintegration and secure the benefits arising out of the CSME.[390]

Another characteristic of the Revised Treaty of Chaguaramas is the recognition of less developed countries among the CARICOM member states and a differential and special treatment, Chapter VII of the Revised Treaty of Chaguaramas. Although the Caribbean legislator does not refer to the international definition of least developed countries,[391] it is acknowledged that the CARICOM member states are unequally developed and that regional integration should therefore proceed at different paces.[392] Special and differential treatment is not only provided for disadvantaged countries, but similarly to disadvantaged regions or sectors.[393] The acknowledgment of preferential treatment is paralleled by rules that provide a certain flexibility to adapt to the special needs of disadvantaged countries or sectors.

Chapter IV of the Revised Treaty of Chaguaramas deals with policies for sectorial development and *inter alia* strives for cross-border employment of natural and human resources, for the promotion of regional economic enterprises or an enhanced and diversified production of goods and services.[394] Chapter 52(1) lit. f) of the Revised Treaty sets out that "production integration" shall be advanced in order to

---

[387] Preamble of the Revised Treaty of Chaguaramas.

[388] *CARICOM Secretariat,* Competition Policy and Law in the CSME, 2010, p. 4.

[389] *Stewart,* in: *Drexl/Bakhoum/Fox/Gal/Gerber,* Competition Policy and Regional Integration in Developing Countries, 2012, p. 161, 171: "Integration is not an option for these territories; it is a necessity for survival in the world-economy.". See also *Beckford,* in: *Drexl/Bakhoum/Fox/Gal/Gerber,* Competition Policy and Regional Integration in Developing Countries, 2012, p. 185, 187: "Market integration is one of the central objectives of competition policy under the RTC".

[390] Article 169(1) of the Revised Treaty of Chaguaramas.

[391] Since 1971, United Nation has recognized the category of "Least Developed Countries" (LDCs) for States that are disadvantaged with regard to their development progress and which therefore are particularly vulnerable to poverty. For more information see <http://unctad.org/en/Pages/ALDC/Least%20Developed%20Countries/Research-and-Policy-Analysis-on-LDCs.aspx> accessed 11 November 2018.

[392] See for example Preamble of the Revised Treaty of Chaguaramas: "Acknowledging further that some Member States, particularly the Less Developed Countries, are entering the CSME at a disadvantage by reason of size, structure and vulnerability of their economies; and (…) [c]onscious further that disadvantaged countries, regions and sectors will require a transitional period to facilitate adjustment to competition in the CSME; [c]ommitted to establish effective measures, programmes and mechanisms to assist disadvantaged countries, regions and sectors of the Community".

[393] Article 1 of the Revised Treaty of Chaguaramas.

[394] Article 51(2) lit. a), lit. c), lit. e) of the Revised Treaty of Chaguaramas.

achieve the objectives of the Caribbean industrial policy. In Article 51(8) of the Revised Treaty production integration includes the "complementary production involving collaboration among several economic enterprises operating in one or more Member State to produce and use required inputs in the production chain" and "cooperation among economic enterprises in areas such as purchasing, marketing, and research and development". While collaboration among economic enterprises could fall within the scope of the prohibition regarding anticompetitive agreements, Article 177(1) lit. a) and Article 51(8) of the Revised Treaty are in line with the exception in Article 177(4) lit. a), according to which agreements contributing to "the improvement of production or distribution of goods and services; or the promotion of technical or economic progress while allowing consumers a fair share of the resulting benefit" are not prohibited. The Caribbean legislator made an effort to avoid contradicting provisions. The industrial policy objectives also aim at the creation of a "balanced economic and social development in the CSME bearing in mind the special needs of disadvantaged countries, regions and sectors (…)."[395] It is not clear how this balancing requirement will be applied with regard to industrial policy. Possibly, disadvantaged sectors will be allowed to collaborate on more areas, thereby however possibly challenging the prohibitions set out in the regional competition law chapter.

The same situation is apparent as regards to the agricultural sector. Articles 56ff. of the Revised Treaty of Chaguaramas provide for a differentiated legal framework for the agricultural sector. Generally the Revised Treaty of Chaguaramas envisages a "transformation of the agricultural sector towards market-oriented, internationally competitive (…) sound production of agricultural products (…) bearing in mind the differences in resource endowment and economic development of the Member States."[396]

Chapter VII establishes a regime for disadvantaged countries, regions and sectors. Article 146(1) of the Revised Treaty establishes that the COTED may adopt effective measures "to arrest or mitigate adverse effects on economic activity". Article 146(2) of the Revised Treaty then clarifies that such measures may also "provide for temporary derogations from rights and obligations set out in the treaty". Article 146(2) thus enables the COTED to suspend the application of Chapter VIII. Actually, this regulation is also contained in Article 183 of Chapter VIII of the Revised Treaty, according to which COTED may exempt sectors or enterprises from the application of regional competition law in the public interest.

Chapter VIII is logically embedded in the special and differential treatment approach in the CARICOM. In particular the provisions on exemptions take this approach into account. By providing for the establishment of sectorial rules by the COTED, which may override regional competition law, Chapter VIII can be applied flexibly. It remains open how this flexibility and large discretion of COTED is going to be used with regard to competition law. CARICOM has burdened itself with a

395 Article 51(2) lit. h) of the Revised Treaty of Chaguaramas.

396 Article 56(1) of the Revised Treaty of Chaguaramas.

difficult but appropriate balancing act: bearing in mind the needs for the disadvantaged countries on the one hand, and achieving the imperative of regional economic integration on the other hand.

State of Progress of the Common Market

As the regional competition law in the CARICOM is closely entwined with the creation of a common market, the state of progress will be dealt with separately. While the enforcement of regional competition law constitutes a fundamental pillar of the maintenance of a common market, this is not a one-sided equation, but reflects the interaction between the common market and regional competition law. The removal of trade barriers by the member states and increased intra-community trade furthers the application of regional law.

Although all member states are obliged to apply the Common External Tariff (CET), there has been evidence for insufficient compliance of some member states by applying unauthorized import duties and discriminatory internal taxes.[397] These member states are among the economically weaker states within the CARICOM. There seems to be a causal link between weak economic performance of member states and a tendency to adopt discriminatory actions. Clearly, these factors, including diverging levels of economic development among member states, impede the level of intra-community trade.[398] Generally, exceptions from the application of the CET can be granted according to Article 83 of the Revised Treaty of Chaguaramas. The possible suspension by the COTED even resulted in two cases before the Caribbean Court of Justice, in which Trinidad Cement Limited[399] tried to challenge decisions of COTED, in which it had granted a suspension of the CET.[400]

Furthest developed within the CSME are the rights of free movement of goods and skills.[401] Yet, far from being completely implemented, the principle of free

---

397 There was evidence for such actions in St. Kitts and Nevis, St. Vincent and the Grenadines and in Suriname; see *Smith-Hillman,* The Prospect of a Caribbean Competition Policy, 40 J. W. Trade 405, 415 (2006).

398 *Smith-Hillman,* The Prospect of a Caribbean Competition Policy, 40 J. W. Trade 405, 415 (2006).

399 The same cement company, which also filed a complaint against the CARICOM Competition Commission. In total, there were three cases involving the TCL company before the Court of Justice.

400 *Trinidad Cement Limited v The Caribbean Community*, Caribbean Court of Justice Application No. OA 1 of 2009; *Trinidad Cement Limited v The State of the Co-operative Republic of Guyana*, Caribbean Court of Justice Application No. OA 2 of 2009. Another case before the Caribbean Court of Justice concerning the *Common External Tariff is Hummingbird Rice Mills Ltd v Suriname and The Caribbean Community*, Caribbean Court of Justice Application No. OA 1 of 2011.

401 According to studies conducted by the CARICOM Secretariat from 2009 to 2012, the CSME is operating at about 64% level of compliance, the free movement of skills at 66% and the free movement of goods at 80%, <http://www.csmeonline.org/en/news/item/137-csme-operating-at-about-64-level-of-compliance> accessed 11 November 2018.

movement of people is largely restricted to skilled labour and sports. The principle of free movement of goods is still hampered by restrictions imposed by member states, for example by diverging standards. Similarly, the right of establishment and the free movement of services struggle under diverging national administrative procedures and requirements.[402]

Generally, intra-regional trade in the CARICOM is relatively low and integration has not led to a "discernible trend of increase".[403] Petroleum constitutes 60% of the intra-regional trade.[404] Another sector of overarching importance for the Caribbean countries is the tourism sector.[405] Due to its high relevance, the Caribbean countries were also heavily struck by the financial crisis. The process of establishing an internal market is slow and the harmonization of standards and relevant policies partly "appear to be piecemeal and hesitant".[406]

Limping intra-community trade and the slow implementation of the common market justify the special competition law provisions in Chapter VIII of the Revised Treaty of Chaguaramas that provide for differential treatment. Accordingly, the possibility to exempt certain sectors or regions from regional competition law is in line with the state of progress of the Caribbean market. Yet, one has to hope that the proceeding development of the common market will render country-specific exceptions less necessary. This preconditions that the common market in the CARICOM leads to an approximation of the levels of development of the member states. The more such an approximation takes place, the less competition law provisions for differential treatment should be included in Chapter VIII.

---

[402] According to studies conducted by the CARICOM Secretariat from 2009 to 2012, the right of establishment operates at about a 64% level of compliance and the free movement of services at 37%, <http://www.csmeonline.org/en/news/item/137-csme-operating-at-about-64-level-of-compliance> accessed 11 November 2018. A representative of the CSME-Unit of the CARICOM Secretariat argued that the lack of compliance in these areas was in particular due to the difficulties to monitor compliance.

[403] Executive Summary of the Caribbean Trade and Investment Report 2010, p. 1 <http://www.caricom.org/jsp/community_organs/ctir_2010_executive_summary.pdf> accessed 11 November 2018.

[404] Executive Summary of the Caribbean Trade and Investment Report 2010, p. 2 <http://www.caricom.org/jsp/community_organs/ctir_2010_executive_summary.pdf> accessed 11 November 2018.

[405] *Stewart*, An Empirical Examination of Competition Issues in Selected Caricom Countries, 2004, pp. 112ff. For more information on anti-competitive practices in the tourism sector of small market economies, see *Rodriguez/Murdy*, Anti-Competitive Practices in the Tourism Industry: The Case of Small Economies, 4/10 J. Business & Economics Research 43, 43ff. (2006).

[406] *Pollard*, in: *Hall/Chuck-A-Sang*, CARICOM Single Market and Economy Genesis and Prognosis, 2007, p. 91, 97.

The CARIFORUM-EC Economic Partnership Agreement

The negotiations of the *CARIFORUM-EC EPA* already started in 2004 and are forged in the context of the broader *EU-ACP Cotonou Partnership Agreement*, which was signed in 2000 between the European Union and several regional groups.[407] Signatories to the *CARIFORUM-EC EPA* are all member states of the CARICOM and the Dominican Republic.[408]

The *CARIFORUM-EC EPA* is a broad agreement, covering not only aspects of trade and promoting economic growth, but taking into account the development objectives and the "reduction and eventual eradication of poverty".[409] The *CARIFORUM-EC EPA* demonstrates a comprehensive approach, because it is embedded within the general framework and objectives of the CARICOM. It is explicitly based on the principle of regional economic integration, thereby expressing the underlying conviction that increased economic integration furthers economic growth and sustainable development.[410] Moreover, the *CARIFORUM-EC EPA* is also dedicated to a differential and special treatment approach, allowing transition periods or safeguard clauses with regard to the implementation.[411]

Similar to the Preferential Trade Agreement between Peru and Colombia and the European Union, the *CARIFORUM-EC EPA* includes a competition law chapter that obliges the signing states to adopt national competition laws.[412] With regard to the respective institutions, the agreement contains the obligation to install the CARICOM Competition Commission as competent enforcing organ.[413] Article 128 of the *EPA* explicitly mentions that the member states of CARICOM have to comply with Chapter VIII of the Revised Treaty of Chaguaramas within 5 years. Additionally, it includes provisions on cooperation between competition agencies, which are however rather "soft"[414] and not phrased as obligation in contrast to the provisions regarding the implementation of substantive competition law.[415]

---

[407] Article 2 of the CARIFORUM-EC Economic Partnership Agreement.

[408] For more information on the status and incorporation of the Dominican Republic, see *Stewart*, in: *Drexl/Bakhoum/Fox/Gal/Gerber*, Competition Policy and Regional Integration in Developing Countries, 2012, p. 161, 181.

[409] Article 1 lit. a) of the CARIFORUM-EC Economic Partnership Agreement.

[410] Article 4 of the CARIFORUM-EC Economic Partnership Agreement.

[411] See for example: Article 17: "Modification of Tariff commitments", Article 25: "Safeguard clause", of the *CARIFORUM-EC Economic Partnership Agreement*.

[412] Article 127(1) of the CARIFORUM-EC Economic Partnership Agreement.

[413] Article 127(1) of the CARIFORUM-EC Economic Partnership Agreement.

[414] Article 127 of the *CARIFORUM-EC Economic Partnership Agreement* only uses the term "may" instead of "shall". Article 130 of the *CARIFORUM-EC Economic Partnership Agreement* does not refer to specific enforcement cooperation, but cooperation in the sense of technical assistance and capacity building.

[415] Article 128: "Exchange of information and enforcement cooperation", Article 130: "Cooperation", of the *CARIFORUM-EC Economic Partnership Agreement*.

Irrespective of the raised criticism regarding the *CARIFORUM-EC EPA*'s effectiveness,[416] there is an obvious complication between the provisions in the Revised Treaty of Chaguaramas and its objectives. It is based on the same underlying convictions and utilizes similar mechanisms to achieve these objectives. This consistent embeddedness might be surprising. The *CARIFORUM-EC EPA* was criticized for suffering from a "negotiating deficit".[417] The former Regional Negotiating Machinery,[418] a permanent body composed by its own staff, was allegedly authorized to initiate the Agreement before all member states had the chance to express their views on the *EPA*.[419] According to *Duke Pollard*[420] the EPA demonstrates "a depressing cacophony of responses" in CARICOM, as Barbados and Jamaica insisted on the positive and Guyana only on the negative aspects of the agreement and most of the member states expressed no opinion at all.[421] In fact, *Duke Pollard*'s description mirrors the different economic influences of countries in the Caribbean.

Nevertheless, member states are in the process of complying with the provisions set out in the *Economic Partnership Agreement* regarding the implementation of national competition legislation. They thereby simultaneously fulfil their obligations set out in the regional competition law chapter of CARICOM. This is no coincidence, because the persons that are competent for regional competition law enforcement in the CARICOM, namely *Kusha Haraksingh,* the current chairman of the CARICOM Competition Commission, participated actively in the drafting of the competition law chapter of the *EPA*. The *EPA* thus constituted a "push factor"[422] for the compliance of member states with Chapter VIII of the Revised Treaty of Chaguaramas.

---

[416] The provisions on cooperation are only drafted in non-mandatory term, albeit this would help developing countries to enforce competition law bearing in mind their lack of resources and lack of expertise. Developing countries are especially struggling with anticompetitive practices by international firms with "deep pockets". In the CARICOM, this "power asymmetry" is particularly visible in the tourism sector, which is the leading economic sector in the Commonwealth Caribbean region. However, the sector is dominated by international and partly Jamaican tour operators, see *Stewart,* An empirical examination of competition issues in selected Caricom countries, 2004, pp. 114ff. The *CARIFORUM-EC EPA* does not cover the issue of jurisdictional constraint to investigate foreign firms, see *Stewart,* in: *Drexl/Bakhoum/Fox/Gal/Gerber,* Competition Policy and Regional Integration in Developing Countries, 2012, p. 161, 183.

[417] *Pollard,* in: *Hall/Chuck-A-Sang,* CARICOM: Policy Options for International Engagement, 2010, p. 467, 476.

[418] In 2009, the Regional Negotiating Machinery was transformed into a specialized department of the Secretariat General and was renamed Office of Trade Negotiations. For more information see <http://www.crnm.org/> accessed 11 November 2018.

[419] *Pollard,* in: *Hall/Chuck-A-Sang,* CARICOM: Policy Options for International Engagement, 2010, p. 467, 476.

[420] Honourable Judge at the Caribbean Court of Justice.

[421] *Pollard,* in: *Hall/Chuck-A-Sang,* CARICOM: Policy Options for International Engagement, 2010, p. 467, 476.

[422] *Stewart,* in: *Drexl/Bakhoum/Fox/Gal/Gerber,* Competition Policy and Regional Integration in Developing Countries, 2012, p. 161, 184.

5.3.3 *Vertical Embeddedness: Congruence with National Interests and Economic Policies*

The efficacy of regional competition law enforcement also depends on the congruence with the national policy framework. As competition policy is an integral part of economic policy, national economic interests and policies also have to be taken into account. This in particular applies to a situation, in which member states have still not implemented a domestic competition law regime. Governments might be inclined to favour short-term measures, such as antidumping measures over implementing a domestic competition policy.[423] Moreover, as the necessity to implement competition policy is closely entwined with the degree of market liberalization, the political will to implement competition policy will only evolve with the expansion of national liberalization programs.

Diverging details of national and regional substantive competition laws—wording or even anticompetitive matters that are addressed—do not constitute major obstacles to effective long-term enforcement of a regional competition law. However, national and regional competition law systems that aim at different objectives are prone to lead to inconsistent enforcement. Consequently, national and regional competition laws do not have to be identical, but have to be consistent in their underlying objectives and economic conceptions. Therefore, even more important than analysing the national anticompetitive provisions in detail, is to analyse the compatibility and interaction of underlying competition objectives and underlying economic and trade policies.[424]

5.3.3.1 National Competition Law Objectives and Policies Within WAEMU

The centralized competition law system in WAEMU replaced national competition law provisions. However, general national economic and trade policies should still promote the objectives included in the WAEMU competition provisions in order to enhance efficiency and consequent application of competition law within the entire region. One can thus analyse prior competition law objectives and whether the implementation of the regional competition law system created incentives for member states to reform their legal frameworks in accordance with the establishment of open and competitive national markets, with the ultimate goal of the establishment of a competitive common West African market.

In the WAEMU, all member states theoretically rely on the principle of a free market economy and subsequent freedom to set prices. Many of them have even

[423] *Jenny/Horna,* in: *Brusick/Alvarez/Cernat,* Competition Provisions in Regional Trade Agreements, 2005, p. 281, 320.

[424] *Horna/Kayali,* in: *Alvarez/Wilse-Samson,* Implementing Competition-Related Provisions in Regional Trade Agreements, 2007, p. 21, 31.

manifested the freedom of prices free from state intervention as a legal principle in their laws.[425] However, complete deregulation is still to become a reality. In fact the state as economic actor is still very present in many of WAEMU's member states.[426] This explains the fact that much national legislation still contains exception clauses that provide for possible intervention by the state (on specific sectors) to regulate prices.[427] Such state involvement partly explains the WAEMU Commission's case law, in which the state often constitutes the plaintiff or defendant.

However, the freedom of setting prices also entails a different perspective. In many member states of the WAEMU, the fixing of prices by the state is not considered problematic or anticompetitive. In fact, the national populations in some instances even seemed to prefer prescribed prices, because they believe them to be fair and more stable.[428]

The overall national economic and competition law objectives comply with the principles set out in the Treaty of Dakar and do not hamper the enforcement of regional competition law. Despite salvatory clauses, which in special situations of crises might allow state intervention and price-fixing by the state, all member states are in the process of liberalizing and opening their domestic markets.[429]

Another feature of WAEMU's member states is the preponderance of sector regulators that are also competent for applying competition law. Sectorial control might not adequately protect competition, as the relevant authorities often lack specific competition knowledge or independence.[430] *Inter alia* due to these deficiencies,

---

[425] Burkina Faso: Article 1 of Loi n° 15/94 du 15 Mai 1994 relative à la concurrence; Senegal: Article 1 and 2 of Loi n° 1994/63 du 22 Août 1994 sur les prix, la concurrence et le contentieux économique; Mali: Article 3 of L'Ordonnance n° 07-025 du 18 Juillet 2007 portant organisation de la concurrence; Togo: Article 1 of Loi n° 99-011 du 28 Décembre 1999 portant organisation de la concurrence au Togo; Bénin: Article 3 of L'Ordonnance n° 20/PR/MFAEP du 5 Julillet 1967 portant réglementation des prix et des stocks; Ivory Coast: Article 1 of Loi n° 91-999 du 27 Décembre 1991 relative à la concurrence.

[426] In particular in the form of state-owned enterprises and (natural) monopolies, *CUTS CCIER*, A Time for Action, 2010, pp. 17f.

[427] Burkina Faso: Article 1 of Loi n° 15/94 du 15 Mai 1994 relative à la concurrence, Decree n° 2003-615/PRES/PM/MCOEMFB du 13 Novembre 2003 portant réglementation des prix et produits, biens et services soumis à contrôle; Senegal: Article 23 of Loi n° 1994/63 du 22 Août 1994 sur les prix, la concurrence et le contentieux économique; Mali: Article 3 of L'Ordonnance n° 07-025 du 18 Juillet 2007 portant organisation de la concurrence; Togo: Article 1(2) of Loi n° 99-011 du 28 Décembre 1999 portant organisation de la concurrence au Togo; Bénin: Article 4 of L'Ordonnance n° 20/PR/MFAEP du 5 Julillet 1967 portant réglementation des prix et des stocks; Niger: Article 5 of Ordonnance n° 92-025 du 7 Juillet 1992 portant réglementation des prix et de la concurrence; Ivory Coast: Article 2(1) of Loi n° 91-999 du 27 Décembre 1991 relative à la concurrence.

[428] For example in Senegal: *CUTS*, Vers des régimes efficients de la concurrence par le renforcement des capacités dans des pays sélectionnés d'Afrique de l'Ouest, 2009, p. 28 <http://www.cuts-ccier.org/7up4/pdf/PCP-Senegal.pdf> accessed 11 November 2018.

[429] *CUTS CCIER*, A Time for Action, 2010, pp. 4ff.

[430] "[M]ost of their [sector regulators] staff are former employees of the related Ministry or of the SOE [state-owned enterprise] monopolising the market before liberalisation, thus seriously compromising independence of the regulator." See *CUTS CCIER*, A Time for Action, 2010, p. 52.

there is evidence of anticompetitive practices in regulated sectors.[431] In the absence of hierarchical governance between national sectorial rules and regional competition law, stringent application of the latter might be easily undermined.[432]

Several member states of the WAEMU incorporated provisions on consumer protection in their national competition laws.[433] Civil society's awareness regarding national consumer protection laws is typically higher than awareness regarding national competition laws.[434] This indicates that benefits of consumer protection laws are easier to explain than benefits that arise from competition law enforcement.[435] While the demarcation of national consumer protection and regional competition law might create difficulties, national provisions for consumer protection do not necessarily have to interfere with the WAEMU competition law. Rather the WAEMU Commission might profit from the perception of consumer policy by encouraging cooperation with national consumer associations and authorities.[436]

5.3.3.2 National Competition Law Objectives and Policy Within AndeanC

The Colombian and Peruvian competition law objectives are largely in compliance with the objectives set out in Decision 608, market efficiency and consumer welfare.[437] Article 2 of the Colombian Law 1340 of 2009 determines that the purposes of competition law are the "free participation of businesses in the market, consumer welfare, and economic efficiency". In the Peruvian competition law, Article 1 of Legislative Decree N° 1034 promulgates the objective of the promotion of economic efficiency in the markets for the welfare of the consumers, thereby emphasizing the connection between economic efficiency and consumer welfare even more explicitly than Decision 608.[438]

The Bolivian and Ecuadorian competition law objectives also seem to follow a consumer welfare approach. Art. 1 of the Bolivian Supreme Decree N° 29519 declares as the object the regulation of competition and protection of consumers

---

431 *CUTS CCIER,* A Time for Action, 2010, p. 53.

432 *UNCTAD,* Voluntary Peer Review on Competition Policies of WAEMU, Benin and Senegal, 2008, p. 35.

433 For example: Burkina Faso: Articles 23 and 24 of Loi relative à la concurrence, Loi 33-2001 du 4 décembre 2001; Mali: Articles 36ff. of L'Ordonnance n° 07-025/P-RM du 16 Juillet 2007 portant Organisation de la concurrence.

434 *CUTS CCIER,* A Time for Action, 2010, p. 46.

435 This for example corresponds to the experiences of the Jamaican Fair Trading Commission, see above Part II, Dimension I: Sect. 5.2.3.1.

436 See above Part II, Dimension I: Sect. 5.2.3.1.

437 Article 2 of Decision 608 of 2005.

438 Article 1 of Legislative Decree N° 1034: "Finalidad de la presente Ley.- La presente Ley prohibe y a sanciona las conductas anticompetitivas con la finalidad de promover la eficienciy económica en los mercados para el bienestar de los consumidores".

against harmful practices. Going even further than the wording, representatives from the Bolivian competition agency stated that they were not interested in undertakings as competitors at all, but only if they exercised an impact on consumers.[439] Art. 1 LORPCM in Ecuador declares market efficiency, just commerce, the general welfare and welfare of consumers and users, or the establishment of a social, solidary and sustainable economic system as main competition law objectives. However, the utilization of the notion of "just competition" in Ecuador leaves room for state intervention and state control.[440] A similar situation exists in Bolivia, where the Constitution only addresses private monopolies.[441] In Ecuador, the current Superintendent of the competition authority has at different instances emphasized the importance of abolishing the monopolistic structure of the Ecuadorian market and of creating economic structures that empowers the Ecuadorian people to participate in the market and improve dynamics of entrepreneurship.[442] In his view not only state investments, but private investments guarantee for a sustainable market.[443]

---

[439] Statement made during several interviews conducted with representatives of the Bolivian competition agency by the author in January/February 2012 in La Paz, Bolivia.

[440] See also *National Development Plan of the Republic of Ecuador*: National Plan for Good Living, 2009 to 2013, Building a Plurinational and Intercultural State, p. 24: "The Fundamental Law strengthens the State by recovering its planning, regulating and redistributing role, and as a guarantor of public matters. It is not a simplistic statist vision in which the role of the market is merely replaced by the role of the State. On the contrary, by strengthening and expanding rights and recognizing participation as an essential element in the construction of the new society, the Constitution seeks to strengthen *society* and not merely the State.". See also Article 304 of the *New Constitution of Ecuador of 2008*: "La política comercial tendrá los siguentes objetivos: Evitar las prácticas monopólicas y oligopólicas, particularemente en el sector privado, y otras que afecten el funcionamiento en los mercados.". See also Article 335 of the *New Constitution of Ecuador of 2008*: "El Estado regulará, controlará e intervendrá, cuando sea necesario, en los intercambios y transacciones económicas; y sancionará la explotación, usura, acaparamiento, simulación, intermediación especulativa de los bienes y servicios, así como toda forma de perjuicio a los derechos económicos y a los bienes públicos y colectivos. El Estado definirá una política de precios orientada a proteger la producción nacional, establecerá los mecanismos de sanción para evitar cualquier práctica de monopolio y oligopolio privados, o de abuso de posición de dominio en el mercado y otras prácticas de competencia desleal.". For general information on the Ecuadorian competition law, see *Quevedo,* El Derecho de la Libre Competencia en el Nuevo Marco Constitucional del Ecuador, 2011 and *Andrade,* Lineamientos para un Régimen Jurídico de la Competencia en el Ecuador, 16/2 Rev. Jur. Univ. Católica 13, 13ff. (2003).

[441] Article 314 of the Bolivian Constitution of 2009: "Se prohíbe el monopolio y el oligopolio privado, así como cualquier otra forma de asociación o acuerdo de personas naturales o jurídicas privadas, bolivianas o extranjeras, que pretendan el control y la exclusividad en la producción y comercialización de bienes y servicios."

[442] *El Telégrafo,* 25 March 2013, "Hay intereses muy poderosos que quieren evitar un cambio – Entrevista con Pedro Páez, Superintendente de control del poder de mercado" <http://www.telegrafo.com.ec/economia/item/hay-intereses-muy-poderosos-que-quieren-evitar-un-cambio.html>.

[443] *Revista Gestión,* Economía y Sociedad, N° 225, March 2013, pp. 22–26, "La codicia no puede ser el único moto del país: Pedro Páez" <http://scpm.gob.ec/entrevista-a-pedro-paez-superintendente-de-control-de-poder-del-mercado-revista-gestion/>.

After the crisis of the Washington Consensus[444] many AndeanC's member states strengthened the role of state intervention on national markets.[445] Some governments even re-introduced price control systems.[446] The differing underlying economic approaches to a certain extent explain the stagnated commitment towards regional competition law enforcement.[447] Nevertheless, national competition law policies are generally in line with Decision 608's objectives, albeit they are capable of creating loopholes for state intervention. Article 36 Decision 608 allows for national regulatory measures as long as they do not distort competition in the sub-regional market. Yet, the general complementarity of national and regional objectives guarantees that there actually is a political will to support regional competition law enforcement and that national economic policies support economic integration overall. In this context, one should in particular mention the ambiguous commitment of Bolivia[448] as regards the AndeanC. Generally, it will be difficult to reconcile regional competition law enforcement, which is aimed at increasing the competitiveness of the regional market with approaches of national governments that restrict national liberalization attempts and that favour other regional integration groups that are not reconciled with the AndeanC.[449]

5.3.3.3 National Competition Law Objectives and Policy Within CARICOM

Generally, all member states of CARICOM are open economies based on free markets. However, liberalization has been a slow process and the state often intervened as an economic agent. In Trinidad and Tobago, price regulation of the state on the poultry market was the only instrument to deal with price variations, which arose

---

[444] The Washington Consensus refers to a package of economic policy prescriptions that were promoted by institutions located in Washington D.C., such as the World Bank and the International Monetary Fund, in order to enhance economic stability and growth of developing countries that had been under economic crises.

[445] *Botta,* The Role of Competition Policy in the Latin American Regional Integration: A Comparative Analysis of Caricom, Andean Community and Mercosur, 21–22 October 2011, St. Gallen, p. 22; see also *Peña,* in: *Marsden,* Handbook of Research in Trans-Atlantic Antitrust, 2006, pp. 732, 743f.

[446] *Peña,* in: *Marsden,* Handbook of Research in Trans-Atlantic Antitrust, 2006, p. 732, 744. According to *Peña,* indirect price control even took place in Peru.

[447] For example, before Ecuador enacted its domestic competition law, it actually supported the adoption of a regional competition policy. After the implementation of the national competition law, Ecuador refrained from further supporting Decision 608.

[448] In 2012, Bolivia also joined the MERCOSUR. It also holds close economic relations with Venezuela. It is to be noted that Venezuela was willing to "abandon" the AndeanC (it withdrew from the AndeanC in 2006) to become a member of the MERCOSUR. For more information see *The New York Times,* 8 December 2005, "South American Trade Blocs Moves to Admit Venezuela" <http://www.nytimes.com/2005/12/08/business/worldbusiness/08trade.html?_r=0>.

[449] In contrast to the WAEMU, in which there are attempts to reconcile the WAEMU with the ECOWAS and OHADA, because the memberships of participating states overlap.

from anticompetitive behaviour.[450] In Barbados, Antigua and Barbuda and Jamaica governments introduced stabilized prices for selected basic food items.[451] Generally the small size of the Caribbean economies makes them vulnerable to concentrations and the process of liberalization and privatization often resulted in the creation of natural monopolies.[452] This creates a dilemma, in which the CSME has to reconcile objectives of regional competition law enforcement with growth ambitions of small market economies.[453] Positive examples in this regard are the Trinidad and Tobago telecommunications sector, whose monopoly was abolished in 2005, or the Jamaican telecommunications sector, which was liberalized in 2003.[454]

The convergence between national and regional competition law and policy in CARICOM is particularly important to analyse, because parallel investigations on the national and regional level are generally possible according to the provisions of the Revised Treaty of Chaguaramas.[455] Convergence was widely achieved, *inter alia* because representatives of Jamaica, Barbados and Trinidad and Tobago belonged to the task force for the drafting of the regional competition provisions. These countries are among the economically most developed jurisdictions.

When Chapter VIII of the Revised Treaty of Chaguaramas entered into force, Jamaica and Barbados were the only member states with a domestic competition law regime. Trinidad and Tobago had published a green and a white paper on a domestic competition law, however the implementation process stagnated after that. In Jamaica and Barbados, special weight was attributed to consumer welfare. Guyana followed the model of Barbados and installed a mixed national authority. Clearly, Chapter VIII of the Revised Treaty also takes a consumer welfare approach. While Article 2 of the Revised Treaty of Chaguaramas also mentions other objectives, the inclusion of consumer protection provisions in Part Two of Chapter VIII is a strong indicator for its importance.[456]

Finally, one has to highlight that except Jamaica, all member states' national competition legislations (or legislative drafts)—where they exist—make reference

---

[450] *Stewart,* An Empirical Examination of Competition Issues in Selected Caricom Countries, 2004, p. 5.

[451] *Lee,* Caricom Competition Commission: Enhancing Competition Enforcement in the Caribbean Community, 3–5 June 2009, Zurich, p. 16.

[452] *Gal,* Competition Policy for Small Market Economies, 2003, pp. 31ff.

[453] *Smith-Hillman,* The Prospect of a Caribbean Competition Policy, 40 J. W. Trade 405, 405 (2006).

[454] Competent for these sectors are regulatory bodies, the Telecommunication Authority in Trinidad and Tobago and the Office of Utility Regulation in Jamaica. See generally on the telecommunications sectors in CARICOM member states *Stewart,* in: *Schatan/Avalos,* Condiciones y Políticas de Competencia, 2006, p. 331, 375.

[455] See below Part II, Dimension IV: Sect. 8.1.2 and Part II, Dimension V: Sect. 9.2.4.

[456] The probable superior relevance of the consumer welfare approach in CARICOM competition law was also highlighted by the Chairman of the CARICOM Competition Commission, Kusha Haraksingh in an interview with the author in Port-of-Spain, Trinidad and Tobago, 29 October 2012. The future actions of the CARICOM Competition Commission will demonstrate how the objectives set out in Article 2 of the Revised Treaty of Chaguaramas will be balanced and applied.

to the regional competition law framework and especially to the CSME. Although, ultimate implementation, enforcement and effective cooperation are still slow, this does not result from unwillingness. Rather, it seems that the CARICOM member states are committed to the CSME. Despite existing distrust among each other, particularly against the economically strong Trinidad and Tobago, the member states display a general believe in the benefits of regional economic integration within the CSME and agree with the objectives of regional competition policy.[457]

5.3.3.4 Summary of Regional Competition Law Objectives and Embeddedness

Generally, one can conclude that regional competition policy is always embedded in other regional and national economic and competition policies. Yet, four main challenges to regional competition law appeared in all three RTAs, albeit with different intensities: First, the competition policy implementation process is slow due to insufficient resources and weak national administrative bodies. Second, national interventionist tendencies prevail. Nationally relevant sectors are partially exempted from competition law application, but fall under the surveillance of regulatory bodies.[458] Third, divergences in economic prosperity between member states are capable of creating distrust among member states and are capable of reducing national support for the common market, because member states profit differently from it.[459] Fourth, intra-community trade has remained relatively weak.

[457] Feature Address by the Honourable David Thompson Q.C., M.P., Prime Minister of Barbados at the Opening Ceremony of the Convocation of the CSME, Lloyd Erskine Sandiford Conference Centre, Bridgetown, Barbados, 9 October 2009: "(…) I believe this capacity constraint, and not disinterest in the CSME, is responsible for any examples of irregular application of the provisions across the Community." He further mentions particular problems in the field of the free movement of labour and the different levels of development. For more details on the "State of play in economic integration" in the CARICOM, see *Stewart,* in: *Drexl/Bakhoum/Fox/Gal/Gerber,* Competition Policy and Regional Integration in Developing Countries, 2012, pp. 161, 173ff.

[458] This is the case in the financial sector of Trinidad and Tobago, see *Stewart,* in: *Drexl/Bakhoum/Fox/Gal/Gerber,* Competition Policy and Regional Integration in Developing Countries, 2012, p. 161, 179.

[459] The most drastic example for the unequal economic power among member states within a RTA is the CARICOM, in which Trinidad and Tobago and respective firms (to a certain extent also Barbados) constitute the economically most powerful players within the CSME, see *Smith-Hillman,* The Prospect of a Caribbean Competition Policy, 40 J. W. Trade 405, 407 (2006). For a general overview of CARICOM intra-regional trade, see *Ibid.,* p. 414.

Chapter 6
Dimension II: Legislative Competence on Competition Law

The vertical allocation of material competences is not only determined by the substantive law and its scope of application. It also comprises the question of legislative competence, meaning the institutional organ that is entitled to legislate on competition matters ("legislative primacy" on competition matters). An obligation for the national legislator to completely harmonize its national competition laws withdraws national legislative discretion. At the same time, the impact of the scope of application of a regional law is reduced if the national and regional law's content is actually the same. On the other hand, complete legislative sovereignty of a member state of an RTA to draft its competition law would be rendered obsolete by an extremely narrow scope of application of national competition law.

There are different degrees of legislative competence of the regional entity, ranging from a complete unification of the substantive competition law to loose, non-binding guidelines provided by the regional level.

6.1 Unification of Laws Through a Wide Definition of the Territorial Scope of Application: The Case of WAEMU

Complete unification of national and regional laws is the most drastic allocation of legislative competences. There are different instruments to achieve such unification: either by full harmonization imposed by the regional level or by complete withdrawal of national legislative competences on a specific matter. Remaining parallel national legislative competence can also be rendered obsolete by a wide scope of application of regional law that leaves no room for the application of national

J. Molestina, *Regional Competition Law Enforcement in Developing Countries*, Munich Studies on Innovation and Competition 9,
https://doi.org/10.1007/978-3-662-58525-2_6

provisions. This however concerns the allocation of competences via the substantive laws' content.[1]

In the centralized competition law system of the WAEMU the advisory opinion no. 003/2000[2] led to the complete deprivation of national legislative competences regarding agreements, abuse of dominant position and state aids. The regional Court was asked to interpret the Articles 88, 89 and 90 of the Treaty of Dakar and thereby to define the competences of the Commission. The Court's decision was based on three main elements. First, Articles 88, 89 and 90 of the Treaty of Dakar were considered to entail exclusive competence of the WAEMU Commission to apply regional competition law. Second, it was held that the community competition law was a centralized system, which covered the matters of agreements, concerted practices and abuse of dominant position capable of distorting or restricting competition in the area of the community. Member states could only exercise formally assigned competences. Third, the legislative competences of the member states were limited to criminal dispositions regarding anticompetitive practices, rules concerning transparency of the market and rules regarding the organization of competition agencies and procedural rules.[3] This distinction is of crucial importance, because whereas the unification of substantive competition law and legislative competences by themselves can be useful instruments in developing countries, it was the combination with the exclusive enforcement competence of the WAEMU Commission that led to a large number of inefficiencies.

In other words, while the competition law's substantive content has been unified via replacement by regional law, the national institutions and their organization remain within national competences. In fact, national competition authorities vary in their organizational design, independence, competences and functions.[4]

Moreover, the regulation of unfair competition and restrictive practices[5] remains within national legislative competence, as well as the penalization of competition law infringements and the according procedures.[6] Likewise, the centralization of

[1] See above Dimension I: Chap. 5.

[2] Advisory Opinion no. 03/2000/CJ/WAEMU of 27 June 2000, "Demande d'avis de la Commission de l'UEMOA relative à l'interprétation des articles 88, 89 et 90 du Traité relatifs aux règles de concurrences dans l'Union".

[3] Advisory Opinion no. 03/2000/CJ/WAEMU of 27 June 2000, "Demande d'avis de la Commission de l'UEMOA relative à l'interprétation des articles 88, 89 et 90 du Traité relatifs aux règles de concurrences dans l'Union"; Directive no. 02/2002/CM/WAEMU; Regulation no. 03/2002/CM/WAEMU.

[4] For more information see *Bakhoum,* Étude sur la Révision du Cadre Institutionnel de Mise en Oeuvre des Règles de Concurrence de l'UEMOA, 2011.

[5] French law distinguishes between competition provisions against anticompetitive practices and provisions covering restrictive practices. Competition law is generally associated with the notion of restraints to competition and is in line with the European competition law, covering cartels and abuse of dominance. Restrictive practices generally relate to "individual" restraints that arise from uneven bargaining power between contracting parties. They are prohibited per se without establishing a specific effect on the market. The ordinary judiciary has jurisdiction over restrictive practices.

[6] "Les Etats membres ne sont compétents que pour prendre les dispositions pénales réprimant les pratiques concurrentielles, les infractions aux règles de transparence du marché et à l'organisation de la concurrence."; Advisory Opinion no. 03/2000 of 27 June 2000.

competition law does not touch upon national sector regulation. Several regional sectorial Directives have been enacted, most prominently are the Directives, Regulations and Decisions on the telecommunications sector,[7] however apart from that, there has been little activity to harmonize the different national sectorial systems.[8]

Existing national competition laws become inapplicable through the direct effect and supremacy of community law and related national provisions have to be reformed in accordance with community rules.[9] Where national provisions did not exist, member states are solely held to refrain from enacting laws that could counteract the objectives of community laws.[10] This is codified in Art. 6(1) of Directive no. 02/2002/CM/UEMOA.[11] In the same vein, Art. 6(2) of Directive no. 02/2002/CM/UEMOA sets out that national competition law structures have to be organized in accordance with their competences that are now limited to the surveillance of the market and the assistance to the regional competition authority.

Again, the centralization of legislative competences regarding competition law matters, as well as the accentuation of the supremacy of regional law clearly strive at the aim of guaranteeing a convergent competition law application in the WAEMU. Nevertheless, national institutions, norms and institutional bodies are supposed to complete the regional framework. This leaves room for possible conflicts and divergences. The following section sheds some light on the impact of the centralization on national competition law systems and evaluates whether unification actually took place.

---

[7] Décision n° 09/2006/CM/UEMOA portant création du comité des regulateurs nationaux de télécommunications des états membres de l'UEMOA; Directive n° 01/2006/CM/UEMOA relative à l'harmonisation des politiques de contrôle et de régulation du secteur des télécommunications, Directive n° 02/2006/CM/UEMOA relative à l'harmonisation des régimes applicables aux operateurs de réseaux et fournisseurs de services; Directive n° 03/2006/CM/UEMOA relative à l'interconnexion des réseaux et services de télécommunications; Directive n° 04/2006/CM/UEMOA relative au service universel et aux obligations de performance du réseau; Directive n° 05/2006/CM/UEMOA relative à l'harmonisation de la tarification des services de télécommunications; Directive n° 06/2006/CM/UEMOA organisant le cadre général de coopération entre les autorités nationales de régulation en matière de télécommunications. All legal documents are of 23 March 2006.

[8] *Weick*, Competition Law and Policy in Senegal, 33/3 W. Comp. 521, 535 (2010).

[9] *Bakhoum*, Delimitation and Exercise of Competence between the West African Economic and Monetary Union (WAEMU) and its Member States in Competition Policy, 29/4 W. Comp. 653, 669 (2006); *Bakhoum*, L'articulation du droit communautaire et des droits nationaux de la concurrence dans l'Union Economique et Monétaire Ouest Africaine, 2007, p. 151.

[10] See Article 7 of Treaty of Dakar; *Bakhoum*, Delimitation and Exercise of Competence between the West African Economic and Monetary Union (WAEMU) and its Member States in Competition Policy, 29/4 W. Comp. 653, 669 (2006).

[11] See considerations of Directive n° 02/2002/CM/UEMOA relative à la coopération entre la Commission et les structures nationales de concurrence des états membres pour l'application des articles 88, 89 et 90 du traité de l'UEMOA.

6.1.1 Implications on Member States with Existing and Operative National Competition Law Systems

For the principles of direct effect and applicability[12] and the principle of primacy[13] of regional law, national competition law provisions are automatically superseded by the regional competition provisions and can no longer be applied.

Although Senegal has so far not changed its substantive competition law,[14] the jurisdiction generally accepted the centralization of legislative competition competences. The refraining from reforming national law may also be attributed to the complementary between the Senegalese and WAEMU provisions on cartel agreements and abuse of dominant position.[15] While prior to 2003 pending cases were still resolved under national competition law,[16] the Senegalese competition authority abstained from making decisions on later cases.[17] However, despite the operability of the Senegalese competition system, cooperation and collaboration between the national competition authority and the WAEMU Commission does not take place. Although a relatively large number of requests was submitted before the national authority in Senegal, none of them was resolved by the WAEMU Commission.[18] This is mainly due to the Senegalese competition authority's reluctance to refer cases to the WAEMU Commission. In the decision *DHL C/ la Société Nationale la Poste* of 13 October 2003, the case was referred to the WAEMU Commission, but *DHL* withdrew its complaint after being informed about the referral to the regional agency.[19]

---

[12] See below Part II, Dimension V: Sect. 9.1.

[13] See below Part II, Dimension V: Sect. 9.2.

[14] Explanation of the impact of the advisory opinion no. 003/2000 of the 27th of June, 2000 on the Senegalese competition law n° 04-63 of the 22 August 1994, see *Commission Nationale de la Concurrence*, De la loi n° 94-63 du 22 août 1994 sur les prix, la concurrence et le contentieux économique, aux Directives et Règlements de l'UEMOA.

[15] *UNCTAD,* Voluntary Peer Review on Competition Policies of WAEMU, Benin and Senegal, 2008, p. 93.

[16] DHL C/ la Société Nationale la Poste (plainte du 13 octobre 2003); Fallou Fall, Directeur des Boulangeries Sokhna Mame Diarra Bousso C/ l'arrêté 42/GRZ du 29 avril 1994 du Gouverneur de la Région de Ziguinchor fixant les modalités de distribution du pain dans la commune de Ziguinchor, according to *Commission Nationale de la Concurrence du Sénégal,* Rapport Public 2002–2003, p. 23.

[17] One of the still pending cases was the case "Syndicat des Agences de Voyages et de Tourisme du Sénégal C/ la Compagnie Air France (lettre du 29 mai 2001)". On 25 September 2003 the Senegalese decision (Décision n° 02/D-02 of 27 December 2002) was referred to the Court of Justice of WAEMU by the Council of States for annulment, see Arrêt des Sections Réunies n° 12/03, *Commission Nationale de la Concurrence du Sénégal,* Rapport Public 2002–2003, p. 24. See also *UNCTAD,* Voluntary Peer Review on Competition Policies of WAEMU, Benin and Senegal, 2008, pp. 107f.

[18] *UNCTAD,* Voluntary Peer Review on Competition Policies of WAEMU, Benin and Senegal, 2008, pp. 104f.; *Bakhoum,* Étude sur la Révision du Cadre Institutionnel de Mise en Oeuvre des Règles de Concurrence de l'UEMOA, 2011.

[19] *Commission Nationale de la Concurrence du Sénégal,* Rapport Public 2002–2003, p. 60, Annex 5: "Objet: Plainte du 13 Octobre 2003 de DHL Sénégal C/ La Société de la Poste".

In the same vein, there has not been cooperation in the conduct of investigations regarding potentially anticompetitive practices. Interestingly, it seems that the WAEMU was however cooperating with the Senegalese Directorate of Internal Trade,[20] which is part of the organisation of the Ministry of Commerce.[21] The Directorate of Internal Trade has dealt with several competition cases since 2003 in accordance with WAEMU community law.[22] The reluctance of the Senegalese competition law authority to cooperate clearly emanates from the withdrawal of all competition law competences caused by the centralized system.[23] Already during the legislative process and adoption of the regional competition law system, representatives of the Senegalese state and national interest groups had been vehement opponents of the centralized system arising out of the narrow definition by the WAEMU Court of Justice.[24] However, one has to carefully differentiate between the centralization through the withdrawal of competences to legislate on competition law matters and the centralization through the exclusive competence of the WAEMU Commission to apply regional competition law.

Likewise, the WAEMU Commission has not fulfilled its cooperation task arising out of the new competition law system. According to the report of the Senegalese Competition Commission, the WAEMU did not inform it about investigations on the Senegalese cement sector and did not invite the domestic authority to the regional seminar of WAEMU on the community competition legislation held in Dakar on 5–9 May 2003.[25]

In Burkina Faso legal reforms after the implementation of the exclusive regional competition law system did not take place. It was only recognized that the Law no. 15/94, in particular its competition rules, becomes inapplicable. However, national consumer rights provisions still remain valid. This creates ambiguities for the application of national substantive law with regard to the remaining applicable provisions under the centralized system and possible conflicts with regional competition law. Nevertheless, Burkina Faso's competition authority is the most active national

---

[20] Direction du Commerce Intérieur.

[21] *UNCTAD,* Voluntary Peer Review on Competition Policies of WAEMU, Benin and Senegal, 2008, p. 103; *Bakhoum,* Étude sur la Révision du Cadre Institutionnel de Mise en Oeuvre des Règles de Concurrence de l'UEMOA, 2011.

[22] *UNCTAD,* Voluntary Peer Review on Competition Policies of WAEMU, Benin and Senegal, 2008, pp. 102ff. These cases not only concern competition matters, but also consumer protection, unfair competition, counterfeit trade and anti-dumping actions.

[23] *CUTS,* Vers des régimes efficients de la concurrence par le renforcement des capacités dans des pays sélectionnés d'Afrique de l'Ouest, 2009 <http://www.cuts-ccier.org/7up4/pdf/PCP-Senegal.pdf> accessed 11 November 2018.

[24] See *Commission Nationale de la Concurrence du Sénégal,* Rapport Public 2002–2003, pp. 35, 36; *Commission Nationale de la Concurrence du Sénégal,* Avis n° 01. –A.02 du 15 mars 2002, De la Commission Nationale de la Concurrence en date du 15 mars 2002 relatif à une demande d'observation du Ministre des Petites et Moyennes Entreprises et du Commerce sur le projet de loi communautaire de la Concurrence; Lettre n° 0717/MPMEC/ITA du 23 mai 2002 du *Ministre des PME et du Commerce* au Président de la Commission économique de l'UEMOA, Objet: Observations sur le projet de loi communautaire de la concurrence.

[25] Commission Nationale de la Concurrence du Sénégal, Rapport Public 2002–2003, p. 33 (Fn).

authority in cooperating with the WAEMU Commission. In fact, three reports regarding anticompetitive practices were submitted to the Commission on its request.[26] Furthermore, the national authority has been very active by assisting the Commission in the exercise of investigations.[27] The location of the WAEMU Commission in Burkina Faso's capital city most probably constitutes one of the main reasons for the strong interrelation. Moreover, the relatively elaborated competition law experience of Burkina Faso also attributes to efficient vertical cooperation.

Mali reformed its national laws in accordance with the newly implemented community law in 2007, thereby expressly recognizing the exclusive competence of the WAEMU Commission regarding competition matters in Article 43 of the Ordinance no. 07-025. However, the national Decree no. 08-260 still includes provisions on price-setting of undertakings with monopoly power. Mali has kept national provisions on unfair competition, which are difficult to distinguish from "classical" competition law rules. They cover matters, such as predatory pricing, discriminatory pricing or refusal to supply.[28] Generally, antitrust enforcement was and remains weak in Mali.[29] The main reasons that are brought forward for the loose enforcement are the lack of adaptability of the national competition law to the socio-economical context. The latter is explained by the lack of a competition culture, the lack of political willingness to make competition law enforcement a priority, the lack of competition in several economically important sectors, such as electricity, and finally the magnitude of the informal sector constituting approximately 60% of the entire domestic market and the prevailing poverty.[30] Further reasons are the weakness of the general regulatory and institutional framework and the lack of resources and expertise of the national authority.[31] With regard to the cooperation with the regional organs, two competition law cases have been submitted to the WAEMU Commission, among them the regional case *SOTELMA-Malitel v Orange Mali*,[32] which deals with an abuse of dominant position.[33]

In Ivory Coast, the national competition law system builds on a relatively old system, originating from 1991, and several competition law cases had been dealt

[26] *Bakhoum*, Étude sur la Révision du Cadre Institutionnel de Mise en Oeuvre des Règles de Concurrence de l'UEMOA, 2011.

[27] *Bakhoum*, Étude sur la Révision du Cadre Institutionnel de Mise en Oeuvre des Règles de Concurrence de l'UEMOA, 2011.

[28] Articles 7ff. of L'Ordonnance n° 07-025 du 18 Juillet 2007 *portant organisation de la concurrence*.

[29] *CUTS*, Document Préliminaire du Mali sur les Scénarios de Concurrence, 2009 <http://www.cuts-ccier.org/7up4/pdf/PCP-Mali.pdf> accessed 11 November 2018.

[30] *Ibid.*

[31] *Ibid.*

[32] For more information on the case, see *Bakhoum/Molestina*, in: *Drexl/Bakhoum/Fox/Gal/Gerber*, Competition Policy and Regional Integration in Developing Countries, 2012, pp. 89, 102.

[33] The case is still ongoing.

with under the Law no. 91-999.[34] However since 2002, the national authority has remained relatively inactive due to the socio-political and economic crisis.[35] Consequently, for this inactivity, cooperation or collaboration with the WAEMU competition law bodies does not exist. Nevertheless, the Law no. 2013-662 of 2013 explicitly recognizes the WAEMU competition legislation.

It goes without saying that even the more developed national competition law systems in the WAEMU suffer from severe resource constraints, such as a lack of independence of the competition authority, the exposition to corruption and political pressure, political and social instability and the absence of a competition culture.[36] These constraints impact the level of cooperation with the WAEMU Commission, which is generally low. However, cooperation is particularly important for competition law enforcement, because the regional WAEMU Commission itself suffers from severe resource constraints.[37] Even worse, the little existing national competition law experience that Senegal, Burkina Faso, Mali and Ivory Coast have gained is 'wasted' in the centralized enforcement system, in which cooperation remains limited. Again, this does not primarily relate to the centralization of the legislative competences, but is caused by the exclusive competence of the WAEMU Commission to apply competition law in the WAEMU territory.

While the degree of efficiency of a national competition authority expands to the degree of efficiency of cooperation, the decisive component appears to be the political will and the will of the domestic authority to cooperate. The example of Senegal demonstrates that the will to cooperate can be reduced through a complete withdrawal of decision-making and legislative competences on competition matters. On the other hand, the functioning cooperation between the WAEMU and Burkina Faso authority adds an additional element that determines vertical cooperation. The same geographical location of the WAEMU Commission and the Burkina Faso competition authority has supported the awareness of regional competition law enforcement. To sum up, the more general acceptance the WAEMU Commission obtains in a member state, the more vertical cooperation is likely to take place. On the other hand, reforms of national laws do not take place automatically, albeit regional law might set out a formal obligation to do so. Unification of laws cannot replace incentives for domestic competition authorities to reform national laws and to cooperate and collaborate with the Commission effectively. Incentives lack in particular if the WAEMU Commission itself does not fulfil its obligations, namely its information obligation.[38]

Moreover, member states have found 'loopholes' to regulate 'classical' competition law practices nationally. In accordance with French legal tradition, the law

---

[34] Loi n° 91-999 du 27 Décembre 1991 *relative à la concurrence*.

[35] *Bakhoum,* Étude sur la Révision du Cadre Institutionnel de Mise en Oeuvre des Règles de Concurrence de l'UEMOA, 2011.

[36] The Senegalese Competition Commission lacks human and financial resources. See *Commission Nationale de la Concurrence du Sénégal,* Rapport Public 2002–2003, pp. 19ff.

[37] See below, Part II, Dimension III: Sect. 7.1.3.

[38] See below Part II, Dimension IV: Sect. 8.2.

distinguishes between provisions on anticompetitive practices and restrictive practices. Restrictive practices still remain within the legislative competences of the member states. In the same vein, member states have retained the competence to regulate unfair competition. This parallel system bears potential for contradiction, as the provisions for unfair competition in Mali demonstrate. Mali's legal chapter on unfair competition[39] covers practices that would usually constitute 'classical' competition law provisions and practices. Similarly, the provisions on restrictive practices in Burkina Faso cover competition law practices, such as predatory pricing or the refusal to supply.[40] Although a clear-cut differentiation between restrictive practices and competition matters is thus unrealistic, national law is nevertheless to a large extent convergent with the regional laws' substance. Moreover, the Court of Justice of WAEMU's decision no. 003/2000 explicitly stated that community law takes precedent over national laws if a practices falls under the scope of Article 88 lit. a) and b) of the Treaty of Dakar.[41]

Another obstacle to harmonization of substantive law arises from the national exceptions for state intervention despite the on-going process of deregulation and liberalization. Domestic governments can under certain circumstances fix prices, provide subsidies and are still very present economic players. Surprisingly, this fact has not counteracted regional competition law, but on the contrary, has to a certain extent justified the centralized system.[42]

---

[39] Chapter 1 of L'Ordonnance n° 07-025 du 18 Juillet 2007 *portant organisation de la concurrence.*

[40] Titre 4 de la Loi n° 15/94 du 15 Mai 1994 *relative à la concurrence.*

[41] *Bakhoum* raises the question whether such a broad understanding of exclusivity is feasible or justified. However he highlights that a parallel national application of practices with regard to their relevance to national law creates a risk of collision, namely in the form of contradicting solutions or duplication of sanctions. Although, one could avoid this risk by requiring national competition authorities to seek the advice of the WAEMU Commission before a decision, *Bakhoum* states that the exclusive application of community law even on practices is more in conformity with the legislative unification, set out in the Advisory Opinion no. 003/2000/CJ/UEMOA. It avoids diverging sanctions and guarantees that a violation of the law is ceased after a procedure in accordance with community law. For more information see *Bakhoum,* L'articulation du droit communautaire et des droits nationaux de la concurrence dans l'Union Economique et Monétaire Ouest Africaine, 2007, pp. 82f.

[42] In fact, the regional provisions on state aids and other state-related practices have turned out as the most utilized and most prominent regional competition law provision. This has to be pointed out, because the abolishment of state-related trade barriers constitutes an important pillar of a common regional market. For the case law of the WAEMU Commission, see below Part II, Dimension III: Sect. 7.1.3.2.

6.1.2 Implications on Member States Without Prior or Operative National Competition Law Systems, Including Member States with Prior Sectorial Regulation

In Guinea-Bissau, the least developed national competition law system within WAEMU, cooperation with the WAEMU Commission does not take place. With regard to legislative actions, there have only been legal initiatives to lessen the administrative burden to engage in business in the country.[43] One also has to highlight that the official language in Guinea-Bissau is Portuguese and not French.

Competition law enforcement in Togo through its national competition authority is hampered by the lack of resources and the legislation is characterized by a strong state control on prices. Cooperation with the WAEMU Commission does not take place.

In Niger, price regulation is also still very prominent. Nevertheless, there circulates a national draft legislation that aims at the installation of a more open and more competitive domestic market.[44] Organized according to Decree no. 2010-740/PCSRD/MCI/PJE,[45] the Direction of Competition, Competitiveness and Consumer Protection[46] deals with potential anticompetitive practices in Niger. Partly explicable by the still prevailing price regulation by the state, cooperation on competition law matters with the WAEMU Commission has not taken place. There are though ongoing projects regarding the creation of a national competition law authority, thereby taking into account the assisting function of national authorities in the competition enforcement procedures initiated by the regional level.[47]

Benin's national competition law was only enacted in 2016. Nevertheless, Benin has already previously taken measures based on WAEMU law. For example, there has been collaboration during an investigation in the *CANAL+Horizon* case.[48] Moreover, in the case *GAZODUC de l'Afrique de l'Ouest* of 6 May 2004 Benin and Togo sought a negative clearance from the WAEMU Commission.[49] In another case on 30 January 2006, the Ministry of Finance and Economy of Benin lodged a

---

43 Decreto-Lei n° 01/2005.

44 *Bakhoum,* Étude sur la Révision du Cadre Institutionnel de Mise en Oeuvre des Règles de Concurrence de l'UEMOA, 2011.

45 Décret n° 2010-740/PCSRD/MCI/PJE du 04 novembre 2010 portant organisation des Directions Générales et des directions nationales du Ministère du Commerce, de l'Industrie et de la Promotion des Jeunes Entrepreneurs et déterminant les attributions de leurs responsables.

46 Direction de la Concurrence, de la Compétitivité et de la Protection du Consommateur.

47 *Bakhoum,* Étude sur la Révision du Cadre Institutionnel de Mise en Oeuvre des Règles de Concurrence de l'UEMOA, 2011.

48 *Bakhoum,* Étude sur la Révision du Cadre Institutionnel de Mise en Oeuvre des Règles de Concurrence de l'UEMOA, 2011.

49 *UNCTAD,* Voluntary Peer Review on Competition Policies of WAEMU, Benin and Senegal, 2008, p. 150.

complaint against Burkina Faso for having illegally restrained tobacco imports from Benin.[50]

6.1.3 *Summary of the Unification of Substantive Laws in the WAEMU*

The unification of substantive laws in the WAEMU through the Court of Justice's Decision intends to achieve convergent application of competition law within the region. Two main considerations underlie this uniform application: First, WAEMU-wide competition law enforcement would automatically lead to competition law enforcement in all member states. Second, the harmonisation of national competition laws and policies would lead to convergent application of them. In consequence, harmonization would also include an assimilation of enforcement measures.[51] Third, a uniform single competition law would facilitate and encourage cooperation in competition law enforcement. Unfortunately, the unification has not lived up to its aims.

The impact of the unification of substantive laws in the WAEMU on member states without prior competition law experience was very limited, as liberalizing reforms and economic growth are proceeding at a slow pace. More than 10 years after the instalment of the centralized system member states without a prior domestic competition-law system still lack national competition agencies, and competition culture in the private or public sector was not fostered significantly. This leads to a situation, in which theoretically all member states fall under the scope of regional competition law, but enforcement stagnates.

Similarly, harmonization of existing national competition laws in order to create more legal certainty has not been achieved. The regional competition law directives and regulations require legislative reforms. However they are neither controlled nor enforced.

Moreover, the bundling of competences on the regional level has increased the amount of resources required on the community level. Consequently, the cooperation of national competition authorities, in particular in the form of their monitoring and transferring function, is of paramount importance to safeguard actual WAEMU-wide competition law application. Yet cooperation does not take place effectively, mostly due to resource constraints of national authorities, lack of domestic

---

[50] *UNCTAD*, Voluntary Peer Review on Competition Policies of WAEMU, Benin and Senegal, 2008, pp. 150f.

[51] The Court of Justice of WAEMU in its decision particularly highlights the danger of confusion that can arise from parallel application of national and regional law, namely in the form of diverging interpretations and cumulative sanctions. It is to be pointed out that the regional Court specifically refers to undertakings. It considers them the main victims of such confusion, see Advisory Opinion no. 03/2000/CJ/WAEMU of 27 June 2000, "Demande d'avis de la Commission de l'UEMOA relative à l'interprétation des articles 88, 89 et 90 du Traité relatifs aux règles de concurrences dans l'Union".

competition law expertise and lack of competition culture. This in particular concerns member states without prior competition law experience. On the other hand, withdrawn from all competences, in particular member states with prior competition law systems do not have the according political will to cooperate with the regional level. In this context, the WAEMU contrasts the development of the European competition law system, in which especially member states with prior competition law expertise[52] constituted the engine for the community competition system. In the WAEMU, the unified competition law system was imposed from the regional level, even against the will of some member states.[53] However, the cooperation with Burkina Faso demonstrates that a close geographic location of national authorities with the regional authority can constitute a positive factor that increases the general awareness of the regional legal framework for domestic economies and politics. Sporadic cooperation with national ministries of other member states demonstrates that the will to cooperate is not generally absent.

Finally, the unification of substantive competition law does not touch upon the member states' competence to legislate on criminal and civil law liability.[54] Thus, although the substantive provisions are harmonized, criminal sanctions and civil law liability for competition law infringements can still differ between the member states.[55]

Despite ongoing reform initiatives,[56] the introduction of more discretion to national competition law structures does not constitute an easy procedure due to the requirement of unanimity to make changes to the Treaty of Dakar and the deep-rooted ideology of centralization in West Africa.[57]

---

[52] For example Germany.

[53] Most predominantly Senegal.

[54] More information on investigations and procedural autonomy, see below Part II, Dimension IV: Sect. 8.1.3.2. In general on the principle of procedural autonomy see Part II, Dimension V: Sect. 9.5.

[55] See below Part II, Dimension IV: Sect. 8.1.3.3.

[56] UNCTAD also engages in a project regarding a reform of the WAEMU system, "Le Projet de renforcement des capacités de la Commission et des Etats membres de l'UEMOA", see <http://unctad.org/en/pages/newsdetails.aspx?OriginalVersionID=333UNCTAD> accessed 11 November 2018.

[57] *Weick*, Competition Law and Policy in Senegal, 33/3 W. Comp. 521, 538 (2010). According to *Weick*, Senegal is the only member state that would want more flexibility in competition law.

6.2 Convergent Standards Through Minimum or Partial Harmonization of Substantive Laws: The Case of CARICOM

A different legal framework for the domestic competition law offers the approach of minimum harmonization. Minimum harmonization only sets binding standards instead of unifying the national and regional laws completely. These standards can dictate minimum standards directly or create convergence indirectly by harmonizing other aspects of the law or specific sectors.

The modern European competition law system creates convergence of the results of application between Article 101 TFEU and national competition laws, as Article 3(2) of Regulation 1/2003/EC prescribes. The application of national competition laws may not lead to the prohibition of agreements that may affect cross-border trade, but that do not restrict competition or fulfil the conditions of Article 101(3) TFEU. National provisions and according enforcement measures may be stricter than Article 102 TFEU and might therefore differ. One has to highlight however, that at the moment of the entry into force of Regulation 1/2003/EC, member states already had domestic competition law structures, including substantive laws and authorities. Moreover, the substantive domestic competition laws of the young competition law regimes[58] were largely harmonized with the European provisions.[59] The restriction on the harmonization of results thus leaves sufficient space for national discretion and purely autonomous decisions of national competition agencies.[60] On the other hand, "soft harmonization" has the potential to excerpt a strong harmonizing incentive on the interpretation of national law.[61]

[58] For Germany, which had already introduced a domestic competition law system in 1958 (*Gesetz gegen Wettbewerbsbeschränkungen* of 27 July 1957, BGBl. I, S. 1081), Regulation 1/2003 signified a paradigmatic change. Consequently, in 2005 Germany reformed its domestic substantive and procedural competition laws in order to adapt to the new European framework, see *Drexl,* Perspectives européennes sur la politique de la concurrence dans l'espace OHADA, XXV R.I.D.E. 281, 293 (2011).

[59] *Dreher* already notices an explicit adaption of European provisions and of European standards in domestic competition law regimes in 1993, which he calls "Harmonisierung von unten", see *Dreher,* Kartellrechtsvielfalt oder Kartellrechtseinheit in Europa?, AG 437, 444 (1993).

[60] *Drexl,* Perspectives européennes sur la politique de la concurrence dans l'espace OHADA, XXV R.I.D.E. 281, 290f. (2011).

[61] *Brokelmann,* Enforcement of Articles 81 and 82 EC under Regulation 1/2003, 29/4 W. Comp. 535, 553 (2006). *Monti* has a very critical view on the modernization of the European enforcement system through Regulation 1/2003, see *Monti,* EC Competition Law, 2007, pp. 392ff.

6.2.1 *Obligation to Enact National Substantive Competition Laws and a National Competition Authority for the Member States as Subjects of International Law in the CARICOM*

There are several provisions in the Revised Treaty of Chaguaramas that entail obligations on the member states regarding their domestic competition law structures. Article 170 of the Revised Treaty of Chaguaramas represents the central provision. In general, Article 170(1) lit. b) RTC obliges the member states to "take the necessary legislative measures to ensure consistency and compliance with the rules of competition and provide penalties for anti-competitive business conduct" and to "establish and maintain institutional arrangements and administrative procedures to enforce competition laws".[62] The latter institutional obligation is specified in Article 170(2) RTC, which states that "[E]very Member State shall establish and maintain a national competition authority for the purpose of facilitating the implementation of the rules of competition." Thus the Caribbean competition system comprises particular, namely institutional as well as substantive law obligations.[63]

Regarding the domestic substantive competition law, Article 170(5) RTC stipulates a notification requirement within the 24 months of the entry into force of the Revised Treaty for the member states, according to which they shall inform the COTED of existing legislation, agreements and administrative practices inconsistent with the provisions of Chapter VIII. The COTED shall also establish a program providing for the repeal of such legislation, agreements and administrative practices within 36 months of entry into force of the Revised Treaty of Chaguaramas.[64] The Articles 177 to 179 of the Revised Treaty entail specifications on the content of domestic substantive competition laws. The required competition law prohibitions cover illicit agreements between enterprises, abuse of dominant position and other like conduct by enterprises whose object or effect is to frustrate the benefits of the establishment of a common market, namely the CSME.[65] Articles 177(2) to 179 of the Revised Treaty of Chaguaramas further define the notions of anti-competitive business conduct, such as agreements or abuse of dominant position.

The obligation to implement national competition laws for the member states requires clarification. Although member states feel obliged to establish national competition law regimes, the Revised Treaty of Chaguaramas is actually unclear on

[62] Article 170(1) lit. b)(i), (iii) of Revised Treaty of Chaguaramas.

[63] The general obligation of member states of CARICOM to follow and implement the obligations arising out of the Revised Treaty of Chaguaramas is set out in Article 9 of the Revised Treaty of Chaguaramas: "Member States shall take all appropriate measures, whether general or particular, to ensure the carrying out of obligations arising out of the Treaty or resulting from decisions taken by the Organs and Bodies of the Community. They shall facilitate the achievement of the objectives of the Community. They shall abstain from any measures which could jeopardize the attainment of the objectives of the Treaty."

[64] Article 170(5) of Revised Treaty of Chaguaramas.

[65] Article 177(1)(a) to (c) of the Revised Treaty of Chaguaramas.

this point. Article 170(1) lit. b)(i) RTC determines that "member states shall take necessary legislative measures to ensure consistency and compliance with the *rules of competition*". The latter is defined in the Preamble of the Revised Treaty of Chaguaramas and only refers to prohibitions of anticompetitive practices that distort competition within *the Community or frustrate* benefits expected from the establishment of the *CSME*, as set out in Article 177(1) lit. a) to lit. c) and Article 179(1) of the Revised Treaty of Chaguaramas.[66] The Preamble however explicitly mentions the objective of harmonization of national competition policies, thereby presupposing that such national competition policies exist. In the same vein, Article 170(1) lit. b)(i) requires member states to ensure "consistency and compliance" with the regional rules of competition. Moreover, Article 170(1) lit. b)(iii) of the Revised Treaty of Chaguaramas obliges member states to "establish and maintain institutional arrangements and administrative procedures to enforce competition laws". The broad formulation indicates that the Caribbean legislator aimed at referring to the implementation of laws that prohibit *national* and *regional* competition law infringements.[67]

In the same vein, the Revised Treaty of Chaguaramas does not provide for specific requirements for the content of national substantive competition law for national competition law infringements. However again, Article 170 lit. b) (i) of the Revised Treaty of Chaguaramas refers to "consistency" and the general underlying objective of harmonization of national competition policies, which implies that the anticompetitive practices within the Community as set out in Article 177 to 179 RTC, shall be incorporated accordingly for national infringements in national legislation. While the Articles 177 to 179 RTC thus set standards for the content of national legislation with regard to the regional competition-law infringements, they also allow flexibility for the national legislators in the implementation of more stringent competition rules.[68]

Additionally to substantive-law-related requirements, the Revised Treaty of Chaguaramas also entails provisions concerning the institutional arrangements in the member states. Article 170(1) lit. b)(iii) of the Revised Treaty of Chaguaramas determines that member states shall establish and maintain institutional arrangements to enforce competition laws and Article 170(2) RTC explicitly states that member states shall establish a national competition authority. In Article 170(3) and Article 170(1) lit. b)(iv) RTC, the Treaty even defines the required powers of such a national competition authority and necessary access to it. While the Revised Treaty of Chaguaramas does not set out specific requirements for the design of the national

---

[66] The definition of "rules of competition" also refers to Article 166(1)(a)(i), but Article 166 does not have any subparagraphs and concerns the use of technological and research facilities. The blind reference to Art. 166(1)(a)(i) RTC is another indicator for the partially inconsistent drafting of the Revised Treaty of Chaguaramas.

[67] The CARICOM follows a system of international law, in which regional legislation requires the incorporation into domestic law through national legislators.

[68] *Beckford*, in: *Drexl/Bakhoum/Fox/Gal/Gerber*, Competition Policy and Regional Integration in Developing Countries, 2012, pp. 185, 187.

competition authority, one can draw some conclusions from the structure of the provisions in Chapter VIII.

The Treaty refers to institutional arrangements twice, namely in Article 170(1) lit. b)(iii) and Article 170(2) of the Revised Treaty. While the former provision relates to enforcing institutional and administrative structures in general, the latter, explicitly refers to a national competition authority. From a systematic analysis of the Revised Treaty of Chaguaramas one can conclude that the regional drafters in the CARICOM wanted the member states to install a complete domestic competition law structure, including institutional and substantive law arrangements. Article 170(1) lit. b) RTC refers to vertical and horizontal cooperation obligations of the national competition agencies. The Treaty thus envisages the national agencies to be more than mere executing authorities for the regional competition law and the creation of a regional competition authority does not displace the establishment of national authorities.[69] In fact, the Treaty aims at creating a network of national and regional competition law structures.

The set out obligations in Chapter VIII for the member states are partly worded with insufficient precision. This could on the one hand be attributed to negligence of the Caribbean legislator. On the other hand it reflects that the Revised Treaty is conceived as an "unfinished agenda".[70] Some mechanisms that are incorporated in the Treaty are supposed to work on the basis of "mutual respect".[71] The general compliance provision in Article 9 of the Revised Treaty of Chaguaramas also reflects this.

Apart from the provisions set out in Chapter VIII, the lack of precision in the CARICOM is also caused by three other elements: First, the Revised Treaty of Chaguaramas does not entail specific deadlines regarding the implementation of the competition provisions; second, the large discretion conferred to the COTED with regard to sectorial exemptions; and third and predominantly, the Revised Treaty of Chaguaramas only creates rights and obligations for the CARICOM member states as subjects of international law and thus lacks direct effect for individuals.

---

[69] *O'Keefe,* Latin American and Caribbean Trade Agreements, 2009, p. 377.

[70] Kusha Haraksingh, current chairman of the CARICOM Competition Commission, described the Revised Treaty of Chaguaramas as an "unfinished agenda" in an interview with the author in Port-of-Spain, Trinidad and Tobago, 29 October 2012.

[71] Kusha Haraksingh, current chairman of the CARICOM Competition Commission, stated that some things in the CARICOM were to function based on "mutual respect", in an interview with the author in Port-of-Spain, Trinidad and Tobago, 29 October 2012.

6.2.1.1 CARICOM Model Law on Competition

The CARICOM partial standards approach offers opportunities to harmonize existing or newly implemented national competition laws. Harmonization clearly constitutes one of the objectives of the Revised Treaty.[72] The *CARICOM Model Law on Competition* further incites this opportunity for convergence.[73]

The substantive law prohibitions regarding anticompetitive agreements and abuse of dominant position in the *CARICOM Model Law on Competition* comply with the state of art in competition law.[74] Despite ongoing initiatives to implement a merger control regime on the regional level, the *CARICOM Model Law* does not include such a regulation. Instead, it incorporates a very detailed chapter on resale price maintenance.[75] Its inclusion reflects that the *CARICOM Model Law* relied on the Jamaican Fair Competition Act of 1993.[76] The Caribbean model law proposes a three-folded objectives approach, which strives at economic efficiency, market protection and consumer welfare.[77] In congruence with a consumer protectionist approach, the model law also includes non-competition law provisions, such as on misleading advertising.

The *CARICOM Model Law on Competition* places special weight on the establishment of national competition authorities.[78] In order to guarantee independence of the national competition agency, the *Model Law* vests the authority with the power to charge fees and use them to cover its expenses.[79] Similarly, the agency's personal shall be appointed by the authority itself or its Executive Director.[80] Apart from general investigative powers, the authority is encouraged to fulfil an advocacy function.[81] Regarding its institutional design, the Caribbean model law drafters learned from the experiences of the Jamaican competition law authority.[82] By attributing the respective national courts with the power to enforce the authority's decisions, the *CARICOM Model Law on Competition* respects the principle of separation of powers and avoids an infringement of natural justice.

---

[72] Preamble of the Revised Treaty of Chaguaramas: "Convinced further that the application and convergence of national competition policies and the cooperation of competition authorities in the Community will promote the objectives of the CSME".

[73] CARICOM Model Law on Competition, The Fair [Trading] [Competition] Act, CPC/2003/6/REP, 16 October 2003.

[74] "Anti-competitive Agreements, Abuse of Dominant Position", Part III of the *CARICOM Model Law on Competition*; see also *UNCTAD,* Model Law on Competition, 2004.

[75] "Resale Price Maintenance", Part IV of the *CARICOM Model Law on Competition.*

[76] "Resale Price Maintenance", Part IV of the Fair Competition Act, Jamaica 1993.

[77] "Objects of the Act", Section 3 of Part I of the *CARICOM Model Law on Competition.*

[78] "The Fair Trading Commission", Part II of the *CARICOM Model Law on Competition.*

[79] Sections 8ff. of Part II of the *CARICOM Model Law on Competition.*

[80] Section 12 of Part II of the *CARICOM Model Law on Competition.*

[81] Section 6 Subsection 2 of Part II of the *CARICOM Model Law on Competition.*

[82] The institutional design of the Jamaican competition authority was challenged in *Jamaica Stock Exchange v Fair Trading Commission,* Supreme Court Civil Appeal No. 92/97 of 2001. For more information see above Part II, Dimension I: Sect. 5.2.3.1.

Finally, the *CARICOM Model Law on Competition* takes into account regional integration and the regional and national network of competition law regimes. The national competition authority shall cooperate with the CARICOM Competition Commission and with other national competition authorities.[83] Moreover, Part VIII of the *Model Law* governs the obligatory references to the CARICOM Competition Commission and the powers of the latter during an investigation. Most importantly, Section 56 of Part VIII determines that "[a] decision of the Community Competition Commission under this Act is binding on all parties."

6.2.1.2 Lack of Implementation Deadline

Although the competition related obligations indicated in the Revised Treaty of Chaguaramas are phrased in mandatory terms, the Treaty does not incorporate any deadline for the implementation of these obligations.[84] Bearing in mind the little competition law expertise among CARICOM member states and the lack of resources, the absence of deadlines appears as a deliberate choice of the Caribbean legislator. It aims at the special treatment of less developed countries by allowing them to implement national competition law structures at their own pace. It thus seems counter-intuitive that the *CARIFORUM-EC Economic Partnership Agreement* does include a timeframe for the implementation of a competition policy in the CARICOM member states. One has to recall that all contracting parties of the Revised Treaty of Chaguaramas are also parties of the *CARIFORUM-EC EPA*. Article 127 of the *CARIFORUM-EC Economic Partnership Agreement* requires that member states of the CARICOM shall enact competition laws within 5 years of the entry into force of the agreement. While Article 127(1) only requires the establishment of the CARICOM Competition Commission, with regard to substantive competition laws it explicitly requires the implementation of national competition laws and determines Chapter VIII as the regional competition set of rules.[85] The *CARIFORUM-EC EPA* also includes provisions related to cooperation in the implementation phase. In this regard, Article 130 offers technical assistance in the drafting of guidelines or legislation in order to facilitate capacity building and to ensure "sound competition policies and rule enforcement".

---

[83] Section 6 Subsection 3 lit. a) and lit. b) of Part II of the *CARICOM Model Law on Competition.*

[84] Article 240(2) of the Revised Treaty of Chaguaramas generally postulates "expeditious" action of the member states to give effect to decisions of competent Organs and Bodies in their domestic law. The provision is phrased in such an imprecise way that it can only represent an empty phrase or declaration of intent, in contrast to a specific obligation.

[85] Article 125(3): "'competition laws' includes: (...)

(b) for the CARIFORUM States, Chapter 8 of the Revised Treaty of Chaguaramas of 5 July 2001, national competition legislation complying with the Revised Treaty of Chaguaramas and the national competition legislation of The Bahamas and the Dominican Republic. Upon entry into force of this Agreement and thereafter, the enactment of such legislation shall be brought to attention of the EC Party through the CARIFORUM-EC Trade and Development Committee."

6.2.1.3 The Possible Erosion of Minimum Competition Law Standards Through the Establishment of Special Sectorial Rules and Policies

The minimum standards set out in Chapter VIII demonstrate the attempt of the regional legislator to increase convergence regarding the handling of possible anti-competitive practices in the region.[86] Nevertheless, the application of sectorial rules may still limit the matters covered by regional competition law.

According to Articles 182 and 183 of the Revised Treaty of Chaguaramas, the COTED may develop specific provisions on certain sectors or exempt sectors or undertakings. While the exemption-competence of COTED relates to the enforcement of regional law,[87] the competence to establish and develop appropriate policies and special rules for particular sectors within the CARICOM concerns the legislative powers. Considering that the COTED[88] consists of ministers designated by the member states, this attributes member states with wide discretion to circumvent the implementation of competition provisions in accordance with the Revised Treaty of Chaguaramas. In case the COTED agrees to adopt special rules for a particular sector, the sectorial policy releases member states from the minimum standards set out in the Articles 177 et seqq. RTC regarding the implementation of national competition law. Moreover, by holding the power to develop the Community competition policy in CARICOM, the COTED plays a decisive role in drafting regional and indirectly also national competition provisions. The possibility for the CARICOM Competition Commission to make non-binding recommendations regarding the Community Competition Policy[89] does not attenuate this strong institutional position of COTED.

On the one hand, COTED's central powers in the implementation of the regional competition policy reflect the "governments jealousy guarding their sovereignty".[90] However, COTED's extensive powers do not only relate to an insufficient commitment or political will of the member states to cede sovereignty, it also reflects a fundamental policy-decision and objective of the Revised Treaty of Chaguaramas. Preponderant among the objectives of CARICOM are not only the creation of market integration through harmonization, but also the "operationalization of special and differential treatment".[91] As the realization of the goals of harmonization and special and differential treatment in some instances conflict and diverge, the

---

[86] Preamble of the Revised Treaty of Chaguaramas: "Convinced further that the application and convergence of national competition policies and the cooperation of competition authorities in the Community will promote the objectives of the CSME".

[87] More information on the exemption-competence of COTED, see above Part II, Dimension I: Sect. 5.1.6.

[88] More details on the institutional set-up of the enforcement authorities in the CARICOM, see below Part II, Dimension III: Sect. 7.1.1 and Part II, Dimension IV: Sect. 8.2.2.

[89] Article 173(2) lit. b) of the Revised Treaty of Chaguaramas.

[90] *Stewart*, in: *Drexl/Bakhoum/Fox/Gal/Gerber*, Competition Policy and Regional Integration in Developing Countries, 2012, 161, 180.

[91] *Beckford*, in: *Drexl/Bakhoum/Fox/Gal/Gerber*, Competition Policy and Regional Integration in Developing Countries, 2012, 185, 203.

Caribbean legislator by attributing COTED with far-reaching policy competences has provided for flexibility not only in the application of CARICOM law, but also in the implementation of national competition laws. COTED can quickly apply short-term or interim policy measures without having to amend the Revised Treaty of Chaguaramas. COTED's composition of representatives of all member states also provides for controlling mechanisms, since no member state will agree to jeopardize integration overall out of benevolence without profiting from it. Consensus-finding before the COTED thus constitutes a controlling mechanism. Finally, COTED's decision can be reviewed by the Caribbean Court of Justice.[92] Thus, in the long run, it will be the Caribbean Court of Justice that will have to strike the appropriate balance between harmonization and special and differential treatment.[93]

While COTED can shape regional competition and sectorial policy, it cannot force or direct member states to follow a certain national competition policy or sectorial policy.[94] Especially by exempting many and large sectors from the application of national competition law, member states could *de facto* hamper a harmonized application of competition law throughout the region. In fact, many national competition regimes have exempted important sectors from the application of national competition law.[95]

6.2.1.4 Implications of the Lack of Direct Effect for Competition Law Enforcement

The institutional structure of the CARICOM is marked by the absence of a supranational direct effect. The Revised Treaty of Chaguaramas only creates rights and obligations for the sovereign member states of CARICOM as subjects of international law without binding individuals directly.[96]

The paramount majority of CARICOM member states subscribe to the doctrine of dualism. In fact, only Suriname and Haiti, which are civil law jurisdictions,[97] follow the monist doctrine of international law. Article 240(1) of the Revised Treaty of Chaguaramas codifies the dualist principle of statutory incorporation.[98]

---

[92] Article 211 of the Revised Treaty of Chaguaramas.

[93] More details on COTED see below Part II, Dimension IV: Sect. 8.2.2.

[94] *Beckford,* in: *Drexl/Bakhoum/Fox/Gal/Gerber,* Competition Policy and Regional Integration in Developing Countries, 2012, pp. 185, 190.

[95] However, one has to bear in mind that often Regulatory Bodies cooperate with the national competition authority and in many cases, national regulatory provisions also comprises competition-related provisions.

[96] *Menns/Eversley,* The Appropriate Design of the CARICOM Competition Commission, 20 May 2011, Amsterdam, p. 18; *Pollard,* The CCJ and the CSME, 24 May 2006, Antigua, p. 9.

[97] For more information on the Civil Law System in CARICOM, see *Belle Antoine,* Commonwealth Caribbean, 2008, pp. 44ff.

[98] *Pollard,* in: *Hall/Chuck-A-Sang,* CARICOM: Policy Options for International Engagement, 2010, pp. 467, 477; Article 240(1): "Decisions of competent Organs taken under this Treaty shall be subject to the relevant constitutional procedures of the Member States before creating legally binding rights and obligations for nationals of such States".

The Treaty provisions can either be incorporated in domestic law via direct enactment by drafting similar domestic legislation or indirectly in the form of self-executing operation.[99] Both approaches bear the danger of creating inconsistencies among different laws, because the drafting of the domestic provisions can differ. Similarly, reference to Treaty obligations can be subject "to as many interpretations as there are national jurisdictions in the Caribbean Community."[100] Nearly all member states of CARICOM, following the dualist doctrine, have generally opted for an indirect enactment of the Revised Treaty.[101] Yet member states thereby do not automatically fulfil their obligations arising out of Chapter VIII of the Revised Treaty of Chaguaramas. Some require further legal action of national legislators. For example, although Article 168 of the Revised Treaty of Chaguaramas is sufficiently ratified via indirect enactment, the provisions in Article 170 lit. b), 170(2), 170(3), 170(5), Article 174(6) or Article 177 of Chapter VIII RTC require the drafting of national provisions. This vests national legislators with large discretion. Hence, the minimum standards set out in Chapter VIII and the *CARICOM Model Law on Competition* do not solely appear as incentives for, but necessary elements of harmonization.

It is therefore even more important that the minimum standards are phrased in clear and unambiguous terms. In this context, the bindingness of the CARICOM Competition Commission's decisions requires further examination. Article 174(6) of the Revised Treaty of Chaguaramas postulates that "[t]he Member States shall enact legislation to ensure that determinations of the [CARICOM Competition] Commission are enforceable in their jurisdictions".[102] While the obligation of member states incorporates "determinations" by the CARICOM Competition Commission, as set out in Article 173(3) of the RTC, it is not clear whether collateral

---

[99] *Belle Antoine,* Commonwealth Caribbean, 2008, pp. 215f.

[100] *Pollard,* The CCJ and the CSME, 24 May 2006, Antigua, p. 13; *Pollard,* in: *Hall/Chuck-A-Sang,* CARICOM single Market and Economy Genesis and Prognosis, 2007, pp. 91, 104; *Pollard,* in: *Hall/Chuck-A-Sang,* CARICOM: Policy Options for International Engagement, 2010, pp. 467, 478.

[101] For example: Section 3 of the Caribbean Community Act of Antigua and Barbuda (2004): "Subject to this Act, the Treaty, the text of which is set out in the Schedule, shall have the force of law"; Section 3 of the Barbados Community Act (2003): "Subject to this Act, the Treaty shall have the force of law in Barbados".

[102] Partly, it was even argued that Article 174(6) of the Revised Treaty of Chaguaramas and an explicit implementation of a national norm determining the bindingness of the CARICOM Competition Commission's decisions were superfluous. It was argued that by signing the Revised Treaty of Chaguaramas, a member state would automatically recognize the bindingness of the CARICOM Competition Commission's decisions and that they would automatically exercise direct effect. However, such a view constitutes an infringement of the principles of the dualist system. Even under the monist doctrine the wording of the Revised Treaty of Chaguaramas, in particular Article 174(6), requires further legal action in order to comply with the positive obligations set out in Chapter VIII. An alternative wording of the provisions in Chapter VIII of the RTC would have led to different legal consequences. The wording of Article 174(6) of RTC could have been for example: "The determinations of the Commission are deemed to be enforceable in the jurisdictions of the Member States".

or foregoing powers of the Commission, such as competences during an investigation are covered by this term as well.[103] Nevertheless, a clear-cut definition of the notion of "determinations" in Article 174(6) RTC might be superfluous, because Article 9 RTC generally obliges the member states to "take all appropriate measure (...) to ensure the carrying out of obligations (...) resulting from decisions taken by the Organs and Bodies of the Community." The general undertaking of implementation thus covers decisions of the CARICOM Competition Commission that determine the start of an investigation.

In the same vein, Article 174(6) RTC creates ambiguities, as it does not clarify whether "all" determinations of the regional competition authority should be enforceable in all member states or only those involving an enterprise located in a particular member state.[104] On the one hand, a teleological argument favours a general bindingness as it increases convergence and guarantees a consistent application of Chapter VIII. On the other hand, in line with the special and differential treatment approach, a limited bindingness contributes to enforcement flexibility.[105] Section 56 of the *CARICOM Model Law on Competition* only sets out that the decisions of the CARICOM Competition Commission "under this Act [are] binding on all parties".

Another ambiguity for the national legislator arises in the context of the Articles 175(1) and 174(1) of the Revised Treaty of Chaguaramas. By utilizing the wording of "may", it seems that the referral of cases by the member states to the regional authority in case of transactions with cross-border effects constitutes a voluntary decision. Yet Section 54(1) of the *CARICOM Model law on Competition* utilizes "shall" in the according provision. It remains open whether the national competition laws have to include provisions that oblige the national competition authority to refer cases to the CARICOM Competition Commission in case of a transaction with cross-border effects. So far, all national competition authorities conceived the transferral of cases with cross-border effect as an obligation.[106] The wording in the *Model Law on Competition* supports the view that this national conception corresponds to the Caribbean legislator's intention.

---

[103] *Beckford*, in: *Drexl/Bakhoum/Fox/Gal/Gerber*, Competition Policy and Regional Integration in Developing Countries, 2012, pp. 185, 194.

[104] *Ibid.*

[105] *Ibid.*

[106] Apart from the ambiguity created for the national legislators, the ambiguity might become problematic during the long-term application of Chapter VIII of the Revised Treaty of Chaguaramas. It remains to be seen whether national competition authorities will willingly cooperate with the CARICOM Competition Commission or whether the regional competition law will have to be amended, including disciplining mechanisms with regard to vertical cooperation.

6.2.2 *Implications for National Competition Law Regimes with Existing Competition Laws*

The enactment of Chapter VIII of the Revised Treaty required jurisdictions with existing competition legislation, namely Jamaica and Barbados, to amend their national laws in accordance with the regional provisions. While substantive law was already compliant with the regional law at the time of the entry into force of the Revised Treaty, national procedural provisions had to be added or amended in order to establish the cooperation with the CARICOM Competition Commission and to make its decision enforceable.

In Jamaica, the Fair Trading Act of 1993 has been under revision since 2001 when the Fair Trading Commission's and the Act's constitutional validity had been successfully challenged. Moreover, the inclusion of a national merger control regulation is also envisaged under a reform of the national antitrust provisions. These developments took place irrespective of the Revised Treaty of Chaguaramas. In fact, Jamaica has so far not fulfilled the obligations arising out of the Treaty. It has neither incorporated national provisions that ensure the bindingness of the CARICOM Community Commission's decisions, nor provisions that enable cooperation during competition law cases with cross-border effects. As legislative and governmental procedures are generally slow in Jamaica, Jamaica's reluctance to amend its law does not necessarily represent a lack of commitment towards the enforcement of regional competition law. During the drafting process in the inter-governmental task force regarding Chapter VIII, Jamaica constituted an active supporter of regional competition policy.[107] Nevertheless, the slow pace demonstrates how vulnerable the regional competition law implementation process is to national influences and governmental changes.

Barbados implemented national competition legislation in 2002. Anticipating the entry into force of the Revised Treaty of Chaguaramas, the Barbados Fair Competition Act incorporated Section IX, which refers to the Community Competition Commission. Parallel to the Part VIII of the *CARICOM Model Law on Competition*, the Fair Competition Act governs the relation with the CARICOM Competition Commission. Section 47 of the Fair Competition Act establishes the bindingness of decisions of the regional authority. They are enforceable before the High Court to the same extent as a decision of the national Fair Trading Commission.

In contrast to its regional counterpart, the Barbados competition law also provides for a national merger regulation. Bearing in mind the ongoing reform initiatives to include a merger control system on the regional level,[108] it seems to be the

[107] Statements made during interviews with representatives from the Jamaican Fair Trading Commission and the CARICOM Competition Commission, October 2012 in Kingston, Jamaica and Port-of-Spain, Trinidad and Tobago.

[108] See with regard to the WAEMU, UNCTAD project "Le Projet de renforcement des capacités de la Commission et des Etats membres de l'UEMOA", see <http://unctad.org/en/pages/newsdetails.aspx?OriginalVersionID=333UNCTAD> accessed 11 November 2018.

common understanding throughout the Caribbean region that even small market economies, such as Barbados, should have a merger control regime.

As Barbados has already implemented the obligations arising out of the Revised Treaty of Chaguaramas, later amendments of the national competition law did not become necessary. There has been yet an ongoing revision process of the national competition law since 2005. This revision process applies to all pieces of national legislation, including utility regulation, and did not arise as a consequence of the implementation of regional competition policy.[109]

For the little case law before the CARICOM Competition Commission,[110] it is impossible to analyse the effectiveness of cooperation between the CARICOM Commission and the national authorities. Nevertheless, the Jamaica and Barbados Fair Trading Commissions were actively involved in the legislative process for the implementation of Chapter VIII of the Revised Treaty of Chaguaramas. With regard to the substantive content of national competition laws, Chapter VIII of the RTC also had little impact on the existing competition law regimes. Moreover, Barbados and Jamaica did not remove competition law exemptions of sectors, such as the telecommunications or electricity sector. Nevertheless, there is close cooperation between sectorial and competition agencies during enforcement in Jamaica and Barbados, which might be expanded to the regional level as well.

6.2.3 *Implications for Member States Without Prior National Competition Law Regimes*

The current competition-law enactment initiatives throughout the CARICOM region picture Chapter VIII of the Revised Treaty of Chaguaramas as an effective implementation tool. New national competition laws are drafted in accordance with the *CARICOM Model Law on Competition* and fulfil the obligations set out in Chapter VIII of the Treaty. They particularly include provisions regarding the bindingness of the CARICOM Competition Commission's decisions and provisions regarding the enforcement of cross-border effect transactions. In contrast to Chapter VIII of the Revised Treaty of Chaguaramas, a large number of newly implemented national competition laws also often include merger control.[111]

Trinidad and Tobago's competition-law provisions, albeit not fully proclaimed yet, reach back to enactment initiatives in 1997/1998 prior to the *CARICOM Model Law on Competition*. They are in accordance with the model law. Trinidad and Tobago's competition law exempts banks and non-bank financial institutions, according to Section 3(1) lit. h), and exempts companies that fall under the scope of

[109] Statements made by Antonio Thompson, Chief Economist at the Fair Trading Commission of Barbados, during an interview with the author on 23 October 2012 in Bridgetown, Barbados.

[110] Only one case: *Trinidad Cement Limited v The Competition Commission,* Caribbean Court of Justice Application No. OA 1 of 2012, CCJ 4 (OJ).

[111] See above Part II, Dimension I: Sect. 5.2.3.

the Telecommunications Authority Act,[112] according to Section 3(1) lit. g). In particular the special jurisdiction of the financial regulatory bodies is problematic as the majority of Trinidad and Tobago's investment in the Caribbean region is in the financial sector.[113] Financial institutions of Trinidad and Tobago also frequently used mergers and acquisitions to expand to the regional market.[114]

Suriname encountered problems in implementing its national competition law and dealing with the *CARICOM Model Law on Competition*. First, Suriname follows the monist doctrine and civil law tradition. According to representatives from the Ministry of Trade and Industry in Suriname the regional provisions had to be converted from criminal-sanctions into administrative sanctions. Apart from these technical legal problems, the major difficulties related to a language barrier. Understanding and translating the technical English utilized in the *CARICOM Model Law on Competition* into Dutch and into a civil law formulations was conceived as a difficult obstacle.[115]

Generally, the implementation processes were accompanied by technical assistance by the CARICOM Secretariat. The European Union has also been an active supporter by granting financial and technical assistance and *UNCTAD* has constituted an important experience-sharing platform.[116]

---

[112] The telecommunications sector in Trinidad and Tobago was liberalized in 2004 with the entry into force of the Amendment to the Telecommunications Act 2001. Before that, the telecommunications sector constituted a monopoly, which was dominated by the Telecommunications Services of Trinidad and Tobago Limited ("TSTT"). The latter is jointly owned by National Enterprises Limited (51%), whose majority is in turn owned by the Government of Trinidad and Tobago, and Cable & Wireless (West Indies) Limited. For more information about TSTT see <http://www.tstt.co.tt/> accessed 11 November 2018.

[113] *Stewart,* in: *Drexl/Bakhoum/Fox/Gal/Gerber,* Competition Policy and Regional Integration in Developing Countries, 2012, pp. 161, 175.

[114] *Stewart,* in: *Drexl/Bakhoum/Fox/Gal/Gerber,* Competition Policy and Regional Integration in Developing Countries, 2012, pp. 161, 179.

[115] Statements made by representatives from the Suriname Ministry of Trade and Industry to the author, December 2012. In this context, the representative in particular mentioned Section 18(1) of the CARICOM Model Law on Competition: "No person shall give effect to an exclusionary provision in an agreement.". It took the Ministry some time to come up with a correct representation: "Exclusion clauses in a contract are prohibited and automatically void."

[116] For example Belize received money under the 10th European Development Fund. UNCTAD organized several regional workshops on competition policy, for example on 12 and 13 October 1999 in Trinidad and Tobago.

6.2.4 *Summary of Convergent Standards Through Minimum or Partial Harmonization in a System of International Law*

As the foregoing analysis shows, the minimum standard approach in CARICOM vests national legislators with large discretion. This is particularly due to the lack of mandatory deadlines or other sanctioning mechanisms for non-compliance. The *CARICOM Model Law on Competition* offers guidance on the substantive law, which has been in particular positively received by the young competition law jurisdictions. In the absence of recommendations on whether national competition law agencies should also incorporate consumer protection, some member states have installed mixed authorities, whereas others have established separate competition and consumer commissions. This will most probably not affect the enforcement of Chapter VIII, as the CARICOM Competition Commission is itself a mixed authority and will therefore cooperate with both kinds of competition agencies.

While convergence of existing anticompetitive prohibitions is largely achieved throughout the region, the Revised Treaty of Chaguaramas does not address the issue of national sectorial regulation and does not give any guidance. This is a loophole in the Caribbean minimum standard approach, which is capable of hampering the harmonization process with regard to provisions related to intra-regional trade.

Now, more than 10 years after the entry into force of the Revised Treaty of Chaguaramas, still only a few member states have actually implemented or enforced the national competition law regime. The slow pace of implementation does not rest upon the absence of political commitment. Rather a lack of resources, in particular competition law expertise, and changing and generally slow governments are the main obstacles to stringent implementation. Similar to the national implementation progress, the regional level also suffers from a lack of resources and has thus only proceeded at a slow pace. The CARICOM Competition Commission was only inaugurated in 2008. However recently, there has been considerable competition law activity on the regional level. The CARICOM Competition Commission launched an investigation on the telecommunication sector regarding the acquisition of Columbus International Inc. by Cable and Wireless Communications Plc.[117] Likewise it issued guidelines on the setting of fines.[118]

Whereas regional competition law enforcement is progressing, the question remains open to which extent Chapter VIII of the Revised Treaty of Chaguaramas constitutes(d) an incentive to implement national competition laws and, in a second step, to harmonize them. Rather than relying on institutionalized implementation

---

[117] See Press release of the CARICOM Competition Commission of 27 May 2016, available at <http://www.caricomcompetitioncommission.com/images/pdf/ccc_press_release_27May2016.pdf>.

[118] *CARICOM Competition Commission,* Guidelines for setting fines for anti-competitive business conduct, 2015, available at <http://www.caricomcompetitioncommission.com/images/pdf/guide_setting_fines.pdf>.

mechanisms, the Revised Treaty of Chaguaramas appears to be based on "mutual respect" among its contracting parties. A positive precondition in CARICOM is that competition law was not obtruded on member states without such legislation. The member states concerned actually felt the need and felt sufficiently developed to adopt national competition legislations.[119] Through the representation of national ministers in COTED, the member states participate(d) actively in the shaping of the regional competition policy.

The *CARIFORUM-EC Economic Partnership Agreement* reinforces the objectives set out in the Revised Treaty of Chaguaramas. It sets a clear timeframe and creates an additional incentive besides regional integration, namely by the improved trade relations with the European Union.

However, as the experiences in Jamaica and Barbados show, Chapter VIII of the Revised Treaty of Chaguaramas and the *CARIFORUM-EC EPA* constitute less influential factors on the harmonization of existing laws and policies. Thus in order to change already existing national legislation in the context of a regional competition law regime, it requires more coercive elements, such as deadlines or sanctions for non-compliant member states. On the other hand, timeframes must not be too short, because due to the dualist system, national governments also need to enact according to domestic provisions. In this process, due regard has to be given to the lack of resources and in particular to the typically slow administration in developing countries.

6.3 "Soft" Harmonization Through Non-Binding Guidelines: The Case of the AndeanC

A regional competition law without any kind of obligation for its member states regarding the enactment of substantive competition law rules is difficult to imagine. Loyalty clauses in all three RTAs acknowledge the fact that national and regional rules are interrelated and have to be coordinated. However, the necessary degree of coordination varies. In the AndeanC the implementation of national competition law and institutions, albeit unquestionably being a goal of regional competition law, is not based on an explicit obligation contained in regional competition law.

---

[119] In Trinidad and Tobago initiatives to enact national competition legislation already started in 1996/1997. In Guyana the situation was still different in 1995. Professor Richard Whish, a specialist adviser to the Government of Guyana, argued against the introduction of a national competition law. He argued that technical and economic resources were scarce and that competition law did not constitute a priority to use these resources, see *Malahoo,* Competition Law in Emerging Economies: The Jamaican Experience, 2000, p. 6.

6.3.1 *Obligation to Establish a National Authority in the AndeanC in Charge of the Application of Regional Competition Law*

Decision 608 in the AndeanC does not contain an obligation for member states to enact national substantive laws, nor does it specify the content of the national competition laws. In 2005, the date of the entry into force of Decision 608, this only concerned Ecuador and Bolivia, which neither possessed a national competition law nor a competition authority.

However, Article 37 of Decision 608 explicitly lays down that the member states are required to establish mechanisms that render the common instruments (of the AndeanC) effective and to strengthen their national competition authorities through programs of exchange of information and experiences, of technical expertise, and of collections of jurisprudence and administrative doctrines regarding the defence of free competition.[120] In addition, Article 42 of Decision 608 requires the member states to notify the Secretariat General about national legislation in terms of free competition, as well as about modifications or substitutions to it.[121] Article 36 of Decision 608 comprises the prohibition on member states to distort competition through regulatory measures and vests the Andean Committee on the Defence of Free Competition[122] with the power to give recommendations regarding the elimination of such state practices in order to promote economic freedom and free competition.[123] Whether these provisions entail an obligation for member states to enact national competition laws is doubtful. While Article 37, according to its wording, refers to the strengthening of national competition authorities that already existed, it does not stipulate an obligation to establish national authorities for *national* competition law enforcement. In the same vein, Article 42 presumes the existence of national competition law provisions, but it does not oblige states without them to enact a national system. Article 36 only entails a non-binding recommendation

[120] Artículo 37 de la Decisión 608: "Los Países Miembros establecerán mecanismos para procurar el perfeccionamiento de los instrumentos comunes y el fortalecimiento de las autoridades nacionales competentes en materia de libre competencia, mediante programas de intercambio de información y experiencias, de entrenamientos técnicos, y de recopilación de jurisprudencia y doctrina administrativa, relacionados con la defensa de la libre competencia."

[121] Artículo 42 de Decisión 608: "Los Países Miembros notificarán a la Secretaría General sus legislaciones nacionales en materia de libre competencia. Asimismo, notificarán las modificaciones o sustituciones a la misma."

[122] For more details on the Andean Committee on the Defense of Free Competition, see below Part II, Dimension IV: Sect. 8.2.1.2.

[123] Artículo 36 de la Decisión 608: "En la adopción y aplicación de las políticas y medidas regulatorias de mercado, los Países Miembros no impedirán, entorpecerán ni distorsionarán la competencia en el mercado subregional. El Comité podrá elevar recomendaciones tendientes a eliminar, cuando corresponda, estos trámites y requisitos para promover el ejercicio de la libertad económica y la competencia." *Cortázar* hopes that Article 36 of Decision will be useful and will serve as an inspiration for domestic legislators, see *Cortázar*, Decisión 608 de la Comunidad Andina, 2/2 Rev. Der. Comp. 123, 148 (2006).

power of the Committee. Additionally Article 36 does only comprise recommendations regarding the "elimination" and not regarding the "establishment" of state actions. The deliberate refraining from coercive measures is further accentuated by the lack of deadlines regarding the implementation of national competition law and an according national authority.

Decision 608 and the guidelines regarding the application of Decision 608 are clearly supposed to constitute an incentive for member states to implement or reform national competition laws.[124] Member states are required to notify the latter. The aims are in line with general goals of Andean integration, which *inter alia* strive at the gradual harmonization of economic and social policies and the approximation of respective national legislations.[125] Finally, the "downloading option" constitutes an innovate instrument to enhance the implementation of national competition law structures and to further harmonization. Yet, in line with the non-coercive approach, it remains an "option".

6.3.2 The "Downloading Option" in the AndeanC

The "downloading option" set out in Art. 49 of Decision 608 and Decision 616 offers the possibility for member states without domestic competition law regimes or with solely sectorial control to apply the provisions of Decision 608 even for merely national practices. This signifies that member states may apply the regional law irrespective the actual existence of a "cross-border effect". One has to distinguish the "downloading option" from the decentralized application regime in the European Union according to the Regulation no. 1/2003/EC. According to the latter, member states apply the European law in cases of practices that have an effect on cross-border trade.[126] Merely national activities remain under the scope of national competition law.

Decision 608's "downloading option" was originally only envisaged for Bolivia in Article 49. Decision 616 then expanded the application of the "downloading option" to Ecuador. Decision 616 derogated Article 51 of Decision 608, which had previously stated that Decision 608 would only be applicable for Ecuador after 2 years or in the moment of the enactment of a national competition law. Thus, without Decision 616, in 2005, the former Andean Decision 285 would have been still applicable in Ecuador at that moment, because of the immediate internal effect of the community law.[127]

[124] *Secretaria General de la Comunidad Andina,* Guía Práctica para la aplicación de la Decisión 608 "Normas para la protección y promoción de la libre competencia en la Comunidad Andina", 2007, p. 3.

[125] Artículo 3 lit. b) de Acuerdo de Integración Subregional Andino "Acuerdo de Cartagena".

[126] *Marcos,* in *Fox/Sokol,* Competition Law and Policy in Latin America, 2009, pp. 453, 461.

[127] *Riofrío Martínez-Villalba,* La Ley de Libre Competencia Toca a la Puerta, 2/11 Rev. Novedades Jur. 1, 3 (2005).

Article 50 of Decision 608 and Article 2 of Decision 616[128] include the obligation on Bolivia and Ecuador to have national authorities regarding the application of regional competition law. This institutional obligation does neither extend to general implementation of substantive competition law, nor does it provide for specific requirements regarding the set-up of the authority. It is particularly important to note, that the identification of the competent authority only relates to the enforcement of regional law, and not necessarily of national law. Although, from practical terms, it would be reasonable to design a single authority for both laws, one can conclude that Decision 608 only provides for a minimum standardization concerning the organizational structure for the regional law's enforcement. However, the "loyalty clause" in Article 36 of Decision 608 at least limits the domestic (legislative) discretion to that extent, to which it would distort competition.

The "downloading option" was deliberately conceived as a purely transitory device that was supposed to remain valid until a member state adopts its own domestic competition law regime.[129] Based on the competition law experience in the European Union, where in the moment of the implementation of the early community competition law not all member states possessed domestic competition laws,[130] it was expected that the "downloading option" would constitute an incentive for the implementation of national competition legislations. By serving as a framework, the "downloading option" and Decision 608 were intended to overcome national difficulties in the legislation process of domestic competition laws, such as political or private opposition, lack of financial resources or the lack of competition law expertise. The application of competition law would also enhance the creation of a competition culture.[131] In this vein, the application of similar rules was held to accelerate the harmonization of national competition laws (horizontally, but also vertically) and to facilitate possible cooperation among competition authorities. Moreover, learning directly from the experiences of other member states would be facilitated. The latter argument also applies to member states with existing domestic competition law regimes.

The wording of Article 49 of Decision 608 and Article 1 of Decision 616[132] emphasizes the transitory character of the "downloading option". Bolivia and Ecuador "may", apply the regional norms, but are under no obligation to do so. Decision 608 thus leaves sufficient discretion for the emergence of national

---

[128] Decisión 616 "Entrada en vigencia de la Decisión 608 para la República del Ecuador"; Artículo 1: "Ecuador podrá aplicar lo dispuesto en la Decisión 608, en lo que resulte aplicable, para los casos que se presenten fuera del ámbito descrito en el artículo 5 de la Decisión 608", Artículo 2: "A más tardar el 1 de agosto de 2005, Ecuador designará interinamente a la Autoridad Nacional que será la encargada de la ejecución de la Decisión 608."

[129] *Marcos*, in *Fox/Sokol*, Competition Law and Policy in Latin America, 2009, pp. 453, 460.

[130] At the initial implementation phase of European competition law (in 1959 the first European competition law was enacted) only Germany had a functioning national competition law system. Italy only adopted a domestic competition law in 1990.

[131] *Marcos*, in *Fox/Sokol*, Competition Law and Policy in Latin America, 2009, pp. 453, 461.

[132] "(Bolivia or Ecuador) may apply any dispositions contained in Decision 608, which may be applicable (…)".

competition law regimes. On the other hand, the use of the term "may" is open to interpretation and potentially endangers the aim of Decision 608 as a harmonizing device.[133] In the same vein, the "downloading option" does neither specify which entity can interpret and define the contained rules, nor does it decide whether national interpretations could change the Andean rules.[134] According to *Francisco Marcos*, further issues are also capable of hampering the efficacy of the "downloading option": The incompatibility of the regional with the national system or possible conflicts between the regional norm and other national rules and institutions affecting competition; an unsuccessful "downloading" of the Andean rules may risk the credibility of the regional rules themselves and may even endanger prospects of adopting national competition laws.[135] The next section will try to evaluate in more detail which benefits and risks proved to be true in the member states of the AndeanC and which impact Decision 608 actually had on member states' competition law systems.

6.3.3 Implications for Member States Without Competition Laws

When Decision 608 was implemented, Bolivia did not have a domestic competition law. However, Bolivia enacted Supreme Decree no. 29519 in 2008, which replaced Decision 608 as national law, irrespective the fact that it does not have the rank of a law.[136] The "downloading option" has never been used in Bolivia.

The distinction between prohibitions of absolute and relative anticompetitive practices in the Supreme Decree no. 29519 reflects that the Bolivian system is to a large extent based on the Mexican competition law model. Other parts are in accordance with aspects from the Decision 608 or the European competition law. Irrespective of whether this may cause conflicts between the national and regional norms and affect competition law enforcement in the AndeanC,[137] it becomes clear

---

[133] *Marcos,* in *Fox/Sokol,* Competition Law and Policy in Latin America, 2009, pp. 453, 460; *Lozano,* La Decisión 608 de la CAN y sus Implicaciones en Bolivia, 21 Boletín Latinoamericano de Comp. 43, 47 (2006).

[134] *Marcos,* in *Fox/Sokol,* Competition Law and Policy in Latin America, 2009, pp. 453, 460.

[135] *Marcos,* in *Fox/Sokol,* Competition Law and Policy in Latin America, 2009, pp. 453, 465ff.

[136] This is one of the reason why the Supreme Decree N°2 9519, which is enacted by the Executive, is partly considered as unconstitutional. The laws of the AndeanC have direct effect in the member states and in Bolivia, regional laws have the rank of national law and are hence higher in the legal hierarchy. Further criticism concerns the sanctioning power of the Superintendence of Enterprises, because there does not exist a specific law that provides the authority with such sanctioning powers. The Law n° 2495 of 4 August 2003 only provides for general dispositions on the functions of the Superintendence of Enterprises.

[137] *Ochoa Urioste,* Régimen General del Derecho de la Competencia en Bolivia, 26 Boletín Latinoamericano de Comp. 8, 14 (2009) sees a conflict between Andean or European and the Mexican or Bolivian competition law system. A different opinion is expressed by *Cortázar,* in:

that incentives to enact a competition law system did not mostly originate from the regional level, but from abroad. This finding was affirmed in interviews, in which representatives of the Vice-Ministry of internal commerce and exportations described that assistance in the legislative process was not sought from AndeanC's institutions, but only from the Mexican authority and COMPAL.[138]

Competition law jurisprudence in Bolivia does neither refer to the Decision 608 nor Andean law in general. The Superintendence of Enterprises has published several decisions, so called Administrative Resolutions, since 2011 that deal with anti-competitive practices according to the Supreme Decree no. 29519.[139] Prominent decisions are: Praxair,[140] a global provider for industrial gases, and Cervecería Boliviana.[141] However, the respective decisions were not based on Andean competition law, but solely relied on Supreme Decree no. 29519.[142] Yet surprisingly, the Bolivian competition law authority referred to jurisprudence from Chile and Argentina. Moreover, although *Praxair* is a globally acting firm, the Bolivian authority did not consider or analyse a possible effect on "cross-border" trade, albeit Article 5 of Decision 608 is binding and would have actually obliged them to do so.

Ecuador needed 4 years to enact the Executive Decree no. 1614[143] in 2009, which specified the internal procedures for the application of Decision 608. In 2011, Ecuador finally also enacted a domestic competition law, the Organic Law of

---

Drexl/Bakhoum/Fox/Gal/Gerber, Competition Policy and Regional Integration in Developing Countries, 2012, p. 133.

[138] COMPAL (Competencia y Protección del Consumidor en America Latina/Competition and Consumer Protection for Latin America) is a program to support competition and consumer protection policies in cooperation with the UNCTAD. Interview with Jaime Luna, Vice-Ministry of internal commerce and exportations, conducted by the author, 26 January 2012 in La Paz, Bolivia.

[139] For example: Resolución Administrativa RA/AEMP/DTDCDN/ N° 116/2011, 1 December 2011 and Resolución Administrativa RA/AEMP/DTDCDN/ N°0034/2012, 17 February 2012 against the companies "Praxair Bolivia" and "Hielo Seco" for having abused their dominant position; Resolución Administrativa RA/AEMP/DTDCDN N° 118/2012, 30 November 2012 against the company "Compañía Industrial de Tabacos" ("CITSA"); Resolución Administrativa RA/AEMP/DTDCDN N° 003/2013, 11 January 2013 against the company "PIL ANDINA" because of price discrimination; Resolución Administrativa RA/AEMP/DTDCDN N° 072/2013, 15 August 2013 against the company "Instituto Boliviano del Cemento y del Hormigón (IBCH)". Available at <http://www.autoridadempresas.gob.bo/direccion-tecnica-de-defensa-de-la-competencia-y-desarrollo-normativo/resoluciones> accessed 11 November 2018.

[140] Resolución Administrativa RA/AEMP/DTDCDN/ N° 0030/2013, 11 April 2013; Resolución Administrativa RA/AEMP/DTDCDN/N°0034/2012, 17 February 2012; Resolución Administrativa RA/AEMP/DTDCDN/ N° 116/2011, 1 December 2011. In Bolivia, firms have to register a national company before engaging in business. Thus the case only concerned the company PRAXAIR in Bolivia. This does not exclude the existence of a cross-border effect.

[141] Resolución Administrativa RA/AEMP/N° 054/2011, 20 September 2011; Resolución Administrativa RA/AEMP/N° 052/2011, 13 September 2011.

[142] The Resolution regarding the "cervecería" case does mention Decision 608 at two instances. Nevertheless, the final decision of the case is only based on legal considerations arising from Supreme Decree n° 29519. During the analysis only the provisions of the Supreme Decree's are mentioned. The mentioning of Decision 608 remains a formality.

[143] Decreta n° 1614, Normas para la aplicación de la Decisión 608 de la CAN, 14 March 2009.

Regulation and Control of Market Power.[144] The new Ecuadorian competition law partly resembles European competition law and the provisions of Decision 608. It distinguishes between the object and effect of an agreement in Article 11 LORPCM and the determination of a dominant position, Article 9 LORPCM, relies on the same elements as Decision 608 or European competition law. Whereas, this partial resemblance might originate from the immediate influence of Decision 608 and 616 on domestic Ecuadorian competition law, the inclusion of non-technical terms, such as "just competition" and "economic dependency", also reflects other influences.

Ecuador had already been engaging in an internal drafting process when Decision 608 was adopted.[145] In 2002, the Law on the Promotion and Defence of Economic Competition[146] was discussed and approved before the National Congress of Ecuador. This law project already followed the state-of-the-art of competition laws, including rules on illicit agreements and abuse of dominant position. However, on 13 November 2002, the Constitutional Vice-President of the Republic, in the name of the President, *Pedro Pinto* Rubianes, rejected the ratification of the draft law claiming that the competition-law project required further preparation and examination.[147] According to him, competition law, being one of the elements that are part of the freedom of enterprises, required a thorough analysis of the fundamental laws as a whole. Unfortunately, he neither mentioned which provisions of the draft law did not meet this requirement, nor did he suggest any improvements.[148]

Legal initiatives regarding a domestic competition law revived under the new economic paradigm "Socialism of the 21st Century" in Ecuador, which was introduced by President *Raffael Correa* as part of the new Constitution in 2008. It refers to a neoliberal economic model based on social and ethical principles.[149]

Ecuador has applied Decision 608 as national law in several cases before enacting its own domestic competition law in 2011.[150] While the first decision, concerning predatory pricing of an airline cited Chilean, European, North American and Canadian cases apparently unsystematically and only conducted a superficial

[144] Ley Orgánica de Regulación y Control del Poder de Mercado, 29 September 2011.

[145] Other drafts of Ecuadorian competition law prior to the LORPCM are available from the author.

[146] Ley de Promoción y Defensa de la Competencia Económica, 31 October 2002.

[147] Presidencia de la Republica, Oficio No. T. 1913-DAJ-2002-6484, 13 November 2002.

[148] For more information on the legislative process and history in Ecuador, see *Marcos,* ¿Una Política de Competencia para la República de Ecuador?, 21 Boletín Latinoamericano de Comp. 29, 29ff. (2006). Criticism regarding the new law particularly arose from the private sector, which felt excluded from the legislative process. Moreover, it was criticized that the finally enacted competition law entailed lower fines and less strict provisions than actually envisaged by previous versions of the law; see Revista Vanguardia, Article of 27 June 2011, pp. 16–20, "Ley Antimonopolio – Ya viene el lobo…".

[149] *National Development Plan of the Republic of Ecuador*: National Plan for Good Living, 2009–2013, Building a Plurinational and Intercultural State.

[150] MIPRO-COMP-Resolución-001-2010 ("Airline LAN Ecuador"); MIPRO-COMP-Resolución-002-2010 ("Airline LAN Ecuador"); MIPRO-COMP-Resolución-001-2011 ("Pfizer"); MIPRO-COMP-Resolución-002-2011 ("Graiman")

analysis of the circumstances of the case,[151] the more recent *Pfizer*[152] case conducts a thorough analysis of the Andean competition law provisions. It thus provides an interesting example for the application of the "downloading option" in Ecuador.

The *Pfizer* case of the Subsecretariat of Competition, which is part of the Ministry of Industry and Productivity of Ecuador, dealt with a case of abuse of dominance and analysed Ecuadorian as well as Andean law. The pharmaceutical company *Pfizer* was held to have abused its dominant position in Ecuador according to Article 8 lit. g) of Decision 608 by abusively using its procedural and intellectual property rights to the detriment of competition. Firstly, the Subsecretariat of Competence of Ecuador established that Art. 5 of Decision 608 was not applicable, because the alleged anticompetitive conduct originated from and produced effects in Ecuador solely.[153] Unfortunately, the reasons for this conclusion were not specified. Secondly, the Administrative Resolution clarified the "dual character" and applicability of Decision 608 by referring to the principle of "direct effect". It reaffirmed that irrespective of the date of entry into force of the Executive Decree no. 1614, Andean community rules were applicable without requiring any additional legislative measures or other measure of administrative, political, economic, social or educational nature.[154] Thus, the Subsecretariat of Competition stated that due to this principle of "direct effect", Decision 608 had entered into force as domestic law from 25 July 2005 and that a lack of knowledge of this norm did not excuse any person for an infringement from that date on.[155] The *Pfizer* case thereby illustrates the theoretical framework of the "downloading option".

In the *Pfizer* case the Subsecretariat had to decide whether an abuse of a granted intellectual property right could also constitute an abuse of a dominant position in the vein of Article 8 of Decision 608. The Subsecretariat of Competition firstly established the character of Article 8 of Decision 608 as "general prohibition clause" and its broad interpretation.[156] In this context, the decision relied on a literal argument. Article 8 of Decision 608 was considered as a non-exhaustive enumeration of anticompetitive conducts because it utilizes open expressions, such as "are presumed to be"[157] and lit. g) mentions all "practices that exclude actual competitors from the market, or prevent potential competitors from entering the market, for reasons other than economic efficiency".[158] Secondly, the Subsecretariat of

[151] MIPRO-COMP-Resolución-001-2010 ("Airline LAN Ecuador"); MIPRO-COMP-Resolución-002-2010 ("Airline LAN Ecuador").

[152] MIPRO-COMP-Resolución-001-2011 ("Pfizer").

[153] MIPRO-COMP-Resolución-001-2011 ("Pfizer"), p. 26.

[154] MIPRO-COMP-Resolución-001-2011 ("Pfizer"), p. 36. Andean community rules are directly applicable "sin requerir de medidas legislativas adicionales o de otra naturaleza –administrativas,. Políticas, económicas, sociales, educativas-".

[155] MIPRO-COMP-Resolución-001-2011 ("Pfizer"), p. 37.

[156] MIPRO-COMP-Resolución-001-2011 ("Pfizer"), p. 52.

[157] Article 8 of Decision 608: "se presumen".

[158] Article 8 lit. g) of Decision 608: "Aquellas conductas que impidan o dificultan el acceso o permanencia de competidores actuales o potenciales en el mercado por razones diferentes a la eficiencia económica". See MIPRO-COMP-Resolución-001-2011 ("Pfizer"), p. 53.

Competition applied a systematic analysis of Article 8 of Decision 608. On the one hand, it tried to interpret the provision in accordance with the regional legal framework and in the context of other global antitrust policies. On the other hand, it tried to define the norm in the light of the national Ecuadorian constitution.[159] In this context, the Subsecretariat mentioned Article 335 of the New Ecuadorian Constitution, which sets the state's obligation to establish mechanisms to sanction any practice of abuse of dominant position. This dual fold systematic interpretation reveals a problematic aspect of the "downloading option". The "downloaded" regional norm (even in its function as national norm) has to correspond to the regional or international context. Especially in the AndeanC, this is difficult because of the lack of competition law cases. Even more problematic is the interpretation of the "downloaded" norm in its function as a national legal provision. Decision 608 aims at preventing obstacles to market access by public or private entities and underlines the confidence in the market as an economic regulatory tool.[160] This particularly highlights that also public entities exercising governmental or administrative faculties fall within the subjective scope of application of Decision 608.[161] Interestingly, the Subsecretariat of Competition in its analysis explicitly referred to Article 335 of the New Constitution of Ecuador, which states that "the state defines a price policy orientated towards the protection of national production, and that the state shall establish sanctioning mechanisms in order to avoid any monopolistic or oligopolistic practices by the private sector and to avoid abuse of dominant position".[162] Whereas, the danger stemming from abuse of a dominant position through the private sector is acknowledged, this Article lays the basis for the possibility of state intervention. Nevertheless, for the lack of legal precedents of Decision 608, one cannot evaluate whether this contradiction regarding the underlying aims of national and regional law had an impact on the credibility or coherent application of Decision 608.[163] In the consultation SG-C/D.1.7177-2011 of 18 January 2011 the General Secretary of the AndeanC, *Santiago Cembrano Cabrejas*, reaffirmed the "dual character" of Decision 608. He reasserted the broad interpretation of Article 8 of Decision 608 in its function as national and as regional norm.

A remarkable particularity of the *Pfizer* case in contrast to former decisions by the Subsecretariat of Competition is that it also referred to sentences from the

159 MIPRO-COMP-Resolución-001-2011 ("Pfizer"), p. 53.

160 *Secretaria General de la Comunidad Andina,* Guía Práctica para la aplicación de la Decisión 608 "Normas para la protección y promoción de la libre competencia en la Comunidad Andina", 2007, p. 4.

161 *Secretaria General de la Comunidad Andina,* Guía Práctica para la aplicación de la Decisión 608 "Normas para la protección y promoción de la libre competencia en la Comunidad Andina", 2007, p. 7.

162 Article 335 of the New Constitution of Ecuador of 2008:"(…) El Estado definirá una política de precios orientada a proteger la producción nacional, establecerá los mecanismos de sanción para evitar cualquier práctica de monopolio y oligopolio privados, o de abuso de posición de dominio en el mercado y otras prácticas de competencia desleal."

163 *Marcos* highlights this danger in: *Marcos,* in *Fox/Sokol,* Competition Law and Policy in Latin America, 2009, p. 462.

Peruvian competition law authority, the INDECOPI and to Chilean competition-law judgments.[164]

Although the "downloading option" has to a certain extent allowed Ecuador to deal with competition-law cases without being able to invoke extensive competition law experience, some even involving multinational firms, such as *Pfizer*, it has also demonstrated its flaws. The Bolivian authorities apparently ignored Articles 49 and 50 of Decision 608. In the absence of an obligation to "download", the Superintendence of Enterprises did not apply Decision 608 until 2008, when domestic competition laws had already been adopted. The mentioning of Decision 608 in the respective decisions hence only seemed to have occurred as a mere formality.

On the other hand, the Ecuadorian Subsecretariat of Competition utilized the "downloading option". However, the "download" was handled very superficially and the Administrative Resolutions focused mainly on international jurisprudence, such as European or US decisions. The lack of Andean precedents on competition law matters surely explains this external orientation, however, it does not explain, why in most cases the focus remains on jurisdictions outside the AndeanC, irrespective of the developed competition law systems in Colombia and Peru.[165]

Furthermore, the Ecuadorian *Pfizer* case also revealed problematic aspects of interpreting a regional norm as domestic norm. While the broad interpretation of the notion of an abuse of dominant position corresponds to the state of the art in competition law, more complex issues will create greater difficulties, when they have to fit the regional as well as the national legal framework. This is especially the case if the respective member state follows a different fundamental economic policy. Again, for the relatively superficial analysis of Decision 608, such problems or conflicts did not arise, but the "downloading option" cannot replace the implementation of domestic competition law and can only function as a transitory device.

The "downloading option" does not constitute a harmonization mechanism for member states that are only in the primary implementation phase of domestic competition law. Although Decision 608 as a whole represented an incentive to develop a national competition law system at all, the Ecuadorian national competition legislation still differs from the Andean substantive law in important aspects such as merger control or abuse of economic dependency. Moreover, other influences, such as national political interests or other bilateral trade agreements outside the AndeanC, also fostered the enactment of a national competition law regime. Hence, the application and actual use of a "downloading option", which might accelerate the implementation of domestic competition law systems, has to be accompanied by additional endeavours to implement national competition laws.

---

[164] MIPRO-COMP-Resolución-001-2011 ("Pfizer"), p. 55.

[165] In this context, the *Pfizer* case constitutes an exception.

6.3.4 Implications for Existing Competition Law Systems in the Member States

In 2009, Colombia reformed its national competition law by adopting Law no. 1340.[166] In the context of these legislative reforms the function of the Superintendence of Industry and Trade as competition law authority was strengthened. Furthermore, the reforms introduced the possibility to impose more severe sanctions on firms and private persons. Initiatives to reform the existing law had already started in 2005.

Also due to the legislative improvements, the Superintendence of Industry and Trade has managed to significantly improve its competition-law enforcement record since 2008. From 2008 to 2014 the competition authority imposed sanctions totalling USD 24.47 million in 22 horizontal agreement cases, of which 18 were prosecutions of hard core cartels.[167] In the same period, it fined undertakings for the abuse of dominance in five cases and dealt with a large number of notified mergers.[168] Finally, the overall procedure was rendered more efficient. On average, the Superintendence of Industry and Trade now takes 7–15 months to finalize a procedure.[169] For the first time, Article 7 of the new Law no. 1340 has also introduced a competition advocacy-related provision in the Colombian legal framework. Despite the young age of the law, the Superintendence of Industry and Trade has tried to prioritize investigations in the areas of healthcare, public utilities and public procurement. In this context, it also published opinions on ongoing regulation proposals, such as with regard to the transportation and energy and gas sector.[170]

Decision 608's impact on these legal reforms remains limited. The Colombian competition law even prior to the reforms already corresponded to state of the art of competition-law rules. It even included a merger control system. Thus, the reforms geared more to a fine-tuning and sharpening of administrative and procedural rules, instead of aiming at creating convergence with regional rules.[171] However, the inclusion of a national competition advocacy provision reflects an additional and new function for the national competition law authority. In fact, Articles 36 and 37 of Decision 608 clearly accentuated the importance of competition advocacy. While competition advocacy has been already discussed thoroughly on the global and international level, it was identified as a new priority in the Andean region. Furthermore, Articles 36 and 37 of Decision 608 intend to avoid conflicts with national sectorial regulation and acknowledge the potential of conflicts between

[166] "Normas en materia de protección de la competencia", see above Part II, Dimension I: Sect. 5.2.2.1.

[167] *OECD,* Colombia: Assessment of Competition Law and Policy, OECD 2016, p. 20.

[168] *OECD,* Colombia: Assessment of Competition Law and Policy, OECD 2016, pp. 25 et seq.

[169] *SIC,* Competition Bulletin – First Quarter 2012, 2012.

[170] *SIC,* Competition Bulletin – First Quarter 2012, 2012, p. 11.

[171] This finding was also expressed by representatives from the SIC and the ANDI (*Asociación Nacional de Empresarios de Colombia*) during interviews with the author conducted in January/ February 2012 in Bogota, Colombia.

such sectorial regulation and the free competition on the common market.[172] Article 7 of Law no. 1340 responds to this potential conflict and creates a link between the national competition authority and state-imputed regulation. Decision 608 thereby emphasized the notion of competition advocacy on the national level.

So far, there has been neither cooperation during investigations nor information-sharing between the Colombian and the Andean competition authority. Moreover, the Superintendence of Industry and Trade has not referred a single case to the Secretariat General based on a practice with cross-border effect.[173]

The impact of Decision 608 on Peruvian competition law and national enforcement is similarly limited. Peru reformed its competition law in 2009 with Legislative Decree no. 1034. The latter aims at a clarification of the competition law prohibitions. Interestingly, the Legislative Decree no. 1034 was enacted in the context of the implementation of the "Peru Trade Promotion Agreement", which was signed between the United States and Peru on 2 April 2006 and ratified by the Peruvian Congress in June 2006. The agreement entered into force in 2009. Chapter 13 of the Agreement comprises the obligation to enact national competition legislation and Chapter 13(5) of the agreement particularly refers to the prohibition of monopolies that impair trade and investment.[174] Therefore, the agreement signed with the United States might also have had an impact on the reform of national competition law.

Vertical cooperation in competition law investigations or enforcement does not take place. Accordingly, the INDECOPI has never referred a competition-law case to the Secretariat General of the AndeanC. One explanation might be that the INDECOPI does generally not engage in "joint inspections or down raids in conjunction with another competition authority".[175] On the other hand, informal cooperation and dialogues bilaterally, as for example between the Peruvian INDECOPI and the Colombian Superintendence of Industry and Trade, have taken place.[176]

In sum, the impact of Decision 608 remains very limited on member states with prior competition law experience. While cooperation during the enforcement of competition law does not take place at all, the content of Decision 608 was capable of inciting the conduct of competition law advocacy. However, the actual weight of Decision 608 on a legislative process in relation to legislative initiatives arising

---

[172] *Secretaria General de la Comunidad Andina,* Guía Práctica para la aplicación de la Decisión 608 "Normas para la protección y promoción de la libre competencia en la Comunidad Andina", 2007, p. 42.

[173] This aspect actually concerns the enforcement of regional law.

[174] For more information on the "Peru Trade Promotion Agreement", see <http://www.ustr.gov/trade-agreements/free-trade-agreements/peru-tpa>.

[175] *OECD,* Improving International Co-operation in Cartel Investigations – Contribution from Peru, 2012, p. 3 <http://www.oecd.org/daf/competition/ImprovingInternationalCooperationInCartelInvestigations2012.pdf> accessed 11 November 2018.

[176] Representatives from both authorities confirmed this during interviews conducted with the author in Bogota, Colombia and Lima, Peru in January/February 2012. Likewise, see *OECD,* Improving International Co-operation in Cartel Investigations – Contribution from Peru, 2012 <http://www.oecd.org/daf/competition/ImprovingInternationalCooperationInCartelInvestigations2012.pdf> accessed 11 November 2018.

from bilateral trade agreements or internal reforms cannot be determined. Generally, Decision 608, irrespective of its little relevance for specific enforcement measures of national authorities with prior competition law experiences, it creates a catalogue of prohibitions of standardized anticompetitive conducts and thereby establishes a basis for consistent competition law enforcement in the AndeanC.[177]

The lack of vertical cooperation between national and regional level has two main explanations. The Colombian and Peruvian authorities are more interested in fostering bilateral cooperation agreements, in particular with agencies that have competition law experience, such as Chile[178] or Mexico. On the other hand, the Secretariat General has not been proactive in establishing regular cooperation mechanisms, nor has it insisted on its assisting role in the enforcement of national competition laws.

6.3.5 Summary of "Soft Harmonization" Through Non-Binding Guidelines in the AndeanC

The Decision 608, including its "downloading option", *de facto* functions as non-binding guidelines for the member states. Although by 2011 all member states have enacted domestic competition law provisions, this outcome was not brought about by sanctions taken on the regional level or by other informal pressure. Member states were only obliged to assign a domestic authority that is in charge for the application of regional competition law. It may seem contradictory to assume the existence of national authorities that are capable of enforcing regional antitrust law without having national competition law provisions before that. While this ambiguity remained a theoretical inconsistency in the European Union,[179] in the AndeanC this fact might have contributed to the lack of use of Decision 608 and the slow national competition law implementation process.[180] The analysis of the national legislative and reform processes of national competition law in the AndeanC demonstrates that many difficulties arose from institutional ambiguities and from difficulties to determine the competent competition law authority.[181]

Decision 608 created an incentive for member states without prior competition law to adopt domestic competition legislation. Even for member states with prior experience, Decision 608 emphasized the relevance of competition advocacy. Decision 608 thus contributed to the emergence and progress of a national competition culture. Yet the exact weight of its influence cannot be determined as Decision

[177] *Cortázar,* Decisión 608 de la Comunidad Andina, 2/2 Rev. Der. Comp. 123, 136 (2006).

[178] There is also considerable exchange between the Peruvian and Chilean competition jurisdictions regarding the ongoing process of introducing national merger control regimes.

[179] See *Drexl,* Perspectives européennes sur la politique de la concurrence dans l'espace OHADA, XXV R.I.D.E. 281–304 (2011).

[180] See below on the enforcement record, Part II, Dimension III: Sect. 7.1.2.2.

[181] See above Part II, Dimension I: Sect. 5.2.

608 was implemented in a context where all member states had already been engaging in their own legislative implementation processes or reform initiatives. Furthermore, the significant impact of bilateral preferential trade agreements apart from the AndeanC cannot be underestimated. Namely the bilateral trade agreements between Colombia and the US, Peru and the US, as well as between the countries and the European Union also entail competition law provisions.[182]

Decision 608 was explicitly conceived as a harmonization tool.[183] Not only was this harmonization aimed at the substantive law, but it was also expected that a supranational norm would in a medium-term lead to the harmonization of the national competition policies.[184] Contrary to the European experience, in which the "soft-harmonization" led to a "spontaneous harmonization"[185] of national laws, the AndeanC's member states adopted diverging concepts of competition policy. Especially, the Colombian and Peruvian liberal market approach contrasts with the still existing tendencies towards state-interventionism in Bolivia and Ecuador.

National willingness to accept harmonization thus correlates to the coerciveness of economic integration for member states, in particular the preponderance of the economic benefits of a common market.[186] While in the European Union, traditionally cross-border trade between member states has always been very important, Andean states are more engaged in trade with the United States.[187] This creates a vicious circle. The lack of harmonization diminishes the efficacy of the common market and decreases initiatives for member states to integrate. On the other hand, far-reaching harmonization facilitates integration. Although harmonization in the European Union also took almost 30 years until all member states possessed a national competition law regime, the prognosis of Andean competition law is nevertheless more negative. Cross-border trade remains low and member states are ignoring the Andean competition law framework. Furthermore, it has been argued that in the European Union legal professionals and national business associations advocated the "Europeanization" of national competition laws.[188] In the AndeanC,

[182] The trade agreement between Peru and the US was Signed on 12 April 2006 and entered into force on 1 February 2009; for more information see <http://www.sice.oas.org/ctyindex/PER/PERagreements_e.asp> accessed 11 November 2018. The trade agreement between Colombia and the US was signed on 22 November 2006 and entered into force on the 15 May 2012; for more information see <http://www.sice.oas.org/ctyindex/COL/COLagreements_e.asp> accessed 11 November 2018. The trade agreement between Colombia, Peru and the European Union was signed on 21 December 2012 and entered into force on 1 March 2013 in Peru and on 1 August 2013 in Colombia; for more information see <http://www.fdcl.org/wp-content/uploads/2012/04/CELEX_22012A122101_EN_TXT.pdf>.

[183] Proyecto COMPETENCIA, Instrumentos de Apoyo al Sector Agropecuario y Competencia en la Comunidad Andina, SG/di 775, 9 December 2005.

[184] Informe de la Primera Reunion de Expertos Gubernamentales en Materia de Libre Competencia, SG/REG.LC/I/Informe/Rev.1, 29 October 1998, p. 2 (available from the author).

[185] *Monti,* EC Competition Law, 2007, p. 402.

[186] See *Marcos,* in *Fox/Sokol,* Competition Law and Policy in Latin America, 2009, p. 453.

[187] On the role of bilateral trade agreements with the United States, see above Part I, Sect. 1.1.2.

[188] *Monti,* EC Competition Law, 2007, p. 402.

regional competition law has not made it to the basic economic and legal university curriculum. Similarly, private business associations[189] in the AndeanC do not show interest in regional competition law. In particular small and medium-sized enterprises "face various dilemmas" when dealing with competition law.[190] The initiation of a competition-law investigation bears economic and financial risks. To submit a complaint requires legal advice and a financial investment, while the complaining party might suffer from repressive measures by the accused competitor(s) or company. These dangers are even aggravated by legal uncertainty due the lack of legal precedents regarding Decision 608. At last, no member state of the AndeanC has been willing to take a leading role in the promulgation of regional competition law. To the contrary, competition law enforcement remains national and the economic importance of a common Andean market as trading space seems to be diminishing for the member states.

[189] For example: the "Asociación Nacional de Empresarios de Colombia" and the "Confederación de Empresarios Privados de Bolivia". In interviews with the author these business associations stated that they were not interested in regional competition law for the lack of use.

[190] *Cortázar*, in: *Drexl/Bakhoum/Fox/Gal/Gerber*, Competition Policy and Regional Integration in Developing Countries, 2012, pp. 133–160.

Chapter 7
Dimension III: Organization of Enforcing Agencies

The institutional design of and the interplay between the competent competition law authorities and other bodies of law that are involved in regional competition law enforcement is of crucial importance in order to understand enforcement processes in the WAEMU, the AndeanC and the CARICOM. One thus has to identify the actors that participate in the enforcement process in the narrow sense, in particular the decision-making process. Moreover, one should also consider and evaluate the impact and reach of possible controlling mechanisms by other organs, such as judicial review or mandatory cooperation mechanisms.

7.1 Regional Competition Law Authorities

In the WAEMU, the community competition law system relies on two main organs: the WAEMU Commission,[1] more specifically the Directorate of Competition, and the Consultative Committee of Competition.[2] Other relevant enforcement institutions are the national competition law authorities and the Court of Justice of WAEMU.

The main competition law organs in the AndeanC are the Secretariat General and the Andean Committee for the Defence of Free Competition. Other relevant institutions are the Andean Tribunal,[3] the Commission,[4] which is the main legislative body and expresses itself through decisions, and the national competition authorities.[5]

[1] Commission de l'UEMOA.

[2] Comité Consultatif de la Concurrence.

[3] Art. 30 Agreement of Cartagena; *Marwege,* Der Andengerichtshof, 1994.

[4] Articles 21ff. Agreement of Cartagena.

[5] Also relevant for the development of competition policies in Latin America is the UNCTAD-led programme COMPAL. The COMPAL programme is a technical assistance programme on compe-

J. Molestina, *Regional Competition Law Enforcement in Developing Countries*,
Munich Studies on Innovation and Competition 9,
https://doi.org/10.1007/978-3-662-58525-2_7

In the CARICOM the organs enforcing competition law are the CARICOM Competition Commission and the COTED. National competition law authorities, although only a few exist so far, also hold an important role in the enforcement of regional competition law. Further relevant organs in the drafting or revision process constitute the Conference of Heads of Government and the Caribbean Court of Justice.

The three RTAs vary in essential organizational aspects: ranging from a completely independent supranational competition authority, to a general regional authority that either has a specific department for competition or just assigns certain employees on a project basis.

7.1.1 Specialized Independent Commission Model: The CARICOM Example

7.1.1.1 The General Structure

The CARICOM Competition Commission was inaugurated on 18 January 2008 in Paramaribo, Suriname in accordance with Article 171 of the Revised Treaty of Chaguaramas. It is responsible for the application of the regional competition rules, the coordination of the implementation of the community competition policy and competition advocacy.[6] According to Article 173(1) lit. c) RTC, the CARICOM Competition Commission shall also perform other functions conferred to it by any competent body of the Community. The notion of "competent body of the Community" is open to some ambiguity and requires further specification with regard to the hierarchy and its definition. The definition in the preamble of the Revised Treaty of Chaguaramas explains that a "competent authority means the authority legally authorised to perform a function". In the case of Chapter VIII, this would primarily concern the COTED that may request an investigation, Article 175(2) RTC. However the notion of "any competent body of the Community" might be broader and cover other institutions as well. In order to regulate the procedures before the CARICOM Competition Commission, the regional competition authority enacted the CARICOM Competition Commission Rules of Procedure in 2011, in accordance with Article 174(7) of the Revised Treaty of Chaguaramas.

The CARICOM Competition Commission is not only a competition agency, but is also supposed to support the member states with regard to the promotion of consumer welfare and the protection of consumer interests, Article 186 of the Revised Treaty of Chaguaramas. However, one has to highlight that the CARICOM Competition Commission does not hold an enforcement role in the field of consumer

---

tition and consumer protection for Latin America, supported by SECO Switzerland. The programme is especially relevant for Bolivia, but it is also active in other member states of the AndeanC such as Ecuador and Peru.

[6] Article 173(1) of the Revised Treaty of Chaguaramas.

protection, but is limited to technical assistance and other consumer welfare promoting activities.[7]

In accordance with Article 172(1) of the Revised Treaty of Chaguaramas, the CARICOM Competition Commission is composed of seven members, which are appointed by the Regional Judicial and Legal Service Commission.

7.1.1.2 The Constitutional Design of the CARICOM Competition Commission: The Regional Judicial and Legal Service Commission

The Regional Judicial and Legal Service Commission was created with the Agreement Establishing the Caribbean Court of Justice.[8] The appointment of CARICOM Competition Commission's members via the Regional Judicial and Legal Service Commission constitutes a "de-politicized appointment process".[9] A crucial element to this de-politicized appointment is the composition of the Regional Judicial and Legal Service Commission by a wide range of members to avoid captures by single interest groups, namely two lawyers, the chairman of the Judicial Services Commission and the chairman of a Public Service Commission, two academics, two Bar representatives and two persons from civil society.[10] The underlying conception is that a broad membership creates a "collective identification" of the members with the objectives of the Regional Judicial and Legal Service Commission itself, rather than representing the group from which they have been elected.[11] Moreover, the chairmen are not elected, but rotate, which reinforces the creation of an identity of the Regional Judicial and Legal Service Commission itself. Codifying the Regional Judicial and Legal Service Commission's operational independence, Article V(12) of the Agreement Establishing the Caribbean Court of Justice determines that the Commission "shall neither seek nor receive instructions from any body or person external to the Commission". The high degree of political and operational independence in the appointing organ simultaneously guarantees that the members of the CARICOM Competition Commission are appointed independently and solely on the basis of their qualifications.

---

[7] The only action that could be considered an "active" enforcement action is Article 186(1) (b) of the Revised Treaty of Chaguaramas, according to which the Commission can "take such measures as it considers necessary to ensure that the Member States discourage and eliminate unfair trading practices, including misleading or deceptive conduct, false advertising, bait advertising, referral selling and pyramid selling".

[8] Article V of the Agreement Establishing the Caribbean Court of Justice, 2001.

[9] *Malleson,* Promoting Judicial Independence in the International Courts, 58 I. C. L. Q. 671, 680 (2009).

[10] *Malleson,* Promoting Judicial Independence in the International Courts, 58 I. C. L. Q. 671, 680 (2009); Article V(1) of the Agreement Establishing the Caribbean Court of Justice, 2001.

[11] *Malleson,* Promoting Judicial Independence in the International Courts, 58 I. C. L. Q. 671, 680 (2009).

The members of the CARICOM Competition Commission are appointed for a renewable 5-year term and elected based on their expertise or experience in commerce, finance, economics, law or other competition-policy-related fields.[12] A Commissioner may only be removed from office for inability to perform its functions or "misbehaviour" and may be subject to disciplinary procedures.[13] Although the undefined notion of "misbehaviour" leaves room for potential abuse in order to exercise pressure on the Commissioners, Article 172(5) RTC also determines that a Commissioner can only be removed on the vote of the Regional Judicial and Legal Service Commission and moreover only if the latter is represented by three-quarters of its members.

The financial independence of the CARICOM Competition Commission is more limited. It is primarily financed by contributions from the member states.[14] In a supranational system, the influence by national political interest groups is reduced by the possibility of the regional authority to collect fines for competition law breaches. Neither the Revised Treaty of Chaguaramas, nor the Rules of Procedure of the CARICOM Competition Commission incorporate provisions regarding the calculation of possible fines in case of violations of competition law. Although the CARICOM Competition Commission has the competence to impose fines for breaches of regional competition law,[15] due to the dualist system, the fines have to be enforced by the national agencies. Even if the CARICOM Competition Commission's determinations are binding in the member states or if the CARICOM Competition Commission has appealed to the Caribbean Court of Justice for an order,[16] which binds the member states according to Article XV and Article XVI of the Agreement Establishing the Caribbean Court of Justice, it is still dependent on the member state's cooperation. As enforcement takes place in accordance with national procedural laws, despite the CARICOM Competition Commission's competence to impose fines, the limits of a fee remain determined by national authorities or by national courts, when cases are appealed.[17] This does not only cause the danger of inconsistencies among member states with regard to the amount of possible fines, but also creates uncertainty for the CARICOM Competition Commission to estimate its available budget.

The CARICOM Competition Commission also suffers from resource constraints.[18] Competition law expertise is generally scarce throughout the region and recruitment remains difficult for various reasons. Competition law and policy have not been incorporated in the Caribbean universities' general curriculum and the location of the CARICOM Competition Commission in Suriname, one of the

[12] Article 172(2) and Article 172(3) of the Revised Treaty of Chaguaramas.

[13] Article 172(4) of the Revised Treaty of Chaguaramas.

[14] *CARICOM Secretariat,* The CARICOM Competition Commission, 2008, p. 6.

[15] Article 174(4) (j) of the Revised Treaty of Chaguaramas.

[16] Article 175(11) of the Revised Treaty of Chaguaramas.

[17] *CARICOM Secretariat,* The CARICOM Competition Commission, 2008, p. 6.

[18] Statement made by Kusha Haraksingh, Chairman of the CARICOM Competition Commission, in an interview with the author in Port-of-Spain, Trinidad and Tobago, on 29 October 2012.

lesser-developed countries in the CARICOM, might constitute an obstacle to finding skilled personal.

The Revised Treaty of Chaguaramas does not give guidance on the appointment with regard to the nationality of the members. It is possible that Article 23(2) RTC, which prescribes that the recruitment of Community staff shall bear in mind the principle of equitable geographical distribution, might further complicate the appointment process. While according to the current chairman of the CARICOM Competition Commission "equitable geographical distribution" was achieved by chance, this might not always be given in the future for the limited number of experts in the region.

The CARICOM Competition Commission has drawn conclusions from the experiences during procedures of the Fair Trading Commission in Jamaica. The Rules of Procedure of the CARICOM guarantee that the persons carrying out investigations are separated from those adjudicating on the case.[19] Accordingly, the Rules of Procedure of the CARICOM Competition Commission differentiate between an Investigating Panel[20] (Sections 5 to 9) and an Adjudicating Panel[21] (Sections 10 to 56).

The CARICOM Competition Commission is generally operationally independent, because it can carry out its investigations and enquiries based on its procedural rules without political interference or guidance.[22] Article IV of the Agreement between the Government of the Republic of Suriname and the Caribbean Community establishing the seat and the office of the Competition Commission of 2007 and the Protocol on the Privileges and Immunities of the Competition Commission of 2007 guarantee immunities for the Commission and its staff. Notwithstanding the virtues of independence, in order to comply with principles of a representative democracy, institutional independence has to be balanced with some form of accountability.[23] This accountability does not only adhere to the legitimacy of the authority, but it also attributes to consistent and transparent competition law enforcement. Accounting processes should be transparent and non-discriminatory.

The CARICOM Competition Commission is accountable to the COTED. It has to make recommendations to the COTED[24] and conflicts of jurisdiction are resolved

---

[19] CARICOM Competition Commission Rules of Procedure, 2011.

[20] Definition according to the CARICOM Competition Commission Rules of Procedure, 2011: "Investigating Panel means a panel of the Commission designated by the Chairman pursuant to Rule 4(2) to conduct an investigation".

[21] Definition according to the CARICOM Competition Commission Rules of Procedure, 2011: "Adjudicating Panel means a panel of the Commission designated by the Chairman pursuant to Rule 10(2) to conduct an enquiry, with a view to making a determination pursuant to Article 174(3) of the Treaty and, if appropriate, to make an order, direction or imposition pursuant to Article 174(4) of the Treaty".

[22] For more information on the enforcement procedure in CARICOM, see below Part II, Dimension IV: Chap. 8.

[23] *Trebilcock/Iacobucci*, Designing Competition Law Institutions, 41 Loy. U. Chi. L.J. 455, 457 (2010).

[24] Article 173(2) (b) of the Revised Treaty of Chaguaramas.

by the COTED.[25] The COTED is also competent for making competition policy and rules[26] that will guide the overall orientation of the CARICOM Competition Commission. Furthermore, the COTED can request an investigation[27] and can also limit the Commission's enforcement powers through exemptions.[28] Yet the CARICOM Competition Commission does not have to report to the COTED concerning the content of an enquiry, but only about the fact that it has started an investigation.

The COTED retains a strong influence generally on the orientation of the authority and specifically during the enforcement process. This is problematic, because the COTED is composed of ministers of the member states,[29] thereby being more vulnerable and loyal to national interests and national political interests groups. Consequently, the decision-making processes in the COTED, being a political and policy-establishing body, is less transparent than in an institution that is guided by stringent procedural rules. The COTED could therefore indirectly impact the CARICOM Competition Commission's accountability and transparency depending on how excessively it will use its powers.

The CARICOM Competition Commission conducts its investigations in accordance with applicable national laws.[30] The enterprise that is the target of such an investigation can resort to domestic courts in order to vindicate its rights if it felt injured by the Commission's investigative actions.[31] Alternatively, an affected party can exercise its right of defence and the right to be heard before the Caribbean Court of Justice, to which the CARICOM Competition Commission is thus accountable.[32] In fact, the first matter, on which the CARICOM Competition Commission issued a decision, was submitted to the Caribbean Court of Justice by the affected party.[33]

7.1.1.3 Conclusion on the CARICOM Competition Commission

The CARICOM Competition Commission can largely operate independently, which is also guaranteed by its institutional structure and the internal Rules of Procedure. However, external hierarchical relations with some Community organs are still unresolved. In particular regarding the relationship between the CARICOM

---

[25] Article 176(5) of the Revised Treaty of Chaguaramas.

[26] Article 182 of the Revised Treaty of Chaguaramas.

[27] Article 175(2) of the Revised Treaty of Chaguaramas.

[28] Article 183 of the Revised Treaty of Chaguaramas.

[29] Article 15 of the Revised Treaty of Chaguaramas.

[30] Article 174(2) of the Revised Treaty of Chaguaramas.

[31] *Trinidad Cement Limited v The Competition Commission,* Caribbean Court of Justice Application No. OA 1 of 2012, CCJ 4 (OJ), [26].

[32] On different controlling mechanisms before a regional Court of Justice, see below Part II, Dimension IV: Sect. 8.3.

[33] *Trinidad Cement Limited v The Competition Commission,* Caribbean Court of Justice Application No. OA 1 of 2012, CCJ 4 (OJ).

Competition Commission and the COTED, purely political policy questions might clash with competition law enforcement actions.[34]

Yet the future outlook can be optimistic: First, the CARICOM Competition Commission, despite insufficient resources, has started operation with a "good case" against a large and famous company on a basic economic industry, namely cement. It demonstrated its ability to conduct a thorough analysis of the common market, in which it recognized the cement sector a key sector for economic development. Definitively, its high degree of independence contributed positively to this. At the same time, the case against Trinidad Cement Limited demonstrates the commitment and willingness of the CARICOM Competition Commission's staff to attack large and influential enterprises in the region. It demonstrates that the number of personnel in young competition law agencies is not the determining factor of the agency's effectiveness, but rather the commitment and ambition of the agency's staff.[35] Second, the Caribbean Court of Justice has reemphasized its active role as "guardian of the treaty" also in the area of competition law and has given a reasonable judgment that provides for a framework of effective competition law enforcement within CARICOM while sufficiently respecting the interests at stake.

7.1.2 Non-Specialized Directorate Model: The Andean Example

7.1.2.1 The General Structure

The Secretariat General constitutes the executive organ of the general integration system in the AndeanC.[36] Article 30 lit. a) of the Agreement of Cartagena entrusts the Secretariat General with the task of ensuring that the regional legal norms and decisions adopted by the supranational institutions are obeyed. In order to enforce compliance, the Secretariat General has *ex officio* power to bring non-compliance proceedings before the Andean Court of Justice and plays an important role in the mandatory prejudicial administrative phase of a non-compliance proceeding.[37] Furthermore, the Secretariat General works as a technical secretariat for the enforcement of the Andean Commission's Decisions. The Secretariat General is an

[34] *Beckford,* in: *Drexl/Bakhoum/Fox/Gal/Gerber,* Competition Policy and Regional Integration in Developing Countries, 2012, pp. 185, 191.

[35] *Kovacic,* Creating New Competition Policy Institutions in Transition Economies, 23 Brook. J. Int'l. Law 403, 431 (1997).

[36] Articles 29ff. Agreement of Cartagena.

[37] Action for non-compliance is divided into two parts: administrative part and judicial part. The administrative part takes place before the Secretariat General, where the affected parties can bring forward their standing regarding the matter. Artt. 23ff. of Treaty of the Creation of the Andean Tribunal of Justice, Decisión 623, "Reglamento de la Fase Prejudicial de la Acción de Incumplimiento".

independent authority: it possesses its own staff[38] and budget.[39] However, it has to publish an annual program, based on which the Andean Commission decides the annual budget.[40]

The Secretariat General's functions are organized in five different areas: environment, social issues, politics and external relations, institutional issues, economics and trade.[41] Competition law related matters are generally accounted to the economic and commercial area. The Secretariat General is governed by a General Secretary and several General Directors, which are responsible for a particular subdivision, so called "directorates". Although the directorates cover different topics, these topics do not necessarily correspond to the general five function areas of the Secretariat General.

In fulfilling its functions the Secretariat General forms different groups, usually composed of five to six persons, who deal with a specific project.[42] These persons can be part of various project groups. In 2003, two groups worked on regional competition policy, of which one concerned the cooperation between the AndeanC and the European Union.[43] Although this project-based group structure contributes to a structural flexibility of the Secretariat General,[44] the lack of staff that is exclusively assigned to deal with competition law matters risks that other topics might prevail over competition law matters. In fact, with the member states' decreasing support of regional competition law the Secretariat General also refrained from making Decision 608 a priority. The resources assigned to competition law enforcement reflect this development: Only one functionary is currently directly assigned to deal with competition law issues. The assigned staff member in particular highlighted the lack of technical equipment as main obstacle to efficient competition law enforcement. During the implementation phase of Decision 608, the Secretariat General only employed a limited number of lawyers and they were under constant time pressure. The staff member responsible for competition law also had to deal with other topics. The Secretariat General is forced to set priorities in a stringent manner. In the absence of support by the member states, it has to do this on its own initiative.

Generally, the Generally Secretariat is composed of approximately 190 staff members, of which half are professionals. The large part of the staff is employed

---

[38] Articles 23ff. of Decision 409.

[39] Generally, the AndeanC's institutions are financed by the member states. However, Ecuador and Bolivia pay smaller shares. The AndeanC also relies on external funding, as for example provided by the European Union.

[40] Articles 33ff. of Decision 409.

[41] There is a 6th area, which deals with technical support by programmes such as the INTERCAN programme <http://www.comunidadandina.org/transparencia/organigrama.htm> accessed 11 November 2018.

[42] *Krakowski,* El ambiente institucional de las autoridades de competencia en la Subregión Andina, 2003, p. 16.

[43] *Krakowski,* El ambiente institucional de las autoridades de competencia en la Subregión Andina, 2003, p. 16.

[44] *Ibid.*

and more than half of the professionals work on substantial areas instead of administrative topics.[45] The Secretariat General acts through resolutions, so called "resoluciones motivadas" and "informes"; the latter are mainly designed for internal procedures and do not constitute a final decision.[46] In contrast to the European Commission the internal procedure of the Secretariat General, as regulated by Decision 425, does not differentiate between merely preparatory measures and non-routine measures that have to be agreed upon by the General Secretary of the Secretariat General.[47] According to Article 6 of Decision 425 any determination made by the Secretariat General, including "resoluciones motivadas", have to be dictated by the General Secretary.[48] The General Secretary has to be "a person of high representation".[49] He or she solely works for the Secretariat General and always has to take into consideration the interests of all member states and the Andean Community as a whole.[50] He is elected by the Andean Council of Ministers of Foreign Relations and can only be withdrawn by this body based on consensus in case of a severe mistake as set out in the rules of the Secretariat General.[51]

Because of the lack of competition law expertise of the General Secretary, he or she has to rely on technical assistance. This assistance can originate from a Directorate[52] or from external experts, ideally originating from different member states based on an equal number.[53] The usual procedure involves that the internal and external experts agree on the matter, before they submit their results to the General Secretary, who ascertains the final content of the specific decision. According to Article 38 of the Agreement of Cartagena the staff of the Secretariat General has to abstain from any actions that are incompatible with the character of its function and must not accept any instructions of governments or any national or international entity. According to interviews with employees of the Secretariat General this consensus based internal process generally works well and the General Secretary relies on the opinion presented by the experts and the directorates.

---

[45] *Krakowski,* El ambiente institucional de las autoridades de competencia en la Subregión Andina, 2003, p. 16.

[46] During the prejudicial phase of an action of non-compliance of the Andean Tribunal of Justice, the General Secretary expresses itself through "Dictamen".

[47] On the internal procedure for the adoption of decisions of the European Commission, see *Ortiz Blanco,* EC Competition Procedure, 2006, pp. 49ff.; Rules of Procedure of the Commission [2000] OJ L308/26 (last amendment [2003] OJ 2003 L92/14).

[48] *Secretaria General de la Comunidad Andina,* Guía Práctica para la aplicación de la Decisión 608 "Normas para la protección y promoción de la libre competencia en la Comunidad Andina", 2007, p. 15.

[49] Article 32 of Agreement of Cartagena.

[50] Article 8 of Decision 409.

[51] Articles 5, 13, 15 of Decision 409.

[52] The Secretariat General mostly employs economists and only very few lawyers, of which only one is currently assigned to deal with competition law matters exclusively.

[53] Articles 36ff. of Agreement of Cartagena.

7.1.2.2 Competition Law Cases Dealt with by the Secretariat General

The Secretariat General is the competent body to enforce Decision 608 and to issue related decisions, as well as to apply sanctioning measures. Yet, so far, it has not released a single resolution under the regional competition law norm.[54] Nor has any investigation before the Secretariat General been initiated by an individual or a national competition law authority.[55]

Yet as set out in Art. 30 of Agreement of Cartagena and Decision 425, the Secretariat General is generally responsible for guaranteeing the application of regional law, which also includes Decision 608. The Secretariat General has never challenged decisions of national competition authorities regarding the non-existence of a cross-border effect, although for the principle of direct effect of regional law and its primacy over national law, the national authority would be obliged to apply Decision 608 if cross-border effect is actually present.[56]

7.1.2.3 Conclusions on the Secretariat General of the AndeanC

The Secretariat General is structurally independent. This is supported by its autonomy regarding its own staffing and the internal distribution of its annual budget.[57] The general internal decision-making process, despite the lack of competition expertise of the General Secretary, provides for sufficient knowledge of competition law professionals or other related experts. Yet the flexible structure in the non-specialized project-based structure of the AndeanC has led to resources constraints regarding competition law enforcement. The non-attribution of resources to regional competition law enforcement on the one hand reflects the declining interest in regional competition law enforcement, but also generally demonstrates that the Secretariat General with regard to competition law sees itself as a reactive organ that relies on the initiative of member states.

---

[54] Under the former Decision 285, the Secretariat General dealt with three cases, of which two were rejected on the basis that they did not fall within the scope of application. The only case, which was actually prosecuted and led to the imposition of a sanction concerned a price cartel among palm oil producers in Colombia; see below Resolution 892, Part II, Dimension IV: section "Resolutions Concerning the National Confederation of Palm-Growers and Palm Oil Enterprises (Peru) vs. Fund for Price Stabilisation for Palm-Oil and Its Fractions (Colombia)". For more information on the two other non-competition law cases under Decision 285, see *Botta,* The Role of Competition Policy in the Latin American Regional Integration: A Comparative Analysis of Caricom, Andean Community and Mercosur, 21–22 October 2011, St. Gallen, p. 21.

[55] For more information on the enforcement procedures see Part II, Dimension IV: Sect. 8.1.

[56] There are national cases from Bolivia, Colombia, Ecuador and Peru that consider Article 5 of Decision 608, but all cases come to the conclusion that there was no cross-border effect.

[57] According to the Commission of the AndeanC, 46% of the Secretariat General's budget is spend on salaries. The budget of the Secretariat General has been stable between 1993 and 2002. Even when some member states were late with their financial contributions, the Secretariat General was capable to pay salaries on time because of installed funds. See *Krakowski,* El ambiente institucional de las autoridades de competencia en la Subregión Andina, 2003, pp. 16f.

7.1.3 *Specialized Directorate Model: The Case of the WAEMU*

7.1.3.1 The General Structure

In the WAEMU, the competent competition law entity is the Directorate of Competition, which is part of the larger regional authority, the Commission, which is responsible for dealing with all matters regarding community integration. The Commission is the general executive body of the WAEMU. Other general functions encompass the carrying out of decisions taken by the Conference of the Heads of States or the Council of Ministers, the distribution of the budget of the Union, the assurance of the publication of the official bulletin of the Union and the publication of an annual general report on the activities and evolution of the Union.[58] The Commissioners are appointed by the Conference of Heads of States based on criteria of competence and integrity.[59] The Treaty of Dakar provides for the Commissioners' independence.[60] A mandate can only be revoked in the case of a serious mistake or incapacity of the Commissioner.[61]

The Commission is structured in Departments.[62] The Department of the Regional Market, Trade, Competition and Cooperation is in charge of the competition law in the region. The Department of the Regional Market, Trade, Competition and Cooperation itself is divided into several Directorates. The Directorate of Competition is the competent regional competition authority. It is divided into two sections: the first deals with anticompetitive practices and public interventions on the market, the other one deals with legislation, training and external relations. While the former deals more with the enforcement of competition law in the narrow sense, the latter is concerned with general competition law related queries.[63]

The Directorate of Competition is only sparsely staffed, with three permanent employees. The authority employs one chief for each direction and a director for the Directorate. Further provisions regarding administrative or technical staff are not contained in the decision regarding the organization of the department of the regional market, trade, competition and cooperation.[64] This sparse personal composition causes serious resource constraints. One has to recall that due to the wide territorial scope of the regional competition law, and above all the exclusive enforcement competence of the authority, the Directorate of Competition in WAEMU is in

---

[58] Article 26 of the Treaty of Dakar.

[59] Article 27 of the Treaty of Dakar.

[60] Article 28 of the Treaty of Dakar.

[61] Article 27 of the Treaty of Dakar.

[62] Decision n° 0157/2007/PCOM/UEMOA, portant création et organisation des services de la Commission de l'UEMOA.

[63] Decision n° 345/2008/PCOM/UEMOA, portant organisation du département du marché régional, du commerce, de la concurrence et de la coopération.

[64] Decision n° 345/2008/PCOM/UEMOA, portant organisation du département du marché régional, du commerce, de la concurrence et de la coopération.

charge of all possible competition law-related queries that arise in the common market, irrespective the existence of a cross-border effect.

Furthermore, the Directorate of Competition does not dispose of a sufficient financial resources. Organizationally belonging to the Department of the Regional Market, the budget of the Directorate of Competition depends on the internal distribution of the funds. Hence, the Directorate of Competition does not enjoy financial discretion, but has to rely on the goodwill of the President of the Commission, who is in charge for the distribution of the funds. Although, in theory the direction might be provided with sufficient financial resources, the lack of flexible utilization hinders effective competition law enforcement. This is especially the case, where an urgent or rapid intervention would be required.

The decision-making process does not solely lie with the Directorate of Competition itself.[65] Firstly, before making a decision, the Directorate of Competition has to invoke the Consultative Committee on Competition to submit an opinion.[66] This opinion however does not bind the Commission or the Directorate of Competition.[67] Its impact on the internal decision-making power thus remains limited. The Commission is not even obliged to publish the Consultative Committee's opinion and does not have to fear possible public resentments.

The Directorate of Judicial Affairs[68] is entitled to intervene even more drastically in the decision-making process. The Directorate of Judicial Affairs is tied to the Presidency of the Commission. Before making a decision, the Directorate of Competition has to invoke the Directorate of Judicial Affairs to make observations regarding the decision. Based on the observations, the Directorate of Competition then has the possibility to revise and return its decision to the President of the Commission. The decision only becomes valid and enforceable with the signature of the President of the Commission. The involvement of the President of the Commission, *inter alia* through its attached Directorate of Judicial Affairs, bears certain inefficiencies. Firstly, the division of decision-making powers slows down the decision making process. On the other hand, and more importantly, the participation of the Commission's presidency also regarding the content of a decision, limits the operational discretion of the Directorate of Competition. While it is theoretically possible that the Direction of Competition does not follow the observations made by the Directorate of Judicial Affairs, it does not seem practical, since the President of the Commission will be more inclined to follow the observations made by the Directorate of Judicial Affairs because of its structural attachment to the Presidency. However, the signature of the President is a necessary element to create a binding decision. This mandatory signature does not only apply to the final decision, but every procedural step. The involvement is also problematic for the lack of

[65] More details on the enforcement process of regional competition law in the WAEMU, see below Part II, Dimension IV: Chap. 8.

[66] More details on the Advisory Committee on Competition in the WAEMU, see below Part II, Dimension IV: Sect. 8.2.1.1.

[67] Articles 28(3), 22 and 23 of Regulation no. 03/2002/CM/UEMOA.

[68] Direction des Affaires Juridiques.

competition law expertise in the Directorate of Judicial Affairs or the Presidency of the Commission. Consequently, the structure of the internal decision-making process of the Directorate of Competition does not guarantee a decision based on mere competition-related considerations, but decisions might be pervaded by political considerations. Prior to the creation of the specified Directorate of Competition in 2007 the Department of the Regional Market, Trade, Competition and Cooperation dealt with competition-related matters, however without making competition a particular focus of its activities.[69]

The complex administrative arrangements extends the duration of processing competition law cases. Moreover, the involvement of the Directorate of Judicial Affairs impairs the transparency of competition law procedures in WAEMU. For parties outside the Commission, it may be difficult to understand the considerations of a decision of the Commission for the lack of visibility of all persons and public entities involved during the enforcement process.

Finally, the Commission decisions can be subject to judicial review before the WAEMU Court of Justice. Member states, the Council of the WAEMU as well as private and judicial persons have to right to initiate such proceedings before the Court.[70] This also includes the right to initiate a judicial review of a Commission's decision that imposes a fine in order to reach a modification or annulment of that decision.[71]

7.1.3.2 Competition Law Cases of the WAEMU Commission

In contrast to the AndeanC, the WAEMU Commission has decided several cases, of which however only a few cases constituted competition law matters.[72] An evaluation of those legal cases reveals certain characteristics. Most cases involve state-related practices. Either member states are accused of distorting competition through the use of state aids or they are accused of interfering with the market by violating obligations set out by community law.[73] In the cases *SOCOCIM v the State*

[69] *Bakhoum/Molestina,* in: *Drexl/Bakhoum/Fox/Gal/Gerber,* Competition Policy and Regional Integration in Developing Countries, 2012, pp. 89, 94.

[70] Article 31 of Regulation no. 03/2002/CM/UEMOA; Article 8 of the Additional Protocol no. 1.

[71] For more information on the judicial control in the WAEMU, see in particular Part II, Dimension IV: Sect. 8.3.2.4.

[72] For example: Affaire ASKY or Affaire GAZODUC de l'Afrique de l'Ouest. *Tchapga,* La politique de la concurrence dans la CEMAC et l'UEMOA, 1 Conc. 237, 244 (2013). According to *Tchapga,* 23 of the 33 cases between 2007 and 2011 constituted tariff and non-tariff related trade barriers that affected the commercialization of several products on the common market and only 9 cases dealt with restrictive practices to competition.

[73] Examples for state aid related cases in WAEMU are: Affaire CAMEG; Décision invitant du Sénégal à retirer la norme NS 03-072.

of Senegal and Cement of Sahel[74] and *RUFSAC v the State of Senegal*,[75] the Commission held that the state of Senegal had infringed the Treaty of Dakar by granting exonerations from taxes to local enterprises.[76] Other cases deal with requests to clear a potential anticompetitive practice.[77] Three cases dealt with illicit agreements and abuse of dominance.[78]

There are only few cases coming from private initiatives.[79] The limited number can be explained by the centralized system on the one hand, which requires private parties to submit an enquiry in Ouagadougou. Especially for small and medium-sized enterprises geographical distance constitutes an obstacle, which increases costs. Moreover, a number of complaints by the private sector were withdrawn after notification by the national authorities that they would be referred to the WAEMU Commission.[80] It seems that the private sector still associates regional competition law enforcement with a high level of legal uncertainty. On the other hand, the private sector in general lacks a competition culture.

The largest number of cases involve state-imputed anticompetitive behaviour. Despite ongoing liberalization the WAEMU is still marked by state interventionism, national trade regulations and the activity of public monopolies and enterprises that are granted special rights by states, but conflict with WAEMU provisions.[81] This is in particular problematic with regard to the establishment of a common market, which relies on the abolition of trade barriers between the member states. The Commission's decisions that address state-imputed anticompetitive practices reflect the Commission's commitment to the creation of a common market. In this sense, the Commission acknowledges that effective enforcement of the regional competition

[74] Décision n° 05/2005/COM/UEMOA portant interdiction d'exonérer le clinker importe, rendered on 21 October 2005.

[75] Décision n° 08/2010/COM/UEMOA invitant l'Etat du Sénégal à mettre fin aux exonérations accordées sur les importations d'emballages en papier kraft, rendered on 1 August 2010.

[76] For a brief summary see *Bakhoum/Molestina*, in: *Drexl/Bakhoum/Fox/Gal/Gerber*, Competition Policy and Regional Integration in Developing Countries, 2012, pp. 89, 101.

[77] Affaire concentration entre SIFCA, COSMIVOIRE et al... et UNILEVER CI.

[78] Affaire Sotelma-Malitel contre Orange Mali (agreement), Affaire STAF contre SONAPOST et Etat du Burkina (abuse of dominance), Affaire CANAL OVERSEAS (abuse of dominance). For a brief summary see *Bakhoum/Molestina*, in: *Drexl/Bakhoum/Fox/Gal/Gerber*, Competition Policy and Regional Integration in Developing Countries, 2012, pp. 89, 102.

[79] Example for cases based on private initiative: Affaires SOCOCIM contre Etat du Sénégal et CIMENTS du Sahel.

[80] See, for instance, the Senegalese case *DHL v Société Nationale la Poste* (complaint of 13 October 2003) was forwarded to the WAEMU Commission; Annex 5 of *Commission Nationale de la Concurrence du Sénégal*, Rapport Public 2002–2003, p. 60; *UNCTAD*, Voluntary Peer Review on Competition Policies of WAEMU, Benin and Senegal, 2008, p. 149.

[81] *Goretti/Weisfeld*, Trade in the WAEMU: Developments and Reform Opportunities, 2008, p. 8 <http://www.imf.org/external/pubs/ft/wp/2008/wp0868.pdf> accessed 11 November 2018; *Bakhoum*, Delimitation and Exercise of Competence between the West African Economic and Monetary Union (WAEMU) and its Member States in Competition Policy, 29/4 W. Comp. 653, 679 (2006); *Bakhoum/Molestina*, in: *Drexl/Bakhoum/Fox/Gal/Gerber*, Competition Policy and Regional Integration in Developing Countries, 2012, pp. 89, 101f.

law and policy constitutes a fundamental pillar for the functioning of such a common market.

7.1.3.3 Conclusions on the Directorate of Competition in the WAEMU

While the number of decisions does not reflect the "real state of the art of competition on the territory of the union",[82] one has to acknowledge the progress that the WAEMU Commission, in particular the Directorate of Competition has made. External and internal factors limit the efficacy of the WAEMU Commission.

Internally the regional authority suffers from a strong administrative burden surrounding the presidency of the Commission. In a similar vein the involvement of the Directorate of Judicial Affairs makes the competition law related decision-making process prone to merely political influences. These internal factors are even aggravated by a lack of human and financial resources, in particular with regard to the large territory to which regional competition law applies.

External factors comprise insufficient cooperation with national competition law authorities, which are hesitant to refer cases to the regional authority. This is partly due to "psychological" considerations, as member states might be "frustrated" and not willing to cooperate.[83] On the other hand, national competition authorities merely lack the experience and know-how regarding the procedure to submit cases to the WAEMU authority.[84] Most probably for similar reasons, neither professional organisations nor consumer associations have altered their practice of addressing complaints directly to national agencies.[85] The uncertainty is even intensified by the remaining ambiguities of the centralized system in the WAEMU. As non-competition-related matters still remain within national legislative competence and outside of the exclusive competence of the WAEMU Commission, a clear-cut demarcation of competences between different authorities is very difficult and might often not be possible at all.

The large number of state-related complaints justifies a centralization regarding state aids and state-related anticompetitive practices. To discipline member states that still rely on price regulation and on an interventionist trade policy, a strong centralized entity completely detached from national structures seems preferable.[86]

[82] *UNCTAD,* Voluntary Peer Review on Competition Policies of WAEMU, Benin and Senegal, 2008, p. 64.

[83] *UNCTAD,* Voluntary Peer Review on Competition Policies of WAEMU, Benin and Senegal, 2008, p. 65.

[84] *UNCTAD,* Voluntary Peer Review on Competition Policies of WAEMU, Benin and Senegal, 2008, p. 63: The report refers to the case "MALITEL against Orange", in which the complaint was first lodged before the Mali competition authority and then referred to the WAEMU Commission. It was not clear whether the file was transmitted for simple information, opinion or in order to receive a decision.

[85] *UNCTAD,* Voluntary Peer Review on Competition Policies of WAEMU, Benin and Senegal, 2008, p. 109.

[86] *Bakhoum/Molestina,* in: *Drexl/Bakhoum/Fox/Gal/Gerber,* Competition Policy and Regional Integration in Developing Countries, 2012, pp. 89, 101.

The preponderance of cases that involve state-initiated practices implies the existence of cross-border effects. Hence, one can conclude that the majority of cases dealt with on the regional level also involved cross-border effects. In practice, the centralized system is thus to a certain extent attenuated.

7.2 National Competition Authorities Prior and After the Installation of the Regional Competition Authority

A common feature in the WAEMU, the AndeanC and the CARICOM is the variation of national institutional competition law landscape before the implementation of the regional competition law system. Each RTA comprised member states with an existing national competition legislation and operative authority, as well as member states without competition laws or an operative authority. After the implementation of the regional competition policy, the number of states without a national competition law has overall decreased and many of them are in the process of or have installed national competition authorities.[87]

7.2.1 National Competition Law Structures

First, the biggest differences lie within the distinction between common law and civil law systems. While national competition authorities in the CARICOM are mostly designed in accordance to the US model, in form of a judicial system, the domestic authorities in the WAEMU and the AndeanC follow an administrative model, similar to the European system, in which an authority enforces competition law.[88] The Peruvian competition authority, the INDECOPI, displays another particularity, as it is divided into an executive Technical Secretariat and the INDECOPI Tribunal, which functions as second and final administrative instance.

Second, national competition law authorities vary in their degree of independence. In some member states the national competition law authority, if existent at all, largely depends on public administration or forms a directorate in a national ministry of trade.[89] As the independence of a competition law authority is structurally reduced under such an institutional set-up, it bears the risk that competition law enforcement will be biased by political considerations or even adopts very interventionist measures, such as a direct price-control. Even in the case of a

[87] For more details on the impact of regional competition law on the national competition law system, see above Part II, Dimension II: Sect. 6.1 (WAEMU), Sect. 6.2 (CARICOM) and Sect. 6.3 (AndeanC).

[88] *De León*, An Institutional Assessment of Antitrust Policy, 2009, p. 537.

[89] *Bakhoum/Molestina*, in: *Drexl/Bakhoum/Fox/Gal/Gerber*, Competition Policy and Regional Integration in Developing Countries, 2012, pp. 89, 100.

structurally independent authority, this does not guarantee for independence from national governments.[90] It is a frequent practice that the staff of the competition agency also works for the ministry and that decisions have to be taken in the general ministry's interest or are of merely of an advisory nature.[91]

Finally, competition law authorities can also be designed as mixed authorities, covering not only competition law, but also other areas of law, such as consumer law or intellectual property.[92] For example, the Barbados Fair Trading Commission is also responsible for consumer protection and the Peruvian INDECOPI also constitutes the competent authority for the protection of intellectual property rights.

Despite the differences with regard to the institutional structure of national competition law agencies, one can discern certain features that are paradigmatic of competition authorities in developing countries. The lack of resources constitutes the main problem for competition agencies. This does not only incorporate financial resources and the lack of autonomy regarding an authority's budget, but mainly relates to the attraction of sufficient and adequately skilled personal. The Senegalese authority, which has been working relatively efficient and which was able to even discipline international companies such as *Air France*,[93] only had nine members at that time, of which only six were permanent agents and three deputies.[94] The lack of resources is even accentuated by political instabilities or corruption. In the Ivory Coast, political turbulences led to the termination of the national Commission's

---

[90] Investigation into the acquisition of Oceanic Digital (Jamaica) Limited by Digicel Jamaica Limited, Pursuant to Section 17 of the Fair Competition Act Staff Report December 8, 2011, Case no. 6997-11; Part II, Dimension I: Sect. 5.2.3.1.

[91] This was the case in Senegal, Benin and Mali; see *Bakhoum/Molestina*, in: *Drexl/Bakhoum/Fox/Gal/Gerber*, Competition Policy and Regional Integration in Developing Countries, 2012, pp. 89, 100. The situation is similar in Niger, see *Bakhoum*, A Developing-Country Perspective on "Global Competition", 28 October 2011, Chicago, pp. 8, 12.

[92] Generally on the integration of consumer law in a competition authority, see *Cseres*, Integrate or Separate. Institutional Design for the Enforcement of Competition Law and Consumer Law, 11 April 2013 <http://ssrn.com/abstract=2200908> accessed 11 November 2018.

[93] Decision no. 02-D-02, *Syndicat des agences de voyage contre Air France*: *Air France* was held in 2002 by the Senegalese Competition Commission to have abused its dominant position on the market of connections between Senegal and France by unilaterally imposing lower commission rates for travel agencies, which they had to accept because of their economic dependence. For more information see *CUTS*, Vers des régimes efficients de la concurrence par le renforcement des capacités dans des pays sélectionnés d'Afrique de l'Ouest, 2009, pp. 30f. Yet the case also demonstrates difficulties with regard to the qualification of the practice and the adoption of economic dependence approach. An appeal was submitted to the Council of State. However it was withdrawn in 2009. See *UNCTAD*, Voluntary Peer Review on Competition Policies of WAEMU, Benin and Senegal, 2008, p. 108; *Weick*, Competition Law and Policy in Senegal, 33/3 W. Comp. 521, 531 (2010).

[94] Senegal's Competition Commission, The Handbook of Competition Enforcement Agencies 2014, p. 271.

activities.[95] Similarly, the Peruvian INDECOPI[96] or the Colombian Superintendent of Industry and Trade have been subject to strong governmental influences.[97]

Other enforcement-related obstacles arise from a poor drafting of procedural and institutional provisions regarding a competition authority. This was the case of the Jamaican Fair Trading Commission, whose institutional structure was held to be in breach of the Jamaican constitution, because it did not sufficiently separate the adjudicating from the investigating power.[98]

7.2.2 National Competition Law Enforcement and National Sectorial Regulation[99]

In the progress of liberalization of sectors that are considered as strategic by member states state-owned monopolies or state-owned enterprises were privatized, but remained subject to sectorial regulation. Many member states in the WAEMU, the AndeanC and the CARICOM have created sector regulators and related regulatory laws.[100] In some instances, the lack of a national competition authority was

---

[95] *Bakhoum,* A Developing-Country Perspective on "Global Competition", 28 October 2011, Chicago, p. 10.

[96] Under the presidency of Alejandro Toledo "all of the members of INDECOPI's Antidumping Commission resigned on the same day and were replaced four days later by a Commission whose President was an oil executive and an official in Peru's National Industries Society. Shortly thereafter, the Commission's Technical Secretariat resigned.", see *OECD,* Competition Peer Review Report of Peru, 11/1 OECD J. Comp. L. Policy 177, 184 (2009); *OECD,* Peer Review on Competition Law and Policy in Colombia, 2009, p. 21.

[97] See the experiences of Emilio José Archila, former Superintendent for Industry and Trade, who had ruled against the merger of the airlines Avianca (state-owned) and Aces airlines in 2001. He was then replaced after the airlines had questioned his impartiality; see Airline Business, 1 October 2001, "Aces-Avianca faces new obstacles" <http://www.flightglobal.com/news/articles/aces-avianca-faces-new-obstacles-136853/> accessed 11 November 2018; El Tiempo, 02 July 2001, "Avianca gana el pulso" <http://www.eltiempo.com/archivo/documento/MAM-469166> accessed 11 November 2018. See also *Fox/Healey,* When the State harms Competition – The Role for Competition Law, 2013, p. 44 <http://ssrn.com/abstract=2248059> accessed 11 November 2018.

[98] For more information on the Jamaican competition law system, see above Part II, Dimension I: Sect. 5.2.3.1.

[99] The diversity of national sectorial regulation is only dealt with briefly in this study, because it would go beyond its scope. Yet the study highlights the implications that arise out of national sectorial regulation on regional competition law enforcement.

[100] With regard to Benin, Burkina Faso and Senegal in the WAEMU, see *UNCTAD,* Voluntary Peer Review on Competition Policies of WAEMU, Benin and Senegal, 2008, pp. 34f., 44f., 78ff., 137ff. With regard to Senegal, see *Weick,* Competition Law and Policy in Senegal, 33/3 W. Comp. 521, 534ff. (2010). With regard to Colombia and Peru, see *De León,* An Institutional Assessment of Antitrust Policy, 2009, pp. 441ff. With regard to Barbados and the OECS in the CARICOM, see *Sampson/Sampson,* in: *Mehta/Evenett,* Politics Triumphs Economics?, 2009, pp. 327, 336ff.

compensated by regulatory authorities that apply competition rules, above all merger control regulation in specific sectors.[101]

However, although national competition law enforcement and sectorial control overlap regarding their objectives, by defending "the public interest against monopoly power (...) they vary in scope and types of intervention."[102] As a consequence, co-existence of national sectorial regulation and national competition laws requires clear horizontal demarcation criteria. A lack of clear-cut demarcation criteria might lead to forum shopping and possible enforcement loopholes.[103] In the three RTAs, these demarcation criteria vary. In fact, in Jamaica, the Privy Council held that competition law also applied to the regulated telecommunication sector. In some instances, national competition laws—if existent at all—always override national sectorial regulation or vice versa. Other national jurisdictions apply a concurrent system.[104] Barbados adopted a mixed authority for the administration of competition policy and utility regulation.[105]

Without going into the pros and cons of sectorial regulation and competition policy or possible synergies of both, in a regional competition law the diversity of national sector regulation and competition policy causes difficulties. In the absence of clear-cut provisions that govern the hierarchy between national sectorial regulation and regional competition law national sector regulation can be used to circumvent the application of regional competition law. This creates obstacles for convergent application of regional competition law, because member states will be inclined to mainly incorporate national interest considerations in the application of national sectorial regulation. This phenomenon is relatively new and there have not been open conflicts between regional competition law and national sectorial regulation so far.[106]

---

[101] *De León*, An Institutional Assessment of Antitrust Policy, 2009, p. 453. This was for example the case in Bolivia. See above Part II, Dimension I: Sect. 5.2.2.2 and Part II, Dimension II: Sect. 6.3.3.

[102] *De León*, An Institutional Assessment of Antitrust Policy, 2009, p. 420.

[103] For examples of unsynchronised Regulations and Competition Laws, see *Mehta/Agarwal/Singh*, Politics Trumps Economics, 2007, pp. 29ff.; *De León*, An Institutional Assessment of Antitrust Policy, 2009, pp. 456ff.

[104] *De León* provides a brief overview of the competence demarcation criteria in some states of Latin America, see *De León*, An Institutional Assessment of Antitrust Policy, 2009, pp. 441ff.

[105] *Sampson/Sampson*, in: *Mehta/Evenett*, Politics Triumphs Economics?, 2009, pp. 327, 344ff.

[106] According to the Peer review of the *UNCTAD* with regards to the WAEMU, "it might be that in the absence of confirmation by future decisions of the national and community competition authorities, in case of conflict of jurisdiction, the specific regulation might have precedence over community law." See *UNCTAD*, Voluntary Peer Review on Competition Policies of WAEMU, Benin and Senegal, 2008, p. 35. Yet, all practices that fall under Article 88 of the Treaty of Dakar also underlie the principle of primacy of regional law; see above Part II, Dimension II: Sect. 6.1.

7.2.3 Conclusions on National Competition Law Enforcement and Institutional Structures

The lack of sufficient resources and the lack of sufficient independence are omnipresent obstacles for competition law enforcement that exist, irrespective of the adopted institutional form and design of a national authority. Determining for the efficiency of competition law enforcement in member states is mostly the commitment of a national agency's staff. Although the installation of regional competition law regimes has led to a spread of newly created national competition agencies, it only had a limited impact on domestic competition authorities that had already existed prior to the implementation of the regional system. Moreover, the adopted institutional structure of a newly established national competition law authority seems to be more influenced by legal tradition than by the regional authority's design.[107]

With regard to sectorial regulation, one can make two observations based on the experiences of the member states of the WAEMU, the AndeanC and the CARICOM: (1) In addition to regional competition policy, there have been attempts to harmonize sectorial regulation, for example in the form of regional sectorial Directives.[108] (2) The introduction of a regional competition-law framework has to some extent incited the implementation of specialized national competition law structures, as specialized competition authorities were established and specialized competition laws were adopted in addition to national sectorial agencies and regulation.[109] Some member states had attributed their national sectorial regulation authorities with competences as regards regional competition law enforcement.[110] Likewise, in some member states both sector agencies and national competition authorities assist the regional competition authority in regional competition law enforcement.[111]

---

[107] Regarding the diversity of institutional design among European competition authorities, see *Cseres,* Integrate or Separate. Institutional Design for the Enforcement of Competition Law and Consumer Law, 11 April 2013 <http://ssrn.com/abstract=2200908> accessed 11 November 2018.

[108] In the WAEMU, sector regulation harmonization was attempted in the agriculture, transport, banking and financial, insurance companies, energy and telecommunications sector. See *UNCTAD,* Voluntary Peer Review on Competition Policies of WAEMU, Benin and Senegal, 2008, p. 34. In the AndeanC, harmonization of economic policies is considered essential for the increase of intra-community trade; see in this regard Secretariat General, "Armonización de Políticas Económicas en la Comunidad Andina", document of 18 September 1998, <http://www20.iadb.org/intal/catalogo/PE/2011/07349.pdf> accessed 30 August 2017. In the CARICOM, harmonization of laws includes a harmonisation of provisions related to companies, intellectual property, as well as to economic, fiscal and monetary measures that are supposed to strengthen the CSME <http://www.caricom.org/jsp/single_market/single_market_index.jsp?menu=csme> accessed 11 November 2018.

[109] See above Part II, Dimension II: Sect. 6.1 (WAEMU), Sect. 6.2 (CARICOM) and Sect. 6.3 (AndeanC).

[110] This was the case in Benin as a member state of the WAEMU.

[111] This is the case in Barbados and Jamaica in the CARICOM.

Chapter 8
Dimension IV: Enforcement Procedures of Regional Competition Law in the Narrow Sense

In order to draw conclusions on the vertical allocation of competences, the enforcement in the narrow sense of regional competition law is of vital importance.[1] Enforcement is a multi-layered process, which at each stage might attribute competition law competences to different entities.

The assessment of an enforcement procedure's effectiveness is difficult. Different measurements to evaluate a performance are at hand:[2] The mere number of investigated cases does not appear as a valid evaluation criterion.[3] The mere focus on the duration of an investigation is not representative either, as it does not express whether legitimate interests and rights of the participating parties have been sufficiently taken into account in the evaluation of a case. Rather, an analysis of enforcement procedures of regional competition law has to bear in mind several aspects of legal certainty, but also specific competition-related issues. A competition law process has to respect the right of defence, adequate time limits and has to adhere to the principles of transparency and accountability.[4]

---

[1] Under the three examined Regional Trade Agreements enforcement of national competition law (in the WAEMU the legislative competence on competition law related matters is concentrated on the community level) takes place without any involvement of the regional entity. Enforcement is a merely national process, shaped by national procedural provisions. Consequently, this study only focuses on the enforcement of regional competition law.

[2] *Kovacic,* Using Ex Post Evaluations to Improve the Performance of Competition Policy Authorities, 31 J. Corp. L. 503, 506ff. (2006).

[3] *Kovacic/Hollman/Grant,* How does your competition agency measure up?, 7 Eur. Comp. J. 25, 26ff. (2011); *ICN,* Seminar on Competition Agency Effectiveness, 2009, p. 10.

[4] This is in particular relevant in order to increase public support for an agency's functions, *Kovacic/Hollman/Grant,* How does your competition agency measure up?, 7 Eur. Comp. J. 25, 31 (2011).

J. Molestina, *Regional Competition Law Enforcement in Developing Countries*, Munich Studies on Innovation and Competition 9,
https://doi.org/10.1007/978-3-662-58525-2_8

8.1 Regional Competition Law Enforcement Procedures

Competition law enforcement entails several steps. It does not only encompass the conduct of a specific competition law investigation, which includes the decision regarding the initiation of an investigation, the handling of the investigation itself and finally the decision-making. The final decision can take the form of a fine or a settlement or non-monetary measures. The decision then has to be enforced in its specific form. Competition law authorities ideally also conduct market studies regarding specific sectors and engage in competition advocacy. The latter has gained increasing importance for its capacity to proliferate awareness of competition policy, to establish a competition culture and to attribute to competition law deterrence in the long run.[5]

8.1.1 Regional Competition Law Investigations

In the WAEMU, Regulation no. 03/2002/CM/UEMOA[6] distinguishes four types of proceedings: a notification procedure aiming at the granting of a negative clearance or individual exemption under Article 88 lit. a) and b) of the Treaty of Dakar,[7] proceedings based on a complaint,[8] proceedings relative to the adoption of a block exemption[9] and proceedings relative to state-related practices.[10]

The WAEMU Commission has issued several negative clearance decisions, namely on the realization of the *GAZODUC* project[11] and on a project of

[5] *De León*, An Institutional Assessment of Antitrust Policy, 2009, p. 384.

[6] With regard to the procedural powers of the WAEMU Commission, Regulation no. 03/2002/CM/UEMOA is largely modelled after the European Regulation 17/62/CE.

[7] Articles 3, 7 and Chapter I of Regulation no. 03/2002/CM/UEMOA.

[8] Articles 4, 5 and Chapter II of Regulation no. 03/2002/CM/UEMOA.

[9] Article 6 of Regulation no. 03/2002/CM/UEMOA.

[10] Regulation n° 02/2002/CM/UEMOA, relatif aux pratiques anticoncurrentielles à l'intérieur de l'UEMOA, 23 May 2002; Regulation n° 04/2002/CM/UEMOA, relatif aux aides d'Etat à l'intérieur de l'UEMOA et aux modalities d'application de l'article 88 (c) du Traité, 23 May 2002.

[11] Décision n° 06/2004/COM/UEMOA portant Decision de ne pas soulever d'objections à l'égard des lois portant diverses dispositions relatives au regime juridique et fiscal unique et harmonise applicable dans la République du Bénin et dans la République Togolaise dans le cadre de la réalisation du projet GAZODUC de l'Afrique de l'Ouest, 23 December 2004 (Actually this case concerned a notification of a state aid according to Article 5 of Regulation 04/2002/CM/UEMOA) and Décision n° 002/2005/COM/UEMOA portant attestation negative à l'égard des accords créant des entreprises communes dans le cadre de la réalisation, de l'exploitation du GAZODUC de l'Afrique de l'Ouest et de la vente du gaz naturel sur les marchés du Bénin et du Togo, 21 January 2005. For more information on the details of the latter case, see also *Bakhoum*, L'articulation du droit communautaire et des droits nationaux de la concurrence dans l'Union Economique et Monétaire Ouest Africaine, 2007, pp. 172ff.

concentration between several enterprises in the palm oil industry.[12] In both cases, member states (Benin and Togo) had requested a prior negative exemption.[13]

In the former European Community the inclusion of prior notification requirements was considered necessary in order to provide for more legal certainty[14] because of the lack of a competition culture and in order to guarantee uniform application of community competition law.[15] On the other hand, a notification requirement was held capable of overcoming an information deficit regarding business practices.[16] These aspects clearly also apply to the situation in the WAEMU and justify a centralization of procedural powers.[17] On the other hand, the European experience demonstrates that centralization of procedural powers is highly resource consuming and in the long run counteracted the goal of legal certainty.[18] Whereas in young competition law jurisdictions there might exist a greater necessity for legal certainty, the complete withdrawal of national competition law competences does not constitute the only instrument to achieve this goal. Moreover, in particular the combined effects of the large territorial scope of application, the exclusive application competence of the regional authority, the notification requirement and the scarce human resources in the WAEMU Commission with regard to competition law matters render competition law enforcement in the WAEMU inefficient.[19]

The WAEMU Commission can initiate an investigation *ex officio* or on demand of an enterprise, an association of enterprises, of a private party or a member state.[20]

---

[12] Décision n° 009/2008/COM/UEMOA portant attestation negative à l'egard du Projet de Concentration entre les Sociétés UNILEVER-CI, SIFCA, COSMIVOIRE, PALMCI, NAUVU, PHCI, SHCI et, SANIA, 22 October 2008.

[13] Décision n° 06/2004/COM/UEMOA portant Decision de ne pas soulever d'objections à l'égard des lois portant diverses dispositions relatives au regime juridique et fiscal unique et harmonise applicable dans la République du Bénin et dans la République Togolaise dans le cadre de la réalisation du projet GAZODUC de l'Afrique de l'Ouest, 23 December 2004.

[14] Regulation 17/62 was criticized for not adequately contributing to an increase in legal certainty and for on the other hand creating administrative inefficiencies with regard to the workload of the Commission. The practice of non-binding comfort letters did not create legal certainty and even agreements with little or no effect on competition were still illegal; see *Wißmann,* Decentralised Enforcement of EC Competition Law and the New Policy on Cartels, 23/2 W. Comp. 123, 130 (2000); *Venit,* The Modernization and Decentralization of Enforcement under Articles 81 and 82 of the EC Treaty, 40 C. M. L. Rev. 545, 550 (2003).

[15] *Wesseling,* The Modernisation of EC Antitrust Law, 2000, p. 21.

[16] *Wesseling,* The Modernisation of EC Antitrust Law, 2000, p. 20.

[17] *Bakhoum,* L'articulation du droit communautaire et des droits nationaux de la concurrence dans l'Union Economique et Monétaire Ouest Africaine, 2007, p. 175.

[18] The Commission was unable to deal rapidly and efficiently with the enormous amount of notifications. The granting of comfort letters was unable to compensate for a Commission's decision for the lack of bindingness and the relatively little reasoning, as well as their low degree of publicity; see *Montag,* The Case for a Reform of Regulation 17/62, 22 Fordham Int'l. L.J. 819, 826ff. (1998); see also *Ehlermann,* Implementation of EC Competition Law by National Anti-Trust Authorities, 17 ECLR 88 (1996).

[19] For a final analysis of the inclusion of a prior notification requirement in regional competition law in developing countries, see Part III, Dimension IV: Sect. 12.4.1.2.

[20] Articles 8 to 14 of Regulation no. 03/2002/CM/UEMOA.

Any physical or moral person can submit a complaint.[21] The majority of the Commission's cases had been initiated following a submitted request, of which most were submitted by member states. Directive no. 02/2002/CM/UEMOA accordingly states that the national structures exercise permanent market surveillance. They assure a general inquiry mission, either based on national initiative or on an express mandate by the Commission.[22] Thus, despite the adoption of a centralized system, the task of market surveillance is still shared between the Commission and the national competition law authorities.

Moreover, submitting a request does not depend on difficult formalities: a notification regarding a negative clearance or individual exemption only requires the submission of a single formula "N" and its annexes,[23] complaints can be submitted in a written or oral form.[24] However, the final decision regarding the initiation of a process lies solely within the Commission. The internal procedural rules of the Commission also apply to this initiating decision, thus the Directorate of Competition has to get the signature of the President of the Commission. More than submitting a request to the Commission, member states of the WAEMU can also engage in an investigation on their proper initiative. However, they are obliged to inform the WAEMU Commission immediately and the investigations have to be based on community competition law.[25] Apart from instances, in which regional law is used by a member state against another member state, it is improbable that national authorities will be active investigators of potential breaches of Community competition law. They often lack sufficient resources and the political will to cooperate with the WAEMU Commission.[26]

A special type of *ex officio* proceeding of the WAEMU Commission is the possibility to conduct sectorial investigations. According to Article 19 of Regulation no. 03/2002/CM/UEMOA, in the case that the evolution of trade or price rigidity in an economic sector indicates a distortion of competition, the Commission can conduct sectorial investigations or market studies on competition and is generally held to incite discussions among the affected economic actors and regional and national institutions. According to Article 19(2) of Regulation no. 03/2002/CM/UEMOA, the Commission also publishes an annual report on the status of competition in the WAEMU. More generally, the Department of the regional market, trade, competition

---

[21] Article 12 of Regulation no. 03/2002/CM/UEMOA.

[22] Article 3(1) of Directive no. 02/2002/CM/UEMOA: "Les structures nationales de concurrence assurent une mission générale d'enquête, sur initiative nationale ou sur mandate esprès de la Commission, conformément aux pouvoirs et aux procedures d'investigation prévus par le droit communautaire et les droits nationaux. A ce titre, elles mènent une activité permanente de surveillance du marché afin de déceler les dysfonctionnements lies aux pratiques anticoncurrentielles."

[23] Article 10 and Articles 18ff. of Regulation no. 03/2002/CM/UEMOA.

[24] Article 13 of Regulation no. 03/2002/CM/UEMOA.

[25] Article 3(1) of Directive no. 02/2002/CM/UEMOA; *Bakhoum,* L'articulation du droit communautaire et des droits nationaux de la concurrence dans l'Union Economique et Monétaire Ouest Africaine, 2007, p. 220.

[26] *Bakhoum,* L'articulation du droit communautaire et des droits nationaux de la concurrence dans l'Union Economique et Monétaire Ouest Africaine, 2007, p. 221.

and cooperation is responsible for supervising common policies in the Union, such as competition related policies.[27]

In the AndeanC, national authorities that are competent for competition matters, national organizations of integration and every natural or judicial person of public or private law or consumer organization can initiate an investigation, too.[28]

The *ex officio* competence of the Secretariat General was only introduced by Decision 608.[29] During the meetings of governmental experts it was even discussed whether such a competence would contradict Article 93 of the Agreement of Cartagena and infringe the principle of subsidiarity.[30] Article 93 of the Agreement of Cartagena deals with economic competition and sets out the legislative mission to enact provisions that protect competition in the region. The article determines that the Secretariat General has to guarantee the application of such norms in particular cases, which are brought to it.[31] From this it was partly deduced, that the Secretariat General's activities were limited to cases of complaints. However, Article 93 has to be interpreted as "attributive" and not "prohibitive" norm, thereby only "attributing" the Secretariat General with additional competences, rather than limiting it to specific cases.[32] Additionally, an *ex officio* competence of the Secretariat General was also held to be compatible with the principle of subsidiarity, since it only touched upon matters of concern of the region and not of the individual member states.[33] However so far, the Secretariat General has neither initiated an investigation under Decision 608, nor has it conducted a sectorial analysis.

The requirements for a positive decision on the initiation of an investigation are set out in Article 11 of Decision 608. While Article 11 lit. a) through c) mostly concern formal requirements, lit. d) and lit. e) call for a description of the affected goods or services and sufficient evidence of proof. In the case of a request, the Secretariat General can grant 15 or even 20 additional days in order for the applicant to fulfil these requirements.[34] At this stage of a competition-law procedure, it is not necessary to conclusively prove the anticompetitive practice entirely, but a moderate level of evidence is sufficient.[35] According to Article 13 of Decision 608, the

---

[27] On the functions of the Department of the regional market, trade, competition and cooperation in WAEMU <http://www.uemoa.int/Pages/UEMOA/Commission%20de%20L_UEMOA/commissaires_dmrc.aspx> accessed 11 November 2018.

[28] Article 10 of Decision 608.

[29] Article 10 of Decision 608.

[30] Informe de la Cuarta Reunion de Expertos Gubernamentales en Materia de Libre Competencia, SG/REG.LC/IV/INFORME, 1 August 2003, pp. 3ff.

[31] Art. 93 Agreement of Cartagena: "Corresponderá a la Secretaría General velar por la aplicación de dichas normas en los casos particulares que se denuncien".

[32] Informe de la Cuarta Reunion de Expertos Gubernamentales en Materia de Libre Competencia, SG/REG.LC/IV/INFORME, 1 August 2003, p. 3.

[33] Informe de la Cuarta Reunion de Expertos Gubernamentales en Materia de Libre Competencia, SG/REG.LC/IV/INFORME, 1 August 2003, p. 3.

[34] Article 13 of Decision 608.

[35] *Stucchi López Raygada,* La Integración en la Comunidad Andina y su Sistema de Protección y Promoción de la Libre Competencia, 2 Rev. Comp. Propriedad Intelectual 71, 91 (2006).

Secretariat General has 15 days after the submission of a complete request to decide on an opening of an investigation. The decision of the Secretariat General, in the form of a Resolution, has to be published in the Official Journal of the Agreement of Cartagena[36] and has to be communicated to the affected parties, namely the applicant for investigation, the denunciated or concerned national competition law authorities.[37] The Resolution has to contain a description of the concerned practice, a time frame for the submission of information and has to identify the national competition law authorities that will have to cooperate with the regional authority for the undertaking of the investigation.[38]

In contrast to the former European and the WAEMU system, the Andean competition law does not include a prior notification requirement. Moreover, only member states can request the Secretariat General to grant an individual exemption.[39]

In the CARICOM,[40] the CARICOM Competition Commission[41] shares the competence to request the initiation of an investigation with the COTED[42] and the member states.[43] The term "member state" in Article 175(1) RTC includes national governments, as well as national competition authorities and national consumer protection authorities. However, Article 175(1) RTC only entitles a member state to request an investigation under the premise that the respective enterprise is located in another member state and "prejudices trade and prevents, restricts or distorts competition in the territory of the requesting member state". The provision thus excludes a general monitoring task of member states regarding anticompetitive practices on the common market.

Private parties, such as individuals or firms, cannot address the CARICOM Competition Commission directly in order to request an investigation regarding regional anticompetitive practices. They must address their governments or national competition authority, which then at their discretion request an investigation of the CARICOM Competition Commission.[44] It is questionable whether Chapter VIII likewise intended to exclude national consumer associations or manufacturers associations to address the CARICOM Competition Commission directly. Although they represent private entities, they enhance efficient surveillance of the regional market. Notwithstanding a clear cut answer, private entities and their representative associations can still find "creative ways"[45] to bring a matter to the notice of the

[36] "Gaceta Oficial del Acuerdo de Cartagena".

[37] Article 13 of Decision 608.

[38] Article 14 of Decision 608.

[39] Article 6 of Decision 608.

[40] In the CARICOM, one has to carefully differentiate between the preliminary assessment phase, the investigation phase conducted by the Investigating Panel and the enquiry conducted by the Adjudicating Panel of the CARICOM Competition Commission.

[41] Article 174 of the Revised Treaty of Chaguaramas.

[42] Article 175(2) of the Revised Treaty of Chaguaramas.

[43] Article 175(1) of the Revised Treaty of Chaguaramas.

[44] *CARICOM Secretariat,* Competition Policy and Law in the CSME, 2010, p. 17.

[45] This statement was made by the current chairman of the CARICOM Competition Commission, Kusha Haraksingh, in an interview with the author in Port-of-Spain, Trinidad and Tobago on 26 October 2012.

CARICOM Competition Commission, thereby invoking its *ex officio* investigation initiation right. One can thus hope that the CARICOM Competition Commission will establish collaborative working relations with civil society organizations and will rely on their voluntary compliance, thereby using them as "watchdogs" for the competition authority.[46]

Article 180 of the Revised Treaty of Chaguaramas covers negative clearance rulings.[47] Article 183(2) RTC provides for exemption mechanisms. Yet similar to the AndeanC, negative clearance rulings are only available for member states and exemptions by the CARICOM Competition Commission may only be granted on request of the COTED or a member state.

Regarding the *ex officio* initiation right in the CARICOM, it is interesting to note that Article 175(2) RTC, which governs COTED's requesting right, is differently worded than Article 175(1) RTC, which governs the member states' requesting right. Article 175(2) RTC requires a conduct of an enterprise in the CSME that "distorts competition within the CSME and has or is likely to have cross-border effects", whereas Article 175(1) RTC does not include "likely" effects. It is unclear whether the slight difference in wording refers to different required degrees of probability in order to request an investigation. In any event, Article 175(3) RTC requires both—member states and the COTED—to provide the CARICOM Competition Commission with sufficient information to make a preliminary assessment. Such information will also have to include arguments in favour of the likelihood of a cross-border effect. Additionally, it is the CARICOM Competition Commission that ultimately decides on the appropriate measures that will be adopted.[48]

A potential hurdle to effective monitoring of the Caribbean market arises from possible exemptions of national competition laws through (partially exempted) national sectorial regulation. While competition authorities and regulatory bodies in member states have often managed to cooperate and communicate horizontally, this does not automatically apply to vertical cooperation with the CARICOM Competition Commission. Cross-border supervision and collaboration among sectorial institutions, such as among the financial institutions, are lacking.[49] Interestingly, the *CARIFORUM-EC Economic Partnership Agreement* has recognized this flaw and has incorporated Article 129(5), according to which the CARIFORUM-EC Trade and Development Committee has to be informed about sectorial rules. The

---

[46] *CARICOM Secretariat,* Competition Policy and Law in the CSME, 2010, p. 20.

[47] The negative clearance ruling has in many instances been criticized for being very resource consuming, see *Stewart,* in: *Drexl/Bakhoum/Fox/Gal/Gerber,* Competition Policy and Regional Integration in Developing Countries, 2012, pp. 161, 180. The future experiences of the CARICOM Competition Commission will show how often member states will actually use Article 180 of the Revised Treaty of Chaguaramas.

[48] Article 174(1) of the Revised Treaty of Chaguaramas, see also below Part II, Dimension IV: Sect. 8.1.1.2.

[49] *Stewart,* in: *Drexl/Bakhoum/Fox/Gal/Gerber,* Competition Policy and Regional Integration in Developing Countries, 2012, pp. 161, 179.

Revised Treaty of Chaguaramas in Article 170(5) sets out the obligation that "member states shall notify COTED of existing legislation (...) inconsistent with the provision [of Chapter VIII]". However, for the lack of regional provisions that govern the relation between competition law and national sectorial regulation,[50] Article 170(5) RTC does not sufficiently guarantee that the COTED (not mentioning the CARICOM Competition Commission) is comprehensively informed about national sectorial legislation and related practices.

Subject to a request of the COTED or a member state, the CARICOM Competition Commission "may in respect of cross-border transactions or transactions with cross-border effects, monitor, investigate, detect, make determinations or take action to inhibit and penalise enterprises whose business conduct prejudices trade or prevents, restricts or distorts competition within the CSME".[51] The utilization of the verb "may" instead of "shall" demonstrates that the CARICOM Competition Commission is vested with discretion to take the steps that it considers necessary and appropriate. The CARICOM Competition Commission is however obliged to consult the "interested parties", namely the COTED or the involved member state(s).[52] This consultation shall be concluded within 30 days of the date of receipt of the request of investigation, but parties can agree to extend the period.[53]

Requests for an investigation by the COTED and by the member states have to be in writing and disclose sufficient information for the CARICOM Competition Commission to make a preliminary assessment of the matter.[54] In *Trinidad Cement Limited v The Competition Commission* the Caribbean Court of Justice specified some requirements for a request by the COTED, but also underlined the particularities in case the Commission wants to initiate an investigation based on its *ex officio* power, in accordance with Article 176(1) RTC.

The use of the word "may" in Article 175(1) RTC demonstrates that member states are not obliged to refer cases to the regional competition authority. In the same vein, Chapter VIII lacks sanctioning mechanisms, but relies on the general willingness of national structures to cooperate. Yet many member states have enacted national provisions and also the *CARICOM Model Law on Competition* includes a provision that replicates Article 175(1) RTC as an obligation.[55] Article 175(1) RTC therefore reflects an underlying presumption of Chapter VIII that

---

[50] See above Part II, Dimension II: Sect. 6.2.

[51] Article 174(1) of the Revised Treaty of Chaguaramas.

[52] Article 175(4) of the Revised Treaty of Chaguaramas.

[53] Article 175(5) of the Revised Treaty of Chaguaramas.

[54] Article 175(3) of the Revised Treaty of Chaguaramas.

[55] For example Article 48(1) of the Fair Trading Act of Trinidad and Tobago: "Where an inquiry or investigation by the Commission involves anti-competitive conduct in another Member State, which has the effect of lessening competition in Trinidad and Tobago, the Commission shall (...) refer the matter to the Community Competition Commission." See also Article 54(1) of the CARICOM Model Law on Competition: "Where the Commission seeks to determine whether conduct by an enterprise in another Member State prejudices trade and prevents, restricts or distorts competition in (...), the Commission shall refer the matter to the Community Competition Commission".

national competition authorities are generally willing to cooperate with the CARICOM Competition Commission.

If the CARICOM Competition Commission wants to conduct an investigation based on its *ex officio* competence, Article 176(1) RTC obliges it to request a preliminary assessment by the according national competition authority within a time determined by the CARICOM Competition Commission. It is only if the regional competition authority is unsatisfied with the outcome of the preliminary examination that it shall conduct its own preliminary examination. One should stress the underlying conception, that ideally the *ex officio* investigation right of the CARICOM Competition Commission is conducted solely by the respective national competition authority. However, some jurisdictions of the member states have not amended national legislation and still do not provide for rules that allow preliminary examination at the request of an external body.[56] Furthermore, it is not defined how extensive this preliminary assessment by the member states ought to be. While Article 176(1) RTC is broadly formulated, the introduction of the CARICOM Competition Commission Rules of Procedure indicates that the preliminary assessment is primarily supposed to deal with the determination of the jurisdiction of the Commission.[57]

After the preliminary examinations of the national and regional competition authorities, the Commission and member state shall jointly identify the competent authority to investigate—if such investigation is required based on the preliminary examination.[58] In case of arising disputes, the CARICOM Competition Commission cannot continue with the investigation, but has to await a decision of the COTED in accordance with Article 176(5) lit. a) and lit. b) of the Revised Treaty.[59] The COTED can thereby limit the *ex officio* investigation initiation right of the CARICOM Competition Commission. The CARICOM Competition Commission's expertise on potential preventions, restrictions or distortions within the CSME might thus be overruled by a merely political institution, such as the COTED, which is composed of representatives from national governments.

On the other hand, in case of the requesting competence of member states and the COTED,[60] the CARICOM Competition Commission is entitled to decide on the jurisdiction after consultation with the interested parties.[61] However, the Revised Treaty does not provide for a resolution by the COTED in case of conflicts between

---

[56] On Jamaica see *Stewart*, in: *Drexl/Bakhoum/Fox/Gal/Gerber*, Competition Policy and Regional Integration in Developing Countries, 2012, pp. 161, 194.

[57] "By Article 176 of the Treaty it was agreed that where the Commission has reason to believe that business conduct by an enterprise in the CSME prejudices trade and prevents, restricts or distorts competition within the CSME and has cross-border effects, the Commission shall request the national competition authority to undertake a preliminary examination, *as a result of which it may be determined that the Commission has jurisdiction to conduct an investigation.*" (emphasis added), CARICOM Competition Commission Rules of Procedure, 2011.

[58] Article 176(4) of the Revised Treaty of Chaguaramas.

[59] Article 176(5) of the Revised Treaty of Chaguaramas.

[60] Article 175(1) and (2) of the Revised Treaty of Chaguaramas.

[61] Article 175(4) of the Revised Treaty of Chaguaramas.

the Commission and a member state regarding the initiation of an investigation. Although Article 176(6) RTC determines that member states can initiate a judicial proceeding before the Caribbean Court of Justice at any time, the provision does not resolve whether such judicial control would halt a Commission's investigation or parts of it.[62] The same ambiguity arises with regard to Article 175(12) RTC, which establishes that "[a] party which is aggrieved by a determination of the Commission under paragraph 4 of Article 174 in any matter may apply to the Court for a review of that determination".

In the *Trinidad Cement Limited v The Competition Commission* decision the Caribbean Court of Justice highlighted the Rule 74 of the CARICOM Competition Commission Rules of Procedure, according to which the Adjudicating Panel[63] of the Commission "may adjourn the whole or any part of the enquiry pending the determination of the question or issue".[64] Irrespective of the absence of a mandatory nature of Rule 74, it is thus probable that the CARICOM Competition Commission will conduct investigations, but halt the enquiry and await a possible Caribbean Court of Justice's decision. The Caribbean Court of Justice held that TCL could have awaited a decision of the Adjudicating Panel of the CARICOM Competition Commission and that ordinarily, the regional Court would not control procedural steps before an enquiry of the Commission.[65]

8.1.1.1 Trinidad Cement Limited v CARICOM Competition Commission: Judgement of the Caribbean Court of Justice[66]

In the judgement *Trinidad Cement Limited v CARICOM Competition Commission*, the Caribbean Court of Justice had to deal with several issues of competition law enforcement, which arose in the context of the first case of the CARICOM Competition Commission. The first case concerned an alleged abuse of dominant position by Trinidad Cement Limited.[67]

---

[62] *Beckford* already raised this question prior to the *Trinidad Limited Cement v Caricom Competition Commission* Judgement of the Caribbean Court of Justice; see *Beckford*, The Appropriate Design and Enforcement of Competition Law and Policy in Countries at Different Stages of Market Development, 26–28 May 2010, Brasilia, p. 7. However, the problem only arises in situations, in which member state is trying to circumvent the conduct of an investigation contrary to the request of another member state or the COTED, in which it might have been overruled.

[63] The CARICOM Competition Commission is divided in an investigative and adjudicating panel. See below Part II, Dimension IV: Sect. 8.1.2.

[64] *Trinidad Cement Limited v The Competition Commission*, Caribbean Court of Justice Application No. OA 1 of 2012, CCJ 4 (OJ), [17].

[65] *Ibid.*

[66] For clarification purposes, the judgement of the Caribbean Court of Justice is already briefly dealt with at this point of the study. The details of the arguments by the parties and the Caribbean Court of Justice, if not analysed directly at this point, can be found in the according chapter of the study. References to the according chapters will be indicated in the footnotes.

[67] Guyana had already in a prior case before the Caribbean Court of Justice made allegations against Trinidad Cement Limited arguing that it had abused its dominant position in the regional

On the 26th meeting of COTED on 24–25 November 2008, COTED requested the Commission to "advise" whether there was sufficient evidence to conduct a preliminary assessment of an alleged anticompetitive business practice by the Trinidad Cement Limited Group.[68] The Caribbean Court of Justice held that this request did not fulfil the requirements set out in Article 175(3) RTC. On 15 December 2009, the Secretary General, who had also attended COTED's meeting in his former function as Assistant Secretary General for Trade and Economic Integration, send a request to the CARICOM Competition Commission to investigate against the TCL Group, also citing the resolution made by COTED and stating that it would act on behalf of COTED.[69] The CARICOM Competition Commission answered the Secretary General on 10 February 2010 pointing out the ambiguities between COTED's first resolution and the Secretary General's request.[70] The latter replied by acknowledging the Commission's concern and proposed to the COTED to expressly request the Commission to initiate an investigation on 26 March 2010 and 13 April 2010.[71] However, before the COTED actually complied with the proposition, the CARICOM Competition Commission initiated investigations on 16 April 2010. After the conclusion of the preliminary assessment of the matter by the Investigating Panel of the CARICOM Competition Commission, the Commission decided to conduct an enquiry. After being informed about this decision, Trinidad Cement Limited filed a declaration on 1 February 2012 that the CARICOM Competition Commission's decisions to initiate an investigation and to hold an enquiry were void.[72]

Trinidad Cement Limited's first argument referred to the definition of "interested party" in the meaning of Article 175 of the Revised Treaty of Chaguaramas. It argued that it should already have been consulted and informed during the initial stages, during the preliminary assessment, of the investigation by the Investigating Panel of the CARICOM Competition Commission. However, the Caribbean Court of Justice mainly declined TCL's argument, because the interest of the Commission in safeguarding an effective investigation outweighed the early notification interest

cement market through price discrimination in terms of Article 179(1) lit. g) of the Revised Treaty of Chaguaramas. *Trinidad Cement Limited and TCL Guyana Incorporated v The State of the Co-operative Republic of Guyana,* Caribbean Court of Justice Application No. OA 2 of 2009, CCJ 5 (OJ), [17]; *Trinidad Cement Limited v The Competition Commission,* Caribbean Court of Justice Application No. OA 1 of 2012, CCJ 4 (OJ), [47].

[68] *Trinidad Cement Limited v The Competition Commission,* Caribbean Court of Justice Application No. OA 1 of 2012, CCJ 4 (OJ), [31].

[69] *Trinidad Cement Limited v The Competition Commission,* Caribbean Court of Justice Application No. OA 1 of 2012, CCJ 4 (OJ), [32].

[70] *Trinidad Cement Limited v The Competition Commission,* Caribbean Court of Justice Application No. OA 1 of 2012, CCJ 4 (OJ), [34].

[71] *Ibid.*

[72] *Trinidad Cement Limited v The Competition Commission,* Caribbean Court of Justice Application No. OA 1 of 2012, CCJ 4 (OJ), [2].

of TCL.[73] It found in principle that "a party complained of does not fall within the expression "an interested party" as that expression is used in the Revised Treaty."[74]

The second substantive claim brought forward by the Trinidad Cement Limited concerned the absence of a proper request from the COTED in order for the CARICOM Competition Commission to initiate an investigation, Article 175(2) of the Revised Treaty of Chaguaramas. An investigation based on a request made by the COTED was problematic, because the COTED had at first only asked the Commission to "*advise* whether there was evidence sufficient to enable a preliminary assessment of whether there was anti-competitive business conduct by the TCL Group".[75] An explicit request was only sent later by the Secretary General, which quoted COTED's first resolution. The Commission referred to this clear request of the Secretary General, as well as to the indications made by the Caribbean Court of Justice in a prior judgement, *TCL Group v the Co-operative Republic of Guyana* and to its *ex officio* power to initiate an investigation.[76]

The Caribbean Court of Justice took a generous approach, although it acknowledged the defect in COTED's resolution. First, the observations made in the prior judgment were taken as sufficient ground to initiate an investigation for the CARICOM Commission. Second, the Commission was held to have not acted on its *ex proprio motu* competence, because this would have required a previous preliminary assessment by a national competition authority, Article 176(1) RTC. Third, the Caribbean Court of Justice acknowledged that the request of the Secretary General was not sufficient to request an investigation. Yet it was satisfied with a later ratification of the COTED, which validated the request made by the Secretary General. This was only allowed, because the evidence had sufficiently shown COTED's intention to request an investigation from the Commission against the TCL Group.[77] One can thus conclude that the formal requirements for a request are mandatory. However errors can be cured retrospectively and do not automatically render a started investigation of the Commission void or unlawful.

In order to convince the Court to dismiss TCL's claim, the CARICOM Competition Commission also argued that it lacked the necessary juridical personality and could therefore not constitute a proper party in a Caribbean Court of Justice proceeding.[78] Yet the Caribbean Court of Justice argued that the provisions that enable the legal standing of the Commission, as active or passive party before

[73] *Trinidad Cement Limited v The Competition Commission,* Caribbean Court of Justice Application No. OA 1 of 2012, CCJ 4 (OJ), [25].

[74] *Trinidad Cement Limited v The Competition Commission,* Caribbean Court of Justice Application No. OA 1 of 2012, CCJ 4 (OJ), [26].

[75] *Trinidad Cement Limited v The Competition Commission,* Caribbean Court of Justice Application No. OA 1 of 2012, CCJ 4 (OJ), [31] (emphasis added).

[76] *Ibid.*

[77] *Trinidad Cement Limited v The Competition Commission,* Caribbean Court of Justice Application No. OA 1 of 2012, CCJ 4 (OJ), [36, 37].

[78] *Trinidad Cement Limited v The Competition Commission,* Caribbean Court of Justice Application No. OA 1 of 2012, CCJ 4 (OJ), [10ff.].

the Court of Justice preconditioned its juridical personality.[79] Article 174 of the Revised Treaty of Chaguaramas vests the Commission with extensive powers in respect of cross-border transactions or transactions with cross-border effect. Moreover, the Commission is entitled to appeal to the Court for an order, Article 175(11) RTC and to address the Caribbean Court of Justice to review a decision, Article 180(3) RTC. On the other hand, affected parties by a determination of the Commission may apply to the Court for a judicial review of the determination, Article 175(12) RTC. Finally, the Agreement between Suriname and the Community Establishing the Seat of the Commission and the Protocol on the Privileges and Immunities of the Competition Commission explicitly states that the Commission "shall possess full juridical personality".[80]

The CARICOM Competition Commission further argued that the Caribbean Court of Justice had no competence to review the decision of the Commission regarding the initiation and conduct of an investigation regarding an allegedly anti-competitive practice.[81] The Commission in particular argued that the decision to initiate an investigation did not constitute a "determination" in the sense of Article 174(4) RTC.[82] The Court decided in favour of the CARICOM Competition Commission's argument, stating that the Court would ordinarily not take cognizance of allegations that certain procedural steps taken by the Commission during the investigation stage were unlawful or void.[83] It also held that it was not unreasonable for Trinidad Cement Limited to await the decision of the Adjudicating Panel.[84]

---

[79] *Trinidad Cement Limited v The Competition Commission,* Caribbean Court of Justice Application No. OA 1 of 2012, CCJ 4 (OJ), [13].

[80] Article II.1 of the Agreement between the Government of the Republic of Suriname and the Caribbean Community establishing the Seat and the Office of the Competition Commission, 2007; Article II.1 of the Protocol on the Privileges and Immunities of the Competition Commission, 2007. *Trinidad Cement Limited v The Competition Commission,* Caribbean Court of Justice Application No. OA 1 of 2012, CCJ 4 (OJ), [11].

[81] *Trinidad Cement Limited v The Competition Commission,* Caribbean Court of Justice Application No. OA 1 of 2012, CCJ 4 (OJ), [14ff.].

[82] *Trinidad Cement Limited v The Competition Commission,* Caribbean Court of Justice Application No. OA 1 of 2012, CCJ 4 (OJ), [14].

[83] *Trinidad Cement Limited v The Competition Commission,* Caribbean Court of Justice Application No. OA 1 of 2012, CCJ 4 (OJ), [17].

[84] *Trinidad Cement Limited v The Competition Commission,* Caribbean Court of Justice Application No. OA 1 of 2012, CCJ 4 (OJ), [17]. For more information on the judicial review of determinations of the CARICOM Competition Commission, see below Part II, Dimension IV: Sect. 8.3.2.

8.1.1.2 The Caribbean Court of Justice's obiter dictum on the CARICOM Competition Commission's Rules of Procedure

The Court's judgement is moreover interesting, because it reflects the Caribbean Court of Justice's function and understanding as "guardian of the Treaty".[85] In this sense, the Caribbean Court of Justice, in this first case involving Chapter VIII and the CARICOM Competition Commission, took the opportunity to analyse the Rules of Procedure of the CARICOM Competition Commission in an *obiter dictum*.

First, the Caribbean Court of Justice criticised that the Rules of Procedure did not replicate the requirements set out in Article 175(3), 175(4), 175(5) and 175(8) of the Revised Treaty of Chaguaramas.[86] While the lack of replication does not discharge the Commission of these requirements, incorporation in the Rules of Procedure could serve as reminder.[87] In fact, while Article 175 RTC sets out time and consultation obligations for the Investigating Panel, the Rules 2–9 of the Rules of Procedure only entail powers of the Investigating Panel. The Caribbean Court of Justice in particular mentions a possible contradiction between Article 174(4) RTC and the Rules 8 and 9 of the Rules of Procedure.[88] While Article 174(4) lit. a) RTC stipulates that "upon receipt of a request" consultations with interested parties shall determine whether the investigation is within the jurisdiction of the Commission, Rules 8 and 9 of the Rules of Procedure only require a determination on the Commission's jurisdiction "upon completion of its investigation", thereby at a later stage of the investigation by the Investigating Panel.[89]

Possible contradictions might also arise between Rule 8 and Rule 55(1) lit. b) of the Rules of Procedure according to the Court. Rule 8 requires the Investigating Panel to state "whether an offence has been committed" and the "nature of that offence", albeit Rule 55(1) lit. b) of the Rules of Procedure determines that the Executive Director can only start an enquiry if his notice establishes "a prima facie case that an offence has been committed".[90]

Likewise, Rule 4(1) of the Procedural Rules regulates the competence of the Commission to conduct an investigation "provided the Commission has jurisdiction pursuant to Articles 174, 175 and 176 of the Treaty". This also includes the *proprio motu* competence of the Commission to start an investigation in the sense of Article 176(1) RTC. However, the Rules of Procedure do not mention the requirement of

---

[85] *Trinidad Cement Limited v The Competition Commission,* Caribbean Court of Justice Application No. OA 1 of 2012, CCJ 4 (OJ), [45].

[86] *Trinidad Cement Limited v The Competition Commission,* Caribbean Court of Justice Application No. OA 1 of 2012, CCJ 4 (OJ), [46]. These provisions deal with the requirements for a request for an investigation and set out the procedure for an investigation by the Commission.

[87] *Ibid.*

[88] *Trinidad Cement Limited v The Competition Commission,* Caribbean Court of Justice Application No. OA 1 of 2012, CCJ 4 (OJ), [47].

[89] *Ibid.*

[90] *Trinidad Cement Limited v The Competition Commission,* Caribbean Court of Justice Application No. OA 1 of 2012, CCJ 4 (OJ), [47].

the CARICOM Competition Commission to request the national competition authority to undertake a preliminary examination as Article 176(1) RTC sets out.[91]

Finally, the *Trinidad Cement Limited v CARICOM Competition Commission* judgement highlights difficulties arising out of the dualist doctrine and reveals that there seem to exist ambiguities with regard to the enforcement of the regional competition provisions as set out in Article 177(1) of the Revised Treaty of Chaguaramas. Rule 4(1) of the CARICOM Competition Commission's procedure state that "[t]he Commission may conduct an investigation if it has reasonable grounds for suspecting that there has been an infringement of *national provisions* implementing Article 177(1)(a), (b) or (c) of the Treaty, provided the Commission has jurisdiction pursuant to Articles 174, 175 and 176 of the Treaty". The difficulty arises out of the ambiguity which legislative measures of national legislators are necessary.[92] The wording of Article 177 RTC, "A member State shall, within its jurisdiction, prohibit as being anti-competitive business conduct the following: (a) agreements (…) which have as their object or effect the prevention, restriction or distortion of competition *within the Community* (…)"could indicate that member states should enact national provisions that prohibit anti-competitive infringements with national effect and should enact additional national provisions that prohibit anti-competitive infringements with regional effect. On the other hand, it is arguable that the mere ratification of the Revised Treaty of Chaguaramas is sufficient to enact Article 177 RTC as regional provision for anti-competitive practices with an effect on the Community. It seems that the Investigating Panel of the CARICOM Competition Commission followed the latter opinion, because its report only focused on a possible infringement of the Treaty provisions themselves.[93] Yet a direct breach of regional competition law provisions is actually not in line with its nature as piece of international law, which lacks direct effect and applicability. Similarly, the Caribbean Court of Justice in its *obiter dictum* observes "that it is difficult to see how an investigation of the regional Competition Commission could deal with cross-border anti-competitive business conduct by focusing on the infringement of national provisions."[94] It also highlights the difficulty of choosing the applicable national provision.[95] For the requirement of cross-border effect or cross-border transaction, there will be at least two national laws applicable. The Caribbean Court of Justice suggests that the Commission revises its procedural rules. In the same vein, the *CARICOM Model Law on Competition* only incorporates provisions regarding infringements on the national market and provisions regarding the cooperation among the competition law authorities. On the other hand, one cannot ignore the wording of Article 177 RTC, which is directed at the member states and from its

[91] This point of criticism was not raised by the Caribbean Court of Justice.

[92] See in this regard Part II, Dimension II: Sect. 6.2.

[93] *Trinidad Cement Limited v The Competition Commission*, Caribbean Court of Justice Application No. OA 1 of 2012, CCJ 4 (OJ), [48].

[94] *Trinidad Cement Limited v The Competition Commission*, Caribbean Court of Justice Application No. OA 1 of 2012, CCJ 4 (OJ), [48].

[95] *Ibid.*

explicit wording requires further action.[96] Notwithstanding, the interpretation, which the Caribbean Court of Justice hinted at, a different wording, such as "(a)s constituting anti-competitive business conduct and thereby prohibit, shall be deemed the following", would have been more unambiguous regarding the preponderant dualist system within the CARICOM.[97]

8.1.2 Conduct of and Powers During Investigations

In the WAEMU, investigative functions are shared between national authorities and the Commission.[98] However, behaviour related to state aids, anticompetitive practices by public monopolies and state-owned enterprises as well as anticompetitive practices that affect trade between member states lies within the exclusive competence of the WAEMU Commission.[99] This is mostly attributed to the anticipatory procedure, according to which all state aids have to be notified to the WAEMU Commission.[100] The shared investigation can either be based on a direct mandate of the Commission or, if the Commission conducts the investigation, on the basis of cooperation with the national competition law structures.[101] Additionally, there exists a reciprocal obligation to inform about ongoing investigations between the Commission and national competition law agencies.[102] For example, the Commission

---

[96] *Beckford,* Effecting cooperation to resolve cross-border anti-competitive conduct affecting CARICOM, XV Competition Matters – Fair Trading Commission 6, 7 (2011).

[97] The *Trinidad Cement Limited v The Competition Commission* judgement of the Caribbean Court also comments on decisions of the European Court of Justice that had been referred to by the Trinidad Cement Limited Group. However, the Court explicitly highlights the danger of using precedents from the European Court, because between the CARICOM and European competition regimes existed "considerable dis-similarities that flow from the significant differences in the wording, nature and effect of underlying legal instruments and the overarching governing system of law". Furthermore, the CCJ determines that the two cited European cases did not apply to the actual case, because the CARICOM Competition Commission had not exercised investigative powers to the prejudice of the Trinidad Cement Limited Group; see *Trinidad Cement Limited v The Competition Commission,* Caribbean Court of Justice Application No. OA 1 of 2012, CCJ 4 (OJ), [27, 28].

[98] Articles 3 and 5 of Directive no. 02/2002/CM/UEMOA; Article 28(1) of Regulation no. 03/2002/CM/UEMOA.

[99] Article 5(2) of Directive no. 02/2002/CM/UEMOA. There are four different procedures regarding state aids: procedure regarding notification of state aids, Articles 5 to 12 of Regulation no. 04/2002/CM/UEMOA, procedure regarding illegal aids, Articles 13 to 17 of Regulation no. 04/2002/CM/UEMOA, procedure regarding abusive aids, Article 18 of Regulation no. 04/2002/CM/UEMOA and procedure regarding existing aid, Articles 19 to 21 of Regulation no. 04/2002/CM/UEMOA.

[100] Article 5(1) of Regulation no. 04/2002/CM/UEMOA. For more details on the procedures with regard to state aids, see *Bakhoum,* L'articulation du droit communautaire et des droits nationaux de la concurrence dans l'Union Economique et Monétaire Ouest Africaine, 2007, pp. 129ff.

[101] Article 3(1) of Directive no. 02/2002/CM/UEMOA.

[102] Article 3 and Article 5(4) of Directive no. 02/2002/CM/UEMOA

has to send a copy to the competent national competition authority of the member state, in which it requests information of an enterprise or person.[103] The final decision of the Commission also has to be transmitted to the national competition authority of that member state, in which the targeted enterprise is located or of which the targeted private person is a citizen.[104] National competition authorities can express their observations on the investigation, but the decision-making and the enforcement power remain within the community level. The national competition authorities' role is limited to cooperation. Nevertheless, the applicable procedural provisions, Directive no. 02/2002/CM/UEMOA and Regulation no. 03/2002/CM/UEMOA, set out that this cooperation between national and the regional authority ought to be "close and constant".[105]

Generally the WAEMU Commission has the right to collect all necessary information from governments, competent authorities of the member states, of undertakings and associations of undertakings as well as from individuals.[106] The Commission has different measures at hand to conduct its investigation and to gather relevant information for the assessment of the potentially anticompetitive conduct. First, it can gather information via the request for information as set out in Article 18 of Regulation no. 03/2002/CM/UEMOA (informal inquiry). An informal inquiry cannot be enforced by sanctions, but false or incomplete responses can lead to sanctions.[107] If the addressed undertaking or person does not comply, the Commission can initiate a request in form of a Decision, which also includes sanctions for the case of non-compliance (formal inquiry).[108] Finally, the Commission has to send a copy of the decision to the member state, where the respective undertaking or person is located.[109]

A second alternative measure concerns inspections, set out in the Articles 20 and 21 of Regulation no. 03/2002/CM/UEMOA. Article 21(2) of Regulation no. 03/2002/CM/UEMOA determines that the inspection has to be based on an "authorisation in writing" containing the objective of the action. Similarly, Article 21(3) of Regulation no. 03/2002/CM/UEMOA foresees a prior notification to the national competition law agencies of the investigation. These provisions hinder "strong enforcement actions"[110] of the Commission, in particular with regard to information gathering, as undertakings are informed beforehand of upcoming investigations. In

---

[103] Article 18(2) of Regulation no. 03/2002/CM/UEMOA.

[104] Article 18(6) of Regulation no. 03/2002/CM/UEMOA.

[105] Article 28(2) of Regulation no. 03/2002/CM/UEMOA.

[106] Article 18(1) of Regulation no. 03/2002/CM/UEMOA.

[107] Article 18(3) of Regulation no. 03/2002/CM/UEMOA.

[108] Article 18(5) of Regulation no. 03/2002/CM/UEMOA. A formal inquiry is consecutive, not alternative, to an informal inquiry, see *Bakhoum,* L'articulation du droit communautaire et des droits nationaux de la concurrence dans l'Union Economique et Monétaire Ouest Africaine, 2007, p. 162.

[109] Article 18(6) of Regulation no. 03/2002/CM/UEMOA.

[110] *Bakhoum,* A Developing-Country Perspective on "Global Competition", 28 October 2011, Chicago, p. 12.

the WAEMU, the Commission has the power to make copies of all documents and books of the firm, make oral examinations on the spot and access all facilities according to provisions of the applicable national law.

Article 20 of Regulation no. 03/2002/CM/UEMOA allows national authorities to conduct the investigation on request of the Commission. Agents of the Commission can still grant assistance, Article 20(2) of Regulation no. 03/2002/CM/UEMOA. Vice versa, national agents can offer assistance to agents of the Commission during an investigation, Article 21(4) of Regulation no. 03/2002/CM/UEMOA.[111] Finally, the Commission can conduct inquiries of entire economic sectors according to Article 19 of Regulation no. 03/2002/CM/UEMOA.

WAEMU's procedural laws regarding competition law enforcement envisage strong cooperation between national and regional antitrust agencies and idealistically a reciprocal exchange of information. In practice however, such close cooperation did not take place for various reasons.[112]

In the AndeanC the anticompetitive investigation is conducted through the national competition authorities of the member states, in which the concerned firms have their seat, or in which the firms realize their economic activity and, if it is the case, in which the effects of the practices take place or the complaining party is located.[113] Article 15 of Decision 608 refers to several involved member states, which recites the underlying requirement of a cross-border effect, as set out in Article 5 of Decision 608. As regards the enforcement of a regional norm there will always be at least two national competition law authorities involved in addition to the Secretariat General.

The national investigations underlie at all times the permanent coordination of the Secretariat General.[114] In particular, the enforcement through the national competition authorities relies on a "plan of investigation", which however has been elaborated by the Secretariat General in cooperation with competent national competition authorities.[115] The "plan of investigation" has to contain the actions that are planned to be adopted, a proposal for the timeframe, the responsible organs and the concerned economic agents and the information at reach regarding the concerned products or services and possible relevant market.[116] In order to guarantee harmonized enforcement among the member states the "plan of investigation" the

---

[111] More details on the procedural powers of Commission in WAEMU, see *Bakhoum*, L'articulation du droit communautaire et des droits nationaux de la concurrence dans l'Union Economique et Monétaire Ouest Africaine, 2007, pp. 159ff.

[112] See Part II, Dimension II: Sect. 6.1.1.

[113] Article 15 of Decision 608.

[114] Article 18 of Decision 608.

[115] Article 15 of Decision 608.

[116] *Secretaría General de la Comunidad Andina,* Guía Práctica para la aplicación de la Decisión 608 "Normas para la protección y promoción de la libre competencia en la Comunidad Andina", 2007, p. 27. <http://intranet.comunidadandina.org/Documentos/DTrabajo/SGdt396.doc> accessed 11 November 2018.

investigation should only follow the measures set out in the plan.[117] Simultaneously, the Secretariat General can also conduct its own investigations, parallel to national procedures.[118] The detailed procedural measures in the "plan of investigation" bear a great danger, because according to Article 15 of Decision 608 it has to be notified to all interested parties, including the accused firms. This may lead to inefficiencies during enforcement, in particular with regard to the gathering of information.[119] Despite this weakness, the detailed "plan of investigation" might be justified for the need to coordinate the different procedural norms in the member states. The AndeanC relies on a principle of parallel application of procedural norms. Article 16 of Decision 608 sets out an extensive list of competences of the investigating authority during the competition law proceedings, such as the right to interrogate persons or conduct inspections with or without prior notification.[120] Nevertheless, without prejudice to these competences, the national competition law authorities conduct their investigations based on national legislation. The latter in particular determines the kind of procedure that has to be applied, the investigative powers of the authority, the gathering of evidence and other proceedings. The potential of legal conflicts or diverging procedural rights or even different enforcement results is in theory diminished by the "plan of investigation" and Article 16 of Decision 608. On the one hand, the AndeanC's legislator thus assumed the necessity to harmonize procedural norms in case of decentralized enforcement. On the other hand, it has relied on existing national procedural provisions from experienced competition law jurisdictions.[121] Due to the doctrine of direct application and superiority of regional law, Article 16 of Decision 608 can be interpreted as setting out minimum procedural standards for national competition authorities.[122]

Finally, in order to facilitate cooperation between the Secretariat General, the national competition law authorities and the Andean Committee for the Defence of Competition a functionary is assigned who serves as coordinating mediator.[123]

---

[117] Article 17 of Decision 608.

[118] Article 18 of Decision 608.

[119] *Stucchi López Raygada,* La Integración en la Comunidad Andina y su Sistema de Protección y Promoción de la Libre Competencia, 2 Rev. Comp. Propriedad Intelectual 71, 93 (2006).

[120] Article 16 lit. a) to c) of Decision 608. Regional procedural rules allow for the requirement of natural or judicial persons to exhibit all relevant documents, including accounting and corporate books, receipts for payments, commercial transactions and correspondence, magnetic data carriers and the necessary programs to read them, also including information regarding the firm's organization, trade partners, stock options and the structure of the property of the firm. Article 16 of Decision 608 also provides for interrogations of economic agents or their employees, representatives etc., as well as for inspections with or without prior notification and examination of books, registers and other documents. The investigating entity is also entitled to make photocopies or take pictures.

[121] The list in Article 16 of Decision 608 corresponds to the competences of the Peruvian competition authority, the INDECOPI as set out in Article 2 of Legislative Decree N° 807.

[122] *Novak Talavera,* in: *Fondo Editorial,* Derecho Comunitario Andino, 2003, pp. 57, 68ff.

[123] *Secretaría General de la Comunidad Andina,* Guía Práctica para la aplicación de la Decisión 608 "Normas para la protección y promoción de la libre competencia en la Comunidad Andina", 2007, p. 15 <http://intranet.comunidadandina.org/Documentos/DTrabajo/SGdt396.doc> accessed 11 November 2018.

According to Article 17 of Decision 608 the national authorities have 90 days to conduct the investigation. The Secretariat General then has 45 additional days to conduct its own evaluations and can complement the results by requesting more information.[124] After 10 additional days the Secretariat General has to elaborate an "informe" on the results of the investigation to the members of the Andean Committee for the Defence of Free Competition, the respective national authorities and the interested parties.[125]

In the CARICOM, the most important feature of the conduct of an investigation is the clear separation of investigating and adjudicating functions of the authority. In practice, namely in the case against the Trinidad Cement Limited Group, the Executive Director received the complaint by COTED and then informed the Chairman of the Commission. The latter then assigned two Commissioners to conduct an investigation.[126] At this point, these were the only Commissioners knowing about the details of the case. At the end of their investigation, the two Commissioners wrote a report recommending a formal enquiry against Trinidad Cement Limited.[127] The report was submitted to the Executive Director of the Commission, who issued a Notice, which identified the relevant concerns and material facts for the Adjudicating Panel.[128] The Chairman of the Commission however was only informed about the general recommendation without knowing the detailed outcome of the investigation. He then assigned an Adjudicating Panel to conduct the enquiry, from which the former two Commissioners were excluded.[129] Only at this point was the Trinidad Cement Limited informed, which was one of the main points for discussion in the *TCL v The Competition Commission* case.[130] This is also in accordance with Article 175(7) RTC, which only stipulates that after the decision to conduct an enquiry, any party complained against shall be afforded with the opportunity to defend its rights. This is only possible if the concerned party is informed about the initiation of the enquiry.[131] At the end of an enquiry, the CARICOM Competition Commission then makes its determination regarding an infringement of regional competition law.[132]

The investigation by the Investigating Panel takes place in accordance with national laws.[133] Accordingly, the powers of the Investigating Panel are governed by

---

[124] Article 19 of Decision 608.

[125] Article 20 of Decision 608.

[126] Rule 4(2) of the CARICOM Competition Commission Rules of Procedure, 2011.

[127] Rule 8 of the CARICOM Competition Commission Rules of Procedure, 2011.

[128] Rule 11 of the CARICOM Competition Commission Rules of Procedure, 2011.

[129] Rule 10(2) of the CARICOM Competition Commission Rules of Procedure, 2011.

[130] See above *Trinidad Cement Limited v Caricom Competition Commission*, Part II, Dimension IV: Sect. 8.1.1.1.

[131] Rule 12 of the CARICOM Competition Commission Rules of Procedure, 2011.

[132] Part VII "Deliberation and Determination" of the CARICOM Competition Commission Rules of Procedure, 2011.

[133] Article 174(2) of the Revised Treaty of Chaguaramas.

the requirement to apply for a warrant under relevant national provisions.[134] This presupposes that the CARICOM Competition Commission cooperates with national authorities during the investigation phase. In particular, powers such as regarding the searching of premises or the taking in possession of documents require support by the national authorities.[135] If the Investigating Panel decides against the jurisdiction of the Commission, the latter shall discuss with the concerned member state(s), whether the national competition authority should pursue the matter.[136] While the investigation is conducted in close cooperation with the national competition authorities, the enquiry is solely governed by the Adjudicating Panel of the CARICOM Competition Commission and in accordance with its Rules of Procedure.

According to Article 175(6) lit. b) RTC, the Commission has to complete the investigation within 120 days. Yet extensions are possible. It is interesting to note is that the time frames set out in the Revised Treaty of Chaguaramas are not replicated in the CARICOM Competition Commission Rules of Procedure. Regarding the length of the enquiry, Chapter VIII does not state any requirements. Because of the limited number of competition cases, it still remains to be seen whether the Commission will be able to respect its time limits. In particular the time frame for the investigation might be problematic, as the investigation phase relies on close cooperation between the partly unexperienced national and regional competition authorities. The lack of deadlines for the CARICOM Competition Commission might contribute to an inappropriately long uncertainty for the targeted enterprise by having to cope with very lengthy procedures. On the other hand, the lack of time frames for the enquiry phase gives the CARICOM Competition Commission large discretion and sufficient time to thoroughly examine the matter. The ultimate average duration of regional competition law enquiries will to a large extent depend on the commitment and workload of the Commission's staff.

The CARICOM Competition Commission has far-reaching powers during an investigation, once it has reasonable grounds for suspecting that there has been a breach of competition law, Rule 4(1) of CARICOM Competition Commission Rules of Procedure. Article 174(2) RTC determines that the Commission can oblige any person involved in an allegedly anticompetitive conduct to appear in person for interrogation and to provide any requested document or it can take other actions that are necessary to further the investigation.

However, these powers can only be exerted in accordance with the "applicable national laws". Rule 39(1) of the CARICOM Competition Commission Rules of Procedure for example requires that "[a]ll persons appearing before the Adjudicating Panel in any oral hearing shall conform to the conduct required in the High Court of the jurisdiction in which such oral hearing is being conducted." During the investigating and adjudicating phase, the powers of the CARICOM Competition Commission always have to conform to the procedural rights in the concerned jurisdiction. The introduction of the CARICOM Competition Commission Rules of

[134] Rule 6(1) of the CARICOM Competition Commission Rules of Procedure, 2011.

[135] *Ibid.*

[136] Rule 9(2) of the CARICOM Competition Commission Rules of Procedure, 2011.

Procedure correspondingly reemphasises the principles of (i) separation of adjudicating and investigating functions, (ii) the right of defence and (iii) the protection of confidential and propriety information of the parties concerned. Article 170(4) RTC and Rule 6(4) of the Rules of Procedure also limit the investigation powers of the CARICOM Competition Commission regarding the protection of confidential information of member states or enterprises, whose disclosure "would be prejudicial to the public interest or to the legitimate commercial interests of enterprises, public or private".[137]

It is expected that the CARICOM Competition Commission will cooperate with national competition agencies, not only during the investigating phase, but also during the adjudicating phase. This is not only due to the limited resources, but Article 170(3) of the Revised Treaty of Chaguaramas explicitly determines that national competition authorities shall cooperate with the Commission, investigate any allegations referred to by the Commission and generally cooperate with other national competition authorities. Yet this envisaged network of cooperation between regional and national competition authorities is neither formalized[138] nor codified in the CARICOM Competition Commission Rules of Procedure.

8.1.3 *Decision-Making Power and Its Implementation*

8.1.3.1 Decisions and Possible Measures

In the WAEMU, the regional Commission holds the final decision-making power.[139] The Commission, in its final decision, can either grant the negative clearance[140] or an individual or block exemption or it can find an infringement of regional competition.[141] Even before making a decision, the Commission can already impose provisional measures, according to Article 5 of Regulation no. 03/2002/CM/UEMOA. In case the Commission finds an infringement, it can impose a fine[142] or a periodical fine per day until the respective practice is terminated.[143] In order to guarantee legal certainty and to offer the affected party the possibility to appeal, decisions of the

[137] Article 170(4) of the Revised Treaty of Chaguaramas.

[138] *Menns/Eversley,* The Appropriate Design of the CARICOM Competition Commission, 20 May 2011, Amsterdam, p. 25. In the European Union the European Competition Network (ECN) constitutes a formalized cooperation and enforcement mechanism.

[139] One also distinguishes between non-contradictory (Article 15 of Regulation no. 03/2002/CM/UEMOA) and contradictory procedures (Article 16 of Regulation no. 03/2002/CM/UEMOA) in the WAEMU.

[140] Articles 3, 6 and 7 of Regulation no. 03/2002/CM/UEMOA.

[141] Article 4 of Regulation no. 03/2002/CM/UEMOA.

[142] Article 22 of Regulation no. 03/2002/CM/UEMOA.

[143] Article 23 of Regulation no. 03/2002/CM/UEMOA.

Commission have to be sufficiently reasoned, according to Article 44 of the Treaty of Dakar.[144]

According to Article 28(4) of Regulation no. 03/2002/CM/UEMOA the Advisory Committee on Competition has to be consulted prior to decisions of the WAEMU Commission.[145]

In the AndeanC the decision-making is vested in the Secretariat General. It has to express its conclusions in a "motivated resolution". However, in order to guarantee a certain participation of the member states, the Committee for the Defence of Free Competition also has the right to express its opinion during the final evaluation process.[146] The Andean Committee can express its opinion on the preliminary "informe" of the Secretariat General, thereby expressing its own conclusions on the evaluated practice. However, the Committee's opinion is not binding for the Secretariat General. The latter only has to justify a diverging opinion. Thus the decision-making competence lies solely within the Secretariat General and the member states are only consulted.[147]

Decision 608 offers different measures, which the Secretariat General can decide upon: the adoption of a settlement (Artt. 27 ff. of Decision 608), of protective measures, such as the provisional suspension of the conduct or the submission of a guarantee (Artt. 31 ff. of Decision 608), or the order to immediately cease the conduct and the adoption of corrective and/or punitive actions (Art. 34 of Decision 608).[148] The extent of the decided measure has to take into account several aspects, such as the gravity of the infringement, the countervailing benefits, the affected relevant market etc.[149]

In the CARICOM, according to Article 174(3) of the Revised Treaty of Chaguaramas and Rules 51 and 52 of the CARICOM Competition Commission Rules of Procedure, only the Adjudicating Panel of the Commission can decide upon the anticompetitiveness of an examined practice and its compatibility with the rules of competition. Nevertheless, Rule 4(1) of the Rules of Procedure has caused discussions with regard to the definition of the notion of "rules of competition" in Article 174(3) of the RTC. Instead of referring to an infringement of regional competition law, Rule 4(1) mentions an "infringement of *national provisions*

---

[144] *UNCTAD,* Voluntary Peer Review on Competition Policies of WAEMU, Benin and Senegal, 2008, p. 50.

[145] For more information on the Advisory Committee on Competition in the WAEMU, see below Part II, Dimension IV: Sect. 8.2.1.1.

[146] Article 21 and 22 of Decision 608. More information on the Andean Committee for the Defence of Free Competition see below Part II, Dimension IV: Sect. 8.2.1.2.

[147] This consultation procedure has been named the "co-decision" phase by *Stucchi López Raygada,* La Integración en la Comunidad Andina y su Sistema de Protección y Promoción de la Libre Competencia, 2 Rev. Comp. Propriedad Intelectual 71, 96 (2006).

[148] This study refrains from explaining each possible measure separately, because their specific requirements are irrelevant for the allocation of competences between the national and the regional level.

[149] Article 34 of Decision 608.

implementing Article 177" (emphasis added).[150] Article 174(4) of the RTC determines that the CARICOM Competition Commission has different actions at hand "to remedy or penalise anti-competitive business conduct referred to in Article 177". This wording referring to Article 177 RTC supports the Caribbean Court of Justice's view that Rule 4(1) of the Rules of Procedure is unluckily worded and should be understood in the sense that it refers to the regional competition law provisions.[151]

The CARICOM Competition Commission can in accordance with Article 174(4) lit. b) to lit. j) of the Revised Treaty of Chaguaramas order the termination or nullification of an agreement, conduct etc., order the targeted enterprise to take the necessary steps to overcome possible effects of the anticompetitive conduct, order a payment of compensation or impose fines.

8.1.3.2 Enforcement of Measures

In accordance with the centralized system, the WAEMU Commission determines the amount of a fine that is imposed on enterprises or association of enterprises.[152] Yet enforcement of the specific measures takes place decentrally. Member states and national competition authorities are indirectly involved in the imposition of fines. First, the Consultative Committee on Competition has to be consulted on the determination of the amount of a fine.[153] Second, the WAEMU Commission's decisions do not have criminal character and civil law liability and indemnities are only enforceable before national courts.[154] Third, Article 3(3) lit. c) of Directive no. 02/2002/CM/UEMOA establishes the decentralized enforcement before national competition law structures of pecuniary sanctions for all persons other than states.[155]

However, in the framework of enforcement of measures, the rules governing provisional measures create some inefficiency. The mechanism of provisional measures is an instrument to prevent serious and irreparable damages and eventually

[150] *Trinidad Cement Limited v The Competition Commission,* Caribbean Court of Justice Application No. OA 1 of 2012, CCJ 4 (OJ).

[151] *Trinidad Cement Limited v The Competition Commission,* Caribbean Court of Justice Application No. OA 1 of 2012, CCJ 4 (OJ), [48].

[152] Articles 22 and 23 of Regulation no. 03/2002/CM/UEMOA.

[153] Article 28(4) of Regulation no. 03/2002/CM/UEMOA.

[154] Article 22(4) of Regulation no. 03/2002/CM/UEMOA.

[155] Regulation no. 04/2002/CM/UEMOA provides for rules on state aids. As the WAEMU decision in this context is directed at member states and can either clear or prohibit a state aid, questions of civil or criminal law liability, which are relevant for anticompetitive practices by legal or natural persons, do not arise. Yet, if a member state does not comply with a decision, the WAEMU Commission has several instruments at hand to enforce it, see Article 24 of Regulation no. 04/2002/CM/UEMOA. A drastic measure at hand is for example the suspension of financial aid granted by the Union to the member state, Article 24(1) alt. 4 of Regulation no. 04/2002/CM/UEMOA or the Commission can fine the undertaking, which has been benefiting from the state aid, Article 24(2) of Regulation no. 04/2002/CM/UEMOA.

guarantees that the decision on a competition matter is efficiently implemented.[156] The determination on the application of provisional measures is completely centralized, lying solely within the discretion of the WAEMU Commission. Bearing in mind the large administrative burden of the WAEMU Commission and the often perceived (geographical) remoteness of the regional authority from the location of the targeted company, enforcement through national authorities would in a large number of cases constitute a faster and more efficient way to apply interim measures. While in the European competition law system interim measures can be ordered from national courts and national competition law authorities,[157] the WAEMU system does not provide for such decentralized mechanisms.[158]

Although in the AndeanC the Secretariat General decides on the measures that will be adopted, the execution and enforcement of the measures is decentralized.[159] The executing member state(s) has to be explicitly appointed in the final "motivated resolution" of the Secretariat General at the end of an investigation.[160] The member state that implements the measure has to report the enforcement to the Secretariat General, the other involved member states and the concerned persons in the process.[161] Despite this information requirement, Decision 608 does not set out a specific procedure in case of non-fulfilment or insufficient enforcement of the measures. However, the Secretariat General is supposed to supervise the implementation of the measures periodically and can initiate an action of non-compliance before the Andean Tribunal in case it is unsatisfied with the implementation of the member state.[162]

The CARICOM Competition Commission is the competent organ to make determinations regarding an infringement of the competition law rules and other related provisions of the Revised Treaty of Chaguaramas, Article 174(3) RTC. However, the measures have to be enforced by the national competition agencies. Article 174(6) RTC requires member states to implement according legislation to ensure that the determinations of the Commission are enforceable in their jurisdiction, as they lack direct effect and application. Moreover, if persons or an undertaking do

---

[156] Article 5(4) of Regulation no. 03/2002/CM/UEMOA. On the European system on interim measures, see mainly Article 8 of Regulation 1/2003, *Ortiz Blanco,* EC Competition Procedure, 2006, pp. 529ff.

[157] Commission Notice on the handling of complaints by the Commission under Articles 81 and 82 of the EC Treaty, OJ C 101/65, 27 April 2004, pp. 65–77, para. 80; *Ortiz Blanco,* EC Competition Procedure, 2006, p. 531.

[158] *Bakhoum,* L'articulation du droit communautaire et des droits nationaux de la concurrence dans l'Union Economique et Monétaire Ouest Africaine, 2007, p. 171.

[159] Article 35 of Decision 608.

[160] *Secretaria General de la Comunidad Andina,* Guía Práctica para la aplicación de la Decisión 608 "Normas para la protección y promoción de la libre competencia en la Comunidad Andina", 2007, p. 40.

[161] Article 35 of Decision 608.

[162] *Secretaria General de la Comunidad Andina,* Guía Práctica para la aplicación de la Decisión 608 "Normas para la protección y promoción de la libre competencia en la Comunidad Andina", 2007, p. 41.

not comply with the determination, the Commission can also request an order from the Caribbean Court of Justice, whose original jurisdiction has been recognized in most domestic laws of the CARICOM member states, Article 175(11) of the Revised Treaty of Chaguaramas.[163] Yet Article 175(11) of the Revised Treaty might require additional enforcement steps with regard to an order of the regional Court. As *Delroy S. Beckford* in this context highlights "Article 175(11) RTC does not stipulate whether the order (...) is limited to a declaration of breach of the competition provisions in the RTC or would encompass an order for compliance."[164] In the latter case, in which the regional Court declares an order for compliance, the actual enforcement in member states will depend on the stage of ratification of provisions that render the determinations of the CARICOM Competition Commission binding.[165] Moreover, *Delroy S. Beckford* underlines that "the existing governance mechanism does not *require* a decision of the CCJ to have direct effect and be enforceable within a CARICOM member and against a CARICOM national found to have breached the competition provisions of the RTC."[166]

Yet the indirect enforcement of the CARICOM Competition Commission's decision depends on the pace of the implementation process of national competition law structures. Moreover, the indirect enforcement of decisions endangers consistent application of regional competition law. The pivotal role of the Caribbean Court of Justice becomes apparent. It is not only a body that guarantees the right of defence but it constitutes an important element to the harmonization of competition policy within CARICOM under the premise that private parties or member states invoke its jurisdiction.

8.1.3.3 Claims for Damages, Declarations and Injunctions and Criminal Law Liability for Breaches of Regional Competition Law

The emphasis of individuals' rights protection is not only conceived for its own sake, but also as a pillar for the effectiveness of a supranational competition law system overall, contributing to decentralized enforcement of it in the form of private damage claims before national courts.[167] At least in the European Union, the recognition of private damage claims for the breach of European law emanated from the *effet utile* doctrine. Whereas in the European Union private enforcement is

---

[163] *CARICOM Secretariat,* The CARICOM Competition Commission, 2008, p. 11.

[164] *Beckford,* in: *Drexl/Bakhoum/Fox/Gal/Gerber,* Competition Policy and Regional Integration in Developing Countries, 2012, pp. 185, 192.

[165] Article 174(6) of the Revised Treaty of Chaguaramas: "The Member States shall enact legislation to ensure that determinations of the Commission are enforceable in their jurisdictions."

[166] *Beckford,* in: *Drexl/Bakhoum/Fox/Gal/Gerber,* Competition Policy and Regional Integration in Developing Countries, 2012, pp. 185, 192.

[167] *Drexl,* in: *Drexl* (Ed.), The Future of Transnational Antitrust, 2003, pp. 311, 333; see also ECJ, Judgement of the Court of 20 September 2001, C*ourage Ltd v Bernard Crehan,* Case C-453/99, [2001] ECR I-6297, ECLI:EU:C:2001:465

undergoing further developments, in particular with the enactment and implementation of the private damage claim directive[168] private enforcement of regional law in the WAEMU and the AndeanC has not taken place so far.

In the WAEMU, according to Article 22(4) of Regulation no. 03/2002/CM/UEMOA, the WAEMU Commission's decision is without prejudice to damage claims before national courts. While this implies that national judges are autonomous in their decision, they are bound to the Commission's decision and possible exemption. As a consequence of the exclusive competence of the WAEMU Commission, its declaration of an antitrust infringement is a precondition for compensation under civil law or criminal sanctions, if applicable in the case of competition law infringements.[169]

In case of a "stand alone action", individuals have to seek a decision of the WAEMU Commission, whose headquarters are located in Ouagadougou in Burkina Faso.[170] Due to poor infrastructure in West Africa this can be a time consuming and costly venture.[171] Moreover, the notification requirement is capable of increasing the duration of procedures. In the European Union, the prior notification requirement was used frequently by defendants in injunctive relief procedures in order to delay the national court procedure.[172] This inefficiency was abolished through the enforcement modernization regulation in the European Union, according to which national courts are now competent to apply European competition law provisions and, given that the Commission has not decided on the matter, to make autonomous decisions on an infringement and possible exemption.[173]

The Andean Tribunal of Justice in a decision in 1996 reemphasised the direct applicability and direct effect of Andean norms.[174] The close relation of direct applicability and direct effect had as immediate effect that Andean citizens would feel protected by the rights that Andean law confers to them.[175] Moreover, citizens

---

[168] Directive on Antitrust Damages Actions of 24 October 2014, 2013/0185 (COD), signed into law on 26 November 2014 and adopted on 10 November 2014.

[169] For more information see also *Bakhoum,* L'articulation du droit communautaire et des droits nationaux de la concurrence dans l'Union Economique et Monétaire Ouest Africaine, 2007, pp. 246ff.

[170] *Bakhoum,* Delimitation and Exercise of Competence between the West African Economic and Monetary Union (WAEMU) and its Member States in Competition Policy, 29/4 W. Comp. 653, 675 (2006).

[171] *Ibid.*

[172] *Wils,* Ten Years of Regulation 1/2003, 4 J. Eur. Comp. L. Practice 293, 297 (2013).

[173] Articles 1, 3 and 6 of Regulation no. 1/2003. See also Articles 15 and 16 of Regulation no. 1/2003, which deal with cooperation between national courts and the Commission during the enforcement of European competition law.

[174] Proceso 3-AI-96.

[175] Proceso 3-AI-96, p. 14: "En otras palabras que sus efectos 'generan derechos y obligaciones para los particulares al igual que ocurre en las normas de los ordenamientos estatales', *permitiendo la posibilidad de que aquellos puedan exigir directamente su observancia ante sus respectivos tribunales* (emphasis added).(...) R. Lecourt, Ex Presidente del Tribunal de Justicia de las Comunidades Europeas definió este principio, diciendo que 'es el derecho de cualquier persona de pedir al Juez la aplicación de los Tratados, los Reglamentos, las Directivas o las Decisiones

needed to have the possibility to claim the compliance with regional norms before national judiciary.[176] Hence, in the absence of specific private damage claims procedures in the case of a breach of Andean community law breach, they are enforced nationally.

Decision 608 does not determine whether the decision of the Secretariat General constitutes a mandatory precondition to private enforcement of Andean law before national courts. On the one hand, Article 4 of Decision 608 generally sanctions and prohibits conducts that are set out in Article 7 and 8 of Decision 608. Although Decision 608 does not declare anticompetitive practices as being *ipso iure* "null and void",[177] this should not create an obstacle to private claims. The Andean Tribunal of Justice has in line with the European *effet utile* doctrine emphasized that competition infringers should not profit from their unlawful behaviour.[178] On the other hand, the "practical guidelines"[179] on the application of Decision 608 describe the general enforcement conception under the Decision as a centralized system with regard to administration and application of the rules on the protection and promotion of free competition in the AndeanC.[180] The underlying understanding as centralized

comunitarias, es la obligación del Juez de hacer uso de esa norma cualquiera que sea la legislación del País al que pertenece. Es el respeto de ese derecho y de esa obligación no sólo en las relaciones de los particulares entre sí, sino también en las relaciones entre los particulares y el Estado miembro del que son ciudadanos.' Dámaso Ruiz-Jarabo, Obra "El Juez Nacional como Juez Comunitario", pág. 53. Entre el principio de la aplicabilidad directa y del efecto directo existe una conexión estrecha: la norma comunitaria andina al ser directamente aplicable en los Países Miembros tiene como efecto inmediato que los ciudadanos de la Subregión se sientan protegidos con y en los derechos que esas normas les confieran. Es la forma legal de abrirles la posibilidad de exigir su cumplimiento ante las justicias nacionales."

[176] Proceso 3-AI-96, p. 14.

[177] See for example Article 101(2) TFEU. *Temple Lang* states in this context with regard to the competition actions under the former Articles 85 and 86 EEC Treaty: "Articles 85 and 86 are directly applicable and create rights and duties on which national courts must act. Logically, this must mean that firms and individuals injured as a result of infringements of articles 85 and 86 have a right to sue, and not merely that agreements which are contrary to those articles are invalid and unenforceable. Moreover, articles 85 and 86 in their entirety are directly applicable, not merely article 85(2)." *Temple Lang*, EEC Competition Actions in Member States' Courts, 7 Fordham Int'l. L.J. 389, 403 (1983).

[178] See also Tribunal de la Justicia de la Comunidad Andina, Sentencia 1-AN-97, pp. 6f.: "El carácter obligatorio del acto administrativo contenido en la Resolución 397, que señalaba como restricción al comercio la prohibición de importación de café tostado de Colombia por razones de broca de café y la denegación de los permisos fitosanitarios de importación respectivos, creó por sí mismo, sin necesidad de apoyo en otra actuación administrativa la obligación de acatamiento derivado no solamente de su contenido intrínseco sino también de la fuerza que le confiere la obligación fundamental impuesta a los Países Miembros por el artículo 5° del Tratado de Creación del Tribunal, en el sentido de no 'adoptar, ni emplear medida alguna que sea contraria' al ordenamiento jurídico andino o que 'de algún modo obstaculice su aplicación'.

[179] *Secretaría General de la Comunidad Andina,* Guía Práctica para la aplicación de la Decisión 608 "Normas para la protección y promoción de la libre competencia en la Comunidad Andina", 2007.

[180] *Secretaría General de la Comunidad Andina,* Guía Práctica para la aplicación de la Decisión 608 "Normas para la protección y promoción de la libre competencia en la Comunidad Andina", 2007, p. 14.

administration and application system suggests that a decision of the Secretariat General is a binding precondition for private claims for damages and injunctions for breach of regional competition law. It should also be noted that the requirement of a prior decision of the Secretariat General had been considered as disadvantage of the former Decision 285.[181] Nevertheless, granting national judges with full jurisdiction regarding the existence of an anticompetitive practice in the sense of Article 4 of Decision 608 would undermine uniform application in the AndeanC. This is particularly the case, because the national judge will also be obliged to apply a *rule of reason* regarding possible exceptions without having specific evaluation criteria at hand. Moreover, the requirement of a competition authority's decision for successful damage claims does not reflect the common practice in the member states in the AndeanC. In fact, in Colombia recent discussions emphasized the judges' independence.[182] Judicial actions for damages are independent of the pronouncement of the Secretariat of Industry and Trade.[183] Moreover, even class actions for damages are possible under Colombian law.[184] However, there have not been private civil cases so far and civil litigation based on competition law breaches is only emerging.[185] This applies even more to Decision 608. It appears that the attributed degree of independence to national judges with regard to competition law enforcement does not relate to the frequency of private enforcement, but is rather explained by the lack of competition law expertise. As Decision 608 has remained without application, private enforcement of regional competition law remains a merely theoretical possibility.

The preamble of the Revised Treaty of Chaguaramas[186] and several Caribbean Court of Justice judgments[187] reaffirmed the importance of the private sector's par-

---

[181] *Böttcher*, Kartell- und Lauterkeitsrecht in den Ländern der Andengemeinschaft, 2004, pp. 64, 66.

[182] *Perilla Castro,* Propuestas para la Protección de la Libre Competencia ante los Jueces Civiles, 21 Boletín Latinoamericano de Comp. 78, 84 (2006). See also *Cortázar,* Curso de Derecho de la Competencia, 2011, pp. 139ff.; *Miranda Londoño,* La Indemnización de los Perjuicios causados por las Prácticas Restrictivas de la Competencia, 7/7 Rev. Der. Comp. 15, 26ff. (2011).

[183] One explanation for the "decentralized" enforcement of civil and criminal law actions in case of competition law breaches in Colombia could be found in the U.S. American model. The U.S., in its function as trading partner, is considered of paramount economic importance and granted technical assistance with regard to competition law enforcement in Colombia; see *Cortázar,* Curso de Derecho de la Competencia, 2011, p. 141.

[184] Article 4 of Law 472 of 1998, which provides that one of the "collective rights" eligible for vindication in a collective legal action is the right to free economic competition, *OECD,* Colombia: Assessment of Competition Law and Policy, OECD 2016, p. 80.

[185] *Perilla Castro,* Propuestas para la Protección de la Libre Competencia ante los Jueces Civiles, 21 Boletín Latinoamericano de Comp. 78, 78 (2006); *OECD,* Colombia: Assessment of Competition Law and Policy, OECD 2016, p. 80.

[186] Preamble of the Revised Treaty of Chaguaramas: "*Desirous* of restructuring the Organs and Institutions of the Caribbean Community and Common Market and redefining their functional relationships so as to enhance the participation of their peoples, and in particular the social partners, in the integration movement".

[187] *Trinidad Cement Limited TCL Guyana Incorporated v The State of the Co-operative Republic*

ticipation in the CSME. In this vein, the Caribbean Court of Justice applied a purposive interpretation of the Revised Treaty of Chaguaramas and stated that "private entities", "and in particular the social partners", are to play a major role in fulfilling the object and goals of the RTC and that "[t]he CSME is intended to be private sector driven."[188]

The CARICOM Competition Commission's decisions, in order to become binding, require additional implementation under national law.[189] Article 177(3) of the Revised Treaty of Chaguaramas sets out that prohibited agreements in Chapter VIII shall be "null and void" in jurisdictions of member states. One can conclude from this provision that the regional legislator envisaged that member states should guarantee for the right of private parties to rely on competition law as a defence, i.e. as a "shield", in contractual disputes.[190] It is yet not clear from this provision whether member states additionally have to provide for national legislation that guarantees that individuals can also claim damages for competition law breaches before national courts, thereby using competition law infringements proactively, as a "sword". It is only in a second step that one can ask whether member states have enacted domestic provisions that safeguard the possibility for individuals to make damage claims for breaches of Chapter VIII before national courts. Actually, individuals would then be making claims on the basis of an infringement of national law, because the absence of direct effect in CARICOM law requires member states to incorporate treaty provisions[191] and to render the decisions of the CARICOM Competition Commission binding.[192] The efficiency principle set out in Article 9 of the RTC does not reveal whether Article 176(4) RTC also incorporates the obligation for member states to guarantee the use of competition law as a "sword".[193] Yet the broad wording of Article 170(1) lit. b)(i)–(iv) RTC at least indicates that the

---

of Guyana, Caribbean Court of Justice Application No. AR 1 of 2008, CCJ 1 (OJ), [13ff.]; *Trinidad Cement Limited v The Competition Commission*, Caribbean Court of Justice Application No. OA 1 of 2012, CCJ 4 (OJ), [20].

188 *Trinidad Cement Limited TCL Guyana Incorporated v The State of the Co-operative Republic of Guyana*, Caribbean Court of Justice Application No. AR 1 of 2008, CCJ 1 (OJ), [13].

189 See also the obligation for member states to render the CARICOM Competition Commission's determinations enforceable, Article 174(6) of the Revised Treaty of Chaguaramas.

190 The debate on private enforcement in the European Union has been resolved by the Directive on Antitrust Damages Actions of 24 October 2014, OJ L 349, 5 December 2014, pp. 1–19. Regarding the now out-dated debate on the use of European competition provisions as a defence (as a "shield") or proactively (as a "sword") to claim damages or injunctive relief in national courts, see *Temple Lang*, EEC Competition Actions in Member States' Courts, 7 Fordham Int'l. L.J. 389, 403ff. (1983); *Wils*, Should Private Antitrust Enforcement Be Encouraged in Europe?, 26/3 W. Comp. 473–488 (2003).

191 The transformation into domestic law prevails irrespective the application of direct or indirect enactment of international law. Moreover, with the exception of Suriname and Haiti, all Member States of the CARICOM adhere to the dualist doctrine; see *Belle Antoine*, Commonwealth Caribbean, 2008, pp. 44, 215ff.

192 Article 174(6) of the Revised Treaty of Chaguaramas.

193 *Davies/Das*, Private Enforcement of Commission Commitment Decisions, 29 Fordham Int'l. L.J. 917, 927ff. (2005).

obligation should also be interpreted broadly. In particular Article 170(1) lit. b)(iv) of the RTC sets out that "Member States shall: (…) take effective measures to ensure access by nationals of other Member States to competent enforcement authorities including the courts on an equitable, transparent and non-discriminatory basis."[194] The wording indicates that courts are generally vested with a broad competition-law-related-enforcement function. This is also in line with the generally preponderant common law tradition among member states of the CARICOM, which is generally more litigation-based than civil law jurisdictions.[195]

It does not follow from the lack of direct effect of Chapter VIII that civil or criminal law damage claims before national courts require a prior decision of the CARICOM Competition Commission.[196] Nevertheless, private damage claims for the infringement of regional competition law require a national legal framework that implements the provisions of Chapter VIII in domestic law. The obligation to provide a national legal framework in order to guarantee civil and criminal law compensation for competition law infringements is yet left open in the Revised Treaty of Chaguaramas. Under international law, individuals would have to address the Caribbean Court of Justice to force member states to obey and fulfil any obligation that arises out of the Revised Treaty of Chaguaramas. In this context, the possible judicial action could be hollowed out, because individuals will have to seek special leave from their home state, against which they are planning to file a complaint.[197]

Furthermore, it has been questioned whether determinations of the CARICOM Competition Commission will have direct effect in all member states or solely in those that had been involved in the specific regional decision.[198] In the context of private damage claims this question can usually remain unanswered, because private parties will make their claim before courts located in the member state that was also involved in the decision. Similarly, in case of criminal law liability, individuals will usually face charges in the member state in which the offense has been committed.

---

[194] *A fortiori*, this must also apply to the nationals of the Member States, to whose court access is sought.

[195] *Ehlermann*, Implementation of EC Competition Law by National Anti-Trust Authorities, 17 ECLR 88, 89 (1996).

[196] *Beckford* in this context refers to the Jamaican case *Olint Corp Ltd. v National Commercial Bank Jamaica Ltd.*, Supreme Court Civil Appeal No. 40/2008 from the 12, 13, 14 May & 18 July 2008, [65], in which Judge Morisson, J.A. states: "While it is obviously correct that the only reference to an injunction in the Act is Section 47 (1)(b) which gives the court the power to grant an injunction at the instance of the Fair Trading Commission, in respect of uncompetitive conduct in breach of certain provisions of the Act, it does not necessarily follow from this in my view that a citizen whose statutory rights have been infringed is precluded from seeking injunctive relief under the court's general equitable jurisdiction in a proper case (See *Duchess of Argyll v Duke of Argyll* (1967) Ch 302 per Ungoed Thomas J at page 346: "I see no reason why the court should refuse to protect a right by injunction, merely because it is a statutory right.")." See *Beckford*, Enforcement of Competition Law in CARICOM, 35/2 W.I.L.J. 109, 117f. (2010).

[197] See below on the judicial control in the CARICOM, Part II, Dimension IV: Sect. 8.3.2.

[198] *Beckford*, in: *Drexl/Bakhoum/Fox/Gal/Gerber*, Competition Policy and Regional Integration in Developing Countries, 2012, pp. 185, 194.

Private enforcement before national courts might be problematic, because many allegedly anticompetitive practices are attributed to state behaviour. Relying on an European precedent,[199] the Caribbean Court of Justice with its exclusive competence to interpret the Treaty has explicitly recognized the principle of state liability in damages in the CARICOM.[200] Although the "threshold for eligibility for damages [caused by breaches by a member state] is (...) a high one",[201] at least the Caribbean Court of Justice provides for a legal organ, before which private entities can claim breaches of regional law committed by member states. The Caribbean Court of Justice's impact on the shaping of regional competition law enforcement and policy remains to be seen. It is at least theoretically possible, that the Caribbean Court of Justice's accessibility for individuals, if granted special leave, could constitute a vital counterweight to the strong discretion of the member states in competition law enforcement.

As a last resort, individuals can find "other creative ways"[202] to bring an alleged breach to the CARICOM Competition Commission's attention in order to invoke its *ex officio* competence to investigate.

One can conclude from the WAEMU's and the AndeanC's experiences that private enforcement does not constitute a fundamental pillar of enforcement of supranational competition law.[203] This might change in the long run with an increasing competition culture and awareness. Yet it also requires more specific rules, similar to the European damage claim Directive, as well as a number of regional competition law precedents in order to guarantee consistency of enforcement. It also requires special competition law training of national and regional judges. In particular, regional courts might play a determining role, as they might be called upon in order to force member states to obey to community obligations and enforce certain provisions regarding the protection of individuals' rights.

National courts on the other hand will depend on sufficient information. In the WAEMU, Article 22(4) of Regulation no. 03/2002/CM/UEMOA specifically provides for information requests by national judges. Nevertheless, this WAEMU provision on cooperation between the national judiciary and the Commission is not as far reaching as under European law. Apart from assistance of the Commission and information sharing obligations, the national courts can also ask the European

[199] ECJ, Judgement of the Court of 19 November 1991, *Francovich v Italian Republic,* C-6/90 and C-9/90, [1991] ECR 1991 I-05357, ECLI:EU:C:1991:428.

[200] *Trinidad Cement Limited TCL Guyana Incorporated v The State of the Co-operative Republic of Guyana*, Caribbean Court of Justice Application No. OA of 2009, CCJ 5 (OJ), [27f.].

[201] Trinidad Cement Limited TCL Guyana Incorporated v The State of the Co-operative Republic of Guyana, Caribbean Court of Justice Application No. OA of 2009, CCJ 5 (OJ), [28].

[202] Statement made by Kusha Haraksingh, current chairman of the CARICOM Competition Commission, made during an interview with the author in Port-of-Spain, Trinidad and Tobago, on 29 October 2012.

[203] In contrast, with regard to the European Union, see the Directive on Antitrust Damages Actions of 24 October 2014, 2013/0185 (COD), signed into law on 26 November 2014 and adopted on 10 November 2014.

Commission to provide for an opinion regarding the civil case on damages.[204] Even more importantly, national judges can always refer a case to the Court of Justice of the European Union.

Decision 608 does not provide for information sharing mechanisms between the Secretariat General and national courts. However, as Articles 23 to 25 of Decision 608 govern the exchange of information between national competition authorities and the Secretariat General, they could be applied accordingly to the relation between national courts and the regional competition authority. Similarly, Chapter VIII of the Revised Treaty of Chaguaramas does not entail an information sharing provision for national Courts. Article 173(2) lit. e) of the Revised Treaty of Chaguaramas however sets out that the Commission is obliged to cooperate with "competent authorities in the Member States". Competent authorities might also include national courts, because they are competent for enforcing criminal and civil law liabilities that arise out of breach of regional competition law.

The requirement of a prior regional competition authority's decision does not hinder effective private enforcement of regional competition law. It rather reflects a deliberate centralized conception of the regional competition law enforcement structure.[205] While such a precondition enhances uniform competition law enforcement of regional competition law, one should not neglect potential hurdles for private damage claims that can result out of it. Potential obstacles to private enforcement cover difficulties concerning the accessibility of the regional competition authority or the increased duration of private claims procedures.

Irrespective of the discussion on whether private enforcement also functions as an instrument for competition law deterrence[206] and whether it is feasible for regional competition law systems in developing countries, one should not neglect that the right to private damages touches upon core constitutional issues of the affected individuals. Hence, the absence of adequate protection of individual rights will challenge the constitutional and democratic justification of an integration movement overall, irrespective the degree of centralization or decentralization.

Although the different degrees of centralized or decentralized competition law enforcement within the WAEMU, the AndeanC and the CARICOM are visible in

---

[204] Article 15 of Regulation no. 1/2003/EU.

[205] In the WAEMU, this precondition is based on the exclusive enforcement competence of the WAEMU Commission, Advisory Opinion no. 003/2000/CJ/UEMOA, 27 June 2000, "Demande d'avis de la Commission de l'UEMOA relative à l'interprétation des articles 88, 89 et 90 du Traité relatifs aux règles de concurrences dans l'Union", Article 22 of Regulation no. 03/2002/CM/UEMOA. In the AndeanC, Decision 608 is held to establish a centralized system of administration and application of rules on the protection and promotion of free competition, *Secretaría General de la Comunidad Andina,* Guía Práctica para la aplicación de la Decisión 608 "Normas para la protección y promoción de la libre competencia en la Comunidad Andina", 2007, p. 14.

[206] On the discussion with regard to the functions of private and public antitrust enforcement in Europe see: European Commission, Green Paper on Damages Actions for breach of the EU antitrust rules, COM(2005)672, 19 December 2005; see also *Wils,* Ten Years of Regulation 1/2003, 4 J. Eur. Comp. L. Practice 293 (2013); *Wils,* The Relationship between Public Antitrust Enforcement and Private Actions for Damages, 32/1 W. Comp. 3–26 (2009); *Wils,* Should Private Antitrust Enforcement Be Encouraged in Europe?, 26/3 W. Comp. 473–488 (2003).

the framework of actual enforcement procedures, the latter are mostly characterized by shared enforcement competences. All three systems rely on cooperation with national competition authorities, although their degree of discretion varies. While the CARICOM attributes national competition authorities with most far-reaching discretion, which even limits the *ex officio* right of the CARICOM Competition Commission,[207] the WAEMU and the AndeanC regional competition authority still depend on the transferral of cases by national competition authorities. Moreover, in all three systems the actual enforcement of decisions in the narrow sense taken by the regional level with regard to breaches of regional competition law is decentralized.

8.1.4 Advocacy Function and Competition Promotion

Irrespective of the discussion on whether competition advocacy or competition enforcement can be substitutes or which one should be applied first in developing countries, competition advocacy and enforcement are at least mutually dependent. The more competition culture exists in the private sector and the public sector, the more cases and complaints will be submitted to the according competition law authorities. This section will briefly outline how the regional authority engages in competition advocacy directly and to what extent the regional framework incites the conduct of competition advocacy by competition-related bodies in the region.

The centralization of the competition law system in WAEMU, which imposed a uniform competition law on all member states, was expected to force member states to address competition law issues and engage in competition advocacy. The WAEMU Commission has organized workshops and seminars in order to spread knowledge about the regional legislation.[208] In accordance with Article 19(2) of Regulation no. 03/2002/CM/UEMOA it conducted studies and research on competition in order to initiate debates between economic actors. The provision *inter alia* mentions the Regional Consultative Chamber of the Union, national consultative chambers and consumer organisations. Moreover, the WAEMU Commission publishes annual reports, which are available on the WAEMU webpage.[209] While the sections on the state of competition remained relatively superficial in the early years, the WAEMU Commission started to summarize specific complaints and investigations.[210] Generally, the WAEMU Commission is obliged to publish its

---

[207] Article 176(1) of the Revised Treaty of Chaguaramas.

[208] For more details see *Bakhoum*, L'articulation du droit communautaire et des droits nationaux de la concurrence dans l'Union Economique et Monétaire Ouest Africaine, 2007, p. 268.

[209] Annual Reports of the Commission on the functioning and evolution of the Union (2000–2011) <http://www.uemoa.int/Pages/UEMOA/Commission%20de%20L_UEMOA/RapportsCommissiondelUEMOA.aspx> accessed 11 November 2018.

[210] See in this regard in particular the reports from 2009–2011, Rapport Annuel de la Commission sur le fonctionnement et l'évolution de l'Union 2009, p. 29 <http://www.uemoa.int/Documents/

competition law decisions.[211] Other advocacy measures are participation in international conferences. Moreover, the WAEMU Commission has organized seminars regarding capacity building in the member states and also for the judiciary. In this sense, the WAEMU Commission assists member states in the fulfilment of their obligation to reform national competition and sectorial laws and institutional structures in compliance with the community legislation, namely Article 6 of the Directive no. 02/2002/CM/UEMOA.[212]

Competition advocacy aimed at private businesses yet remains limited. The centralized system has impaired the accessibility of the competent competition authority and has created an obstacle for the private sector and the public to submit complaints based on breach of community competition law. Private enforcement obstacles run counter to the expected benefits of competition advocacy, which *inter alia* aims at an improvement of a competition culture in the private sector.

The focus of advocacy of the WAEMU Commission is so far mainly aimed at the creation of a competition culture among member states and public institutions. We can assume that the WAEMU attempts to cover a holistic competition advocacy approach in the long run, because Article 19(2) of Regulation no. 03/2002/CM/UEMOA makes explicit reference to professional organizations and consumer associations. So far, competition advocacy aimed at the private business sector relies on the member states' and national authorities' initiatives. Especially the national competition law authorities from Senegal, Benin and Ivory Coast have been and still remain active advocators.[213] However, competition advocacy regarding regional competition law has remained weak due to the deprival of all competition law enforcement powers. The Advisory Committee on Competition can also be defined as an indirect contributor to competition advocacy by organizing debates and discussing general questions on competition law matters according to Article 10 of the Executive Regulation no. 07/2005/CM/UEMOA regarding the internal procedures of the Committee.

A novelty for regional Andean competition law is the inclusion of the competition advocacy provisions in Chapter V of Decision 608.[214] Article 37 of Decision

Commission_de_L_UEMOA/Activites/Rapport2009Com.pdf> accessed 11 November 2018; Rapport Annuel de la Commission sur le fonctionnement et l'évolution de l'Union 2010, pp. 21f. <http://www.uemoa.int/Documents/Commission_de_L_UEMOA/Activites/Rapport2010com.pdf> accessed 11 November 2018; Rapport Annuel de la Commission sur le fonctionnement et l'évolution de l'Union 2011, pp. 20f. <http://www.uemoa.int/Documents/Commission_de_L_UEMOA/Activites/Rapport2011Com.pdf> accessed 11 November 2018.

211 See Article 29 of Regulation no. 03/2002/CM/UEMOA.

212 See Annual Reports of the Commission on the functioning and evolution of the Union (2000–2011) <http://www.uemoa.int/Pages/UEMOA/Commission%20de%20L_UEMOA/RapportsCommissiondelUEMOA.aspx> accessed 11 November 2018.

213 For more information, see *Bakhoum*, L'articulation du droit communautaire et des droits nationaux de la concurrence dans l'Union Economique et Monétaire Ouest Africaine, 2007, pp. 270ff.

214 Article 36 of Decision 608 sets out that national regulatory policy may not hinder or distort competition in the common market. The Dictamen no. 01-2007 of the Secretariat General specifies that only national policies with an effect on cross-border trade, as set out in Article 5 of Decision

608 entails an obligation for member states to enhance competition advocacy measures.[215]

The AndeanC also engages in informal competition advocacy, in form of seminars and capacity building measures. The guide on Decision 608 is also supposed to promote a competition law culture and to inform on the regional law.[216] In this context, the Secretariat General published booklets on the aspects of competition law and anticompetitive practices.[217]

Especially during the initial implementation phase of Decision 608, during the "Proyecto Competencia", the Secretariat General organized seminars for Bolivia and Ecuador in order to assist them during the implementation process of a national competition law system.[218] However, since then the Secretariat General has remained merely reactive in the field of informal competition advocacy in particular after 2006 when Venezuela withdrew from the AndeanC. The lack of precedents in combination with the limited amount of specific competition-related advocacy actions of the Secretariat General has even led to the negative image of the regional institution by national competition authorities of not handling "real" competition law cases, but only engaging in the publishing of "cute little leaflets on the ABC of competition".[219]

The relatively experienced national competition law authorities, namely the Peruvian INDECOPI and the Colombian Superintendence of Industry and Trade, regularly organise seminars in order to proliferate a competition culture nationally; this did not change with the enactment of Decision 608.

In the CARICOM, Article 173(1) lit. b) of the Revised Treaty mentions the promotion and protection of competition in the Community as one of the functions of the Commission. More specifically these functions are set out in Article 170 lit. a) ii) and Article 173(2) lit. h) of the Revised Treaty. The CARICOM Competition Commission is supposed to "establish and maintain an information system to enable enterprises and consumers to be kept informed about the operation of markets within the CSME" (Article 170 lit. a) ii)) and to "develop and disseminate informa-

---

608, fall within the scope of application of Article 36 of Decision 608. See above Part II, Dimension I: Sect. 5.1.5.2.

[215] For more information on "soft" harmonization through non-binding guidelines, see above Part II, Dimension II: Sect. 6.3.

[216] *Secretaria General de la Comunidad Andina,* Guía Práctica para la aplicación de la Decisión 608 "Normas para la protección y promoción de la libre competencia en la Comunidad Andina", 2007, p. 3.

[217] See for example *Secretaría General de la Comunidad Andina,* el ABC de la competencia, 2004.

[218] Comision de la Union Europea and Secretaria General de la Comunidad Andina, "Proyecto Competencia", Armonizacion de las Reglas de Competencia en la Region Andina, (ASR/B7-3100/IB/98/0099), Informe de Actividades Periodo: Febrero de 2003 a Abril de 2003, 9 May 2003.

[219] This statement was made by a representative of a national competition law authority in the AndeanC, who was referring to a brochure published by the AndeanC and the European Commission "el ABC de la competencia" in the framework of the "Proyecto Competencia" in 2004. The representative of the national competition authority made this statement during an interview conducted with the author in January/February 2012.

tion about competition policy, and consumer protection policy" (Article 173(2) lit. h)). Although these provisions entail information and advocacy functions directly aimed at businesses and consumers, the regional CARICOM Competition Commission has so far only conducted advocacy actions that targeted state entities, such as judges or the national competition law agencies. The CARICOM Competition Commission for example conducted training sessions with judges in St. Lucia under a funding of the European Union.

Yet advocacy actions aimed at businesses and consumers are in practice mostly exercised by national competition authorities with competition law expertise, mainly Jamaica's and Barbados' Fair Trading Commissions. While the Revised Treaty of Chaguaramas does not entail explicit competition advocacy duties for national competition authorities, Jamaica's and Barbados' legislations include according provisions. Section 5(2) of the Jamaican Fair Competition Act[220] and Section 5(1) lit. a), b) of the Barbados Fair Competition Act[221] spell out specific information and cooperation duties of the Commissions with regard to businesses, consumers and their associations. The Fair Trading Commission in Barbados was able to increase awareness of competition law by organizing annual training workshops and meetings with representatives from the business sector and consumers.[222]

Mostly for the lack of resources on the regional level, competition advocacy in all three regional trade agreements remains predominantly national. In the WAEMU, the situation is different because of the strong centralization of competences. The

---

[220] Section 5(2) of the Fair Competition Act:

It shall be the duty of the Commissioner-
(a) to make available
(i) to persons engaged in business, general information with respect to their rights and obligations under this Act;
(ii) for the guidance of consumers, general information with respect to the rights and obligations of persons under this Act affecting the interests of consumers;
(b) to undertake studies and publish reports and information regarding matters affecting the interest of consumers;
(c) to co-operate with and assist any association or body of persons in developing and promoting the observance of standards of conduct for the purpose of ensuring compliance with the provisions of this Act.

[221] Section 5(1) lit. a) and b) of the Fair Competition Act:

The Fair Trading Commission shall
(a) be responsible for the promotion and maintenance of fair competition;
(b) carry out, on its own initiative or at the request of any person that has an interest in the matter, such investigations or inquiries in relation to the conduct of trade
(i) as will enable it to prevent the use of trading practices in contravention of this Act;
(ii) as it may consider necessary or desirable in connection with any matters falling within the provisions of this Act.

[222] See for example the workshop entitled "Competition Law & Policy", 30 and 31 March 2011, organized by the Fair Trading Commission of Barbados for business people, administrators and legal professionals; for more information see <http://www.ftc.gov.bb/index.php?option=com_content&task=view&id=206&Itemid=96> accessed 11 November 2018.

limited activity by regional competition authorities with regard to competition advocacy has mainly addressed public institutions, such as national competition authorities or other governmental institutions. The division of the addresses of advocacy between the private[223] and the public sector[224] targeted advocacy is an efficient distribution of competition advocacy duties, because it is easier for national agencies to address private domestic businesses and consumers. Nevertheless, the separation of "private and government advocacy" exercised by national and regional competition authorities respectively has also created a gap. Regional competition law tends to remain solely applied by member states, but not by private parties.

Generally, advocacy targeting the private sector remains scarce. This creates a vicious circle: the less awareness among businesses and consumers of regional competition law, the less will they address and try to enforce regional competition law.[225] In the CARICOM, the institutional situation is different. Private parties cannot address the CARICOM Competition Commission directly, but through their national competition authorities.[226] However, apart from taking the procedure via the national agency, they can also find "creative ways"[227] of bringing allegedly anticompetitive practices to the attention of the regional Commission. Additionally, given that awareness of the benefits of regional competition law and policy exists, consumers and businesses could function as controlling entities that can exercise public pressure in order to force national competition authorities and other related domestic institutions to transfer cases to the regional level.

It is thus not sufficient to vest the regional agency only with a "government advocacy" task. While this might be appropriate at the initiation stage of a regional authority because of the resources constraints, in the long run, regional agencies should also directly address private businesses and consumers or oblige national competition authorities to engage in competition advocacy in the private sector with regard to regional competition law and policy. The latter solution however requires that national competition authorities are sufficiently aware and convinced of the benefits of having a regional competition law system.

---

[223] Competition advocacy aimed at the private sector.

[224] Competition advocacy aimed at the public sector.

[225] Similarly *Cortázar*, in: *Drexl/Bakhoum/Fox/Gal/Gerber*, Competition Policy and Regional Integration in Developing Countries, 2012, pp. 133, 150ff.

[226] Article 175 and Article 176 of the Revised Treaty of Chaguaramas.

[227] Statement of the Kusha Haraksingh, Chairman of the CARICOM Competition Commission in an interview with the author conducted on 29 October 2012 in Port of Spain, Trinidad and Tobago.

8.2 Cooperation Mechanisms with National Structures

There are different possible forms of cooperation mechanisms with and among member states.[228] Inter-governmental networks can provide for compulsory or voluntary cooperation structures. They can be marked by high or low level of formalism. They can be specialized and only competent in certain policy areas, such as competition policy, or vested with general competences. A network can be vested with policy enforcement functions solely, or it can (possibly additionally) be assigned to contribute to policy-making.[229] As inter-governmental networks create a platform in which national competition authorities and the regional competition authority share information, they are inclined to not only discuss the issues at stake, but also debate general competition policy issues.

With regard to competition law enforcement, possible functions of inter-governmental networks predominantly comprise the exchange of information. Depending on the institutional design of an RTA overall it can also be responsible for the allocation of cases among the regional and national competition authorities. The allocation of competition competences among competition authorities can be a general task or an extraordinary function when conflicts arise in this respect. Moreover, cooperation mechanisms are often used during competition law investigations. This can take the form of assistance regarding the conduct of an investigation or a network can participate in the decision-making process.

8.2.1 Specialized Inter-governmental Cooperation Bodies

The WAEMU and the AndeanC adopted similar cooperation mechanisms to the European Competition Network, by creating specialized inter-governmental cooperation organs, which are comprised of representatives from the national competition authorities and the regional competition authority.

---

[228] Generally one could define inter-governmental cooperation mechanisms as "cross-border cooperation between public authorities, with or without the participation of private actors and/or international organizations, in a forum other than a traditional international organization (process informality), and/or as between actors other than traditional diplomatic actors (such as regulators or agencies) (actor informality), and/or which does not result in a formal treaty or legally enforceable commitment (output informality)"; see *Pauwelyn,* in: *Pauwelyn/Wessel/Wouters*, Informal International Lawmaking, 2012, pp. 13, 22.

[229] With regard to the ECN, *Cengiz* states that it is marked by a high degree of formalism, that it includes compulsory information obligation for national competition authorities and that despite being designed as a policy-enforcement network, it has acted as policy-making network. On the other hand, he describes that communication between members of the ECN takes place on an informal basis. *Cengiz,* The European Competition Network, 2009, pp. 8ff. <http://cadmus.eui.eu/bitstream/handle/1814/11067/MWP_2009_05.pdf?sequence=1> accessed 11 November 2018.

8.2.1.1 The Advisory Committee on Competition in the WAEMU

The WAEMU Advisory Committee on Competition was created via Article 28 of Regulation no. 03/2002/CM/UEMOA and its structure is governed in the Internal Procedures of the Advisory Committee on Competition Regulation of Execution no. 07/2005/COM/UEMOA.[230] The Committee is composed by two persons representing each member state, who are experts in the field of competition.[231] The members of the Advisory Committee are nominated for 3 years, which can be prolonged once, and act in the function as members of the Committee in full independence and discretion.[232] According to Article 5 of the internal procedures a president is appointed for 1 year following the alphabetical order of member states. The Committee renders its opinion based on a majority vote.[233] It is assisted by an administrative and technical secretariat.[234]

Neither Article 3 of the Internal Procedures of the Advisory Committee on Competition, nor Article 28(3) of Regulation no. 03/2002/CM/UEMOA clarify, whether appointed members necessarily have to be employees of the national competition authority. However, a narrow interpretation could exclude member states that do not possess national competition authorities or rely on sectorial regulation. In fact, Article 28(3) of Regulation no. 03/2002/CM/UEMOA and Article 4 of the internal procedures of the Committee point out that in case of issues that touch upon sectors of general economic interests the delegation of the member state has to comprise a representative of the national regulatory authority or a representative of the professional association of the respective sector.

The Committee meets once per semester in the headquarters of the WAEMU Commission.[235] Meetings only take place after convocation by the WAEMU Commission. The latter fixes the date and determines the agenda of the next meeting.[236] At least 15 days before the meeting member states are informed about the

---

[230] Reglement de L'Exécution n° 007/2005/COM/UEMOA portant Reglement interieur du Comite Consultatif de la Concurrence.

[231] Art. 28(3) of Regulation no. 03/2002/CM/UEMOA and Article 3 of Internal Procedures of the Advisory Committee on Competition Regulation of Execution n° 007/2005/COM/UEMOA *portant Reglement interieur du Comite Consultatif de la Concurrence.*

[232] Article 3 of Internal Procedures of the Advisory Committee on Competition Regulation of Execution n° 007/2005/COM/UEMOA *portant Reglement interieur du Comite Consultatif de la Concurrence.*

[233] Article 30 of Internal Procedures of the Advisory Committee on Competition Regulation of Execution n° 007/2005/COM/UEMOA *portant Reglement interieur du Comite Consultatif de la Concurrence.*

[234] Article 11 of Internal Procedures of the Advisory Committee on Competition Regulation of Execution n° 007/2005/COM/UEMOA *portant Reglement interieur du Comite Consultatif de la Concurrence.*

[235] Articles 12, 13 of Internal Procedures of the Advisory Committee on Competition Regulation of Execution n° 007/2005/COM/UEMOA *portant Reglement interieur du Comite Consultatif de la Concurrence.*

[236] Articles 15, 16 of Internal Procedures of the Advisory Committee on Competition Regulation of Execution n° 007/2005/COM/UEMOA *portant Reglement interieur du Comite Consultatif de la Concurrence.*

agenda.[237] Half of the members of the Committee (eight members) have to agree in order to issue a recommendation of the Advisory Committee on Competition.[238] Thus, the structure of the Committee does not guarantee that all member states are equally represented in the final recommendation. Moreover, extraordinary sessions can only be initiated by the Commission or two thirds of the Committee's members.[239] It appears that the impact of the centralization of competition competences also extends to the Advisory Committee. While member states can under certain circumstances demand a session of the Advisory Committee on Competition, the main initiation power is vested in the WAEMU Commission. Similar to the multi-level and hierarchical procedures within the Commission, the internal structure of the Advisory Committee of Competition features a high degree of formalism. In this context, *Mor Bakhoum* points out that the required formal convocation by the WAEMU Commission for the meetings establishes a potential obstacle to the efficiency of the Advisory Committee on Competition, in particular in situations where fast decisions are at stake.[240] Yet written procedures are possible if no specific case is at stake.[241] This does not only save time, but also simplifies participation of all representatives of national authorities.

On the other hand, one has to acknowledge that member states of the WAEMU, despite limping collaboration in investigations and enforcement of community competition law in the narrow sense and despite their different levels of competition law experience, have been participating regularly in meetings of the Advisory Committee. The formalistic procedure regarding the hearings of the Advisory Committee hence did not provide an obstacle to participation. One could even argue that the formalities, such as the provision of the agenda at least 15 days before the meeting and the convocation by the Commission, represented an incentive for member states to deal with competition law matters and thereby enhanced horizontal cooperation or information sharing between national competition or related authorities.

The Advisory Committee on Competition has to be consulted prior to decisions regarding a competition law infringement.[242] Furthermore, its prior consultation is

---

[237] Article 16 of Internal Procedures of the Advisory Committee on Competition Regulation of Execution n° 007/2005/COM/UEMOA *portant Reglement interieur du Comite Consultatif de la Concurrence.*

[238] Article 22 of Internal Procedures of the Advisory Committee on Competition Regulation of Execution n° 007/2005/COM/UEMOA *portant Reglement interieur du Comite Consultatif de la Concurrence.*

[239] Article 13(2) of Internal Procedures of the Advisory Committee on Competition Regulation of Execution n° 007/2005/COM/UEMOA *portant Reglement interieur du Comite Consultatif de la Concurrence.*

[240] See *Bakhoum,* L'articulation du droit communautaire et des droits nationaux de la concurrence dans l'Union Economique et Monétaire Ouest Africaine, 2007, p. 226.

[241] Article 14 of Internal Procedures of the Advisory Committee on Competition Regulation of Execution n° 007/2005/COM/UEMOA *portant Reglement interieur du Comite Consultatif de la Concurrence.*

[242] Article 28(4) of Regulation no. 03/2002/CM/UEMOA.

mandatory with regard to decisions that concern state-imputed practices and regarding the amount of a fine.[243] In contrast to its large scope of involvement, the impact on the WAEMU Commission's decisions remains limited. The submitted opinions of the Advisory Committee do not bind the Commission. According to Article 28(7) of Regulation no. 03/2002/CM/UEMOA the WAEMU Commission is not even obliged to publish the opinion. While this provision might aim at protecting confidential information considerations, it also reduces the pressure on the Commission to explain its considerations on the Advisory Committee's opinion.[244] On the other hand, there has not been a single case so far, in which the WAEMU Commission did not follow the Advisory Committee's recommendation.

As a good example, the *CAMEG* case[245] initiated by the WAEMU Commission in 2010 illustrates the involvement of the Advisory Committee on Competition in regional competition law enforcement procedures. The *CAMEG* case is based on a complaint submitted by private distributors of pharmaceuticals in Burkina Faso, the *Société de Distribution Pharmaceutique du Burkina* and the *Société Multi M*. The company's' headquarters are located in Ouagadougou. The complaint was lodged against the state of Burkina Faso, which had granted special rights to *CAMEG* (*Centrale d'Achat des Médicaments Génériques*). *CAMEG* is a non-profit entity of private law, which is charged with the public service obligation to provide the public with pharmaceuticals at the best possible conditions. Accordingly, *CAMEG* also engages in import and buying activities regarding pharmaceutical products. The state of Burkina Faso is a stakeholder of *CAMEG*. The two private pharmaceutical distribution companies argued that the preferential treatment by the state led to distortions in the market and was thus infringing Regulation no. 02/2002/CM/UEMOA regarding anticompetitive practices and Regulation no. 04/2002/CM/UEMOA regarding the control of state aids. After having submitted the complaint at first before the national competition law authority of Burkina Faso,[246] it was submitted to the WAEMU Commission on 31 March 2010. The Commission then initiated proceedings on 20 April 2010.[247]

After having heard the respective parties to the complaint, *inter alia* the Minister of Economics and Finances in Burkina Faso and *CAMEG*, the opinion of the Advisory Committee was requested. However, instead of asking for a general recommendation regarding the case, the WAEMU Commission specified its demand. It specifically asked whether, in view of the social objectives that support a special treatment of trade for generic products it is relevant to require that the distribution channels of these products obey the same rules as for other pharmaceutical products. It also wanted to know whether the status of *CAMEG*, being a non-profit association, was sufficient to reserve it the advantages that the plaintiff denounced. The

[243] Article 28(4) of Regulation no. 03/2002/CM/UEMOA.

[244] Article 28(7) of Regulation no. 03/2002/CM/UEMOA.

[245] The case is not published.

[246] The national authority dealt with the case in the period from 14 June 2006 until 7 July 2008, when it rejected the complaint based on its lacking competence.

[247] Lettre n° 4004/DC/DMRC/DCONC of 20 April 2010.

answers to these questions were held to be relevant in order to decide on the existence of an anticompetitive practice related to the state of Burkina Faso according to Article 6 of Regulation no. 02/2002/CM/UEMOA and on the applicability of Regulation no. 04/2002/CM/UEMOA.

While the case indicates that the Advisory Committee on Competition is attributed a decisive role in the procedure, it also demonstrates that the Committee's opinion is mainly taken into account in view of the two above-mentioned questions. On the one hand, specific questions facilitate the recommendation process for members of the Committee. This in particular applies to member states with limited competition law experience, but also affects the overall efficiency. Specific questions accelerate the decision-making process among the representatives of the member states. Simultaneously, they increase the utility of the recommendation for the WAEMU Commission. It becomes more probable that the Commission will actually respect the recommendation in its decision. On the other hand, it is unclear whether the WAEMU Commission will only consider the parts of the recommendation, which answer the specific question(s). Such a scenario would limit the Advisory Committee's discretion considerably. In fact, the Advisory Committee would then resemble more a technical body of assistance, whose activity, though formally codified, depends on the motivation of the WAEMU Commission. The Advisory Committee on Competition is formally conceived as a policy-enforcement network and not as policy-making network.[248] At least, this appears to be the conception of the WAEMU Commission.

Generally the Advisory Committee on Competition establishes an intergovernmental cooperation mechanism. It embodies a link between national and regional authorities. The involvement of representatives of the member states justifies the decisions made by the regional authority by increasing its support. The more member states participate in the decision-making process, the more probable will the regional decision be applied and enforced by the agencies of the member states. Nevertheless, the non-binding character of issued opinions of the Advisory Committee of Competition is not capable of adequately balancing the centralized enforcement system in the WAEMU. While the obligation of prior hearing of the Committee guarantees that member states are informed about ongoing procedures, it does not guarantee that it actually exercises an influence and actually contributes to the decision regarding the procedures.

All in all, the Advisory Committee on Competition is restrained to its advisory function. Despite regular participation of member states, it does not guarantee collaboration of national authorities with the WAEMU Commission in the direct enforcement of regional competition law, nor does it significantly enhance horizontal cooperation between domestic competition authorities.

---

[248] Regarding the European Competition Network, see *Cseres,* Questions of Legitimacy in the Europeanization of Competition Law Procedures of the EU Member States, 7 February 2013, p. 24 <http://ssrn.com/abstract=2213192> accessed 11 November 2018.

8.2.1.2 The Andean Committee on the Defence of Free Competition

The Andean Committee on the Defence of Free Competition was created through Articles 38ff. of Decision 608. It is a permanent technical organ, whose objectives are to fulfil the tasks assigned by the community norms, as well as the development of any other measure that contributes to the promotion and protection of competition in the Andean Community.[249] To be more specific, according to Art. 6 of Decision 608 the Committee has to give recommendations regarding possible exceptions to Decision 608 and it entails an advocacy function, by making recommendations on the possible elimination of regulatory measures taken by member states according to Article 36 of Decision.[250] One of its most important functions is the formulation of opinions regarding the results of a specific investigation on possible anticompetitive behaviour according to Article 21 of Decision 608. In the latter case, the invocation of the Andean Committee of Defence of Free Competition is mandatory for the Secretariat General.

The Andean Committee of Defence of Free Competition comprises a representative of each national competition law authority of the member states.[251] According to Article 3 of the Internal Regulation of the Committee, these representatives have to be accredited by the National Organs of Integration. However, Article 3 does neither give further requirements for the qualification of a representative or specifies the accreditation requirements, nor does it explain the notion of "National Organs of Integration".[252]

The Committee expresses itself through "informes". Although these "informes" do not bind the Secretariat General, the Secretariat has to reason any deviation from the Committee's results expressed in the "informe".[253] The Andean Committee of Defence of Free Competition is hence a cooperative but non-supranational body. It allows cross-border cooperation between the national and regional competition law authorities. These authorities work on an independent basis in the Committee.

---

[249] Reglamento Interno del Comité Andino de Defensa de la Libre Competencia, Annexo II de la Acta de la Segunda Reunion Ordinaria del Comité Andino de Defensa de la Libre Competencia, SG/R.CDC/II/ACTA, 3 October 2005.

[250] Further obligations and rights of the Committee are included in the Articles 13, 20, 22, 26, 27 and Chapter VI of Decision 608.

[251] Art. 3 of Reglamento Interno del Comité Andino de Defensa de la Libre Competencia, Annexo II de la Acta de la Segunda Reunion Ordinaria del Comité Andino de Defensa de la Libre Competencia, SG/R.CDC/II/ACTA, 3 October 2005.

[252] One has to highlight that so far also representatives from the Secretariat General have participated in each Reunion of the Committee. According to Article 7 of the Reglamento Interno del Comité Andino de Defensa de la Libre Competencia, the Committee can agree upon the participation of specialists or other observers and attribute them with the right to vote.

[253] Article 22 of Decision 608. The importance of this requirement was emphasized by the Colombian State in the Second Reunion of the Governmental Experts on Competition Law, Informe de la Segunda Reunion de Expertos Gubernamentales en Materia de Libre Competencia, 16 and 17 February 2000, p. 10.

The Andean Committee for Defence of Free Competition is supposed to meet regularly in ordinary and extraordinary reunions.[254] Ordinary sessions are scheduled preferably in the first and third trimester of each year, thus at least twice a year, by convocation of the President of the Committee.[255] Extraordinary sessions on the other hand can be called upon either by the Committee's President or the Secretariat General.[256] The President is even obliged to do so if at least two representatives of member states request a session of the Committee.[257]

Decisions of the Committee are taken by consensus by the present parties, except in the cases of Article 21 of Decision 608, when the Secretariat General publishes an "informe" regarding an investigation in the context of a possible anticompetitive regional practice. In the latter case, the Committee's decision has to be supported by at least three member states. The underlying minority still has the possibility to express and clarify its diverging position.[258]

---

[254] Article 8 of Reglamento Interno del Comité Andino de Defensa de la Libre Competencia, Annexo II de la Acta de la Segunda Reunion Ordinaria del Comité Andino de Defensa de la Libre Competencia, SG/R.CDC/II/ACTA, 3 October 2005.

[255] Article 8 lit. a) of Reglamento Interno del Comité Andino de Defensa de la Libre Competencia, Annexo II de la Acta de la Segunda Reunion Ordinaria del Comité Andino de Defensa de la Libre Competencia, SG/R.CDC/II/ACTA, 3 October 2005. It is to be noted that all sessions of the Andean Committee for the Defence of Competition were convened by the General Secretary, although not envisaged for ordinary sessions. However, one should not overestimate this fact, because the Secretariat General in interviews with the author stated that its convocation also relied on national initiatives. Thus the Secretariat General in fact did not take a proactive role in the meetings of the Andean Committee.

[256] Article 8 lit. b) Reglamento Interno del Comité Andino de Defensa de la Libre Competencia, Annexo II de la Acta de la Segunda Reunion Ordinaria del Comité Andino de Defensa de la Libre Competencia, SG/R.CDC/II/ACTA, 3 October 2005.

[257] Article 8 lit. b) Reglamento Interno del Comité Andino de Defensa de la Libre Competencia, Annexo II de la Acta de la Segunda Reunion Ordinaria del Comité Andino de Defensa de la Libre Competencia, SG/R.CDC/II/ACTA, 3 October 2005.

[258] Article 13 of Reglamento Interno del Comité Andino de Defensa de la Libre Competencia, Annexo II de la Acta de la Segunda Reunion Ordinaria del Comité Andino de Defensa de la Libre Competencia, SG/R.CDC/II/ACTA, 3 October 2005. It is to be noted that the Internal Rules for the Andean Committee were adopted in 2005, before Venezuela left the AndeanC. However, the majority vote based on three member states envisaged in Article 13 was not changed after the withdrawal of Venezuela.

Resolutions Concerning the National Confederation of Palm-Growers and Palm Oil Enterprises (Peru) vs. Fund for Price Stabilisation for Palm-Oil and Its Fractions (Colombia)

Resolutions 892[259] and 910[260] (concerning the initiation of an investigation), 984[261] (concerning the investigation itself) and 1040[262] (concerning a reconsideration of the correcting measures) deal with a price cartel and demonstrate the involvement of the Andean Committee on the Defence of Free Competition in Andean competition law enforcement. In the case, an association of Peruvian enterprises of palm-oil growers accused Colombian palm oil producers of distorting competition by concertedly fixing prices of Colombian palm oil for exportation and for the internal market by using the mechanisms set out in the Colombian Fund for the Stabilization of Prices for Palm oil (FEDEPALMA).[263] FEDEPALMA had been established according to the Colombian Law no. 101 of 1993 and *inter alia* offers financial compensations for producers, sellers or exporters in order to regulate national production and to increase exportations to the respective market.[264]

Although the proceeding started under former Decision 285, Resolution 984 also includes the newly created Andean Committee on the Defence of Free Competition and the Secretariat General took into consideration its opinion on the examined practice. In the present case, the Andean Committee disagreed with the Secretariat General by opposing an investigation and correcting measures or sanctions.[265]

---

[259] Resolución 892 de la Secretaría General de la Comunidad Andina, Solicitud de la Confederación Nacional de Palmicultores y Empresas de Palma Aceitera del Perú y de las empresas Industrial del Espino S.A., Industrial Alpamayo S.A., Alicorp S.A. y Ucisa S.A. "...sobre aplicación de medidas para corregir perjuicios causados por prácticas restrictivas a la libre competencia", presentada al amparo de la Decisión 285, 14 January 2005.

[260] Resolución 910 de la Secretaría General de la Comunidad Andina, Recurso de Reconsideración contra la Resolución 892 presentado por la Federación Nacional de Cultivadores de Palma de Aceite de Colombia (Fedepalma) y las empresas Acegrasas S.A. y C.I. Grandinos S.A. EMA, 12 April 2005.

[261] Resolución 984 de la Secretaría General de la Comunidad Andina, Investigación iniciada mediante Resolución 892, al amparo de la Decisión 285, relativa a la solicitud de la Confederación Nacional de Palmicultores y Empresas de Palma Aceitera del Perú, y de las empresas Industrial del Espino S.A., Industrial Alpamayo S.A., Alicorp S.A. y Ucisa S.A. para la "...aplicación de medidas para corregir perjuicios causados por prácticas restrictivas a la libre competencia", 15 December 2005.

[262] Resolución 1040 de la Secretaría General de la Comunidad Andina, Recurso de Reconsideración contra la Resolución 984 presentado por el Gobierno de Colombia, la Federación Nacional de Cultivadores de Palma de Aceite de Colombia (Fedepalma) y la empresa Acegrasas S.A., 25 July 2006.

[263] "Fondo de Estabilización de Precios para el Palmiste, Aceite de Palma y sus Fracciones".

[264] Mechanisms for the stabilization of prices are contained in the Decree 2354 of 1996.

[265] Anexo IV de la Acta de la Segunda Reunion Ordinaria del Comité Andino de Defensa de la Libre Competencia, "Informe del Comité Andino de Defensa de la Libre Competencia sobre la Investigación iniciada mediante Resolución 892", SG/R.CDC/II/ACTA, 3 October 2005.

While Article 21 of Decision 608 clearly states that the Committee has to be called upon 5 days after the remission of the "informe" of the Secretariat General, the Secretariat General released its "informe" on 31 August 2005 and only called upon the members of the Committee on 3 October 2005. Still, this delay did not signify a curtailment of the Andean Committee's rights since it had sufficient time to read the Secretariat General's "informe" and the Secretariat General did not dissent from its previous analysis. However, such delays led to a prolongation of the process. Due to a procedural error, the Andean Committee was even called upon a second time. However, it only repeated its prior opposition to the Secretariat General's "informe".[266]

In Informe 984, the Secretariat General sanctioned the Colombian palm-oil producers for fixing prices and for engaging in concerted practices.[267] It thus did not follow the Andean Committee's unanimous recommendation, which had opposed several arguments in the Secretariat General's informe. First, the Committee remarked that the Secretariat General had overlooked the production efficiencies that the Colombian undertakings achieved through the fund. It also postulated benefits for small and medium-sized enterprises arising out of it. On these arguments, the Secretariat General generally agreed with the Committee. However, it questioned a particular benefit for small and medium-sized firms. Secondly, and even more remarkable were the arguments by the Andean Committee that were based on the member states' sovereignty. It denied the presence of a concerted practice because the Colombian enterprises lacked a "free will" to enter into the restrictive agreement or to engage in the concerted practice. It eluded in its recommendation that the fund was based on a sovereign decision of a member state, for which the participants of the fund were obliged by law to comply with it. By definition, this would exclude the existence of an agreement.[268] Going even further, the Committee in its recommendation stated that the right to free competition was not absolute and

---

[266] Resolución 984 de la Secretaría General de la Comunidad Andina, Investigación iniciada mediante Resolución 892, al amparo de la Decisión 285, relativa a la solicitud de la Confederación Nacional de Palmicultores y Empresas de Palma Aceitera del Perú, y de las empresas Industrial del Espino S.A., Industrial Alpamayo S.A., Alicorp S.A. y Ucisa S.A. para la "aplicación de medidas para corregir perjuicios causados por prácticas restrictivas a la libre competencia", 15 December 2005, p. 3; Anexo IV de la de la Acta de la Segunda Reunion Ordinaria del Comité Andino de Defensa de la Libre Competencia, "Informe del Comité Andino de Defensa de la Libre Competencia sobre la Investigación iniciada mediante Resolución 892", SG/R.CDC/II/ACTA, 3 October 2005.

[267] The sanctioning of this case still followed Decision 285. The Secretariat General granted Peru the right to limit the import of palm oil originating from Colombia for one year. The sanctioning mechanisms under Decision 285 constituted a major point of criticism. First, temporary blockage of imports, resembling a model of anti-dumping duties, had the effect of limiting intra-regional trade. Second, it did not guarantee compliance by Colombian oil producers, because they were actually not directly sanctioned for their behaviour. See *Botta,* The Role of Competition Policy in the Latin American Regional Integration: A Comparative Analysis of Caricom, Andean Community and Mercosur, 21–22 October 2011, St. Gallen, pp. 21f.

[268] Anexo IV de la de la Acta de la Segunda Reunion Ordinaria del Comité Andino de Defensa de la Libre Competencia, "Informe del Comité Andino de Defensa de la Libre Competencia sobre la Investigación iniciada mediante Resolución 892", SG/R.CDC/II/ACTA, 3 October 2005, p. 18.

could not interfere with legitimate state intervention that was aimed at the protection of socially vulnerable sectors.

The Secretariat General generally recognized the sovereign decision of Colombia to create the fund in order to protect socially vulnerable sectors. However, it made it very clear that such national protection could not be sustained if other economic agents of other member states were disadvantaged by such protection, namely when intra-regional trade is affected. Referring to the arguments based on the member states' sovereignty, the Secretariat General concluded that the right to free competition was only valid to the extent to which member states have agreed upon it. Decision 285, based on the consent of all member states, did not contain any exceptions relevant for the case. Finally, the Andean Committee also unsuccessfully referred to formal inconsistencies of the Secretariat General's informe, which would lead to its invalidation.

The Secretariat General did address all the arguments made in the Andean Committee's recommendation. Yet, regarding the Committee's argument based on the lack of a "free will" of the Colombian undertakings, it rebutted the argument only by referring to the existence of a concerted practice. To some extent explained by the lack of regional competition law precedents, the Secretariat General's allegations on the Committee's substantive arguments, in contrast to formality arguments, seem to be partially superficial. Although, it is difficult to discern a regular pattern from the above-mentioned resolutions for the lack of other Andean competition law references, one can draw certain conclusions regarding the relationship between the Andean Committee on the Defence of Free Competition and the Secretariat General.

During the process of reforming Decision 285 and the reunions of governmental experts,[269] one of the main points for discussion was whether the Andean Committee on the Defence of Free Competition's recommendations should be binding for the Secretariat General. The Secretariat General argued that such far-reaching powers would contradict and undermine its executive powers.[270] On the other hand, the member states argued in favour of a binding character in order to benefit from the existing competition law experience to its largest possible extent and to enhance dynamic participation of national competition authorities.[271] The position of the member states clearly emanated from a resentment to cede sovereignty. This concern is also reflected in the Andean Committee's recommendation regarding Resolutions 892 and 910, in which it aimed at the rejection of the complaint *inter alia* based on arguments of national sovereignty. Interestingly, during that time,

---

[269] Prior to the creation of the Andean Committee for the Defence of Free Competition in 2005, four Reunions of Governmental Experts in the field of free competition took place: SG/REG.LC/I/Informe/Rev.1, 29 October 1998; SG/REG.LC/II/INFORME, 16 and 17 February 2000; SG/REG.LC/III/INFORME 24 and 25 October 2011; SG/REG.LC/IV/INFORME, 1 August 2003.

[270] Informe de la Segunda Reunion de Expertos Gubernamentales en Materia de Libre Competencia, SG/REG.LC/II/INFORME, 16 and 17 February 2000, pp. 7ff. Other interesting points of discussion were the scope of Article 5 of Decision 608 and the "ex-officio" powers of the Secretariat General to initiate an investigation.

[271] Informe de la Segunda Reunion de Expertos Gubernamentales en Materia de Libre Competencia, SG/REG.LC/II/INFORME, 16 and 17 February 2000, pp. 3ff.

Colombia held the presidency of the Andean Committee on the Defence of Free Competition. Accordingly, a Colombian representative, namely the President of the Colombian Superintendence of Industry and Trade, wrote the recommendation, albeit he acted in his function as president of the Andean Committee. However, the Committee's recommendation to reject the case was taken in consensus and not even the Peruvian representative dissented.

The Andean Committee on the Defence of Free Competition has not lived up to its expectations. Meanwhile, activities have even ceased completely; the last meeting took place in November 2010.[272] During this period, Bolivia held the presidency of the Committee. Peru, which held the presidency of the Committee in 2011/2012, did not show interest in the convocation of a meeting. In an interview with the author, a representative of the INDECOPI even stated that the Peruvian authority generally had no interest in advancing the regional competition law or regional cooperation. The INDECOPI was more interested in keeping its protagonist role as one of the most experienced competition authorities in Latin America; especially since Brazilian, Chilean or Mexican competition law authorities had gained more experience and increased efficacy. Representatives from the Colombian Superintendence of Commerce argued in a similar vein.[273]

Finally, representatives of domestic competition law agencies had criticized the bureaucratic obligations postulated by the Secretariat General.[274] They in particular complained about the Secretariat General's insistence on the sufficient authorization of the national representatives, which partly hindered governmental experts' meetings.[275]

---

[272] Acta de la Primera Reunión Extraordinaria del Comité Andino de Defensa de la Libre Competencia, SG/R.CDC/I-EX/ACTA, 30 November 2010.

[273] Statements of representatives from the Colombian Superintendence of Commerce made in an interview with the author conducted in Bogota, Colombia on 1 February 2012.

[274] Statements of representatives from the Colombian Superintendence of Commerce made during an interview with the author in Bogota, Colombia on 1 February 2012.

[275] Acta de la Primera Reunión Ordinaria del Comité Andino de Defensa de la Libre Competencia, SG/R.CDC/I/ACTA/Rev.1, 13 September 2005, p. 3. However, in this case the Venezuelan representative was not a member of the Venezuelan competition authority and thus did not comply with Article 38 of Decision 608, see Anexo 2.a "Informe I Seminario Subregional de Reflexión" of *European Commission,* "Proyecto Competencia", Armonización de las Reglas de Competencia en la Region Andina, (ASR/B7-3100/IB/98/0099), 3–5 March 2003, p. 8: "cabe anotar que no pudo realizarse la revision de la propuesta de norma comunitaria por (…) no haberse podido reunir a las expertos gubernamentales en la materia responsables de realizar la negociación correspondiente." "Los participantes al evento (…) no estaban facultados por sus países para negociar la norma comunitaria en materia de competencia." See also *De León*, An Institutional Assessment of Antitrust Policy, 2009, p. 82. According to *De León* development of antitrust rules were hindered by a formalistic interpretation of Andean rules by the Secretariat General, which emerged from its internal bureaucracy.

Conflicts of Competence Between the Andean Committee on the Defence of Free Competition and the Secretariat General in the Context of Article 36 of Decision 608

There is no doubt that the Andean Committee on the Defence of Free Competition has to be consulted by the Secretariat General in the context of specific investigations and decisions according to Article 21 of Decision 608. Conflicts of competence between the Andean Committee on Competition and the Secretariat General however arose during an action for non-compliance initiated by the Colombian flower companies on the ground that Colombia had infringed Article 36 of Decision 608.[276] Related to the powers of the Andean Committee's powers, Colombia had argued that the prejudicial phase of an action for non-compliance before the Secretariat General was inadmissible in the context of Article 36 of Decision 608.[277] The Colombian government argued that the Andean Committee was competent for making recommendations on regulatory measures by member states as set out in Article 36.[278]

The Secretariat General acknowledged that Article 36 of Decision 608 generally includes an obligation for member states and that the Andean Committee on the Defence of Free Competition can make recommendations on behalf of the member states in order to comply with this obligation. Nevertheless, according to the Secretariat General, this power of the Andean Committee is limited to situations, in which no legal consequences are created.[279] It held that the Andean Committee's recommendation power was located in a "competition sphere" which was distinct from a judicial action, such as an action for non-compliance.[280] However, the Committee's recommendation could still constitute the ground, on which the Secretariat General accelerates preliminary proceedings to a judicial trial.[281]

The Secretariat General's restrictive view on the powers of the Andean Committee on Competition is based on two considerations. First, it holds the view that the legal action of non-compliance according to Article 23 of the Treaty regarding the Creation of the Tribunal of Justice of the AndeanC is the only appropriate procedural path to determine whether a member state has not complied with community obligations, such as Article 36 of Decision 608 or other Andean legal norms.[282] Second, it relies on its exclusive competence during an action for non-compliance, in which the Secretariat General holds the right of initiative, either on an *ex officio* or complaint basis. Since this exclusive right emanates directly from the Treaty regarding the Creation of the Tribunal of Justice, which constitutes part of primary

---

[276] Dictamen N° 01-2007, Secretaría General de la Comunidad Andina.

[277] Dictamen N° 01-2007, Secretaría General de la Comunidad Andina, p. 8.

[278] *Ibid.*

[279] Dictamen N° 01-2007, Secretaría General de la Comunidad Andina, p. 11.

[280] *Ibid.*

[281] *Ibid.*

[282] *Ibid.*

Andean law, secondary law, such as Decision 608, could not restrain it.[283] The Secretariat General thereby establishes a concurrence between the "competition-sphere"-procedure as set out in Article 36 of Decision 608 and the judicial procedure of an action of non-compliance, which is upheld in the Guidelines regarding the application of Decision 608.[284] Yet this signifies that in the case that affected parties have initiated an action for non-compliance against a member state, the Andean Committee's recommendation powers are completely undermined. It would be desirable to require the Tribunal of Justice of the AndeanC to ultimately decide on the participation of the Andean Committee during an action for non-compliance involving an infringement of Article 36 of Decision 608. In fact, it will have to clarify whether the Andean Committee on the Defence of Free Competition is designed as a competition-law-enforcement body only or whether it is also has the role of participating in regulatory policy decisions.

The Andean Committee on the Defence of Free Competition creates a link between the Secretariat General and the national competition authorities. In this sense, it is generally capable of enhancing the exchange of information during competition law enforcement. The actual impact on competition decisions by the Secretariat General is yet questionable. Although the Secretariat General has to respond to the recommendations of the Andean Committee, it has fulfilled this obligation very superficially. Moreover, the Andean Committee's impact on national market regulatory measures and the scope of application of Article 36 of Decision 608 are still unclear. Yet the Andean Committee on the Defence of Free Competition had once been able to bring together national and regional policy-makers, namely in the drafting process of Decision 608. Considering that Decision 608 is based on the consent of the governmental experts of the Andean member states, its insufficient use is even more surprising. Generally, the institutional design of the Committee would allow it to also constitute a general competition advocacy and policy organ. Nevertheless, in the absence of a strong national political will to support regional competition law enforcement, one could consider a restructuration of the Andean Committee on the Defence of Free Competition into an informal horizontal information exchange platform. So far, horizontal cooperation between national competition authorities has mostly taken place between authorities of a similar level of experience and development and irrespective the membership in the AndeanC.[285]

---

283 *Ibid.*

284 *Secretaria General de la Comunidad Andina,* Guía Práctica para la aplicación de la Decisión 608 "Normas para la protección y promoción de la libre competencia en la Comunidad Andina", 2007, pp. 43f.

285 For example, the Peruvian INDECOPI engages in bilateral competition law cooperation with the competition authorities from Chile, El Salvador, Panama or Colombia. Statements made by Miguel Ángel Luque Oyarce, president of the Indecopi, in an interview with the author in Lima, Peru on 19 January 2012.

8.2.1.3 Summary of Specialized Inter-governmental Cooperation Organs

The Andean Committee on the Defence of Free Competition and the Advisory Committee on Competition in the WAEMU can both be considered as specialized inter-governmental cooperation networks. Yet the different outcomes of the Andean and the WAEMU cooperation bodies are striking. The mere number of publications such as “informes” in the AndeanC or opinions in the WAEMU does not serve as an adequate reference in order to evaluate their efficiency. Instead, the results produced by the two bodies have to be weighted in the light of the general institutional design of the RTA and general legal, political and economical considerations.

The former Reunion of Governmental Experts, the predecessor of the Andean Committee on the Defence of Free Competition, was an active participant during the legislative process of Decision 608. After its implementation, three ordinary and one extraordinary session of the Andean Committee on the Defence of Free Competition took place. In the latter, the Andean Committee was called upon to express its opinion regarding an ongoing competition case. However, after 2010 activities completely ceased.

The WAEMU Advisory Committee on Competition has given recommendations on a large number of regional cases.[286] Remarkably, even member states without prior or limited competition law experience have been attending the meetings of the Committee regularly.

Internal Structure of the Committees

Given the legal provisions regarding the internal structure of the Andean Committee on the Defence of Free Competition and the Advisory Committee on Competition, the two bodies do not differ significantly from each other. Especially their composition with representatives of the member states and circulating presidency among member states are similar. In the WAEMU and the AndeanC, representatives from the regional authority can also attend meetings of the Committees. Moreover, a minimum quorum exists in order to take decisions.[287] Internal regulations of both Committees provide for accountability rules, according to which members in case

[286] In 2010 the Advisory Committee on Competition for example participated in the following cases: “OMA-SENISOT”, “FARINE au Mali”, “Textile au Mali”, “Canal Overseas”, “Affaire STAF contre SONAPOST”, “Affaire ASKY”, “Affaire CAMEG” (the opinions are not published).

[287] While in the AndeanC at least three of the four member states have to be present, in the WAEMU half of the members have to attend a hearing. Decisions of the Advisory Committee on Competition are taken by a majority vote. As regards the Andean Committee of Defence of Competition, Article 13 of the Internal Regulations clarifies that in the context of a regional competition law procedure (Article 21 of Decision 608) a recommendation of the Committee requires a majority vote by at least three of its members. However, members that do not agree have the possibility to publish and express their diverging opinion separately. Other decisions by the Andean Committee have to be taken unanimously by all attending members.

of infringement of their obligations are liable according to the national laws.[288] Similarly, both Committees being part of the regional framework also have to report to the regional competition authorities, thereby being accountable to the regional level.

Main differences arise regarding the right of initiative. The main invocation right in the WAEMU system is vested in the WAEMU Commission. On the other hand, in the AndeanC the president initiates ordinary sessions. The WAEMU Advisory Committee's internal structure is more formalized and leaves less initiating rights to the member states. Consequently, the WAEMU system requires more initiative from the regional level for the Advisory Committee to become active. On the other hand, the Andean Committee relies more on the initiative from the member states, in particular from the country that holds the presidency of the Committee at a given point in time.

Having described the basic structures of the Andean Committee and the Advisory Committee, one can highlight certain aspects. First, in the WAEMU and the AndeanC the focus of inter-governmental Committees remains on their *advisory* function during the decision-making phase, rather than on cooperation mechanisms during the enforcement of the decision. The focus on the advisory function might be justified, because in the AndeanC as well as in the WAEMU, enforcement structurally takes place in close cooperation with the member state(s) concerned.[289] In the long run, regular meetings of the advisory committees can still enhance bonding of national agencies, thereby furthering horizontal cooperation.

The decision-making power of the regional authority remains untouched by the rights and obligations of the Advisory Committee in the WAEMU and the Andean Committee. This is principally attributed to the non-binding character of the opinions issued by the Committees. The obligation of the regional competition authorities to ask for a recommendation from the Committees does not guarantee that the latters' recommendations are taken into account in their content and not only as a mere formality. Yet the system of mandatory consultation provides for an adequate information structure for member states regarding ongoing regional cases.

The underlying question whether the Advisory Committee on Competition and the Andean Committee's internal structure had an impact on regional competition law enforcement's effectiveness cannot be answered *per se*. This is in particular due to the difficulty to measure the effectiveness of a cooperative or advisory body whose functions often encompass informal and non-binding activities. Nevertheless, the WAEMU Advisory Committee's and the Andean Committee's institutional designs might have enhanced the achievement of the objectives of such networks.

---

[288] Article 3 of Internal Procedures of the Advisory Committee on Competition Regulation of Execution n° 007/2005/COM/UEMOA *portant Reglement interieur du Comite Consultatif de la Concurrence* (WAEMU); Article 4 of Reglamento Interno del Comité Andino de Defensa de la Libre Competencia, Annexo II de la Acta de la Segunda Reunion Ordinaria del Comité Andino de Defensa de la Libre Competencia, SG/R.CDC/II/ACTA, 3 October 2005.

[289] See above on regional competition law enforcement procedures, Part II, Dimension IV: Sect. 8.1.

While information sharing is enhanced,[290] an expansion of regulatory reach or a filling of loopholes in national jurisdictions was not achieved. The main reason is that such expansions of national sovereignty were not intended by the creation of the cooperation body. Instead, cooperation mechanisms become a necessary link between national and regional authorities in a regional competition law system in which national sovereignty is transferred and the decision-making power is centralized. This is distinct to a situation, in which horizontal cooperation between national competition law authorities had emerged beforehand and in which member states strive for greater regulatory autonomy.

One can thus draw the conclusion, that the overall regional competition law system's design, centralized or decentralized, also contours the internal structure of the cooperation body. In case of the centralized West African and the mixed Andean internal structures, they are consistent with the cooperation body's institutional design.

Requirement of National Initiatives and Commitment

Political Will to Participate

The more the operability of an inter-governmental cooperation body depends on the initiative of member states, the more important is the political will of the latter to support the cooperation body and the regional competition law system overall. The experiences of the Andean Committee on the Defence of Free Competition highlight the importance of the member states' commitment to the RTA and the Committee on the Defence of Free Competition. The Andean Committee was very active at its initiation phase during 2005 and 2006. Just during that period, Ecuador had a strong interest in the development of a regional competition law framework, because since 2002, it had been struggling to enact a domestic legislation.[291] The Committee was reactivated in 2010. Interestingly, this was shortly after reforms of national competition policies took place or had taken place.[292]

In the WAEMU, on the other hand, member states participated regularly in the sessions of the Advisory Committee on Competition. Members could thereby try to recover their last participation possibilities in competition law decision-making. They might also feel pressured by other member states, as the majority of cases in the WAEMU concern state-related behaviour and often involve disputes between member states. The participation in the Committee might thus prevent member

[290] At least, vertical information-sharing between regional and national authorities is enhanced. Horizontal information-sharing might be enhanced in the long run.

[291] Proyecto de Ley de Promoción y Defensa de la Competencia Económica. Discussed in Congress, 28 August 2002, 1 and 2 and 30 October 2002. The project was however rejected in Congress. It was only in 2011 when Ecuador implemented a domestic competition law.

[292] Colombia and Peru reformed their competition laws in 2009 and 2008. In Bolivia the former sectorial SIRESE law was replaced in 2008/2009. Ecuador was in the legislation process of a competition law, which entered into force in 2011. See above Part II, Dimension I; Sect. 5.2.2.

states to be disadvantaged. Finally, another possible explanation might be the convocation right, which is exercised by the WAEMU Commission, which exerts more pressure than convocations by other member states.

Impact of the Level of Experience

In the WAEMU, even member states with no or limited competition law experience attended the meetings of the Advisory Committee regularly. Given the actual experience of the Andean Committee for the Defence of Free Competition, it is to be highlighted that a member state with limited or no competition law experience stimulated the first impulse for regional cooperation, however then shifted the focus towards national enforcement. On the other hand, for competition law-experienced member states, the commitment towards regional cooperation depends on the relevance of regional competition law, which is closely linked to the relevance of the common market for that state.[293]

The general will of member states to participate in an advisory body is thus not proportionate to its level of competition experience. On the contrary, in particular member states with little experience can profit from cooperation mechanisms. Inexperienced jurisdictions can gain from the more experienced members of the RTA, especially at an early implementation phase of domestic competition law. Nevertheless, after having surpassed this first implementation stage, the cooperation mechanism has to provide for different incentives for participation. The main incentives arise out of the general acceptance of the regional competition law system and the commitment of member jurisdictions to it. The more this general political will is missing, the more important are additional incentives set by the regional level.

Rules on Confidentiality

An important aspect influencing the commitment of member states to participate in an inter-governmental cooperation body is the existence of sufficient rules protecting confidential information. Member states will be reluctant to share (confidential) information that might lead to an investigation against national undertakings. Moreover, the lack of confidential information provisions bears potential for conflict with a member state's mandate of national accountability and political responsibility. In particular national provisions protecting confidential information that are embedded in the larger national constitutional framework could be circumvented. This would in the long run decrease civil society's support and reputation of the regional competition law system.

The Andean Committee on the Defence of Free Competition generally obliges members of the Committee to respect the confidentiality of information that is being exposed in the exercise of their functions and to refrain from disseminating

---

[293] Regarding the relevance of the creation of a common market for a regional competition law system, see below Part III, Sect. 11.3.1.

information.[294] According to Article 10 of the Internal Regulations, sessions are generally public.[295] In the WAEMU, meetings of the Advisory Committee on Competition are generally not public and it lies within the discretion of the WAEMU Commission to publish the Committee's recommendation.[296] Moreover, the Internal Regulations of the Advisory Committee in Article 28 do not only incorporate general confidentiality obligations for its members, but also refer to Article 30 of Regulation no. 03/2002/CM/UEMOA and Article 25 of Regulation no. 04/2002/CM/UEMOA, which include special provisions on the exploitation of business secrets.

The Need for Regional Initiative

The most direct and possibly strongest incentive set by a regional authority is mandatory participation of the inter-governmental cooperation body in the context of specific regional competition law cases. Yet it must not necessarily be the most efficient incentive. While in the WAEMU the Advisory Committee on Competition has therefore been called upon frequently, the stagnation of reunions of the Andean Committee on the Defence of Free Competition is also attributed to the lack of regional legal decisions. The Secretariat General did not react on the stagnation of the Committee either and did not consider institutional changes to the body, which appears to have become obsolete.

Does Timing Matter?

Given the internal rules of the Advisory Committee on Competition in the WAEMU and the Andean Committee on the Defence of Free Competition, one can conclude that both integration systems have established inter-governmental bodies with a high degree of formalism and accountability at a stage in which neither on the national nor on the regional level existed extensive competition law experience.

The formalistic framework might be surprising, because there is a frequently made assumption that networks "generally emerge naturally between actors who need each other's cooperation in search of a common goal".[297] However, clarifying the notion of "natural emergence" of networks, two aspects are important to highlight. First, even naturally grown networks required a common goal supported by the members of the networks at its initiation phase. Effective competition law

[294] Article 4 lit. d) and e) of Reglamento Interno del Comité Andino de Defensa de la Libre Competencia, Annexo II de la Acta de la Segunda Reunion Ordinaria del Comité Andino de Defensa de la Libre Competencia, SG/R.CDC/II/ACTA, 3 October 2005.

[295] It is probable that Colombia was aiming at the rejection of the Secretariat General's Resolutions 892 and 910 for the lack of specific provisions on confidential information.

[296] Article 28(7) of Regulation no. 03/2002/CM/UEMOA.

[297] *Cengiz*, Multi-level Governance in Competition Policy, 35 Eur. L.Rev. 660, 663 (2010).

enforcement constitutes such a goal. However, the experiences in the WAEMU and the AndeanC have shown that member states tend to underestimate the necessity of cooperation during competition law enforcement. Generally, they tend to prefer national enforcement. Second, it is unclear whether efficient networks can also be created on the regional level without some level of prior horizontal cooperation. Without prior cooperation in place a high level of formality and accountability of a regional cooperation network might constitute a discouragement to participation. National competition authorities might feel "pressured" by a high degree of formalism, instead of building trust in the leeway of informal information-sharing.

Yet the experiences of the Andean Committee on the Defence of Free Competition and the Advisory Committee on Competition show that horizontal cooperation between national competition authorities does not happen spontaneously.[298] Rather informal and formal cooperation is facilitated in a formalized framework.[299] In the same vein *Firat Cengiz* argues that "the weakness of common discourse between the competition authorities of Europe pre-Modernisation largely explains the choice of formalism in the design of the ECN."[300] Yet the efficiency gains should not be overrated. In the WAEMU, the centralized system national authorities are limited to a cooperation function in competition law enforcement, thereby solely relying on vertical cooperation. Horizontal cooperation without the involvement of the regional level has by definition become obsolete in the centralized competition law system in the WAEMU. Similarly, the activities of the Andean Committee on the Defence of Free Competition have ceased.

Prior horizontal cooperation is not a necessary element to the installation of an inter-governmental specialized cooperation network. The main aspect to such a network's efficiency remains the political will of participating member states. However, in order not to hinder this political will, the level of existing cooperation and the level of formality of the network have to be balanced.

Creating Vertical and Horizontal Cooperation Via Inter-governmental Cooperation Bodies

Furthermore, cooperation mechanisms within an RTA always comprise two dimensions: the vertical and horizontal network. While the horizontal network can entail direct cooperation between national competition authorities, the vertical network encompasses the cooperation between the regional and national level, and also a possible coordinating function of the regional level that intertwines both dimensions. The Andean Committee on the Defence of Free Competition has so far been mostly focused on the vertical cooperation. Reunions so far have always been

---

[298] *Jenny/Horna,* in: *Brusick/Alvarez/Cernat,* Competition Provisions in Regional Trade Agreements, 2005, pp. 281, 289.

[299] *Ibid.*

[300] *Cengiz,* The European Competition Network, 2009, pp. 9f. <http://cadmus.eui.eu/bitstream/handle/1814/11067/MWP_2009_05.pdf?sequence=1> accessed 11 November 2018.

attended by representatives of the Secretariat General and have dealt with specific regional cases (such as resolutions 894, 910, 984, 1040) or the internal procedures of the Committee. Only in 2010, in the first extraordinary reunion of the Andean Committee, the member states exchanged general information concerning on-going national competition law reforms or legislative progress. Peru's representative even shared conducted investigations by the INDECOPI. After that reunion, horizontal cooperation however ceased.

The same applies to the Advisory Committee on Competition in the WAEMU, which has so far only dealt with specific cases. One can thus conclude that it seems to be easier to establish vertical cooperation in an inter-governmental network. Moreover, experiences of both Committees so far lead to the conclusion that vertical cooperation mechanisms do not automatically further horizontal cooperation and do not by itself lead to convergence of national competition laws.

8.2.2 General Cooperation and Policy Coordination Policy Bodies: CARICOM's Council of Trade and Economic Development

The CARICOM in its organization differs from the institutional design in the WAEMU and the AndeanC. The Council of Trade and Economic Development (COTED) constitutes a Community organ of the CARICOM that is generally responsible for the promotion of trade and economic development within the region.[301] It assists the Conference of Heads of Governments with its work by monitoring the evolution of the CSME, including the possibility to exempt less developed countries of intra-regional free trade or the common external tariff.[302]

The COTED influences regional competition law enforcement of the CARICOM Competition Commission in several ways. It is the competent body for developing the competition policy within the Caribbean Community[303] and for resolving jurisdictional conflicts regarding the jurisdiction of the CARICOM Competition Commission or a member state to investigate an allegedly anticompetitive conduct.[304] Furthermore, the COTED can request the CARICOM Competition Commission to carry out an investigation[305] and it can determine exemptions for the application of Chapter VIII.[306] Thus, the COTED is an institutional body that is

[301] Article 15(2) of the Revised Treaty of Chaguaramas.

[302] *O'Keefe,* Latin American and Caribbean Trade Agreements, 2009, pp. 366f.; see also Chapter VII of the Revised Treaty of Chaguaramas on disadvantaged countries, regions and sectors.

[303] Article 182 of the Revised Treaty of Chaguaramas.

[304] Article 176(5) of the Revised Treaty of Chaguaramas.

[305] Article 175(2) of the Revised Treaty of Chaguaramas.

[306] Article 183 of the Revised Treaty of Chaguaramas.

involved at the policy-making level[307] and that impacts the enforcement of regional competition law in specific cases.

8.2.2.1 Internal Structure

The COTED is composed by ministers designated by the member states.[308] It is thus not a permanent body with a consistent staff, but due to political changes in the member states or at their discretion the representatives in the COTED can change.[309]

In order to form a quorum a simple majority of member states has to be present.[310] While each member state has one vote, decisions require a qualified majority vote of at least three quarters of the membership of the CARICOM.[311] Although decisions have a binding effect, subscribing to the dualist doctrine, rights and obligations can only be created for states as subjects of international law.[312] Decisions of the COTED thus require national arrangements in order to establish the bindingness for individuals.[313] In exceptional cases in which a matter is held to be of "critical importance to the national well-being of a member state" decisions can only be reached by affirmative vote by all member states. A two thirds majority of the member states is sufficient to determine whether a matter is of "critical importance".[314] Decisions regarding procedural matters only require a simple majority.[315]

Minutes of the COTED meetings or even videos of it are partly published. This guarantees a certain level of transparency. Nevertheless, one has to reemphasize the political character of the COTED. It is composed by politicians originating from the national trade ministries and usually deals with policy-shaping matters. Political positions might be traded against each other without always giving the specific reasons for a decision.[316] Moreover, the members of the COTED always have to achieve a balance between decisions furthering economic development and decisions that are realistic and can be implemented by the member states concerned.[317] Moreover,

[307] The COTED is currently discussing the introduction of a regional merger regulation.

[308] Article 15(1) of the Revised Treaty of Chaguaramas.

[309] Article 15(1) of the Revised Treaty of Chaguaramas.

[310] Article 27(1) of the Revised Treaty of Chaguaramas.

[311] Article 29 of the Revised Treaty of Chaguaramas.

[312] *Pollard,* in: *Hall/Chuck-A-Sang,* CARICOM Single Market and Economy Genesis and Prognosis, 2007, pp. 91, 94.

[313] *Beckford,* The Appropriate Design and Enforcement of Competition Law and Policy in Countries at Different Stages of Market Development, 26–28 May 2010, Brasilia, p. 10.

[314] Article 29(4) of the Revised Treaty of Chaguaramas.

[315] Article 27(3) of the Revised Treaty of Chaguaramas.

[316] See *Trinidad Cement Limited v The Caribbean Community*, Caribbean Court of Justice Application No. AR 3 of 2008, CCJ 2 (OJ), [15]: "It is not clear what prompted COTED's decision as no reasons were provided".

[317] See statements made by Maxine McClean, Minister of Foreign Affairs and Foreign Trade, Barbados and Chair of COTED at the opening of the Thirty-Second Meeting of the COTED in Georgetown, Guyana: "The agenda before us is a long and serious one. Alarmingly, it is one that

the CARICOM member states are heavily marked by a "continuing jealous guarding of sovereign rights",[318] which enhances distrust among each other. This kind of "island mentality" and the concentration of economic power in Trinidad and Tobago, Barbados and Jamaica increase the difficulty to reach a common decision on economic matters. Furthermore, national administrative procedures and changing governments have often led to lengthy procedures achieving an agreement only on the smallest nominator of an issue.[319]

Finally, the Caribbean Court of Justice is competent to control decisions taken by the COTED.[320] A review of COTED's decision based on the argument that it has acted *ultra vires* is restricted to situations, in which the COTED exercised discretion.[321] Nevertheless, it is questionable whether purely political matters such as competition policy considerations are justiciable at all.[322] Arguably, the CARICOM Competition Commission could appeal to the Caribbean Court of Justice on the grounds that the COTED's exemption in accordance with Article 183(2) RTC was not in the "public interest".[323] As the reputation of the Caribbean Court of Justice is high and member states are hence wiling to appeal to the Court, it is also probable that in the decisions taken before the COTED, member states will try to anticipate and consider the reasoning and judgments of the Caribbean Court of Justice. This preconditions that there exist legal precedents of the Caribbean Court of Justice that define the notion of "public interest".

---

we have seen before, (...) we cannot continue to take decisions simply for the record and not take steps to implement them". See also statements made by Carolyn Rodrigues-Birkett, Minister of Foreign Affairs, Guyana at the same meeting: "Our agenda is populated with some critical institutional and infrastructural issues, some of which have been with the COTED for over a decade. While we must exercise great care to fashion efficient and acceptable arrangements, we have to be cognizant of the increasingly competitive global environment we are operating in and the demand on the Community from within and without to act with utmost urgency." CARICOM Press Release 185/2011, 19 May 2011, "Effectiveness of COTED, CARICOM on the line – COTED chair".

318 *Stewart,* in: *Drexl/Bakhoum/Fox/Gal/Gerber,* Competition Policy and Regional Integration in Developing Countries, 2012, pp. 161, 173.

319 Statement made by Gayla St. Clair Poyles, Chief Economist at the Ministry of Trade, Trinidad and Tobago, during an interview with the author in Port-of-Spain, Trinidad and Tobago, on 30 October 2012.

320 *See Trinidad Cement Limited v The Caribbean Community,* Caribbean Court of Justice Application No. OA 1 of 2009, CCJ 4 (OJ). In this case a private enterprise challenged a decision of COTED to suspend the CET before the Caribbean Court of Justice.

321 *Trinidad Cement Limited v The Caribbean Community,* Caribbean Court of Justice Application No. OA 1 of 2009, CCJ 4 (OJ), [41].

322 *Beckford,* The Appropriate Design and Enforcement of Competition Law and Policy in Countries at Different Stages of Market Development, 26–28 May 2010, Brasilia, p. 18.

323 Statement made by Kusha Haraksingh, current Chairman of the CARICOM Competition Commission, during an interview with the author in Port-of-Spain, Trinidad and Tobago, on 29 October 2012.

8.2.2.2 Requirement of National Initiative

Being a body of the CARICOM with general economic policy-making power, the requirement of national initiative regarding competition law matters has to be analysed slightly differently. Meetings of the COTED take place regularly and deal with a broad range of economic and trade-related issues.

Political Will of Member States to Participate in the COTED

The political will to participate in the COTED is generally given among member states of the CARICOM. As decisions are binding and concern basic economic and trade related matters, member states are directly concerned by decisions and would act against their own interest by staying away from meetings.[324] Moreover, bearing in mind the suspicions brought forward against each other, but in particular against economically preponderant Trinidad and Tobago, member states are regular participants at the COTED meetings.

It remains to be seen how active member states will be regarding specific competition law enforcement, for example by requesting investigations by the CARICOM Competition Commission or by determining exemptions of the application. It is important to point out though that the first case the CARICOM Competition Commission dealt with was initiated following a request of the COTED.[325]

Influence of the Level of Competition Law Experience in the COTED

The composition of national trade ministers also brings with it a certain degree of competition law expertise. In countries where a competition law authority exists, national ministries are partly still involved in competition law enforcement.[326] In case a national competition law authority is still not existent at all, the ministry of trade and industry often constitutes the competent competition law enforcing entity.[327] Furthermore, the COTED frequently relies on reports or recommendations of external experts.[328]

---

[324] Article 15 and Article 29(1) of the Revised Treaty of Chaguaramas.

[325] *Trinidad Cement Limited v The Competition Commission,* Caribbean Court of Justice Application No. OA 1 of 2012, CCJ 4 (OJ).

[326] For example in Jamaica, the government finally granted the acquisition of Claro by Digicel, see above Part II, Dimension I: Sect. 5.2.3.1.

[327] See for example the current situation in Suriname, see above Part II, Dimension I: Sect. 5.2.3.2.

[328] See for example the "Report on the Audit of the Supply Capacity and Demand for Cement in the Region" of 10 October 2008. This report was a working document at the 26th COTED meeting in Georgetown on 24–25 November 2008. See *Trinidad Cement Limited v The Caribbean Community,* Caribbean Court of Justice Application No. AR 3 of 2008, CCJ 2 (OJ), [12].

In the framework of a general inter-governmental cooperation body the lack of specific competition law expertise is not as problematic as in specific competition law cooperation bodies, such as the Advisory Committee on Competition in the WAEMU or the Andean Committee on the Defence of Free Competition. The knowledge of the ministers suffices to request investigations. Whether it suffices to grant exemptions for certain sectors is yet questionable, although only transitory exemptions might not create irrevocable distortions to the common market. The composition of ministers also guarantees that the regional competition policy is embedded in general industrial policy and trade considerations. It further allows for certain flexibilities in the application of regional competition law, as special treatment can be provided for certain sectors or enterprises.[329]

Yet the combination of political decision-making and exercise of legal functions could be considered problematic. Although the COTED represents a political body, according to Chapter VIII it also has to deal with specific legal questions such as the resolution of a conflict of jurisdiction between the CARICOM Competition Commission and a member state.[330] Moreover, granting an exemption, the COTED is inclined to primarily contemplate industrial and trade policy considerations, instead of deciding the matter on merely legal and efficiency-based considerations.[331]

The conception of the COTED as a political body also touches on issues of confidentiality. Participating member states are not forced to disclose information during a meeting. Moreover, Article 170(4) of the RTC provides for a norm that protects confidential information of member states.

8.2.2.3 The Need for Regional Initiative for Cooperation Through the COTED

Bearing in mind the strong institutional position of the COTED and its diverse ways of exercising influence on the CARICOM Competition Commission, initiatives originating from the CARICOM Competition Commission to support the meetings of the COTED are improbable. In fact, the current chairman of the CARICOM Competition Commission, *Kusha Haraksingh,* highlighted the importance for the Commission to remain independent from the COTED.[332] Moreover, the representa-

[329] This competition-law-related competence of COTED is in line with other competences that it is vested with. The COTED can suspend the application of the Common External Tariff, Articles 82, 83 of the Revised Treaty of Chaguaramas or it can suspend the community origin treatment to any description of imports, Article 164(1) of the Revised Treaty of Chaguaramas.

[330] Article 176(5) of the Revised Treaty of Chaguaramas.

[331] *Beckford,* The Appropriate Design and Enforcement of Competition Law and Policy in Countries at Different Stages of Market Development, 26–28 May 2010, Brasilia, p. 8.

[332] Statements made by Kusha Haraksingh during an interview with the author in Port-of-Spain, Trinidad and Tobago, on 29 October 2012. In this context he stated as an example that he did not have to report to the COTED in the appointment of juridical staff of the CARICOM Competition Commission.

tion of the member states' interests are sufficiently safeguarded in the process of competition law enforcement.[333]

8.2.2.4 Timing and the Creation of Vertical and Horizontal Cooperation

The COTED is one of the assisting bodies of the Community Council of Ministers[334] and replaced a former Ministerial Committee. It was installed with the enactment of the Revised Treaty of Chaguaramas. It constitutes a formalized body, which was in place prior to the entry into force of the CARICOM Competition Commission in 2008. Logically, the CARICOM Competition Commission was established within the existing institutional framework of CARICOM. To a certain extent, the history and sequencing of the institutions' establishment also explains the strong accountability of the CARICOM Competition Commission to the COTED.

As the COTED does not represent a competition specific organ, it does not directly contribute to the enhancement of vertical or horizontal cooperation between national and regional competition authorities. However, it constitutes an information-sharing platform, in which concerns regarding potentially anticompetitive practices can be brought forward to the attention of other member states. Moreover, the COTED can also work as an information-sharing platform for private stakeholders that are affected by regional competition and other economic policies. In this vein, representatives of the Barbados Manufacturer Association were entitled to regularly participate at meetings of the COTED.[335] Nevertheless, it remains open, whether such concerns brought forward in the COTED will then be resolved politically or will be forwarded to the CARICOM Competition Commission for an investigation. In this sense, the powers of the two bodies could overlap, however each applying a different approach. With the referral by the COTED of the first competition law matter to the CARICOM Competition Commission, one has to highlight the peculiarity that actually the Caribbean Court of Justice had called for the request of the regional Competition Commission.[336] It remains unanswered whether the COTED would have been more inclined to deal with such matters on a political basis without the Court's judgment. Bearing in mind the initial hesitation of member states to bring disputes to the Caribbean Court of Justice, it has been even argued that there seems to exist "a general reluctance amongst politicians in the region to move

---

[333] Member states or the COTED have the right to request an investigation from the CARICOM Competition Commission, Article 175(1) of the Revised Treaty of Chaguaramas, and the *ex officio* competence of the Commission is limited by the requirement to conduct a preliminary examination from a national competition authority, Article 176(1) of the Revised Treaty of Chaguaramas.

[334] Article 10(1) lit. b), Article 13 of the Revised Treaty of Chaguaramas.

[335] Statement made by Joel Richards, representative of the Barbados Manufacturer Association, during an interview with the author in Bridgetown, Barbados, on 25 October 2012.

[336] *Trinidad Cement Limited TCL Guyana Incorporated v The State of the Co-operative Republic Of Guyana*, Caribbean Court of Justice Application No. OA 2 of 2009, CCJ 5 (OJ), [17].

conflicts from the political to the legal arena".[337] It appears to remain a common feature of Caribbean politics that "[t]o date, disputes over trade, services and regional migration have generally been negotiated behind closed doors in the political corridors".[338]

Nevertheless, there seems to be a general commitment of the COTED towards regional competition law enforcement through the regional competition authority. One should also point out that in the *TCL* case the targeted enterprise originated from Trinidad and Tobago, the economically dominant member state within the CARICOM. Hence, there is no evidence of any bias in competition law enforcement based on economic strength of a member state. One can thus hope that also Article 176(5) of the Revised Treaty of Chaguaramas, which vests the COTED with far-reaching powers in case of a dispute between the CARICOM Competition Commission and national competition authorities, will not be used excessively solely in favour of the national jurisdictions. The COTED is structurally capable of "virtually tying the hands of the Community Commission".[339]

8.2.2.5 Summary on General Cooperation Bodies in Regional Competition Law Enforcement

The strong institutional position of the COTED represents the decentralized competition law enforcement approach in the CARICOM. In particular the prescribed unanimity rule for determinations on substantive issues reflects the reluctance of member states to cede sovereignty and the underlying distrust that is preponderant within the CARICOM.[340] *Duke Pollard* even argues that the status of the Community as an association of sovereign and equal states "has imposed practical constraints on the pace of economic integration."[341] Moreover, while a political bargaining process allows for informal coordination, it also comes at certain accountability costs. The balancing requires that a regional Court of Justice protects constitutional rights. The Caribbean Court of Justice has demonstrated its capacity to fulfil this role also regarding competition law enforcement in the *TCL* case.[342]

Arguably, at an early stage of a regional competition law enforcement regime, the utilization of a political body as cooperation platform might be appropriate. In national implementation procedures political considerations and cooperation are

---

[337] *Malleson,* Promoting Judicial Independence in the International Courts, 58 I.C.L.Q. 671, 684 (2009).

[338] *Malleson,* Promoting Judicial Independence in the International Courts, 58 I.C.L.Q. 671, 681 (2009).

[339] This argument was made by *Stewart. Jenny/Horna,* in: *Brusick/Alvarez/Cernat,* Competition Provisions in Regional Trade Agreements, 2005, pp. 281, 307.

[340] *Pollard,* The CARICOM System, 2003, p. 436.

[341] *Pollard,* The CARICOM System, 2003, p. 460.

[342] *Trinidad Cement Limited v Caricom Competition Commission,* Caribbean Court of Justice Application No. OA 1 of 2012, CCJ 4 (OJ).

most probably more relevant than actual enforcement issues. Yet, in a more developed stage of a regional competition law regime, practical issues such as the sharing of information during specific competition law cases will become more relevant. Accordingly, a regional competition law system has to provide for flexibility that allows for the installation of new cooperation mechanisms and organizations. In the CARICOM, at a more developed stage, the COTED should either provide for the participation of all national competition authorities at meetings that concern competition law enforcement. Alternatively, an additional but distinct competition law enforcement network comprised of national competition law authorities could be created. If one considers that national competition authorities are held to conduct preliminary investigations in cases the CARICOM Competition Commission wants to initiate an investigation,[343] the creation of a network of national competition authorities might achieve efficiency gains and enhance convergent application of competition law in the CARICOM.

8.3 Control of Regional Competition Law Enforcement

The principles of fair trial and due process require that a party affected by an official decision has to be able to defend itself against a negative decision. Judicial or administrative controls have to guarantee that competition authorities follow adequate standards of rule-making and decide based on the principles of predictability and transparency.[344]

8.3.1 Administrative Appeal

In the WAEMU, decisions of the Commission cannot be revised via an internal administrative procedure. Article 90 of the Treaty of Dakar explicitly states that the Commission, which is in charge of making decisions in competition law matters, underlies the control of the Court of Justice. Parties that are negatively affected by a decision thus have to seek relief before the Court of Justice of the WAEMU.

In contrast to the WAEMU in the AndeanC, there exists an administrative controlling mechanism before the Secretariat General. A complaint against a decision or act of the Secretariat General has to be submitted within 45 days after its publication.[345] This recourse of reconsideration does not postpone the implementation of the respective act of the Secretariat General.[346] However, under certain conditions

[343] Article 176(1) of the Revised Treaty of Chaguaramas.

[344] *De León,* Latin American Competition Law and Policy, 2001, p. 218.

[345] Article 44 of Decision 425. Generally the complaining procedure is called "Recurso de Reconsideración", Article 37 of Decision 425.

[346] Article 41 of Decision 425.

the Secretariat General may suspend the enforcement.[347] It is important to note that the deadline of 30 days, provided for this recourse, inhibits the initiation of an action for annulment before the Andean Tribunal of Justice.[348] The administrative review procedure thus has to precede judicial control. The latter action can be initiated within 2 years after the publication of the Secretariat General's decision.[349]

In the CARICOM, an internal recourse in the CARICOM Competition Commission does not exist. Complaints against specific enforcement measures of the CARICOM Competition Commission can be conducted in accordance with national laws, either before the national competition authority or the national courts depending on the legislative framework in each jurisdiction, because investigations take place in accordance with domestic laws.[350]

8.3.2 Judicial Appeal Through a Regional Court of Justice

The Court of Justice of the European Union was held to function as an "engine to integration".[351] The European Courts are considered to further legal integration, in particular the gradual penetration of European law into the domestic law of the member states. Yet a regional judicial body does not serve as an isolated engine of integration, but can only be analysed in its relation with other institutions, such as national courts and governments, specific national or other regional authorities or the private or academic sector. Finally, a regional Court of Justice also has to be evaluated based on the doctrines of supremacy of regional law and direct applicability.[352] These doctrines directly influence the implementation of regional into domestic law and thereby also shape the range of possible competences of a regional court.[353]

Since the WAEMU, the AndeanC and the CARICOM have followed the model of the Court of Justice of the European Union in the design of their regional Court

---

[347] Article 41 of Decision 425.

[348] Article 43 of Decision 425. See below on Actions for annulment, Part II, Dimension IV: Sect. 8.3.2.4.

[349] Art. 20 of the Treaty Creating the Court of Justice of the Cartagena Agreement.

[350] *CARICOM Secretariat,* The CARICOM Competition Commission, 2008, p. 10. Actually such complaints constitute purely national procedures, because they are directed against national enforcement measures.

[351] *Saldías,* Supranational Courts as Engines of Disintegration, 2007, p. 9 <http://ssrn.com/abstract=1092797> accessed 11 November 2018. See generally on the impact of the Court of Justice of the European Union on integration in the European Union: *Burley/Mattli,* A Political Theory of Legal Integration, 47 Int. Organization 41 (1993); *Weiler,* The European Court of Justice and its Interlocutors, Comparative Political Studies 510 (1994).

[352] See in this context on the general legal principles governing the allocation of competences in RTAs, Part II, Dimension V: Chap. 9.

[353] *Saldías,* Supranational Courts as Engines of Disintegration, 2007, p. 4 <http://ssrn.com/abstract=1092797> accessed 11 November 2018.

of Justice, it is interesting to compare the European Court's experiences with those in developing countries. Certain background conditions and mechanisms appear to be *sine qua non* for judicial control mechanisms in a regional integration system with regard to competition law enforcement.[354]

The WAEMU and the AndeanC have installed supranational courts. In the CARICOM, all member states have signed the Agreement Establishing the Caribbean Court of Justice and have thereby submitted to its exclusive and compulsory original jurisdiction. The regional court's decisions are enforced like decisions of domestic superior courts. The Court of Justice of WAEMU, the Andean Tribunal of Justice and the Caribbean Court of Justice[355] constitute the supranational courts within the RTAs. The courts mirror institutionalized dedication to legal unity and the will to create a new legal system. Since supranational courts hand down binding decisions an escape of its jurisdiction is only possible by withdrawing membership from the RTA.

The regional courts are similarly structured. They are composed by legal representatives of each member state, with the exception of the Caribbean Court of Justice, which consists of fewer judges than member states. Neither the WAEMU, the AndeanC nor the CARICOM have followed the Chilean model and have installed a specialized competition law tribunal. Thus the magistrates are no competition law experts. However, they are usually considered persons of great honour and have gained considerable reputation during their practices as national judges.[356] The magistrates in their function as regional judge are completely independent.[357]

The appointment process varies between the three regional courts. While in the WAEMU and the AndeanC the judges are elected by national governments, either directly by the national governments in the AndeanC[358] or indirectly through their regional representation in the Conference of Heads of States and Governments in the WAEMU,[359] in the CARICOM the appointment process is de politicized. The judges of the Caribbean Court of Justice are appointed by the Regional Judicial and Legal Service Commission (RJLSC) based on open competition among the

---

354 *Ibid.*

355 In the CARICOM some member states still appeal to the Privy Council as court of last instance.

356 WAEMU: Article 2 of Protocole Additionnel n°1 *relatif au organe de contrôle de l'UEMOA* Additional Protocole no. 1. AndeanC: Article 6(1) of the Treaty Creating the Court of Justice of the Cartagena Agreement. CARICOM: Article IV(11) of the Agreement Establishing the Caribbean Court of Justice.

357 WAEMU: Article 3 Règlement n° 1/96/CM *portant Règlement des procédures de la Cour de Justice de l'UEMOA*, 5 July 1996. AndeanC: Article 6(2) of the Treaty Creating the Court of Justice of the Cartagena Agreement. CARICOM: Article V(12) of the Agreement Establishing the Caribbean Court of Justice.

358 AndeanC: Article 7 of the Treaty Creating the Court of Justice of the Cartagena Agreement; Article 7 of Decision 500, Statute of the Court, 22 June 2001.

359 Current court members were appointed under the act no. 03/2007/CCGE/UEMOA portant renouvellement de mandat, nomination et fin de mandats de membres de la cour de justice de l'Union Économique et Monétaire Ouest Africaine (UEMOA) on 20 January 2007.

candidates.[360] Moreover, the independence of the judges with regard to their salaries and the overall sustainability of the Caribbean Court are secured by a Trust Fund, which covers its costs.[361] From a negative point of view, these special preconditions, installed to safeguard the Caribbean Court of Justice's impartiality, certainly also reflect the deep-rooted suspicion of political influences in the region's legal system.[362]

The Court of Justice of the WAEMU is located in Ouagadougou (Burkina Faso), the Andean Court of Justice is permanently seated in Quito (Ecuador) and the Caribbean Court of Justice is actually a travelling court with its headquarters in Trinidad and Tobago.

8.3.2.1 Original and Appellate Jurisdiction of a Regional Court

WAEMU's Court of Justice and the Andean Tribunal of Justice do not encompass an appellate jurisdiction for legal procedures emanating from the member states. The Court of Justice of the WAEMU and the Andean Tribunal fulfil an original jurisdiction by solely resolving cases that are based on community norms.

The Caribbean Court of Justice entails both, original and appellate jurisdiction. With regard to the latter, it functions as court of last instance in regular legal procedures of the member states. A common instance of appeal in an RTA has the potential to harmonize legal standards by creating binding legal precedents for all member states. This judicial mechanism is particularly important in systems without direct effect of regional norms, which structurally inherit a larger risk of non-convergence of national legislations.[363] Hence the submission of all member states to the appellate jurisdiction of the Caribbean Court of Justice is capable of enhancing the harmonization of competition law in the member states. Through the judicial path, the Caribbean Court of Justice could additionally to its original jurisdiction attribute to the creation of common competition law standards.

Yet the impact of a court of last instance remains limited, as it can usually only decide on specific aspects of a case and the possibility of appeal underlies restricted conditions or has to be explicitly conferred.[364] Above all, the Caribbean Court of

---

[360] For more information on the Regional Judicial and Legal Services Commission (RJLSC) in the CARICOM, see above Part II, Dimension III: Sect. 7.1.1.2.

[361] *Pollard,* The CARICOM System, 2003, p. 436.

[362] *Malleson,* Promoting Judicial Independence in the International Courts, 58 I.C.L.Q. 671, 677 (2009).

[363] See above Part II, Dimension II: Sect. 6.2.1.

[364] *Belle Antoine,* Commonwealth Caribbean, 2008, p. 310. The Privy Council took a very restrictive view towards its appellate jurisdiction. It remains open, if the Caribbean Court of Justice will follow this restrictive approach. Generally, Article XXV of the Agreement Establishing the Caribbean Court of Justice says: "In the exercise of its appellate jurisdiction, the Court is a superior Court of record with such jurisdiction and powers as are conferred on it by this Agreement or by the Constitution or any other law of a Contracting Party."

Justice's appellate jurisdiction is not acknowledged throughout the region.[365] While the large majority of member states have accepted the Caribbean Court of Justice's original jurisdiction by signing the Agreement Establishing the Caribbean Court of Justice,[366] only Barbados (2005), Guyana (2005) and Belize (2010) refer to the Caribbean Court of Justice as the final appellate court. The other member states (except for the civil law jurisdictions) still appeal to the Privy Council, which is a court based in Great Britain and a relic from colonial times.[367] Thus presently, the CARICOM encompasses two courts of last instance. The Caribbean Court of Justice in this regard still faces severe political opposition. Interestingly, one of the major concerns is that the Caribbean Court of Justice will not dispense impartial justice, because larger countries would exercise more influence on decisions.[368] Other concerns are the costs for the creation of a new regional court, the legal knowledge of the magistrates and national difficulties to constitutionally entrench the appellate jurisdiction of the Caribbean Court of Justice.[369]

The diverging recognition of the Caribbean Court of Justice's appellate function reflects a deeply rooted distrust of member states in the CARICOM against each other. The strongly perceived heterogeneity among Caribbean member states results in a situation, in which they are more suspicious towards their neighbour than towards the former colonial master. To a certain degree, it also demonstrates the lacking confidence in their own legal culture and knowledge.

8.3.2.2 Preliminary Reference Rulings and Their Impact on Regional Competition Law

The Court of Justice of the European Union's impact on integration in the European Union relies on its procedural mechanisms. The largest number of cases has come before the CJEU through preliminary references from national courts, even of

---

365 Its appellate jurisdiction is incorporated in the Caribbean Court of Justice (Appellate Jurisdiction) Rules 2005 (Amendments in 2006) <http://www.caribbeancourtofjustice.org/court-instruments/rules-of-the-court/the-appellate-jurisdiction-rules> accessed 11 November 2018.

366 The Heads of Government approved the Agreement Establishing the Caribbean Court of Justice in 1999. It was signed by Antigua and Barbuda, Barbados, Belize, Grenada, Guyana, Jamaica, St. Kitts and Nevis, St. Lucia, Suriname and Trinidad and Tobago on 14 February 2001. Dominica and St. Vincent and the Grenadines singed the Agreement on 15 February 2003. The Agreement Establishing the Caribbean Court of Justice came into force on 23 July 2003, and the Caribbean Court of Justice was inaugurated on 16 April 2005 in Port of Spain, Trinidad and Tobago. Haiti, the Bahamas and Montserrat have not signed the Agreement Establishing the Caribbean Court of Justice. For more details on the history of the Caribbean Court of Justice <http://www.caribbeancourtofjustice.org/about-the-ccj/ccj-concept-to-reality> accessed 11 November 2018.

367 *Belle Antoine,* Commonwealth Caribbean, 2008, p. 307.

368 *Belle Antoine,* Commonwealth Caribbean, 2008, p. 307.

369 *Belle Antoine,* Commonwealth Caribbean, 2008, p. 307; *Malleson,* Promoting Judicial Independence in the International Courts, 58 I.C.L.Q. 671, 684 (2009).

younger member states.[370] Many fundamental legal doctrines of European integration, such as the doctrine of direct effect of EU law, were shaped through an expansive interpretation in preliminary reference cases, even despite initial opposition from member states.[371] A great number of preliminary references arose from litigation in which individuals tried to enforce a right granted by EU law before a national court.[372] Hence, another important element is the willingness of national courts, typically lower courts, to refer cases to the CJEU, which thereby expressed their recognition of the jurisdiction of the European Court and of the supremacy of European law in general. Phrased differently, one could appropriately argue that the success of preliminary rulings before a regional court depends on the existence of "constitutional constituencies at [the] national level"[373] supporting the regional law. It remains open, whether this link between national judiciary and individuals, on the one hand, and regional judiciary, on the other hand, could also be established in the WAEMU, the AndeanC or the CARICOM.

Unquestionably, the CJEU has also played an important role in the development of European competition law, for example by clarifying the requirement of a possible "effect on trade" between member states[374] or by defining the notion of an "undertaking".[375] The CJEU is limited to the specific question in light of the specific circumstances of the case and an infringement of EU law only. The CJEU's impact on the development of EU competition law depended on several aspects: (1) the awareness of individuals regarding their rights arising out of community law, (2) the willingness of national (lower) courts to refer cases to the regional level, (3) the variety of matters referred and a broad formulation of referred questions and (4) the application of an extensive interpretation of the regional court itself.

It thus remains questionable whether preliminary reference rulings can be similarly influential for regional competition law policies in developing countries and the examined RTAs. Typically, public institutions in developing countries lack the necessary resources or suffer from corruption.[376] Public confidence in state institutions is generally low.[377] Furthermore, a competition culture still has to evolve and

---

[370] Annual report regarding the judicial activity of the Court of Justice 2016, p. 81 <https://curia.europa.eu/jcms/upload/docs/application/pdf/2017-03/ra_jur_2016_en_web.pdf> accessed 30 August 2017.

[371] *Saldías,* Supranational Courts as Engines of Disintegration, 2007, p. 9 <http://ssrn.com/abstract=1092797> accessed 11 November 2018.

[372] *Weiler,* The European Court of Justice and its Interlocutors, Comparative Political Studies 510, 518 (1994).

[373] *Saldías,* Supranational Courts as Engines of Disintegration, 2007, p. 5 <http://ssrn.com/abstract=1092797> accessed 11 November 2018.

[374] Judgment of the Court of 30 June 1966, Case 56/65, *Société Technique Minière (L.T.M.) v Maschinenbau Ulm GmbH (M.B.U.),* [1966] ECR 235, ECLI:EU:C:1966:38.

[375] Judgment of the Court of 23 April 1991, Case C-41/90, *Klaus Höfner and Fritz Elser v Macrotron GmbH,* [1993] ECR I-01979, ECLI:EU:C:1991:161.

[376] See above Part II, Dimension III: Chap. 7.

[377] See above Part I, Sect. 2.2.2.

regional law in general is not sufficiently recognized neither by individuals, the private business sector nor academia.[378]

In the WAEMU, the rules concerning preliminary reference rulings are included in Article 12 of the Additional Protocol no. 1 regarding the institutions of control in the WAEMU[379] and Article 15(6) of Regulation no. 1/96/CM/UEMOA regarding the procedures of the Court of Justice of WAEMU.[380] The West African provisions also differentiate between mandatory and voluntary referral of a legal question regarding the community law, depending on the judicial instance in which the legal question arises.[381]

There has been one decision arising out of preliminary reference ruling. The reference ruling was submitted from the Senegalese Council of State, the supreme administrative court, in the case of *Air France* against the Syndicate of Travel and Tourism Agencies of Senegal, requesting the Court of Justice to decide on the competent jurisdiction.[382] However, the WAEMU Court of Justice rejected the request based on the argument that it would only be competent for interpreting community law and not for the allocation of competences. This case reflects the willingness of national courts to further regional integration, even despite possible opposition of other national agencies, such as in this case the Senegalese competition authority.

As in the European system, Andean law also differentiates between obligatory and voluntary submissions to the Tribunal for preliminary interpretations depending on the instance of the national court and the majority of the Andean Tribunal's cases also arose from references for preliminary rulings. However the large majority concerned intellectual property matters.[383] The lack of legal precedents regarding Decision 608 certainly reflects the little awareness of regional competition law. National courts might therefore constitute inadequate actors in order to enhance preliminary reference rulings with regard to competition law matters. In fact,

[378] See above Part I, Sect. 2.2.3.2.

[379] La Conférence des Chefs d'État et de Gouvernement de l'Union Économique et Monétaire Ouest Africaine (UEMOA), Protocole Additionnel n°1 *relatif au organe de contrôle de l'UEMOA*.

[380] Le Conseil des Ministres de l'Union Économique et Monétaire Ouest Africaine (UEMOA), Règlement n° 1/96/CM *portant Règlement des procédures de la Cour de Justice de l'UEMOA*, 5 July 1996.

[381] Article 15 Section 6 of Regulation no. 01/96/CM/UEMA regarding the procedures of the Court of Justice of WAEMU.

[382] *UNCTAD,* Voluntary Peer Review on Competition Policies of WAEMU, Benin and Senegal, 2008, pp. 63f.; *Compagnie Air France v. Syndicat des Agents de Voyage et de Tourisme du Sénégal*, Cour de Justice de l'UEMOA, Arrêt n° 1/2005, 12 January 2005.

[383] In interviews with the author, the following reasons for the national awareness regarding regional intellectual property provisions were given: The national legislators were involved in the regional legislation process, national and regional intellectual property rules are almost completely harmonized, intellectual property is a highly technical matter and member states in the AndeanC perceive the protection of intellectual property rights as a very important and sensitive matter. However even in the case of IP matters, the judges needed persuasion to refer IP cases to the regional court, see *Helfer/Alter,* The Andean Tribunal of Justice and its Interlocutors, 41 N.Y.U. Journal of Int'l. L. & Pol. 871, 923 (2009) <http://ssrn.com/abstract=1334733> accessed 11 November 2018.

national intellectual property and competition agencies, such as the Peruvian INDECOPI or the Colombian Superintendence of Trade, regularly sought the Andean Tribunal's guidance and habitually requested its decisions.[384] In the cases 130-IP-2007[385] and 14-IP-2007[386] the Andean Tribunal defined the notion of 'national judge' in the context of preliminary reference rulings according to Article 33 of the Treaty Creating the Court of Justice of the Cartagena Agreement. It argued that the term had to be interpreted broadly and shall be interpreted in such way to include institutions that carry out judicial functions. These institutions should also have standing to request a preliminary interpretation when they resolve a controversy where Andean Law is at issue in the exercise of their powers.[387] Whereas the Andean Tribunal on this basis rejected a reference from the INDECOPI, a request from the Colombian Superintendence of Trade was accepted.

Finally, the influence of preliminary reference rulings on legal integration depends on the variety of legal matters and the width of the referred questions. In the AndeanC, the majority of preliminary reference rulings concern unfair competition and intellectual property issues.[388]

In the Andean case 87-IP-2002[389] though, the Andean Tribunal of Justice had to make a preliminary reference ruling regarding the former competition law norm, Decision 285. The case concerned a dispute between the Bolivian private phone company TELECEL and the Bolivian telecom sector regulator and dealt with discriminatory pricing.[390] The parties to the case disagreed on the applicability of Decision 285. The submitted questions regarding the interpretation of Decision 285 were broadly formulated. The Andean Tribunal was *inter alia*[391] asked to analyse the objectives of the norms designed to correct distortions to free competition, as set out in Article 1 of Decision 285. The Tribunal was furthermore asked to define the

---

[384] *Helfer/Alter,* The Andean Tribunal of Justice and its Interlocutors, 41 N.Y.U. Journal of Int'l. L. & Pol. 871, 912 (2009) <http://ssrn.com/abstract=1334733> accessed 11 November 2018.

[385] Tribunal de la Justicia de la Comunidad Andina, Proceso 130-IP-2007, 17 October 2007.

[386] Tribunal de la Justicia de la Comunidad Andina, Proceso 14-IP-2007, 21 March 2007.

[387] Tribunal de la Justicia de la Comunidad Andina, Proceso 130-IP-2007, 17 October 2007, pp. 8f.; Tribunal de la Justicia de la Comunidad Andina, Proceso 14-IP-2007, 21 March 2007, pp. 7f.: "el término 'Juez Nacional' debe interpretarse incluyendo a los organismos que cumplen funciones judiciales, siempre que cumplan las condiciones mínimas señaladas por la ley interna; para de esta manera tenerlos como legitimados para solicitar la interpretación prejudicial, cuando en el ejercicio de dichas funciones conozcan de un proceso en el que deba aplicarse o se controvierta algunas de las normas que integran el Derecho Comunitario Andino."

[388] Cases see <http://www.tribunalandino.org.ec/sitetjca/index.php>; Intellectual Property Subjects form about 86% of all Preliminary Rulings in the period from 1987 to 2007 according to *Helfer/Alter,* The Andean Tribunal of Justice and its Interlocutors, 41 N.Y.U. Journal of Int'l. L. & Pol. 871, 894 (2009) <http://ssrn.com/abstract=1334733> accessed 11 November 2018.

[389] Tribunal de Justicia de la Comunidad Andina, Proceso 87-IP-2002, 16 October 2002.

[390] The case took place under the former system of sectorial regulation in Bolivia under the SIRESE law. More on the Bolivian competition law system see above Part II, Dimension I: Sect. 5.2.2.2.

[391] The Tribunal was also asked to interpret Articles 4 lit. a) and 5 lit. a) and d) of Decision 285; Articles 17 and 18 of Decision 439; Articles 28, 29, 34 of Decision 462; Articles 4, 5, 6 of Resolution 432.

scope of application (Article 2 of Decision 285) and to define the concepts regarding restrictive practices to free competition in the region.

Yet the broad wording of the questions in the case 87-IP-2002 appears to be an exemption within the pattern of cases that were referred to the Andean Tribunal of Justice. Recent findings regarding non-IP cases demonstrate that national judges referred narrow and specific technical questions to the Andean Tribunal of Justice that adhere closely to the letter of the specific law.[392] According to *Helfer and Alter*[393] in the period from 1987 to 2007, out of 1338 Andean preliminary rulings, only 35 dealt with issues other than intellectual property rights. Another finding is that only few common market-related disputes were litigated in national courts.[394] Moreover, there exists a strong cross-national variation with regard to the referral of national courts. Colombian courts are the most willing to refer cases to the Andean Tribunal.[395] Finally, the examples of referred cases also revealed that national courts tend to submit the same or similar questions.[396]

In the case 87-IP-2002, the Andean Tribunal underlined that in a preliminary ruling its function was to interpret the community norm generally instead of applying the norms to the facts of the case.[397] Based on this principle the Andean Tribunal took the opportunity to generally define the requirements and elements regarding the territorial and subjective scope of application of Decision 285 and to elaborate on the objectives of the regional competition law provisions. The latter were analysed in the context of the objectives of the Agreement of Cartagena. The Andean Tribunal explicitly mentioned the creation of a regional market and the instrument of legal harmonization of economic and social policies as objectives of regional law. Decision 285 aimed at protecting free competition and the exercise of economic freedom, which was a right but also responsibility of all.[398] Regarding the scope of application, the Tribunal determined that regional law applied only to cases that involved at least one company located in the Andean Community and in which the (anticompetitive) practice had an effect on the region, thus relying strongly on the wording of Article 2 of Decision 285. The Tribunal clarified that the latter requirement included a transcending element of the effect, thereby excluding practices whose effects remained limited to the territory of single a member state.[399] In particular, the Andean Tribunal outlined the requirements for the inclusion of public undertakings under the scope of regional competition law and in a very detailed way, delineated justified state intervention that did not fall within the scope of

[392] *Helfer/Alter,* The Andean Tribunal of Justice and its Interlocutors, 41 N.Y.U. Journal of Int'l. L. & Pol. 871, 897 (2009).

[393] *Helfer/Alter,* The Andean Tribunal of Justice and its Interlocutors, 41 N.Y.U. Journal of Int'l. L. & Pol. 871, 871ff. (2009) <http://ssrn.com/abstract=1334733> accessed 11 November 2018.

[394] *Ibid.*, p. 898.

[395] *Ibid.*, p. 899.

[396] *Ibid.*, p. 887.

[397] Tribunal de Justicia de la Comunidad Andina, Proceso 87-IP-2002, 16 October 2002, p. 5.

[398] Tribunal de Justicia de la Comunidad Andina, Proceso 87-IP-2002, 16 October 2002, pp. 12f.

[399] Tribunal de Justicia de la Comunidad Andina, Proceso 87-IP-2002, 16 October 2002, p. 13.

competition law.[400] The Tribunal particularly highlighted that under specific circumstances within the limits of the laws and in order to serve a broader social interest it was allowed to restrict individuals' freedom. However, if such regulatory state action infringed community law, judicial control could be initiated via an action of non-accomplishment against the member state.[401]

The very sensitive differentiation between restraints of competition, on the one hand, and justified state intervention, on the other hand, is in line with the restrictive interpretation in the context of the Andean Liberalization Programme.[402] The Tribunal in the preliminary ruling 1-IP-90 set out the member states' autonomy to decide on tariffs and restrictions regarding exempted goods.[403] It held that: "One must not forget that according to a universally accepted principle of interpretation norms that limit freedom must be interpreted restrictively, as they are the exception to the general rule."[404]

For the lack of precedents under Decision 608, it remains to be seen, whether the Tribunal of Justice of the Andean Community will continue its restrictive interpretation regarding competition law matters and whether it can play an as important role for regional competition law as the CJEU did. Especially the absence of cases referred to the Andean Tribunal and the repetitive and narrow formulation of submitted legal questions might impede national and Andean Courts from becoming "engines of integration". However, national competition authorities could have the potential to overtake this role by obtaining an active standing in the context of preliminary reference rulings. The case 87-IP-2002 shows that the Tribunal is generally willing to define provisions regarding competition law matters in preliminary reference rulings and to apply a teleological interpretation, in the specific case by placing Decision 285 in the context of the broader objectives of the Agreement of Cartagena.

In the CARICOM, any national court or tribunal of a contracting party can address the Caribbean Court of Justice.[405] The question has to involve the

---

[400] Tribunal de Justicia de la Comunidad Andina, Proceso 87-IP-2002, 16 October 2002, pp. 13, 14.

[401] Tribunal de Justicia de la Comunidad Andina, Proceso 87-IP-2002, 16 October 2002, p. 14.

[402] "Programa de Liberación de la Comunidad Andina", Article 72 of the Agreement of Cartagena: "El Programa de Liberación de bienes tiene por objeto eliminar los gravámenes y las restricciones de todo orden que incidan sobre la importación de productos originarios del territorio de cualquier País Miembro"; *Saldías,* Supranational Courts as Engines of Disintegration, 2007, p. 13 <http://ssrn.com/abstract=1092797> accessed 11 November 2018.

[403] Tribunal de Justicia de la Comunidad Andina, Proceso 1-IP-90, 19 September 1990, p. 8: "Interpretación prejudicial de los Artículos 45 y 54 del Acuerdo de Cartagena". "Los Países Miembros son autónomos para decidir sobre gravámenes y restricciones en relación con productos reservados o exceptuados".

[404] Tribunal de Justicia de la Comunidad Andina, Proceso 1-IP-90, 19 September 1990, "Interpretación prejudicial de los Artículos 45 y 54 del Acuerdo de Cartagena, p. 8: "No debe olvidarse, finalmente, que las normas que limitan la libertad deben ser interpretadas restrictivamente, como excepción que son a la regla general, según un principio de interpretación universalmente aceptado".

[405] According to Article XIV and Article XII lit. c) of the Agreement Establishing the Caribbean Court of Justice "the national court or tribunal shall, if it considers that a decision on the question is necessary to enable it to deliver judgment, refer the question to the Court for determination

interpretation or application of the Treaty. The Caribbean legislator has refrained from differentiating between different instances of national courts. Instead national courts have to decide at their own discretion whether a decision by the Caribbean Court of Justice "is necessary to enable [the national court or tribunal of a Contracting Party] to deliver judgement."[406] Consequently, despite the use of "shall" in the Article XIV of the Agreement establishing the Caribbean Court of Justice, the decision on referrals to the regional Court of Justice remains voluntary under the discretion of the national judiciary. Whereas this is also an expression of the lack of direct effect of regional law, national legislators and member states as subjects of international law, are still bound to the regional law based on the principles of public international law. It is important to highlight that the Caribbean legislator in Article XII of the Agreement Establishing the Caribbean Court of Justice deals with the Organization of Eastern Caribbean States as a member state. Article XII(2) of the Agreement Establishing the Caribbean Court of Justice states that for the purpose of this part, "national courts" include the Eastern Caribbean Supreme Court. So far, there have not been referrals regarding competition law issues by national courts.

8.3.2.3 Advisory Opinions by the Regional Court

The possibility to give advisory opinions is closely linked to the responsibilities of a regional court during a preliminary reference ruling. A regional court is ordered to give his opinion on the interpretation of regional law on a request of a community or possibly also national organ. Although an advisory opinion is not binding, it can be assumed that a regional court will follow its own opinion if a question of the interpretation of regional law arises in a later case.

Neither in the AndeanC nor in the European Union are the regional courts provided with the right to give advisory opinions on regional law.[407] In the WAEMU Advisory Opinion no. 003/2000 in the context of the drafting of competition law directives and regulations actually established the centralized competition law system and the Commission's exclusive competence.[408] The Court of Justice of WAEMU can give recommendations during two stages: the Commission can already submit a request in the drafting stage of a legal text or the Commission, the Council of Ministers, the Conference of Heads of States or a member state can

before delivering judgment". See also Rule 11(2)(1) of the Caribbean Court of Justice (Original Jurisdiction) Rules, 2006: "Where a national court is seized of an issue whose resolution involves a question concerning the interpretation or application of the Treaty, the court concerned shall, if it considers that a decision on the question is necessary to enable it to deliver judgment, refer the question to the Court for determination before delivering judgment."

406 Article XIV of Agreement establishing the Caribbean Court of Justice; Rule 11(2)(1) of the Caribbean Court of Justice (Original Jurisdiction) Rules, 2006.

407 The Court of Justice of the European Union can nevertheless give advisory opinions on the compatibility of international agreements with European law, Article 218(11) TFEU.

408 Regarding more detail on the Advisory Opinion no. 003/2000 of the Court of Justice of WAEMU, see above Part II, Dimension I: Sect. 5.1.5.1.

request an advisory opinion in case of ambiguities regarding the application or interpretation of community provisions.[409] The Additional Act no. 10/96 also includes the possibility to give recommendations on existing international treaties or treaties under negotiation. This peculiarity of the court's power to render advisory opinions could become especially relevant in Africa, because all member states of the WAEMU are also members of ECOWAS and OHADA.[410] ECOWAS intends to implement competition law provisions as well and OHADA comprises provisions on commercial law; the hierarchical order with WAEMU's competition provisions in case of legal conflict still remains unclear.[411] Theoretically, the Court of Justice of WAEMU could give an advisory opinion on this topic with regard to the compliance with the Treaty of Dakar.

In the CARICOM, advisory opinions by the regional court are regulated in Article XIII of the Agreement Establishing the Caribbean Court of Justice and Article 11(3) of the Caribbean Court of Justice Rules of 2006. Any member state or the Community can request that the Caribbean Court of Justice delivers its opinion on the interpretation and application of the Revised Treaty of Chaguaramas.[412] In comparison to the far-reaching rights of the Court of Justice of WAEMU, the right to give advisory opinions of the Caribbean Court of Justice does not include the court's participation in the drafting stage of a regional law.

8.3.2.4 Actions for Annulment

Actions for annulment are aimed at the declaration of a community act to be void. Such community acts might also include a regional competition law authority's decision on the existence of an anticompetitive practice. The action for annulment can thus have a direct effect on the enforcement results in a regional competition law regime.

In the WAEMU, an annulment of a Commission's competition law decision is generally possible via a recourse of legality according to the Articles 8 to 11 of the Additional Protocol no. 1, Article 15(2) of Regulation no. 1/96/CM and Article 31 of Regulation no. 03/2002/CM/UEMOA. While judicial reviews of individual decisions taken by the Council or the Commission are open to all private parties,

---

[409] Article 27 of the Regulation no. 10/96, 10 May 1996.

[410] For more information, see <http://www.ecowas.int> and <http://www.ohada.org>.

[411] Different views on the hierarchical organization of ECOWAS and WAEMU competition law provisions include the opinion that the WAEMU should be considered as a member state of ECOWAS, on the one hand, and to look at every member state individually, on the other hand, in order to achieve far-reaching convergence and/or to install consultative mechanisms to resolve eventual conflicts. See *Bakhoum,* Perspectives Africaines d'une Politique de la Concurrence dans l'Espace OHADA, XXV R.I.D.E. 351, 370ff. (2011); *Fau-Nougaret,* La concurrence des organisations régionales en Afrique, 2012, pp. 296ff.; *Ngom,* Intégration Régionale et Politique de la Concurrence dans l'Espace CEDEAO, XXV R.I.D.E. 333, 342ff. (2011); *UNCTAD,* Voluntary Peer Review on Competition Policies of WAEMU, Benin and Senegal, 2008, p. 20.

[412] Article XIII of the Agreement Establishing the Caribbean Court of Justice.

directives, regulations and decisions can only be revised on the initiative of member states, the Council or the Commission.[413]

Four WAEMU Commission's decisions have been submitted to the Court of Justice of WAEMU for annulment so far. The first submission concerned the Commission's decision on Ciment Togo.[414] Ciment Togo had demanded from the Commission to intervene against WACEM (West African Cimento), a competitor on the cement market, whose practices Ciment Togo considered as infringing regional law. However, the Court of Justice rejected the request on 20 June 2001 on procedural grounds.[415] The other case was submitted by Gdeiri SA (Groupement de Développement Economique d'Intervention et de Réalisation des Investissements), which had requested the Commission to intervene against the state of Niger to comply with contractual obligations with respect to social dwellings on the construction market.[416] Gdeiri SA argued that the state of Niger was holding a dominant position and that the Commission's refusal to intervene was illegal. Nevertheless, on 12 January 2005 the Court of Justice rejected the claim. It held that although the state of Niger could generally constitute an "enterprise" in the sense of community law, it did not commit an abuse of dominant position.[417] Two other cases concerned the palm oil sector in Senegal and Ivory Coast. Senegal had introduced a provision requiring certain quality standards for palm oil, which resulted in the exclusion of palm oil products from Ivory Coast. The WAEMU Commission had obliged Senegal to withdraw the provision, as they hindered the free circulation of goods within the common market.[418] The other case concerned the WAEMU Commission's decision that allowed a concentration between Ivorian palm oil undertakings.[419] Senegal had submitted two complaints before the WAEMU Court of Justice against the Commission's decisions, of which the former was withdrawn by Senegal in 2017 and the latter was resolved through an interim injunction.[420]

---

[413] Article 15(2) of Regulation no. 1/96/CM.

[414] ARRÊT N° 1, *Société des Ciments du Togo c/ Commission de l'UEMOA*, 20 June 2001. For a summary see <http://www.izf.net/upload/Documentation/Rapports/CourJusticeUEMOA/Recueil1996_2001.pdf> pp. 133–160.

[415] *UNCTAD,* Voluntary Peer Review on Competition Policies of WAEMU, Benin and Senegal, 2008, p. 63; *Demba,* L'Activité de la Cour de la Justice de l'UEMOA, Rev. de la Faculté des Sciences Juridiques et Politiques (2006).

[416] *UNCTAD,* Voluntary Peer Review on Competition Policies of WAEMU, Benin and Senegal, 2008, p. 63.

[417] *Demba,* L'Activité de la Cour de la Justice de l'UEMOA, Rev. de la Faculté des Sciences Juridiques et Politiques (2006).

[418] *WAEMU Commission* decision no. 007/2010/COM/UEMOA inviting the State of Senegal to withdraw its modified provision NS03-072 and to withdraw any enforcement measures taken in this regard of 4 June 2010.

[419] *WAEMU Commission* decision no. 009/2008/COM/UEMOA granting a negative clearance regarding the planned concentration between Unilever-Ci, Sifca, Cosmivoire, Palmci, Nauvu, PHCI, SHCI and Sania of 22 October 2008.

[420] Regarding *WAEMU Commission* decision no. 007/2010/COM/UEMOA inviting the State of Senegal to withdraw its modified provision NS03-072 and to withdraw any enforcement measures taken in this regard of 4 June 2010, the WAEMU Court of Justice allowed Senegal to withdraw the

The revision of competition law decisions of the Commission by the Court of Justice bears a peculiarity in the WAEMU. According to Article 31 of Regulation no. 03/2002/CM/UEMOA the Court of Justice of WAEMU has full jurisdiction to modify and annul decisions of the Commission, but also to reduce or increase a fine. Article 15 of Regulation no. 1/96/CM/UEMOA clarifies that the Court can be called upon to comment on decisions and sanctions of the Commission with regard to enterprises that have not respected the principal of free competition or have abused a dominant position. It even has full jurisdiction to impose particular obligations.[421]

Yet the Court cannot oblige the Commission to take a specific action. Generally, the Court's far-reaching controlling rights could contribute to a balancing in the centralized competition law system in the WAEMU.[422] However, for the lack of specific competition law expertise, judges might be reluctant to depart from the Commission's decision. On the other hand, very active and interventionist judges could undermine the Commission's decision-making. In this context, the far-reaching competence to define the amount of fines could collide with the Commission's competence to decide on a potential breach of regional competition law. Generally, fines have to be calculated based on difficult economic and legal analysis. It is not clear how judges without specific competition law expertise would be capable of determining the appropriate amount of a fine. Similar to the European experience, the WAEMU Commission could issue guidelines and communications on the calculation of fines.

In the AndeanC, actions for annulment are governed by Articles 17 to 22 of the Treaty Creating the Court of Justice of the Cartagena Agreement and Articles 101 to 106 of Decision 500, including the internal rules of the Andean Tribunal. The right to initiate an action for annulment is very broad, covering the Council of States, the Commission of the AndeanC, the Secretariat General, member states, but also natural or judicial persons.[423] The latter, however, have to demonstrate the impairment of a subjective right or legitimate interest.[424] The Andean action for annulment remains an instrument of objective control. Instead of focusing on the rights of the person at stake, the Tribunal of Justice of the AndeanC undertakes an abstract control of the Andean norm and controls its conformity with the community law framework.[425] This provides individuals with a certain influence on controlling regional norms' legality and could constitute an instrument to review Decision 608 as well. Moreover,

---

complaint on 21 February 2017. Regarding *WAEMU Commission* decision no. 009/2008/COM/UEMOA granting a negative clearance regarding the planned concentration between Unilever-Ci, Sifca, Cosmivoire, Palmci, Nauvu, PHCI, SHCI and Sania of 22 October 2008, the WAEMU Court of Justice issued an interim injunction decision no. 01/2012 on 2 March 2012.

[421] Article 31 of Regulation no. 03/2002/CM/UEMOA.

[422] *Bakhoum,* L'articulation du droit communautaire et des droits nationaux de la concurrence dans l'Union Economique et Monétaire Ouest Africaine, 2007, pp. 178f.

[423] Article 17 of the Treaty Creating the Court of Justice of the Cartagena Agreement.

[424] Article 19 of the Treaty Creating the Court of Justice of the Cartagena Agreement.

[425] *Vigil Toledo,* La Estructura Jurídica y el Futuro de la Comunidad Andina, 2011, p. 97.

the action for annulment is perceived as a fundamental instrument to achieve institutional stability and legal certainty in the legal framework of the AndeanC.[426] In the vein of the principle of separation of powers, the Tribunal of Justice is however limited to (partially) annul a regional norm, without prescribing directly its legal content. Yet, in case of irreparable damages, the Tribunal may also order provisional measures.[427]

There have not been annulments of resolutions under Decision 608 in the AndeanC. However, the joined cases 01-AN-2006, 02-AN-2006 and 01-AN-2007[428] concern the resolutions 892, 910, 984, 1040 of the Secretariat General, which identified an infringement of the former Andean competition law provision, Decision 285, on the basis of price fixing of crude palm oil.[429]

In accordance with Article 17 of the Treaty Creating the Court of Justice of the Cartagena Agreement and Articles 101 to 196 of the Statute of the Tribunal of the AndeanC, a Colombian enterprise of palm oil production (GRANDINOS) and the National Federation of Palm Oil Producers of Colombia and the Colombian State itself requested the annulment of the above-mentioned resolutions. The Andean Tribunal of Justice overruled the resolutions of the Secretariat General based on a very detailed examination of the competition law provisions set out in Decision 285, but also based on a detailed analysis of the facts of the case, such as the legal nature of the Colombian Fund. The Tribunal highlighted that the state could also be subject to competition law, as long it intervened on the market for the fulfilment of its regulatory functions.[430] The Tribunal went on by clarifying the notions of "concerted practices" and "parallel behaviour" as set out in Article 3 of Decision 285. The Tribunal held that an autonomous will was necessary in order to engage in concerted practices, however, that the Colombian palm oil producers lacked this

[426] *Tangarife Torres,* Derecho de la Integración en la Comunidad Andina, 2002, p. 225.

[427] Articles 21 and 22 of the Treaty Creating the Court of Justice of the Cartagena Agreement.

[428] Tribunal de Justicia de la Comunidad Andina, Procesos Acumulados 01-AN-2006, 02-AN-2006 y 01-AN-2007, "Acción de nulidad incoada por la sociedad C.I. Grandinos S.A. contra la Resolución N° 984 de la Secretaría General de la Comunidad Andina; acción de nulidad incoada por la Federación Nacional de Cultivadores de Palma de Aceite (FEDEPALMA) contra las Resoluciones n° 984, 910 y 892 de la Secretaría General de la Comunidad Andina; acción de nulidad incoada por la República de Colombia contra las Resoluciones N° 984 y 1040 de la Secretaría General de la Comunidad Andina".

[429] On the Resolutions 892, 910, 984 and 1040 of the Secretariat General, see above Part II, Dimension IV: Section "Resolutions Concerning the National Confederation of Palm-Growers and Palm Oil Enterprises (Peru) vs. Fund for Price Stabilisation for Palm-Oil and Its Fractions (Colombia)".

[430] Tribunal de Justicia de la Comunidad Andina, Procesos Acumulados 01-AN-2006, 02-AN-2006 y 01-AN-2007, "Acción de nulidad incoada por la sociedad C.I. Grandinos S.A. contra la Resolución N° 984 de la Secretaría General de la Comunidad Andina; acción de nulidad incoada por la Federación Nacional de Cultivadores de Palma de Aceite (FEDEPALMA) contra las Resoluciones n° 984, 910 y 892 de la Secretaría General de la Comunidad Andina; y, acción de nulidad incoada por la República de Colombia contra las Resoluciones N° 984 y 1040 de la Secretaría General de la Comunidad Andina", pp. 35, 36.

autonomy due to the obligation by Colombian law.[431] It is important to highlight that the Tribunal in this context explicitly referred to the findings of the Andean Committee for the Defence of Free Competition. The Tribunal even went further than the mere annulment of the resolutions of the Secretariat General, but blamed the latter for not having initiated investigations against the Colombian state during the prejudicial phase of the action of annulment in accordance with the Andean norms.[432]

One can draw several conclusions regarding the impact of the Andean Tribunal on Andean competition law matters from the case. The Andean Tribunal is generally willing to overrule resolutions of the Secretariat General. Although the magistrates of the Tribunal lack specific competition law knowledge, they were capable of dealing in a very precise and adequate manner with a complex competition issue. On the other hand, one also has to point out that the Tribunal can only generally overrule or approve of a resolution. It is not entitled to estimate an adequate compensation or sanction. Finally, it is to be noted that the Tribunal in its judgment also referred to the decision of the Andean Committee of Defence of Free Competition. Thus the latter does not only have to be limited to its cooperative function during the decision-finding process, but its opinion might continue to be considered until the judicial revision phase.

The Revised Treaty of Chaguaramas in Article 175(12) provides for an action for annulment regarding determinations of the CARICOM Competition Commission. Yet a private entity trying to enforce Article 175(12) RTC has to obtain special leave[433] to commence original jurisdiction proceedings. According to the provision, "[a] party which is aggrieved by a determination of the Commission under paragraph 4 of Article 174 in any matter may apply to the Court for a review of that determination". In *TCL v CARICOM Competition Commission*[434] the wording of Article 175(12) RTC was clarified. Based on a literal interpretation of Article 175(12) of the RTC the CARICOM Competition Commission argued that the reference to Article 174(4) RTC excluded the initiation of an investigation from falling under the term "determination". Notwithstanding, the Caribbean Court of Justice underlined its compulsory and exclusive original jurisdiction. It stated that "[i]n light of (…) the transformation of the CSME into a "regional system under the rule of law", no conduct or exercise of power by a treaty created institution (especially one charged with essential function and endowed with relevant powers under the treaty) should escape the judicial scrutiny of the Court".[435] The Caribbean Court of Justice also incorporated the possibility to declare actions of the Commission

---

[431] *Ibid.*

[432] *Ibid.*

[433] Article 222 of the Revised Treaty of Chaguaramas; *Trinidad Cement Limited v The Competition Commission,* Caribbean Court of Justice Application No. OA 1 of 2012, CCJ 4 (OJ), [2].

[434] *Trinidad Cement Limited v The Competition Commission,* Caribbean Court of Justice Application No. OA 1 of 2012, CCJ 4 (OJ).

[435] *Ibid.*, [16].

unlawful or void.[436] Yet the Caribbean Court of Justice also determined that TCL in this case could have awaited a decision of the Adjudicating Panel of the CARICOM Competition Commission and that ordinarily, the regional Court would not control procedural steps before an enquiry of the Commission.[437]

Irrespective of the specific circumstances of the case, the Caribbean Court of Justice in *TCL v CARICOM Competition Commission* took a broad approach to its interpreting and reviewing competence. It particularly justified its far-reaching powers with the creation of the CSME and thereby underlined its role as an integrationist judicial body. Given this broad self-conception of the Caribbean Court of Justice, it is also possible that parties in accordance with Article 175(12) RTC may not only challenge an entire determination given by the CARICOM Competition Commission, but also the particular findings that constituted the basis of the respective order.[438]

8.3.2.5 Non-compliance Actions

Non-compliance actions in the European Union are directed against member states that do not fulfil their obligations under community law. An action for non-compliance can also become relevant for regional competition law matters, because it can function as an instrument to force member states to enact or ratify national or regional competition laws or establish the respective competition law authorities. It can thus constitute a general controlling mechanism for the implementation of the competition-law-related obligations; either vertically by the regional competition authority, or horizontally if member states have the right to initiate such an action against each other or even initiated by private parties against a member state.

In the WAEMU actions for non-compliance against member states are regulated in Articles 5 to 7 of the Additional Protocol no. 1 and Article 15(1) of Regulation no. 1/96/CM. According to Article 15(1) of Regulation no. 1/96/CM, an action for non-compliance is actually provided for the Commission only. However, also a member state can initiate an action against another member state after a prior referral to the Commission. Consequently, an action for non-compliance could constitute a horizontal deterrence device, for example regarding the application of regional competition law or the refusal to reform national laws.

The reluctance of member states to initiate such legal actions before the WAEMU Court of Justice against other member states is surprising. Regional competition law, enforced by the WAEMU Commission, is frequently used between member states to discipline each other. It seems that a judicial complaint for not having complied with regional law has a different connotation to it than addressing the WAEMU Commission for potentially anticompetitive state behaviour.

---

[436] *Ibid.*, [17].

[437] *Ibid.*, [17].

[438] *Beckford,* The Appropriate Design and Enforcement of Competition Law and Policy in Countries at Different Stages of Market Development, 26–28 May 2010, Brasilia, p. 11.

The reluctance to sue member states before the regional Court may also be explained since such action directly targets national sovereignty.

In the AndeanC not only community bodies or member states, but also legal and natural persons can bring an action of non-compliance before the Andean Tribunal of Justice, if the person can claim to be affected in a subjective right.[439] Member states and individuals however have to address the Secretariat General in a first administrative stage, after which the Secretariat General will issue a decision.[440] This decision does not bind the Tribunal. Only if the Secretariat General does not proceed with the action, persons or member states can address the Tribunal directly.[441]

The Treaty Creating the Tribunal of Justice of the Cartagena Agreement in Article 31 also provides for the possibility for legal or natural persons to address national courts instead of complaining to the regional institutions. In this case, the plaintiff has to argue that the member state has infringed Article 4 of the Treaty Creating the Court of Justice of the Cartagena Agreement. According to Article 4, member states are obliged to adopt all measures, in particular the implementation of according provisions that are necessary for the establishment of the legal system of the AndeanC. In both cases the legal or natural person can also seek compensation in case the member state is held to have disrespected Andean rules. For reasons of geographical distance, one might expect a large number of persons that prefer initiating an action before national courts. Surprisingly, the majority of natural and legal persons have submitted their complaints directly to the Andean Tribunal in Quito.[442] This decision indicates general awareness of individuals of the benefits of regional institutions. Moreover, in the context of filing a complaint against a member state, chances might be considered higher before a regional court, which might be considered less prone to national policy considerations. Yet there have not been any cases of non-compliance before the Andean Tribunal regarding the non-compliance of member states with Decision 608. Nevertheless, during the administrative first stage of a non-compliance action, the Secretariat General released two decisions that involved Decision 608.[443]

Decision no. 03-2009 of the Secretariat General[444] was challenged before the Andean Tribunal of Justice and thus demonstrates the interplay of these two institutions. In conformity with Article 25 of the Treaty Creating the Court of Justice of the

---

[439] Articles 23, 25, 31 of the Treaty Creating the Court of Justice of the Cartagena Agreement.

[440] Articles 24 and 25 of the Treaty Creating the Court of Justice of the Cartagena Agreement.

[441] Articles 24 and 25 of the Treaty Creating the Court of Justice of the Cartagena Agreement.

[442] All cases of non-compliance submitted by natural or legal persons before the Andean Tribunal have referred to non-compliance of member states with the liberalization programme and with the application of intellectual property rights, mainly regarding pharmaceuticals patents, see *Vigil Toledo,* La Estructura Jurídica y el Futuro de la Comunidad Andina, 2011, p. 112.

[443] Dictamen N° 01-2007; see above on Article 5 of Decision 608, Part II, Dimension I: Sect. 5.1.5.2; see also on Dictamen N° 03-2009 in this chapter.

[444] Dictamen N° 03-2009 de la Secretaría General de la Comunidad Andina, "Conforme al artículo 25 del Tratado de Creación del Tribunal de Justicia de la Comunidad Andina", 8 June 2009.

Cartagena Agreement, an Ecuadorian citizen, *Alejandro Ponce Villacís*, claimed that Ecuador had neither implemented nor enforced the Andean Decisions 608 and 616.[445] He particularly referred to Article 2, which included Ecuador's obligation to designate a competent national competition authority. Furthermore he argued that the mere omission of compliance by Ecuador infringed his subjective right, because he was deprived from the rights set out in Decision 608.[446]

On this case, Colombia, via its Ministry of Trade, Industry and Tourism, also expressed its opinion in the prejudicial phase before the Secretariat General and emphasized the importance of establishing national competition authorities in order to prevent distortions in the region. Colombia based its opinion on provisions of Decision 608 directly and on the provisions of the Agreement of Cartagena concerning regional integration, as well as on objectives of the AndeanC, namely the gradual harmonization of national economic and social policies and the creation of a common Latin American market. Article 38 of Decision 608 expressly referred to the obligation of member states to establish a national competition authority and Article 93 of the Agreement of Cartagena, which prohibits distortions of competition in the region through manipulation of prices or other practices with an equivalent effect. By supporting the complaint of *Alejandro Ponce Villacís*, Colombia sought to convince the Secretariat General or Andean Tribunal to take actions against Ecuador in order to accelerate the establishment of an Ecuadorian competition authority.[447]

However, the Secretariat General in its decision rejected the claim as illegitimate. The existence of a subjective right, in contrast to a legitimate interest, presupposed that the claimant received a specific advantage by the normative framework.[448] The Secretariat General argued that while Article 2 and 3 of Decision 608 were generally capable of affecting a subjective right, in the particular case non-compliance with neither Decision 608 nor Decision 616 constituted an infringement of a specific right of the claimant. Finally the Secretariat General also held that the provisions of the Treaty Creating the Court of Justice of the Cartagena Agreement, in particular Art. 2, 3, 4 and 25 could not sufficiently justify an affected subjective right of the claimant. Although individuals in the AndeanC generally held the right to initiate an action for non-compliance, this right was limited by the requirement of an impairment of a personal subjective right. The Secretariat General, during the prejudicial phase, also limited its evaluation of the matter to this requirement, leaving aside other legal questions raised by the claimant.

---

[445] One has to recall that Decision 616 provided for special implementation requirements of Decision 608 for Ecuador.

[446] Dictamen N° 03-2009 de la Secretaría General de la Comunidad Andina, "Conforme al artículo 25 del Tratado de Creación del Tribunal de Justicia de la Comunidad Andina", 8 June 2009, p. 3.

[447] Technically, Colombia could have also initiated an action of non-compliance on its own directly against Ecuador according to Article 24 of the Treaty Creating the Court of Justice of the Cartagena Agreement.

[448] Tribunal de Justicia de la Comunidad Andina, Proceso 75-AI-2001, 29 May 2002.

In the CARICOM, the Agreement Establishing the Caribbean Court of Justice does not differentiate between actions against member states and actions against community institutions. Article XII is formulated in a broad way, stipulating that "(...) the Court shall have exclusive jurisdiction to hear and deliver judgment on: (a) disputes between Contracting Parties to this Agreement; (b) disputes between any Contracting Parties to this Agreement and the Community; (...)." According to Article II of the Agreement Establishing the Caribbean Court of Justice "Contracting Parties" are either member states of CARICOM or any other Caribbean country that is invited by the Conference to become a Party to the agreement. Hence, Article XII lit. a) deals with any dispute among member states, while Article XII lit. b) deals with disputes between member states and community institutions. Individuals can also seize the Caribbean Court of Justice under the precondition that they are granted special leave in accordance with Article 222 of the Revised Treaty of Chaguaramas.[449]

For the lack of deadlines and specific requirements in the Revised Treaty of Chaguaramas regarding the member states' ratification obligations, a non-compliance action against a member state for the failure to adopt national competition laws and institutions does not appear feasible. However, an omission action before the Caribbean Court of Justice for the non-enforcement of regional competition law is generally possible under the regulatory framework of the CARICOM. Yet the impact of judicial actions in competition law enforcement would probably remain very limited. First, member states have been hesitant to enforce the respect of Treaty obligations before the Caribbean Court of Justice.[450] Partly this is due to a lack of capacities to monitor or evaluate possible breaches of the Revised Treaty of Chaguaramas committed by other member states.[451] Furthermore, member states might be more inclined to solve disputes before the COTED, because this might be conceived as a more direct and possibly faster way. Second, in the framework of competition law enforcement, it will be difficult for individuals to claim special leave and to demonstrate that the "interest of justice requires"[452] an action by the Caribbean Court of Justice. The outcome of a specific competition law investigation as well as possible prejudices to rights of the private actor can only be determined after the conduct of such an investigation.[453] Moreover, private actors can also

[449] See for example *Trinidad Cement Limited v The Caribbean Community,* Caribbean Court of Justice Application No. ART 3 of 2008, CCJ 2 (OJ), [22ff.]; *Trinidad Cement Limited v The Caribbean Community,* Caribbean Court of Justice Application No. OA 1 of 2009, CCJ 4 (OJ), [15ff.].

[450] *Pollard,* in: *Hall/Chuck-A-Sang,* CARICOM: Policy Options for International Engagement, 2010, pp. 467, 475.

[451] *Ibid.*

[452] *CARICOM Secretariat,* Caribbean Court of Justice, 2005, p. 7; *Trinidad Cement Limited v The Caribbean Community,* Caribbean Court of Justice Application No. OA 1 of 2009, CCJ 4 (OJ), [16].

[453] *Trinidad Cement Limited* showed that a decision to suspend or lower the Common External Tariff on cement had a prejudicial impact on it, *Trinidad Cement Limited v The Caribbean Community,* Caribbean Court of Justice Application No. OA 1 of 2009, CCJ 4 (OJ), [18]. In the *Trinidad Cement Limited TCL Guyana Incorporated v The State of the Co-operative Republic Of*

address the national competition law agency and then the CARICOM Competition Commission indirectly.

8.3.2.6 Failure to Act Complaints

Failure to act complaints in the European Union are directed against EU institutions that do not fulfil their obligations according to EU law. Such complaints can either be initiated by another EU institution or a member state. This controlling instrument against regional institutions might also become relevant in the context of competition law enforcement.

In the WAEMU, Article 16 of the Additional Protocol no. 1 merely states that the Court of Justice provides for litigations between the Union and its agents. Generally, one could subsume complaints against community organs under this provision. However, so far, there have not been any such cases regarding competition law enforcement.

In the AndeanC, Article 37 of the Treaty Creating the Court of Justice of the Cartagena Agreement and Article 129 of the according statute deal with complaints regarding the failure to act. While this instrument could also be utilized against the Secretariat General, it has so far not been used regarding competition law matters. Private parties are required to demonstrate a legitimate interest or the violation of a subjective right. Generally, the reluctance of the Secretariat General to act on the submission of recourse of reconsideration can also be subject of an action for omission.[454] While this might create demarcation difficulties as regards actions for annulment, the Tribunal accepts this overlap because of the different aims of an action for annulment and an action for failure to act.[455] In fact, while the Secretariat General can change its decision after having been found guilty of a failure to act, the Tribunal of Justice, in the context of an action for annulment, can only (partially) annul the decision. A failure to act complaint against a regional institution contains a preliminary administrative stage: The respective organ has to be demanded to act in written form. Only after not responding within 30 days, in exceptional cases within 45 days, is an action for failure to act admissible.[456]

In the CARICOM, according to Article XII lit. b) of the Agreement Establishing the Caribbean Court of Justice, the Court holds the exclusive jurisdiction to deal

Guyana, Caribbean Court of Justice Application No. OA 2 of 2009, CCJ 5 (OJ), [27], the CCJ required that "[a] party will have to demonstrate that the provision alleged to be breached was intended to benefit that person, that such breach is serious, that there is substantial loss and that there is a causal link between the breach by the State and the loss or damage to that person.", [28]: "The threshold for eligibility for damages is therefore a high one".

454 Tribunal de Justicia de la Comunidad Andina, Proceso 70-RO-2003, "Recurso por omisión interpuesto por la República del Perú contra la Secretaría General de la Comunidad Andina por no haber emitido pronunciamiento sobre el recurso de reconsideración de la Resolucion 576 solicitado por el Gobierno peruano", 22 October 2003, p. 5.

455 *Ibid.*, p. 6.

456 *Ibid.*, p. 4.

with disputes between member states and community organs. This does not clarify the ambiguities that arise in the context of Article 176(6) of the Revised Treaty of Chaguaramas, according to which member states are entitled "to initiate proceedings before the Court at any time". Although the Caribbean Court of Justice and the CARICOM Competition Commission are held to have "concurrent jurisdiction",[457] this does not describe their hierarchical relation in case of conflicts between them.[458]

In the context of failure-to-act complaints, one could also raise the question whether individuals or private enterprises might invoke such an action in order to force community bodies to initiate a competition law investigation. Yet, according to Article 222 of the Revised Treaty of Chaguaramas and Article XXIV of the Agreement Establishing the Caribbean Court of Justice, private entities have to request special leave. They have to establish "that the Treaty intended that a right or benefit conferred by or under the Treaty on a Contracting Party shall ensure to the benefit of such persons directly (…)."[459] Yet with regard to the competence to initiate competition proceedings private parties are explicitly prevented from approaching the CARICOM Competition Commission directly. It might also be difficult to actually enforce such a right, because the outcome of competition law proceedings is uncertain and might not lead to specific legal consequences.

8.3.2.7 Summary of Control of Regional Competition Law Decisions

Constituting an integral element of accountability of a RTA system, the WAEMU, the AndeanC and the CARICOM have established regional courts, which can issue binding decisions without being dependent on the prior consent of member states. Moreover judges of the regional courts act on an independent basis. Yet the degree of independence during the appointment process of regional judges varies; the process in the CARICOM being the most independent and de-politicized process and in the WAEMU and the AndeanC appointing regional judges through national governments. Nevertheless, independent judgments of regional judges seem to be guaranteed in the WAEMU and the AndeanC as well. Hence, a de politicized appointment procedure is not an indispensable precondition in order to guarantee the independence of judges, but it guarantees that the election process remains impartial. This appears to be a particular concern in a situation, in which fewer magistrates than the number of member states compose the regional Court of Justice.[460]

With regard to regional competition law enforcement, the procedures of preliminary reference rulings, advisory opinions and actions for annulment had the greatest impact in the WAEMU, the AndeanC and the CARICOM. Yet preliminary reference

---

[457] *CARICOM Secretariat,* The CARICOM Competition Commission, 2008, p. 10.

[458] For more details on the ambiguities arising out of Article 176(6) of the Revised Treaty of Chaguaramas, see above Part II, Dimension IV: Sect. 8.1.1.2.

[459] *Trinidad Cement Limited v The Competition Commission,* Caribbean Court of Justice Application No. OA 1 of 2012, CCJ 4 (OJ), [7].

[460] This is the case in the CARICOM.

rulings should not be expected to be as influential as preliminary reference rulings in the European Union with regard to regional competition law. This is not only due to the low private sector involvement in regional competition law, but also due to the limited willingness of national courts to refer cases.[461]

Therefore, national competition authorities should be vested with the power to refer cases to a regional court.[462] In fact, in a few cases national competition authorities were already granted a right of referral. Vesting national competition authorities with an active standing in preliminary reference rulings certainly requires a relatively progressed state of implementation of national competition laws. It moreover depends on the commitment of national competition authorities towards regional competition law enforcement. Legal systems also have to safeguard that the duration of regional competition law proceedings is not unreasonably extended through constant referrals. Yet given the frequent focus on national enforcement, this risk is of minor importance, as member states have often been reluctant to address the regional competition authority anyway. It is thus not determining whether preliminary reference rulings are mandatory or not, as there is evidence that points out the commitment of the referring entity, court or possibly national competition authority as decisive factor.

Another concern relates to the diversity of submitted referrals. The procedure for a preliminary reference ruling does not avoid the referral of similar and repetitive questions and does not avoid unequal referral activity of member states. The latter scenario in particular arises if national competition authorities are vested with transferral rights as competition law expertise differs drastically between member states.

The possibility to give advisory opinions only has been acknowledged in the WAEMU and the CARICOM. While the WAEMU Court of Justice can even issue an opinion during the legislative process, the Caribbean Court of Justice can only give opinions on enacted law. Although one cannot make assumptions regarding the effectiveness of the different approaches, one can discern that in the WAEMU and the CARICOM, there is a proportionate relation between the centralization of regional law enforcement and the range of powers of the regional Court of Justice.

Actions for annulment constitute the most direct way to intervene in competition law decisions of the regional competition authority. This is especially the case if the regional Court of Justice has the competence to alter the regional authority's decision, instead of merely annulling it.[463] For private parties it can moreover provide the possibility to defend themselves in case they were found liable for a breach of regional competition law. In this context, the WAEMU, the AndeanC and the CARICOM differ as regards the requirements that private parties have to fulfil in order to seize the regional Court of Justice.[464] Restrictions are generally justified because they balance the individuals' right of defence and accountability of the

---

461 In the WAEMU, national courts were more willing to refer competition law cases to the regional Court of Justice than in the AndeanC.

462 This was discussed in the AndeanC, see above Part II, Dimension IV: Sect. 8.3.2.2.

463 This is the case in the WAEMU.

464 For example requirements such as the infringement of a subjective right or special leave.

regional competition authority, on the one hand, and considerations of legal certainty and duration of an enforcement procedure, on the other hand.

Actions for non-compliance seem mostly to remain an instrument for member states and regional competition authorities against member states. Requirements, such as the infringement of subjective rights or special leave, prevent individuals from exercising general control over the compliance of member states with their regional obligations. With regard to regional competition law enforcement, member states have not initiated actions for non-compliance against other member states. In the same vein, actions for failure to act against regional institutions have not been submitted with regard to regional competition law enforcement.

Regional courts of Justice are generally willing to participate in the development of regional competition law in the WAEMU, the AndeanC and the CARICOM. Moreover, the RTAs contain sufficient and adequate procedures to provide for an *ex post* control of a regional competition authority's decision. Despite partly insufficient competition law expertise, judges have generally displayed a capacity to deal efficiently and adequately with competition law matters. This is not only attributed to the high qualification of judges, but also relates to the functions of a regional court. Instead of solving individual cases based on the circumstances in a specific case, regional judges are in most procedures held to interpret regional law and to answer a legal question based on the principles of the legal framework of the RTA. The latter does not apply in a situation, in which a regional court can even alter a specific and individual decision, as in the WAEMU. In the same vein, a possible participation in the legislative process of regional competition law will require regional judges to be vested with larger competition law expertise. Consequently, in particular in the WAEMU, seminars and competition law training for regional judges are of crucial importance.

Nevertheless, one should not overestimate the impact of a regional court on regional competition law enforcement in developing countries. Addressing a regional court usually involves costs and, especially in young institutions of a RTA among developing countries, correlates to a large degree of legal uncertainty. Hence, regional courts' procedures will in particular in the initiation phase of regional competition law enforcement system remain an instrument used by member states or by large undertakings with "deep pockets". Moreover, requirements for individuals to seize the regional court, such as the impairment of a subjective right[465] or special leave from the home state,[466] restrict access of private parties to the courts.

---

[465] This is the case in the AndeanC.

[466] This is the case in the CARICOM.

Chapter 9
Dimension V: General Legal Principles Governing the Allocation of Competences in RTAs and the Notion of Time

Regional integration is often automatically associated with the concept of supranationality. However, while supranationality might have constituted a key driver in the European competition and general economic system, it is not an indispensable condition for a regional competition law regime's success. Moreover, the concept of supranationality can materialize in different forms, reflecting different degrees of integration and centralization. As the interplay of regional bodies, substantive law and enforcement competences has shown, inter-governmentalism and supranationality do not appear as alternative forms of regional integration, but cumulative factors that shape the overall design of an agreement. Yet, the existence of both factors also bears potential for conflicts and calls for a balancing act. A regional competition law system in particular has to provide for mechanisms and principles that resolve conflicts that might arise from an ambiguous allocation of competences.

Regarding the degree of centralization of an RTA, it is generally assumed that strong centralization of competition law powers prevents problems of multi-level governance and does not require legal rules on the vertical allocation of competences.[1] However, the necessity to implement principles that resolve normative conflicts also applies to unified and centralized competition law systems as in the WAEMU. Not all WAEMU member states have reformed their national competition legislation so far. Moreover, competition law-related areas of law are still under the member states' legislative competence and can thus lead to legal conflicts.

Supranationality is linked to a decision-making process, in which the power is conferred to an autonomous regional authority. In contrast to an intergovernmental system, the decision-making powers are withdrawn from the member states. The

[1] *Cengiz*, Regulation 1/2003 Revisited, 2009, pp. 26, 30 <http://ssrn.com/abstract=1512527> accessed 11 November 2018; *Cseres*, Questions of Legitimacy in the Europeanization of Competition Law Procedures of the EU Member States, 7 February 2013, p. 6 <http://ssrn.com/abstract=2213192> accessed 11 November 2018.

J. Molestina, *Regional Competition Law Enforcement in Developing Countries*,
Munich Studies on Innovation and Competition 9,
https://doi.org/10.1007/978-3-662-58525-2_9

most prominent expressions of supranational normativism in the European Union are the doctrine of direct application and effect as well as the supremacy of community law.[2] In contrast, international law binds sovereign member states without having a direct effect.

9.1 The Principles of Direct Application and Direct Effect of Regional Competition Law

In the WAEMU, regional directives and regulations enter into force with their publication in the Official Bulletin of the Union according to Article 45 of the Treaty of Dakar. Article 43 of the Treaty of Dakar determines the mandatory nature of regulations, which are directly applicable in all member states. The article also sets out that directives bind member states, which have to implement the goals set out in the directive into municipal law.

In the AndeanC, regional law has direct effect and applicability once it is published in the Official Gazette, Articles 2 and 3 of the Treaty regarding the Creation of the Tribunal of Justice of the AndeanC. Article 15 of Decision 425 provides for the direct effect of resolutions and they do not require an additional administrative act, unless the resolution determines differently.[3] A direct application of community law was emphasised by the Andean Tribunal of Justice.[4] According to the latter, direct application is derived from jurisprudence and positive norms, bearing in mind the imperative character of the Agreement of Cartagena and general legal framework.[5]

In the CARICOM, the Revised Treaty of Chaguaramas only binds member states as subjects of international law. As all member states have ratified the Revised Treaty of Chaguaramas and the original jurisdiction of the Caribbean Court of Justice, its judgements have direct effect. In accordance with national law they have the rank of a judgement of a domestic high court.[6]

[2] Judgment of the ECJ, 5 February 1963, Case 26-62, *NV Algemene Transport- en Expeditie Onderneming van Gend & Loos v Netherlands Inland Revenue Administration,* ECR 1, ECLI:EU:C:1963:1; see also *Drexl,* in: *Drexl* (Ed.), The Future of Transnational Antitrust, 2003, p. 311, 331.

[3] Tribunal de Justicia de la Comunidad Andina, Processo 3-AI-96, 27 October 1999.

[4] See for example Tribunal de Justicia de la Comunidad Andina, Processo 3-AI-96, 27 October 1999.

[5] *Tangarife Torres,* Derecho de la Integración en la Comunidad Andina, 2002, p. 208.

[6] See also Article 215 of the Revised Treaty of Chaguaramas.

9.2 Primacy of Regional Law in Exclusive, Concurrent or Parallel Competition Law Enforcement

In the WAEMU and the AndeanC, community law prevails over national law. Parallel to the European prevalence of community law, Article 6 of the Treaty of Dakar sets out that member states are obliged to apply community norms, irrespective of contrary national legislation. In the AndeanC, the Tribunal of Justice stated in the same vein that national norms in contradiction to regional norms would not become invalid, but remain unapplied.[7]

The notion of primacy of community competition law over national law is an essential pillar to the establishment and maintenance of a common market. In order to facilitate intra-community trade and to benefit from the reduction of transaction costs, it is very important that community competition law is applied uniformly and consistently. It has to be applied unconditionally and irrevocability, in order to avoid a fragmentation of the common market by national legislations.[8] The primacy of regional competition law is moreover closely linked to the mandatory nature of a regional legal framework. Yet the question of primacy of regional law only arises in the situation, in which two legislations actually apply to the same matter. Thus, one also has to analyse whether competition law is applied concurrently or parallely by national and regional authorities and in which situations conflicts of legislations are possible to arise.

9.2.1 Exclusive, Concurrent or Parallel Competition Law Enforcement in RTAs

Exclusive competence of a regional competition authority as used in the WAEMU refers to its exclusive competence to apply competition law generally within the RTA. This creates the most centralized form of competition law enforcement. However, exclusivity can also refer to the competence to apply either national or regional competition law exclusively, thereby creating a situation in which national and regional competition law are enforced alternatively. Moreover, exclusive competences might be restricted to some elements of regional competition law, such as the competence to grant exemptions.[9]

---

[7] Tribunal de Justicia de la Comunidad Andina, Processo 3-AI-96, 27 October 1999.

[8] *Drexl,* in: *Drexl* (ed.), The Future of Transnational Antitrust, 2003, p. 311, 339; *Bakhoum,* L'articulation du droit communautaire et des droits nationaux de la concurrence dans l'Union Economique et Monétaire Ouest Africaine, 2007, p. 106.

[9] This was the case under the former European system, in which the European Commission had the exclusive competence to apply the former Article 85(3) of the EC Treaty. Regarding the discussion on a reform of the Commission's monopoly on Article 85(3) of the EC Treaty, see *Ehlermann,* Implementation of EC Competition Law by National Anti-Trust Authorities, 17 ECLR 88, 92ff. (1996).

In a system of concurrent application of substantive regional and national competition law, the applicable law might be either determined by the substantive scope of application, or concurrent competition law enforcement might refer to a system, in which either the regional or national competition authorities are competent to make a decision regarding a possible regional competition law breach. A regional competition authority might be vested with prerogative powers to withdraw national competition authorities from their competences.[10]

In the context of parallel competition law enforcement, one can differentiate between parallel enforcement, in which substantive regional and national competition authorities apply regional and national competition law in parallel but separately.[11] A different understanding of parallel enforcement relates to parallel enforcement of regional competition law by national competition authorities, thereby referring to the enforcement competence in the narrow sense in regional competition law enforcement.[12]

Thus, systems of exclusive, concurrent or parallel competition law enforcement actually do not constitute competence allocation criteria and thus are not descriptive of the degree of centralization or decentralization of regional competition law enforcement. They might overlap and be present cumulatively in a system of regional competition law enforcement.

9.2.2 *Primacy of Community Competition Law in a System of Centralized and Exclusive Application*

Although the exclusive and centralized competition law enforcement in the WAEMU has abolished vertical conflicts between the national and the regional competition law, horizontal and cross-vertical conflicts between national competition-related laws and community law might still arise. In this context, the Court of Justice of WAEMU in the Advisory Decision no. 003/2000 decided that the principal of exclusivity entailed that domains of the member states' competence, such as unfair competition, remained inapplicable if the examined practice fell within the scope of Article 88 lit. a) and lit. b) of the Treaty of Dakar. Although the regional Court only explicitly refers to the legal field of unfair competition, one can conclude that the Court wanted to make a general statement on the scope of the principle of exclusivity, also covering other fields that remain within the national legislative competence, such as stricter national provisions on the restriction of competition or national sectorial regulation.[13] The actual enforcement of primacy of community competition

---

[10] See Article 11(6) of Council Regulation (EC) 1/2003.

[11] Such a parallel application is probable in the CARICOM, see Part II, Dimension V: Sect. 9.2.4.

[12] This kind of parallel application of regional competition law enforcement is applicable in the European Union. For an overview of the reform of EC Competition Law, see *Korah*, in: *Lianos/ Kokkoris* (Eds.) The Reform of EC Competition Law, 2010, pp. xxiii–xxviii.

[13] *Bakhoum*, L'articulation du droit communautaire et des droits nationaux de la concurrence dans l'Union Economique et Monétaire Ouest Africaine, 2007, pp. 82f.

law will also depend on national Courts, which will have to apply community competition law instead of national sectorial law or national unfair competition law.[14] This will depend on their regional competition law knowledge as well.

9.2.3 *Primacy of Community Competition Law in a System of Concurrent Application*

In contrast to the European system, the Andean competition law regime does not provide for parallel application of regional competition law, but for a system of concurrent application of either regional or national law.[15] Hence, conflicts between national and regional laws do not arise through a specific enforcement measure, but revolve around the (preceding) assumption of a cross-border effect of a practice. For the obligatory character and direct effect and application of Andean law, it is the task of national authorities to evaluate whether a cross-border effect in the sense of Article 5 of Decision 608 is actually present. National competition law authorities have to do this evaluation on the basis of criteria that are set out by Decision 608 instead of relying on national criteria. However, despite contrary indications, national competition agencies have always denied the existence of cross-border effects. This hampers convergent application of competition law in the AndeanC, as member states have wide discretion in the drafting of their national competition legislation and structures.[16]

The Andean system does not provide for an institution that supervises the application of Decision 608. For the Secretariat General's exclusive decision-making power, national courts in the AndeanC cannot decide on a potential breach of Decision 608. Yet, they could theoretically exercise an implicit *ex post* control regarding the respect of the principle of primacy when they review decisions of a national competition authority. Community organs, in particular the Secretariat General and the Andean Tribunal will have to supervise the application of the principle of primacy of community law.[17] So far, this has not happened and in particular the Secretariat General does not seem to intend to do so in the near future. It there-

[14] In the European Union, in the course of the installation of decentralized competition enforcement, national judges have been *inter alia* attributed the role of guaranteeing the supremacy of community competition law; see Judgment of the Court of 9 March 1978, Case 106/77, *Simmenthal II*, ECR 1978 - 629, ECLI:EU:C:1978:49.

[15] Even in the case of the utilization of the "downloading option", the AndeanC did not constitute a system of parallel competition law enforcement. On cases with cross-border effect solely Decision 608 was applicable in its function as regional norm. In case of practices with solely national effects, Decision 608 applied as national norm.

[16] In contrast to the European system, regional competition law in the AndeanC does not comprise specific requirements concerning the domestic competition laws' content; see above on "soft" harmonization through non-binding guidelines Part II, Dimension II: Sect. 6.3.

[17] For example through the judicial mechanisms of actions of non-compliance or failure to act, see above Part II, Dimension IV: Sects. 8.3.2.5 or 8.3.2.6.

fore remains open whether the application of Decision 608 allows a parallel enforcement of national competition laws as in the EU. According to the existing Andean legal framework, this is however not the case, as provisions similar to those in the European Regulation no. 1/2003 do not exist.

9.2.4 Primacy in a System of Parallel Competition Law Enforcement and in a Dualist System

The Revised Treaty of Chaguaramas does not contain primacy provisions with regard to regional competition law. The doctrine of implied repeal, as principle of common law, determines that in case two pieces of legislation conflict, one must repeal the other.[18] This presupposes that national and regional law are actually irreconcilable and "fundamentally inconsistent".[19] It is irrelevant, which body issued or applies the legislation and also the date of entry into force is not always a convincing criterion.[20] Consequently, the incorporation of regional competition law in domestic law does not prevent a repeal by other pieces of national legislation. Therefore, the doctrine of implied repeal cannot unambiguously solve a jurisdictional conflict between national and regional law.

As the applicability of Chapter VIII requires that an alleged anticompetitive conduct has cross-border effect or involves a cross-border transaction, this seems to sufficiently differentiate between national and regional competition law breaches and seems to sufficiently avoid jurisdictional conflicts. Nevertheless, it does not stipulate whether in CARICOM regional and national competition legislations are applied alternatively or parallely. Chapter VIII does not incorporate provisions that in case of a cross-border effect or transaction exclude parallel national competition law enforcement based on the breach of national competition laws.

Article 176 RTC deals with the procedures in case of potential anticompetitive business conduct according to regional competition law. Article 176(5) RTC[21] specifies in case of conflicting opinions between the Commission and Member States regarding the business conduct that the Commission has to cease any examination of the matter. A dispute resolution through the COTED only refers to the application of regional competition law, irrespective of a parallel investigation based on national competition law. In fact, no provision of the RTC refrains national competition authorities to engage in an investigation regarding the national anticompetitive

[18] *Beckford*, in: *Drexl/Bakhoum/Fox/Gal/Gerber*, Competition Policy and Regional Integration in Developing Countries, 2012, p. 185, 197.

[19] *Ibid.*, p. 198.

[20] *Ibid.*, p. 201.

[21] Article 176(5) RTC: "5. If there is a difference of opinion between the Commission and the Member State regarding the nature and effects of the business conduct or the jurisdiction of the investigating authority, the Commission shall: (a) cease any further examination of the matter; and (b) refer the matter to COTED for its decision."

effects of the same matter. In the same vein, Chapter VIII remains mute on the resolution of potentially conflicting decisions of national and regional competition authorities. Rather, Article 174(6) RTC sets out that the determinations of the Commission are enforceable in the national jurisdictions. This provision might also cover the resolution of actual conflicting decisions in favour of the regional decision.

The current chairman of the CARICOM Competition Commission, *Kusha Haraksingh*, stated that he did not see a problem in parallel investigations, which may also involve parallel sanctions.[22] He did not even see a need for reconciling parallel decisions, because they were based on different offences, namely national on the one hand and regional on the other.[23] The risk of diverging decisions, which would attribute to the creation of uncertainty for businesses and possible investments in the region and could also hamper the underlying aim of harmonization of competition policies, could be resolved through the cooperation between national and regional competition authorities.

Despite the absence of an explicit provision that allows member states to apply national competition law in parallel to regional law, the strong discretion attributed to the member states in the design and enforcement of national competition law seems to suggest that member states are at least not prevented from such parallel application. In this vein, Article 175(1) RTC only sets out that member states "may" request an investigation, thereby relying on the willingness of national competition authorities to support regional competition law enforcement. Despite the absence of a formal rule on reconciliation, conflicts could still be resolved based on the underlying principles of cooperation and coordination in the framework of CARICOM. In contrast to the European system, the Caribbean legislator did not see a necessity to harmonize national with community provisions in a system of parallel application of national and competition law.[24]

The Revised Treaty of Chaguaramas in this sense constitutes an "unresolved agenda based on mutual respect".[25] This is also codified in the general clause of Article 9 of the Revised Treaty of Chaguaramas. Ideally, national competition authorities, but also national sectorial authorities will coordinate the enforcement of competition law with the CARICOM Competition Commission based on efficiency considerations. This is also relevant with regard to the pooling of scarce resources

[22] Statements made by Kusha Haraksingh during an interview with the author in Port-of-Spain, Trinidad and Tobago, 29 October 2012.

[23] Statements made by Kusha Haraksingh during an interview with the author in Port-of-Spain, Trinidad and Tobago, 29 October 2012.

[24] In *Wilhelm v Bundeskartellamt* the CJEU held that "(…) parallel application of the national system can only be allowed in so far as it does not prejudice the uniform application throughout the common market of the community rules on cartels and of the full effect of the measures adopted in implementation of these rules."; Judgment of the Court of 13 February 1969, Case 14-68, *Walt Wilhelm and others v Bundeskartellamt,* ECR 1, ECLI:EU:C:1969:4, para. 4.

[25] Statements made by Kusha Haraksingh during an interview with the author in Port-of-Spain, Trinidad and Tobago, 29 October 2012.

in order to avoid a duplication of required resources on the national and regional level through parallel national and regional competition law application.

9.3 The Principles of Effectiveness and Equivalence

The principle of effectiveness has been of particular importance in European competition law and applies in situations, in which national law is applied in order to enforce regional law. Member states are for example entitled to design detailed national procedural rules to guarantee the implementation of individual rights granted by community law as long as they "respect the principles of equivalence and effectiveness".[26] Whereas the principle of effectiveness stipulates that EU law has to be effectively implemented in the member states, the principle of equivalence requires national legislation to be designed in such a way as to provide for an equivalent effective standard[27] to the regional provisions.

A codified principle of effectiveness is a relevant element in the allocation of competence within an RTA, as it may grant and broaden competences of the regional level. In this vein, it has provided for the obligation of courts in the EU to develop new techniques in competition law enforcement, most importantly to compensate the victims of an infringement by recognizing damage claims.[28] The involvement of national courts seems to reflect an understanding in the EU that effective competition law enforcement can only be achieved through constant balancing of regional and national competences on the grounds of efficiency considerations.[29] This understanding generally fits in with the principles of proportionality and subsidiarity.

All three RTAs have recognized the need to codify the principle of effectiveness. In the WAEMU Article 7 of the Treaty of Dakar, and in the CARICOM Article 9 of the Revised Treaty of Chaguaramas copy the former Article 10 EC, which laid the ground for the principle of effectiveness in the EU. In the AndeanC Article 36 or 37 of Decision 608 provide for competition law specific loyalty clauses. Article 53 of the Agreement of Cartagena generally sets out that member states shall progressively adopt a strategy to achieve the envisaged development objectives of the Agreement.

---

[26] *Drexl*, in: *Drexl* (Ed.), The Future of Transnational Antitrust, 2003, p. 311, 338. Judgment of the CJEU of 20 September 2001, Case C-453/99, *Courage v Crehan*, ECR I-06297, ECLI:EU:C:2001:465.

[27] Principle of equivalence.

[28] *Drexl*, in: *Drexl* (Ed.), The Future of Transnational Antitrust, 2003, p. 311, 338.

[29] See for example Protocol (No 2) on the Application of the Principles of Subsidiarity and Proportionality, [2010] OJ 83/206, 30 March 2010.

9.4 The Principle of Subsidiarity

All three RTAs included subsidiarity clauses. The West African Treaty of Dakar includes a subsidiarity clause in Article 5 of the Treaty of Dakar,[30] in which the institutions of the community are restricted in the use of their legislative competences. In the same vein, Article 60 of the Revised Treaty of Chaguaramas sets out that the Conference of Heads of States shall identify *priority domains*, in which harmonization of national legislation is necessary to achieve the objectives of the union.[31]

In the AndeanC, the wording of Article 93 of the Agreement of Cartagena, which determines that the Secretariat General has to *monitor* the application of the rules of competition, was partly interpreted as including a subsidiarity principle with regard to the competence of the Secretariat General on the field of competition.[32] Yet, this view was rebutted based on the argument that Article 93 of the Agreement of Cartagena provided the Secretariat General with powers instead of refraining it from exercising competences.[33] Moreover, the interest of a common subregional market required an efficient allocation of competences, on the national level as well as on the regional level.[34]

It is interesting to point out that the concepts of the principle of subsidiarity between the WAEMU and the CARICOM, on the one hand, and the AndeanC, on the other hand—given the premise that one actually interprets the AndeanC's and CARICOM's provisions as subsidiarity clause, differ. While in the WAEMU and the CARICOM the subsidiarity is conceived as a concept of legislative powers of the supranational institutions, the AndeanC's subsidiarity principle refers to the executive powers of the Secretariat General in the context of actual competition law enforcement. Given the WAEMU's emphasis on subsidiarity of legislative powers of the WAEMU organs, one might question whether the WAEMU Court of Justice in its judgement actually took into account the principle set out in Article 5 of the Treaty of Dakar. In the European Union, the scope of the principle of subsidiarity was limited and has never been applied to the fundamental freedoms of the European Union nor to competition policy according to Article 5(3) TEU and Article 3(1) lit.

---

[30] Article 5 of the Treaty of Dakar: "Dans l'exercice des pouvoirs normatifs que le présent Traité leur attribue et dans la mesure compatible avec les objectifs de celui-ci, les organes de l'Union favorisent l'édiction de prescriptions minimales et de réglementations-cadres qu'il appartient aux Etats membres de compléter en tant que de besoin, conformément à leurs règles constitutionnelles respectives."

[31] Article 60 of the Treaty of Dakar: "(…) [la Conférence des Chefs d'Etat et du Gouvernement] identifie les domaines prioritaires dans lesquels, conformément aux dispositions du présent Traité, un rapprochement des législations des Etats membres est nécessaire pour atteindre les objectifs de l'Union."

[32] Informe de la Cuarta Reunion de Expertos Gubernamentales en Materia de Libre Competencia, SG/REG.LC/IV/INFORME, 1 August 2003, pp. 3ff (available from the author).

[33] *Ibid.*, p. 3.

[34] *Ibid.*, p. 3.

b) TFEU.[35] In the absence of such treaty provisions, the principle of subsidiarity in the WAEMU thus appears to be perceived as a mainly political principle, which does not prevent Court of Justice from exercising discretion with regard to it. In contrast, the enforcement focus of the AndeanC's principle of subsidiarity to a certain extent explains the reactive and passive competition law enforcement position of the Secretariat General. In the CARICOM, subsidiarity is also accomplished through the dualist system.[36] Yet, in all three systems, interpretative leeway of principles of subsidiarity and effectiveness leave sufficient room for centralized or decentralized regional competition law enforcement.

9.5 The Principle of Procedural and Institutional Autonomy in the Application of Regional Competition Law and Policy

Whereas Article 3(2) of the European Regulation no. 1/2003/EC sets out rules for national competition law enforcement parallel to applicable European competition law, it does not impede the procedural and institutional autonomy of member states.[37] Yet, *inter alia* the participation in the European Competition Network has accelerated the harmonization of national procedures, of which the harmonization of the national and European leniency programs probably constitutes the most prominent achievement.[38]

---

[35] *Tridimas,* The General Principles of EU Law, 2006, pp. 184ff.; see also Judgment of 23 October 2003, Case T-65/98, *Van den Bergh Foods v Commission*, ECR II-04653, ECLI:EU:T:2003:281, paras. 197–199, in which the Court rejected the principle of subsidiarity as an argument against the prerogative enforcement right of the Commission.

[36] In the CARICOM, the CARICOM Heads of State and Government in 2005 established a Technical Working Group on Governance of the Caribbean Community in order to review the current institutional governance structure. The Technical Working Group in its report of the 23 October 2006 argued in favour of the introduction of the "collective exercise of sovereignty" in agreed areas by member states. The agreed areas of such "shared sovereignty" are supposed to be determined on the basis of the principles of "proportionality" and "subsidiarity", Report of the Technical Working Group on Governance appointed by CARICOM Heads of Government, p. 14. "On this basis, it would be possible to reconcile the twin imperatives of nationalism and regionalism, based on a division of responsibility between the two levels of decision-making."

[37] *European Commission,* Communication from the Commission to the European Parliament and the Council, Report on the functioning of Regulation 1/2003, 2009, p. 8; *Cseres,* Questions of Legitimacy in the Europeanization of Competition Law Procedures of the EU Member States, 7 February 2013, pp. 7, 13 <http://ssrn.com/abstract=2213192> accessed 11 November 2018.

[38] *Cengiz,* The European Competition Network, 2009, p. 19 <http://cadmus.eui.eu/bitstream/handle/1814/11067/MWP_2009_05.pdf?sequence=1> accessed 11 November 2018; *Cengiz,* Regulation 1/2003 Revisited, 2009, p. 33 <http://ssrn.com/abstract=1512527> accessed 11 November 2018; *Cseres,* Questions of Legitimacy in the Europeanization of Competition Law Procedures of the EU Member States, 7 February 2013, p. 4 <http://ssrn.com/abstract=2213192> accessed 11 November 2018.

In the WAEMU, institutional autonomy with regard to the domestic competition law enforcement bodies is set out in Directive no. 02/2002/CM/UEMOA, which does neither require the member states to adopt a national competition authority nor a specific structure.[39] Article 6(2) of Directive 02/2002/CM/UEMOA sets out that member states are obliged to reform their national competition law structures in accordance with their now limited competence, as set out in Article 3 and 4 of the same Directive. However, as Articles 3 and 4 of Directive 02/2002/CM/UEMOA only refer to monitoring and transferral functions of national competition authorities, it follows from this that member states are not even obliged to create authorities that actually have controlling functions.[40] This could create a situation, in which national competition authorities lack sufficient competences to effectively assist the WAEMU Commission during competition law investigations.[41] Furthermore, the institutional autonomy creates difficulties to discern the competent national authority that has to cooperate with the WAEMU Commission. Directive no. 02/2002/CM/UEMOA does not incorporate a provision that obliges member states to appoint the competent authority.[42] Procedural autonomy also exists in the WAEMU.[43] However it only arises in the context of cooperation with the WAEMU Commission, as national competition authorities are limited to a supporting function in the framework of competition law enforcement.[44]

In the AndeanC Article 16 of Decision 608 explicitly sets out that investigations take place in accordance with national legislation and national competition law procedures. Yet Article 16 of Decision 608 contains specific investigation competences that serve as a minimum legal standard.[45] Although procedural autonomy of member states is generally respected, Decision 608 has created a legal framework for procedural rules during an investigation in the context of Decision 608.

In the CARICOM, member states have large discretion to legislate on national competition and corresponding procedural laws. Although the internal rules of procedure regulate the procedures before the CARICOM Competition Commission, the actual investigations are carried out in accordance with national procedural

[39] Article 1 of Directive no. 02/2002/UEMOA: "Structure nationale de concurrence: toute institution nationale, à compétence générale ou sectorielle, intervenant dans le domaine du contrôle de la concurrence." In fact, the national competition law authorities in the WAEMU differ in their composition and range of functions and competences. See above Part II, Dimension II: Sect. 6.1.

[40] *Bakhoum,* L'articulation du droit communautaire et des droits nationaux de la concurrence dans l'Union Economique et Monétaire Ouest Africaine, 2007, p. 215.

[41] *Bakhoum,* L'articulation du droit communautaire et des droits nationaux de la concurrence dans l'Union Economique et Monétaire Ouest Africaine, 2007, p. 215.

[42] The competent national authority does not necessarily have to be the national competition authority, but can constitute a ministry or sectorial agency or even several national authorities. See for example the cooperation between the ministries in Senegal with the WAEMU Commission. See above Part II, Dimension II: Sect. 6.1.1.

[43] See for example Article 21(1) of Regulation no. 03/2002/CM/UEMOA.

[44] See above on the conduct of investigations, Part II, Dimension IV: Sect. 8.1.2.

[45] See above on the initiation and conduct of an investigation, Part II, Dimension IV: Sect. 8.1.2.

laws.[46] In this vein, Article 170(1) lit. b)(iii), (iv) of the Revised Treaty of Chaguaramas determines that member states have to enact national procedural laws in order to enforce regional competition laws.

9.6 Mandatory Lead Jurisdiction

In the context of the discussion of a globalized competition law, it is proposed to designate a supranational entity in order to decide on the competent jurisdiction.[47] This organ is entitled to determine the jurisdiction that will have exclusive competence to enforce regional competition law. In the three RTAs at stake such a solution would only resolve remaining conflicts of jurisdiction, because the legal criteria provided for are supposed to delimit the competent authority objectively. Moreover, the assignment of an exclusive competence to enforce regional competition law within a RTA creates an incentive problem, as the competent jurisdiction will be inclined to mainly take into account its own interests.[48] Generally, a biased competence allocation is more probable to occur through national competition authorities than through a regional authority. On the other hand, if the regional competition authority holds the prerogative power and abusively detains all competences and cases, this would consume an unproportionate amount of resources. If the competent jurisdiction is chosen based on the impact of the allegedly anticompetitive practice, usually the same jurisdictions, namely the larger ones or economically more relevant ones, will be chosen to enforce competition law. This creates a disadvantage for the smaller and economically weaker member states that might be similarly affected by the anticompetitive practice.[49]

Yet even in an RTA in some instances the existence of an institution that is responsible for deciding on the competent institution and/or applicable law might be useful. In the European Union, the Commission maintains its prerogative power to enforce European competition law.[50] After consultation with the member states, it is even entitled to stop a domestic competition law investigation.[51] So far, the Commission has not used this power to intervene. As *Firat Cengiz* appropriately concludes, this can be weighted as indicator for functioning communication between

[46] Rule 6(1) of the CARICOM Competition Commission Rules of Procedure, 2011, "Power to enter premises under warrant".

[47] See on the discussion, *Budzinski,* The Governance of Global Competition, 2008, pp. 203ff., 166f.; *Bätge,* Wettbewerb der Wettbewerbsordnungen?, 2009, pp. 268ff.

[48] *Budzinski,* The Governance of Global Competition, 2008, pp. 166f., 203f.; *Bätge,* Wettbewerb der Wettbewerbsordnungen?, 2009, pp. 268f.

[49] *Budzinski,* The Governance of Global Competition, 2008, pp. 166f., 203f.; *Bätge,* Wettbewerb der Wettbewerbsordnungen?, 2009, pp. 268f.

[50] Article 11(6) of Regulation no. 1/2003.

[51] Article 11(6) of Regulation no. 1/2003.

the national and regional authorities within the European Competition Network.[52] Moreover, the ECN demonstrates that close and frequent communication in a network can overcome the above-mentioned incentive problems.

Whether it is recommendable to vest a body with such prerogative enforcement powers depends on two preconditions: First, the probability and frequency of multiple competent jurisdictions despite the competence allocation through a substantive demarcation criterion. Second, the necessity to reconcile possible diverging decisions. The latter is usually given in a regional competition law system, which *inter alia* aims at harmonizing competition policies and the creation of a common market.

In the WAEMU, the centralization of competition law enforcement renders a possible prerogative of the WAEMU Commission obsolete, as it constitutes the exclusive institution to enforce regional competition law. This preconditions that the scope of application of regional competition law actually applies. The Court of Justice of the WAEMU does not feel competent to control this. Although it is generally assigned to solve jurisdictional disputes, it rejected a case based on the argument that it was not competent to decide on the allocation of competences.[53]

In the AndeanC, Article 5 of Decision 608 provides for a competence-demarcation criterion regarding the application of Andean competition law. Unfortunately, competition law cases were so far found to have solely national implications. Possible conflicts might still arise between the Secretariat General and national sectorial agencies that deal with areas related to trade and competition. Yet, bearing in mind the broad field of competence of the Secretariat General, which is designed as an administrative body of the integration process, the recognition of a mandatory lead jurisdiction is not the only solution to avoid multiple jurisdictions or conflict of competences. The Secretariat General could also encourage discussions, in which conflicts of competences could be reconciled through communication with the respective authorities as happened in the ECN. In the same vein, the Andean Committee for Defence of Free Competition could function as an adequate institution to solve competition-law-related disputes of competences. Remaining conflicts that cannot be reconciled would ultimately have to be resolved by the Andean Tribunal of Justice.

In the CARICOM, multiple jurisdiction conflicts actually only arise between national competition authorities, as investigations take place decentrally on a national level. Yet, the regional CARICOM Competition Commission and the assigned national competition authority might hold diverging views on the substantive analysis of the respective business practice. It is possible that a national competition authority might conclude that the practice at stake only has national effects and thereby only national competition law applies. According to Article 176(5) RTC

[52] *Cengiz,* The European Competition Network, 2009, p. 17 <http://cadmus.eui.eu/bitstream/handle/1814/11067/MWP_2009_05.pdf?sequence=1> accessed 11 November 2018.

[53] See *Compagnie Air France v. Syndicat des Agents de Voyage et de Tourisme du Sénégal*, Cour de Justice de l'UEMOA, Arrêt n° 1/2005, 12 January 2005. In more detail discussed above Part II, Dimension IV: Sect. 8.3.2.2.

the COTED is the competent body to resolve the dispute. The COTED, composed by national representatives might be more inclined to the national agency's view, thereby contributing to a *de facto* prerogative power of national competition authorities. As the Caribbean Court of Justice can revise decisions of the COTED[54] and generally entails the exclusive competence to interpret the Revised Treaty of Chaguaramas,[55] it will also depend on the regional Court whether the COTED will be able to exercise a prerogative power at its own discretion.

To sum up, there is neither a clear tendency in favour of vesting a body with prerogative powers regarding competition law enforcement within an RTA among developing countries, nor with regard to the appropriate national or regional body. Yet one should acknowledge the risk for abuse that a prerogative power involves, and the prevalent distrust among member states. Objective competence allocation criteria therefore remain more feasible and prerogative power mechanisms should remain *ultima ratio* for specific and limited situations of jurisdictional conflicts. Objective competence allocation criteria also support the development of a set of consistent regional case law. With the exception of the WAEMU, the AndeanC's and the CARICOM's institutional frameworks already provide for potential institutional bodies with prerogative powers, namely the Andean Committee for Defence of Free Competition and the COTED. Yet, in order to minimize the above-mentioned potential for abuse, it is necessary that the regional courts actually exercise their monitoring powers.

9.7 Quantitative Thresholds

Applying a quantitative threshold regarding the allocation of competence requires careful differentiation. The European *de minimis* clause is not a competence allocation criterion, but determines that business practices might not amount to a competition law infringement due to their insufficient effect.[56] Yet, the clause also specifies the scope of application of regional competition law by requiring an appreciable effect on trade between member states. The European merger law includes a quantitative threshold. This however does not constitute a competence demarcation criterion either, but specifies the scope of application of regional merger law.[57] Solely relying on a quantitative threshold in order to determine a competent authority appears as non-feasible. Yet, the European experience has shown that a *De minimis*

[54]Article 176(6) of the Revised Treaty of Chaguaramas.

[55]Article 211 of the Revised Treaty of Chaguaramas.

[56]Commission Notice on agreements of minor importance that do not appreciably restrict competition under Article 81(1) of the Treaty establishing the European Community (de minimis), C 368/07, 22 December 2001, OJ C 291/1, 30 August 2014, p. 1–4.

[57]Council Regulation (EC) No. 139/2004, 20 January 2004 on the control of concentrations between undertakings (the EC Merger Regulation), 29 January 2004, OJ L 24, 29 January 2004, p. 1–22.

clause can contribute to a more efficient use of resources by limiting the scope of application of regional competition law.

Generally, the WAEMU competition law and policy does not provide for a *de minimis* rule. This increases the workload of the WAEMU Commission.[58] In the AndeanC, the scope of application of Decision 608 solely depends on the territorial effect of a practice. Article 181 of the Revised Treaty of Chaguaramas provides for a *de minimis rule* in the CARICOM. In contrast to the European Union, practices of insignificant impact on trade within the CSME are not exempted *per se*, but the CARICOM Competition Commission has discretion to exempt such business conduct.[59]

Regarding the current process of adopting a regional merger control system in the CARICOM, it remains open whether it will adopt a similar approach to the European merger control system, in which a *one-stop-shop* principle[60] avoids parallel application of regional and national merger control. However, the establishment of such a principle in a dualist system will also depend on the implementation into domestic law by national legislators.

Although, a *de minimis* rule is not codified in the WAEMU or the AndeanC, it appears useful to limit the scope of application of regional competition law to anti-competitive practices with an appreciable effect. This does not only enhance a more efficient use of resources of the regional authority, but would also target those anti-competitive practices that are actually the most harmful for a common market.

9.8 Conclusions on the General Legal Principles Governing the Allocation of Competences in RTAs

Clearly the principle of direct effect and application of regional competition constitutes the main difference between the WAEMU and the AndeanC on the one hand and the CARICOM on the other hand. Nevertheless, conflicts of competences and questions regarding the scope of application of regional law arise similarly, which have to be solved. It is not a feasible solution to allow conflicting decisions by regional and national authorities, as this would undermine the functioning of a common market and would waste resources. Such a situation would thus require either the assignment of an institutional organ with prerogative powers or a codified

[58] In fact, the inter-governmental group of experts regarding competition law and policy at a conference in 2008, argued in favour of an auto-limitation of the WAEMU Commission regarding its competences. The adoption of a *de minimis* rule was brought forward as possible solution; *Groupe Intergouvernemental d'experts sur le Droit et de la Politique de la Concurrence,* Répartition des Compétences entre les Autorités Communautaires et les Autorités Nationales, 16–18 July 2008, Geneva.

[59] Article 181 of the Revised Treaty of Chaguaramas.

[60] Article 21 of Council Regulation (EC) No. 139/2004, 20 January 2004 on the control of concentrations between undertakings (the EC Merger Regulation), 29 January 2004, OJ L 24, 29 January 2004, p. 1–22.

framework for extensive cooperation. Most importantly, in particular young regional competition law regimes need a clear definition of the scope of application of regional law. Bearing in mind the limited resources, this scope of application of regional law might be moreover limited to the anticompetitive business practices that have the most harmful effect on the common market. In the absence of case law on general legal principles, such as the principles of effectiveness, equivalence and subsidiarity these can only assist in the identification of the competent authority or applicable law.

Chapter 10
Dimension VI: The Notion of Time—Adaptability and Sustainability of Regional Competition Law Enforcement

Regional integration is a dynamic process in the first place.[1] RTAs and their competition laws do not represent rigid legal constructions, but constitute dynamic systems that need to adapt to changing circumstances. This in particular applies to a regional competition law, because ideally with the emergence of domestic competition law structures, also cultural and political awareness and commitment towards competition law will increase. Therefore, the question is whether the legal systems of the WAEMU, the AndeanC and the CARICOM are generally capable of (quickly) adapting to changes. Have the competition law systems of the WAEMU, the AndeanC and the CARICOM changed over time? In a second step one should then evaluate whether the regional competition policies were introduced at a "good" moment and whether changes to the regional competition law system led to efficiency gains.

10.1 General Legal Adaptability of the Regional Competition Law System

The WAEMU system in its centralized form is the oldest regional competition law regime of the three RTAs. While it was held that the exclusive competence of the Commission would contribute to the uniform application of competition law and thereby support the common market[2] the inefficiencies of the centralized system have become more and more apparent. Currently, there are ongoing reform

[1] *Ziller,* The Challenges of Governance in Regional Integration, 2005, p. 9.

[2] Advisory Opinion no. 003/2000/CJ/WAEMU, 27 June 2000, "Demande d'avis de la Commission de l'UEMOA relative à l'interprétation des articles 88, 89 et 90 du Traité relatifs aux règles de concurrences dans l'Union".

J. Molestina, *Regional Competition Law Enforcement in Developing Countries*, Munich Studies on Innovation and Competition 9,
https://doi.org/10.1007/978-3-662-58525-2_10

initiatives with regard to the competition law system.[3] They plead for a moderate decentralization, as well as enhanced cooperation between competition and sectorial agencies.[4] The reform proposals do not refer to specific provisions that ought to be changed. In fact, Articles 88, 89, 90 of the Treaty of Dakar do not explicitly refer to the extensive scope of application, but the regional court's advisory decision determined the exclusive competence. Thus they would "only" need to be interpreted differently, and would not require an amendment of the Treaty.[5] In particular, the requirements of Article 88 of the Treaty of Dakar on the effect on the interior of the Union[6] and the effect on the common market[7] leave sufficient leeway to be interpreted as being limited to effects on trade between member states. On the other hand, the Court did not consider any different interpretation of the provision. Article 90 of the Treaty of Dakar does not establish a general exclusive competence of the WAEMU Commission on any competition law practices, but refers to the application of Article 88 and 89 of the Treaty of Dakar, hence to the application of regional competition law. Article 89 of the Treaty of Dakar allows the Council of Ministers[8] to enact Regulations under certain majority vote conditions with regard to the application of community competition law.[9] Thus only Regulations and Directives would have to be changed. The WAEMU system hence provides for certain flexibility. As *Mor Bakhoum* aptly states, in the course of deepening the integration process, the provisions of the Treaty of Dakar have so far only been amended instead of being completely replaced or deleted. This demonstrates that the Treaty of Dakar "is marked by both pragmatism and realism".[10] Yet the reform process is slow.[11]

---

[3] See in particular the UNCTAD project "Le Projet de renforcement des capacités de la Commission et des Etats membres de l'UEMOA", see <http://unctad.org/en/pages/newsdetails.aspx?OriginalVersionID=333UNCTAD> accessed 11 November 2018.

[4] *Bakhoum,* Étude sur la Révision du Cadre Institutionnel de Mise en Oeuvre des Règles de Concurrence de l'UEMOA, 2011.

[5] A different opinion has *Weick* who questions an overturning of the Court of Justice decision in the near future *inter alia* because of the required unanimity to alter the Treaty of Dakar, see *Weick,* Competition Law and Policy in Senegal, 33/3 W. Comp. 521, 538 (2010).

[6] Article 88 lit. a) of the Treaty of Dakar: "(…) ayant pour objet ou pour effet de restreindre ou de fausser le jeu de la concurrence *à l'intérieur de l'Union*;" (emphasis added).

[7] Article 88 lit. b) of the Treaty of Dakar: "(…) un abus de position dominante *sur le marché commun ou dans une partie significative* de celui-ci;" (emphasis added).

[8] "Le Conseil des Ministres de l'Union", Articles 20 to 25 of the Treaty of Dakar.

[9] Article 89 of the Treaty of Dakar requires a 2/3 majority for the adoption of Regulations. If the adoption of a legal act by the Council is based on the proposition of the Commission, the Council has to decide on an unanimous vote.

[10] *Bakhoum,* Delimitation and Exercise of Competence between the West African Economic and Monetary Union (WAEMU) and its Member States in Competition Policy, 29/4 W. Comp. 653, 655 (2006).

[11] According to *Weick*, reforms of the centralized system in the WAEMU are unlikely to be implemented in the near future. He *inter alia* explains this with the ideology of centralization in the WAEMU. Furthermore, he doubts whether Senegal "would want its trading partners to have independent competition laws that could be used for protectionism." *Weick,* Competition Law and Policy in Senegal, 33/3 W. Comp. 521, 538 (2010).

The AndeanC is the second oldest regional competition law regime, if one takes Decision 608 as the point of reference.[12] Decision 608 of 2005 reformed the regional competition law regime and introduced the "downloading option". Yet, with the emergence of national competition law structures, also in Bolivia and Ecuador, this "downloading option" has lost its relevance. Decision 608 *inter alia* aims at creating incentives for member states to establish domestic competition law structures. The "downloading option" was deliberately perceived as a transitory device. Yet, with regard to Decision 608, time seems to have been a negative factor. Since 2005 there have not been any regional competition law cases. It appears that with the establishment of domestic competition law structures in all member states, competition law enforcement has shifted towards solely national enforcement based on breaches of national antitrust law. The longer the Andean Decision 608 remains unapplied, the more general awareness of regional competition law will decrease, not only within the private sector or civil society, but also among national public institutions. Moreover, the Andean Secretariat General does not intend to revive its competition law enforcement powers. This is not due to the lack of specific legal mechanisms, but due to its self-conception as a reactive organ that awaits initiatives from the member states. This also diminishes the Secretariat General's reputation regarding competition law enforcement.

The CARICOM is the youngest regional competition law regime of the three RTAs if one considers that the CARICOM Competition Commission was only inaugurated in 2008.[13] The CARICOM competition law system is still in a transition phase, because a great number of member states are still struggling with the establishment of domestic competition law structures and the adoption and implementation of regional competition law norms in their national legislation. It is thus even more remarkable that the CARICOM Competition Commission was able to start to investigate against the Trinidad Cement Limited Group, a very large and economically strong company in the region. The Caribbean Court of Justice demonstrated with its reasonable judgment that it is generally capable of dealing with competition law matters. Hence, it is probable that the Caribbean Court of Justice in its original jurisdiction will contribute to an interpretation of regional competition law provisions that takes into account changing circumstances and interests. Although the wording of Chapter VIII is partly ambiguous and creates legal uncertainty, this open wording simultaneously provides for a high degree of flexibility. In the same vein, the COTED with its far-reaching competition law powers can be regarded negatively, but it offers possibilities to adopt exceptional measures for disadvantaged enterprises, sectors, regions or countries. The concrete interplay of the CARICOM Competition Commission, the Caribbean Court of Justice and the COTED still evolves and will to a large extent depend on the pace of the implementation of

[12] Actually, the AndeanC already provided for a regional competition law norm with Decision 285, which entered into force in 1991, but was hardly applied. For more information on Decision 285 see *Böttcher*, Kartell- und Lauterkeitsrecht in den Ländern der Andengemeinschaft, 2004, pp. 64f.

[13] The Revised Treaty of Chaguaramas and Chapter VIII already entered into force in 2001.

national competition law systems. Yet, so far one can consider the first regional competition law enforcement steps as successful.

10.2 Timing of Regional Competition Law Implementation

The determination of the right timing for the introduction of regional competition law firstly requires the identification of the relevant points of reference. In regional competition law enforcement, these points relate to the general integration process, in particular the progress of the common market, and the stage of development of national competition law expertise and structures.

The stage of regional integration varies between the WAEMU, the AndeanC and the CARICOM. The WAEMU constitutes the furthest integrated system. It even comprises a monetary union, which predates the economic union.[14] Moreover, the WAEMU relies on a tradition of centralization, because of the former French colonial tradition.[15] While the AndeanC and the CARICOM can similarly be traced back to an old integration movement,[16] the creation of a common market was only initiated more recently.[17] In the WAEMU, the AndeanC and the CARICOM, the introduction of a common market thus precedes the implementation of a regional competition policy. Having said that, if one understands a common market as a geographical area, in which trade does not underlie any tariff barriers and in which the free movement of goods, services, capital and persons is guaranteed, one has to acknowledge that the common markets in all three RTAs are yet still to emerge. Bearing in mind that the protection of the common market constitutes one of the main regional competition law objectives in the WAEMU, the AndeanC and the CARICOM, the establishment phase of a common market appears to be the adequate moment for the introduction of regional competition law.

This finding does not determine whether the introduction of regional competition law in its specific form was well timed. Interestingly, the economically most integrated RTA, namely the WAEMU, attributes the member states with the least competition law competences. In fact, the Advisory Opinion no. 003/2000 of the WAEMU Court of Justice justifies the exclusive competence of the Union by

---

[14] The common market was introduced with the Treaty of Dakar in 1994, however was in particular supported by the preferential tariff regime in 1996, see <http://www.uemoa.int/Pages/UEMOA/L_UEMOA/Historique.aspx>.

[15] On the economic and political context in Sub-Saharan Africa, see *Gerber*, Global Competition, 2010, pp. 248ff.

[16] They can be traced back to the Andean Pact/Acuerdo de Cartagena and the West Indies Federation/CARIFTA, see Part I, Sects. 1.1.1, 1.1.2 and 1.1.3.

[17] In the AndeanC, the common market was specifically established by the Protocolo Modificado del Acuerdo de Cartagena in 1987. Until 2005 the principle of the free circulation of goods was established. In the CARICOM, the CSME was introduced in 2001 with the Revised Treaty of Chaguaramas. See above Part I, Sects. 1.1.1, 1.1.2 and 1.1.3.

referring to the latter's integrationist function in the common market.[18] In the same vein, the Court argues that diverging interpretations of competition law would come at the expense of undertakings.[19] Recalling that the strong centralization has proven to be inefficient, one must conclude that the emerging stage of a common market by itself does not justify strong centralization in the introductory phase of regional competition law.[20] Rather than being a direct result of relatively advanced regional economic integration in the WAEMU, one should also acknowledge the strong impact of the "French" tradition of centralization and the conception of the common market that "ignores any stratification of national and community markets."[21]

The second point of reference for the right timing of the introduction of regional competition law is the state of competition law expertise and structures among member states and the level of liberalization. The WAEMU, the AndeanC and the CARICOM resemble each other in this regard, as they comprise few member states with competition law expertise, but the majority of member states lacks such experiences and state intervention is still prevalent in national markets.[22] Moreover, the existing domestic competition law regimes vary in scope of application and taxonomy.[23] It is only the AndeanC that incorporated a specific transitory device that addresses the preponderant lack of domestic competition law structures in the form of the "downloading option".[24] In a similar vein, the CARICOM competition taxonomy offers a certain degree of flexibility that allows the COTED and the CARICOM Competition Commission to adopt transitory rules for less developed and disadvantaged regions or sectors.[25]

The absence of domestic competition law structures can be an argument in favour of centralizing competition law enforcement.[26] Yet with regards to the dynamics of

---

18 Advisory Opinion no. 003/2000/CJ/WAEMU, 27 June 2000, "Demande d'avis de la Commission de l'UEMOA relative à l'interprétation des articles 88, 89 et 90 du Traité relatifs aux règles de concurrences dans l'Union", p. 6.

19 *Ibid.*

20 Even the European centralized competition law system under Regulation no. 17/62/EC was less centralized than the WAEMU system by refraining from substituting national competition laws and by providing for the parallelism of regional and national competition law application. In general on the situation of national and regional competition laws in the European Union in 1995 with regard to the progress of a common European market, see *Dreher,* in: *Forschungsinstitut für Wirtschaftsverfassung und Wettbewerb E.V.*, Umbruch der Wettbewerbsordnung in Europa, 1995, p. 1.

21 Advisory Opinion no. 003/2000/CJ/WAEMU, 27 June 2000, "Demande d'avis de la Commission de l'UEMOA relative à l'interprétation des articles 88, 89 et 90 du Traité relatifs aux règles de concurrences dans l'Union", p. 5: "Le Traité de Dakar consacre ainsi un nivellement par le haut du marché de l'Union où les différents marchés nationaux sont confondus dans *un marché unique qui ignore toute stratification des marchés nationaux et communautaires*" (emphasis added).

22 See above Part II, Dimension I: Sect. 5.2.

23 See above Part II, Dimension I: Sect. 5.2.

24 See above Part II, Dimension II: Sect. 6.3.2.

25 Articles 182 and 183 of the Revised Treaty of Chaguaramas; See also Chapter 7 "Disadvantaged Countries, Regions and Sectors", Articles 142 to 167 of the Revised Treaty of Chaguaramas.

26 See Part III, Dimension V: Sect. 12.6 and Part III, Sect. 14.6.

regional competition law enforcement, one has to pay careful attention to the right timing of the implementation and the specific form at the moment of implementation of regional competition law. The European competition law is a positive example, because at an early stage, in which few member states possessed a functioning national competition law system, there was no obligation for member states to introduce national regimes.[27] Today, with an integral common market and a relatively well spread competition culture, domestic competition laws of EU member states are almost largely harmonized.[28] The WAEMU system, on the other hand, ignored the dynamics of regional competition law by completely preventing a national learning process. It also ignored the prior existing competition law expertise from which the regional level could have learned. At the same time it required a high level of commitment of national authorities towards regional competition law enforcement, namely through cooperation obligations. Although economic integration in the WAEMU was relatively advanced, in comparison to the AndeanC and the CARICOM the notion of competition and liberalized markets was similarly young. The WAEMU experience thus demonstrates that economic integration cannot replace the development of a national competition culture and experience.

Finally, in the AndeanC and the CARICOM regional competition laws were introduced at a stage in which a large number of member states were engaging in the implementation and development of national competition law structures.[29] Even more, there was explicit support from member states for the establishment of the regional competition law framework.[30] In contrast, the centralization of regional competition law in the WAEMU proceeded against the will of some member states, namely against Senegal, which also constitutes the member state with most competition law expertise. A parallel national and regional implementation process saves resources, because regional and national entities can assist each other and may simultaneously profit from member states with more competition law experience. The AndeanC's, the CARICOM's as well as the EU's experiences moreover demonstrate that regional competition law should not be imposed on member states, neither by the regional level nor from abroad. Rather, member states should make use of internal driving forces for supporting the implementation of regional competition law.

Interestingly, in the CARICOM and the EU, such national incentives stemmed from the more competition law-experienced member states, while in the AndeanC,

---

[27] *Drexl,* Perspectives européennes sur la politique de la concurrence dans l'espace OHADA, XXV R.I.D.E. 281, 292ff. (2011).

[28] *Drexl,* Perspectives européennes sur la politique de la concurrence dans l'espace OHADA, XXV R.I.D.E. 281, 293ff. (2011).

[29] In the AndeanC, Ecuador and Bolivia were in the process of a competition law legislation process. In the CARICOM, Trinidad and Tobago has been engaging in legislative initiatives since 1997/1998. Jamaica and Barbados reformed and enacted national competition laws in 2001and 2002. See above Part II, Dimension I: Sect. 5.2.

[30] In the AndeanC: Ecuador and Bolivia. In the CARICOM: Jamaica, Barbados and Trinidad and Tobago (despite the absence of domestic competition law structures, it was an active participant in meetings concerning the implementation of a regional competition law regime).

member states in the process of implementing domestic competition law regimes constituted the main driving forces of regional competition law implementation. The lack of use of Decision 608 in the AndeanC yet demonstrates that even a good implementation moment for regional competition law does not guarantee for its application in the long run. This seems to suggest that there is a difference with regard to the quality and impact of support depending on the member state. The support by more competition law-experienced member states, which are usually also the economically stronger member states, appears to be more important for the implementation and long-term enforcement of regional competition law than the support of less experienced and economically weaker member states.[31]

---

[31] Although Germany was once an insisting supporter of the introduction of a decentralized enforcement in the EU, it had already at an early stage consulted the European Commission regularly when dealing with the former Articles 81 and 82 of the EU Treaty; see *Jenny/Horna,* in: *Brusick/Alvarez/Cernat,* Competition Provisions in Regional Trade Agreements, 2005, pp. 281, 288; *Ehlermann,* Implementation of EC Competition Law by National Anti-Trust Authorities, 17 ECLR 88, 90 (1996).

Part III
The Optimal Degree of Centralization and Decentralization: Evaluation of the Three Regional Competition Law Systems with Regard to the Enforcement of Competition Law in Developing Countries

Chapter 11
General Conclusions on the Efficacy of a Regional Competition Law System

Before evaluating the different degrees of centralization or decentralization, this section sheds some light on the main difficulties and incentives for the implementation of national competition law structures and regional competition law enforcement that arose in the context of a regional competition law system.

11.1 The Dynamic Relationship Between Regional and National Competition Policy

The analysis of competition law implementation as part of regional competition law enforcement raises two questions: Does the existence of national competition law structures constitute a precondition for efficient regional competition law enforcement? If this is the case, does regional competition law incite the implementation of national competition law structures?[1]

Rather than being interchangeable substitutes or independent legislative frameworks with different objectives[2] national and regional competition policies complement and cross-fertilize each other. The subsidiarity of one legislation to the other depends mainly on economic and to some extent political circumstances. Accordingly, the enactment of regional competition law in addition to national competition law does not always create enforcement efficiency gains. Efficiency gains from regional competition law will particularly remain limited in situations in which most anticompetitive practices have purely national effects and/or cross-border trade is weak. In

[1] See below Part III, Chap. 12.

[2] One of the main differences between regional and national competition policy objectives is the relevant market. While national competition law protects national markets, regional competition law primarily aims at the protection of the regional market.

J. Molestina, *Regional Competition Law Enforcement in Developing Countries*, Munich Studies on Innovation and Competition 9,
https://doi.org/10.1007/978-3-662-58525-2_11

such a scenario one will also have to critically assess the appropriateness of economic regional integration overall.

In the same vein, the existence of national competition law structures does not constitute an indispensable precondition for the adoption of a regional competition law system. The absence of national competition law structures obviously abolishes the necessity to reconcile national and regional competition laws.[3] Moreover, the absence of national competition law enforcement might even allow a regional competition authority to develop regional competition case law more easily.[4] On the other hand, in the absence of pre-existing national competition law systems, the regional competition authority is deprived of learning and profiting from local knowledge and expertise. The lack of a national competition culture might also hamper the regional competition law endeavour.

Having briefly outlined the interdependencies between regional and national competition policy, one can raise the question whether and under which conditions a regional competition law system can replace national structures. There are three possible scenarios for replacement: by substituting the national authority, by replacing the national competition law provisions, or by replacing both.

At first glance, the proposition of having only one competition authority seems tempting, because it reduces the amount of resources required to set up and maintain a competition authority. Yet the WAEMU's experiences show that one sole regional competition authority[5] is not capable of appropriately providing for effective competition law enforcement, especially when national markets are affected. The existence of a single regional competition authority creates problems with regard to its accessibility for private businesses or individuals and with regard to the monitoring of allegedly anticompetitive practices within the territory of the RTA.[6] This being said, if the territory that has to be supervised is very small, because of a limited number and limited territorial size of the participating states, a single authority could provide for sufficient monitoring and accessibility. The OECS is in the process of establishing a sub-regional competition authority that is supposed to function as the national authority for each member state of the OECS.[7] One has to emphasize that the member states are microstates and, moreover, have similar economic infrastructures. Yet in this scenario, the "shared" authority cannot be expected to apply different substantive competition laws depending on the issue at stake.

[3] However, the regional competition law system still has to be reconciled with the general domestic legal framework and possibly with other existing national competition-related provisions, such as sector regulation, price control or unfair competition.

[4] *Jenny/Horna*, in: *Brusick/Alvarez/Cernat*, Competition Provisions in Regional Trade Agreements, 2005, pp. 281, 287.

[5] In fact, the WAEMU system is actually not a system of a single regional authority, because national competition authorities are supposed to assist the WAEMU Commission. Yet, as the WAEMU Commission monopolizes all decision-making powers and national agencies have been reluctant to cooperate, one can still draw certain conclusions at this point.

[6] See above WAEMU's experiences, Part II, Dimension IV: Sect. 8.1. In addition, the large territorial scope of application increases the workload of the regional competition authority and thereby increases the amount of resources the authority needs in order to enforce competition law.

[7] See above OECS, Part II, Dimension I: Sect. 5.2.3.3.

Consequently, the replacement of national competition authorities through a common regional authority has to be accompanied by a unification of substantive competition law provisions.

Applying only one substantive competition law can be achieved either through full harmonization[8] or through an extensive scope of application of regional competition law.[9] In the European Union, the territorial scope of application of Community competition law is interpreted broadly and substantive competition law rules have almost reached a stage of full harmonization.[10] The approaches of "soft" harmonization and parallel application of competition law in the European Union allowed member states to gain their own competition law experience and develop a domestic competition culture.[11]

The situation is different in the case of RTAs that consist of developing countries. First, the efficiency of competition law enforcement is closely linked to the general economic development and the status of liberalization in a state. Moreover, the analysis of the three RTAs examined in this study shows that the stage of economic development within an RTA typically varies between different member states. Thus, in order to adjust the economic conditions, it might be necessary to include special and differential treatment provisions, which allow for a flexible application of competition law.[12] Even in the European Union, member states retain discretion with regard to stricter rules on unilateral conduct.[13] Second, the previous analysis of the WAEMU, AndeanC and the CARICOM revealed that political distrust among members of an RTA is a determining factor. Consequently, in order to respect national concerns of sovereignty, member states should not be completely excluded from the legislative process of competition policy, in particular because competition policy is a field of law that touches upon core economic and industrial policy matters. In order to enable close cooperation between national and regional competition authorities, one cannot underestimate the importance of the creation of a competition culture on the local ground.[14] However, the emergence of a competition culture, not only within the private sector, but also among public institutions, presupposes that they are involved in the process of competition law implementation. The extent of substitution of national substantive competition law by regional law is thus proportionate to the level of competition law experience and competition law culture in the member states.[15]

[8] See also the relevance of harmonization below, Part III, Sect. 11.4.1.

[9] See the example of the WAEMU, Part II, Dimension II: Sect. 6.1.

[10] *Drexl*, Perspectives européennes sur la politique de la concurrence dans l'espace OHADA, XXV R.I.D.E. 281, 290 (2011).

[11] On the experiences of Germany with "soft" harmonization, see *Drexl*, Perspectives européennes sur la politique de la concurrence dans l'espace OHADA, XXV R.I.D.E. 281, 293 (2011).

[12] See competition law objectives in the CARICOM, Part II, Dimension I: Sect. 5.3.1.3.

[13] See Art. 3(2) Council Regulation (EC) 1/2003.

[14] For more details see below, Part III, Sect. 11.7.

[15] In the European Union, decentralized enforcement of the broadly interpreted scope of application of EU competition law was only possible because member states had developed a proper competition culture.

The previous arguments similarly apply to the last scenario, in which regional institutions replace both national substantive competition law and national competition authorities. Such a broad replacement is only practical in very exceptional situations in which the political commitment of member states towards regional integration is unusually strong. One precondition for the latter will be the member states' participation in the legislative process and ideally their participation in the enforcement process.

One can thus conclude that while the absence of national competition law structures does not prevent the adoption of a regional competition law system, the implementation of national competition law structures is a precondition for effective competition law enforcement in the long run, irrespective of the degree of centralization or decentralization applied within the RTA.

11.2 From Regional to International Economic Integration: Creating a Common Market

In theory, a general RTA in the form of a tariff union entails the lowering of entry barriers of the domestic markets. The general goal is to create a common market with intensive trade between the member states. A regional competition policy aims at protecting and maintaining this newly created economic area by preventing the establishment of entry barriers to the market by private actors, thereby protecting intra-community trade.[16]

11.2.1 Redefining the Common Market in Developing Countries

In the case of the European Union, the protection of economic integration has been one of the prime drivers for the enactment of a community competition law.[17] The creation and protection of a common market is still today one of the objectives of European competition law, even if the objectives of economic efficiency and consumer welfare are nowadays considered as primary goals. Articles 101 and 102 TFEU are held to be better equipped than national competition law provisions to

[16] While there are different forms and stages of integration, economic integration can generally be understood as the abolition of all barriers to trade, such as tariff barriers, in order to increase trade between nations. Thus, according to this definition, the most advanced stage of economic integration leads to the creation of a common market. A common market usually also imposes a common external tariff on imports from non-member states, thereby aiming at creating an economic advantage for the participating states.

[17] *Monti*, EC Competition Law, 2007, p. 39.

deal with cross-border issues. This argumentation presumes the existence of trade between member states.

In RTAs consisting of developing countries, however, cross-border trade is relatively low.[18] This is mainly attributed to an interplay of preponderant small-scale enterprises producing similar products, and to dispersed demand, which results in a fragmentation of the market and localized production.[19] It is in particular the lack of diversity in the range of products that emphasizes the relevance of external trade with countries outside the RTA, especially with developed countries.[20] A further reason for the lack of cross-border trade is that there are typically very few technology industries in developing countries.

Trade statistics support the outcome that there is only a slight increase in intra-community trade within the framework of an RTA.[21] In the WAEMU, despite a common currency and regional institutions and framework, cross-border trade is low relative to trade with countries outside the RTA.[22] However, from 2000 to 2006, the share of intra-regional trade remained relatively stable at around 11%, making WAEMU the African RTA with the highest share of intra-community trade.[23] Nevertheless, this number should be treated with caution, because the informal and unrecorded market is very large.[24] According to data from the Andean Community, its inter-state trade has increased from USD 75 million to USD 7.81 billion in its 41 years of integration.[25] Intra-community trade generally rose at an annual average

---

[18] There are also exceptions to this general assumption: the economic activities of beer brewers indicate that trade between the African States (at least between Kenya and Tanzania) is actually high. See on this case, *Drexl,* Perspectives européennes sur la politique de la concurrence dans l'espace OHADA, XXV R.I.D.E. 281, 288 (2011).

[19] *Gerber,* Global Competition, 2010, p. 258.

[20] *Gerber,* Global Competition, 2010, p. 258.

[21] For statistics regarding the Andean community, see *Trotignon,* L'impact des accords de libre-commerce entre pays latino-américains, LXI Economie Appliquée 95–120 (2008); regarding the intra community trade in the CARICOM, see *Egoumé-Bossogo/Mendis,* Trade and Integration in the Caribbean, 2002 <http://www.imf.org/external/pubs/ft/wp/2002/wp02148.pdf> accessed 11 November 2018. On the importance of Ivory Coast regarding intra community trade in WAEMU, see *Egoume/Nayo*, Feeling the Elephant's Weight: The Impact of Côte d'Ivoire's Crisis on WAEMU Trade, 2011 <http://www.imf.org/external/pubs/ft/wp/2011/wp1180.pdf> accessed 11 November 2018.

[22] *Egoume/Nayo*, Feeling the Elephant's Weight: The Impact of Côte d'Ivoire's Crisis on WAEMU Trade, 2011, p. 7.

[23] *Goretti/Weisfeld,* Trade in the WAEMU: Developments and Reform Opportunities, 2008, p. 5 <http://www.imf.org/external/pubs/ft/wp/2008/wp0868.pdf> accessed 11 November 2018; *Van den Boogaerde/Tsangarides,* Ten Years After the CFA Franc Devaluation: Progress Toward Regional Integration in the WAEMU, 2005, p. 17.

[24] *Agbodji,* Intégration et Échanges commerciaux Intra Sous-régionaux: le Cas de l'UEMOA, 1/1 Rev. Afr. de l'Intégration 161, 162f. (2007).

[25] On intra-community trade and general export numbers increased except in 2008 and 2009 during the international financial crisis, see *Secretaría General de la Comunidad Andina,* Comunidad Andina: Principales Indicadores 41 años de Integración y Desarrollo, 2011 <http://estadisticas.comunidadandina.org/eportal/contenidos/1638_8.pdf>.

rate of 13.5%.[26] In the CARICOM, intra-regional trade did not increase significantly in the periods between 1995–2000 and 2000–2005 according to the Caribbean Trade and Investment Report 2005.[27] Although data suggest that intra-community trade has grown, this was mostly related to the increased price of petroleum.[28] Trinidad and Tobago's exports due to its petroleum resources accounted for 78% of intra-regional exports in 2009, whereas all the OECS' combined share amounted to only 5.5%.[29] Still, imports from outside the regional market continue to account for more than 80% of CARICOM's trade.[30]

What then, if not the protection of intra-community trade, is the chief task of a regional competition law in developing countries?[31] The creation of a common market in developing countries does not directly serve as an end in itself, but should be regarded as a "response to economic globalization".[32] In fact, the creation of a common market and regional economic integration appear to be a necessary intermediate step to further the international and global economic integration of the participating member states of the RTA.[33] A common market creates a level playing field throughout the region, which offers enhanced opportunities for undertakings to increase their productivity and to achieve economies of scale. However, not all domestic firms are capable of using these opportunities. Given the inefficiencies arising out of the small size of the markets and the suboptimal level of production, only a limited number of firms, usually originating from the same member state(s), have sufficient financial capital to invest in entering a foreign market, even though this foreign market might be the direct neighbouring country. Investment costs also correlate with the stage of development of the infrastructure in a country.[34] Moreover,

---

[26] Press release from the Secretariat General of the 26 May 2010 <http://www.comunidadandina.org/ingles/press/press/np26-5-10.htm>; see also publication of the Secretariat General on Trade Integration through the Trade Area in the Andean Community <http://www.comunidadandina.org/ingles/comercio/fta.htm>.

[27] Caribbean Trade and Investment Report 2005 <www.caricom.org>.

[28] *Stewart,* in: *Drexl/Bakhoum/Fox/Gal/Gerber,* Competition Policy and Regional Integration in Developing Countries, 2012, pp. 161, 173f.

[29] *CARICOM Secretariat,* Caribbean Community Regional Aid for Trade Strategy 2013–2015, 2013, p. 9 <http://cms2.caricom.org/documents/5269-caribbean_community_aft_strategy_final.pdf> accessed 13 September 2017.

[30] *Ibid.*, p. 10.

[31] *Prada,* Wettbewerbspolitik und Wirtschaftsintegration in den Amerikas, 2001, p. 34. *Prada* even states that regional provisions regarding regional competition are unnecessary if the regional trade volume is low as regards the trade volume of the member states.

[32] *Drexl,* in: *Drexl/Bakhoum/Fox/Gal/Gerber,* Competition Policy and Regional Integration in Developing Countries, 2012, 231, 238f.

[33] Integration of developing countries in the global economy is extremely poor. According to the UNCTAD, Africa is the least integrated regional in the world economy, at 2 per cent; *UNCTAD,* Voluntary Peer Review on Competition Policies of WAEMU, Benin and Senegal, 2008, p. 2.

[34] See for example the deficiencies in the transport and transit system in Benin: *Goretti/Weisfeld,* Trade in the WAEMU: Developments and Reform Opportunities, 2008, p. 8 <http://www.imf.org/external/pubs/ft/wp/2008/wp0868.pdf> accessed 11 November 2018. In an RTA consisting of islands, such as the CARICOM, the problem of poor infrastructure is even more severe, because

exporting firms of developing countries may have to compete with other firms that do not have to cover such large transportation costs and are not exposed to currency fluctuations. Thus, the augmented potential demand that a common market holds in store is only targeted by medium-scale or even larger enterprises; often, those that possessed a dominant or large market share in a member state before the common market was created.[35] Moreover, developing countries' markets are marked by the preponderance of an informal economy. The enterprises in the informal sector tend to be small and only active on the local level.

At this point, regional competition law enforcement takes on an important protectionist function with regard to smaller enterprises faced with the new competition that arises from the creation of a common market. Namely, the regional competition law authority is likely to be better equipped to deal with anticompetitive practices originating from another member state or third states outside the RTA. This is not only due to the greater political influence a regional competition authority can exercise on member states, but ideally also based on an improved system of information-gathering that is facilitated by cooperation and other related enforcement mechanisms.[36]

Although intra-community trade in RTAs between developing countries is less significant than its counterpart in the developed world, the benefits of the creation of a common market, even from an inward-looking perspective, should not be underestimated. It enables at least some firms dealing with tradable goods to enhance their productivity and maybe even to act globally.[37] Additionally, it contributes to an increased competitiveness in the overall RTA and its member states.[38] This constitutes an integral part of a strategy to guarantee relatively low costs and a

---

inter-state trade solely relies on ships and aircrafts. These sectors have been prone to high levels of concentration; regarding ports and cargo shipping, see *Brusick/Evenett*, Should Developing Countries Worry about Abuse of Dominant Power?, 2 Wis. L. Rev. 269, 275f. (2008).

[35] The legal competition precedents in the WAEMU, the AndeanC and the CARICOM support this finding: undertakings targeted by regional competition law tend to be of larger size. Even in the WAEMU, which does not rely on the requirement of cross-border trade, the examined undertakings were large.

[36] In this context, the first competition case of the CARICOM Competition Commission against Trinidad Cement Limited demonstrates a positive start, though the case's success is not primarily attributed to the greater political weight and enhanced information gathering by a regional competition authority. Rather, it is a demonstration of the determination of the regional competition authority to also attack large businesses with deep pockets. Yet it is a demonstration of the efficiency of horizontal cooperation on the regional level between different regional integration organizations, which in particular facilitates the surveillance of the common market; *Trinidad Cement Limited v The Competition Commission,* Caribbean Court of Justice Application No. OA 1 of 2012, CCJ 4 (OJ). In fact, the competition-related issues of the case against Trinidad Cement Limited first came up in a judgement of the Caribbean Court of Justice, and COTED requested the CARICOM Competition Commission to investigate; *Trinidad Cement Limited and TCL Guyana Incorporated v The State of the Co-operative Republic of Guyana,* Caribbean Court of Justice Application No. OA 2 of 2009, CCJ 5 (OJ), [17].

[37] *Mateus*, Competition and Development: What Competition Law Regime?, 2010, p. 285 <http://ssrn.com/abstract=1699643> accessed 11 November 2018.

[38] *Ibid.*

wide range of products to the consumers. Small market economies can profit from a regional common market by offering comparative advantages, for example in the form of lower wage costs.[39] Finally, a vital regional market also attracts FDI, which constitutes not only a regional, but an equally national consideration. International firms will be more inclined to invest in a larger economic space than smaller national markets.

11.2.2 Public vs. Private Restraints to Inter-state Trade Between Developing Countries

The early case-law in the field of competition in the WAEMU, the AndeanC and the CARICOM revealed that a large number of anticompetitive practices are related to state actions or state-owned companies.[40] The preponderance of state-related practices reflects weak market integration in the RTAs that has not reached a level comparable to the EU market.[41] When liberalization in developing countries is slow to materialize, it often leads to a situation in which firms within an economy derive their relatively large size and strong market position—which enables them to become active on a common market—from state-ownership or current or past state subsidies.[42]

There are yet further explanations for the state-imputed regional competition case law. On the one hand, private anticompetitive practices are structurally more difficult for a regional authority to detect, because private businesses and parties are still reluctant to submit complaints to the regional competition authority.[43] At the same time, national competition authorities have been reluctant to refer cases to the regional authority.[44] Recalling the limitation of resources, a regional competition authority might thus lack sufficient instruments to challenge private anticompetitive behaviour. This concern mainly relates to the information-gathering phase, during which a regional authority still has to rely on the cooperation of national authorities.

---

[39] *Van den Boogaerde/Tsangarides,* Ten Years After the CFA Franc Devaluation: Progress Toward Regional Integration in the WAEMU, 2005, p. 17.

[40] Even Trinidad Cement Limited, against which the CARICOM Competition Commission conducted its first investigation, was only privatized in 1990, and before that it was completely owned by the Government of Trinidad and Tobago; see Trinidad Cement Limited homepage, see <http://www.tcl.co.tt/about-tcl>.

[41] *Jenny/Horna,* in: *Brusick/Alvarez/Cernat,* Competition Provisions in Regional Trade Agreements, 2005, pp. 281, 313.

[42] On the capacity of a regional competition law system to deal with state-related anticompetitive practices, see below, Part III, Sect. 11.3.

[43] See also below Part III, Sect. 11.8.

[44] See below Part III, Dimension IV: Sect. 12.4.6.

Although one can expect that with the development of a common market the number of private anticompetitive practices will increase, the preponderance of public restraints calls for certain competition policy considerations. Primarily, public actions should not *per se* be exempted from competition law. Rather, both private and public constraints must be prohibited in a convergent way.[45] One can thus acknowledge positively that the WAEMU, the AndeanC and the CARICOM all provide for sanctions covering anticompetitive practices performed by the state.[46] Moreover, these regional competition policies were embedded in a broad regional legislative framework, one aim of which is the enhancement of "competitive neutrality".[47]

11.2.3 The Overarching Incentive of a Common Market for Regional Competition Law Enforcement

The link between trade and competition has been acknowledged in all three RTAs.[48] The competition laws of the WAEMU, the AndeanC and the CARICOM rely on the conviction that regional competition supports the creation and maintenance of a common market.[49] Thus, the more intra-community trade exists in an RTA and the more relevant the common market is for national economies, the higher the relevance of regional competition law is.[50] This is particularly, but not exclusively, the case if the regional competition policy makes explicit reference to the creation of a common market. This finding concerns the overall awareness of and support for regional competition law, for example in the form of cooperation. Moreover, if a common market gains in importance, this represents an incentive for national legislators not only to implement national competition law structures, but also to align and harmonize national competition law legislations with the regional framework. Assuming that the common market creates business opportunities for national

---

45 Convergence of prohibitions against private and public restraints to competition were necessary in the European Union's initial market-integrationist approach in order to create a single common market; *Fox/Healey,* When the State harms Competition – The Role for Competition Law, 2013, p. 12 <http://ssrn.com/abstract=2248059> accessed 11 November 2018.

46 See above Part II, Dimension I: Sect. 5.1.3.

47 See above Part II, Dimension I: Sect. 5.1.3 and Part II, Dimension I: Sect. 5.3.

48 See above Part II, Dimension I: Sect. 5.3.

49 With regard to the factors that impact the intensity of inter-state trade and those that impact the national support of a common market, see above Part III, Sect. 11.2.1. Possibly, divergences between economic powers of member states require the introduction of compensatory or transitory special and differential treatment provisions, for example the suspension of the Common External Tariff.

50 This statement is based on the precondition that regional competition law applies to cross-border practices. This is the case in the WAEMU, the AndeanC and the CARICOM.

industries, national legislators will tend to make an effort to facilitate trade and thereby increase efficiency of these local industries.

In the CARICOM, all member states without prior national competition laws are in the process of implementing domestic competition law structures. The explicit alignment of Chapter VIII with economic integration and the simultaneous progress of the CSME have supported this movement. Since 2008 the CARICOM Competition Commission has offered support in the form of technical assistance, seminars and workshops. The progress of the CSME thereby clearly provided incentives for spreading national competition law implementation. However, its incentivizing function with regard to enforcement, in particular in the form of vertical cooperation, can only be judged on the basis of further development of the competition case law in the future.

In the AndeanC on the other hand, intra-community trade is relatively insignificant for member states. This offers a plausible explanation for the lack of use of Decision 608. Although all member states have enacted national competition laws,[51] the common market was not as motivating as in the CARICOM. The implementation of national legislation seems to be traced back to a large extent to national legislative incentives that had been emerging irrespective of the Andean competition law. An indicator for this finding is the limited harmonization of national laws with regional law.

When community competition law was introduced in the WAEMU, legal integration was already relatively well developed, and the WAEMU is marked by a tradition of centralization. Yet in the absence of an obligation to establish a national competition authority,[52] some member states still lack functioning national competition law structures. Even more problematic, national institutions are reluctant to cooperate with the WAEMU Commission.

From these experiences, one can conclude that even though the common market and economic integration have an incentivizing function for the implementation of domestic competition legislation, it does not by itself suffice for cooperation as regards regional competition law enforcement. The common market, in a similar vein, does not abolish the task of a regional authority to promote competition law implementation and application, for example in the form of technical assistance. Moreover, the actual impact on the national implementation of competition law structures depends on the political will of the member states. The necessity to integrate economically has to be translated politically and the benefits arising out of a common market have to become visible among national governments and civil society.

---

[51] Bolivia is an exception. Although a national Supreme Decree with regard to competition law exists, there are still ambiguities concerning the competent authority. See above Part II, Dimension I: Sect. 5.2.2.2.

[52] Currently there is no obligation under the regional law for member states to establish a national competition authority. In the same vein, the institutional design is left to national autonomy. This might undergo a change with the current reform of the WAEMU competition law system.

11.2.4 Larger Integration and Open Regionalism: Opportunities or Threats to RTAs in Developing Countries?

While in the WAEMU, the AndeanC and the CARICOM the common market is explicitly incorporated as a goal of economic integration, economic integration is yet positioned in a larger framework. The WAEMU and the AndeanC are even geared towards larger integration, being part of ECOWAS or larger South American integration.[53] Despite potential conflicts of law, placing an RTA within a larger integration movement does not seem to menace the regional integration movement itself. However, more problematic appears to be the concept of "open regionalism", in which member states are free to engage in bilateral trade negotiations.[54]

Bilateral agreements do not necessarily create conflicts with the regional competition law system. This is especially the case if they refer to the regional competition institutions and laws and include similar competition law provisions.[55] Bilateral agreements might thereby even incentivize the implementation of domestic competition law structures and the application of regional competition law.[56]

However, bilateral trade agreements have a different focus than RTAs by striving for the attainment of market access instead of the creation of a common market.[57] The question whether this affects the creation and development of a common market within the RTA actually reveals a "chicken-and-egg" dilemma. On the one hand, the initiative to engage in bilateral trade agreements reflects the limping intra-community trade in RTAs in developing countries, which retain industrialized nations, in particular the US, as the most important trading partners. On the other hand, letting bilateral agreements replace *en bloc* negotiations in the long run can undermine the importance of economic and political integration within the RTA.[58] The importance of the creation of a common internal market in an RTA thus correlates with the incentive to conduct trade negotiations *en bloc*.[59] The factors are linked in a reciprocal relationship.

---

[53] See on the concept of "open regionalism" in the AndeanC, Part II, Dimension I: Sect. 5.3.2.2 and on advisory opinions by the regional court, Part II, Dimension IV: Sect. 8.3.2.3.

[54] Part II, Dimension I: Sect. 5.3.2.2.

[55] See for example the US–Peru preferential trade agreement; see *Horna/Kayali*, in: *Alvarez/Wilse-Samson*, Implementing Competition-Related Provisions in Regional Trade Agreements, 2007, pp. 21, 51ff.

[56] See for example the CARIFORUM-EC Economic Partnership Agreement, Part II, Dimension I: Section "The CARIFORUM-EC Economic Partnership Agreement".

[57] On the interplay between bilateral trade agreements, international trade and competition law, see *Bakhoum*, Commerce International, Politique de Concurrence et Accords de Partenariat Economique, 1/2 Rev. Afr. de l'Intégration 3–7 (2010).

[58] Part II, Dimension I: Sect. 5.3.2.2.

[59] In the CARICOM, the common market (CSME) constitutes the centre of gravity of the RTA. CARIFORUM-EC Economic Partnership Agreement negotiations took place *en bloc*. See Part II, Dimension I: Section "The CARIFORUM-EC Economic Partnership Agreement".

11.3 Creating a Credible Threat: In Particular with Regard to International Anticompetitive Practices

Developing countries are marked by a vulnerability towards international anticompetitive practices, namely, from internationally operative or multinational firms usually originating from developed jurisdictions. As national enforcement measures against international anticompetitive practices are held to function inefficiently,[60] this section examines the efficiency of regional competition law enforcement against international anticompetitive practices.

11.3.1 The Relevance of the Creation of a Common Market

Generally, by increasing the number of people within a RTA, the undertakings' incentives to exit a (common) market decrease. *Michal Gal* in this context describes this as the creation of a "critical mass" that is capable of coping with power asymmetries.[61]

In the CARICOM the tourism sector is dominated by international tour operators. The application of restrictive distribution agreements, such as exclusive dealing and tying arrangements, and the dependence of the Caribbean countries on the tourism sector have led to a segmentation of the Caribbean market.[62] Enforcement through a regional authority would be able to constitute a credible threat to the international tour operators, not only due to the region's size, which would make the "exit" option less attractive, but also and more importantly through consistent competition law enforcement throughout the region.[63]

Yet the ability to create a "critical mass" and to lower an enterprise's incentive to exit a market are linked to the degree of development of a common market.[64] A common market that still does not provide for free movement of goods and people will

---

[60] *Evenett/Levenstein/Suslow*, International Cartel Enforcement, 2001, pp. 1, 21; *Evenett*, in: *Hoeckman/Mattoo/English*, Development, Trade and the WTO: A Handbook, 2002, pp. 456, 462. For more information on the increased deterrent effect of cumulative sanctions, see below Part III, Sect. 11.6.4.

[61] *Gal/Faibish Wassmer*, in: *Drexl/Bakhoum/Fox/Gal/Gerber*, Competition Policy and Regional Integration in Developing Countries, 2012, pp. 291, 295; *Stewart*, An Empirical Examination of Competition Issues in Selected Caricom Countries, pp. 126ff.

[62] *Gal/Faibish Wassmer*, in: *Drexl/Bakhoum/Fox/Gal/Gerber*, Competition Policy and Regional Integration in Developing Countries, 2012, pp. 291, 295.

[63] Without describing the specific enforcement mechanism, but also supporting the potential benefit of creating a credible threat, see *Gal/Faibish Wassmer*, in: *Drexl/Bakhoum/Fox/Gal/Gerber*, Competition Policy and Regional Integration in Developing Countries, 2012, pp. 291, 295.

[64] Even in developed countries or within a developed common market, the actual weight of the "exit option" is doubtful. The higher sunk or investment costs for entering a market (even a small one) are, the lower are the incentives to exit in case of competition-law-related sanctions.

not be able to create a uniform and consistent "critical mass". As highlighted previously, the establishment of a common market within RTAs among developing countries is slow and often suffers from the lack of trade liberalization by the member states.[65] This is particularly the case in the initiation phase of a common market.

11.3.2 Increasing the Political Weight of a Competition Authority's Decisions

Anticompetitive practices of international firms are *inter alia* difficult to tackle because foreign governments often intend to protect the economic interest of national firms. As long as the presumption that a country's GDP and its state of development have an impact on its political influence is not rebutted, one can assume that the combined appearance of states within an RTA has more weight in the global political environment.[66] The spread of economic partnerships to negotiate trade agreements *en bloc* with developed countries seems to follow this understanding.[67] As a case in point, the *CARIFORUM-EC Economic Partnership Agreement* includes competition law provisions that provide for cooperation.[68] It explicitly acknowledges the regional authority, the CARICOM Competition Commission, as competent addressee to implement the agreement's provisions and cooperation.[69] Regional competition law structures thus theoretically incite and simplify intensified cooperation between developed and developing competition law systems. First, the other party of the trade agreement, mostly a developed trading partner, will only have one contact point. Second, there seems to be a perception that regional competition authorities are better positioned to deal with international anticompetitive practices than national ones. Arguably, regional competition authorities are regarded as more independent than their domestic counterparts. Generally, an increased competition law enforcement record, in particular with regard to international anticompetitive practices, increases developing countries' "bargaining position in reaching international cooperative solutions".[70]

---

[65] See above Part II, Dimension I: Sect. 5.3.2.

[66] *Gal*, The Unique Enforcement Challenges Faced by Small Economies, 33 Fordham Int'l. L.J. 1, 23 (2009). *Gal* presumes that a country's size or level of development is positively correlated with its political power.

[67] The European Union also engaged in *en bloc* negotiations with the AndeanC. It was only when these negotiations failed that the EU agreed to continue to negotiate bilaterally with the member states of the AndeanC; see above Part II, Dimension I: Sect. 5.3.2.2.

[68] Article 128 of the CARIFORUM-EC Economic Partnership Agreement.

[69] The Agreement also refers to the authority of the Dominican Republic (Comisión Nacional de Defensa de la Competencia), see Article 125(1) of the *CARIFORUM-EC Economic Partnership Agreement*.

[70] *Gal*, The Unique Enforcement Challenges Faced by Small Economies, 33 Fordham Int'l. L.J. 1, 35 (2009).

Cooperation agreements with developed nations structurally aim at the facilitation of information gathering and the increased probability of detecting international anticompetitive behaviour. Yet the latter benefit remains rather theoretical, mainly because the actual record of cooperation between RTAs in developing countries and developed competition law jurisdictions during actual competition law enforcement remains weak. Incentives to share information for a developed competition law jurisdiction are only strong if the jurisdiction is affected by the anticompetitive practice as well or has a related interest in its prosecution. Generally, this will exclude pure export cartels, which developing countries are particularly vulnerable to. *David Gerber* aptly states in this context: "Extra-regional" influences tend to provide far less support for enforcement at the regional level than they do for formal regionalization of competition law.[71] One should not stumble into the pitfall of believing that solely regional competition authorities are capable of creating a credible threat in developing countries. Rather, the impact of a competition authority's actions depends on its operational capacities. Senegal in this context provides a good example. Before the introduction of the exclusive competences of the WAEMU Commission, the Senegalese had successfully dealt with large foreign enterprises, such as *Air France*.[72]

11.3.3 Necessity to Provide Regional Competition Authority with Sufficient Enforcement Powers

In order to become proficient domestic competition agencies have to gain proper competition law enforcement experience.[73] An agency's perception and reputation primarily depend on its actions and its efficiency.[74] Consequently, a regional competition law system has to provide a regional authority with sufficient enforcement and sanctioning powers. The specific attribution of such powers depends on the institutional design and the vertical allocation of competences.[75]

---

[71] *Gerber*, in: *Drexl/Bakhoum/Fox/Gal/Gerber*, Competition Policy and Regional Integration in Developing Countries, 2012, pp. 253, 269.

[72] Affaire Syndicat des Agences de Voyage et de Tourisme du Sénégal contra Air France, Décision n° 02-D-02 of 27 December 2002; for a summary see Weick, Competition Law and Policy in Senegal, 33/3 W. Comp. 521, 531 (2010), see Part II, Dimension I: Sect. 5.2.1.1.

[73] *Kovacic*, Institutional Foundations for Economic Legal Reform in Transition Economies, 77 Chi.-Kent L. Rev. 265, 285 (2001).

[74] This is not only a concern with regard to international anticompetitive behaviour. Rather, generally the emergence of a competition culture among private businesses and member states in an RTA depends on the reputation and efficacy of the regional competition authority.

[75] In this regard, the AndeanC serves as an example. The former Decision 285 did not vest the regional authority with sanctioning power. As a consequence, competition culture at the national level and cooperation was lacking; see *Jenny/Horna*, in: *Brusick/Alvarez/Cernat*, Competition Provisions in Regional Trade Agreements, 2005, pp. 281, 314.

It is yet unclear whether vesting a regional competition authority with sufficient enforcement powers requires a specific standard of regional substantive competition law. The WAEMU, the AndeanC and the CARICOM have all incorporated the classical competition law provisions, namely on anticompetitive agreements and abuse of dominant position.[76] The situation is even more problematic as regards the adoption of a regional merger regime.

The adoption of merger control in developing countries has often been criticized because of the lack of technical skills and the required advanced economic understanding, which might induce a high administrative burden.[77] On a more practical basis, the adoption of a regional merger control regime has been hampered by the struggle of member states to find a consensus.[78] Especially the fear of member states regarding a possible reduction of national welfare explains why they are slow in establishing a regional merger control regime, as the latter will usually adopt a total-welfare approach.[79] However, there is empirical evidence that anticompetitive mergers have involved firms that pursued a regional strategy and were present in several member states within an RTA.[80] This offers a large field for the application of regional merger control. This does not necessarily argue in favour of replacing the national merger control regime by a regional one. Rather, especially in RTAs with very heterogeneous markets of different sizes, national merger control constitutes an efficient supplement for purely national mergers. In view of the often mentioned concerns, instead of adopting a regional *ex ante* merger control from the beginning of the regional competition law system, one could at least apply regional competition laws *ex post* to mergers. The regional competition law authority can thereby gain experiences in the field of mergers by applying regional competition law on a flexible basis without having to face the potential difficulties of installing a merger control system from scratch.

11.4 Increasing Legal Certainty and Convergence

Developing countries, which are often marked by a high level of corruption, are struggling to create a legal framework that not only the private business sector, but also consumers can rely upon. Respect of the rule of law and hence legal certainty are important features of a functioning competition law system.

Especially for the private business sector, in order to make investments, it is necessary to be able to predict the legal consequences and to be protected against

---

[76] It has already been noted that both public and private restraints should be addressed. See above Part III, Sect. 11.2.2.

[77] See on regional merger regulation, Part II, Dimension I: Sect. 5.1.4.

[78] This was the case in the AndeanC, Part II, Dimension I: Sect. 5.1.4.

[79] *Evenett,* Analytical Considerations in the Design of Regional Rules on Competition Law, 2005, p. 9.

[80] *Jenny,* Cartels and Collusion in Developing Countries, 29/1 W. Comp. 109, 134 (2006).

arbitrary or even contradictory public decisions. A common argument in favour of regional competition law enforcement presumes that it will lead to harmonization and thereby increase legal certainty. In developing countries, which are moreover very dependent on foreign direct investment, the notion of legal certainty becomes even more important. Finally, one also has to analyse the particular role of harmonization in the context of the creation of a common market.[81]

11.4.1 The Relevance of Harmonization of Competition Law and Policy Within an RTA Among Developing Countries

In the European Union, "soft harmonization" has successfully created a European economic space with convergent laws.[82] The objective of regional competition law to harmonize national competition policies is therefore often taken for granted and its benefits are presumed as a matter of fact. Nevertheless, its benefits should be handled with care with regard to the special needs of developing countries. To this end, this section will define the concept and purpose of harmonization.

Harmonization of laws describes the process of creating common standards within a certain geographical[83] and subject-matter area. Typically, harmonization is used as a direct instrument of the regional law to change national laws.[84] Arguments based on welfare-economics are often put forward in favour of harmonizing competition law, namely, the reduction of transaction costs, the internalization of external effects or the establishment of a "level playing field".[85] Harmonization is under-

[81] When discussing the notion of harmonization, one has to carefully distinguish between the incentives for competition law implementation and enforcement arising out of harmonization and, on the other hand, incentives that further harmonization itself. Only after affirming that harmonized competition law promotes competition law implementation and enforcement should one analyse whether a regional competition law framework can create incentives for competition law harmonization.

[82] The European competition law system never entailed an obligation for the Member States to adopt a national competition law. However, through the process of "soft harmonization" most of the Member States have to a large extent harmonized their national competition laws with the European provisions. For more details on "soft harmonization" see *Drexl,* Perspectives européennes sur la politique de la concurrence dans l'espace OHADA, XXV R.I.D.E. 281–304 (2011). For more details on the development of the national competition laws in the framework of the development of the European competition law, see *Monti,* EC Competition Law, 2007, pp. 401ff.

[83] For example in a common market.

[84] Other forms of harmonization are formal and substantive harmonization. While the former refers to the supremacy and the direct applicability and effect of regional law, the latter describes spill-over effects of regional legal rules from one economic area to another. The forms of harmonization are subsumed under the term of legal integration; *Möschel,* Wettbewerb der Wettbewerbsordnungen, WuW 599, 600ff. (2005); *Bätge,* Wettbewerb der Wettbewerbsordnungen?, 2009, pp. 53, 241.

[85] *Bätge,* Wettbewerb der Wettbewerbsordnungen?, 2009, pp. 48ff.; *Müller,* Systemwettbewerb, Harmonisierung und Wettbewerbsverzerrung, 2000, pp. 121ff.; *Möschel,* Wettbewerb der Wettbewerbsordnungen, WuW 599, 601ff. (2005).

stood as an instrument to avoid enforcement conflicts concerning the requirements and sanctions of competition law, to close possible enforcement loopholes and to achieve an efficient allocation of competences between the authorities that apply competition law. Yet the function of harmonization as indispensable condition for effective enforcement can be questioned. The inclusion of clear-cut competence-allocation criteria identifies the competent enforcement body and the applicable competition rules. Ideally, such an allocation of competence should be based on efficacy considerations.[86] Moreover, the harmonization of competition laws within a regional competition regime does not exclude conflicts with sectorial or competition-related provisions.[87] Similarly, harmonized competition laws do not provide for a guarantee that all anticompetitive practices are covered and prosecuted.[88] Possibly, a framework of cooperation is capable of substituting the requirement to harmonize competition policies.[89] Another argument in favour of harmonization of competition laws is the prevention of a "race to the bottom".[90] Yet what constitutes the "bottom" of competition law is difficult to define. Generally, for the business sector the implementation of competition law represents an incentive for investing in a country.[91]

Apart from the general doubts as regards harmonization as a benefit as such,[92] one must also analyse the benefits of harmonization in the light of the special needs of developing countries.[93] Most importantly, in developing countries the idea of competitive markets without the intervention of the state is generally a new one. Consequently, the emergence of a competition culture in developing countries is extremely slow in contrast to industrialized countries. The interrelation between

[86] See above on mandatory lead jurisdictions and quantitative thresholds, Part II, Dimension V: Sects. 9.6 and 9.7.

[87] On the actual conflicts that have arisen in WAEMU, AndeanC and CARICOM see below Part III, Sect. 11.4.3.1.

[88] *Möschel,* Wettbewerb der Wettbewerbsordnungen, WuW 599, 603 (2005).

[89] *Bätge,* Wettbewerb der Wettbewerbsordnungen?, 2009, p. 48.

[90] *Bätge,* Wettbewerb der Wettbewerbsordnungen?, 2009, p. 50. In contrast, *Möschel* argues that the intention to set common standards creates the risk of watering down the content of competition law, because it is difficult to find a common denominator, see *Möschel,* Wettbewerb der Wettbewerbsordnungen, WuW 599, 604 (2005).

[91] *Sokol* argues that "(c)ompetition policy chapters may be a signal of a credible commitment to potential foreign investors that a country is market-oriented and pro-investment", see *Sokol,* Why Countries Enter into Non-Enforceable Competition Policy Chapters in Free Trade Agreements, 83 Chi.-Kent L.Rev. 101, 142 (2008). *Fox* argues in a similar vein that "there is no perceptible race to the bottom (…) and the argument – We pay the costs of antitrust; therefore you should too – is based on the false premise that antitrust in essence imposes costs on business". See *Fox,* Why Must the Central European Nations Adopt the Competition Law of the European Union?, 23 Brook. J. Int'l. Law 351, 358 (1997).

[92] Regarding the discussion surrounding the harmonization of Central Eastern European Community law and EC law, see *Fox,* Why Must the Central European Nations Adopt the Competition Law of the European Union?, 23 Brook. J. Int'l. Law 351, 357 (1997).

[93] With regard to the introduction of the principle of competition in Europe, see *Dreher,* Kartellrechtsvielfalt oder Kartellrechtseinheit in Europa?, AG 437, 443 (1993).

harmonization and the creation of a competition culture is however ambiguous. On the one hand, harmonizing competition laws in an RTA facilitates the implementation of domestic competition law in the first place and enhances consistent competition law enforcement throughout the region. This increases legal certainty and predictability.[94] This is especially the case as national laws that are harmonized with the regional framework will increase the latter's acceptance. Hence it is fair to say that "harmonization tends to facilitate market integration".[95] On the other hand, a competition culture does not emerge automatically with the implementation of competition law. Rather, competition law has to be adapted to the prevailing circumstances in a country and ideally will have been legitimated by local stakeholders and interest groups.[96] It is crucial for the development of a competition culture that benefits arise out of competition law enforcement and that these are also transmitted to civil society and the business sector as well as public institutions. Consequently, the benefits that arise from intra-community trade are more relevant than the harmonization of competition laws by itself.

However, harmonization of competition policies within an RTA appears as an element of the overarching common economic policy in the regional integration process.[97] A common market that is already very competitive and integrated can more easily compensate for transaction and investment costs arising out of diverging (competition) laws than a common market that is still in the creation phase, or national markets that are still in the process of increasing their competitiveness.[98] Differently phrased, the task of competition policy to enhance competitive market structures is more relevant in developing than in developed countries.[99] The increase of competitiveness of member states within an RTA is a crucial element in the attainment of economic and sustainable development.

Harmonization is a process with two directions: it can take place upwards or downwards.[100] The absence of competition law experience usually exists on the national as well as on the regional level. Thus, harmonization should not be construed as a one-way mechanism. Rather, the regional competition law regime should be designed in such a way that it enables national and regional competition law authorities to learn from each other. Especially at the moment of implementation of

---

[94] According to *Dreher*, the implementation of a regional competition law directive is not suitable in a situation, in which a competition culture is emerging nationally, because such a directive could impede the ongoing process of parallel development of national competition laws; see *Dreher*, Kartellrechtsvielfalt oder Kartellrechtseinheit in Europa?, AG 437, 445 (1993).

[95] *Fox*, Why Must the Central European Nations Adopt the Competition Law of the European Union?, 23 Brook. J. Int'l. Law 351, 357 (1997).

[96] *Alvarez/Horna*, Implementing competition law and policy in Latin America: The role of Technical Assistance, 83 Chi.-Kent L. Rev. 91, 98 (2008).

[97] *Dreher*, Kartellrechtsvielfalt oder Kartellrechtseinheit in Europa?, AG 437, 439 (1993).

[98] The common economic policy of an RTA between developing countries usually also entails the objective to attract foreign direct investment.

[99] *Baetge*, Globalisierung des Wettbewerbsrechts, 2009, p. 51.

[100] *Dreher*, Kartellrechtsvielfalt oder Kartellrechtseinheit in Europa?, AG 437, 445ff. (1993).

a regional competition law regime, it might be appropriate for the regional entity to learn from existing national competition law authorities.[101] With the advancement of the regional competition law regime, the downward learning direction might become more relevant and present. Moreover, forced harmonization comes at national sovereignty costs, thereby possibly challenging the national political will to support the regional authority in competition law enforcement. In this sense, the centralized and unified competition law in the WAEMU constitutes a negative example. By unifying competition law and policy on the regional level, the regional authority was unable to benefit from national experience, and national authorities were unable to develop a proper competition culture. On the other hand, in the CARICOM, the regional competition law is partly based on existing national competition law regimes.[102] Although member states have large discretion in the drafting and enforcement of national competition law, especially the young competition law jurisdictions voluntarily followed the *CARICOM Model Law on Competition*. Vertical harmonization might also contribute to the support of regional competition law, thereby enhancing its long-term application. In the AndeanC, regional IP laws are well received by member states and applied regularly.[103] Explanations given for the frequent application involved the developed stage of vertical harmonization and the nature of IP law as a highly technical matter.[104] Actually, if vertical harmonization was achieved, the latter argument would similarly apply to competition law.

Despite its high relevance especially for regional competition law regimes in developing countries, in particular with regard to increasing the competitiveness of the common and national markets,[105] harmonization should thus not be understood as a final goal by itself. It is important that a regional competition law system sets incentives for the implementation and enforcement of competition law, on the national as well as on the regional level. Harmonization to some extent facilitates this and can constitute a tool to set such incentives. Yet it cannot compensate for a lack of national political commitment to regional competition law enforcement. The constraints created by harmonization have to be carefully balanced with the need for adaptability and flexibility.[106] There is no "one size" of harmonization that fits all, but rather, benefits of harmonization depend on the appropriateness of its degree.

---

[101] *Dreher*, Kartellrechtsvielfalt oder Kartellrechtseinheit in Europa?, AG 437, 448 (1993).

[102] Chapter VIII mirrors in many parts the Jamaican competition law, Part II, Dimension I: Sect. 5.2.3.1.

[103] See in this context the pattern of preliminary reference rulings in the AndeanC, which overwhelmingly concerned intellectual property, notwithstanding the fact that Andean law spans a wide array of regional trade and investment issues. See *Helfer/Alter*, The Andean Tribunal of Justice and its Interlocutors, 41 N.Y.U. Journal of Int'l. L. & Pol. 871, 887 (2009), <http://ssrn.com/abstract=1334733> accessed 11 November 2018.

[104] Interview with representatives of the Superintendence of Industry and Trade in Colombia conducted by the author in Bogota, Colombia, on 1 February 2012.

[105] See also below on the importance of harmonization in attracting foreign direct investment and the intensification of intra-community trade, Part III, Sect. 11.4.2.

[106] *Ziller*, The Challenges of Governance in Regional Integration, 2005, p. 9; *Gal*, Competition Policy for Small Market Economies, 2003, p. 260.

The more competition law culture and experiences exist among member states, the more harmonization can be required of national laws by the regional level.

11.4.2 The Importance of Harmonization in Attracting Foreign Direct Investment (FDI) and the Intensification of Intra-community Trade

A foreign undertaking may be willing to invest in several member states.[107] Diverging competition law systems with different requirements will increase its investment costs.[108] A regional competition law, if applicable in the case of this FDI, could convey a larger level of certainty and could thereby decrease the investment costs. This argument similarly applies to firms within the RTA that want to expand to another member state, thereby intensifying inter-state trade.[109] Yet one should not ignore the fact that attracting FDI is also positively correlated with the level of education and financial stability.[110] Moreover, given the diverging infrastructures between member states in an RTA, FDI is unlikely to be equally distributed among member states.[111] In the same vein, the distribution of benefits of intra-community trade depends on the level of economic integration and a similar level of economic development of the member states. This might hamper the support of all member states for regional competition law and enforcement.

The argument of reducing transaction and investment costs especially applies to mergers.[112] However, this benefit depends heavily on the specific design of the RTA. In the absence of harmonized regional and national merger regulation or in the absence of a centralized system, such as the "one-stop shop" doctrine in the EU, a

---

[107] "FDI involves a non-negligible set-up cost which generates increasing returns to scale and makes larger markets a more profitable investment opportunity than smaller markets". *Jaumotte,* Foreign Direct Investment and Regional Trade Agreements: The market size effect revisited, 2004, p. 3 <http://www.imf.org/external/pubs/cat/longres.aspx?sk=17770.0> accessed 11 November 2018.

[108] *Gal,* The Unique Enforcement Challenges Faced by Small Economies, 33 Fordham Int'l. L.J. 1, 34 (2009).

[109] Generally the overarching achievement of macroeconomic stability in an RTA, including a high level of infrastructure, education and financial stability, is a determining factor for the attraction of FDI; see *Jaumotte,* Foreign Direct Investment and Regional Trade Agreements: The market size effect revisited, 2004, p. 5 <http://www.imf.org/external/pubs/cat/longres.aspx?sk=17770.0> accessed 11 November 2018.

[110] *Jaumotte,* Foreign Direct Investment and Regional Trade Agreements: The market size effect revisited, 2004, p. 5.

[111] *Jaumotte,* Foreign Direct Investment and Regional Trade Agreements: The market size effect revisited, 2004, pp. 4, 15.

[112] See above Part II, Dimension I: Sect. 5.1.4. Regional merger regulation, there is empirical evidence that firms penetrate a market via mergers. See also *Budzinski,* Toward an International Governance of Transborder Mergers?, 41 N.Y.U. Journal of Int'l. L. & Pol. 1–52 (2004).

regional competition law could even turn out as an obstacle to FDI originating from outside or inside the RTA. If regional and national merger laws diverge, regional law creates an additional administrative burden to the already existing national regimes. This appears to be a realistic danger in RTAs among developing countries. In the AndeanC and the CARICOM, member states struggled to find a consensus on regional merger control, which in consequence remained national.

11.4.3 Different Forms and Consequences of Imperfect Harmonization

In the WAEMU, the unification of competition laws has created a situation of *de facto* harmonization. In the CARICOM, national and regional competition laws are to a large extent harmonized. Even in the AndeanC where the underlying market concepts differ, competition laws converge.[113] A common feature of all three RTAs is however that certain areas remained non-harmonized. In this context, one has to highlight the lack of hierarchical regulation of regional competition law and national sectorial regulations or sectorial exemptions from competition law. Furthermore, the organization of national competition authorities is left to the national legislature in all three RTAs. Finally, national procedural autonomy is ensured by leaving the enforcement of criminal and civil law liability under national discretion. This leaves room for collisions between regional and national competition law enforcement in all three RTAs. The potential for conflicts is yet reduced through the adoption of a "loyalty clause". Moreover, the principle of primacy of regional law solves conflicts in favour of the regional law. Although in the WAEMU, the AndeanC and the CARICOM decisions regarding breaches of regional competition law are taken on the regional level,[114] inconsistencies can still occur in the form of a duplication of sanctions or differing enforcement measures, for example through criminal sanctions. In addition, the framework for private enforcement might vary. Given these areas of national discretion, there might also be enforcement loopholes, for example due to a lack of sufficient investigative powers of a national competition authority.

---

[113] Bolivia and Ecuador have different underlying market concepts than Colombia and Peru. This leaves room for possible state intervention; see above Part II, Dimension I: Sect. 5.3.3.2.

[114] In the CARICOM, the member states, respectively the COTED, hold more competences, as they are expected to conduct preliminary investigations on behalf of the CARICOM Competition Commission. The principle of mutual respect is of prevalent importance in the CARICOM. However, with regard to conflicts of final decisions on the breach of regional competition law, the CARICOM Competition Commission remains the body with decision-making power.

11.4.3.1 Actual Record of Conflicting National and Regional Enforcement

Actual incidents of national and regional enforcement conflicts are yet rare. One explanation applicable in the WAEMU and the CARICOM refers to the relatively advanced degree of harmonization, which reduces the risks of conflicting decisions and sanctions. Moreover, rigorous centralization of competition law competences in the WAEMU abolished the risk of conflicting decisions between competition authorities.

On the other hand, a lack of transparency and a lack of data also explain the apparent absence of open conflicts between national and regional enforcement measures. Regional competition authorities are often unaware of all cases that have a regional impact but are dealt with nationally. They might also lack the sufficient resources or legal instruments to supervise all ongoing cases or to enforce the consequent transferral of cases to the regional level by national competition authorities. The experience of the Secretariat General in the AndeanC exemplifies this finding. Although the regional competition authority suspects that cases with cross-border effects are dealt with by the national authorities, it does not force their transferral to the regional level despite the existence of means for this purpose.[115] Similarly, in the WAEMU, the cooperation with and transferral of cases through national competition authorities or related public authorities such as ministries is dysfunctional. One can thus conclude that the lack of harmonization is not primarily a problem of diverging decisions or enforcement measures. It rather constitutes an obstacle to the application of regional competition law and to close and constant cooperation between the regional and national authorities. In this regard *Eleanor Fox* aptly summarizes: "The differences in formulation of principle virtually never produce trade friction, even though the differences are often based on different values (*e.g.*, whether the law should protect fairness and small business). The friction is most commonly produced by non-enforcement of existing law."[116]

11.4.3.2 Lack of Harmonization of Competition Law Procedures and Institutions: Harmonization as a Precondition for Cooperation?

Another field of non-harmonization that already caused concerns in the context of the establishment of the European Competition Network is the colourful landscape of national competition authorities.[117] On the one hand, one has to ask whether the

[115] The Secretariat General could initiate a complaint for non-compliance before the Andean Tribunal according to Art. 25 of the Treaty Creating the Court of Justice of the Cartagena Agreement. See above Part II, Dimension IV: Sect. 8.3.2.5.

[116] *Fox,* Why Must the Central European Nations Adopt the Competition Law of the European Union?, 23 Brook. J. Int'l. Law 351, 358 (1997).

[117] *Cengiz,* The European Competition Network, 2009, p. 14 <http://cadmus.eui.eu/bitstream/handle/1814/11067/MWP_2009_05.pdf?sequence=1>.

effective functioning of a network requires "a certain degree of harmony in the resources, powers, experiences and independence"[118] of the incorporated competition authorities. On the other hand, the necessity of harmonized competition procedures and institutions with regard to cooperation also needs to be taken into account.[119]

In particular the lack of independence of national competition authorities might be problematic with regard to the exchange of information and collaboration.[120] Recalling the remaining preponderance of state intervention, national competition authorities in developing countries might be prone to national interest groups and tendencies to protect the national industry. The more decentralized enforcement of regional competition law is, the more independent from such national interest considerations the national authorities have to be.[121] A regional institutional and legal framework, which sets standards for national procedures or requires a certain degree of institutional independence, can only have a limited impact, because independence of competition authorities cannot be established "objectively".[122] Rather, its impact depends on the relevance and autonomy of the general regional institutional framework.[123] The more committed a member state is to regional integration, the more it will make an effort to incite horizontal and vertical cooperation between its agencies and other national or regional authorities. Likewise, an assimilation of its procedures and institutional design of authorities facilitates cooperation. Yet this finding only applies to member states that actually depend on cross-border trade. Economically dominant member states have lower incentives to cooperate.[124]

---

[118] *Ibid.*

[119] As the discussion regarding the harmonization of national competition law procedures and diverging national competition authorities has been advanced extensively on the European level, I will try to limit myself to those considerations that are particularly relevant for RTAs in developing countries. With regard to the European discussion, see *Cengiz,* The European Competition Network, 2009 <http://cadmus.eui.eu/bitstream/handle/1814/11067/MWP_2009_05.pdf?sequence=1>; *Cengiz,* Regulation 1/2003 Revisited, 2009 <http://ssrn.com/abstract=1512527>; *Cseres,* Questions of Legitimacy in the Europeanization of Competition Law Procedures of the EU Member States, 7 February 2013 <http://ssrn.com/abstract=2213192>; *Gauer,* in: *Ehlermann/Atanasiu,* Eur. Comp. L. Ann. 2002, 2004, pp. 187ff.; *Thyri,* in: *Hummer,* Neueste Entwicklungen im Zusammenspiel von Europarecht und nationalem Recht der Mitgliedstaaten, 2010, pp. 379ff.

[120] According to *Cengiz,* in terms of resources and independence national competition authorities of the Eastern European States were a matter of concern; *Cengiz,* The European Competition Network, 2009, p. 14 <http://cadmus.eui.eu/bitstream/handle/1814/11067/MWP_2009_05.pdf?sequence=1>; See also *Cseres,* Multi-Jurisdictional Competition Law Enforcement, 3 Eur. Comp. J. 465, 473 (2007).

[121] *Gauer,* in: *Ehlermann/Atanasiu,* Eur. Comp. L. Ann. 2002, 2004, pp. 187, 192.

[122] *Ibid.*

[123] It will in particular depend on the powers and functions of a regional court of justice.

[124] With regard to the attainment of political stability in member states within a RTA, one must note that a regional framework only has a limited impact. The AndeanC and the WAEMU in a couple of instances struggled with political turmoil in their member states, for example in Peru, Mali and Ivory Coast. In 1992, Peru even suspended its membership to the AndeanC. See Part I, Chap. 1.

Moreover, in the three RTAs at stake many member states are still in the process of creating domestic competition law structures. This leads to a situation in which national competition authorities often lack competition law expertise or resources. The analysis moreover shows that national competition law authorities often only exist in the form of a ministry or a sector regulator.[125] On the one hand, in the absence of a competition authority with general jurisdiction, the regional competition authority might struggle to identify the competent and most efficiently placed national authority to cooperate with. On the other hand, such a situation creates asymmetries in the efficacy and number of competition law investigations and other enforcement measures among member states within an RTA. Given the differing requirements for complaints, the number of submitted (national and regional) cases would generally differ between member states.[126] These difficulties are particularly problematic in RTAs among developing countries. The foregoing analysis of the WAEMU, the AndeanC and the CARICOM revealed that the overall integration process is often hampered by distrust among the member states. Typically, the member states with more competition law expertise and resources will also constitute the economically stronger states. Weaker member states might thus feel insufficiently represented in regional competition law enforcement.

Yet the harmonization of national procedural laws as well as the institutional design of national authorities does not appear politically feasible, nor necessary.[127] Even in the European Union, national procedural autonomy does not only stem from the subsidiarity principle.[128] Rather, it is derived "from one of the residual competences reserved to the Member States and it accordingly constitutes a manifestation of their sovereignty."[129] The impact of incongruent competition law enforcement is further attenuated by the principles of loyalty and effectiveness, which have been acknowledged by the WAEMU, the AndeanC and the CARICOM.[130] Consequently, instead of forcing member states to harmonize national procedures, enforcement difficulties should be solved on the basis of commitment and political will to cooperate.[131] A precondition for mutual trust, however, is a certain degree of interdependence between member states. While in the EU economic interdependen-

[125] See above on the national competition law structures, Part II, Dimension I: Sect. 5.2.

[126] With regard to the situation in the EU, see *Cseres*, Questions of Legitimacy in the Europeanization of Competition Law Procedures of the EU Member States, 7 February 2013, pp. 17f. <http://ssrn.com/abstract=2213192>.

[127] *Thyri*, in: *Hummer*, Neueste Entwicklungen im Zusammenspiel von Europarecht und nationalem Recht der Mitgliedstaaten, 2010, pp. 379, 398.

[128] *Schroeder*, Nationale Maßnahmen zur Durchführung von EG-Recht und das Gebot der einheitlichen Wirkung, AöR 3, 13f. (2004).

[129] Rebutting this view, see *Kakouris*, Do the Member States possess Judicial Procedural "Autonomy"?, 34 CML.Rev. 1389, 1389ff. (1997).

[130] On the principles of effectiveness and equivalence, see Part II, Dimension V: Sect. 9.3.

[131] Even the European Competition Network has been held to work efficiently on the basis of "mutual trust and solidarity", *Cengiz*, The European Competition Network, 2009, p. 19 <http://cadmus.eui.eu/bitstream/handle/1814/11067/MWP_2009_05.pdf?sequence=1>.

cies exist through intensive inter-state trade, in the WAEMU, the AndeanC and the CARICOM they are only established through the regional framework and in particular through the creation of a common market.[132] In consequence regional competition law requires a certain degree of formalization of cooperation.[133] One possible measure in order to achieve such formalization is the inclusion of minimum standards of enforcement powers and the clear definition of tasks of national competition authorities. Similarly, constitutional and democratic considerations call for the codification of fundamental private rights, such as the right of defence or the codification of a common minimum standard for the submission of complaints.[134]

11.5 The Competition Authority's Independence with Regard to Competition Law Enforcement in Developing Countries

Experiences show that developing countries struggle to establish efficient basic administrative infrastructures. Democracy is unstable due to frequent governmental changes, corruption or sometimes even revolutions.[135]

11.5.1 Furthering Greater Independence in Regional and National Competition Law Enforcement

Typically, an RTA and in particular the creation of a common market presume the existence of provisions on equal treatment irrespective of nationality. While national markets are generally very concentrated in developing countries, it is less frequent that these private groups also enjoy the same market power in the common market. Moreover, a regional competition authority, which consists of several nationalities, avoids too much bonding between political and business elites. This makes the exercise of unilateral influence by one member state or its government on the regional authority difficult. Rather, regional authorities are structurally bound to take into

---

[132] However, the withdrawal of the United Kingdom from the EU (expected in 2019) demonstrates that even economic interdependencies cannot compensate for lacking political will or a population's support to maintain and further regional integration.

[133] See below on cooperation mechanisms with national competition law structures, see Part III, Dimension IV: Sect. 12.4.5.

[134] *Gauer,* in: *Ehlermann/Atanasiu,* Eur. Comp. L. Ann. 2002, 2004, pp. 187, 197. Decision 608 provides a positive example as it requires minimum investigative powers on the national level.

[135] See for example the internal conflict in Peru from 1980 to 2000, in which the country was shaken by terrorist attacks from the "Shining Path" and counter actions by the Fujimori government.

account the interests of all member states or the common interest of the integration movement.

Benefits from regional competition law enforcement in particular arise with regard to state aids. In member states, disciplining a state regarding anticompetitive behaviour can be a schizophrenic act if the national competition authority itself is part of a ministry and has no autonomous decision-making power.[136] Even "independent" competition authorities may suffer repercussions when trying to apply competition law to state-protected enterprise.[137] Especially the supervision of state aids appears to be problematic and prone to political influences.[138] A regional authority can offer a degree of independence that is detached from the national governments.[139] It can impose sanctions on a state without facing a conflict of interests. In sum, a regional competition law is more suitable to deal with state-imputed anticompetitive practices, thereby lowering barriers to entry. This is demonstrated by the WAEMU cases examined in this study, in which regional competition law was used by the member states to discipline each other, but also the CARICOM Competition Commission's first case against TCL[140] offers a positive example.

Yet the impact of a regional competition law system on the degree of independence of the national competition authorities remains limited. Indeed, the adopted institutional model depends on prevailing "legal administrative traditions, stage of economic development and political realities"[141] among member states. While the WAEMU and the AndeanC rely on a civil law system, most of the Caribbean countries belong to the common law world. The latter explains the strong emphasis of a separation of adjudicative and investigative powers in the CARICOM Competition Commission. In the same vein, the existence of a specialized regional competition authority did not prevent member states from keeping competition law enforcement in the framework of sectorial regulation or enforcement through a public ministry. With regard to actual domestic enforcement, the regional competition law regime

---

[136] See for example on the national competition agencies in West Africa, see *Bakhoum/Molestina,* in: *Drexl/Bakhoum/Fox/Gal/Gerber,* Competition Policy and Regional Integration in Developing Countries, 2012, pp. 89, 100.

[137] See the experiences of Emilio José Archila, former Superintendent for Industry and Trade in Colombia, who had ruled against the merger of the airlines Avianca (state-owned) and Aces airlines in 2001. See on the national competition law structures, Part II, Dimension III: Sect. 7.2.1.

[138] *Cseres* notes this with regards to the Central and Eastern European States (CEECS): "Political independence is not guaranteed in all the countries. This is especially true in the case of state aid monitoring."; *Cseres,* Multi-Jurisdictional Competition Law Enforcement, 3 Eur. Comp. J. 465, 486 (2007).

[139] On the effects resulting from a certain institutional design of the regional competition authority and the benefits of attaining greater independence in competition law enforcement, see below Part III, Dimension III: Sect. 12.3.

[140] *Trinidad Cement Limited v The Competition Commission,* Caribbean Court of Justice Application No. OA 1 of 2012, CCJ 4 (OJ).

[141] *Cseres,* Integrate or Separate. Institutional Design for the Enforcement of Competition Law and Consumer Law, 11 April 2013, p. 18 <http://ssrn.com/abstract=2200908> accessed 11 November 2018.

was supposed to create a counterweight to national political or economic interest groups.

When examining the experience of the WAEMU, the AndeanC and the CARICOM, it is generally difficult to discern an overall effect of the existence of a regional competition law regime on the national progress of liberalization. While an effective regional framework can stimulate national liberalization programs, the actual enforcement depends on the prevailing national will to support liberalization and the regional integration movement overall. Again, this depends on the economic relevance of regional economic integration for national economies. In the same vein, political ties between the regional and national level will only be established through interdependencies. In consequence, the function of an RTA to enhance political stability in member states correlates with the member states' perception of it and their commitment to it.

11.5.2 The Difficult Notion of Independence of Competition Authorities in Developing Countries

The independence from political intervention has been highlighted as an essential part of the functioning of a competition authority. However, in developing countries not only the countries' economies, but also their political structures differ from the general conditions in developing countries. According to the often-cited phrase that "one size does not fit all", the appropriate degree of independence has to be clarified for developing countries and young competition law jurisdictions.

Regarding the structural independence of a competition agency, two aspects can be distinguished: the external view of the agency and the internal functioning of it. Competition law culture is weak in developing countries and the idea of competition still encounters scepticism from the private sector and consumers.[142] Therefore a completely structurally independent and detached competition law agency may not have the necessary civil support. The weight of an authority's sanctions also depends on the view of the citizens. In the absence of a competition culture, the weight of sanctions of the authority will be higher if the sanction can be traced back to a public authority or a ministry with sufficient degree of political importance.[143]

Embedding a competition authority within a ministry creates advantages as well as disadvantages. Clearly, employees that are assigned to competition law enforcement may be prone to general political influences within the ministry. In a similar vein, staff within a ministry may not be exclusively assigned to competition law but might have to fulfil several tasks. This might drive persons with particular competition law expertise

---

[142] In the member states of WAEMU it is for example very common that consumers and businesses accept and prefer prices that are fixed by the government, see *Bakhoum,* A Developing-Country Perspective on "Global Competition", 28 October 2011, Chicago, p. 8.

[143] This is for example the case in Niger, see *Bakhoum,* A Developing-Country Perspective on "Global Competition", 28 October 2011, Chicago, p. 14.

away, as they might prefer to work in a more technical, purely competition-law-related institution. On the other hand, a complete detachment from a ministry may cause information problems.[144] Insufficient cooperation with other decision-makers in the executive, legislative or judicative branches may create inefficiencies or even hinder the efficient functioning of the agency completely.[145] This is particular the case, because competition law enforcement is closely linked to general trade and industrial policy considerations within a country.

There are several dimensions of institutional independence that are interrelated and overlap. One can differentiate between types of independence related to the composition of a competition authority, such as financial independence or discretion with regard to the selection and withdrawal of staff etc. Other kinds of independence relate to the application of competition law, mainly the operational independence and the decision-making power, including the discretion of a competition agency. Bearing in mind the importance of public perception of an agency and respecting democratic principles of "checks and balances", independence of an authority cannot signify complete absence of any controlling mechanism, either by the judiciary or other public institutions.[146] In the same vein, the notion of independence does not rule out that a competition authority is subject to mechanisms of internal and external review.[147] To find the appropriate level of independence for a competition law agency is thus a balancing act. Yet a legal framework should provide for a guarantee that the competition law authority is capable of enforcing competition law on merely competition-related considerations.[148] This legal framework should also guarantee transparency and accountability. These aspects are of crucial importance, especially for gaining public support and reputation of the agency.[149]

---

[144] *Clark,* Competition Advocacy: Challenges for Developing Countries, 6/4 OECD J. Comp. L. Policy 69, 71 (2005).

[145] *Alvarez/Horna*, Implementing competition law and policy in Latin America: The role of Technical Assistance, 83 Chi.-Kent L.Rev. 91, 97 (2008); *Trebilcock/Iacobucci* tend towards an integrated agency model, in which a specialized competition agency undertakes investigative, enforcement, and adjudicative functions irrespective of concerns regarding the agency's independence. See *Trebilcock/Iacobucci*, Designing Competition Law Institutions, 41 Loy. U. Chi. L.J. 455, 467ff. (2010); *Menns/Eversley* argue for the need to separate the enforcement, investigative and adjudicative personnel or bodies within the agency from the realm of political influence: *Menns/Eversley,* The Appropriate Design of the CARICOM Competition Commission, 20 May 2011, Amsterdam, p. 8.

[146] *Mehta/Agarwal/Singh*, Politics Trumps Economics, 2007, pp. 36f.

[147] *Menns/Eversley,* The Appropriate Design of the CARICOM Competition Commission, 20 May 2011, Amsterdam, p. 11.

[148] *Clark,* Competition Advocacy: Challenges for Developing Countries, 6/4 OECD J. Comp. L. & Policy 69, 71 (2005). Along the same lines, according to *De León* "the institutional independence of competition agencies rests on four pillars: possession of an independent legal charter; financial autonomy in the provision of funds and management of its own resources; tenure stability in the appointment of policy officials; and involvement of several government bodies in the appointment of the competition authorities". See *De León*, An Institutional Assessment of Antitrust Policy, 2009, pp. 24ff.

[149] See on the creation and the promotion of a competition culture also Part III, Sect. 11.7.

What does this mean for a regional competition authority? The structurally higher degree of independence in a democratically legitimized system has to be accompanied by some form of accountability.[150] The question in an RTA is however to whom a regional competition authority should be accountable. On the one hand, the WAEMU, the AndeanC and the CARICOM rely on the principle of procedural autonomy, retaining at least the adjudication of criminal and civil law liability under the of the domestic judiciary. On the other hand, the core regional decision is subject to judicial review before the regional court of justice. This is an appropriate institution, because it enhances convergent application of regional competition law. Moreover, its decisions are, ideally, based solely on legal considerations and it is usually vested with qualified personnel of high reputation. It is interesting to highlight that the WAEMU Court of Justice even has the power to modify decisions taken by the WAEMU Commission. While this might constitute an appropriate instrument to balance the far-reaching powers of the WAEMU Commission,[151] it does not signify that the centralized system constitutes an efficient solution.

Given the lack of competition culture, in particular regarding regional competition law, a regional competition authority has to make an additional effort to publish and spread information on its actions and the benefits arising from these actions.[152] This does not only concern consumers and private businesses, but also cooperation will benefit from enhanced transparency of regional competition law enforcement. At the same time, transparency cannot supersede provisions on the protection of confidential information, because this would also hamper cooperation with other public agencies. In the same vein, a regional competition authority's decision should be predictable.[153] Yet the importance of preserving flexibility in competition law enforcement in developing countries also has to be highlighted.[154] The balancing of predictability and flexibility in regional competition law enforcement will often require a decision by the regional court of justice.

Generally, the regional competition authorities should be operationally independent. While advisory bodies can be of a political nature, decision-making competition authorities should be largely detached from political influences and be able to make determinations based on economic and efficiency considerations.

[150] *Trebilcock/Iacobucci*, Designing Competition Law Institutions, 41 Loy. U. Chi. L.J. 455, 457 (2010).

[151] *Bakhoum,* L'articulation du droit communautaire et des droits nationaux de la concurrence dans l'Union Economique et Monétaire Ouest Africaine, 2007, p. 178f.

[152] *Trebilcock/Iacobucci*, Designing Competition Law Institutions, 41 Loy. U. Chi. L.J. 455, 458 (2010).

[153] *Ibid.*

[154] On the importance of preserving flexibility in the framework of a regional competition law structure, see Part III, Sect. 11.10.

11.6 Overcoming the Lack of Resources in RTAs Consisting of Developing Countries

Regional integration and competition policy is an issue of multilevel governance.[155] Pooling the resources available at the regional level seems to be an attractive solution, as it enables an authority to reach economies of scale with regard to competition law enforcement. Enhanced effectiveness can mainly be achieved in the context of dealing with anticompetitive practices that involve several member states. In such a case, the regional authority can in theory gather information more easily while being less exposed to political influences. Effective competition law enforcement affects not only the regional, but also national markets. Efficiency gains do not come about by themselves in a regional competition law regime, but require careful allocation of competences. Phrased differently, one has to distinguish "between effective networks and bureaucratic black holes".[156] Moreover, the reduction of administrative bureaucracy cannot be forced at the expense of constitutional rights.[157] Efficiency gains have to be balanced with the principles of transparency, legal certainty, accountability and due process.

11.6.1 The Interdependence Between the Attribution of Competences and the Required Resources

In addition to an agency's costs regarding its functioning and maintenance, a regional competition authority can also avoid costs that arise with its creation.[158] Micro-jurisdictions, such as St. Kitts and Montserrat in the Caribbean, do not have to establish a national authority, but can only rely on a common authority.[159] Since a common authority raises issues of accessibility, it either has to be a flexible travelling authority or has to offer easy digital or electronic access.

Organisation costs are yet duplicated if a regional competition agency is created in addition to domestic structures. In consequence, systems of parallel competition law enforcement will only save resources if national and regional competition authorities engage in close and constant cooperation. The actual reduction depends on the authority's institutional design and the competences and tasks attributed to it.

---

[155] *Ziller,* The Challenges of Governance in Regional Integration, 2005, p. 8.

[156] *Anderson,* Squaring the Circle? Reconciling sovereignty and global governance through global government networks, 118 Harv. L. Rev. 1255, 1278 (2005).

[157] *Trebilcock/Iacobucci*, Designing Competition Law Institutions, 41 Loy. U. Chi. L.J. 455, 457 (2010).

[158] *Gal* and *Faibish* distinguish between direct and indirect costs of regional competition agreements, see *Gal/Faibish Wassmer,* in: *Drexl/Bakhoum/Fox/Gal/Gerber,* Competition Policy and Regional Integration in Developing Countries, 2012, pp. 291, 301.

[159] See example of OECS in the Caribbean, though the issue arises of how to treat the OECS within the CARICOM.

An authority that suffers from a large administrative burden or that is responsible for many different functions will not be able to reduce the amount of resources it requires. Unfortunately, the centralized system in the WAEMU is marked by a high administrative burden in the WAEMU Commission combined with an extensive territorial scope of application of regional competition law. The inefficiencies are even aggravated if enforcement measures are duplicated on the national level despite coverage by regional law. In the WAEMU, although competition powers have been withdrawn from the national competition authorities, national ministries or sectorial agencies might still engage in investigations with regard to competition law infringements. Similarly, the decentralized system in the CARICOM requires national competition authorities to undertake a preliminary investigation in case of the *ex officio* initiation right of the CARICOM Competition Commission.[160] Despite the newly created regional authority, the decentralized system thus still requires member states to provide for sufficient competition law structures and to invest resources in regional competition law enforcement.[161]

The allocation of competences in RTAs comprised of developing countries appears as "a balancing act between the protection of national sovereignty issues and effectiveness of competition law enforcement"[162] in which the former in many instances prevails unfortunately.[163] In particular, distrust among member states is a common feature that hampers the adoption of effective cooperation and information exchange mechanisms. Therefore, regional competition law systems in developing countries will generally save fewer resources than their counterparts constituted by developed countries.

11.6.2 The Lack of Skilled Staff

Competition law authorities in developing countries typically struggle with a high fluctuation of experts, who are hired away by the private sector with more attractive offers.[164] Theoretically, a regional competition authority has the capacity to develop a proper agency's expertise faster than a national entity by learning from the experiences in the member states and by pooling the expertise of the national authorities.[165] Generally, it has been found that it requires about 10 years for countries to

---

[160] Article 176(1) of the Revised Treaty of Chaguaramas.

[161] *Jenny/Horna,* in: *Brusick/Alvarez/Cernat,* Competition Provisions in Regional Trade Agreements, 2005, pp. 281, 322.

[162] *Ibid.*

[163] This is even the case in the WAEMU, in which the protection of national competences has caused national competition authorities to refrain from cooperating with the WAEMU Commission.

[164] *Gal,* Institutional Solutions when Antitrust Enforcement Resources are Scarce, 41 Loy. U. Chi. L.J. 417, 426 (2010).

[165] *Gal,* Institutional Solutions when Antitrust Enforcement Resources are Scarce, 41 Loy. U. Chi. L.J. 417, 430 (2010).

collect the necessary expertise and experience in order to enforce competition law effectively.[166] Another precondition for effective enforcement is that the regional authority offers more attractive career opportunities than the private sector. Without this precondition, the lack of expertise merely extends on the regional level. In this context, one has to acknowledge that the location of a regional authority also impacts its attractiveness as a working environment. Finally, careful attention should be paid to the selection of staff in a regional competition authority. National diversity and equilibrated representation of member states in the authority's staff will increase and facilitate national support in the long-term competition law enforcement.

As the number of staff in the regional competition authorities at stake varies, it is indispensable to substantiate the necessary resources for efficient competition law enforcement. According to *Abel Mateus*, as a rule of thumb about 5–7 professionals should be working in a competition agency for each 1 million of population.[167] However, there might also be economies of scale for countries with a very large population.[168] For small economies he estimates 8–10 professionals for each million.[169] On the other hand, some countries *Abel Mateus* studied were doing more than expected with regard to the number of staff.[170] An agency's effectiveness does not mainly depend on quantitative resources, but the individuals' commitment constitutes the determining factor.[171] The lack of resources is thus not merely a quantitative, but more importantly a qualitative issue.

---

[166] *Singh*, Competition and Competition Policy in Emerging Markets, 2002, p. 6; *Scherer*, Competition Policies for an Integrated World Economy, 1994, pp. 32ff.

[167] *Mateus*, Competition and Development: What Competition Law Regime?, 2010, p. 8 <http://ssrn.com/abstract=1699643> accessed 11 November 2018.

[168] *Ibid.*

[169] *Ibid.*

[170] *Ibid.*, p. 9.

[171] This finding corresponds to the experiences of the Peruvian competition law authority, the INDECOPI. The agency was very active and conducted many investigations, inquiries and prosecutions in the period from 1995 to 2000, in which Beatriz Boza was the INDECOPI's president. Working at the INDECOPI was regarded highly; see *Kovacic*, Lessons of Competition Policy Reform in Transition Economies for U.S. Antitrust Policy, 74 St. John's L. Rev. 361, 371 (2000). However, after she resigned, from 2000–2004 the new Peruvian government limited the INDECOPI's powers significantly and curtailed its political independence. The competition authority was further marked by a lack of competition law expertise; *OECD*, Peer Review on Competition Law and Policy in Peru, 2004, pp. 15ff. <http://www.oecd.org/daf/competition/prosecutionandlawenforcement/34728182.pdf> accessed 11 November 2018.

11.6.3 Preconditions for Network Efficiencies

The absence of purely decentralized application of regional competition law renders the allocation of cases within a regional competition law network less urgent in the WAEMU, the AndeanC and the CARICOM.[172] In the CARICOM system of parallel competition law application Article 176(1) of the Revised Treaty of Chaguaramas still provides for a dispute resolution mechanism between regional and national competition authorities.

Despite clear criteria in all three RTAs[173] regarding the scope of application of regional law, savings in resources are only achieved if the competition authority that actually takes competition law enforcement measures is the most efficient and thus the appropriate body to do so. However, identifying the most efficient authority is a difficult task. Not only does one encounter measuring difficulties in determining "efficiencies", but within a regional competition law regime "efficiency" also encompasses broader aspects, such as long-term and dynamic effects of regional competition law enforcement.[174]

The determination of the "best" competition authority requires that a regional competition law system allows for its identification. This can only be achieved through constant vertical and horizontal cooperation. More precisely, the regional competition law system has to allow for and promote exchange of information. Rather than measures of a "suboptimal" competition authority, ineffective cooperation constitutes the main cause for waste of resources within a regional competition law regime.

Horizontal cooperation between national competition authorities does not occur spontaneously. This is particularly the case in the absence of intensive inter-state

[172] In the same vein, a prerogative to decide cases, as the European Commission is vested with according to Article 11(6) of Regulation 1/2003, is not similarly pressing.

[173] Irrespective of remaining ambiguities with regard to the specific definition in the CARICOM, all three RTAs rely on a case-allocation criterion that is based on the territorial effect of a conduct.

[174] Efficiency can arise out of geographical closeness or existing data or information gathered at a competition authority. In case of targeted practices that involve several member states or take place in the entire common market the regional competition authority might be the appropriate authority under the condition that it accumulates the information on the practice. On the other hand, the European Commission demonstrates that decentralized enforcement can also constitute an efficient alternative even in the case of cross-border practices if sufficient competition law culture exists on the national level and if the national commitment to the common market is strong. Competition law enforcement by a regional competition authority can contribute to long-term or dynamic effects and enhance convergent application. As a consequence, practices that touch upon economically important sectors (for example telecommunications and transportation) for the maintenance of a common market might be dealt with more efficiently by the regional authority. In the framework of promoting balanced social standards within an RTA, this could require anti-competitive practices in socially relevant sectors (for example the health sector) to be addressed regionally. This might be particularly relevant in developing countries.

trade or economic interdependencies.[175] The WAEMU, the AndeanC and the CARICOM have formalized cooperation by creating cooperation bodies. However, even in such a formalized framework of cooperation, the latter mostly takes place vertically.

11.6.4 Cumulative Sanctions as an Increased Deterrent Effect?

Enforcement without deterrence creates costs.[176] An enforcement regime produces more deterrence when the probability of detection and punishment for companies is bigger than the gains of carrying out the illegal conduct.[177] The probability of detection depends on a sociological factor, namely the perceived effectiveness of the functioning of the competition law agency. Further influencing factors are the functioning of the judicial system and of the public institutions in general.[178] Thus, there exists a positive correlation between the amount of resources spent, or the agency's overall effort, and the probability of detection. In addition, the degree of independence of the authority and the powers it possesses are relevant factors.[179] A regional competition law infrastructure that adds to the improvement of these cited elements consequently furthers the level of deterrence.[180]

Has the bundling of sanctions on the regional level in the WAEMU, the AndeanC and the CARICOM created greater deterrence than the cumulative effect of several sanctions imposed by national competition authorities?[181] Although there have not been apparent incidents in which national and regional sanctioning complemented or conflicted with each other,[182] bundled sanctions imposed by the regional authority are generally held to achieve efficiency gains with regard to international anticom-

---

[175] According to *Jenny/Horna*, despite developed harmonization of national laws, spontaneous cooperation between national competition authorities on enforcement issues does not even take place between countries that are important trading partners or geographically close; *Jenny/Horna*, in: *Brusick/Alvarez/Cernat*, Competition Provisions in Regional Trade Agreements, 2005, pp. 281, 289.

[176] *Buccirossi/Ciari/Duso/Spagnolo*, Deterrence in Competition Law, 2009, p. 2.

[177] *Evenett/Levenstein/Suslow*, International Cartel Enforcement, 2001, p. 22; *Buccirossi/Ciari/Duso/Spagnolo*, Deterrence in Competition Law, 2009, pp. 11ff.

[178] *Buccirossi/Ciari/Duso/Spagnolo*, Deterrence in Competition Law, 2009, p. 18.

[179] *Buccirossi/Ciari/Duso/Spagnolo*, Deterrence in Competition Law, 2009, p. 27.

[180] More specifically on efficient sanctions and fines in Latin America, see *Tapia*, Increasing Deterrence in Latin American Competition Law Enforcement, 1–2 July 2011, London.

[181] See *Evenett/Levenstein/Suslow*, International Cartel Enforcement, 2001, p. 21.

[182] The situation is different with regard to mergers. Cumulative sanctions are not possible, because a merger is either granted (possibly with conditions) or denied; see *Bätge*, Wettbewerb der Wettbewerbsordnungen?, 2009, p. 136.

petitive practices.[183] However, a precondition for increased deterrence through regional enforcement is that the fines be adequately large and actually enforced.[184] A study conducted by *John Connor* demonstrates that sanctions for international hard-core cartels, with the exception of the USA, are generally lower than the profits achieved by the cartel.[185] The effective and adequate sanctioning of an enterprise that engages in anticompetitive conduct also contributes to the credibility of the agency, which in turn adds to deterrence. The study by *John Connor* indicates that the risk of over-deterrence with regard to hard-core cartels can in any case be neglected.[186] There is thus no clear preference for bundled regional sanctioning over cumulative national sanctions, although regional sanctions might be more efficiently imposed on international firms.

11.7 Creating and Promoting a Competition Culture

While the Western hemisphere has in most parts internalized competition as something positive that protects the citizens' rights and contributes to the overall welfare, this sentiment is largely inexistent in developing countries. The notion of competition is either unknown or in some instances even conceived as a threat.[187]

11.7.1 The Necessity to Establish a National Competition Law Culture

The regional experiences, as well as the member states' experiences in the WAEMU, the AndeanC and the CARICOM, have shown that the mere implementation of a competition law does not automatically enhance a competition culture. The benefits of competition law have to become visible for consumers and the private sector,[188]

[183] Sanctioning of international firms located abroad is only enhanced indirectly, through the pooling of resources or increased political weight of the RTA in the international context. First, a regional competition authority is less vulnerable to pressure from lobbying groups. Second, a regional competition law authority is structurally more effective with regard to the enforcement of measures against anticompetitive practices that concern several member states of the RTA.

[184] *Evenett,* Analytical Considerations in the Design of Regional Rules on Competition Law, 2005, p. 9. Regarding the adequate level of fines in Latin America, see *Tapia,* Increasing Deterrence in Latin American Competition Law Enforcement, 1–2 July 2011, London, pp. 8ff.

[185] *Connor,* Le Droit de la Concurrence de l'Union Économique et Monétaire Ouest Africaine, 6 J. Industry, Comp. Trade 195, 211ff. (2006).

[186] See also *Baetge,* Globalisierung des Wettbewerbsrechts, 2009, p. 138.

[187] *Bakhoum,* A Developing-Country Perspective on "Global Competition", 28 October 2011, Chicago, pp. 13ff.

[188] For example in the form of low prices.

as well as for the academic world, professional associations and consumer associations as groups that usually contribute to the promotion of a competition culture.

Placing competition policy on the regional agenda may signal its importance to the member states, thereby inciting academia as well as professional and consumer associations to engage in competition advocacy.[189] Vice versa, active participation of the before-mentioned institutions enhances competition law enforcement of the national and regional competition authorities.[190] Competition advocacy functions could be shared between the two levels, thereby also saving resources.

Although regionalizing competition law enforcement can prompt the promotion of a competition culture, there is also the danger of impeding national development of the latter. *Josef Drexl* in this context stresses that "regional competition policy is less well equipped to establish a competition culture on the ground".[191] In fact, regional competition law in the WAEMU, the AndeanC and CARICOM has been hardly perceived by private businesses and has not yet become present in the citizens' every day life; accordingly, accessing the regional authority is conceived as difficult.[192] Moreover, competition policy considerations, if national competition law still does not exist, might not be included in areas of economic legislation and regulation by national legislators.[193]

One has to differentiate between the promotion of competition culture among individuals and public political institutions. A regional competition authority is better equipped to establish a competition culture among governments and ministries because, being part of the larger regional integration framework, it can exercise strong political influence. It can constitute a neutral information-sharing and discussion platform for national governments.[194] As the share of governmental regulation and state intervention in recently liberalized markets is still relatively large, competition advocacy directed at public institutions and governments should be in the focus of regional competition agencies.[195] The focus on "governmental" advocacy functions might be in particular justified at the beginning of the establishment of a

---

[189] With regard to the experiences in the EU, see *Jenny/Horna,* in: *Brusick/Alvarez/Cernat,* Competition Provisions in Regional Trade Agreements, 2005, pp. 281, 286.

[190] In CARICOM and the AndeanC, the RTAs have created regional universities, which inter alia include integration-related topics in their curriculum. In CARICOM, the University of West Indies has campuses in Barbados, Jamaica and Trinidad and Tobago. The AndeanC created the Simón Bolívar Andean University, whose main campus is located in Bolivia.

[191] *Drexl,* in: *Drexl/Bakhoum/Fox/Gal/Gerber,* Competition Policy and Regional Integration in Developing Countries, 2012, pp. 231, 243.

[192] *Drexl,* in: *Drexl/Bakhoum/Fox/Gal/Gerber,* Competition Policy and Regional Integration in Developing Countries, 2012, pp. 231, 243f. *Alvarez/Horna* argue that regional law cannot replace a national law that is considered as legitimate by local stakeholders; see *Alvarez/Horna,* Implementing competition law and policy in Latin America: The role of Technical Assistance, 83 Chi.-Kent L.Rev. 91, 98 (2008).

[193] *Drexl,* in: *Drexl/Bakhoum/Fox/Gal/Gerber,* Competition Policy and Regional Integration in Developing Countries, 2012, pp. 231, 243f.

[194] See above Part III, Sect. 11.6.3.

[195] *De León,* An Institutional Assessment of Antitrust Policy, 2009, p. 383.

regional competition law system, when legal regional instruments to address governmental anticompetitive practices are still to be adopted.

And yet it is indispensable that national competition law authorities are left with some leeway to gain their own enforcement experiences. In a centralized system such as in the WAEMU, in which national competition authorities are completely excluded from the decision-making process even for national cases, this might constitute a particularly challenging task. However, even in the centralized competition law system in the WAEMU, member states are obliged to participate and cooperate in the competition law enforcement process.[196] An obligation to cooperate does not correlate with the competition culture that might emerge from proper competition law enforcement. This is especially the case if a withdrawal of proper competences decreased the general commitment of the member states and national authorities to regional competition law enforcement.

11.7.2 The Necessity to Establish a Competition Law Culture with Regard to Regional Competition Law

Although a regional competition law enforcement framework can promote the emergence of a general competition culture, the experience of the WAEMU, the AndeanC and CARICOM shows that regional bodies have to make an extra effort in order to inform the public about the benefits of regional competition law. This is in particular the case after member states have established national competition law institutions, because they might be inclined to refrain from using the regional competition framework. In the AndeanC, the lack of use of Decision 608 created a vicious circle with regard to its reception. The less Decision 608 was used, the more this was interpreted as a signal of its inefficiency.

The crux of the establishment of a competition culture with regard to regional law seems to be the lack of involvement of the private sector.[197] The sector is either unaware of regional competition law at all or might prefer to deal with national competition institutions.[198] Likewise, difficulties of accessibility[199] or the regional institutional design itself[200] can prevent the private sector from addressing a regional

---

[196] Member states have to participate in meetings of the Consultative Committee on Competition and have to assist the WAEMU Commission in conducting investigations, Part II, Dimension IV: Sect. 8.2.1.1.

[197] *Cortázar,* in: *Drexl/Bakhoum/Fox/Gal/Gerber,* Competition Policy and Regional Integration in Developing Countries, 2012, pp. 133, 154.

[198] See for example the case *DHL v Sonapost* in the WAEMU, in which *DHL* withdrew its complaint after it had been transferred to the WAEMU Commission, Part II, Dimension II: Sect. 6.1.1.

[199] For more details on the difficulties of accessibility and transparency of a regional competition law system, see below Part III, Sect. 11.8.

[200] This is the case in the CARICOM, where individuals are actually excluded from submitting complaints directly to the CARICOM Competition Commission; see above on market surveillance,

competition authority. Moreover, in contrast to advanced economies, the private sector in developing countries does not appear to demonstrate a similar "degree and quality of concern in regional economic decision-making".[201]

An intensification of "public advocacy"[202] measures by the regional competition authority involves resource costs, because competition advocacy aimed at the private sector and consumers has been more efficiently exercised by national competition law institutions.[203] A more efficient way to nurture private business' competition culture with regard to regional competition law is in the production of good case law.[204] These cases then need to be published, thereby revealing the benefits of regional competition law. As private enforcement will be low in the initial phase of regional competition law enforcement, the regional competition authority should conduct *ex officio* investigations on economically relevant sectors, in particular with regard to the common market.[205] Mandatory notification obligations also enhance the private sector's involvement in regional competition law enforcement, but have proven to be resource-consuming in the long run.[206] With regard to regional decision-making, the regional framework should try to enhance participation of private business associations. One might also expect that with an increased enforcement of regional competition law, member states and national authorities will become more active advocates of a "regional competition law culture". Yet it is a dynamic process and regional and national competition authorities will have to constantly work on the promotion of a competition culture.[207]

Finally, in the WAEMU, the AndeanC and the CARICOM, irrespective of the institutional design, private damage claims can be brought before national judges. This requires national judges to gain adequate knowledge about regional competition law. Therefore, special emphasis should also be placed on the creation of a competition culture among national judges.

Part II, Dimension IV: Sect. 8.1.1 and on the initiation and handling of investigations, Part II, Dimension IV: Sect. 8.1.2.

[201] *Pollard,* in: *Hall/Chuck-A-Sang,* CARICOM Single Market and Economy Genesis and Prognosis, 2007, pp. 91, 111.

[202] Competition advocacy, which targets the private sector.

[203] Summary of competition advocacy in the three RTAs, Part II, Dimension IV: Sect. 8.1.4.

[204] On the importance of the evolution of regional case law see below, Part III, Sect. 11.3.3.

[205] A positive example is the decision of the CARICOM Competition Commission to initiate an investigation against a large cement company in the region, *Trinidad Cement Limited v The Competition Commission,* Caribbean Court of Justice Application No. OA 1 of 2012, CCJ 4 (OJ).

[206] This was the case in the European Union and has been improved through Regulation 1/2003.

[207] *Jenny/Horna,* in: *Brusick/Alvarez/Cernat,* Competition Provisions in Regional Trade Agreements, 2005, pp. 281, 320.

11.8 The Problem of Accessibility and Private Enforcement

11.8.1 Accessibility of Regional Competition Authorities in Infringement Procedures of Regional Competition Law

Weak "regional" competition culture creates a discrepancy: Consumers and local businesses constitute potential beneficiaries of regional competition law enforcement without being aware of it. This is particularly problematic if these benefits depend on the initiative to be taken by the affected party, for example by submitting a complaint before the regional authority. A similar discrepancy might arise between awareness of and possible obligations for private businesses arising out of regional competition law, such as notification requirements in order to receive an exemption.[208]

In all three RTAs, in order to claim civil damages or criminal sanctions, the preliminary decision with regard to a breach of regional competition law is probable to constitute a mandatory precondition.[209] Irrespective of the degree of centralization, the decision-making competence resides in the regional authority. Although a regional decision-monopoly enhances convergence and thereby legal certainty,[210] it might also create obstacles to regional competition law enforcement. The regional competition authority might be less accessible than national competition authorities for individuals or private businesses. In particular the procedure to address the regional authority should not be burdensome, for example by involving large expenditures or lengthy procedures.

An obvious obstacle to access to the regional competition authority can result from its geographical distance. One should appreciate the convenient location of the WAEMU Commission and the Secretariat General within their RTA. Burkina Faso is located in a central position within the WAEMU. Peru is similarly centrally located and moreover borders with all other member states. Yet poor infrastructure and costly transportation, which typically prevail in developing countries, can still render a direct submission very costly and burdensome.[211]

---

[208] Interestingly, in the WAEMU, the proposed new regulation makes notifications for exemption optional.

[209] This requirement is not clearly established in the AndeanC; see on Claims for Damages, Declarations, Injunctions and criminal law liability for breaches of regional competition law, Part II, Dimension IV: Sect. 8.1.3.3.

[210] In the absence of such a monopoly, convergent application requires national competition authorities to be highly committed to regional competition law and regional legal precedents. The European system also suggests that controlling mechanisms, such as a reallocation through the prerogative of the European Commission, might guarantee convergence.

[211] See the *DHL/Post* case in the WAEMU. After the Senegalese authority transferred the case to the WAEMU Commission, the enterprise withdrew its complaint, see above Part II, Dimension II: Sect. 6.1.1.

Generally, for bringing complaints mandatory deadlines and the codification of the legal procedure support transparency and legal certainty within a regional competition enforcement procedure. In the same vein, the procedural rules before the regional authority should incorporate provisions regarding the protection of individuals' and private businesses' rights, such as confidentiality issues or the right of defence.[212]

In the CARICOM, although individuals and private businesses can be subject to the regional competition law provisions, they are excluded from submitting complaints before the CARICOM Competition Commission. This makes private businesses dependent on the willingness of national competition authorities to cooperate and transfer cases to the regional level. The same difficulty arises in regional competition law systems that grant direct accessibility of the regional authority to private parties, but private parties choose to address their national competition authority based on an infringement of regional competition law. While in the CARICOM individuals or private business might find "creative ways" to address the regional authority, the question remains whether there exist legal instruments for individuals or private businesses to force a national authority to refer a case to the regional competition authority. An action for non-compliance before a regional court of justice that also individuals can submit under certain circumstances[213] seems to be a possible way to discipline member states and their institutions.[214]

In the WAEMU, the AndeanC and CARICOM infringement procedures initiated by private agents have been rare. This is mainly attributed to relatively weak interstate trade, the large informal sector and weak regional competition law culture. The level of development of the common market and the level of economic integration, as well as the civil society's awareness of them, correlate with the private sector's involvement in regional competition law enforcement. Therefore, a regional competition law authority should facilitate access to the regional competition authority in the long run. This could be achieved through enhanced cooperation with national competition authorities or by providing digital and electronic access to the regional competition authority. Moreover, rights and obligations for individuals and private businesses arising through regional competition law have to be complemented with a sufficient degree of accessibility, transparency and accountability. A very limited

---

[212] In the European Union all Member States have signed the European Convention on Human Rights. Moreover see CJEU, Judgement of 13 April 2000, Case C-292/97, *Karlsson and Others*, ECR I-2760, para. 37 stipulates that "requirements flowing from the protection of fundamental rights in the Community legal order are also binding on Member States when they implement Community rules." See *Wils*, The Relationship between Public Antitrust Enforcement and Private Actions for Damages, 32/1 W. Comp. 3, 17 (2009).

[213] In the CARICOM, individuals need to be granted special leave in order to address the Caribbean Court of Justice. Yet because of the ambiguous wording of Chapter VIII, it is unclear whether national competition authorities actually are subject to an obligation to transfer cases; see above Part II, Dimension IV: Sect. 8.1.1.2. Nevertheless, the CARICOM competition law enforcement structure of a decentralized inter-governmental system demonstrates the increased importance of a regional court also with regard to the protection of individuals' rights.

[214] Part II, Dimension IV: Sect. 8.3.2.5.

scope of application of regional law or a lack of regional sanctioning power could to a certain extent justify a lower standard as regards these elements. Yet in the long run, the lack of accessibility, transparency and accountability will hinder the emergence of awareness of regional competition law among individuals and the private sector. This does not mean that direct accessibility of the regional competition authority for privates is a *sine qua non* condition for the success of regional competition law enforcement. However, insufficient accessibility for private parties should be compensated with mechanisms of institutional control. The more decentralized regional competition law enforcement is, the more important is efficient judicial control before a regional court of justice. Furthermore, in a situation in which national competition authorities are reluctant to fulfil their obligations to assist the regional authority, it might be an appropriate consideration to enhance the private sector's involvement in regional law enforcement.[215]

11.8.2 The Role of National Judges in Private Enforcement of Regional Competition Law

The segmentation of the private enforcement process (decision-making remains centralized while enforcement takes place before the national judiciary) in the WAEMU, the AndeanC and the CARICOM constitutes a system that is based on a balancing of several values and considerations. In an RTA, while the objective of the creation of a common market calls for a uniform application of regional competition law, private parties' rights' protection requires enforcement procedures that are accessible and comply with constitutional values. This also comprises procedural aspects, such as speed and legal certainty of an enforcement procedure.[216] In order to guarantee access to evidence, in case of follow-on actions, a regional competition law framework also needs to include provisions on access to files and information.[217] This also includes rules on confidentiality.

---

[215] *Cortázar*, in: *Drexl/Bakhoum/Fox/Gal/Gerber*, Competition Policy and Regional Integration in Developing Countries, 2012, pp. 133, 154ff.

[216] See on private damages in the European Union, Directive on Antitrust Damages Actions of 24 October 2014, 2013/0185 (COD), signed into law on 26 November 2014 and adopted on 10 November 2014, OJ L 349, 5 December 2014, pp. 1–19.

[217] Information mechanisms between regional competition authorities and national judiciaries are included in the WAEMU in Article 22(4) of Regulation No. 03/2002/CM/UEMOA and Article 30 of the Regulation contains a professional secrecy provision. In the AndeanC Articles 23–25 of Decision 608 deal with confidentiality issues, but do not specifically deal with exchange of information between national courts and the Secretariat General. In the CARICOM, Article 170(4) of the Revised Treaty of Chaguaramas sets out a confidentiality rule for member states and according to Article 173(2) lit. g) of the RTC the CARICOM Competition Commission must facilitate exchange of relevant information and expertise. This provision might also include exchange of information with the national judiciary.

Against the backdrop of the modernization of European competition law enforcement, one can raise the question whether national judges in developing countries should be vested with more competences to apply regional competition law in order to facilitate accessibility and accelerate the development of regional competition law enforcement. Under European competition law, national judges have to apply the community norms directly and to decide on an infringement or a possible exception without a prior decision of the European Commission. The modernization of enforcement has above all achieved an acceleration of enforcement procedures and has achieved to save resources of the Commission.[218] Yet the particularities of developing countries oppose the achievement of similar efficiencies by allowing national judges to apply regional competition law directly. In fact, also in the European Union, modernization would not have been similarly successful in the early 1960s, when only Germany provided for domestic competition law structures.[219] The main disadvantage of endowing national judges with more competences is the inconsistent application of regional competition law. Despite relatively well-qualified judges, competition law enforcement remains a challenging task due to economic and legal considerations, which are entwined and complex. Moreover, given that the overall integration processes in the three RTAs have been relatively slow, it is not realistic to expect judges to apply a common welfare standard and to refrain from promoting purely national interests. The application difficulties even increase in the case of a *rule of reason*, which lacks legal certainty. Moreover, the fear of not being sufficiently represented by a regional competition law authority would be transferred to the national level.

A possible solution could provide for enhanced cooperation obligations and information mechanisms with the regional competition authority. This could alleviate the danger of inconsistent competition law enforcement. Yet at the same time, a mere cooperative function and information exchange between national judges and the regional competition authority raises concerns of transparency and due process. In order to avoid a circumvention of procedural rules that are codified for an infringement procedure the regional competition authority would have to adopt similar rules for cooperation and exchange of information with the national judiciary, for example regarding confidential information. Such codified principles of due process become even more important in a situation in which corruption[220] and

[218] Nevertheless, the predicted increase of individual prohibition decisions by the European Commission did not occur, see *Wils,* Ten Years of Regulation 1/2003, 4 J. Eur. Comp. L. Practice 293, 298ff. (2013).

[219] *Ehlermann,* Implementation of EC Competition Law by National Anti-Trust Authorities, 17 ECLR 88, 89 (1996).

[220] In the course of this study, there was no evidence for or against a high level of corruption among national judges. On the contrary, judges were usually considered as highly competent public officials by civil society. However *Lande* in an early article restates an opinion in the context of the discussion regarding the implementation of competition laws in transition economies that: "many of the enforcers and judges in a number of transition economies are likely to be corrupt and/or inexperienced in competition matters. Corrupt and/or inexperienced decision makers can be a tremendous problem because every antitrust law contains terrifying levels of discretion. (…) [A]

distrust of public administration are common features in a society. Moreover, the allocation of competences should provide for possibilities for the regional authority to gain its own experiences. In this regard, giving national judges too far-reaching competition law competences could hamper the development of regional precedents.[221] One should also recall that a regional competition authority's decision is perceived differently than a decision of a national court. Whereas a regional authority firstly has to gain acceptance within a national jurisdiction, national court decisions form part of the national legal system. One might thus appropriately doubt whether national court decisions on private damages can substitute legal precedents by a regional authority. While private and public enforcement are interrelated, they are not direct substitutes as they follow different goals.[222] Finally, from a technical point of view, the regional legal system also has to provide for a binding effect of national court orders among member states.

To sum up, private litigation based on a breach of regional competition law remains rare in RTAs of developing countries. Granting national judges more decisional competences thus only appears feasible in the long run.[223]

11.9 The Political Dimension of Regional Competition Law Enforcement

An RTA is in its first stage an agreement between member states. The scope of a regional competition law regime and its functions thus depend on the competences attributed to it by the member states.[224] As regards competition law enforcement, in

---

ntitrust enforcers and judges often will be tempted to (mis)use whatever laws they have been given, especially if they come from a country with a tradition of centralized planning or heavy involvement in business affairs by government bureaucrats. The decision makers' learning curves are likely to be slow and painful for the economy.", *Lande,* Creating Competition Policy for Transition Economies, 23 Brook. J. Int'l. Law 339, 345f. (1997).

[221] *Jenny/Horna* rightly argue: "At first, the fact that national authorities and courts did not participate very actively in the enforcement of EU law was not considered problematic as it allowed the European Commission to develop the case law (…) in a more systematic and consistent manner than would have been the case had the inexperienced national authorities been more actively involved.", *Jenny/Horna,* in: *Brusick/Alvarez/Cernat,* Competition Provisions in Regional Trade Agreements, 2005, pp. 281, 288f.

[222] Generally, public enforcement measures are considered to aim at the punishment of anticompetitive practices in the relevant market and entail a deterrent effect, private enforcement measures are considered to primarily aim at the compensation for a specific damage. The European Union, Directive on Antitrust Damages Actions of 24 October 2014, 2013/0185 (COD), OJ L 349 is considered to aim at both.

[223] For more details on the attribution of competences for national judges, see below Part III, Dimension IV: Sect. 12.4.7.

[224] The EU is a highly developed RTA. However, it lacks the so-called "competence-competence", the competence to attribute itself with a competence to legislate or act on a specific matter. This competence remains within the member states. This is also a feature that distinguishes an RTA from a sovereign state.

addition to the will to enforce competition law at all,[225] in the case of an RTA, the national governments must support competition law enforcement on a regional level.[226] This willingness has been declining in the AndeanC.

Given the different layers of competition law enforcement, one can differentiate between the political will to regionalize competition law in the first place and the political will to support regional competition law enforcement in the long run.[227] The experiences of the WAEMU, the AndeanC and the CARICOM illustrate that the political will to establish a regional competition law system is more easily achieved than the political support to guarantee enforcement of regional competition law in the long run.

First, during the implementation phase of regional competition law, difficulties mostly arose in the context of finding a consensus and balancing regional with national interests. Experiences with RTAs show that competition law experiences usually positively correlate with the economic and liberalization development of a country.[228] However, the economic power of member states in the implementation phase of a regional competition law is an ambiguous factor. On the one hand, economically stronger member states are usually aware of the benefits of a common market and the necessity of implementing regional competition law. On the other hand, they can be reluctant to cede competition law competences to the regional level. Participation of states with little or no competition law experience at this stage usually depends on their general interest in and commitment to the regional integration movement overall.

Regular participation of all member states during the legislative process for the adoption of a regional competition law can overcome critics, allows for an exchange of differing views on competition law and enhances the balancing of the different interests at stake. Problematic in this context is that the WAEMU's centralized competition law enforcement was actually determined by the WAEMU Court of Justice. All three RTAs discussed in this study have accomplished the implementation phase of regional competition law and provided the regional authorities with the necessary powers to legislate on internal procedures. Similar levels of economic development are thus not a precondition for a regional competition law regime.[229] Rather, it might

[225] *Mehta/Agarwal/Singh*, Politics Trumps Economics, 2007, pp. 14f.

[226] *Gerber*, in: *Drexl/Bakhoum/Fox/Gal/Gerber*, Competition Policy and Regional Integration in Developing Countries, 2012, pp. 253, 259ff.

[227] In this context, *Gerber* distinguishes between "formal regionalization" (impetus to locate competition law at the regional level) and "actual implementation of competition law". According to *Gerber* "[t]here are many incentives formally to regionalize competition law (…); however, political factors provide far less support for implementation of competition law at the regional level." See *Gerber*, in: *Drexl/Bakhoum/Fox/Gal/Gerber*, Competition Policy and Regional Integration in Developing Countries, 2012, pp. 253, 271.

[228] For example, in the WAEMU: Senegal. In the AndeanC: Peru and Colombia. In the CARICOM: Barbados and Jamaica.

[229] *Drexl*, in: *Drexl/Bakhoum/Fox/Gal/Gerber*, Competition Policy and Regional Integration in Developing Countries, 2012, pp. 231, 240.

just be the combination of different economic levels that fosters the establishment of a regional competition law regime.

The will to support regional competition law enforcement in the long run mainly takes the form of cooperation. In this context, in particular the transferral of cases has been problematic, as has the sharing of information. Moreover, member states participate unequally in regional competition law enforcement. This disparate representation in actual competition law enforcement is not only due to the heterogeneous economic power and structures of the member states, but also demonstrates a partly insufficient political will on the part of the national competition authorities.[230] In the WAEMU, the dearth of will to cooperate is clearly attributable to the withdrawal of national competition law competences. Yet a balanced distribution of powers may not actually be so much a precondition for the initial establishment of a regional competition law regime. R, problems arise when the balance slackens after the regime's implementation and there is no longer continuous support for the system on either level. The institutional design must provide for the ability for the regional institutions to learn from the national level and vice versa. In this context, the dynamics of regional competition law enforcement require the regional competition law enforcement regime to leave sufficient leeway to member states to gather competition law experience with regard to their national markets while creating collaboration channels and adapting to changing circumstances, above all in order to gain proper national competition law expertise.

11.10 The Importance of Preserving Flexibility in the Framework of a Regional Competition Law Structure

When assessing the anticompetitiveness of a practice, a regional competition law refers to the welfare of the common market and does not refer to the consequences for a particular state. *Michal Gal* states in this context that regionalization also requires the sacrifice of some degree of domestic welfare.[231] In theory, the larger the number of member states and the more heterogeneous their level of economic development, the greater is the danger of unequal consideration of local welfare. Consequently, the incorporation of (transitory) differential treatment provisions might compensate for unequal distribution of benefits.

---

[230] In the AndeanC, Peru, despite being one of the economically stronger member states, is more interested in national competition law enforcement. In the WAEMU, Burkina Faso has been cooperating regularly with the WAEMU Commission. Senegal, an economically relatively strong member state, has not been an active cooperation partner in regional competition law enforcement. In the CARICOM, for the lack of sufficient regional legal precedents, it is difficult to draw conclusions at this point.

[231] *Gal/Faibish Wassmer*, in: *Drexl/Bakhoum/Fox/Gal/Gerber*, Competition Policy and Regional Integration in Developing Countries, 2012, pp. 291, 302.

The notion of flexibility in a regional competition law system entails several layers. It not only incorporates flexibility in terms of substantive competition law provisions, but also refers to the overall regional competition law system, including the allocation of competences and the internal structure of a regional competition authority.

In general, the protection of traditionally disadvantaged parts of society and structurally disadvantaged regions or sectors[232] in developing countries requires a flexible and adjustable framework of competition law enforcement.[233] As traditional competition law enforcement is based on economic efficiency considerations,[234] social or cultural policies that have as their object the protection of minorities are likely to clash with competition policy.[235] A competition law system should thus be designed in such a way that it is capable of balancing the interests at stake without leading to fragmented enforcement. In a regional competition law regime, flexibility additionally raises issues of national sovereignty, as one has to assign the competent entity—national or regional—to apply competition law on a flexible basis. With regard to regional competition law enforcement one therefore has to ask whether it results in a loss of flexibility[236] and, if it does, how far this loss affects the efficacy of competition law enforcement.

In this context, flexibility and harmonization should not be perceived as mere opposites. Even within the framework of harmonization of competition law within an RTA, national competition authorities have to be given sufficient leeway to develop their own competition law experience. Even if one acknowledges the efficiency gains that might arise out of very centralized and uniform regional competition law enforcement in developing countries, one should conceive it as a transitory or initial stage device only.[237]

The experiences in the WAEMU, the AndeanC and the CARICOM moreover demonstrate that substantive regional competition law is capable of providing for flexibility. By including exemptions or special and preferential treatment provisions,

---

[232] See above on regional competition law objectives, Part II, Dimension I: Sect. 5.3.1.

[233] *Fox,* Economic Development, Poverty, and Antitrust, 13 Sw. J.L. Trade Americas 101, 121 (2007).

[234] Even the consumer welfare approach does not constitute a social objective of competition law. Rather, it emphasizes the relevance of possible economic consequences for the consumer. South Africa was the first jurisdiction to include and allow non-classical competition law considerations in its competition law enforcement and analysis.

[235] *Fox,* Economic Development, Poverty, and Antitrust, 13 Sw. J. L. Trade Americas 101, 102ff. (2007).

[236] *Ziller* even argues that "flexibility is a condition of success" of regional integration, see *Ziller,* The Challenges of Governance in Regional Integration, 2005, p. 9.

[237] One should thus welcome the reform initiatives in the WAEMU with regard to the centralized competition law enforcement. In the AndeanC, the "downloading option," which led to a situation of complete harmonization of national and regional competition laws, only functioned as a transitory device. Regarding the benefits that arose from centralized competition law enforcement in the European Union, see *Jenny/Horna,* in: *Brusick/Alvarez/Cernat,* Competition Provisions in Regional Trade Agreements, 2005, pp. 281, 287.

regional substantive law can adapt to changing circumstances. Similarly, interim measures can be suitable. Ideally, a regional competition law should provide for guidelines on the special treatment of structurally disadvantaged or particularly vulnerable groups and sectors, such as for SMEs or the agricultural sector, which is typically very large in developing countries. Special and explicit guidelines might also contribute to a more direct and positive perception of the regional competition authority.

Finally, a regional competition law enforcement regime constitutes a dynamic process. Consequently, it has to adapt to changing circumstances and ideally adapt to an increased awareness of competition law.[238] The "downloading option" serves as a positive example, as it allowed member states to use it as a transitory device until the adoption of proper domestic competition laws. Possible adaptation can also take the form of a re-allocation of competition law enforcement competences. This point largely depends on the general legal structure of the RTA and the competence to enact regulations or directives. Moreover, adaptation might include a shift in competition law enforcement priorities. Hence, rules governing the internal structure of a regional competition authority should allow the latter to determine its own enforcement agenda.

11.11 General Conclusions

Some of the often-predicted benefits of setting up a regional competition regime, such as the saving of resources or greater independence of a competition authority, can only be achieved to a limited extent and under specific requirements. A regional competition law regime is a complex construction relying on manifold aspects, ranging from economic to political and socio-cultural implications. Despite the necessity to create incentives for the establishment of national competition law structures—without stipulating a specific form—there are actually no factors that constitute an indispensable precondition for the success of a regional competition law system. Nonetheless, a regional competition law without an underlying economic centre of gravity is difficult to construct. On the other hand, there are no factors whose existence guarantees the success of a regional system. In fact, one has to bear in mind that the notion of "successful" regional competition law enforcement is difficult to measure. Moreover, the changing social, cultural and political context requires flexibility and adaptability in the long run.

The experiences of the WAEMU, the AndeanC and the CARICOM show that a major advantage of a regional competition law framework is its incentive function for member states to implement a domestic competition policy. For very exceptional cases, such as in the OECS, regional competition law is not perceived as an equally efficient substitution for national competition law. As sovereignty issues and distrust

[238] See on the notion of time, Part II, Dimension VI: Chap. 10.

among member states are prominent features of RTAs of developing countries, the inciting function of a regional competition law is even more relevant than specific enforcement measures taken against anticompetitive practices of undertakings. In fact, as cross-border trade is generally weak, one would expect the key area of competition law enforcement to remain local even within a common market. Hence, the dynamics of regional competition law and the objectives will change eventually once member states adopt and apply national competition laws.

One can further conclude that the institutional design, meaning the allocation of competences regarding competition law enforcement in a regional competition law regime, has a strong impact on the efficacy of the system. It is the allocation of competences that determines the institutional design, thereby determining whether the regional competition law structure creates an incentive or an obstacle for competition law enforcement, nationally or regionally.

As in the European Union, in RTAs among developing countries the economic and political paradigms of integration are interdependent and subject to the dynamics of regional integration. Unfortunately, it appears that the implementation of economically justified measures is often hampered by political considerations, which are moreover often difficult to grasp. One must thus appreciate the considerable activity record of the WAEMU Commission, the Secretariat General and the CARICOM Competition Commission despite political hurdles and institutional deficiencies. Generally, it would be too short-sighted to merely limit the creation of RTAs among developing countries to reactions of developing countries to external pressure coming from the international world. In fact, the benefits of RTAs have an inward as well as an outward direction. While they stimulate economic growth and development of member states, mainly through the creation of a common market, they also contribute to a better integration of member states in the global economic and political sphere.

Chapter 12
The Optimal Degree of Centralization or Decentralization: Recommendations for and Implications of Certain Institutional Designs

Having defined the elements that shape the degree of centralization or decentralization of competition law enforcement in the WAEMU, the AndeanC and the CARICOM, the next section will draw general conclusions and discuss the implications for the institutional design of competition law enforcement in developing countries. This mainly raises two questions: (1) Which implications result from a specific institutional design of competition law enforcement? The answer to this question will be given for the specific "dimensions" of competition law enforcement in an RTA. (2) What are the conditions in the sense of "competition constraints"[1] that determine the efficacy of a certain institutional competition law enforcement design?

12.1 Dimension I: Vertical Allocation of Competences Through the Content of Regional Substantive Competition Law

12.1.1 Territorial Scope of Application: The Requirement of Cross-Border Trade

The hub of vertical competence allocation through substantive competition law lies in the territorial scope of application. Relying on the effects doctrine, the requirement of cross-border effects can limit or extend the scope of application of regional

[1] *Drexl* develops several principles of orientation for the design of a regional enforcement system, see *Drexl*, in: *Drexl/Bakhoum/Fox/Gal/Gerber*, Competition Policy and Regional Integration in Developing Countries, 2012, pp. 231–252; see also on competition constraints *Bakhoum/ Molestina*, in: *Drexl/Bakhoum/Fox/Gal/Gerber*, Competition Policy and Regional Integration in Developing Countries, 2012, pp. 89, 108ff.

J. Molestina, *Regional Competition Law Enforcement in Developing Countries*, Munich Studies on Innovation and Competition 9,
https://doi.org/10.1007/978-3-662-58525-2_12

competition law. The specific definition of "cross-border" trade will mostly depend on the envisaged degree of economic integration, varying from a mere cooperation agreement to a custom and economic union. In striving to abolish economic barriers between member states, the scope of application of regional competition law will be broader than in a loose association of sovereign states.[2]

The broadest territorial scope of application was adopted in the WAEMU by leaving no room for the application of national competition laws. This created a single uniform law.[3] In the absence of national competition law that is applied in parallel, businesses operating on several national markets in theory only have to consider one law, which reduces transaction costs. This is an aspect that may particularly attract FDI. Moreover, a uniform regional competition law also covers anticompetitive practices originating from MNEs that are only active in one member state.[4] Yet the unification of substantive competition law is not the only way to achieve these efficiency gains, but such unification might even produce severe negative effects.

There are (at least) four reasons to consider alternatives to territorially uniform law: First, the principle of primacy of regional over national competition law resolves conflicts of laws, which also reduces transaction costs. Second, cross-border activities will lead to the application of regional competition law. Hence, even under a system of parallel application, undertakings will only have to follow regional law and will only have to consider those national particularities that are allowed under the regional legal framework.[5] Third, even an extensive territorial scope of application of regional competition law does not exclude the application of, on the one hand, different national procedural and administrative laws that enforce the regional competition law,[6] and on the other hand, diverging national sectorial laws.[7] Fourth, efficiencies arising from the application of regional competition law as regards practices with purely national effect on a single member state are extremely limited or even tend to be negative. Anticompetitive practices

[2] None of the three, the WAEMU, the AndeanC, or the CARICOM, constitutes such a loose association of sovereign states.

[3] A unification of competition law matters under regional competition law corresponds to the exclusive competence of a regional competition authority to apply competition law within the RTA.

[4] Recalling that a regional competition authority is structurally better positioned to deal with international anticompetitive practices or anticompetitive practices by multi-national enterprises (MNEs). See above Part III, Sect. 11.3.

[5] Implications regarding the regional legal framework actually concern Dimension II, regarding legislative primacy in competition law matters. Full harmonization of competition law leads to a similar situation, in which only one uniform set of competition law rules is applicable throughout the region of an RTA.

[6] The actual enforcement of regional competition law relates to national procedural autonomy (Dimension II) and actual enforcement of regional competition law (Dimension III).

[7] In the WAEMU, the AndeanC and the CARICOM, there have not been obvious cases of conflicts between regional competition law and national sectorial law. This is yet most probably attributed to a lack of transparency, rather than to the lack of actual conflicts. See above Part III, Sect. 11.4.3.1.

originating from multinational firms with a purely national effect limited to one member state within a RTA remain rare. It is unlikely that MNEs and foreign enterprises will be only active in one member state, because investment costs linked to entering a new market will not pay off in small emerging markets, which are frequent in developing countries. Even in the case of the latter, a regional competition law authority is always obliged to set priorities with regard to the large territorial scope of application. It is then questionable whether and under which conditions anticompetitive practices that only concern one state are made a matter of regional priority. Similarly, in an RTA in which there is one economically dominant member state or in which there are high entry barriers between member states it is possible that purely national practices will become a regional priority. Yet in such a scenario, one might aptly question the functioning of the common market and the purpose of regional competition law overall. In fact, applying regional competition law to purely national matters not only consumes large amounts of resources, but also impairs the development of a national competition law culture to the detriment of efficient long-term enforcement of competition law within an RTA.[8]

The main deficiency of an extremely broad scope of application is the large amount of human and financial resources it requires to monitor the entire territory with regard to allegedly anticompetitive practices. Hence, the regional authority will depend on the assistance of national competition authorities. Such assistance, however, also presupposes sufficient resources and is heavily dependent on the agencies' willingness to cooperate, which might be hampered by the unification of laws. This can easily lead to an imbalance in representation or loopholes in enforcement, as some member states are likely to be more active and cooperative than others.

Does there exist a scenario in which the monitoring task of an entire territory does not lead to great resource consumption? The Organization of Eastern Caribbean States offers such a scenario. Arguably, a limited number of member states, the preponderance of microstates with similar economic structures and transparent markets are the factors that facilitate the surveillance by a regional competition authority. Nevertheless, another precondition remains: there must be a generally close relation between states, politically and/or economically.

Competition constraints, such as the limited amount of resources on the regional level, the different sizes of member states and their great number, their economic heterogeneity and a lack of tradition in close political and/or economic cooperation argue in favour of limiting the territorial scope of application based on "cross-border" or "inter-state" effect of anticompetitive practices.

As this creates a system of concurrent competition law enforcement, either regional or national, there are certain aspects to consider. Parallel application requires a clear-cut demarcation criterion to avoid large resource consumption through the competence allocation process itself, in particular at an early stage of regional competition law enforcement. Moreover, a final dispute resolution instance should deal with possible conflicts. Such a resolution mechanism could also be

[8] See on the experiences of the WAEMU, Part II, Dimension II: Sect. 6.1.

informal, for example within a competition network. In order to achieve efficiency gains in competition law enforcement, the competence demarcation criterion should rely on efficiency considerations. This is a legal and economic venture in which legal, institutional, political and economic aspects of the common market and of the integration movement overall should be taken into account. As the definition of a demarcation criterion is a complex task, it is justifiable for RTAs among developing countries to rely on the criteria of more developed counterparts. In the same vein, the adoption of very formalistic competence demarcation criteria might be appropriate at an early stage of regional integration. Nevertheless, regardless of how unambiguous the competence demarcation criterion is, the experiences of the three RTAs examined in this work demonstrate that among developing countries, the regional level might have to monitor and force the consistent application of the competence allocation criterion, as national competition authorities lack expertise or might be prone to pursuing national political interests.[9]

12.1.2 The Notion of Appreciable Effect and the De-Minimis Clause

It is interesting to highlight that only the CARICOM included the possibility for the CARICOM Competition Commission to exempt business practices whose impact on competition and trade is considered minimal (*de minimis* clause).[10] Neither the WAEMU nor the AndeanC adopted a *de minimis* clause. In the context of developing regional legal precedents, one should welcome the fact that generally all practices that have an effect on the common market within a regional competition law system fall under the scope of regional competition law. In RTAs among developing countries, the number of such practices will be lower than in their developed counterparts, in which inter-state trade is higher. Therefore, the requirement of establishing an appreciable effect on the common market is not as pressing as in more developed RTAs such as the European Union. Yet in the long run, regional competition authorities of RTAs among developing countries will also have to develop criteria according to which they can prioritize competition law application. Likewise, a *de-minimis* rule limits the scope of application of regional competition law by excluding practices with limited effect on cross-border trade. Until then, the regional competition authority will have to balance economic efficiencies with market power on a case-to-case basis.

---

[9] Experiences in the AndeanC support this assumption: Despite the formal competence demarcation criterion, member states and according national competition authorities did not apply regional competition law. See above Part II, Dimension II: Sect. 6.3.

[10] Article 181 of the Revised Treaty of Chaguaramas: *de-minimis* Rule.

12.1.3 Dealing with State-Related Anticompetitive Practices

Regional provisions allowing for far-reaching measures against anticompetitive practices of states that are capable of distorting competition in the common market reflect a larger degree of centralization. Especially provisions on state aids or public undertakings touch upon member states' sovereignty and might cause conflicts.[11] The adoption of such regional rules thus requires the commitment of member states to the enforcement of regional competition law and the economic integration movement overall. Likewise, the adoption of such rules reflects national commitment to liberalization. Different stages of the latter and different stages of economic development among member states might thus constitute an obstacle to the implementation and enforcement of regional provisions dealing with state-imputed practices.

Nevertheless, centralized governance and centralized enforcement of the law against state-related anticompetitive practices and state aids, for example through the regional competition agency, should clearly be preferred. As the regional competition authority is vested with greater political neutrality,[12] it is structurally less susceptible to national political interests. Especially in developing countries, in which state-owned and dominant undertakings are still a widespread phenomenon, the process of liberalization and the creation of a common market have to be completed with rigorous and consistent competition law enforcement. In this regard, in the long run, even if state-protectionist measures become less frequent, the regional competition authority will remain the key institution to guarantee "neutral" competition law enforcement.

12.1.4 The Inclusion of Individual Exceptions, Exemptions and Special and Differential Treatment Provisions

The inclusion of individual exceptions, exemptions and provisions that grant special and differential treatment for regions or sectors in competition law systems in developing countries requires careful adjustment. Apart from the question, which institution has the power to request or decide on an exception or exemption, exceptional provisions always entail certain risks. Especially in regional competition law systems, excessive use of the possibility to grant exemptions might hinder the development of regional case law, but also diverging application of exemption possibilities might preclude the development of consistent and uniform regional case law, for example by referring only to cases that arise in a particular member state. It would also affect the transparency of regional competition law enforcement. Due to the lack of competition culture and imperfect liberalization, there is also a justified

[11] On state-related behaviour and public enterprises, see Part II, Dimension I: Sect. 5.1.3.

[12] See above Part III, Sect. 11.5.1.

concern that national competition authorities will grant exceptions in order to protect their national industries, thereby creating potential barriers to inter-state trade.

However, completely excluding exemptions and differential and special treatment clauses in regional competition law does not appear feasible, as regional integration will always create disadvantages for some member state(s). As a rule of thumb, the more heterogeneous the economic development and the national markets and the larger the number of member states, the more exemptions and preferential treatment clauses will be included in the regional competition law framework. However, such exceptions should not be excessive, as they are capable of endangering convergent application and transparency.[13] First, special treatment should only be provided for a transition period. Limiting its duration, however, calls for monitoring mechanisms to supervise the adequacy of special treatment over time. Exemptions, on the other hand, are generally not drafted as part of transition clauses. In order to avoid undermining the regional competition law, exemptions of entire sectors or regions should remain limited and should be abolished over time. Second, the granting of exceptions to regional competition law should follow certain criteria and transparent procedures. In this context, the CARICOM system is problematic, because the COTED, a political organ, can decide upon sectorial exemptions to regional competition law enforcement without relying on codified procedures for such exemptions.[14]

12.1.5 *Objectives of Regional Competition Law*

Generally, regional competition law objectives are neutral regarding the degree of centralization or decentralization. Yet the explicit inclusion of a common market approach reinforces the weight of economic integration. This does not signify that the RTA always favours an economic paradigm over a political one. One might expect the scope of application of regional competition law to be interpreted broadly, as the creation of a common market aims at the abolition of all barriers to trade. The role of competition law objectives determines the prohibition of certain practices, rather than defining the scope of application. Yet competition law objectives define the focus of application by considering certain practices particularly harmful to competition.

None of the RTAs has adopted a formal market approach for the application of regional competition law, according to which market integration constitutes an objective as such. This might create difficulties and thereby require larger amount of resources, because the regional competition authority will always have to engage in an economic analysis. Similar to the development of European competition law

[13] This issue is interrelated to the level of flexibility of regional competition law enforcement. See above Part III, Sect. 11.10.

[14] More information on the enforcement of exceptions, see below Part III, Dimension IV: Sect. 12.4.4

and the case law of the courts, it might be useful and efficient to apply a formal market integration approach in the initial phase of an RTA, in particular among developing countries with little competition law experience. Moreover, the promotion of market integration constitutes a political objective.[15] Due to the low level of inter-state trade among developing countries, the emphasis of the political component to regional integration appears to be necessary to strengthen the common market.

12.1.6 The Inclusion of Regional Merger Policy[16]

The main arguments against the inclusion of a merger control regime in developing countries are based on the lack of sufficient competition law expertise available and the large amount of resources merger control enforcement would require.[17] However, mergers are a common way for MNEs or large enterprises to penetrate developing countries' markets.[18] A regional competition law and regional authorities are better suited to address mergers with cross-border effects[19] than national competition authorities.[20] By providing a uniform control system, regional law also attracts FDI, because businesses will encounter fewer transaction costs when they have to notify mergers to one authority and conform to only one law as opposed to several national competition laws or merger regimes.[21] In balancing efficiency with a possible increase of market power, a regional competition law still allows local firms to reach their optimal competitive size through mergers.[22]

Having outlined the possible efficiencies resulting from a regional merger control system in developing countries, it is yet difficult to define the optimal degree of

---

[15] *Motta,* Competition Policy, 2004, p. 23.

[16] The topic of merger policy in developing countries is deliberately only treated superficially in this study, since it is a controversial matter that requires a discussion and a thorough economic analysis that would go beyond the scope of this study. For more information see *Gal,* Competition Policy for Small Market Economies, 2003, pp. 194ff.

[17] *De León,* An Institutional Assessment of Antitrust Policy, 2009, p. 269: "Merger control drains resources from both applicants and competition agencies." *De León,* Latin American Competition Law and Policy, 2001, pp. 111ff.

[18] With regard to the Common Market for Eastern and Southern Africa (COMESA) *Lipmile* argues: "As trade and investment liberalization reduced entry barriers, firms may have greater incentives to engage in anti-competitive practices and mergers, which would limit market access by other firms." *Lipimile,* in: *Drexl/Bakhoum/Fox/Gal/Gerber,* Competition Policy and Regional Integration in Developing Countries, 2012, pp. 205, 205.

[19] In this context, mergers with cross-border effects can include mergers initiated by MNEs from outside the RTA, or those initiated by larger enterprises from another member state within an RTA.

[20] See Part III, Sect. 11.3.

[21] *Kerber,* in: *Drexl,* The Future of Transnational Antitrust, 2003, pp. 269, 286.

[22] *Gal,* Competition Policy for Small Market Economies, 2003, p. 224.

centralization.[23] Regional merger control should only cover mergers that have a cross-border anticompetitive effect. Consequently, member states, in particular those of a large size, should consider creating their own merger control system in addition to the regional system in order to cover mergers with purely national effect.

From the perspective of the undertakings, in particular those seeking attractive recipient countries for their FDI, legal certainty is of utmost importance. For this reason, it is advisable to refrain from a system of parallel application. On the other hand, an exclusive regional merger without any national control might be inefficient when national markets are very heterogeneous. Regional merger control in RTAs among developing countries therefore requires a clear demarcation criterion, which takes into account the size of the regional market, as well as the specific landscape of national markets.

12.1.7 Competition Advocacy

Competition advocacy can be an instrument to spread a competition culture. The most effective way to spread the benefits of regional competition law is effective enforcement that responds to the needs of the large population. The fewer the number of regional competition cases, because cases with a regional interest are rare, the more the regional competition authority has to engage in competition advocacy. Moreover, one should differentiate between advocacy that targets the private[24] and the government sector.[25] While the former is more efficiently exercised on the national level, a regional competition authority should concentrate on the latter.[26] Competition advocacy activities should thus be shared between national and regional competition authorities and should be used in a flexible way in order to adapt to changing circumstances.

---

[23] See the experiences of the COMESA merger control law, which was enacted on 14 January 2013. On October 2014, it also published merger assessment guidelines. Despite the operability of the system, the regulations do not expressly exclude the parallel jurisdiction of the national competition authorities (i.e.: one-stop-shop principle or parallel applicability). In particular Kenya and Egypt insisted on parallel national filing obligations. By 2017, all national regulators except for the ones in Kenya recognize COMESA as a one-stop-shop system. See statement made by COMESA Competition Commission chief executive George *Lipimile* on 1 September 2017. On ambiguities regarding the competence allocation as regards merger control, see *Rudman/Wilson,* COMESA Competition Law – A New Regional Merger Regime for Eastern and Southern Africa, 4 J. Eur. Comp. L. Practice 368 (2013). Generally on the COMESA merger control, see *Lipimile,* in: *Drexl/Bakhoum/Fox/Gal/Gerber,* Competition Policy and Regional Integration in Developing Countries, 2012, p. 205.

[24] See Part II, Dimension IV: Sect. 8.1.4.

[25] See Part II, Dimension IV: Sect. 8.1.4.

[26] See above Part III, Sect. 11.7.

12.2 Dimension II: Implications for the Vertical Allocation of Competition Law Competences

The taxonomy of the competence to legislate on competition matters entails two elements, both of which need to be considered in examining the efficiency of the degree of centralization. First, how has the regional legislative framework impacted implementation and/or harmonization of national competition law and institutions? Second, what are its implications for competition law enforcement?

As regards the first question, most member states in the three RTAs have adopted proper competition laws or are in the process of doing so.[27] However, the spread of newly implemented competition law regimes, in particular in the developing world, is a general global trend, which has been observed since 1990.[28] Consequently, it is neither possible to figure out the exact impact of a regional competition law system, nor is it possible to make unambiguous statements on the causality between regional and national competition law implementation.

12.2.1 Implementation of National Competition Law Structures: Informal Incentives vs. Obligations

In a regional legislative framework, the development of national competition legislation can be influenced by various means ranging from mere informal incentives to mandatory and enforceable obligations. While mere competition advocacy, non-binding guidelines, a model competition law or technical assistance are informal tools, the inclusion of timeframes and obligations to unify or to harmonize constitute proactive mandatory measures to implement a certain national competition structure. The latter's mandatory character can even be strengthened by sanctioning mechanisms, which operate either indirectly via judicial control mechanisms or directly through surveillance and sanctioning by the regional competition authority. In the same vein, a complete exclusion of national legislative powers in the field of competition law is a form of coerced implementation of competition law. The question is thus, under which circumstances does a specific degree of coercion seem feasible?[29]

---

[27] See on the legislative competence in competition law matters, Part II, Dimension II: Chap. 6.

[28] *Lande,* Creating Competition Policy for Transition Economies, 23 Brook. J. Int'l. Law 339, 339f. (1997).

[29] This question refers to the inclusion of obligations on Member States as such. It thus mainly concerns the question of whether Member States should be "obliged" to enact national competition law structures. The question of whether a regional legislative framework should harmonize to a full or minimum extent is a related, but distinct question. It concerns the range of possible legislative obligations on the member states imposed by the regional level.

An obvious advantage of relying on binding obligations is the acceleration of the development of domestic competition law structures.[30] In this context, a regional legislator might be inclined to include deadlines for the adoption of national competition laws. Additionally, member states are forced to invest resources in the creation of domestic competition law structures. Obligations can in this regard work as an external push factor that can overcome internal political opposition. Yet also in the context of a regional competition law regime, the lack of resources of member states to enact national competition law and to create the corresponding institutions has to be taken into account. Moreover, a domestic competition law regime within an RTA requires "double" embeddedness: It has to be in conformity with the national constitution and national economic policy as well as other provisions arising out of the integration movement. Competition policy that is merely imposed on member states can cause political opposition and may fail to promote the creation of a local competition culture.[31] Hence, the implementation process of domestic competition law structures will be even more resource-consuming. Alternatively, member states might be unable to comply with the obligation, for lack of resources or lack of commitment. Sanctioning mechanisms on the regional level, trying to enforce the obligation, will not only consume resources and decrease the member states' commitment to regional integration overall, they might even be useless.

With the emergence of a common market, the necessity to have effective competition laws in all member states grows as well. Both movements are interrelated and similarly depend on national political support. Rather than forcing member states to implement national competition law structures, the regional level should grant technical assistance and enhance the exchange of competition law expertise. Generally, the inclusion of a loyalty clause to a certain extent also prevents conflicts between national and regional laws and enforcement. In any circumstance, member states should not be entirely prevented from adopting national competition laws. Consequently, complete unification is only feasible in very limited situations.[32] Coercion is only appropriate where economic integration has become a reality and where there is a certain consensus on the standards within the RTA. In this context, it was an appropriate measure to oblige states wishing to gain accession to the EU in 2004 to enact national competition law structures in accordance with the regional law.[33] In the same vein, with the overall progress of economic integration, the loyalty clause might be interpreted more broadly.

---

[30] This argument was advanced in favour of the WAEMU's unification of competition laws. See above Part II, Dimension I: Sect. 5.1.5.1.

[31] Similarly *Jenny/Horna*, who argue that "adopting a national competition law in these cases, particularly when this is principally done to meet an obligation, is not sufficient to make Member States appreciate the benefits of competition either at national level or at the level of the regional grouping." *Jenny/Horna*, in: *Brusick/Alvarez/Cernat*, Competition Provisions in Regional Trade Agreements, 2005, pp. 281, 319.

[32] See Part II, Dimension I: Sect. 5.1.5.1 and Part II, Dimension II: Sect. 6.1.

[33] See *Drexl*, Perspectives européennes sur la politique de la concurrence dans l'espace OHADA, XXV R.I.D.E. 281, 292f. (2011).

12.2.2 *Range of Implementation Obligations and Learning Direction: Top-down and Bottom-up*

Another question relates to the range of possible implementation obligations. Having established that domestic legislative structures have to engage in proper competition law implementation processes, this does not specify to what extent the regional framework should set standards. Although there is no "one-size-fits-all" standard, it is possible to make certain observations and recommendations.

One should carefully identify the lead-jurisdictions[34] of the implementation of regional and national competition law.[35] If initiatives mainly stem from the member states, this is an indicator for ongoing national competition law implementation processes and the existence of political support for a regional competition regime.[36] A regional legislator should try to rely on existing competition laws and experiences (bottom-up), instead of imposing far-reaching harmonization obligations on member states (top-down).[37] However, political support might diminish over time. As the AndeanC demonstrates, initial harmonization movements can be superseded by the adoption of different economic market concepts and changing political leadership and views.[38] The learning process is thus a dynamic process, which in the long run has to take place in both directions.

While "soft harmonization"[39] has characterized the development of national competition laws in the European Union, the situation in RTAs in developing countries is different. As there is less inter-state trade, the regional legislative framework has to set standards for national competition laws. National competition law has to cover illicit agreements and abuse of dominant positions. Apart from this rather

---

[34] One should not overestimate the practice of young competition law jurisdictions in developing countries to cite precedents from developed competition law jurisdictions such as the US or the EU. This does not mean that these jurisdictions actually constitute the pacemakers of national competition law implementation. Rather, their legal precedents are referred to because of the dearth of competition law cases in the younger jurisdictions. Moreover, US and EU competition law cases are often cited in a superficial and non-systematic way. See also the Ecuadorian Pfizer case, which *inter alia* referred to Chilean case law; see Part II, Dimension II: Sect. 6.3.3.

[35] With regard to the leading jurisdictions in the AndeanC, see *De León*, An Institutional Assessment of Antitrust Policy, 2009, p. 82.

[36] According to *De León,* in the EU, the European Commission played the pacemaker role (top–down); *De León*, An Institutional Assessment of Antitrust Policy, 2009, p. 82. In fact, in the early stage of European competition law implementation only Germany possessed a functioning domestic competition law regime, *Monti,* EC Competition Law, 2007, p. 401.

[37] In fact, in the AndeanC and the CARICOM, regional competition law is designed after national competition laws (predominantly Peru, Colombia and Barbados, Jamaica). With regard to the AndeanC, see *De León*, An Institutional Assessment of Antitrust Policy, 2009, p. 82. Arguing in favour of harmonization bottom-up in the European Union at its initial stage, see *Dreher,* Kartellrechtsvielfalt oder Kartellrechtseinheit in Europa?, AG 437, 446f. (1993).

[38] In this context, Ecuador and Bolivia implemented national laws that are not harmonized with Decision 608. See above Part II, Dimension II: Sect. 6.3.3.

[39] For more details on "soft harmonization" see *Drexl,* Perspectives européennes sur la politique de la concurrence dans l'espace OHADA, XXV R.I.D.E. 281–304 (2011).

obvious finding, as regional competition law will mainly be aimed a state-imputed anticompetitive practices, it should also determine non-discriminatory treatment of public and private enterprises under national competition law. In the same vein, it should set out criteria for the granting of exemptions from national competition law in order to avoid circumvention based on merely national industry considerations and to further convergent competition law enforcement.[40] As limping liberalization and a low level of economic development are prominent features of developing countries, special sectorial rules and preferential treatment might still be appropriate.[41] In fact, in the course of balancing adaptability and convergence of regional competition law enforcement, the latter should not prevail at any expense in developing countries. In the course of assimilation of the member states' level of economic development, the range and criteria regarding exemptions from national competition law should become narrower over time. Yet, ideally, a regional legislative framework should also include provisions[42] that govern the relationship of regional competition law and sectorial or other rules that grant special treatment to less developed sectors or regions within the RTA.

12.2.3 Incentives for Member States to Harmonize National Substantive Competition Law

Generally, harmonization by itself in a regional competition law regime cannot compensate for the lack of political will of member states to support and cooperate in regional competition law enforcement. Instead of being taken as a goal by itself in RTAs among developing countries, harmonization is in particular beneficial in the context of a common market and as a means to attract FDI.[43] It will moreover enhance the implementation of competition laws in member states.[44] In developing as well as in developed countries, within an RTA, the determining factor for the progress of harmonization of competition laws is the intensity of inter-state trade and the relevance of the common market for member states. As the determining factors are weaker in developing countries than in their developed counterparts, a regional competition law system should give incentives for member states to further harmonization of national laws. Harmonization and inter-state trade correlate

[40] See also *Dreher*, who lists a number of basic competition law "structures" ("Kartellrechtliche Grundstrukturen") that contribute to the achievement of convergence in a competition law system; *Dreher*, in: *Forschungsinstitut für Wirtschaftsverfassung und Wettbewerb E.V.*, Umbruch der Wettbewerbsordnung in Europa, 1995, pp. 1, 6f.

[41] CARICOM has even made special and differential treatment one of the main principles of the Revised Treaty of Chaguaramas, Part II, Dimension I: Sect. 5.3.1.3.

[42] Apart from the mere primacy of regional law, see Part II, Dimension V: Sect. 9.2.

[43] Part III, Sect. 11.4.2.

[44] Part III, Sect. 11.4.1.

reciprocally, as harmonized national and regional competition laws facilitate cross-border trade.

CARICOM's experience shows that assistance from the regional level for member states during their competition law implementation process enhances harmonization of national laws.[45] Assistance can take the form of regional guidelines or a regional model competition law. In the process of spreading competition law knowledge such guidelines might shift from general competition law guidelines to specific enforcement issues. In particular in RTAs among developing countries, it can be useful to adopt guidelines outlining the most severe competition law infringements. The severity should be determined based on the specific developing countries' considerations, mainly the alleviation of poverty. Consequently, in particular bid-rigging and price-fixing might be considered as most severe anticompetitive practices.[46]

Similarly, cooperation during enforcement of regional competition law spreads knowledge on regional competition law and enhances an exchange of experiences. By learning from each other, horizontally or vertically, this will in the long run also contribute to a harmonization of enforcement measures and results. Close cooperation can be achieved in a formalized cooperation network.[47] Yet it is important for its success that meetings of national competition authorities take place regularly. At this point, it could be recommendable for the regional competition authority to exercise pressure and force the national institution to attend meetings of a cooperation network regularly.

The adoption of a "downloading option" is structurally conceived and capable of enhancing harmonization in member states without prior domestic competition laws. Yet the AndeanC's experience shows that the harmonizing incentive can be easily supressed by national interests and influences. Moreover, the actual application of a "downloading option" is bound by the prevailing national political will and the severity of resource constraints.[48] The concerns about the operational capability of the "downloading option", which *Francisco Marcos* aptly raised, regarding a lack of compatibility with the other national rules and institutions related to competition law, the risk of decreasing the credibility of Andean competition rules and the risk of impeding the adoption of national competition rules,[49] have so far not arisen in the AndeanC. Yet this is mostly attributed to the inconsistent and very superficial use of the "downloading option" in the AndeanC. One should thus not neglect the

---

[45] See above Part II, Dimension II: Sect. 6.2.

[46] *Weick,* Competition Law and Policy in Senegal, 33/3 W. Comp. 521, 539 (2010).

[47] With regard to the impact of the ECN in the European Union and Regulation 1/2003's impact on Spain and Portugal *Brokelmann* states: "What is more, the new regime-in particular Articles 3(2) and 16(2) of the Regulation exerts a strong harmonizing influence on the interpretation of national competition law. This is not only due to the coordination mechanisms foreseen in Regulation 1/2003 but certainly also to the fluent dialogue between competition authorities in the framework of the ECN." *Brokelmann,* Enforcement of Articles 81 and 82 EC under Regulation 1/2003, 29/4 W. Comp. 535, 553f. (2006).

[48] *Marcos,* in *Fox/Sokol,* Competition Law and Policy in Latin America, 2009, pp. 453, 462.

[49] *Marcos,* in *Fox/Sokol,* Competition Law and Policy in Latin America, 2009, pp. 453, 465ff.

potential for conflicts and danger if a "downloading option" is used more consistently and hence interdependencies between the "downloaded" and the "regional" competition law are stronger and more visible.

Finally, preliminary reference rulings regarding definitions of regional law can also promote harmonization. Yet in RTAs among developing countries the impact of preliminary reference rulings should not be overestimated, because here there is yet little private enforcement and little competition law knowledge and expertise among national judges. In this context, in a supranational and concurrent or parallel competition law enforcement system, it might be useful to vest national competition authorities with the power to address a regional court of justice in case they encounter difficulties in interpreting regional law.[50]

12.2.4 Regional Obligations on National Procedural Laws and the National Competition Law Authority's Design

The analysis of the WAEMU's, the AndeanC's and the CARICOM's institutional structure reveals different models with regard to the institutional design of a competition authority. Usually, the legal and institutional tradition of a country will determine the specific design. Although it might be difficult for the regional competition authority to identify the competent national authority among varying national institutional designs, regional competition law should not intervene in the internal structure and require a certain design.[51] Even if the competent national competition authority takes the form of a national regulatory agency or department thereof, internal mechanisms can provide for its operational independence in order to make decisions based on competition and economic efficiency considerations. Ideally, in the long run with the progress of economic development, all member states within an RTA should possess a national authority that is exclusively assigned to enforce competition law.[52]

Procedural autonomy appears to constitute a core area of national sovereignty. There are yet some minimum requirements with regard to the functioning of regional

[50] Actually, these criteria only apply to the AndeanC in the context of this research. See Part II, Dimension IV: Sect. 8.3.2.2. The question regarding the power to initiate a preliminary reference ruling is distinct from the question of which institution is competent to issue a decision in regional competition law. In the AndeanC, this is the Secretariat General's competence.

[51] See above with regard to the implications arising because of a certain institutional design of a competition authority, Part III, Dimension III: Sect. 12.3.

[52] In order to avoid the cost-intensive creation of specialized authorities, one might consider creating a mixed authority. In this context, the Fair Trading Commission in Barbados provides a positive example, in which efficiency gains were achieved through combining consumer and competition protection and utility regulation. On the other hand, mixed authorities can be problematic with regard to competition law enforcement, as other policies and law enforcement might be considered more important than competition law. For more information on the Fair Trading Commission in Barbados, see <http://www.ftc.gov.bb/> accessed 11 November 2018.

competition law enforcement. National institutions have to be endowed with sufficient powers to render competition law effective. On the one hand, this entails sufficient powers to actually enforce a regional competition authority's decision. On the other hand, minimum standards could require the national authority to provide for accessibility of the competition authority for private parties and the protection of their rights.[53] A regional framework could also include the obligation of national competition authorities to cooperate.[54] Yet as distrust among member states is large, the cooperation obligation should not be too far-reaching. In particular sensitive areas, for instance the handling of confidential information, should be regulated explicitly.

12.2.5 Horizontal Demarcation of Competences Between National Sector Regulation and Regional Competition Law

To address the relationship between regional competition law and national sectorial regulation constitutes a field in which the legal principles of primacy of regional law over national law and the primacy of *lex specialis* over *lex generalis* might clash. The same potential of conflict can arise between national competition-law-related fields of law, such as unfair competition, and regional competition law. A regional legislative framework should thus provide for rules to determine the competent jurisdiction. Moreover, national sector regulation agencies and the regional competition authority should in a first step identify potential scenarios in which clashes are likely to arise. In this context, special emphasis should be placed on the potential creation of entry barriers.[55] Generally, national sector regulation that only benefits a national industry and thereby creates entry barriers is capable of circumventing the application of regional competition law and might even hinder the functioning of a common market overall.

A different, but not alternative, approach is to further the development of a regional sector regulation framework that aims at the harmonization of national sector regulation. Minimum enhance their convergent application within the RTA. They might also avoid conflicts with regional objectives, mainly the creation of a common market with convergent rules on trade and economic policy. Moreover, a regional sector regulation framework can assist member states in the process of

[53] As private enforcement remains rare in developing countries, obligations for national legislators to adopt and apply specific procedural rules and provisions granting individuals' rights protection still constitute a theoretical issue.

[54] This is the case in the CARICOM: Article 170(3) of the Revised Treaty of Chaguaramas.

[55] See Recommendation No. 6 of *UNCTAD,* Voluntary Peer Review on Competition Policies of WAEMU, Benin and Senegal, 2008, p. 158.

liberalization by guaranteeing that national sector regulation accepts "certain principles essential to the existence of competition".[56]

Although the introduction of regional competition law furthers the establishment of new, or the strengthening of existing national competition authorities, it does not abolish national sectorial regulation.[57] Hence, with regard to an optimal use of limited resources, in particular technical expertise, a regional competition law framework should also include national sector regulation agencies, as well as other specialized agencies,[58] as possible cooperators in regional competition law enforcement. In the absence of a regional obligation to establish a national specialized competition authority, the national sector regulator might be the only national authority with competition law expertise and corresponding competences.

12.3 Dimension III: Implications Arising Out of the Institutional Design of a Regional Competition Authority

Regional competition law authorities are structurally bound to obtain greater independence in competition law enforcement than national authorities. Yet efficiency gains will depend on the specific institutional design of the regional authority. In the WAEMU, the AndeanC and the CARICOM, the systems vary regarding their institutional degree of independence—being part of a larger regional body or an independent authority—the degree of specification—varying from general, mixed or mere competition law agencies—and the institutions to which they are accountable.[59]

The neutrality of a regional competition authority towards state-related practices is only guaranteed under certain conditions.[60] A regional competition authority that is only composed of national politicians will tend to refer state-related measures to the national level. Such an authority might even refrain from enforcing regional competition law against state-imputed practices in general.[61] Likewise, decentralized

[56] *UNCTAD*, Voluntary Peer Review on Competition Policies of WAEMU, Benin and Senegal, 2008, p. 34.

[57] See above Part II, Dimension III: Sect. 7.2.2.

[58] For example consumer protection authorities, if they exist. In Jamaica, the national consumer protection authority works closely with the national competition authority by exchanging information. Statements made in an interview with the author by representatives from the Fair Trading Commission in Kingston, Jamaica, 17 October 2012.

[59] On the pros and cons of different institutional models of competition laws, see for example *Fox*, Antitrust and Institutions, 41 Loy. U. Chi. L. J. 473 (2010); *Trebilcock/Iacobucci*, Designing Competition Law Institutions, 41 Loy. U. Chi. L. J. 455 (2010).

[60] This is an additional and different difficulty to the struggle to keep political considerations out of competition law enforcement; see Part III, Sect. 11.4.

[61] In this context, the far-reaching enforcement of the COTED, which is composed of national ministers, has been criticized; see above Part II, Dimension IV: Sect. 8.2.2.

enforcement systems do not achieve greater independence as regards anticompetitive practices or state aids. Yet even regional competition authorities are not completely shielded from political pressures. Hence, the achievement of greater independence in competition law enforcement as regards state-related measures is correlated to the general will of the national governments to cede sovereignty (to the regional level).

The experiences of the WAEMU Commission, the Secretariat General and the CARICOM Competition Commission show that even regional competition authorities struggle and have to make an effort to keep political considerations out of competition law enforcement.[62] Although the authorities work relatively independently, they are not shielded from any political consideration in competition law enforcement.[63] Hence, the level of independence does not correlate with the institutional model that is adopted in the design of a regional competition authority, but depends on the interplay of regional institutions and the regional competition authority's commitment. Yet an authority that does not rely on staff exclusively responsible for competition law, as in the directorate model in the AndeanC, is more inclined to let political considerations influence competition law enforcement. Moreover, staff and resources will have to be traded among different fields of activity under a general directorate model. It appears that in the absence of initiatives coming from the member states, regional competition policy is prone to be superseded by other fields of economic and industrial policy, thereby rendering the regional competition authority more reactive than proactive.[64] This creates a vicious circle in which the member states and accordingly the regional authority refrain from furthering regional competition law enforcement.[65] On the other hand, there are efficiencies that stem from embedding regional competition law into broader policies related to the integration process and assigning regional staff to several fields.[66] Information-gathering will be easier, as general economic policy measures and competition law enforcement interrelate.

In the same vein, the decision between a mixed or an integrated competition law authority does not create clear efficiency benefits for regional competition law enforcement in developing countries.[67] This is especially the case because in

[62] This is not a particularity of developing countries, but also European competition enforcement was partly held to be too political; see *Fox,* Antitrust and Institutions, 41 Loy. U. Chi. L.J. 473, 477f. (2010).

[63] In the WAEMU, the WAEMU Commission has to take into account observations of the Directorate of Judicial Affairs and in the CARICOM, the COTED has far-reaching powers to supersede the scope of application of regional competition law.

[64] The Secretariat General had already been criticized under the former Decision 285 for adopting a too formalistic and legalistic interpretation of Andean law, see *De León*, An Institutional Assessment of Antitrust Policy, 2009, p. 82.

[65] With regard to a possible re-definition of the Secretariat General in the AndeanC regarding regional competition law enforcement, see below Part III, Sect. 13.2.

[66] *Fox,* Antitrust and Institutions, 41 Loy. U. Chi. L.J. 473, 484 (2010).

[67] Generally on the pros and cons of an integrated or separated institutional design of competition law and consumer law, see *Cseres,* Integrate or Separate. Institutional Design for the Enforcement

developing countries regional competition policy and consumer policy—if they exist at all—are generally very young. In the case where regional competition law and regional consumer law are implemented at the same time, as part of a broader holistic approach of regional integration,[68] establishment costs might be saved by only creating a mixed authority. This assumption should be handled with care, because long-term consequences have not been examined in developing countries. In the examined member states in this study both systems exist and did not encounter efficiency deficits based on the specific model.[69]

Another relevant factor to consider is the geographic location of a regional competition authority. The larger the number and territory of member states, the more difficult it is to spread the reputation of the regional authority and to provide for its accessibility. The selection should be carefully balanced with sovereignty issues and awareness of distrust among member states. Locating the regional competition authority within an economically dominant member state could even increase the latter's dominance. The selection of the location of the regional authority can also constitute a development measure to support a less developed member state.[70] However, the choice of the location also has to create sufficient incentives to attract qualified staff.

One can conclude that resources of a regional competition authority have to be proportionate to its assigned tasks. The larger the territorial scope of competition law, the more resources and the more commitment of national competition authorities to cooperate are necessary. In the same vein, a mixed authority will require more staff despite possible economies of scale by combining consumer law with competition law.[71] Moreover, a regional competition authority should be capable of setting priorities. This is particularly necessary with regard to limited resources. A regional competition authority in developing countries should prioritize those sectors that are particularly important for economic integration and for the special needs of developing countries. It should among other things conduct sectorial investigations on important sectors such as agriculture, food and beverages, but also infrastructure-related sectors, namely, cement, transportation and communication.[72]

---

of Competition Law and Consumer Law, 11 April 2013, pp. 1–51 <http://ssrn.com/abstract=2200908> accessed 11 November 2018.

[68] This was the case in the CARICOM. See above Part II, Dimension III: Sect. 7.1.1.

[69] The Barbadian competition authority is a mixed authority and is considered as one of the most efficient authorities within CARICOM.

[70] In the case of the CARICOM, the installation of the regional Commission in Suriname created job opportunities for Surinamese citizens.

[71] *Cseres,* Integrate or Separate. Institutional Design for the Enforcement of Competition Law and Consumer Law, 11 April 2013, pp. 33ff. <http://ssrn.com/abstract=2200908> accessed 11 November 2018.

[72] According to *Zoghbi*, the main factors that should be considered by competition authorities in prioritising work and identifying the most damaging practises are also the likelihood of competitive harm, the resources needed for the investigation, the size and the importance of the relevant market, the deterrent value of pursuing, other aggravating factors and policy considerations. See *Zoghbi*, in: *Mehta/Evenett*, Politics Triumphs Economics?, 2009, pp. 89, 93ff.

12.4 Dimension IV: Measures to Shape Competition Enforcement Procedures

12.4.1 Regional Competition Law Investigations

Efficient regional competition law enforcement depends on regular market surveillance with regard to competition law breaches. Depending on the territorial scope of application of regional competition law, on the territory of an RTA or on the economic diversity of member states, this can be a very resource-intensive task.[73] Thus, even under a centralized system, market surveillance should always be shared between regional and national competition authorities and conducted on a constant and parallel basis.[74] This requires that member states—despite the tendency to focus on the monitoring of their own territory with regard to national anticompetitive practices—transfer cases to the regional authority if they consider them to have a regional impact.[75] Vice versa, in the absence of a unified competition law within an RTA, a regional competition authority should transfer cases to national authorities if it considers them to have a solely national effect. How can a regional competition law system incite such shared monitoring and which are the main addressees of such incentives?

12.4.1.1 Right-Holders to Request an Investigation

National competition authorities have to be vested with the right to request investigations from the regional competition authority. A shared monitoring function with national competition authorities further preconditions that they have sufficient knowledge about regional competition law. The latter is either achieved through a detailed and rich regional case law—unfeasible in young regional competition law regimes—or by advocacy and technical training conducted on the regional level. Moreover, participation of national competition authorities in a formalized cooperation network can enhance the sharing of the monitoring task of the common market.[76]

---

[73] Part II, Dimension IV: Sect. 8.1.1.

[74] Even in an RTA with a very small territory and a limited number of member states, such as the OECS, monitoring functions should be shared. If national competition authorities and national competition law systems were completely substituted by the regional competition law system, monitoring functions would still be shared with organisations on the national level.

[75] This could be described as concurrent market surveillance.

[76] See below on differences between institutional designs of cooperation organ, Part III, Dimension IV: Sect. 12.4.6.

Direct Accessibility of the Regional Competition Authority for the Private Sector

Direct accessibility of the regional competition authority for private complainants does not constitute a *sine qua non* condition for enhanced participation of the private sector in regional competition law enforcement.[77] Generally, private parties might prefer to deal with national authorities, even if electronic access to the regional authority is guaranteed and language issues are not a problem. This can create a vicious circle in which reluctant national competition authorities will not refer cases of the private sector to the regional authority and the private sector, in the absence of regional precedents, will not develop a competition culture with regard to regional competition law. This difficulty calls for competition advocacy by the regional authority targeting organizations of the private sector, for instance national manufacturers or consumer associations. There is a strong argument for including these groups in the list of parties that are entitled to bring complaints to the regional authority. As regional competition law culture grows, individuals might be more inclined to contact the regional competition authority directly. The necessity to recognize a right to complain of private parties correlates with the level of regional competition culture in the private sector. Moreover, private parties will only actively seek regional competition law enforcement, if regional competition law affects them at all. This however preconditions a relatively advanced stage of the common market, in which market distortions are not predominantly limited to state-related restraints.

Hence, the weaker the commitment of national competition authorities to cooperate with the regional competition authority, the greater the necessity to provide for direct accessibility of the regional competition authority for private businesses and individuals. Although only few individuals or private businesses will utilize direct access, as most private parties will prefer to deal with competition law matters nationally, direct access has to be guaranteed in order to circumvent national competition authorities' discretion in case they refrain from transferring regional competition law cases. In an ideal scenario, in which national commitment towards regional competition law enforcement is strong, national competition authorities could decide upon the existence of a regional effect of an alleged anticompetitive practice.[78] This will provide for a high degree of accessibility, while saving resources of the regional competition authority at the same time. However, especially in developing countries, competition law expertise and other resources among national competition authorities are scarce. The adequate and correct determination of the actual existence of a potential regional effect can thus not be guaranteed.

[77] See on the problem of accessibility and private enforcement Part III, Sect. 11.8.

[78] Possibly, the national competition authority could also determine whether a different national competition authority should have jurisdiction to deal with the matter. Yet cases with effects limited to the territory of one state will, however, rarely be brought to the authority.

Ex Officio Power of a Regional Competition Authority to Initiate Investigations

It has been highlighted in this study that the regional competition authority has to be vested with sufficient powers in order to function and develop expertise in the field of competition law enforcement. In this context, one has to highlight the importance of vesting the regional authority with an *ex officio* right to initiate investigations. In fact the former Andean Decision 285 did confer such powers to the regional authority[79] and far-reaching interventionist rights of national authorities or organs might similarly hamper a possible *ex officio* right.[80] An *ex officio* right is of particular importance with regard to state-related anticompetitive practices, against which national competition authorities might be reluctant to initiate investigations.

Yet especially young regional competition authorities should handle the *ex officio* investigation power with care. Cautious use is justified in the light of a relatively high degree of uncertainty with regard to the information at hand, but also with regard to the efficiency of cooperation with national competition authorities. This positions a young regional competition authority in a difficult position. In the course of gaining reputation, especially in its early phase of operation, a regional competition authority can risk impeding its long-term functioning through bad cases and inefficient procedures. Moreover, as competition culture will also be undeveloped at an early phase, the required level of justification of its actions is still very high, in contrast to a competition authority that has already gained reputation. It is thus recommendable for young regional competition authorities to rely on complaints or requests from other public bodies.[81] For the lack of private enforcement, such requests are most likely to originate from national competition authorities, national competition-related institutions or other regional institutions. It is thus useful to allow a broad array of national and regional institutions to submit complaints to the regional competition authority.

[79] Article 6 of Decision 285.

[80] In the CARICOM, according to Article 176(1) of the Revised Treaty of Chaguaramas, national competition authorities have to undertake a preliminary examination of a business conduct in case the CARICOM Competition Commission invokes its *ex officio* right. Moreover, in case of disputes, it is the COTED that resolves the matter, see Article 176(5) of the Revised Treaty of Chaguaramas. See also Rule 9(2) of the CARICOM Competition Commission Rules of Procedure 2011.

[81] In the AndeanC, the Secretariat General did not initiate *ex officio* investigations in the absence of submitted requests, in contrast to the European Commission, which investigated a number of delicate cases despite opposition from member states. See *Botta,* The Role of Competition Policy in the Latin American Regional Integration: A Comparative Analysis of CARICOM, Andean Community and Mercosur, 21–22 October 2011, St. Gallen. For an overview of the activities based on the initiative (20%) of the European Commission in 1996, see *Cini/McGowan,* Competition Policy in the European Union, 2008, p. 101. Yet the European Commission had greater support with regard to regional competition law enforcement and the commitment to economic integration was generally larger than in the AndeanC.

Competence to Decide on Cross-Border Effect

Closely linked to the *ex officio* initiation power of a regional competition authority is the allocation of the competence to decide on the existence of cross-border effect.[82] However, one has to be clear that actual conflicts regarding the existence of cross-border effects only arise in the case that a national authority attempts to apply national competition law with a result that conflicts with regional competition law. National authorities might be particularly inclined to apply national competition laws if national interests or issues of sovereignty are at stake. Completely decentralizing this decision, i.e. allowing a national institution to make a decision in case of such a dispute, entails the danger of undermining the regional competition law enforcement. It could in particular hamper uniform and non-discriminatory application of the regional law if the national authority decides every case on the basis of national competition law. Moreover, in a scenario in which an institution composed of several representatives of member states jointly decides, the larger the number of member states, the slower a consensus-finding process will be, thereby slowing down competition law enforcement. On the other hand, generally centralizing the decision-making powers on cross-border effects leads to a situation, in which the regional authority has to decide on every matter related to competition law. This is highly inefficient, as it would waste resources as exemplified by the WAEMU experience.

In order to solve the particular situation of disagreement between a national and the regional competition authority, the separation of decision-making and dispute-resolving competence might constitute a feasible solution. Generally, under the principle of direct application of regional competition law, a national authority should be entitled to autonomously decide on the existence of a cross-border effect. In addition, the RTA should install a separate dispute-resolution mechanism, for example before a regional court of justice. Alternatively, the regional competition law authority could have prerogative power to make a decision, which however can be challenged before the regional court. Ideally, in a regional court of justice all affected parties feel sufficiently and adequately represented and their interests are equally taken into consideration. The regional court of justice can usually only decide whether the regional competition authority has acted *ultra vires*.[83] The regional court of justice or any other independent dispute resolution institution that is recognized by member states could also be vested with the discretion to assign the competent authority directly, rather than merely controlling if the authority concerned was the competent one to deal with the matter.

[82] Given that the scope of application of regional competition law relies on such a condition, as recommended by this study. See above Part III, Dimension I: Sect. 12.1.1.

[83] Part II, Dimension IV: Sect. 8.3.

12.4.1.2 Prior Notification Requirements

The less cooperation takes place between regional and national competition authorities, the more effort the regional authority has to make to acquire information on potentially anticompetitive practices. In this context, the introduction of a prior notification obligation appears as a useful instrument during the initiation phase of a regional competition law authority to gather information directly from market participants.

Prior notification requirements in the European Union were necessary in order to seek an individual exception from regional competition law, for which the European Commission held the exclusive competence before the enactment of Regulation no. 1/2003. However, this European prior notification requirement became inefficient due to the amount of required resources based on the extremely large number of submitted notifications. This did not only result from a large number of practices that fell under the scope of application of European competition law, but particularly resulted from the extensive use of the notification system by undertakings in order to achieve legal certainty.

As regards RTAs among developing countries good arguments can be brought forward in favour of introducing prior notifying requirements for undertakings before engaging in a potentially anticompetitive practice. Yet in particular a high level of required resources as demonstrated by the European experience as well as other disadvantages have to be taken into account. In theory, the larger the geographical area of application of regional competition law, the larger the number of submitted notifications and the larger the required resources will be. Given the relatively low level of intra-community trade within RTAs among developing countries, one might question if a similar scenario is likely to occur in the near future, as interstate trade and the range for the application of regional law remains limited. Moreover, a large territorial scope of application and prior notification procedures must not always be incompatible. Rather, a regional competition authority will then have to develop prioritization schemes that enable it to accelerate decisions. In the EU, block exemptions for unproblematic cases proved to be particularly helpful. Block exemptions should be adopted in cooperation with national competition authorities. Decision 608 demonstrates that a mandatory involvement of a specialized competition law body such as the Andean Committee on the Defence of Free Competition, composed of representatives of member states, can balance regional and national interests at stake and can guarantee that the adopted block exemptions serve the interests of the RTA.[84] Block exemptions could thus be drafted by such an institution. This moreover allows for an efficient use of existing competition law knowledge and learning processes upwards and downwards.

[84] This is clearly set out in the Guidelines regarding the application of Decision 608 in the AndeanC, *Secretaría General de la Comunidad Andina,* Guía Práctica para la aplicación de la Decisión 608 "Normas para la protección y promoción de la libre competencia en la Comunidad Andina", 2007, p. 21.

In the long run, decentralized enforcement as in the European Union, might become more feasible and allow for abolishing prior notification requirements. In the absence of prior notification requirements the private businesses bear the responsibility to assess whether a respective practice is compatible with regional competition law. This requires once again a developed competition culture within the private sector and the existence of a broad array of regional legal precedents of decentralized enforcement. Ideally, it also preconditions a strong commitment by national competition authorities to regional competition law enforcement, which might provide for assistance to private businesses regarding the self-assessment under regional competition law.

12.4.2 Conducting Regional Competition Law Investigations

Generally, it is advisable to share the conduct of competition law investigations and to rely on existing national administrative structures. There are different degrees of centralization and decentralization in regional competition law enforcement regarding the degree of independence and the range of involvement of national competition authorities in investigations on regional competition law.

One has to differentiate the degree of centralization or decentralization in regional competition law enforcement from the possibility to conduct parallel investigations under national competition law.[85] Likewise, the conduct of regional competition law investigations is closely linked to the degree of decentralization or centralization of the decision-making competence.[86] In the absence of decentralized decision-making, national competition authorities are bound by a regional authority's decision and its instructions. National authorities are similarly bound by the final decision-making power of the regional competition authority after the authority has exercised its possible prerogative power to deal with a matter.[87]

Investigations regarding regional competition law without the assistance of national competition authorities are difficult to imagine, in particular in developing countries, in which resources are generally scarce. Ideally, investigations should be carried out in close and constant cooperation between national and regional competition authorities.[88] This requires that regional and national competition authorities share information. It also requires regional and national investigation procedures to be coordinated to a certain extent. While they do not necessarily have to be

[85] For more information on the principle of primacy of regional law in exclusive, concurrent or parallel competition law enforcement, see Part III, Dimension V: Sect. 12.5.4.

[86] The degree of centralization or decentralization of the decision-making competence will be dealt with below, see Part III, Dimension IV: Sect. 12.4.3.

[87] This is the case in the European competition law system; Art. 11(6) of Council Regulation (EC) 1/2003.

[88] In the WAEMU, Article 28(2) of Regulation no. 03/2002/CM/UEMOA.

completely harmonized,[89] two independent investigation procedures concerning a potential breach of competition law should not contradict each other in basic points, which could affect legal certainty. This in particular includes certain time frames for investigations or compliance obligations for the targeted enterprise.

Alternatively, national competition authorities might only be allowed to assist in individual cases with regard to specific investigative measures. Such selective participation might avoid conflicts in procedural requirements and provide a clear time frame. It might also alleviate the investigations carried out by young and inexperienced national competition authorities. Yet depending on the remaining discretion of national authorities, limited assistance in the framework of investigations can conflict with the principle of procedural autonomy and might raise issues of national sovereignty.[90] Reducing national competition authorities to mere auxiliary bodies to the regional competition authority could thus lead to political resentment and reluctance to cooperate in the long run.

For the limited data and case law in the WAEMU, the AndeanC and the CARICOM, in particular with regard to the conduct of specific enforcement measures, it is difficult to make general comments on the optimal degree of discretion attributed to national competition authorities during investigations. In systems in which national competition authorities are vested with general and unspecific investigation powers, regional competition law enforcement will heavily rely on reciprocal information obligations. Information should not only be shared vertically, but also horizontally between member states. This however requires a strong commitment of member states to regional competition law enforcement and the integration process overall. Similarly, the regional competition authority is mandated to respect information obligations in order to safeguard the interests of the member states. In this context, cooperation networks become even more important and useful, because they are able to allow for close and constant cooperation and information sharing between national competition authorities and the regional authority. The more discretion national competition authorities have during investigations on breaches of regional competition law, the more formalized and constant meetings and coordination via a competition cooperation network should take place.[91] As a middle course between decentralized and centralized regional competition law investigations, investigations by national competition authorities should be governed by a regional procedural framework that determines the core investigation powers of national authorities and certain time frames. This increases legal certainty and avoids conflicts of investigation measures while respecting the member states' procedural autonomy.[92]

---

[89] Part III, Sect. 11.4.

[90] See Part II, Dimension V: Sect. 9.4.

[91] See on the cooperation mechanisms with national competition law structures Part III, Dimension IV: Sect. 12.4.6.

[92] In this context, the Plan of Investigation in the AndeanC is a positive example. It is capable of balancing national and regional interests, because it is determined by national and regional competition authorities; see above Part II, Dimension IV: Sect. 8.2.

12.4.3 Decision-Making Power and Enforcement

Decentralizing decision-making competences in the EU took a long time. Its success depended on various preconditions, namely a relatively well-developed competition culture and competition structures in member states throughout the region, an important and strong common market and the corresponding commitment to it by member states, and a large number of regional competition law precedents. While in RTAs among developing countries implementation of national competition law structures is forging ahead, especially the progress of economic integration and the spread of a competition culture takes place at a much slower pace. Decentralizing the decision-making competence thus only appears feasible at a more progressed state of competition culture and economic integration.

One can differentiate between exclusive and parallel decision-making competences with regard to breaches of regional and national competition law. In a system of parallel decision-making of national competition authorities with regard to breaches of national competition law, there is no exclusive area of applicability of regional competition law.[93]

In the context of a strong tendency towards national protectionism and the attempt to achieve convergent competition law application in an RTA, parallel decision-making on national and regional competition law breaches requires coordination of decisions.[94] Undertakings engaging in trade within an RTA depend on legal certainty and should be capable of complying with decisions of all competition authorities.[95] This does not only refer to the decisions as such, on allowing or prohibiting a certain conduct, but also to enforcement measures. Advanced and far-reaching vertical and horizontal harmonization will avoid many conflicts.[96] The principle of primacy of regional law and a loyalty clause can also solve remaining conflicts.[97]

Yet one should not neglect the particular needs of developing countries in competition law enforcement and the importance of maintaining flexibility within regional competition law enforcement.[98] Within the boundaries of the regional

---

[93] *Geradin,* A Legal and Economic Analysis of the Proposed Modernization of the Enforcement of EC Competition Law, 9/1 Colum. J. Eur. L. 1, 11 (2002).

[94] The current chairman of the CARICOM Competition Commission, *Kusha Haraksingh*, does not see the necessity to reconcile national and regional decision-making. Statements made in an interview with the author conducted in Port-of-Spain, Trinidad and Tobago, 29 October 2012.

[95] This is obviously not the case if the national and regional decisions completely contradict each other.

[96] *Geradin,* A Legal and Economic Analysis of the Proposed Modernization of the Enforcement of EC Competition Law, 9/1 Colum. J. Eur. L. 1, 11 (2002).

[97] See Article 3(1)1 of Regulation no. 1/2003/EC and the former judgement, ECJ, Judgment of the Court of 13 February 1969, Case 14-68, *Walt Wilhelm and others v Bundeskartellamt,* ECR 1, ECLI:EU:C:1969:4, para. 9.

[98] On the importance of preserving flexibility in the framework of a regional competition law structure, see Part III, Sect. 11.10.

standards, national competition authorities should be allowed to apply special and differential treatment in the case of competition law breaches. These special provisions should however only be provided for a transitional period in particular with regard to breaches of regional competition law. As in the European Union, national competition law might be stricter or deviate from regional laws as long as efficient regional competition law enforcement is not affected. It might thus be advisable for the regional legislature to adopt rules or guidelines that clarify the scope and application of differential treatment in the case of regional and national competition law infringements.[99]

Despite varying degrees of competition law experience and differing degrees of efficiency of domestic competition law structures, actual conflicts of sanctioning measures or conflicting decisions seem to be of minor concern in RTAs among developing countries. This might be due to the fact that conflicts between regional and national enforcement measures are only possible in competition law enforcement systems in which national and regional competition law can be applied in parallel. In systems, in which decisions under the regional law are enforced on a national level, conflicts of enforcement measures can always arise horizontally, for example sanctions at hand might vary between member states or national competition authorities might even lack sufficient powers or skills to enforce the regional decision. In order to avoid extreme inconsistencies or loopholes, which might backfire to the regional competition authority and are capable of increasing distrust between member states, the regional framework should provide for standards or guidelines. They should in particular set out the core powers of national competition authorities. Guidelines can also clarify possible fining and sanctioning schemes.

12.4.4 The Enforcement of Individual Exceptions

Related to the decision-making power of a regional competition authority is the competence to grant individual exceptions from regional competition law. Yet conflicts can only arise in a system of parallel competition law enforcement, in which national authorities are entitled to apply regional competition law directly. This degree of decentralized competition law enforcement is more feasible at an advanced stage of competition law enforcement of national and regional competition law authorities.

Although good arguments speak in favour of vesting a regional competition authority with exclusive decision-making rights on individual exceptions, one should still refrain from dividing the general application of regional competition law from decisions on possible individual exceptions to it.

Generally, it is argued that vesting the regional competition authority with an exclusive right to decide on individual exceptions enables the authority to develop

[99] In the EU, according to Regulation 1/2003 member states are allowed to adopt stricter laws on unilateral anticompetitive agreements.

clear application criteria with regard to possible exceptions of regional competition law.[100] It can thereby also contribute to the uniform application of exceptions and avoids forum shopping. Member states might lack sufficient expertise and resources to apply individual exceptions adequately. The preponderance of state-owned enterprises moreover increases the vulnerability of national competition authorities and national judges to national political lobbying and corruption. Especially in the absence of clear-cut exception criteria, which have to be developed on the regional level based on regional competition law cases, individual exceptions could be used to create loopholes for national industry protection at the expense of liberalization. Yet these arguments mainly apply to young competition law jurisdictions in which competition culture is generally weak. In such inexperienced jurisdictions the aspect of legal certainty is of paramount importance for market participants, as well as for law-enforcing institutions, which are still in the learning phase.[101] However, recalling that efficient parallel enforcement of regional competition law generally requires a relatively progressed stage of competition law experience, the arguments in favour of centralizing the decision-making power on individual exceptions are less compelling.

More pressing in RTAs between developing countries is the lack of resources. The European experience demonstrated that enterprises tended to refer to the European Commission directly in order to receive an individual exception, which provided them with greater legal certainty. This clearly undermines efficiencies that are supposed to arise under a system of parallel regional competition law enforcement. Moreover, a large territorial scope of application of regional competition law even aggravates the problem of resource constraints.

In the same vein, block exemptions are a possible measure to address resource constraints. They do not only contribute to a faster processing of unproblematic cases, but also offer guidance for national competition authorities that still lack competition law experience. Block exemptions should be formulated in close cooperation between regional and national competition authorities in order to guarantee consistent application.

Generally, close cooperation between the national and regional level regarding the formulation of guidelines on the application of exceptions and exemptions, as well as cooperation regarding the specific enforcement, will also increase the awareness of private parties regarding the regional authority. In fact, addressing a regional authority might constitute an obstacle for requests originating from private businesses, as they might prefer to deal with more familiar national institutions. Cooperation is thus an instrument to legitimize the regional authority's decisions from the perspective of the national private sector.

---

[100] See the development of European competition law, in which the notification requirement was replaced by decentralized self-evaluation in the course of increased competition law culture.

[101] According to *Ehlermann* the Commission's monopoly to grant exemptions constituted a "natural" monopoly for its ability to reconcile several objectives of the EC Treaty, see *Ehlermann*, Implementation of EC Competition Law by National Anti-Trust Authorities, 17 ECLR 88, 95 (1996).

12.4.5 Private Enforcement Before National Judiciary

Systems of direct effect and application of regional law, in which the regional competition law provides for direct nullity of anticompetitive agreements, require clarification.[102] If direct effect incorporates vertical as well as horizontal effects, such systems would actually allow national judges and authorities to directly determine the nullity of a practice based on a breach of regional competition law. However, principles of direct effect and application do not impair regional competition law systems from requiring a decision of the regional competition authority as a constituent condition for the establishment of nullity.[103]

In the case of decentralized damage actions, but centralized decision-making,[104] the national judge will find him—or herself in a situation in which he or she has to take a partly autonomous decision.[105] Despite a breach of regional law, damages are compensated in accordance with national laws. A national judge might face problems of evidence, because he or she has to rely on the decision of another institution to which different procedural rules, especially on producing evidence, apply.[106] National judges should thus be able to request information within the boundaries of appropriate confidentiality rules from the regional authority.[107]

National enforcement of criminal and civil law liability originating from an anticompetitive practice additionally bears the risk of diverging decisions in the member states. In the absence of an obligation to make competition law infringements criminal offences, criminal consequences vary between member states. However, even if member states criminalize competition law infringements, actual enforcement might vary. With regard to criminal offences, the competition law terms such as "agreement" and "abuse of dominant position" have to be translated into terms of domestic criminal law.[108] This might be problematic, because the competition law terms might *inter alia* not comply with the constitutional requirements of criminal

[102] The WAEMU and the EU constitute such systems.

[103] This is the case in the WAEMU, see Part II, Dimension V: Sect. 9.1. For more information see also *Bakhoum,* L'articulation du droit communautaire et des droits nationaux de la concurrence dans l'Union Economique et Monétaire Ouest Africaine, 2007, pp. 56f.

[104] In a regional legal system of direct effect and application, in which regional competition law provides for direct nullity of anticompetitive practices, centralized decision-making only applies to the competence to grant exemptions or issue negative clearance rulings.

[105] For example, a judge has to autonomously estimate the amount of compensation or decide on the intensity of the specific criminal sanction.

[106] With regard to WAEMU see *Bakhoum,* L'articulation du droit communautaire et des droits nationaux de la concurrence dans l'Union Economique et Monétaire Ouest Africaine, 2007, p. 245.

[107] See request for information in the WAEMU, the AndeanC and the CARICOM. For more information on enforcement procedures of regional competition law in the narrow sense, Part II, Dimension IV: Chap. 8.

[108] *Bakhoum,* L'articulation du droit communautaire et des droits nationaux de la concurrence dans l'Union Economique et Monétaire Ouest Africaine, 2007, pp. 86ff.

law offences.[109] Moreover, in order to confirm criminal liability, a person has to fulfil a certain degree of objective and subjective responsibility with regard to the anticompetitive practice. National legislations and authorities might differ in this "translation process". Consequently, in some member states individuals may not be criminally liable for anticompetitive behaviour at all.[110] In others, criminal punishment might be very strict and even lead to imprisonment.[111] In the same vein, preconditions for the attainment of civil law damages might vary.[112] Irrespective of the inclusion of principles such as effectiveness[113] and equivalence,[114] a discrepancy in national procedural requirements for private actions hinders uniform enforcement of a regional authority's decision.[115] If individuals are free to decide on the competent national court, the discrepancy might additionally lead to "forum-shopping" among domestic courts, based on their requirements for private civil or criminal law claims. The discrepancy is even aggravated by different levels of competition law expertise among member states.

Nevertheless, substituting decentralized optional criminal and civil law enforcement based on a breach of regional competition law by regional enforcement does not constitute a politically feasible solution. This is particularly the case in developing countries in RTAs that have been very keen to protect their sovereignty. In addition, it would demolish efficiencies generated by the reliance on existing national procedural and administrative structures. Moreover, from the individuals' or private businesses' perspective, national enforcement of private claims entails certain advantages: national courts are usually easier to access by individuals and, in contrast to an infringement procedure before a regional competition authority, the national judiciary usually provides for cost allocation rules for legal expenses between the winning and the losing party.[116] Having said that, this does not determine the amount of competences national judges should be vested with, in particular whether they should have to await a decision by the regional competition authority.[117]

Dualist systems generally do not allow national judges to apply regional competition law directly, because treaty provisions require its incorporation in domestic

---

[109] *Bakhoum,* L'articulation du droit communautaire et des droits nationaux de la concurrence dans l'Union Economique et Monétaire Ouest Africaine, 2007, pp. 89ff.

[110] *Bakhoum,* L'articulation du droit communautaire et des droits nationaux de la concurrence dans l'Union Economique et Monétaire Ouest Africaine, 2007, pp. 95f.

[111] *Ibid.*

[112] On the different requirements in Member States of the European Union, see *Davies/Das,* Private Enforcement of Commission Commitment Decisions, 29 Fordham Int'l. L.J. 917, 947ff. (2005).

[113] On the principles of effectiveness and equivalence, see Part II, Dimension V: Sect. 9.3.

[114] Part II, Dimension V: Sect. 9.3.

[115] *Davies/Das,* Private Enforcement of Commission Commitment Decisions, 29 Fordham Int'l. L.J. 917, 947 (2005).

[116] *Temple Lang,* EEC Competition Actions in Member States' Courts, 7 Fordham Int'l. L.J. 389, 453 (1983).

[117] On the role of national judges in private enforcement of regional competition law, see Part III, Sect. 11.8.2.

law. Consequently, even in case of a breach of regional competition law, private parties will have to enforce remedies solely on the basis of national procedural and national law. In order to enhance convergent application and remedies for breach of regional competition law, the regional law should oblige member states to adopt certain standards for the private parties' damage claims. Possibly, private parties will have to address the regional court of justice on the grounds that a member state has not complied with its treaty obligations.

Yet the question requires an answer in supranational systems. The attribution of national judges with the competence to decide on regional competition law matters, including exemptions, without any involvement of the regional competition authority should only remain a long-term option under the prerequisite that member states have had the chance to gather their own competition law experience and under the prerequisite that the regional competition authority has developed regional competition law precedents. Generally, the more discretion national judges are vested with in competition law enforcement, the higher the quality and impartiality of judges has to be.[118] Finally, it will also be the prevailing legal tradition and the willingness to recourse to the judiciary that will determine the actual efficiency of private regional competition law enforcement.[119]

12.4.6 Cooperation Mechanisms with National Competition Law Structures

In the context of regional competition law enforcement, cooperation mechanisms mainly aim at enhanced cooperation between national competition authorities on the one hand (horizontal cooperation) and the regional competition authority on the other hand (vertical cooperation). While during investigations, the main functions embrace the exchange and sharing of information on allegedly anticompetitive practices, cooperation networks could also engage in policy-making and could thereby contribute to the development and adaptability of regional competition law. Finally, cooperation mechanisms can enhance convergence of national competition laws and national procedures and sanctioning powers of national competition authorities.[120]

---

[118] In the European Union, the role of national judges with regard to competition law enforcement was promoted from the early 1980s, *Ehlermann,* Implementation of EC Competition Law by National Anti-Trust Authorities, 17 ECLR 88, 88f. (1996).

[119] *Ehlermann* states in this context: "Europeans are not as litigious as Americans: their traditional social and cultural attitudes may even be opposed to recourse to the judiciary." *Ehlermann,* Implementation of EC Competition Law by National Anti-Trust Authorities, 17 ECLR 88, 89 (1996).

[120] This was the case in the context of the ECN and Regulation 1/2003 in the European Union. See *Wils,* Ten Years of Regulation 1/2003, 4 J. Eur. Comp. L. & Practice 293, 296 (2013).

The general degree of centralized or decentralized competition law enforcement contours the internal structure of a cooperation entity and vice versa. In this context, the invocation of cooperation bodies in the WAEMU and the AndeanC correlated to the general degree of centralization or decentralization of regional competition law enforcement.[121] Although the dogma "one size does not fit all" applies to inter-governmental cooperation as well, certain prerequisites for the internal structure can be listed: a minimum quorum, a majority vote in case of recommendations on specific cases, sufficient time to prepare sessions, accountability and liability provisions, an invocation right for the national and regional level, possibly with certain requirements or limitations. While requirements such as a minimum quorum or sufficient preparation time will guarantee that the decision taken within the cooperation forum actually reflects the interests of a large number or majority of present member states, majority votes and conditions for the invocation right avoid an abusive hollowing-out or slowing-down of the functioning of the cooperative body. Another precondition is the inclusion of provisions on the protection of confidential information.

The notion of "cooperation mechanism" in regional competition law enforcement can have many meanings.[122] Hence, instead of making general conclusions on the impact of certain institutional designs of a cooperation mechanism, it is more appropriate to look at specific features that impact the degree of centralization or decentralization.

The most significant feature concerns the bindingness on the regional competition authority of decisions of the cooperation body. While it appears to be by definition that cooperation bodies lack decision-making powers, the degree of bindingness on the regional competition authority can still vary. Obligations for the regional authority to explain divergences from the cooperation entity's decision might increase the weight of the latter's decision, although decision-making remains centralized. Actually, the obligation to explain divergences aims at guaranteeing an element of cooperation that should be intrinsic in a cooperation mechanism: namely, that the regional competition authority actually considers the cooperation body' observations or decisions. The latter will usually reflect considerations and interests of member states. Explanation obligations for the regional competition authority will thus prove useful in situations in which member states fear to not be sufficiently represented in regional competition law enforcement. Such a situation appears to be typically prominent if member states distrust each other, for example based on different levels of economic development or in situations in which economic integration is proceeding at a slow pace. Moreover, if the cooperation entity is the only possibility for member states to express their considerations, this also calls for explanation obligations. In sum, the more centralized the regional competition law enforcement is, the higher is the relevance of the cooperation body. Yet far-reaching

[121] See Part II, Dimension IV: Sect. 8.2.1.3.

[122] This is demonstrated by the different institutional designs and results of such mechanisms in the WAEMU, the AndeanC and the CARICOM, as well as in the EU. See above Part II, Dimension IV: Sect. 8.2.

explanation obligations for the regional competition authority entail the risk of slowing down the overall enforcement process and do not rule out that the regional authority will only fulfil its obligation superficially.[123]

The stagnation of meetings of the Andean Committee on the Defence of Free Competition resulted from the reluctance of member states to invoke the Committee. This raises the question whether extensive formal requirements foster cooperation through a network. Mandatory participation in cooperation networks does not automatically achieve efficient cooperation. Rather, effective incentives for an active participation of national competition authorities in regional competition law enforcement relate to the importance of the common market. For example, member states will usually fear that their absence will lead to insufficient representation of national interests in the decision-making process[124] or indirect economic repercussions. Such a scenario moreover decreases the need for supervision and invocation by the regional authority. On the other hand, a certain degree of formalism appears necessary in order to enhance cooperation. In fact, the less prior horizontal cooperation existed between national competition authorities, the more formal the internal design of a cooperation mechanism should be.[125]

Moreover, while cooperation bodies allow for enhanced vertical cooperation, they do not guarantee the emergence of horizontal cooperation between national competition authorities. This is on the one hand correlated with the lack of interdependencies and prevailing distrust between RTAs among developing countries and on the other hand to the actual inexistence of effective national competition authorities.[126] In the same vein, there is no unambiguous finding with regard to enhanced harmonization of national competition and procedural laws through a cooperation network. While some newly implemented competition law regimes mirrored the regional provisions, the main determinants for harmonization are the prevailing

---

[123] This happened in the AndeanC, in which the Secretariat General treated the Informe of the Andean Committee on Defence of Free Competition only superficially. See above Part II, Dimension IV: Sect. 8.2.1.2.

[124] Another difficulty with regard to insufficient representation within a competition cooperation body concerns the unequal distribution of investigatory assignments among member states. In this context, *Andreas Mundt,* the current president of the German competition authority since 2009, mentioned that in the framework of the ECN the German competition authority is called upon comparably often in order to conduct investigations. According to *Mundt,* this relates to its geographical position at the centre of the European Union. With an increase of intra-community trade, this unequal distribution of investigations assignments based on geographical location of states might also arise in the WAEMU and the AndeanC. In the CARICOM, due to its composition of islands, which requires trade to be conducted by plane or ship, this problem might be less relevant.

[125] *Cengiz,* The European Competition Network, 2009, pp. 9, 10 <http://cadmus.eui.eu/bitstream/handle/1814/11067/MWP_2009_05.pdf?sequence=1> accessed 11 November 2018. For more information on cooperation mechanisms, see also Part II, Dimension IV: Sect. 8.2.

[126] On the creation of vertical and horizontal cooperation via inter-governmental cooperation bodies, see Part II, Dimension IV: section "Creating Vertical and Horizontal Cooperation via Inter-Governmental Cooperation Bodies".

national economic system and the commitment to economic integration, rather than the participation in a cooperation network.[127]

Furthermore, the attributed range of tasks led to different outcomes. General political cooperation entities tend to support and facilitate national implementation processes of competition law and they might participate in competition policy-making. On the other hand, specialized competition cooperation entities in developing countries have been holding an advisory function in the decision-making with regard to breaches of regional competition law. In contrast to the European Competition Network, the Advisory Committee on Competition in the WAEMU and the Andean Committee for the Defence of Free Competition, which are consultative bodies, have not participated in general competition policy discussions. While this can change over time with the emergence of national competition cultures, it can be advisable especially for RTAs and member states with new competition law experiences and little competition law structures to enhance competition law cooperation through a general political institution. This can also enhance embeddedness of regional and national competition policy with other related industrial policies in the framework of economic integration.[128]

Moreover, in the absence of parallel and decentralized competition law enforcement as in the EU, an allocation of cases as in the ECN regarding the authority that actually adopts measures and enforces the decision does not constitute a function of cooperation bodies. However, in the CARICOM, the allocation of the competent authority within a competition network might prove useful in order for the Commission to determine the national authority that conducts the preliminary investigation.[129] Hence, the more decentralized regional competition law enforcement is, the more cooperation networks should also allow for the identification of the most adequate national competition authority to enforce the law, and for a possible (re-)allocation of enforcement competences.

12.4.7 Accountability and Ex Post Control of Regional Competition Law Enforcement

An important element of regional competition law enforcement is to guarantee accountability through judicial control by a regional court of justice. The installation of a regional court of justice as such does not shape the degree of centralization or decentralization of regional competition law enforcement, but reflects the intention to deepen integration overall.

While there is large convergence between the internal procedures and structures of the regional courts of justice in developing countries and the Court of Justice of

---

[127] On the overarching incentive of a common market for regional competition law enforcement, see Part III, Sect. 11.2.3.

[128] Part II, Dimension I: Sect. 5.3.

[129] Article 176(1) of the Revised Treaty Chaguaramas.

the European Union, some aspects still vary and can require different preconditions or can lead to different results. However, due to the little available data and case law on competition law matters, it is not possible to reliably evaluate certain internal procedures and compositions of regional courts with regard to the efficacy of regional competition law enforcement.

Financial funds of a regional court of justice safeguard independent decision-making by the judges. While the appointment process of judges should generally be neutral and objective, it is particularly important in an RTA in which member states tend to be reluctant to cede sovereignty and in which not all member states are represented by a judge. In fact, the larger the number of member states, the more impracticable it is to have an equivalent number of judges. One could thus argue that the more member states an RTA has, the more depoliticized, for example in the form of a separate legal and judicial commission,[130] the appointment process of regional judges should be.

Another concern with regard to an *ex post* control of regional competition law enforcement before a regional court of justice concerns the competition law expertise of regional judges. While regional judges are usually among the most qualified legal personnel and possess high reputation, proportional to the competition law experiences of the member state, they will usually lack competition law expertise. However, the analysis of the experiences in the WAEMU, the AndeanC and the CARICOM has demonstrated their capacity to deal with competition law matters adequately and efficiently. Regional judges will not conduct an analysis based on economic efficiency, but will interpret the law with regard to the general regional framework, principles and legislation. Yet in the case of an action for annulment, in which the regional court may be allowed to alter the regional competition authority's decision, regional judges should also conduct an economic analysis. In the same vein, involvement of a regional court of justice in a legislative drafting process of regional competition law will require it to not only take into account institutional considerations of the overall RTA, but also competition law-specific considerations, such as economic efficiencies.[131] Hence, the further the reach of measures and procedures of a regional court of justice on regional competition law enforcement, the more competition law expertise regional judges must have.

As private competition law enforcement remains the exception and private parties' access to the regional court of justice is restricted, they will not often happen to seize the regional court. Hence, in particular in the initial phase the regional court's procedures will remain an instrument of control used by member states or by large undertakings with deep pockets. For efficiency reasons it is advisable to have an administrative first-control instance before approaching the regional court. Especially individuals or small and medium-sized firms might prefer such a preliminary instance before approaching the regional court. Moreover, they will mostly address the regional court of justice indirectly through preliminary reference rulings.

---

[130] See on this aspect the Regional Judicial and Legal Service Commission (RJLSC) in the CARICOM, Part II, Dimension III: Sect. 7.1.1.2.

[131] This is for example the case with regard to abuse of dominant position thresholds etc.

In this context, the implications arising out of mandatory or voluntary referrals by national courts is still not clear. Yet it is possible that a mandatory referral at least by a national court of last instance will support the development and interpretation of regional competition laws.

12.5 Dimension V: Principles of Regional Competition Law Enforcement

Different legal principles also shape the overall degree of enforcement of regional competition law. The principles of regional law enforcement do not result from a deliberate decision of governments. Rather, the general legal principle of direct effect of regional law is the result of a certain legal tradition. The following section thus does not plead for the adoption of an international law system without direct effect or the adoption of a supranational system. Rather, member states, developed or developing, have to be cautious to understand the peculiarities that arise from certain principles of law within a regional competition law system.

12.5.1 International Law and Supranational Competition Law Systems

In supranational systems, direct effect of regional competition law allows individuals to directly rely on regional law without depending on the decision of national parliaments to incorporate regional provisions into national law.[132] While this can facilitate decentralized enforcement of regional competition law through private damage claims, individuals' rights' protection can similarly be guaranteed in systems of international law.[133] The question of whether and under which conditions a regional competition law system allows individuals to assert private damage claims for the infringement of regional competition law arises under supranational as well as under international law.[134] In both systems, anticompetitive practices might not automatically be null and void by law.[135]

---

[132] Yet it is only in combination with the principle of primacy of regional over national law that a regional legislative framework can create a convergent system of individuals' rights protection in all member states within a RTA.

[133] *Drexl,* in: *Drexl,* The Future of Transnational Antitrust, 2003, pp. 311, 334f.

[134] *Ibid.*

[135] While in the WAEMU, according to Article 88 of the Treaty of Dakar anticompetitive practices are deemed null and void by law, in the AndeanC, Article 4 of Decision 608 only determines that anticompetitive conduct shall be sanctioned and prohibited. In the CARICOM, Article 177(3) of the Revised Treaty sets out the obligation for member states that anticompetitive practices shall be null and void.

In systems of international as well as supranational law, the regional court of justice will play a crucial role in defining provisions of regional or international law. In a system of international law, the regional court of justice will have to exercise a key monitoring function with regard to adequate fulfilment of the member states' ratification obligations.[136] Individuals can only participate indirectly in such monitoring proceedings. In particular, the requirements for individuals to claim a member state's breach of its international law obligations might be difficult to fulfil.[137]

What does this mean for regional competition law systems among developing countries? One has to recall that the main incentive for convergent implementation of national competition laws with regional competition law in RTAs is the intensity of inter-state trade.[138] Irrespective of the existence of a system of international or supranational law, the higher the significance of inter-state trade, the more will member states be inclined to harmonize national laws and apply them convergently with regional law. In the absence of intensive inter-state trade, the regional law has to set legal standards in order to enhance harmonization and convergent application of competition law within the RTA. In both systems harmonization of national and regional competition laws as well as convergent application of them contribute to efficient competition law enforcement, which in turn enhances legal certainty for private parties. Yet the main points of reference differ between international and supranational legal systems. In systems of international law the regional law has to set legal standards regarding the national substantive competition law. In supranational systems, the incorporation of legal standards is advisable with regard to national procedures and powers of national competition authorities according to which infringements of regional competition law are enforced.

12.5.2 The Principles of Effectiveness and Subsidiarity

The principles of effectiveness and subsidiary do not have a specific impact on the degree of centralization or decentralization. Even in the case of an inclusion of a subsidiarity principle, in particular the experience of the WAEMU shows that its interpretation offers sufficient leeway for the adoption of a centralized or decentralized regional competition law system.

---

[136] It is to be remembered that even in supranational systems with direct effect a regional Court of Justice will have to monitor adequate enactment of legal norms, such as directives that lack direct effect.

[137] Consider in this regard the requirement to be granted special leave in the CARICOM, Part II, Dimension IV: Sect. 8.3.2.5.

[138] Part III, Sect. 11.2.3.

12.5.3 *Prerogative Competence Allocation Powers and the Right to Determine the Competent Jurisdiction*[139]

In combination with an objective competence allocation criterion, such as cross-border effect, prerogative competence allocation powers could still be attributed to an authority in case of diverging opinions on the determination of the competent authority.[140] While in the EU, the European Commission's prerogative power to hear competition law cases with cross-border effect remains an element of centralized competition law enforcement, in the CARICOM, the COTED's power to decide on conflicts with regard to the competent jurisdiction[141] reflects decentralized enforcement. Moreover, in the European Union, the ECN constitutes a platform in which allocation of competences between national competition authorities takes place informally, thereby preventing conflicts.

Vesting an entity with prerogative powers is a tricky task, because it entails a psychological element that might raise sovereignty and legitimacy concerns. Moreover, it incorporates the risk of abusive use, thereby undermining the respect of the allocation criterion that is structurally more objective and neutral than a case-by-case decision of a competition authority. If the regional competition authority can determine the competent jurisdiction, it could abusively claim to decide all cases. This would waste resources and would lead to insufficient regional competition law enforcement in the long run. On the other hand, in case an entity composed of member states' representatives, such as the COTED, is entitled to determine the competent jurisdiction, this can create room for non-competition-related considerations and can hamper convergent application of regional competition law in the long run. Although internal voting mechanisms of all member states can prevent abusive use of such prerogative powers, such mechanisms will also come at the cost of transparency. In order to balance the issues at stake, the most effective way is to use a cooperation mechanism in which regional as well as national competition authorities are present. Yet in order to achieve efficiency gains and consistent and transparent enforcement, even such a mixed cooperation mechanism requires the adoption of conflict resolution principles. Moreover, one should not neglect the necessity for young regional competition authorities to develop legal precedents.[142]

---

[139] The question with regard to prerogative competences to assign the competent entity is actually not only a question of underlying principles of regional competition law enforcement, but also relates to potential conflicts that might arise in the context of determining the existence of cross-border effect, as well as in the context of the actual conduct of a regional competition law investigation. For clarity reasons, the subject of prerogative powers is dealt with at the end under Dimension V, because it also reflects a general enforcement principle.

[140] On the possibility to adopt a mandatory lead jurisdiction with the competence to assign the exclusive competence to deal with a case in global competition, see *Budzinski,* The Governance of Global Competition, 2008, pp. 203ff.

[141] Article 176(5) of the Revised Treaty of Chaguaramas.

[142] On the necessity to establish a national competition culture, see above Part III, Sect. 11.7.1.

Hence, the younger the regional competition law system is, the more recommendable is the recognition of prerogative powers of the regional competition law authority with regard to the resolution of jurisdiction conflicts between national and regional competition authorities. A regional court of justice should be installed as the last instance of control and thereby provides for accountability.

12.5.4 Principle of Primacy of Regional Law in Exclusive, Concurrent or Parallel Competition Law Enforcement

The principle of primacy of application of regional competition law has different points of reference depending on the exclusive, concurrent or parallel application of regional and national competition law. The experiences of the WAEMU, AndeanC and the CARICOM have demonstrated that conflicts and ambiguities regarding the applicable law are still possible.

In a system of exclusive and centralized enforcement, there is only one applicable law for competition matters. Yet conflicts can still arise between competition-related national laws and regional competition law. Irrespective of the principle of primacy, regional competition law does not automatically supersede national laws with a competition component. Rather, the principle of *lex specialis* and principle of primacy of regional law can conflict and may require a decision by the regional court of justice.[143]

In a system of concurrent competition law application, such as in the AndeanC in which either regional or national law is applicable, the principle of primacy depends on the interpretation of the competence demarcation criterion. Moreover, one should be aware that the actual respect of the principle of primacy by national authorities requires control and surveillance by the regional level. In fact, the AndeanC's experience demonstrates that member states may disrespect the direct effect and primacy of regional competition law.

Finally, a system of parallel enforcement of national and regional competition law requires the reconciliation of national and regional decisions on breaches and enforcement measures. In order to provide for convergent application of regional law, a principle of primacy of regional law also has to include the primacy of regional enforcement measures.

In all three systems, the objective of economic integration generally led to the adoption of a loyalty clause.[144] More than solving specific jurisdictional conflicts

[143] In the WAEMU, regional competition law prevails over national legislation with a competition component.

[144] See in this regard: Article 7 of the Treaty of Dakar in the WAEMU; Article 9 of the Revised Treaty of Chaguaramas in the CARICOM; the former Article 10(1) of the EC Treaty used to codify the principle of effectiveness in the European Union. Now, Article 4(3) TEU contains the principle of "sincere cooperation" between member states and the European Union. Articles 36 and 37 of Decision 608 entail specific loyalty tasks with regard to regional competition law enforcement in the AndeanC.

between national and regional law, a loyalty clause generally determines that member states actively and passively support the attainment of the objectives of regional integration. It thus not only covers conflicts between the regional and the national law or ambiguities with regard to allocation of competences, but is theoretically also capable of reconciling conflicting enforcement measures. The inclusion of a loyalty clause might be particularly problematic in systems of international law in which the doctrine of implied repeal is not capable of unambiguously solving conflicts between regional and national laws.[145]

12.6 Dimension VI: Dynamics of Regional Competition Law Enforcement

Regional competition law enforcement is a dynamic process, which may change over time. The challenge, in particular for young RTAs and regional competition law systems, is to adapt to changing circumstances while providing for sustainable competition law enforcement and incentivizing competition law enforcement and implementation by the member states. Regional competition law systems' design is thus also a matter of the right timing.

The first element of timing relates to the existing national competition law landscape (vertical dimension). The existence of a (functioning) domestic competition law structure is unquestionably not a precondition for the introduction of a regional competition policy. To the contrary, a regional competition law can work as a key incentive and supportive framework for the implementation of national competition law structures.[146] Nevertheless, the stage of development of domestic competition policy and the level of experience with regard to competition matters in the member states of an RTA at the moment of the implementation of a regional competition law is an important determinant for the regional law's substantive content.[147]

Second, with regard to other regional economic policies, a regional competition law can only be introduced with or after the implementation of economic liberalization policies (horizontal dimension). Regional competition policy is in particular linked to the creation of a common regional market. The question of whether the complete functioning of such a market is a precondition for the successful enforcement of a common market, and vice versa, constitutes a chicken-and-egg problem. However, one can at least expect that with the strengthening and development of the common market the application of regional competition law will expand in practice. This might require a change in the allocation of competences, for example in the form of increased cooperation with national competition authorities—presuming

[145] Part II, Dimension V: Sect. 9.2.4.

[146] In this sense, the WAEMU, the AndeanC and the CARICOM competition law regimes embrace the harmonization of national competition policies as one of the main objectives.

[147] See below Part III, Chap. 14.

that they exist in the member states—in order to cope with the increase of the workload.

The last point of reference constitutes the substantive content of the regional law itself (substantive competition law dimension). The mandatory character of a regional competition law and the complexity of its provisions should adhere to specific periods of competition law development, requiring a level of commitment of national competition authorities adapted to the current status of economic and overall regional integration. The level of commitment also has to consider other non-economic aspects, in other words "soft" competition-related factors, such as the overall acceptance of regional competition law or the emergence of a competition culture within the national jurisdictions. With processing economic integration and the increased presence of other "soft" competition-related aspects, consistent application of regional competition law becomes more important in order to prevent distortions in the common market. As a consequence, the competition law's content can become more sophisticated and require national jurisdictions to display greater commitment to regional competition law.

In this context commitment does not only refer to close cooperation between national and regional competition authorities, but also includes the degree of harmonization, ranging from partial to full harmonization of national laws. On the other hand, in theory application becomes easier, because the regional law is more accepted and its benefits have become more apparent through increased economic integration. It is important to emphasize that this is a dynamic process, too, as the enforcement of regional competition law and economic integration and the development of "soft" competition-related factors are closely related.[148]

Regional competition law enforcement therefore also entails a time component. Generally, there is no evidence that argues against the introduction of regional competition law at an early stage of regional integration. Yet the pace of integration, in particular the relevance of the common market for the member states, and the level of competition law expertise among member states have to be acknowledged in the design of a regional competition law system. A lack of competition law expertise and structures among member states justifies a certain centralization of regional competition law, for example in the form of a large scope of application of regional law. Similarly, a regional competition law could provide for a centralized framework with regard to mandatory standards in domestic competition laws. However, a regional competition law system should never be implemented at the expense of national learning processes with regard to competition law. Some centralized elements might thus be conceived as transitional devices; or the regional competition law system should provide for flexible adaptation provisions. Moreover, the evidence suggests that economically stronger member states with more competition law expertise tend to be more influential with regard to the implementation of a regional competition law system and also with regard to the long-term enforcement

[148] See *Drexl*, Perspectives européennes sur la politique de la concurrence dans l'espace OHADA, XXV R.I.D.E. 281–304 (2011); *Drexl*, in: *Drexl/Bakhoum/Fox/Gal/Gerber*, Competition Policy and Regional Integration in Developing Countries, 2012, pp. 231–252.

of regional competition law. They often constitute the pacemakers in the implementation of a regional competition law system in the first place. One might expect that in the absence of the support of such an experienced and economically strong member state, a regional competition authority will have to engage in greater competition advocacy and will have to make a greater effort to gain the support of the other member states.

Chapter 13
Proposal on Re-Allocation of Competences in the WAEMU, AndeanC, CARICOM

Applying the principles developed above to the WAEMU, the AndeanC and the CARICOM regional competition law system, a partial re-allocation of competences will be recommended in the following section.

13.1 WAEMU: "Controlled Decentralization"[1] with Centralized Standards

In order to avoid the inefficiencies that arise out of the strong centralization of *Dimension I* the substantive competition law, certain aspects call for decentralization. Regional competition law is structurally better placed to deal with practices that affect several member states or international anticompetitive practices[2]; whereas practices with a purely national impact should be handled by national competition authorities. Consequently, the competence demarcation criterion of "effect on the common market"[3] should be revised in the sense that only practices that have an effect on inter-state trade fall under the scope of regional competition law. The inter-state trade criterion would accordingly apply to exemptions of regional competition law, which remain governed by the WAEMU Commission. Certain aspects of substantial competition law have proven to be more efficiently conducted centrally. This mainly concerns state aids, which should remain under the exclusive competence of the regional competition law. However, they should not fall under regional law regardless of their effect on the regional market. Rather, thresholds can govern that only state aids with an appreciable effect on the common market and

[1] In this sense, see also *Bakhoum*, L'articulation du droit communautaire et des droits nationaux de la concurrence dans l'Union Economique et Monétaire Ouest Africaine, 2007, pp. 248ff.

[2] See above on the territorial scope of application, Part III, Dimension I: Sect. 12.1.1.

[3] Part III, Dimension I: Sect. 12.1.1.

J. Molestina, *Regional Competition Law Enforcement in Developing Countries*, Munich Studies on Innovation and Competition 9,
https://doi.org/10.1007/978-3-662-58525-2_13

cross-border trade fall under the regional law's scope of application in order to save resources. In this context, Regulation no. 04/2002/CM/UEMOA generally offers an adequate legal instrument.

A particularity of WAEMU's substantive competition law is the existence of a merger control system based on the rules on abuse of dominance.[4] Hence, having adopted the recommendations, merger control would also be subject to the effect on inter-state trade-criterion. Yet centralizing the control of mergers can bring efficiency gains, in particular with regard to the attraction of FDI. In this context, one should highlight the centralized model in the European Union, namely the "one-stop-shop" doctrine. Applying a different criterion to merger control than to the provisions on abuse of dominant position however only appears feasible if the WAEMU legislature introduces an explicit merger control regime, which is structurally different than a control via the provisions governing abuse of dominant position.

The allocation of legislation competences, *Dimension II*, should allow member states to adopt national competition laws, which govern anticompetitive practices with a purely national effect. Yet the governance of state aids with an appreciable effect on the regional market should remain centralized under the exclusive competence of the WAEMU Commission.[5] Vesting national legislators with the power to legislate on competition law goes further than merely limiting the WAEMU Commission's functions, for example in the form of the requirement of appreciable effects or *de facto* auto-limitation.[6] Such an approach would not sufficiently enhance the adoption and development of national competition laws and institutions.

A second question that arises if one recognizes legislative power for member states on anticompetitive agreements and abuse of dominant position is the question regarding a potential standard. Bearing in mind that coerced harmonization is ineffective, a strategy of "soft harmonization"[7] offers possible solutions. Yet less developed inter-state trade in the WAEMU than in the European Union might not create sufficient incentives to harmonize national laws. This might hamper convergence of competition law enforcement within the WAEMU, because national legislators are inclined to shape national laws towards the protection of domestic interests and industries.[8] On the other hand, differing national competition law might be justified

---

[4] Namely, Article 4 of Regulation no. 03/2002/CM/UEMOA, Articles 4(1) and 4(3) of Regulation no. 02/2002/CM/UEMOA. In contrast to the European merger control, the WAEMU offers a control based on the provisions on abuse of dominant position. For more details see Part II, Dimension I: Sect. 5.1.4.

[5] See also *Bakhoum,* L'articulation du droit communautaire et des droits nationaux de la concurrence dans l'Union Economique et Monétaire Ouest Africaine, 2007, pp. 291f.

[6] On a possible auto-limitation of the WAEMU Commission as a competence demarcation rule, see *Groupe Intergouvernemental d'experts sur le Droit et de la Politique de la Concurrence,* Répartition des Compétences entre les Autorités Communautaires et les Autorités Nationales, 16–18 July 2008, Geneva, p. 7.

[7] On "soft harmonization" see *Drexl,* Perspectives européennes sur la politique de la concurrence dans l'espace OHADA, XXV R.I.D.E. 281 (2011).

[8] *Weick,* Competition Law and Policy in Senegal, 33/3 W. Comp. 521, 538 (2010).

in order to guarantee flexible and preferential treatment for less-developed sectors. The existing loyalty clause guarantees that national provisions do not counteract the overall objective of the creation of a common market with convergent competition law application. Nevertheless, the inclusion of standards generally enhances convergent competition laws without excessively limiting the member states' legislative discretion.[9] Standards should provide for the inclusion of the "classical" competition law prohibitions, but in developing countries should also require the national legislation not to discriminate between public and private enterprises.[10] Regional standards should also avoid an excessive adoption of exemptions and national sector regulation that excludes sectors from competition law application. With regard to member states without a proper domestic competition law the adoption of a "downloading option"[11] can incite national competition law implementation. Non-binding guidelines can serve as an incentive for existing national competition law jurisdictions to harmonize and align their laws.

The institutional and procedural autonomy, which under the current system is already granted to member states, should remain untouched. In the long run, in order to further convergence of competition law application, one can consider the introduction of procedural and institutional standards.[12] The latter should in any case encompass a certain degree of independence for the national competition authority. The national competition authority that cooperates with the WAEMU Commission should be clearly identified and vested with sufficient competences to fulfil its competition law enforcement task.[13] Moreover, guidelines on the amount and kind of sanctions for the most severe competition law infringements[14] facilitate the decentralized application of criminal and/or other competition law sanctions.

Likewise, even under centralized competition law enforcement, the WAEMU should adopt legislative frameworks with regard to national sector regulation, competition-related fields of law, such as unfair competition and concerning international cooperation in the field of competition, namely, with regard to ECOWAS

---

[9] *Drexl* in this context states: "Unlike in the EU, regional integration systems in the developing world should also be concerned about the quality of substantive law in the member states." *Drexl*, in: *Drexl/Bakhoum/Fox/Gal/Gerber*, Competition Policy and Regional Integration in Developing Countries, 2012, pp. 231, 248.

[10] *Bakhoum/Molestina*, in: *Drexl/Bakhoum/Fox/Gal/Gerber*, Competition Policy and Regional Integration in Developing Countries, 2012, pp. 89, 110.

[11] On the "downloading option" in the AndeanC, see Part II, Dimension II: Sect. 6.3.2.

[12] Under the ongoing reform, there is a proposed Directive that defines guidelines for national competition authorities.

[13] On the possibility to establish mixed national competition authorities, see Part III, Dimension III: Sect. 12.3. The competition authority in Barbados, the Fair Trading Commission, offers a positive example. It is a mixed utility regulation, consumer protection and competition policy authority. For more information see *Sampson/Sampson*, in: *Mehta/Evenett*, Politics Triumphs Economics?, 2009, pp. 327, 347ff.

[14] The severity of competition law infringements should of course depend on the particular developing country's problems and its economic or socio-political situation.

and possibly in the future with regard to OHADA.[15] There have been attempts in the WAEMU to harmonize national sector and specialized legislation. Although there have been cases addressing the conflict between national regulatory measures and regional competition law,[16] the WAEMU Court of Justice should assist in the process of clarifying the relation of national regulatory measures and regional competition law. Generally, the WAEMU has jurisdiction to coordinate international cooperation and to further harmonization of legislation, Articles 13 and 60 of the Treaty of Dakar. Coordination of international agreements is a particular concern with regard to competition law enforcement in the WAEMU, as competition legislation of ECOWAS might conflict with WAEMU competition law.[17]

The institutional design of the regional competition authority, *Dimension III*, is marked by a strong administrative burden.[18] This is not so much a question of centralization or decentralization, but rather a general problem of administrative procedure. In fact, having a "centralized" regional authority with its proper staff is important to achieve efficiency gains, such as a greater degree of independence of a regional authority. However, at the WAEMU Commission, one should provide for full-time staff exclusively responsible for competition policy, which will make them financially more independent and less prone to potential non-competition-law-related considerations and will generally increase the attractiveness for qualified personnel.[19] Along the same lines, it might be recommendable to revise the internal bureaucratic procedure that emphasizes the important role of the President of the Commission and to vest the regional authority with greater enforcement competences, in particular with regard to measures taken on short notice.

In order to facilitate a possible reform of the WAEMU competition law enforcement system, the WAEMU should in a first step review regional competition law cases. As a reform will aim at enhancing participation of national competition authorities, it should also review national competition law precedents, probably competition law cases that have arisen in the context of sector regulation. In the long run, the WAEMU Commission should try to engage in *ex officio* investigations of sectors that are of particular relevance for civil society.[20]

The actual enforcement procedures, *Dimension IV*, are shared between national competition authorities and the WAEMU Commission. This requires the WAEMU

[15] OHADA does not have a regional competition law yet.

[16] See above, case regarding the "GAZODUC" project in the WAEMU, during which the WAEMU Commission argued that national public health interests can justify temporary measures by member states, but that they must not distort the common market or create entry barriers to it, Part II, Dimension IV: Sect. 8.1.1.

[17] With regard to potential conflicts and solutions to conflicting jurisdictions, see *Ngom*, in: *Drexl/Bakhoum/Fox/Gal/Gerber*, Competition Policy and Regional Integration in Developing Countries, 2012, pp. 116, 127ff.; *Coulibaly*, Le Droit de la Concurrence de l'Union Économique et Monétaire Ouest Africaine, 43–44 Rev. burkinnabé de droit, 24ff. (2003).

[18] Part II, Dimension III: Sect. 7.1.3.

[19] See also Recommendation No. 10 of *UNCTAD*, Voluntary Peer Review on Competition Policies of WAEMU, Benin and Senegal, 2008, p. 159.

[20] Such sectors encompass nutrition, access to health, transportation etc.

system to further promote the parallel conduct of market surveillance with regard to breaches of regional competition law. A main step is to allow member states to implement and enforce national competition law. Yet the tendency of member states to focus more on national competition law infringements than on breaches of regional law will increase the need for cooperation with the WAEMU Commission. This could be achieved through closer cooperation in the Advisory Committee. While the Committee is currently composed by representatives from member states to give non-binding opinions on competition law matters, its functions could be expanded by transforming it into an information-sharing platform in which also representatives from the WAEMU Commission are present.[21] The widening of the functioning of the Advisory Committee could in the long run also enhance horizontal cooperation between national competition authorities.[22]

Due to the slow establishment of a competition culture and the lack of resources, one of the main problems of regional competition law enforcement remains the information deficit. In order to overcome this deficit, not only an enhanced participation of national competition authorities, but also an intensified involvement of private parties appears a potential solution. Recalling that most of the WAEMU cases so far concerned state-related conduct, it is yet questionable whether, especially at an early stage of regional competition law enforcement, private parties should or could play a determining role in regional competition law enforcement in the WAEMU. With regard to the slow growth of competition law culture among the private sector, the prior notification requirement should be maintained as it concerns the granting of a prior clearance ruling or individual exemption.[23]

Direct accessibility of the WAEMU Commission for private sector representatives should not be abolished. The low number of complaints is mainly explained by the lack of commitment and little competition law expertise of national competition authorities in the WAEMU. As they have to decide upon the existence of a "community effect" and transfer the cases to the regional level, neither complete, nor equal transferral of cases by member states is guaranteed.

In the same vein, one should not adopt a similarly decentralized system as in the European Union, in which national competition authorities directly apply and enforce regional competition law, including exemptions. Such a decentralized enforcement demands a relatively advanced level of national competition law implementation and competition law expertise of national competition authorities. One should also not forget that the introduction of decentralized enforcement in the EU under Regulation no. 01/2003 took place on the basis of a relatively large number of diverse regional competition law precedents. Anticompetitive practices with

---

[21] See above on the Advisory Committee on Competition in WAEMU, Part II, Dimension IV: Sect. 8.2.1.1.

[22] Already under the current legal framework the Advisory Committee on Competition allows for the participation of national sector regulators or professional associations, in case the Committee has to decide on a sector that concerns the before-mentioned groups; see Article 4 of Reglement d'Execution no. 007/2005/COM/UEMOA.

[23] Articles 3, 7 and Chapter I of Regulation no. 03/2002/CM/UEMOA.

a purely national effect should remain under national competition law and national competition authorities' enforcement.

For the principle of direct effect and application of regional competition law, including automatic nullity of anticompetitive practices,[24] national judges are actually competent to directly decide on the nullity. Yet with the exclusive competence of the WAEMU Commission, its decision has been made a constituent condition for private enforcement.[25] The limited competence of national judges should however only remain a transitional situation until member states have sufficient competition law knowledge, until there is increased horizontal cooperation between member states and until the WAEMU Commission has developed diverse regional competition law precedents. Moreover, the regional level will generally have to enhance an increased convergence of the national laws on private enforcement, including procedural standards and rights.

While general legal principles, *Dimension V*, remain untouched by a possible reform of regional competition law enforcement in the WAEMU, the principle of subsidiarity should receive greater emphasis, thereby reinforcing more decentralized competition law enforcement of national cases by the national competition authorities.

Although prerogative powers of the WAEMU Commission have not been necessary in the centralized system, applying the "effect on inter-state trade" as a competence demarcation criterion, the regional authority should have the prerogative power to decide on the actual existence of such an effect. Not only will this accelerate regional competition law procedures and guarantee a certain flexibility, it will also provide the WAEMU Commission with sufficient powers to develop regional competition law precedents, in particular for those matters that are particularly relevant for the entire region. In the long run, the WAEMU legislature should also develop a *de minimis* clause and adopt the requirement of appreciable cross-border effects in order to render regional competition law enforcement more efficient. Yet such a clause is best developed on the basis of extensive regional competition law precedents and sufficient experiences with regard to the patterns of trade in the WAEMU common market.

13.2 AndeanC: Strengthening the Advocacy Function of the Secretariat General

Generally, Decision 608 in the AndeanC is marked by the intention to balance regional and national interests. Yet mostly due to a combination of diverging national economic systems and, more importantly, conceived trading partnerships outside the AndeanC, general scepticism towards Andean integration has emerged. For the

[24] Article 88(1) of the Treaty of Dakar.

[25] Part II, Dimension V: Sect. 9.1.

lack of awareness of regional law in general, weak national and regional competition culture as well as resource constraints, Decision 608 has largely remained unapplied.[26] Possible reforms of the regional competition law system in the AndeanC thus do not primarily target a re-allocation of competences, but should rather focus on the strengthening of awareness regarding the benefits of regional competition law enforcement. Increased efficiency of Decision 608 will also depend on the strengthening of and raised awareness towards the benefits of regional integration as such.[27]

From the considerations above, it follows that possible reforms of the substantive competition law provisions of Decision 608, *Dimension I*, are actually not necessary in order to enhance the efficiency of Andean competition law enforcement.[28] Nevertheless, the previous analysis demonstrated that efficiencies could be gained from centralizing regional competition law enforcement with regard to state aids. However, the latter is improbable, because the exclusion of state aids from Decision 608 constituted a deliberate decision of member states.[29] In particular in the presence of related regional provisions, namely in the Decisions 283, 456 and 457, it might be useful to review whether they sufficiently protect the common market against distortions arising from state actions.[30]

In a similar vein, the inclusion of a regional merger control system is unrealistic given the little commitment of member states. Yet the current provisions allow for a learning process. Similar to the experiences in the EU, the provisions on agreements and abuse of dominance[31] could be used to review mergers *ex post*.[32]

A possible reform reinforces the AndeanC's exemption and exception scheme. Decision 608 actually adopts a *rule of reason* approach, whereas Article 6 of

---

[26] *Cortázar,* in: *Drexl/Bakhoum/Fox/Gal/Gerber,* Competition Policy and Regional Integration in Developing Countries, 2012, pp. 133, 152.

[27] In this context, the projects INTERCAN I and the establishment of an Andean Centre for the Implementation of Policies of Regional Integration (Centro Andino para la Implementación de Políticas de Integración Regional – CAIPIR) should be mentioned as positive developments. Both aim at the facilitation of and the creation of incentives for Member States to apply and implement regional decisions, which are of particular relevance for economic integration in the AndeanC. On INTERCAN I, see <http://www.comunidadandina.org/intercan.htm> accessed 11 November 2018. Also with regard to the CAIPIR, see Commission of the AndeanC, Decision 723 of the 27 November 2009 and 10 December 2009 "Proyecto INTERCAN I de Apoyo a la Integración Económica Regional de la Comunidad Andina". A summary of both projects is given by *Cortázar,* in: *Drexl/Bakhoum/Fox/Gal/Gerber,* Competition Policy and Regional Integration in Developing Countries, 2012, pp. 133, 153.

[28] One has to recall that Decision 608 reforms the former Decision 285, which suffered from several inefficiencies with regard to its substantive competition law provisions. See above Part I, Sect. 1.2.2 Development of regional competition policy in the AndeanC.

[29] Part II, Dimension I: Sect. 5.1.3.

[30] This study only deals with the Decisions 283, 456 and 457 very superficially, because a more detailed analysis would exceed the scope of this research.

[31] Articles 7, 8 and 9 of Decision 608.

[32] *Cortázar,* in: *Drexl/Bakhoum/Fox/Gal/Gerber,* Competition Policy and Regional Integration in Developing Countries, 2012, pp. 133, 144.

Decision 608 provides for the possibility of member states to ask for the adoption of regional block exemptions. The Secretariat General should set out the criteria for allowing certain practices. It could rely on the criteria provided for by Article 6 of Decision 608 and the European exemption criteria.

The "downloading option" was only used as a transitional device and left large discretion to national legislators to enact proper national competition law policies and structures, *Dimension II*. Generally, the legislative competence in the AndeanC is conducted concurrently according to the principle of exclusivity: member states can enact national legislation for practices that do not fall under the scope of Article 5 of Decision 608. All member states have enacted corresponding national legislation. A re-allocation of legislative competences on substantive competition law matters is accordingly neither feasible nor recommendable.

Decision 608 generally provides for institutional and procedural autonomy for national competition authorities in the enforcement of it. Yet for the primacy of regional over national law, Article 16 of Decision 608 sets out standards for investigations regarding potential breaches of Decision 608.[33] A major concern relates to the partly insufficient operational independence of national competition authorities. Moreover, in the immature domestic competition law regimes many difficulties arose in the context of determining the competent national competition authority.[34] This might in particular create inefficiencies with regard to enforcing the law against anticompetitive practices exercised by the state or state-owned enterprises. Although it is impossible to establish operational independence normatively, the regional framework could provide for standards of national competition legislation, in particular with regard to a non-discriminatory treatment of private and public anticompetitive practices. In this context, Article 36 of Decision 608 should be acknowledged positively, because it allows for a challenge of anticompetitive state regulatory measures and policies before the Secretariat General or the Andean Tribunal of Justice.

In the long run, the Secretariat General should also develop guidelines on actual decision-enforcement measures, such as sanctions for breach of competition law. It should also develop guidelines to coordinate national leniency programs, as all member states, but not the AndeanC itself, have by now adopted national leniency programs.[35]

The Secretariat General is the general executive authority, *Dimension III*. With regard to regional competition law enforcement, it would be useful to have at least one person that is exclusively assigned to competition law matters. This would guarantee that regional competition law remains on the agenda of the Secretariat General and would prevent regional competition law enforcement from becoming completely

---

[33] Part II, Dimension V: Sect. 9.2.3.

[34] This was the case in Bolivia and Ecuador, see above Part II, Dimension II: Sect. 6.3.3 and Part II, Dimension I: Sect. 5.2.2.2.

[35] For an overview of the Andean and national competition law regimes in 2012, see *Cortázar*, in: *Drexl/Bakhoum/Fox/Gal/Gerber*, Competition Policy and Regional Integration in Developing Countries, 2012, pp. 133, 143. In addition, the new competition law of Ecuador also covers a leniency program.

dependent on the member states' incentives. Moreover, regional competition law enforcement constitutes a permanent task, which involves constant monitoring of the market. The specially assigned person(s) could also be responsible for gathering and structuring data and information received from national authorities and for the regular convocation of the Andean Committee for the Defence of Competition. The assigned person would also be responsible for the exercise of constant competition law advocacy measures, while placing a special focus on the benefits that arise out of regional competition law enforcement.

For the lack of an actual enforcement record of Decision 608, *Dimension IV*, one needs to inquire into the remaining functions of the Secretariat General with regard to regional competition law enforcement. The Secretariat General in this context has two options, which are not exclusive but complementary. On the one hand, the Secretariat General could make greater use of its *ex officio* right and initiate investigations on its own. This however requires a relatively large amount of staff and resources, because the Secretariat General would have to conduct preliminary sectorial market analyses. In the same vein, it could control the measures taken by national competition authorities with regard to practices that actually fall within the scope of Decision 608.[36] On the other hand, the Secretariat General could place its focus on competition advocacy, in order to increase the awareness of regional competition law in the private business sector, among national judges and national competition and other public authorities.[37]

The latter option appears preferable at the moment. The utilization of the Secretariat General's *ex officio* right constitutes an extremely resource-consuming venture in the absence of the cooperation of national competition authorities and in the absence of thorough information about the markets. Moreover, an increased control of the national competition authorities' actions might be considered as an infringement of their autonomy, thereby creating resistance and resentment, which might hamper regional competition law enforcement in the long run. One should bear in mind that economic integration in the AndeanC has been challenged and is regularly questioned.[38] A focus on competition advocacy could moreover create

---

[36] It has to be pointed out that Decision 608 does not include an explicit prerogative power of the Secretariat General. Yet the Secretariat General can always continue an investigation based on its *ex officio* investigation power. Though unrealistic due to the lack of will of member states and national competition authorities to cede sovereignty, it would be useful to include a prerogative competence of the Secretariat General to conduct investigations based on breach of Decision 608.

[37] In fact, in interviews with the author representatives from national competition authorities mentioned that the Secretariat General's functions have been *de facto* so far limited to competition advocacy functions.

[38] One major crisis arose in the context of the withdrawal of Venezuela in 2006. There is also concern that open regionalism hampers the integration movement of the AndeanC. See above on the notion of "open regionalism" in the AndeanC, Part I, Sect. 1.1.2. With regard to critics of the AndeanC, see among others *Javier Garvich*, "¿Por qué ha fracasado la Comunidad Andina de Naciones?", 24 April 2006 <http://www.terra.com.pe/noticias/articulo/html/act512774.htm> accessed 11 November 2018. Rebutting the general uselessness of the AndeanC, *Cortázar,* in: *Drexl/Bakhoum/Fox/Gal/Gerber,* Competition Policy and Regional Integration in Developing Countries, 2012, pp. 133, 151.

incentives for national competition authorities to increase assistance in the application of Decision 608. The Secretariat General could in particular target representative associations of the private sector in order to enhance private regional competition law enforcement.[39]

Moreover, the Secretariat General should re-activate the already existing Andean Committee on Defence of Free Competition. Regular and possibly even mandatory meetings of national competition authorities' representatives would not only serve as an advocacy mechanism, but could moreover enhance information sharing within the AndeanC. This concerns not only the information sharing between the Secretariat General and national competition authorities, but also horizontal information sharing among national competition authorities. It may also enhance the exchange of expertise and the grating of technical expertise between more and less experienced competition law jurisdictions.

Another reform of the enforcement measures according to Decision 608 would involve the adoption of information obligations for national competition authorities. Practically, all investigations and competition law decisions of national competition authorities should be gathered in a common set of data that is accessible by all authorities.[40] This set of data could be hosted and administered by the Secretariat General. A large set of available information of all member states will in the long run also facilitate the utilization of the *ex officio* right of the Secretariat General.[41] Based on that information it might be able to discern the most relevant sectors with regard to the Andean market and might be able to set priorities of competition law enforcement within the AndeanC.[42]

Although Decision 608 does not provide for automatic nullity of anticompetitive practices, it is questionable whether the decision of the Secretariat General remains a constitutive condition for private damage claims, *Dimension V*. Because of the low awareness of regional competition law, private enforcement of Andean competition law remains a rather theoretical feature. Yet in the long run, private damage claims brought to a national judiciary can be enhanced by refraining from requiring a preliminary decision by the Secretariat General. Again, as in the WAEMU, this preconditions sufficient national competition law expertise and culture, extensive regional competition law precedents and horizontal cooperation between national competition authorities and national judiciary.[43] For the lack of a similarly centralized system of competition law enforcement as in the WAEMU, these components are even more determining in the AndeanC.

---

[39] In the same vein, *Cortázar* argues in favour of greater private-sector involvement in regional competition law enforcement in the AndeanC, *Cortázar*, in: *Drexl/Bakhoum/Fox/Gal/Gerber*, Competition Policy and Regional Integration in Developing Countries, 2012, pp. 133, 154ff.

[40] In the long run, if the Secretariat General actually initiates an investigation or makes a decision, it should also be included as a data provider.

[41] This finding similarly applies to the WAEMU and the CARICOM.

[42] Yet it should not abolish the national competition authorities' discretion. Determined priorities should remain non-mandatory.

[43] This can be achieved through reciprocal information exchange obligations

13.3 CARICOM: Moderate Centralization of Enforcement and Harmonization of Competition Law Standards

Chapter VIII of the Revised Treaty of Chaguaramas contains detailed provisions on anticompetitive agreements and abuse of dominant position, as well as possible infringement procedures, *Dimension I*. Certain notions require clarification, through either the CARICOM Competition Commission or a binding interpretation by the Caribbean Court of Justice. This necessity applies to the notion of "cross-border effect" and the exclusion of non-profit organizations from the subjective scope of application of Caribbean competition law.[44] Ideally, the notion of cross-border effect and the subjective scope of application of Chapter VIII should be interpreted widely in order to provide for convergence in the application of competition law within the CARICOM territory. This is particularly relevant with regard to the strengthening of the CSME.[45] The objective of strengthening the CSME also calls for the introduction of a regional merger control system. In this regard special consideration should be attributed to a centralized system of merger control, vesting the CARICOM Competition Commission with the relevant enforcement powers.[46] As mergers can either be allowed or denied and as some member states provide for national merger regimes, it is important that regional merger control takes precedence over conflicting national merger laws and that national and regional merger regimes are congruent in order to avoid double investigations and decisions. This will increase legal certainty for enterprises engaging in business or intending to do so in the CSME.

Another particularity of Caribbean substantive competition law is the influential position of the COTED, with regard to its far-reaching exemption powers and its competence to adopt special rules on certain sectors.[47] This might be problematic, because the exemption and sectorial powers of the COTED have the potential of undermining the actual application of Chapter VIII. Moreover, the COTED, as a political body, might lack competitive neutrality[48] and thereby replace the evaluation of practices based on economic efficiency by political considerations. This might be particularly problematic in the CARICOM, in which economically weaker states might "gain a favourable hearing, on exemption of sectors that are outcompeted by Trinidad and Tobago firms, or that may be deemed to be in the public interest".[49] Finally, one should not underestimate the transparency costs that arise in the process of finding a consensus within a political body.

---

[44] See Part II, Dimension I: Sect. 5.1.5.3 and Part II, Dimension I: Sect. 5.1.2.

[45] The overarching importance of the CSME is expressed in the preamble of the Revised Treaty of Chaguaramas and with regard to competition policy in Article 169(1) of the Revised Treaty of Chaguaramas.

[46] In order to guarantee uniform application, the COTED should not be vested with decision-making competences.

[47] Articles 182 and 183 of the Revised Treaty of Chaguaramas.

[48] See on the definition of competitive neutrality in Part II, Dimension I: Sect. 5.1.3.

[49] *Stewart,* in: *Drexl/Bakhoum/Fox/Gal/Gerber,* Competition Policy and Regional Integration in Developing Countries, 2012, pp. 161, 180.

On the other hand, positioning Chapter VIII in the overall legal framework of the CARICOM and the Revised Treaty of Chaguaramas, one has to acknowledge that the strong position of the COTED was a deliberate decision. In this vein, Chapter VII similarly stipulates that the COTED can establish, administer and monitor special measures for less developed countries in order to compensate any possible negative impact of the establishment of the CSME or in order to increase their competitiveness.[50] There are thus possible synergies between sectorial and competition policy-making on the one hand and arguments of consistency on the other hand that support COTED's exemption powers also as regards regional competition law enforcement.[51] One should generally recall that preferential treatment and flexible application of regional provisions to less-developed states within CARICOM constitute an overarching principle of Caribbean law application.[52]

Respecting the Revised Treaty's taxonomy, one should thus uphold the exemption power of the COTED. It is to a certain extent limited, because exemptions of the application of Chapter VIII have to correspond to the "public interest".[53] Moreover, the CARICOM system allows for a possible judicial control by the Caribbean Court of Justice.[54] In the course of interpretation of the notion of "public interest", the regional court should also incorporate convergent application of regional competition law as an element of "public interest", in particular with regard to the importance of regional competition law enforcement in the CSME. The Caribbean Court of Justice would thus be capable of balancing different interests at stake. Yet COTED's exemption competences should not exclude the CARICOM Competition Commission, which is in the process of gaining more expertise on competition law matters with cross-border effects. Such participation in exemption procedures should be made mandatory. With an approximation of the levels of economic development within member states, the exemption right should be attributed to the CARICOM Competition Commission.[55] The COTED would retain its right to request to conduct investigations.

The Revised Treaty of Chaguaramas sets out standards for national competition laws within the CARICOM, *Dimension II*. In particular in conjunction with the *CARICOM Model Law on Competition*, this allows member states to adopt

---

[50] See Articles 142, 143, 144, 146 of the Revised Treaty of Chaguaramas. Generally, the COTED is vested with several policy-making and enforcement powers. See Part II, Dimension IV: Sect. 8.2.2.

[51] Generally, the accommodation of competition agencies and industry regulatory authorities has been a problem in the Caribbean. *Sampson/Sampson* in this regard state: "Unlike most developing countries public regulation has been a standard feature in the Caribbean since the 1960s. It has therefore been much easier to accommodate the market changes brought about by liberalisation and wider private participation in the infrastructure industries privatisation. The question in the Caribbean, given the small size of the countries has been what should be the appropriate institutional structures to accommodate competition agencies and industry regulatory authorities?" *Sampson/Sampson,* in: *Mehta/Evenett,* Politics Triumphs Economics?, 2009, pp. 327, 331.

[52] Part II, Dimension I: Sect. 5.3.1.3.

[53] Article 183(2) of the Revised Treaty of Chaguaramas.

[54] Part II, Dimension IV: Sect. 8.3.2.

[55] Part II, Dimension IV: Sect. 8.2.2.5.

convergent national laws that also comply with particularities in the member states. On the other hand, Chapter VIII and the *CARICOM Model Law* rely on Jamaica's competition legislation. The process of competition law harmonization in the CARICOM is thus characterized by flexible and reciprocal learning without the exercise of coercion. It appears to be a particularity of the CARICOM that, far from stringent formal interpretation of regional norms, national ratification is based on cooperation and mutual respect between member states and regional institutions. This explains and justifies the absence of coercive elements, such as short deadlines. Because of their limited resources, member states would most probably not be able to comply with such regional obligations anyway.

Resource constraints, but not slacking commitment to regional integration and regional competition law, are thus the reasons for the slow implementation process of national competition laws and authorities. The economically strongest member states[56] have reformed or implemented or are in an advanced state of implementing national competition laws. The adoption of a transitional "downloading option" would not accelerate the national implementation process and the spread of national competition culture. In the absence of direct effect of regional legislation, member states are still required to conduct a national ratification process, instead of directly "downloading" the regional law. Actually, the *CARICOM Model Law on Competition* constitutes the international law equivalent to the "downloading option" in legal systems with supranationality. One might hope that not only national competition law enforcement but also the frequency of regional competition law enforcement will increase with the progress of the establishment of national competition law structures.

Efficiencies as well as institutional flaws mark the creation of the CARICOM Competition Commission, *Dimension III*. First, the regional competition authority has learned from the experiences of the Jamaican competition authority and has made an effort to separate the adjudicative and investigative powers. Second, its staff is characterized by an equitable geographical diversity, which increases national support. Yet while the geographical diversity was caused more by chance than by design, one could consider codifying the principle of equitable geographical distribution with regard to the Commission's staff. To avoid the CARICOM Competition Commission having to employ people based on their origin rather than skill, one could apply the second phrase of Article 23(2) of the Revised Treaty of Chaguaramas accordingly.[57]

However, the internal procedures of the CARICOM Competition Commission show contradictions and ambiguities that have also been highlighted by the Caribbean Court of Justice.[58] The internal rules on procedure need to be revised by the CARICOM Competition Commission.

---

[56] These are Barbados, Jamaica and Trinidad and Tobago.

[57] Article 23(2) of the Revised Treaty of Chaguaramas: "(…) In the recruitment of such staff, consideration shall be given to securing the highest standard of efficiency, competence and integrity, bearing in mind the principle of equitable geographical distribution."

[58] *Trinidad Cement Limited v The Competition Commission*, Caribbean Court of Justice Application No. OA 1 of 2012, CCJ 4 (OJ), [45ff.].

Generally, one should acknowledge the positive first case of the CARICOM Competition Commission. Although it is difficult to make predictions on the future actions and efficiency of the Commission, one should not expect an intensive application of the *ex officio* investigation right.[59]

The main deficit of the CARICOM's allocation of competences within the regional competition law regime is the strong position of the COTED with regard to the resolution of jurisdictional disputes between the CARICOM Competition Commission and member states during enforcement procedures, *Dimension IV*. The far-reaching powers of the COTED are not only capable of "virtually tying the hands of the Community Commission",[60] but also constitute an impediment to fast enforcement procedures. Given that the COTED is a political body in which all 15 member states are present, consensus finding can become a lengthy process. Most importantly, there is neither the need for the resolution of jurisdictional disputes before the COTED, nor would efficiency gains arise from such dispute resolution. First, in the determination of cross-border effects, solely competition law considerations, such as the determination of the relevant market and the delimitation of the actual effects of the targeted practice, ought to play a role. The CARICOM Competition Commission is provided with competition law experts and is thus sufficiently capable of applying such considerations. Second, the incentives to investigate cases without a cross-border effect regionally are lower than incentives for member states to deal with regional cases nationally. Member states will generally be inclined to protect national industries. Third, the potential harm to the common market caused by the treatment of regional cases by national competition authorities is greater than the harm caused by treatment of national cases by the regional authority. Finally, the CARICOM Competition Commission's decisions can always be controlled before the Caribbean Court of Justice, which has already demonstrated its capacity to efficiently deal with competition law matters.[61] It would thus be most efficient to use the COTED as a competence allocation platform, in which national competition authorities and the CARICOM Competition Commission can discuss jurisdictional issues with regard to a competition law investigation. Yet the ultimate power to decide on the existence of "cross-border effects" should be attributed to the CARICOM Competition Commission.

In the CARICOM, private parties are not allowed to access the CARICOM Competition Commission directly. Although accessibility for individuals is not a precondition, it should be provided in the long run once regional competition culture

[59] Statements made by Kusha Haraksingh, current chairman of the CARICOM Competition Commission, in an interview with the author conducted in Port-of-Spain, Trinidad and Tobago, 29 October 2012.

[60] This argument was made by *Stewart*, cited by *Jenny/Horna*, in: *Brusick/Alvarez/Cernat*, Competition Provisions in Regional Trade Agreements, 2005, pp. 281, 307.

[61] The Caribbean Court of Justice in this context holds that "no conduct or exercise of power by a treaty created institution (especially one charged with essential functions and endowed with relevant powers under the treaty) should escape the judicial scrutiny of the Court" *Trinidad Cement Limited v The Competition Commission*, Caribbean Court of Justice Application No. OA 1 of 2012, [2012] CCJ 4 (OJ), [16].

has sufficiently grown. Yet given that the national competition law implementation is slow and resources among national authorities—if existent at all—are scarce, it would be useful, already under the current system, to allow consumer protection and manufacturer associations to access the CARICOM Competition Commission directly. In fact, now already, the regional Commission has accepted "creative"[62] submissions by individuals.

The provision on the possibility of negative clearance rulings is not expected to cause the same inefficiencies as in the European Union, because it is limited to the member states.[63]

Finally, some aspects of the enforcement procedures in the CARICOM require clarification. Introducing more changes to the regional treaty might not only be cost-intensive, but if these changes involved more obligations on member states it might also cause national resentment. The Revised Treaty of Chaguaramas is perceived as an "unfinished agenda based on mutual respect".[64] In line with this finding, teleological interpretation has often superseded formal literal interpretation of the provisions in Chapter VIII. While this applies to member states, the *TCL v CARICOM Competition Commission* case demonstrates that especially targeted enterprises are inclined to initiate proceedings before the Caribbean Court of Justice. Thus, it is still justified to highlight ambiguities in Chapter VIII: First, the requirements for the right to initiate a competition law investigation, either initiated by the COTED, a member state or the *ex officio* initiation right of the CARICOM Competition Commission, should be clarified. In order to enhance cooperation and transferrals of cases to the regional level, the right to request an investigation by the Commission of the COTED and the member states should generally not be subject to too strict and narrow requirements. The restriction to the CARICOM Competition Commission's *ex officio* initiation right to require a preliminary assessment by a national competition authority reflects the lack of will to cede sovereignty on the part of member states, as well as a certain concern that the regional authority uses its investigation right to the detriment of national industries. Yet bearing in mind the importance to vest the regional competition authority with sufficient enforcement powers,[65] the actual exercise of its powers should not be restricted by limited and narrow conditions. Likewise, in order to enhance submissions by member states and the COTED, a differentiation of requirements between those entities is not justified. One can thus hope that the specific criteria for the initiation rights will be clarified

[62] Statements made by Kusha Haraksingh, current chairman of the CARICOM Competition Commission, in an interview with the author conducted in Port-of-Spain, Trinidad and Tobago, 29 October 2012.

[63] Article 180(1) of the Revised Treaty of Chaguaramas.

[64] Statements made by Kusha Haraksingh, current chairman of the CARICOM Competition Commission, in an interview with the author conducted in Port-of-Spain, Trinidad and Tobago, 29 October 2012.

[65] On the necessity to provide a regional competition authority with sufficient enforcement powers Part III, Sect. 11.3.3.

with progressing enforcement or possibly directly before the Caribbean Court of Justice.

Second, Chapter VIII of the Revised Treaty of Chaguaramas, namely, Article 175(1) and (2) according to their wording only determine a transferral "right" of member states and the COTED, instead of determining an "obligation". Yet given that the CARICOM Competition Commission is entitled to make determinations on breaches of regional competition law by practices with a cross-border effect, transferrals should actually be mandatory. Otherwise, the regional Commission would be exposed to the COTED's and the member states' discretion and limited to its *ex officio* investigation right.[66]

Finally, the use of the term of "concurrent jurisdiction"[67] of the Caribbean Court of Justice and the CARICOM Competition Commission by member states requires clarification.[68] The wording of Article 176(6) of the Revised Treaty of Chaguaramas does not establish a hierarchical order between the two procedures, in particular with regard to the possibility to halt proceedings in competition law procedures.[69] Although it constitutes the legitimate right of member states to initiate judicial reviews of community bodies' acts, Article 176(6) of the Revised Treaty should not be used to sabotage proceedings before the regional competition authority. One should thus hope that the Caribbean Court of Justice makes statements on the admissibility of member states' judicial proceedings according to Article 176(6) of the Revised Treaty of Chaguaramas.

The dominant feature of the general legal system in the CARICOM is the absence of direct effect of regional competition law, *Dimension V*. Although the introduction of supranationality, from a purely competition law perspective, might be efficient, it would surely not be politically acceptable.[70] With regard to individual rights' protection one should thus positively acknowledge that the CARICOM Competition Commission is open for "creative"[71] submissions. As national implementation is still lagging behind, individuals can only address the regional competition authority in case they are affected by a regional competition law breach, although this is actually not intended.

Another general ambiguity refers to parallel or exclusive application of national and regional competition laws. Following the opinion set out in this research,

---

[66] With regard to the disadvantages of applying the ex officio investigation right at an early stage of regional competition law enforcement, see above Part III, Dimension IV: section "Ex Officio Power of a Regional Competition Authority to Initiate Investigations".

[67] Article 176(6) of the Revised Treaty of Chaguaramas, see *CARICOM Secretariat,* The CARICOM Competition Commission, 2008, p. 10.

[68] See above Part II, Dimension IV: Sect. 8.1.1.2.

[69] *Beckford,* The Appropriate Design and Enforcement of Competition Law and Policy in Countries at Different Stages of Market Development, 26–28 May 2010, Brasilia, p. 7.

[70] *Stewart,* in: *Drexl/Bakhoum/Fox/Gal/Gerber,* Competition Policy and Regional Integration in Developing Countries, 2012, pp. 161, 177.

[71] Statements made by Kusha Haraksingh, current chairman of the CARICOM Competition Commission, in an interview with the author conducted in Port-of-Spain, Trinidad and Tobago, 29 October 2012.

national and regional competition laws will be applied in parallel. This however strongly suggests that the CARICOM Competition Commission should adopt guidelines on enforcement measures in order to avoid conflicts. A different possibility could be the enactment of standards for the enforcement measures. Even under the current system, Article 9 of the Revised Treaty of Chaguaramas guarantees some compliance with and convergent application of national laws by the member states. Yet regional guidelines on enforcement measures, more than constituting a mere reconciliation device, could also provide assistance to national competition authorities in the enforcement of national competition laws.

Chapter 14
Guidelines on the Institutional Design of Regional Competition Law Enforcement

Based on a comparison and analysis of regional competition law enforcement in the WAEMU, the AndeanC and the CARICOM, one can identify certain "competition constraints"[1] that impact regional competition law enforcement. In accordance with the slogan "one size does not fit all", the experiences described in this study demonstrate that these competition constraints do not constitute parameters that will never change, but constitute interrelated and dynamic factors that cause different outcomes in different RTAs. As an attempt to summarize the results of the previous analysis, eleven broad policy recommendations regarding the degree of centralization or decentralization of regional competition law enforcement can be formulated.

14.1 Number of Member States and Their Economic Heterogeneity

The larger and the more economically diverse the member states are and the weaker their infrastructure is, the less centralized should the regional competition law structure be (especially Dimension I, IV). The legislative framework (Dimension II) should yet provide for standards of national law in order to enhance convergent competition law enforcement and in order to facilitate the attraction of FDI.

[1] *Drexl* develops several principles of orientation for the design of a regional enforcement system, *Drexl,* in: *Drexl/Bakhoum/Fox/Gal/Gerber,* Competition Policy and Regional Integration in Developing Countries, 2012, pp. 231–252. See also on competition constraints mentioned by *Bakhoum/Molestina,* in: *Drexl/Bakhoum/Fox/Gal/Gerber,* Competition Policy and Regional Integration in Developing Countries, 2012, pp. 89, 108ff.

J. Molestina, *Regional Competition Law Enforcement in Developing Countries*, Munich Studies on Innovation and Competition 9,
https://doi.org/10.1007/978-3-662-58525-2_14

14.2 Intra-Community Trade

The more inter-state trade exists between member states, the more centralized the regional competition law structure can be (Dimension I, II, III, V). Enforcement (Dimension IV) should remain decentralized, in particular if the RTA constitutes of a large number of member states and competition culture is relatively well established in member states.

14.3 Particularities of Prevailing Anticompetitive Practices and Actors

The more state-related anticompetitive practices and state aids exist, the more centralized substantive regional competition law should be (Dimension I). This is usually the case in a young RTA (Dimension V). A centralization of the control of state-related restraints has to be balanced with special and differential enforcement measures or exemptions, for example for the treatment of less-developed member states, regions or sectors. They should however be decided upon on the regional level (Dimension I, IV). Provisions protecting small and medium-sized firms or minorities are more efficiently exercised by national competition law authorities, assuming that national rules are in accordance with regional law and the legislative framework (Dimension I, II, III, V).

14.4 Institutional Capacities and Resources

The more an institution lacks basic resources, the fewer competences should be attributed to it. Yet the notion of "sufficient resources" for competition authorities is not mainly a quantitative question, but a question of commitment of the staff. The fewer resources the regional authority has, the more decentralized a regional competition law system should be (Dimension I, III, IV). In the latter case the regional authority can still be vested with coordinating and advocacy functions or with the function to enhance horizontal cooperation and information sharing between NCAs (Dimension III, IV).

14.5 Existence, Efficacy and Diversity of National Competition Law Systems

The more national competition law systems exist, the less centralized the regional competition law system should be (Dimension I, II). If most member states are still in their implementation or reforming process, the regional competition authority should place special emphasis on competition advocacy and technical assistance offered to national legislators and competition law-enforcing organs (Dimension III, IV). Diversity and a heterogeneous stage of development of national competition law regimes also favour centralized competition law enforcement in order to avoid unequal competition law application that only benefits certain member states (Dimension I, IV).

14.6 Existence of Competition Culture in Member States

The stronger the competition culture in the member states (with regard to general competition and regional competition law), the less centralized the system should be (Dimension II, IV, V). This also preconditions the existence of regional legal precedents. Legal precedents are the most efficient way to spread a regional competition culture. Particular focus should then also be placed on the protection of individuals' rights. It requires special training of national judges and standards for decentralized private or criminal law claims (Dimension II, IV).

14.7 Political Will to Cede Sovereignty

The less willing the member states are to cede sovereignty to the regional level, the more cooperation mechanisms should be included in the RTA and the more advocacy functions should be attributed to the regional level (Dimension I, IV). This *inter alia* entails the strengthening or creation of specialized formal cooperation organs, which are composed of NCAs and the regional competition authority (Dimension III).

14.8 Aspect of Time and Sequencing

The younger the national competition authorities are, the more centralized the regional institution and regional competition law can be (Dimension I, IV). Prior notification requirements for individuals can constitute an instrument to overcome the information deficit of the regional authority (Dimension IV). However, national structures must be given the opportunity to develop their own competition law regimes (Dimension II).

14.9 Goals of Integration and Regional Competition Law

The protection of a common market is the most convincing and incentivizing objective for a uniformly applied regional competition law. Yet, this cannot be achieved solely through the unification of competition law or through completely centralized enforcement (Dimension I, II, IV). In the absence of the creation of a common market as a main objective of economic integration, a regional competition authority can still be vested with coordinating functions or provided with an information-sharing platform to enhance horizontal cooperation and the exchange of information (Dimension III, IV). Yet under such circumstances, competition law enforcement should mainly take place nationally (Dimension I, II, III, IV).

14.10 Existence of a Conflict Resolution Mechanism at the Regional Level

The larger the impact of the appellate instance on competition law decisions or legislation, the more competition law expertise has to be spread among the members of such regional reviewing bodies, most importantly among judges (Dimension III, IV). The greater the reputation and efficacy of a regional court of justice, the more should it be incorporated as a controlling instance for regional competition law decisions. This however requires provisions that govern the demarcation of competences between the regional competition authority and the regional court in case of regional competition law breaches (Dimension I, III).

14.11 Degree and Scope of General Integration (Including Socio-Cultural and Political)

The deeper the general integration of member states in the RTA, the more specific regional competition law can be and the wider its scope of application, irrespective of the question of which entity enforces the regional law (Dimension I). The deeper and broader general integration is, the more cooperation mechanisms with competition-related institutions (national and regional) should be established (Dimension III, IV).

Bibliography

Advocacy Working Group, Advocacy and Competition Policy, Report of the Advocacy Working Group, International Competition Network, paper presented at ICN Conference, 22–23 September 2002, Naples <http://www.internationalcompetitionnetwork.org/uploads/library/doc358.pdf>, (cited as: *Advocacy and Competition Policy*, Advocacy and Competition Policy, 22–23 September 2002, Naples <http://www.internationalcompetitionnetwork.org/uploads/library/doc358.pdf>)

African Competition Forum, Promoting Competition in Benin, Iss. 3 African Competition Forum Report 10 (2014), (cited as: *African Competition Forum*, Promoting Competition in Benin, ACF Report 10 (2014))

Agbodji, Akoété Ega, Intégration et Échanges commerciaux Intra Sous-régionaux: le Cas de l'UEMOA, Vol. 1 No. 1 Revue Africaine de l'Intégration 161–188 (2007), (cited as: *Agbodji*, Intégration et Échanges commerciaux Intra Sous-régionaux: le Cas de l'UEMOA, 1/1 Rev. Afr. de l'Intégration 161 (2007))

Alvarez, Ana María/Evenett, Simon J./Wilse-Samson, Laurence, Anti-competitive Practices and the Attainment of the Millennium Development Goals: Implications for Competition Law Enforcement and Inter-Agency Cooperation, in: *Alvarez, Ana María/Wilse-Samson, Laurence* (Eds.), Implementing Competition-Related Provisions in Regional Trade Agreements: is it possible to obtain development gains?, United Nations, New York and Geneva 2007, pp. 59–95, (cited as: *Alvarez/Evenett/Wilse-Samson*, in: *Alvarez/Wilse-Samson*, Implementing Competition-Related Provisions in Regional Trade Agreements, 2007, p. 59)

Alvarez, Ana María/Clarke, Julian/Silva, Verónica, Negociación y Aplicación de Disposiciones de Competencia en Acuerdos Bilaterales y Regionales de Comercio: Pautas para la Reflexion, No. 2 Revista de la Competencia y la Propriedad Intelectual 5–42 (2006), (cited as: *Alvarez/Clarke/Silva*, Negociación y Aplicación de Disposiciones de Competencia en Acuerdos Bilaterales y Regionales de Comercio: Pautas para la Reflexion, 2 Rev. Comp. Propriedad Intelectual 5 (2006))

Alvarez, Ana María/Horna, Pierre, Implementing competition law and policy in Latin America: The role of Technical Assistance, Vol. 83 Iss. 1 Chicago-Kent Law Review 91–128 (2008), (cited as: *Alvarez/Horna*, Implementing competition law and policy in Latin America: The role of Technical Assistance, 83 Chi.-Kent L. Rev. 91 (2008))

Anderson, Kenneth, Squaring the Circle? Reconciling sovereignty and global governance through global government networks, Vol. 118 Harvard Law Review 1255–1312 (2005), (cited as: *Anderson*, Squaring the Circle? Reconciling sovereignty and global governance through global government networks, 118 Harv. L. Rev. 1255 (2005))

J. Molestina, *Regional Competition Law Enforcement in Developing Countries*, Munich Studies on Innovation and Competition 9,
https://doi.org/10.1007/978-3-662-58525-2

Andrade Ubidia, Santiago, Lineamientos para un Régimen Jurídico de la Competencia en el Ecuador, Vol. 16 No. 2 Revista Jurídica Universidad Católica de Santiago de Guayaquil 13–61 (2003), (cited as: *Andrade*, Lineamientos para un Régimen Jurídico de la Competencia en el Ecuador, 16/2 Rev. Jur. Univ. Católica 13 (2003))

Baetge, Dietmar, Globalisierung des Wettbewerbsrechts, 1st edition, Mohr Siebeck, Tübingen 2009, (cited as: *Baetge*, Globalisierung des Wettbewerbsrechts, 2009)

Bakhoum, Mor, A Dual Language in Modern Competition Law? *Efficiency Approach* versus *Development Approach* and Implications for Developing Countries, Vol. 34 No. 3 World Competition 495–520 (2011a), (cited as: *Bakhoum*, A Dual Language in Modern Competition Law?, 34/3 W. Comp. 495 (2011))

Bakhoum, Mor, Commerce International, Politique de Concurrence et Accords de Partenariat Economique: Réflexions sur les Enjeux et Perspectives d'un Triptyque, Vol. 1 No. 2 Revue Africaine de l'Intégration 3–7 (2010), (cited as: *Bakhoum*, Commerce International, Politique de Concurrence et Accords de Partenariat Economique, 1/2 Rev. Afr. de l'Intégration 3 (2010))

Bakhoum, Mor, Delimitation and Exercise of Competence between the West African Economic and Monetary Union (WAEMU) and its Member States in Competition Policy, Vol. 29 No. 4 World Competition 653–681 (2006), (cited as: *Bakhoum*, Delimitation and Exercise of Competence between the West African Economic and Monetary Union (WAEMU) and its Member States in Competition Policy, 29/4 W. Comp. 653 (2006))

Bakhoum, Mor, Étude sur la Révision du Cadre Institutionnel de Mise en Oeuvre des Règles de Concurrence de l'UEMOA, Working Paper, WAEMU 2011b, (cited as: *Bakhoum*, Étude sur la Révision du Cadre Institutionnel de Mise en Oeuvre des Règles de Concurrence de l'UEMOA, 2011)

Bakhoum, Mor, Interfacing the "Local" with the "Global": A Developing-Country Perspective on "Global Competition", Max Planck Institute for Intellectual Property and Competition Law Research Paper No. 13-02, paper presented at the "Global Competition Law Conference", 28 October 2011c, Chicago, (cited as: *Bakhoum*, A Developing-Country Perspective on "Global Competition", 28 October 2011, Chicago)

Bakhoum, Mor, L'articulation du droit communautaire et des droits nationaux de la concurrence dans l'Union Economique et Monétaire Ouest Africaine (UEMOA), Stämpfli, Berne 2007, (cited as: *Bakhoum*, L'articulation du droit communautaire et des droits nationaux de la concurrence dans l'Union Economique et Monétaire Ouest Africaine, 2007)

Bakhoum, Mor, Perspectives Africaines d'une Politique de la Concurrence dans l'Espace OHADA, Vol. XXV No. 3 Revue Internationale de Droit Économique 351–378 (2011d), (cited as: *Bakhoum*, Perspectives Africaines d'une Politique de la Concurrence dans l'Espace OHADA, XXV R.I.D.E. 351 (2011))

Bakhoum, Mor/Molestina, Julia, Institutional coherence and effectiveness of a regional competition policy: the case of the West African Economic and Monetary Union (WAEMU), in: *Drexl, Josef/Bakhoum, Mor/Fox, Eleanor/Gal, Michal/Gerber, David* (Eds.), Competition Policy and Regional Integration in Developing Countries, Edward Elgar, Cheltenham Northampton 2012, pp. 89–115, (cited as: *Bakhoum/Molestina*, in: *Drexl/Bakhoum/Fox/Gal/Gerber*, Competition Policy and Regional Integration in Developing Countries, 2012, p. 89)

Bakhoum, Mor, Reflections on the concepts of 'economic freedom', 'free competition' and 'efficiency' from the perspective of developing countries, in: *Zimmer, Daniel* (Ed.), The Goals of Competition Law, Edward Elgar, Cheltenham Northampton 2012, pp. 408–440, (cited as: *Bakhoum*, in: *Zimmer*, The Goals of Competition Law, 2012, p. 408)

Bätge, Johanna, Wettbewerb der Wettbewerbsordnungen? Überlegungen zum richtigen Grad von Dezentralität und Harmonisierung im Recht gegen Wettbewerbsbeschränkungen, Nomos, Tübingen 2009, (cited as: *Bätge*, Wettbewerb der Wettbewerbsordnungen?, 2009)

Baumann, Renato/Bustillo, Inés/Heirman, Johannes/Macario, Carla/Máttar, Jorge/Pérez, Esteban, Los procesos de integración de los países de América Latina y el Caribe 2000–2001: avances, retrocesos y temas pendientes, CEPAL – Serie comercio internacional de las Naciones Unidas no. 25, Santiago de Chile 2002 <http://www.eclac.org/publicaciones/xml/5/11175/lcl1780e.pdf>, (cited as: *Baumann/Bustillo/Heirman/Macario/Máttar/Pérez,*

Los procesos de integración de los países de América Latina y el Caribe 2000–2001, 2002 <http://www.eclac.org/publicaciones/xml/5/11175/lcl1780e.pdf>)

Beckford, Delroy S., Effecting cooperation to resolve cross-border anti-competitive conduct affecting CARICOM, Vol. XV Competition Matters – Fair Trading Commission 6–9 (2011), (cited as: *Beckford*, Effecting cooperation to resolve cross-border anti-competitive conduct affecting CARICOM, XV Competition Matters – Fair Trading Commission 6 (2011))

Beckford, Delroy S., Enforcement of competition law in CARICOM: Perspectives on challenges to meeting regional and multilateral obligations, SP/SRCC-PFDALC/Di no. 18-09, paper presented at UNCTAD Regional Seminar on Trade and Competition: Prospects and Future Challenges for Latin America and the Caribbean, 20–21 April 2009, Caracas, (cited as: *Beckford*, Enforcement of competition law in CARICOM: Perspectives on challenges to meeting regional and multilateral obligations, 20–21 April 2009, Caracas)

Beckford, Delroy S., Enforcement of Competition Law in CARICOM: Perspectives on Domestic, Regional, and Multilateral Obligations, Vol. 35 No. 2 West Indian Law Journal 109–143 (2010a), (cited as: *Beckford*, Enforcement of Competition Law in CARICOM, 35/2 W.I.L.J. 109 (2010))

Beckford, Delroy S., Implementing effective competition policy through regional trade agreements: the case of CARICOM, in: *Drexl, Josef/Bakhoum, Mor/Fox, Eleanor/Gal, Michal/Gerber, David* (Eds.), Competition Policy and Regional Integration in Developing Countries, Cheltenham Northampton 2012, pp. 185–204, (cited as: *Beckford*, in: *Drexl/Bakhoum/Fox/Gal/Gerber*, Competition Policy and Regional Integration in Developing Countries, 2012, p. 185)

Beckford, Delroy S., The Appropriate Design and Enforcement of Competition Law and Policy in Countries at Different Stages of Market Development – The Case of CARICOM, paper presented at the II Regional Seminar UNCTAD-SELA on Trade and Competition and Preparatory Meeting for the VI United Nations Conference to Review All Aspects of the Set of Principles and Rules on Competition, 26–28 May 2010b, Brasilia, (cited as: *Beckford*, The Appropriate Design and Enforcement of Competition Law and Policy in Countries at Different Stages of Market Development, 26–28 May 2010, Brasilia)

Behrens, Peter, Integrationstheorie, Internationale wirtschaftliche Integration als Gegenstand politologischer, ökonomischer und juristischer Forschung, Rabels Zeitschrift für ausländisches und internationales Privatrecht 8–50 (1981), (cited as: *Behrens*, Integrationstheorie, Internationale wirtschaftliche Integration als Gegenstand politologischer, ökonomischer und juristischer Forschung, RabelsZ 8 (1981))

Belle Antoine, Rose-Marie, Commonwealth Caribbean – Law and Legal System, Routledge-Cavendish, 2nd edition, New York 2008, (cited as: *Belle Antoine*, Commonwealth Caribbean, 2008)

Berkowitz, Daniel/Pistor, Katharina/Richard, Jean-Francois, Economic development, legality, and the transplant effect, Vol. 47 European Economic Review 165–195 (2003), (cited as: *Berkowitz/Pistor/Richard*, Economic development, legality, and the transplant effect, 47 Eur. Econ. Rev. 165 (2003))

Borrell, Joan Ramon, Choosing among American, European, or no antitrust at all, working paper series, Barcelona February 2005 <http://ssrn.com/abstract=6692882>, (cited as: *Borrell*, Choosing among American, European, or no antitrust at all, 2005 <http://ssrn.com/abstract=669282>)

Bosch, Antonio/García-Montalvo, José, Free and Nondiscriminatory Access to Airports: A Proposal for Latin America, Inter-American Development Bank working paper, Washington 2003 <http://idbdocs.iadb.org/wsdocs/getdocument.aspx?docnum=352782>, (cited as: *Bosch/García-Montalvo*, Free and Nondiscriminatory Access to Airports: A Proposal for Latin America, 2003 <http://idbdocs.iadb.org/wsdocs/getdocument.aspx?docnum=352782>)

Botta, Marco, The Role of Competition Policy in the Latin American Regional Integration: A Comparative Analysis of Caricom, Andean Community and Mercosur, paper presented at the Ninth Annual Conference of the Euro-Latin Study Network on Integration and Trade (ELSNIT) – *Revising Regionalism*, 21–22 October 2011, St. Gallen, (cited as: *Botta*, The Role of Competition Policy in the Latin American Regional Integration: A Comparative Analysis of Caricom, Andean Community and Mercosur, 21–22 October 2011, St. Gallen)

Böttcher, Georg, Harmonisierungsbemühungen der Andengemeinschaft im Bereich des Kartellrechts, Vol. 3 GRUR Int 217–223 (2003), (cited as: *Böttcher*, Harmonisierungsbemühungen der Andengemeinschaft im Bereich des Kartellrechts, GRUR Int 217 (2003))

Böttcher, Georg, Kartell- und Lauterkeitsrecht in den Ländern der Andengemeinschaft, Nomos, Baden-Baden 2004, (cited as: *Böttcher*, Kartell- und Lauterkeitsrecht in den Ländern der Andengemeinschaft, 2004)

Boza, Beatriz, Tailor-Made Competition Policy in a Standardizing World: A Study from the Perspective of Developing Economies, Instituto Apoyo, Lima 2005, (cited as: *Boza*, Tailor-Made Competition Policy in a Standardizing World, 2005)

Brokelmann, Helmut, Enforcement of Articles 81 and 82 EC under Regulation 1/2003: The Case of Spain and Portugal, Vol. 29 No. 4 World Competition 535–554 (2006), (cited as: *Brokelmann,* Enforcement of Articles 81 and 82 EC under Regulation 1/2003, 29/4 W. Comp. 535 (2006))

Brusick, Philippe/Evenett, Simon J., Should Developing Countries Worry about Abuse of Dominant Power?, No. 2 Wisconsin Law Review 269–294 (2008), (cited as: *Brusick/Evenett,* Should Developing Countries Worry about Abuse of Dominant Power?, 2 Wis. L. Rev. 269 (2008))

Buccirossi, Paolo/Ciari, Lorenzo/Duso, Tomaso/Spagnolo, Giancarlo/Vitale, Cristiana, Deterrence in Competition Law, Discussion papers, WZB, Wissenschaftszentrum Berlin für Sozialforschung, Schwerpunkt II Märkte und Politik, Forschungsgruppe Wettbewerb und Innovation, No. SP II 2009-14, Berlin 2009 <http://www.econstor.eu/bitstream/10419/51212/1/614784875.pdf>, (cited as: *Buccirossi/Ciari/Duso/Spagnolo,* Deterrence in Competition Law, 2009 <http://www.econstor.eu/bitstream/10419/51212/1/614784875.pdf>)

Budzinski, Oliver, The Governance of Global Competition – Competence Allocation in International Competition Policy, Edward Elgar, Cheltenham Northampton 2008, (cited as: *Budzinski,* The Governance of Global Competition, 2008)

Budzinski, Oliver, Toward an International Governance of Transborder Mergers? Competition Networks and Institutions between Centralism and Decentralism, Vol. 36 No. 1 N.Y.U. Journal of International Law and Politics 1–52 (2004), (cited as: *Budzinski,* Toward an International Governance of Transborder Mergers?, 41 N.Y.U. Journal of Int'l. L. & Pol. 1 (2004))

Burley, Anne-Marie/Mattli, Walter, Europe Before the Court: A Political Theory of Legal Integration, Vol. 47 Iss. 1 International Organization 41–76 (1993), (cited as: *Burley/Mattli,* A Political Theory of Legal Integration, 47 Int. Organization 41 (1993))

Capobianco, Antonio/Christiansen, Hans, Competitive Neutrality and State-Owned Enterprises, OECD Corporate Governance Working Papers No. 1, OECD Publishing, 2011 <http://www.oecd-ilibrary.org/docserver/download/5kg9xfgjdhg6.pdf?expires=1385377786&id=id&accname=guest&checksum=5544908D37FAB684ADDD3EADCFDF4438>, (cited as: *Capobianco/Christiansen,* Competitive Neutrality and State-Owned Enterprises, 2011 <http://www.oecd-ilibrary.org/docserver/download/5kg9xfgjdhg6.pdf?expires=1385377786&id=id&accname=guest&checksum=5544908D37FAB684ADDD3EADCFDF4438>)

CARICOM Secretariat, Caribbean Community Regional Aid for Trade Strategy 2013-2015, February 2013 <http://cms2.caricom.org/documents/5269-caribbean_community_aft_strategy_final.pdf>, (cited as: *CARICOM Secretariat,* Caribbean Community Regional Aid for Trade Strategy 2013-2015, 2013 <http://cms2.caricom.org/documents/5269-caribbean_community_aft_strategy_final.pdf>)

CARICOM Secretariat, Caribbean Court of Justice – How the Court works – The Original Jurisdiction, Georgetown 2005, (cited as: *CARICOM Secretariat,* Caribbean Court of Justice, 2005)

CARICOM Secretariat, Competition Policy & Law in the CSME, Bridgetown 2010, (cited as: *CARICOM Secretariat,* Competition Policy and Law in the CSME, 2010)

CARICOM Secretariat, The CARICOM Competition Commission: Building Competitive Markets, Bridgetown 2008, (cited as: *CARICOM Secretariat,* The CARICOM Competition Commission, 2008)

Cengiz, Firat, Multi-level Governance in Competition Policy: the European Competition Network, Vol. 35 No. 5 European Law Review 660–677 (2010), (cited as: *Cengiz,* Multi-level Governance in Competition Policy, 35 Eur. L. Rev. 660 (2010))

Cengiz, Firat, Regulation 1/2003 Revisited, TILEC Discussion Paper, DP 2009-042, Liverpool 2009a <http://ssrn.com/abstract=1512527>, (cited as: *Cengiz,* Regulation 1/2003 Revisited, 2009 <http://ssrn.com/abstract=1512527>)

Cengiz, Firat, The European Competition Network: Structure, Management and Initial Experiences of Policy Enforcement, European University Institute Working Paper, MWP 2009/5, Florence 2009b <http://cadmus.eui.eu/bitstream/handle/1814/11067/MWP_2009_05.pdf?sequence=1>, (cited as: *Cengiz,* The European Competition Network, 2009 <http://cadmus.eui.eu/bitstream/handle/1814/11067/MWP_2009_05.pdf?sequence=1>)

Cernat, Lucian, Eager to ink, but ready to act? RTA proliferation and international cooperation on competition policy, in: *Brusick, Phillipe/Alvarez, Ana Maria/Cernat, Lucian* (Eds.), Competition Provisions in Regional Trade Agreements: How to Assure Development Gains, United Nations, New York and Geneva 2005, pp. 1–36, (cited as: *Cernat,* in: *Brusick/Alvarez/Cernat,* Competition Provisions in Regional Trade Agreements, 2005, p. 1)

Cini, Michelle/McGowan, Lee, Competition Policy in the European Union, Palgrave Macmillan, New York 2008, (cited as: *Cini/McGowan,* Competition Policy in the European Union, 2008)

Clark, John, Competition Advocacy: Challenges for Developing Countries, Vol. 6 No. 4 OECD Journal of Competition Law and Policy 69–80 (2005), (cited as: *Clark,* Competition Advocacy: Challenges for Developing Countries, 6/4 OECD J. Comp. L. Policy 69 (2005))

Commission Nationale de la Concurrence du Sénégal, Rapport Public 2002–2003, 14 October 2004, Dakar, (cited as: *Commission Nationale de la Concurrence du Sénégal,* Rapport Public 2002–2003, 2004)

Connor, John M., Effectiveness of Antitrust Sanctions on Modern International Cartels, Vol. 6 Iss. 3–4 Journal of Industry, Competition and Trade 195–223 (2006), (cited as: *Connor,* Le Droit de la Concurrence de l'Union Économique et Monétaire Ouest Africaine, 6 J. Industry, Comp. Trade 195 (2006))

Connor, John M., Latin America and the Control of International Cartels, in: *Fox, Eleanor M./Sokol, Daniel D.* (Eds.), Competition Law and Policy in Latin America, Hart Publishing, Oxford and Portland 2009, pp. 291–323, (cited as: *Connor,* in: *Fox/Sokol,* Competition Law and Policy in Latin America, 2009, p. 291)

Cortázar, Javier, Andean competition law: looking for the private sector, or the quest for the missing link in antitrust, in: *Drexl, Josef/Bakhoum, Mor/Fox, Eleanor/Gal, Michal/Gerber, David* (Eds.), Competition Policy and Regional Integration in Developing Countries, Edward Elgar, Cheltenham Northampton 2012, pp. 133–160, (cited as: *Cortázar,* in: *Drexl/Bakhoum/Fox/Gal/Gerber,* Competition Policy and Regional Integration in Developing Countries, 2012, p. 133)

Cortázar, Javier, Curso de Derecho de la Competencia (Antimonopolios), Pontificia Universidad Javeriana and Editorial Temis, Bogotá 2011, (cited as: *Cortázar,* Curso de Derecho de la Competencia, 2011)

Cortázar, Javier, Decisión 608 de la Comunidad Andina: Un Paso Adelante para el Sistema Antimonopolios de la Regiόn, Vol. 2 No. 2 Revista de Derecho de la Competencia 123–152 (2006), (cited as: *Cortázar,* Decisiόn 608 de la Comunidad Andina, 2/2 Rev. Der. Comp. 123 (2006))

Cortázar, Javier, Hacia un Nuevo Derecho de la Competencia en Colombia – Análisis critico y Prospectiva, Ediciones Doctrina y Ley, Bogotá 2003, (cited as: *Cortázar,* Hacia un Nuevo Derecho de la Competencia en Colombia, 2003)

Coulibaly, Abou Saïb, Le Droit de la Concurrence de l'Union Économique et Monétaire Ouest Africaine, No. 43 – 44 Revue burkinabbé de droit, 1st and 2nd semester 2003, OHADATA D-05-27, (cited as *Coulibaly,* Le Droit de la Concurrence de l'Union Économique et Monétaire Ouest Africaine, 43–44 Rev. burkinnabé de droit (2003))

Cseres, Katalin J., Integrate or Separate. Institutional Design for the Enforcement of Competition Law and Consumer Law, Amsterdam Centre for European Law and Governance, Working Paper Series No. 2013-01, Amsterdam 11 April 2013a <http://ssrn.com/abstract=2200908>, (cited as: *Cseres,* Integrate or Separate. Institutional Design for the Enforcement of Competition Law and Consumer Law, 11 April 2013 <http://ssrn.com/abstract=2200908>)

Cseres, Katalin J., Multi-Jurisdictional Competition Law Enforcement: The Interface between European Competition Law and the Competition Laws of the New Member States, Vol. 3 No. 2 European Competition Journal 465–502 (2007), (cited as: *Cseres,* Multi-Jurisdictional Competition Law Enforcement, 3 Eur. Comp. J. 465 (2007))

Cseres, Katalin J., Questions of Legitimacy in the Europeanization of Competition Law Procedures of the EU Member States, Amsterdam Centre for European Law and Governance, Working Paper Series No. 2013-02, Amsterdam 7 February 2013b <http://ssrn.com/abstract=2213192>, (cited as: *Cseres,* Questions of Legitimacy in the Europeanization of Competition Law Procedures of the EU Member States, 7 February 2013 <http://ssrn.com/abstract=2213192>)

Curiel Leidenz, Claudia, The suppression of the competition policy agenda in the context of an over-regulated economy: the case of Venezuela, in: *Drexl, Josef/Bagnoli, Vicente* (Eds.), State-Initiated Restraints of Competition, Edward Elgar, Cheltenham Northampton 2015, pp. 213–238, (cited as: *Curiel Leidenz,* in: *Drexl/Bagnoli,* State-Initiated Restraints of Competition, 2015, p. 213)

CUTS CCIER, Centre for Competition, Investment & Economic Regulation, A Time for Action – Synthesis Report: Strengthening Constituencies for Effective Competition Regimes in Select West African Countries (7Up4 Project), CUTS C-Cier, Jaipur 2010, (cited as: *CUTS CCIER,* A Time for Action, 2010)

CUTS CCIER, Centre for Competition, Investment & Economic Regulation, Vers des régimes efficients de la concurrence par le renforcement des capacités dans des pays sélectionnés d'Afrique de l'Ouest (Projet 7Up4), Document préliminaire Sénégal sur les scénarios de concurrence, Dakar January 2009 <http://www.cuts-ccier.org/7up4/pdf/PCP-Senegal.pdf>, (cited as: *CUTS,* Vers des régimes efficients de la concurrence par le renforcement des capacités dans des pays sélectionnés d'Afrique de l'Ouest, 2009 <http://www.cuts-ccier.org/7up4/pdf/PCP-Senegal.pdf>)

CUTS, Projet Consumer Unity & Trust Society, Document Préliminaire du Mali sur les Scénarios de Concurrence, January 2009 <http://www.cuts-ccier.org/7up4/pdf/PCP-Mali.pdf>, (cited as: *CUTS,* Document Préliminaire du Mali sur les Scénarios de Concurrence, 2009 <http://www.cuts-ccier.org/7up4/pdf/PCP-Mali.pdf>)

CUTS, Document préliminaire Burkina Faso sur les scénarios de concurrence, Etude de la Concurrence au Burkina Faso, December 2008 <http://www.cuts-ccier.org/7up4/pdf/PCP-Burkina_Faso.pdf>, (cited as: *CUTS,* Document préliminaire Burkina Faso sur les scénarios de concurrence, 2008 <http://www.cuts-ccier.org/7up4/pdf/PCP-Burkina_Faso.pdf>)

Dabbah, Maher M., Competition Law and Policy in Developing Countries: A Critical Assessment of the Challenges to Establishing an Effective Competition Law Regime, Vol. 33 No. 3 World Competition 457–475 (2010), (cited as: *Dabbah*, Competition Law and Policy in Developing Countries, 33/3 W. Comp. 457 (2010))

Davies, John/Das, Manish, Private Enforcement of Commission Commitment Decisions: A Steep Climb not a Gentle Stroll, Vol. 29 Iss. 5 Fordham International Law Journal 917–951 (2005), (cited as: *Davies/Das,* Private Enforcement of Commission Commitment Decisions, 29 Fordham Int'l. L.J. 917 (2005))

Delegation of the European Union of Peru, UE-CAN 2010 - Cooperación Regional con la Comunidad Andina, Lima 2010 <http://issuu.com/ue-delper/docs/cooperacion-ue-can-2010>, (cited as: *Delegation of the European Union of Peru,* UE-CAN, Cooperación Regional con la Comunidad Andina, 2010 <http://issuu.com/ue-delper/docs/cooperacion-ue-can-2010>)

De León, Ignacio, An Institutional Assessment of Antitrust Policy – The Latin American Experience-, International Competition Law Series, Kluwer Law International, The Netherlands 2009, (cited as: *De León*, An Institutional Assessment of Antitrust Policy, 2009)

De León, Ignacio, Institutional Analysis of Competition Policy in Transition and Developing Countries: The Lessons from Latin America, Vol. 3 No. 2 Washington University Global Studies Law Review 405–428 (2004), (cited as: *De León,* Institutional Analysis of Competition Policy in Transition and Developing Countries, 3 Wash. U. Global Stud. L. Rev. 405 (2004))

De León, Ignacio, Latin American Competition Law and Policy – A Policy in Search of Identity, International Competition Law Series, Kluwer Law International, The Netherlands 2001, (cited as: *De León,* Latin American Competition Law and Policy, 2001)

De León, Ignacio, Latin American Competition Policy: From Nirvana Antitrust Policy to Reality-Based Institutional Competition Building, Vol. 83 Iss. 1 Chicago-Kent Law Review 39–65 (2008), (cited as: *De León,* Latin American Competition Policy, 83 Chi.-Kent L. Rev. 39 (2008))

Demba, SY, L'Activité de la Cour de la Justice de l'UEMOA, No. 1 Revue de la Faculté des Sciences Juridiques et Politiques (2006), <http://cyber.law.harvard.edu/credila-ucad/sites/credila-ucad/images/NAF_NOUV_N°1.pdf>, (cited as: *Demba,* L'Activité de la Cour de la Justice de l'UEMOA, Rev. de la Faculté des Sciences Juridiques et Politiques (2006) <http://cyber.law.harvard.edu/credila-ucad/sites/credila-ucad/images/NAF_NOUV_N°1.pdf>)

Dreher, Meinrad, Gemeinsamer Europäischer Markt – einheitliche Wettbewerbsordnung?, in: *Forschungsinstitut für Wirtschaftsverfassung und Wettbewerb E.V.* (Ed.), Umbruch der Wettbewerbsordnung in Europa – Referate des XXVIII. FIW-Symposions, Carl Heymanns, Cologne 1995, pp. 1–22, (cited as: *Dreher,* in: *Forschungsinstitut für Wirtschaftsverfassung und Wettbewerb E.V.,* Umbruch der Wettbewerbsordnung in Europa, 1995, p. 1)

Dreher, Meinrad, Kartellrechtsvielfalt oder Kartellrechtseinheit in Europa?, No.10 Die Aktiengesellschaft 437–448 (1993), (cited as: *Dreher,* Kartellrechtsvielfalt oder Kartellrechtseinheit in Europa?, AG 437 (1993))

Drexl, Josef, Do We Need "Courage" for International Antitrust Law? Choosing between Supranational and International Law Principles of Enforcement, in: *Drexl, Josef* (Ed.), The Future of Transnational Antitrust – From Comparative to Common Competition Law, Stämpfli, Berne 2003, pp. 311–342, (cited as: *Drexl,* in: *Drexl*, The Future of Transnational Antitrust, 2003, p. 311)

Drexl, Josef, Economic integration and competition law in developing countries, in: *Drexl, Josef/Bakhoum, Mor/Fox, Eleanor/Gal, Michal/Gerber, David* (Eds.), Competition Policy and Regional Integration in Developing Countries, Edward Elgar, Cheltenham Northampton 2012, pp. 231–252, (cited as: *Drexl,* in: *Drexl/Bakhoum/Fox/Gal/Gerber,* Competition Policy and Regional Integration in Developing Countries, 2012, p. 231)

Drexl, Josef, Perspectives européennes sur la politique de la concurrence dans l'espace OHADA, Vol. XXV No. 3 Revue Internationale de Droit Économique 281–304 (2011), (cited as: *Drexl,* Perspectives européennes sur la politique de la concurrence dans l'espace OHADA, XXV R.I.D.E. 281 (2011))

Dutz, Mark A./Hayri, Aydin, Does More Intense Competition Lead to Higher Growth?, World Bank Policy Research Working Paper No. 2320, Washington 2000 <http://elibrary.worldbank.org/doi/pdf/10.1596/1813-9450-2320>, (cited as: *Dutz/Hayri,* Does More Intense Competition Lead to Higher Growth?, 2000 <http://elibrary.worldbank.org/doi/pdf/10.1596/1813-9450-2320>)

Edwards, Gail, Legal Transplants and Economics: the World Bank and Third World Economies in the 1980s – a Case Study of Jamaica, the Republic of Kenya and the Philippines, Vol. 9 Iss. 2 European Journal of Law Reform 243–283 (2007), (cited as: *Edwards,* Legal Transplants and Economics, 9 Eur. J. Law Reform 243 (2007))

Egoumé-Bossogo, Philippe/Mendis, Chandima, Trade and Integration in the Caribbean, International Monetary Fund Working Paper, WP/027148, Washington September 2002 <http://www.imf.org/external/pubs/ft/wp/2002/wp02148.pdf>, (cited as: *Egoumé-Bossogo/Mendis,* Trade and Integration in the Caribbean, 2002 <http://www.imf.org/external/pubs/ft/wp/2002/wp02148.pdf>)

Egoume, Philippe/Nayo, Ankouvi, Feeling the Elephant's Weight: The Impact of Côte d'Ivoire's Crisis on WAEMU Trade, International Monetary Fund Working Paper, WP/11/80, Washington April 2011, (cited as: *Egoume/Nayo*, Feeling the Elephant's Weight: The Impact of Côte d'Ivoire's Crisis on WAEMU Trade, 2011 <http://www.imf.org/external/pubs/ft/wp/2011/wp1180.pdf>)

Ehlermann, Claus-Dieter, Implementation of EC Competition Law by National Anti-Trust Authorities, Vol. 17 Iss. 2 European Competition Law Review 88–95 (1996), (cited as: *Ehlermann,* Implementation of EC Competition Law by National Anti-Trust Authorities, 17 ECLR 88 (1996))

Ehlermann, Claus Dieter/Drijber, Berend Jan, Legal Protection of Enterprises: Administrative Procedure, in particular Access to Files and Confidentiality, Vol. 17 Iss. 7 European Competition Law Review 375–383 (1996), (cited as: *Ehlermann/Drijber,* Legal Protection of Enterprises, 17 ECLR 375 (1996))

Espinoza Lozada, Jesús Eloy, Peru: National Institute for the Defence of Competition and the Protection of Intellectual Property, The Antitrust Review of the Americas 138–140 (2016), (cited as: *Espinoza Lozada,* Peru: National Institute for the Defence of Competition and the Protection of Intellectual Property, Antitrust Rev. Americas 138 (2016))

European Commission, Andean Community Regional Strategy Paper 2007–2013, 12 April 2007 (E/2007/678) <http://www.eeas.europa.eu/andean/rsp/07_13_en.pdf>, (cited as: *European Commission,* Andean Community Regional Strategy Paper 2007–2013, 2007 <http://www.eeas.europa.eu/andean/rsp/07_13_en.pdf>)

European Commission, Report on the functioning of Regulation 1/2003, Communication from the Commission to the European Parliament and the Council, COM(2009) 206 final, 29 April 2009, (cited as: *European Commission,* Report on the functioning of Regulation 1/2003, (Communication) COM(2009) 206 final, 2009)

Evenett, Simon J., Analytical Considerations in the Design of Regional Rules on Competition Law, St. Gallen December 2005, (available from the author), (cited as: *Evenett,* Analytical Considerations in the Design of Regional Rules on Competition Law, 2005)

Evenett, Simon J., Competition Advocacy: Time for a Rethink?, Vol. 26 Northwestern Journal of International Law & Business 495–514 (2006), (cited as: *Evenett,* Competition Advocacy, 26 Nw. J. Int'l. L. Bus. 495 (2006))

Evenett, Simon J., Merger and Anticartel Policies in an Era of Integrating Markets, in: *Hoeckman, Bernard/Mattoo, Aaditya/English, Philip* (Eds.), Development, Trade and the WTO: A Handbook, World Bank Publications, Washington 2002, pp. 456–462, (cited as: *Evenett,* in: *Hoeckman/Mattoo/English,* Development, Trade and the WTO: A Handbook, 2002, p. 456)

Evenett, Simon J./Levenstein, Margaret C./Suslow, Valerie Y., International Cartel Enforcement: Lessons from the 1990s, World Bank Policy Research Working Paper No. 2680, Washington 2001, (cited as: *Evenett/Levenstein/Suslow,* International Cartel Enforcement, 2001)

Falla, Alejandro/Quintana, Eduardo, Derecho de la Competencia en la Comunidad Andina, in: *Pontificia Universidad Católica del Perú, Instituto de Estudios Internacionales* (Ed.), Derecho Comunitario Andino, Lima 2003, pp. 143–176, (cited as: *Falla/Quintana,* in: *Pontificia Universidad Católica del Peru,* Derecho Comunitario Andino, 2003, p. 143)

Fau-Nougaret, Matthieu, La concurrence des organisations régionales en Afrique, L'Harmattan, Paris 2012, (cited as: *Fau-Nougaret,* La concurrence des organisations régionales en Afrique, 2012)

Flórez Linero, Daniel Bernardo, La Empresa Colombiana: ¿Una Víctima del Estado? Las Ayudas del Estado a las Empresas y el Debate sobre la Libre Competencia, No. 45 Revista de Derecho Privado 1–36 (2011), (cited as: *Flórez,* La Empresa Colombiana, 45 Rev. de Derecho Privado 1 (2011))

Fox, Eleanor M., Antitrust and Institutions: Design and Change, Vol. 41 Iss. 3 Loyola University Chicago Law Journal 473–488 (2010), (cited as: *Fox,* Antitrust and Institutions, 41 Loy. U. Chi. L.J. 473 (2010))

Fox, Eleanor M., Competition, development and regional integration: in search of a competition law fit for developing countries, in: *Drexl, Josef/Bakhoum, Mor/Fox, Eleanor/Gal, Michal/Gerber, David* (Eds.), Competition Policy and Regional Integration in Developing Countries, Edward Elgar, Cheltenham Northampton 2012, pp. 273–290, (cited as: *Fox,* in: *Drexl/Bakhoum/Fox/Gal/Gerber,* Competition Policy and Regional Integration in Developing Countries, 2012, p. 273)

Fox, Eleanor M., Economic Development, Poverty, and Antitrust: The Other Path, Vol. 13 Southwestern Journal of Law and Trade in the Americas 101–125 (2007), (cited as: *Fox*, Economic Development, Poverty, and Antitrust, 13 Sw. J.L. Trade Americas 101 (2007))

Fox, Eleanor M., The Central European Nations and the EU Waiting Room – Why Must the Central European Nations Adopt the Competition Law of the European Union?, Vol. 23 Iss. 2 Brooklyn Journal of International Law 351–363 (1997), (cited as: *Fox*, Why Must the Central European Nations Adopt the Competition Law of the European Union?, 23 Brook. J. Int'l. Law 351 (1997))

Fox, Eleanor M./Healey, Deborah, When the State harms Competition – The Role for Competition Law, NYU Law & Economics Research Paper Series Working Paper No. 13-11, New York April 2013, <http://ssrn.com/abstract=2248059>, (cited as: *Fox/Healey*, When the State harms Competition – The Role for Competition Law, 2013 <http://ssrn.com/abstract=2248059>)

Francés, Antonio/Palacios, Luisa, Resultados Economicos del Pacto Andino, in: *Molina del Pozo, Carlos Francisco* (Ed.), Integración Eurolatinoamericana, 2nd edition, Ciudad Argentina, Buenos Aires 1998, pp. 485–558, (cited as: *Francés/Palacios*, in: *Molina del Pozo*, Integración Eurolatinoamericana, 1998, p. 485)

Frison-Roche, Efficient and/or effective enforcement, in: *Drexl, Josef/Idot, Laurence/Monéger, Joël* (Eds.), Economic Theory and Competition Law, Edward Elgar, Cheltenham Northampton 2009, pp. 211–217, (cited as: *Frison-Roche*, in: *Drexl/Idot/Monéger*, Economic Theory and Competition Law, 2009, p. 211)

Gal, Michal S., Antitrust in a Globalized Economy: The Unique Enforcement Challenges Faced by Small Economies, Vol. 33 Iss. 1 Fordham International Law Journal 1–42 (2009), (cited as: *Gal*, The Unique Enforcement Challenges Faced by Small Economies, 33 Fordham Int'l. L.J. 1 (2009))

Gal, Michal S., Competition Policy for Small Market Economies, 1st edition, Harvard University Press, Cambridge 2003, (cited as: *Gal*, Competition Policy for Small Market Economies, 2003)

Gal, Michal S., Free Movement of Judgements: Increasing Deterrence of International Cartels Though Jurisdictional Reliance, Law & Economics Research Paper Series Working Paper No. 08-44, New York University School of Law, Economics and Organization, October 2008 <http://ssrn.com/abstract=1291844>, (cited as: *Gal*, Free Movement of Judgements, 2008 <http://ssrn.com/abstract=1291844>)

Gal, Michal S., Size does matter: The effects of market size on optimal competition policy, Vol. 74 No. 6 Southern California Law Review 1437–1478 (2001), (cited as: *Gal*, The effects of market size on optimal competition policy, 74 S. Cal. L. Rev. 1437 (2001))

Gal, Michal S., The 'Cut and Paste' of Article 82 of the EC Treaty in Israel: Conditions for a Successful Transplant, Vol. 9 Iss. 3 European Journal of Law Reform 467–484 (2007), (cited as: *Gal*, The 'Cut and Paste' of Article 82 of the EC Treaty in Israel, 9 Eur. J. Law Reform 467 (2007))

Gal, Michal S., When the Going Gets Tight: Institutional Solutions when Antitrust Enforcement Resources are Scarce, Vol. 41 Iss. 3 Loyola University Chicago Law Journal 417–441 (2010), (cited as: *Gal*, Institutional Solutions when Antitrust Enforcement Resources are Scarce, 41 Loy. U. Chi. L.J. 417 (2010))

Gal, Michal S./Faibish Wassmer, Inbal, Regional agreements of developing jurisdictions: Unleashing the potential, in: *Drexl, Josef/Bakhoum, Mor/Fox, Eleanor/Gal, Michal/Gerber, David* (Eds.), Competition Policy and Regional Integration in Developing Countries, Edward Elgar, Cheltenham Northampton 2012, pp. 291–319, (cited as: *Gal/Faibish Wassmer*, in: *Drexl/Bakhoum/Fox/Gal/Gerber*, Competition Policy and Regional Integration in Developing Countries, 2012, p. 291)

Gal, Michal/Fox, Eleanor, Drafting competition law for developing jurisdictions: learning from experience, Vol. 4 New York University Law and Economics Working Papers, 1–68 (2014), (cited as: *Gal/Fox*, Drafting competition law for developing jurisditions: learning from experience, 4 N.Y.U. L. Econ. Working Papers 2 (2014))

Gal, Michal S./Padilla, Jorge S., The Follower Phenomenon: Implications for the Design of Monopolization Rules in a Global Economy, Vol. 76 Iss. 3 Antitrust Law Journal 899–927 (2010), (cited as: *Gal/Padilla,* Implications for the Design of Monopolization Rules in a Global Economy, 76 Antitrust L.J. 899 (2010))

Gallardo, Ramón García/Domínguez Pérez, Dolores, La Reforma de la Norma de Competencia en la Comunidad Andina, No. 20 Part 1 Boletín Latinoamericano de Comptencia 36–52 (June 2005) <http://ec.europa.eu/competition/publications/blc/boletin_20_1_es.pdf>, (cited as: *Gallardo/Domínguez,* 20 Boletín Latinoamericano de Comp. 36 (2005) <http://ec.europa.eu/competition/publications/blc/boletin_20_1_es.pdf>)

García-Belaunde, José A., El Sueño de Bolívar: De la Federación de los Andes a la Comunidad Andina, Biarritz, 27–28 September 2000 <http://www.comunidadandina.org/documentos/docIA/IA27-9-00.htm>, (cited as: *García-Belaunde,* El Sueño de Bolívar: De la Federación de los Andes a la Comunidad Andina, 2000 <http://www.comunidadandina.org/documentos/docIA/IA27-9-00.htm>)

Gauer, Céline, Does the Effectiveness of the EU Network of Competition Authorities Require a Certain Degree of Harmonisation of National Procedures and Sanctions?, in: *Ehlermann, Claus Dieter/Atanasiu, Isabela* (Eds.), European Competition Law Annual 2002: Constructing the EU Network of Competition Authorities, Hart Publishing, Oregon 2004, pp. 187–201, (cited as: *Gauer,* in: *Ehlermann/Atanasiu,* Eur. Comp. L. Ann. 2002, 2004, p. 187)

Geradin, Damien, Competition between Rules and Rules of Competition: A Legal and Economic Analysis of the Proposed Modernization of the Enforcement of EC Competition Law, Vol. 9 Iss. 1 Columbia Journal of European Law 1–28 (2002), (cited as: *Geradin,* A Legal and Economic Analysis of the Proposed Modernization of the Enforcement of EC Competition Law, 9/1 Colum. J. Eur. L. 1 (2002))

Gerber, David J., Global Competition, Oxford University Press, New York 2010, (cited as: *Gerber,* Global Competition, 2010)

Gerber, David J., Regionalization, development and competition law: exploring the political dimension, in: *Drexl, Josef/Bakhoum, Mor/Fox, Eleanor/Gal, Michal/Gerber, David* (Eds.), Competition Policy and Regional Integration in Developing Countries, Edward Elgar, Cheltenham Northampton 2012, pp. 253–272, (cited as: *Gerber,* in: *Drexl/Bakhoum/Fox/Gal/Gerber,* Competition Policy and Regional Integration in Developing Countries, 2012, p. 253)

Glaeser, Edward L./Shleifer, Andrei, Legal Origins, Vol. 117 Iss. 4 The Quarterly Journal of Economics 1193–1229 (2002), (cited as: *Glaeser/Shleifer,* Legal Origins, 117 Q. J. Econ. 1193 (2002))

Godek, Paul E., One U.S. Export Eastern Europe Does Not Need, Vol. 15 No. 1 Regulation – The CATO Review of Business & Government 20–21 (1992), (cited as: *Godek,* One U.S. Export Eastern Europe Does Not Need, 15 Regulation 20 (1992))

Goretti, Manuela/Weisfeld, Hans, Trade in the WAEMU: Developments and Reform Opportunities, International Monetary Fund Working Paper, WP/08/68, Washington March 2008 <http://www.imf.org/external/pubs/ft/wp/2008/wp0868.pdf>, (cited as: *Goretti/Weisfeld,* Trade in the WAEMU: Developments and Reform Opportunities, 2008 <http://www.imf.org/external/pubs/ft/wp/2008/wp0868.pdf>)

Govaere, Inge, L'Établissement des Règles des Marchés nationaux ou régionaux: De l'état régulateur souverain aux organisations d'intégration régionale promotices, protectrices et intermédiaires, Vol. XVII No. 3 Revue Internationale de Droit Économique 313–337 (2003), (cited as: *Govaere,* De l'état régulateur souverain aux organisations d'intégration régionale promotices, protectrices et intermédiaires, XVII R.I.D.E. 313 (2003))

Grenade, Wendy, Sovereignty, Democracy and Going Regional – Navigating Tensions: The Caribbean Community and the European Union Considered, in: *Hall, Kenneth/Chuck-A-Sang, Myrtle* (Eds.), The Caribbean Community in Transition – Functional Cooperation as a Catalyst for Change, Ian Randle, Kingston 2008, pp. 114–135, (cited as: *Grenade,* in: *Hall/Chuck-A-Sang,* The Caribbean Community in Transition, 2008, p. 114)

Groupe Intergouvernemental d'experts sur le Droit et de la Politique de la Concurrence, Répartition des Compétences entre les Autorités Communautaires et les Autorités Nationales Chargées des Questions de Concurrence et de L'Application des Règles de Concurrence de Union Economique et Monétaire Ouest Africaine (UEMOA), TD/B/COM.2/CLP/69, 15–18 July 2008, Geneva <http://unctad.org/fr/docs/c2clpd69_fr.pdf>, (cited as: *Groupe Intergouvernemental d'experts sur le Droit et de la Politique de la Concurrence,* Répartition des Compétences entre les Autorités Communautaires et les Autorités Nationales, 15–18 July 2008, Geneva <http://unctad.org/fr/docs/c2clpd69_fr.pdf>)

Healey, Deborah, Competitive Neutrality Project, UNCTAD RPP Meeting, New South Wales, 7 July 2013 <http://unctad.org/meetings/en/Presentation/RPP2013_Healey_en.pdf>, (*Healey,* Competitive Neutrality Project, 7 July 2013 <http://unctad.org/meetings/en/Presentation/RPP2013_Healey_en.pdf>)

Helfer, Laurence R./Alter, Karen J., The Andean Tribunal of Justice and its Interlocutors: Understanding Preliminary Reference Patterns in the Andean Community, Vol. 41 No. 4 N.Y.U. Journal of International Law and Politics 2009, 871–930 <http://ssrn.com/abstract=1334733>, (cited as: *Helfer/Alter,* The Andean Tribunal of Justice and its Interlocutors, 41 N.Y.U. Journal of Int'l. L. & Pol. 871 (2009) <http://ssrn.com/abstract=1334733>)

Hollander, Abraham, Competencia en Ecuador, Quito 2001, (available from the author), (cited as: *Hollander,* Competencia en Ecuador, 2001)

Horna, Pierre M./Kayali, Bahri Özgür, National Implementation of Competition-Related Provisions in Bilateral and Regional Trade Agreements, in: *Alvarez, Ana María/Wilse-Samson, Laurence* (Eds.), Implementing Competition-Related Provisions in Regional Trade Agreements: is it possible to obtain development gains?, United Nations, New York and Geneva 2007, pp. 21–57, (cited as: *Horna/Kayali,* in: *Alvarez/Wilse-Samson,* Implementing Competition-Related Provisions in Regional Trade Agreements, 2007, p. 21)

Huntley, Earl, The Treaty of Basseterre & OECS Economic Union, SICE Foreign Trade Information System, Paper No. OECS/AUT/03/38/17, 2003 <http://www.sice.oas.org/ctyindex/OECS/Treaty_e.pdf>, (cited as: *Huntley,* The Treaty of Basseterre & OECS Economic Union, 2003 <http://www.sice.oas.org/ctyindex/OECS/Treaty_e.pdf>)

Immenga, Ulrich/Mestmäcker, Ernst-Joachim (Eds.), Kommentar zum Europäischen Kartellrecht, 4th edition, C.H. Beck, Munich 2007, (cited as: *Immenga/Mestmäcker (Eds.),* Kommentar zum Europäischen Kartellrecht, 2007)

International Competition Network, Seminar on Competition Agency Effectiveness, Summary report, Brussels 2009 <http://ec.europa.eu/competition/information/icn_seminar_2009/report_final_version.pdf>, (cited as: *ICN,* Seminar on Competition Agency Effectiveness, 2009 <http://ec.europa.eu/competition/information/icn_seminar_2009/report_final_version.pdf>)

Jatar, Ana/Tineo, Luis, Competition Policy in the Andean Countries: A Policy in Search of its Place, SICE Foreign Trade Information System, 1997 <http://www.sice.oas.org/compol/articles/cpandea.asp>, (cited as: *Jatar/Tineo,* Competition Policy in the Andean Countries: A Policy in Search of its Place, 1997 <http://www.sice.oas.org/compol/articles/cpandea.asp>)

Jaumotte, Florence, Foreign Direct Investment and Regional Trade Agreements: The market size effect revisited, International Monetary Fund Working Paper, WP 04/206, Washington November 2004 <http://www.imf.org/external/pubs/cat/longres.aspx?sk=17770.0>, (cited as: *Jaumotte,* Foreign Direct Investment and Regional Trade Agreements: The market size effect revisited, 2004 <http://www.imf.org/external/pubs/cat/longres.aspx?sk=17770.0>)

Jenny, Frédéric, Cartels and Collusion in Developing Countries: Lessons from Empirical Evidence, Vol. 29 No. 1 World Competition 109–137 (2006), (cited as: *Jenny,* Cartels and Collusion in Developing Countries, 29/1 W. Comp. 109 (2006))

Jenny, Fréderic/Horna, Pierre M., Modernization of the European system of competition law enforcement: Lessons for other regional groupings, in: *Brusick, Phillipe/Alvarez, Ana Maria/Cernat, Lucian* (Eds.), Competition Provisions in Regional Trade Agreements: How to Assure Development Gains, United Nations, New York and Geneva 2005, pp. 281–327, (cited as: *Jenny/Horna,* in: *Brusick/Alvarez/Cernat,* Competition Provisions in Regional Trade Agreements, 2005, p. 281)

Kaczorowska-Ireland, Alina, Competition Law in the CARICOM Single Market and Economy, Routledge, New York 2015, (cited as: *Kaczorowska-Ireland,* Competition Law in the CARICOM Single Market and Economy, 2015)

Kakouris, C.N., Do the Member States possess Judicial Procedural "Autonomy"?, Vol. 34 Iss. 6 Common Market Law Review 1389–1412 (1997), (cited as: *Kakouris,* Do the Member States possess Judicial Procedural "Autonomy"?, 34 CML. Rev. 1389 (1997))

Kerber, Wolfgang, An International Multi-Level System of Competition Laws: Federalism in Antitrust, in: *Drexl, Josef* (Ed.), The Future of Transnational Antitrust – From Comparative to Common Competition Law, Stämpfli, Berne 2003, pp. 269–300, (cited as: *Kerber,* in: *Drexl,* The Future of Transnational Antitrust, 2003, p. 269)

Korah, Valentine, The Reform of EC Competition Law: The Challenge of an Optimal Enforcement System, in: *Lianos, Ioannis/Kokkoris, Ioannis* (Eds.), The Reform of EC Competition Law – New Challenges, Kluwer Law International, London 2010, pp. xxiii–xxviii, (cited as: *Korah,* in: *Lianos/Kokkoris,* The Reform of EC Competition Law, 2010, p. xxiii)

Kovacic, William E., Getting Started: Creating New Competition Policy Institutions in Transition Economies, Vol. 23 Iss. 2 Brooklyn Journal of International Law 403–453 (1997), (cited as: *Kovacic,* Creating New Competition Policy Institutions in Transition Economies, 23 Brook. J. Int'l. Law 403 (1997))

Kovacic, William E., Institutional Foundations for Economic Legal Reform in Transition Economies: The Case of Competition Policy and Antitrust Enforcement, Vol. 77 Iss. 1 Chicago-Kent Law Review 265–315 (2001) (cited as: *Kovacic,* Institutional Foundations for Economic Legal Reform in Transition Economies, 77 Chi.-Kent L. Rev. 265 (2001))

Kovacic, William E., Lessons of Competition Policy Reform in Transition Economies for U.S. Antitrust Policy, Vol. 74 Iss. 2 St. John's Law Review 361–405 (2000), (cited as: *Kovacic,* Lessons of Competition Policy Reform in Transition Economies for U.S. Antitrust Policy, 74 St. John's L. Rev. 361 (2000))

Kovacic, William E., Using Ex Post Evaluations to Improve the Performance of Competition Policy Authorities, Vol. 31 No. 2 The Journal of Corporation Law 503–547 (2006), available at: http://ssrn.com/abstract=1983339, (cited as: *Kovacic,* Using Ex Post Evaluations to Improve the Performance of Competition Policy Authorities, 31 J. Corp. L. 503 (2006))

Kovacic, William E./Hollman, Hugh/Grant, Patricia, How does your competition agency measure up?, Vol. 7 No. 1 European Competition Journal 25–43 (2011), (cited as: *Kovacic/Hollman/Grant,* How does your competition agency measure up?, 7 Eur. Comp. J. 25 (2011))

Krakowski, Michael, Competition Policy Works: The Effect of Competition Policy on the Intensity of Competition – An International Cross-Country Comparison, Hamburgisches Welt-Wirtschafts-Archiv Discussion Paper No. 332, Hamburg 2005 <http://papers.ssrn.com/sol3/papers.cfm?abstract_id=854908>, (cited as: *Krakowski,* Competition Policy Works, 2005 <http://papers.ssrn.com/sol3/papers.cfm?abstract_id=854908>)

Krakowski, Micheal, El ambiente institucional de las autoridades de competencia en la Subregión Andina, Hamburg Institute of International Economics, Hamburg 2003, (cited as: *Krakowski,* El ambiente institucional de las autoridades de competencia en la Subregión Andina, 2003)

Lachmann, Werner, The Development Dimension of Competition Law and Policy, UNCTAD Series on Issues in Competition Law and Policy, United Nations, New York and Geneva, 1999 <http://unctad.org/en/Docs/poitcdclpm9.en.pdf>, (cited as: *Lachmann,* The Development Dimension of Competition Law and Policy, 1999 <http://unctad.org/en/Docs/poitcdclpm9.en.pdf>)

Lande, Robert H., Creating Competition Policy for Transition Economies, Vol. 23 Iss. 2 Brooklyn Journal of International Law 339–349 (1997), (cited as: *Lande,* Creating Competition Policy for Transition Economies, 23 Brook. J. Int'l. Law 339 (1997))

Lee, Barbara, CARICOM Competition Commission: Enhancing Competition Enforcement in the Caribbean Community, paper presented at the IDRC Pre-ICN Forum on competition and development: competition principles under threat, ICN 8th Annual conference, 3–5 June 2009, Zurich, (cited as: *Lee,* Caricom Competition Commission: Enhancing Competition Enforcement in the Caribbean Community, 3–5 June 2009, Zurich)

Lee, Cassey, Legal traditions and competition policy, Vol. 45 Iss. 2–3 Quarterly Review of Economics and Finance 236–257 (2005), (cited as: *Lee,* Legal traditions and competition policy, 45 Q. Rev. Econ. & Fin. 236 (2005))

Levenstein, Margaret/Suslow, Valerie Y., Contemporary International Cartels and Developing Countries: Economic Effects and Implications for Competition Policy, Vol. 71 Iss. 3 Antitrust Law Journal 801–852 (2004), (cited as: *Levenstein/Suslow,* Contemporary International Cartels and Developing Countries, 71 Antitrust L.J. 801 (2004))

Lewis, David, Enforcing Competition Rules in South Africa: Thieves at the Dinner Table, Edward Elgar, Cheltenham Northampton 2013, (cited as: *Lewis,* Enforcing Competition Rules in South Africa, 2013)

Lipimile, George K., The COMESA regional competition regulations, in: *Drexl, Josef/Bakhoum, Mor/Fox, Eleanor/Gal, Michal/Gerber, David* (Eds.), Competition Policy and Regional Integration in Developing Countries, Edward Elgar, Cheltenham Northampton 2012, pp. 205–228, (cited as: *Lipimile,* in: *Drexl/Bakhoum/Fox/Gal/Gerber,* Competition Policy and Regional Integration in Developing Countries, 2012, p. 205)

Lozano, María Clara, La Decisión 608 de la CAN y sus Implicaciones en Bolivia, No. 21 Part 1 Boletín Latinoamericano de Competencia 43–50 (2006), (cited as: *Lozano,* La Decisión 608 de la CAN y sus Implicaciones en Bolivia, 21 Boletín Latinoamericano de Comp. 43 (2006))

Maharaj, Naraindra, The Trinidad and Tobago Government proposes a Competition Law: What is the purpose of this legislation?, Occasional Papers Series No. 2, Centre of European Law King's College London, London 2000, (cited as: *Maharaj,* The Trinidad and Tobago Government proposes a Competition Law, 2000)

Malahoo, Marlene P., Competition Law in Emerging Economies: The Jamaican Experience, Occasional Papers Series No. 3, Centre of European Law King's College London, London 2000, (cited as: *Malahoo,* Competition Law in Emerging Economies: The Jamaican Experience, 2000)

Malleson, Kate, Promoting Judicial Independence in the International Courts: Lessons from the Caribbean, Vol 58 Iss. 3 International and Comparative Law Quarterly 671– 687 (2009), (cited as: *Malleson,* Promoting Judicial Independence in the International Courts, 58 I. C. L. Q. 671 (2009))

Mancero-Bucheli, Gabriela, Competition Law of Latin America and the European Union – A Comparison and Analysis, Juris Publishing, Huntington 2001, (cited as: *Mancero-Bucheli,* Competition Law of Latin America and the European Union, 2001)

Marcos, Francisco, Do developing countries need Competition Laws and Policy?, paper presented at 23th EALE Conference, 21–23 September 2006a, Madrid, (cited as: *Marcos,* Do developing countries need Competition Laws and Policy?, 21–23 September 2006, Madrid)

Marcos, Francisco, Downloading Competition Law from a Regional Trade Agreement: A Strategy to Introduce Competition Law in Bolivia and Ecuador, in: *Fox, Eleanor/Sokol, Daniel* (Eds.), Competition Law and Policy in Latin America, 1st edition, Hart Publishing, Oxford and Portland 2009, pp. 453–468, (cited as: *Marcos,* in: *Fox/Sokol,* Competition Law and Policy in Latin America, 2009, p. 453)

Marcos, Francisco, ¿Una Política de Competencia para la República de Ecuador?, No. 21 Part 2 Boletín Latinoamericano de Competencia 29–39 (2006b), (cited as: *Marcos,* ¿Una Política de Competencia para la República de Ecuador?, 21 Boletín Latinoamericano de Comp. 29 (2006))

Marwege, Renata, Der Andengerichtshof: Das Rechtsschutzsystem des Andenpaktes mit vergleichenden Bezügen zum Recht der Europäischen Gemeinschaft, Duncker & Humblot, Berlin 1994, (cited as: *Marwege,* Der Andengerichtshof, 1994)

Mateus, Abel M., Competition and Development: What Competition Law Regime?, Working Paper Series, London 26 October 2010 <http://ssrn.com/abstract=1699643>, (cited as: *Mateus,* Competition and Development: What Competition Law Regime?, 2010 <http://ssrn.com/abstract=1699643>)

Mattei, Ugo, Three Patterns of Law: Taxonomy and Change in the World's Legal Systems, Vol. 45 Iss. 1 American Journal of Comparative Law 5–45 (1997), (cited as: *Mattei,* Taxonomy and Change in the World's Legal Systems, 45 Am. J. Comp. L. 5 (1997))

Mehta, Pradeep S./Agarwal, Manish/Singh, V V, Politics Trumps Economics – Lessons and experiences on competition and regulatory regimes from developing countries, CUTS Centre for Competition, Investment & Economic Regulation, Jaipur 2007, (cited as: *Mehta/Agarwal/Singh,* Politics Trumps Economics, 2007)

Menns, KL/Eversley, Decoursey, The Appropriate Design of the CARICOM Competition Commission, paper presented at the ACLE Conference, 20 May 2011, Amsterdam, (cited as: *Menns/Eversley,* The Appropriate Design of the CARICOM Competition Commission, 20 May 2011, Amsterdam)

Ministerio de Desarrollo Productivo y Economía Plural de Bolivia, Política Marco Antimonopolio de Regulación y Ordenamiento de la Economía Plural, COMPAL, La Paz 2011 <http://www.unctadxi.org/sections/DITC/COMPAL/Annual%20Meetings%20docs/ABRIL%202010/PoliticaMarcoAntimonopolio.pdf>, (cited as: *Ministerio de Desarrollo Productivo de Bolivia,* Política Marco Antimonopolio de Regulación y Ordenamiento de la Economía Plural, 2011 <http://www.unctadxi.org/sections/DITC/COMPAL/Annual%20Meetings%20docs/ABRIL%202010/PoliticaMarcoAntimonopolio.pdf>)

Miranda Londoño, Alfonso, Developments and Perspectives in Colombian Competition Law, No. 21 Part 2 Boletín Latinoamericano de Competencia 17–19 (2006), (cited as: *Miranda Londoño,* Developments and Perspectives in Colombian Competition Law, 21 Boletín Latinoamericano de Comp. 17 (2006))

Miranda Londoño, Alfonso, La Indemnización de los Perjuicios causados por las Prácticas Restrictivas de la Competencia, Vol. 7 No. 7 Revista de Derecho de la Competencia 15–42 (2011), (cited as: *Miranda Londoño,* La Indemnización de los Perjuicios causados por las Prácticas Restrictivas de la Competencia, 7/7 Rev. Der. Comp. 15 (2011))

Montag, Frank, The Case for a Reform of Regulation 17/62: Problems and Possible Solutions from a Practitioner's Point of View, Vol. 22 Iss. 3 Fordham International Law Journal 819–852 (1998), (cited as: *Montag,* The Case for a Reform of Regulation 17/62, 22 Fordham Int'l. L.J. 819 (1998))

Monti, Giorgio, EC Competition Law, 1st edition, Cambridge University Press, Cambridge 2007, (cited as: *Monti,* EC Competition Law, 2007)

Möschel, Wernhard, Wettbewerb der Wettbewerbsordnungen, No. 5 Wirtschaft und Wettbewerb 599–605 (2005), (cited as: *Möschel,* Wettbewerb der Wettbewerbsordnungen, WuW 599 (2005))

Mostajo Barrios, Jorge Omar, Prácticas Anticompetitivas y Derecho de la Competencia en Bolivia, No. 32 Extra 2012 Boletín Latinoamericano de Competencia 1–21 (2012), (cited as: *Mostajo,* Prácticas Anticompetitivas y Derecho de la Competencia en Bolivia, 32 Boletín Latinoamericano de Comp. 1 (2012))

Motta, Massimo, Competition Policy – Theory and Practice, Cambridge University Press, Cambridge 2004, (cited as: *Motta,* Competition Policy, 2004)

Müller, Markus, Systemwettbewerb, Harmonisierung und Wettbewerbsverzerrung – Europa zwischen einem Wettbewerb der Gesetzgeber und vollständiger Harmonisierung, 1st edition, Nomos, Tübingen 2000, (cited as: *Müller,* Systemwettbewerb, Harmonisierung und Wettbewerbsverzerrung, 2000)

Ngom, Mbissane, Intégration Régionale et Politique de la Concurrence dans l'Espace CEDEAO, Vol. XXV No. 3 Revue Internationale de Droit Économique 333–349 (2011), (cited as: *Ngom,* Intégration Régionale et Politique de la Concurrence dans l'Espace CEDEAO, XXV R.I.D.E. 333 (2011))

Ngom, Mbissane, Regional integration and competition policy in the Economic Community of West African States (ECOWAS) region, in: *Drexl, Josef/Bakhoum, Mor/Fox, Eleanor/Gal, Michal/Gerber, David* (Eds.), Competition Policy and Regional Integration in Developing Countries, Cheltenham Northampton 2012, pp. 116–132, (cited as: *Ngom,* in: *Drexl/Bakhoum/Fox/Gal/Gerber,* Competition Policy and Regional Integration in Developing Countries, 2012, p. 116)

North, Douglass C., Institutions, institutional change and economic performance, 1st edition, Mohr Siebeck, Tübingen 1992, (cited as: *North,* Institutions, institutional change and economic performance, 1992)

Novak Talavera, Fabián, La Comunidad Andina y su ordenamiento jurídico, in: *Fondo Editorial de la Pontificia Universidad Católica del Perú* (Ed.), Derecho Comunitario Andino, 1st edition, Fondo Editorial PUCP, Lima 2003, pp. 57–100, (cited as: *Novak Talavera,* in: *Fondo Editorial,* Derecho Comunitario Andino, 2003, p. 57)

Ochoa Urioste, Mauricio, Régimen General del Derecho de la Competencia en Bolivia, No. 26 Boletín Latinoamericano de Competencia 8–22 (2009), (cited as: *Ochoa Urioste,* Régimen General del Derecho de la Competencia en Bolivia, 26 Boletín Latinoamericano de Comp. 8 (2009))

OECD, A Follow-Up on Peer Reviews of Competition Law and Policy in Latin America: Argentina, Brazil, Chile, Mexico, Peru, Inter-American Development Bank and OECD, Paris 2007 <http://www.oecd.org/daf/competition/prosecutionandlawenforcement/39472133.pdf>, (cited as: *OECD,* A Follow-Up on Peer Reviews of Competition Law and Policy in Latin America, 2007 <http://www.oecd.org/daf/competition/prosecutionandlawenforcement/39472133.pdf>)

OECD, Colombia: Assessment of Competition Law and Policy, OECD 2016, (cited as: *OECD,* Colombia: Assessment of Competition Law and Policy, OECD 2016)

OECD, Competition Law and Policy in Peru – A Peer Review, Inter-American Development Bank and OECD, Paris 2004 <http://www.oecd.org/daf/competition/prosecutionandlawenforcement/34728182.pdf>, (cited as: *OECD,* Peer Review on Competition Law and Policy in Peru, 2004 <http://www.oecd.org/daf/competition/prosecutionandlawenforcement/34728182.pdf>)

OECD, Competition Peer Review Report of Peru, Vol. 11 No. 1 OECD Journal of Competition Law and Policy 177–181 (2009a), (cited as: *OECD,* Competition Peer Review Report of Peru, 11/1 OECD J. Comp. L. Policy 177 (2009))

OECD, Improving International Co-operation in Cartel Investigations – Contribution from Peru, DAF/COMP/G/WD(2012)38, OECD, Paris 2012 <http://www.oecd.org/daf/competition/ImprovingInternationalCooperationInCartelInvestigations2012.pdf>, (cited as: *OECD,* Improving International Co-operation in Cartel Investigations – Contribution from Peru, 2012 <http://www.oecd.org/daf/competition/ImprovingInternationalCooperationInCartelInvestigations2012.pdf>)

OECD, Merger Control in Latin America and the Caribbean – Recent Developments and Trends, OECD, Managua 2017, (cited as: *OECD,* Merger Control in Latin America and the Caribbean, 2017)

OECD, Peer Review Competition Law and Policy of Colombia, OECD, Paris 2009b <http://www.oecd.org/daf/competition/44110853.pdf>, (cited as: *OECD,* Peer Review on Competition Law and Policy in Colombia, 2009 <http://www.oecd.org/daf/competition/44110853.pdf>)

OECD, Small Economies and Competition Policy: A Background Paper, CCNM/GF/COMP(2003)4, OECD, Paris 2003 <http://vi.unctad.org/windiesst09/docs/presentations/wednesday13/oecdsmalleconomybackground.pdf>, (cited as: *OECD,* Small Economies and Competition Policy: A Background Paper, 2003 <http://vi.unctad.org/windiesst09/docs/presentations/wednesday13/oecdsmalleconomybackground.pdf>)

O'Keefe, Thomas Andrew, Latin American and Caribbean Trade Agreements: Keys to a Prosperous Community of the Americas, Martinus Nijhoff Publishers, Leiden 2009, (cited as: *O'Keefe,* Latin American and Caribbean Trade Agreements, 2009)

Organisation of Eastern Caribbean States, Competition Bill (The Bill) – Explanatory Memorandum, explanatory memorandum presented at the informal meeting of 15th OECS Legal Affairs Committee, 24–25 March 2009, Saint Lucia, (cited as: *OECS,* Competition Bill – Explanatory Memorandum, 24–25 March 2009, Saint Lucia)

Ortiz Blanco, Luis, EC Competition Procedure, Oxford University Press, Oxford 2006, (cited as: *Ortiz Blanco,* EC Competition Procedure, 2006)

Otero, Lorena, El Derecho de la Competencia en Bolivia, Vol. 2 No. 2 Revista de Derecho de la Competencia, 15–31 (2006), (cited as: *Otero,* El Derecho de la Competencia en Bolivia, 2/2 Rev. Der. Comp. 15 (2006))

Owen, Bruce M., Competition Policy in Latin America, paper presented at the conference on Sectoral Reform in Latin America, Stanford Institute for Economic Policy Research, Center for International Development, Working paper No. 268, 13–15 November 2003, Stanford <http://papers.ssrn.com/paper.taf?abstract_id=456441>, (cited as: *Owen,* Competition Policy in Latin America, 13–15 November 2003, Stanford <http://papers.ssrn.com/paper.taf?abstract_id=456441>)

Pardo Cuéllar, María Carolina, Colombia: Overview, The Antitrust Review of the Americas 114–115 (2016), (cited as: *Pardo Cuéllar*, Colombia: Overview, Antitrust Rev. Americas 114 (2016))

Parr, Geoff, The treatment of efficiencies in South African merger consideration, in: *Drexl, Josef/ Idot, Laurence/Monéger, Joël* (Eds.), Economic Theory and Competition Law, Edward Elgar, Cheltenham Northampton 2009, pp. 81–89, (cited as: *Parr,* in: *Drexl/Idot/Monéger,* Economic Theory and Competition Law, 2009, p. 81)

Pauwelyn, Joost, Informal International Law-Making: Framing the Concept and Research Questions, in: *Pauwelyn, J./Wessel, R./Wouters, J.* (Eds.), Informal International Lawmaking, Oxford University Press, Oxford 2012, pp. 13–34, (cited as: *Pauwelyn,* in: *Pauwelyn/Wessel/ Wouters*, Informal International Lawmaking, 2012, p. 13)

Peña, Julián, Competition policies in Latin America, post-Washington Consensus, in: *Marsden, Philip* (Ed.), Handbook of Research in Trans-Atlantic Antitrust, Edward Elgar, Cheltenham Northampton 2006, pp. 732–757, (cited as: *Peña,* in: *Marsden,* Handbook of Research in Trans-Atlantic Antitrust, 2006, p. 732)

Perilla Castro, Carlos Andrés, Propuestas para la Protección de la Libre Competencia ante los Jueces Civiles, No. 21 Part 2 Boletín Latinoamericano de Competencia 78–86 (2006), (cited as: *Perilla Castro,* Propuestas para la Protección de la Libre Competencia ante los Jueces Civiles, 21 Boletín Latinoamericano de Comp. 78 (2006))

Pollard, Duke E.E., Juridical and Constitutional Implications of CARICOM Treaty Practice, in: *Hall, Kenneth/Chuck-A-Sang, Myrtle* (Eds.), CARICOM: Policy Options for International Engagement, Ian Randle Publishers, Kingston 2010, pp. 467–488, (cited as: *Pollard,* in: *Hall/ Chuck-A-Sang,* CARICOM: Policy Options for International Engagement, 2010, p. 467)

Pollard, Duke E.E., The CARICOM System – Basic Instruments, Caribbean Law Publishing Company, Kingston 2003, (cited as: *Pollard,* The CARICOM System, 2003)

Pollard, Duke E.E., The CCJ and the CSME, paper presented at the CSME Business Forum, 24 May 2006, St. John's Antigua <http://chooseavirb.com/ccj/wp-content/uploads/2011/papers_addresses/01-he%20CCJ%20and%20the%20CSME.pdf>, (cited as: *Pollard,* The CCJ and the CSME, 24 May 2006, St. John's Antigua)

Pollard, Duke E.E., The CSME, CCJ and Private Sector, in: *Hall, Kenneth/Chuck-A-Sang, Myrtle* (Eds.), CARICOM Single Market and Economy Genesis and Prognosis, Ian Randle, Kingston 2007, pp. 91–114, (cited as: *Pollard,* in: *Hall/Chuck-A-Sang,* CARICOM Single Market and Economy Genesis and Prognosis, 2007, p. 91)

Prada, Alejandro, Wettbewerbspolitik und Wirtschaftsintegration in den Amerikas, 1st edition, Nomos, Baden-Baden 2001, (cited as: *Prada,* Wettbewerbspolitik und Wirtschaftsintegration in den Amerikas, 2001)

Présidence de la République de Togo, Stratégie de Gestion de la Concurrence au Togo, final report, Lomé-Togo November 2015, (cited as: *Présidence de la République de Togo,* Stratégie de Gestion de la Concurrence au Togo, final report, 2015)

Quevedo, Patricio, El Derecho de la Libre Competencia en el Nuevo Marco Constitucional del Ecuador, Quito 2011, (available from the author), (cited as: *Quevedo,* El Derecho de la Libre Competencia en el Nuevo Marco Constitucional del Ecuador, 2011)

Rambaran, Seema, Competition and Consumer Affairs Commission of Guyana, paper presented at the 12th Session of the Intergovernmental Group of Experts on Competition Law and Policy, 11 July 2012, Geneva, (cited as: *Rambaran,* Competition and Consumer Affairs Commission of Guyana, 11 July 2012, Geneva)

Riofrío Martínez-Villalba, Juan Carlos, La Ley de Libre Competencia Toca a la Puerta, Vol. 2 Iss. 11 Revista Novedades Jurídicas, Ediciones Legales 1-8 (2005), (cited as: *Riofrío Martínez-Villalba,* La Ley de Libre Competencia Toca a la Puerta, 2/11 Rev. Novedades Jur. 1 (2005))

Rodriguez, A.E., Does Legal Tradition Affect Competition Policy Performance?, Vol. 21 Iss. 4 International Trade Journal 417–454 (2007), (cited as: *Rodriguez,* Does Legal Tradition Affect Competition Policy Performance?, 21 Int'l. Trade J. 417 (2007))

Rodriguez, A.E./Murdy, James, Anti-Competitive Practices in the Tourism Industry: The Case of Small Economies, Vol. 4 No. 10 Journal of Business & Economics Research 43–49 (2006), (cited as: *Rodriguez/Murdy,* Anti-Competitive Practices in the Tourism Industry: The Case of Small Economies, 4/10 J. Business & Economics Research 43 (2006))

Rodríguez-Mendoza, Miguel, The Andean Group's Integration Strategy, in: *Inter-American Dialogue* (Ed.), Integrating The Hemisphere: Perspectives from Latin America and the Caribbean, Inter-American Dialogue, Washington 1997, 10–26, (cited as: *Rodríguez,* in: *Inter-American Dialogue,* Integrating The Hemisphere, 1997, p. 10)

Rudman, Desmond/Wilson, Robert, COMESA Competition Law – A New Regional Merger Regime for Eastern and Southern Africa, Vol. 4 Iss. 4 Journal of European Competition Law & Practice 368–374 (2013), (cited as: *Rudman/Wilson,* COMESA Competition Law – A New Regional Merger Regime for Eastern and Southern Africa, 4 J. Eur. Comp. L. Practice 368 (2013))

Sáchica, Luis Carlos, Introducción al derecho comunitario andino, Tribunal de Justicia del Acuerdo de Cartagena, Quito 1985, (cited as: *Sáchica,* Introducción al derecho comunitario andino, 1985)

Salah M.M., Mohamed, La Mise en Concurrence des Systèmes juridiques nationaux – Réflexions sur l'ambivalence des rapports du droit et de la mondialisation, Vol. XV No. 3 Revue Internationale de Droit Économique 251–302 (2001), (cited as: *Salah M.M,* La Mise en Concurrence des Systèmes juridiques nationaux, XV R.I.D.E. 251 (2001))

Salazar Manrique, Roberto, El Derecho Comunitario Andino: De la Teoría Jurídica a la Realidad Actuante del Derecho, Vol. 8 Revista Jurídica 247–296 (1993), (cited as: *Salazar Manrique,* El Derecho Comunitario Andino, 8 Rev. Jur. 247 (1993))

Saldías, Osvaldo, Supranational Courts as Engines of Disintegration, Berlin Working Paper on European Integration No. 5, Berlin 2007 <http://ssrn.com/abstract=1092797>, (cited as: *Saldías,* Supranational Courts as Engines of Disintegration, 2007 <http://ssrn.com/abstract=1092797>)

Salmón Gárate, Elizabeth, Evolución Institucional de la Comunidad Andina: Perspectivas y Problemas, in: *Pontificia Universidad Católica del Perú, Instituto de Estudios Internacionales* (Ed.), Derecho Comunitario Andino, Fondo Editorial PUCP, Lima 2003, pp. 21–56, (cited as: *Salmón Gárate,* in: *Pontificia Universidad Católica del Peru,* Derecho Comunitario Andino, 2003, p. 21)

Sampson, Cezley/Sampson, Faye, Competition and Regulatory Institutional Structures in Micro-states "The Case of the Caribbean", in: *Mehta, Pradeep S./Evenett, Simon J.* (Eds.), Politics Triumphs Economics? Political Economy and the Implementation of Competition Law and Economic Regulation in Developing Countries, Academic Found, New Delhi 2009, pp. 327–359, (cited as: *Sampson/Sampson,* in: *Mehta/Evenett,* Politics Triumphs Economics?, 2009, p. 327)

Scherer, F.M., Competition Policies for an Integrated World Economy, The Brookings Institution, Washington 1994, (cited as: *Scherer,* Competition Policies for an Integrated World Economy, 1994)

Schroeder, Werner, Nationale Maßnahmen zur Durchführung von EG-Recht und das Gebot der einheitlichen Wirkung – Existiert ein Prinzip der "nationalen Verfahrensautonomie"?, Vol. 129 Archiv des öffentlichen Rechts 3–38 (2004), (cited as: *Schroeder,* Nationale Maßnahmen zur Durchführung von EG-Recht und das Gebot der einheitlichen Wirkung, AöR 3 (2004))

Secretaría General de la Comunidad Andina, Comunidad Andina: Principales Indicadores 41 años de Integración y Desarrollo, SG/de 433, Lima 15 July 2011 <http://estadisticas.comunidadandina.org/eportal/contenidos/1638_8.pdf>, (cited as: *Secretaría General de la Comunidad Andina,* Comunidad Andina: Principales Indicadores 41 años de Integración y Desarrollo, 2011 <http://estadisticas.comunidadandina.org/eportal/contenidos/1638_8.pdf>)

Secretaría General de la Comunidad Andina, el ABC de la competencia, Proyecto Armonización de las Reglas de Competencia en la Región Andina, ASR/B7-3110/1B/98/0099, Lima 2004, (cited as: *Secretaría General de la Comunidad Andina,* el ABC de la competencia, 2004)

Secretaría General de la Comunidad Andina, Guía Práctica para la aplicación de la Decisión 608 "Normas para la protección y promoción de la libre competencia en la Comunidad Andina", SG/dt 396, Lima 23 October 2007 <http://intranet.comunidadandina.org/Documentos/DTrabajo/SGdt396.doc>, (cited as: *Secretaría General de la Comunidad Andina,* Guía Práctica para la aplicación de la Decisión 608 "Normas para la protección y promoción de la libre competencia en la Comunidad Andina", 2007 <http://intranet.comunidadandina.org/Documentos/DTrabajo/SGdt396.doc>)

Serrano Pinilla, Felipe, Colombia: Superintendence of Industry and Commerce, The Antitrust Review of the Americas 112–113 (2016), (cited as: *Serrano Pinilla,* Colombia: Superintendence of Industry and Commerce, Antitrust Rev. Americas 112 (2016))

Singh, Ajit, Competition and Competition Policy in Emerging Markets: International and Developmental Dimensions, G-24 Discussion Paper Series, United Nations and Center for International Development Harvard University, No. 18, September 2002, (cited as: *Singh,* Competition and Competition Policy in Emerging Markets, 2002)

Smith-Hillman, First a Glimmer, Now a …? The Prospect of a Caribbean Competition Policy, Vol. 40 Iss. 2 Journal of World Trade 405–422 (2006), (cited as: *Smith-Hillman,* The Prospect of a Caribbean Competition Policy, 40 J. W. Trade 405 (2006))

Sokol, Daniel D., Order without (Enforceable) Law: Why Countries Enter into Non-Enforceable Competition Policy Chapters in Free Trade Agreements, Vol. 83 Iss. 1 Chicago-Kent Law Review 101–163 (2008), (cited as: *Sokol,* Why Countries Enter into Non-Enforceable Competition Policy Chapters in Free Trade Agreements, 83 Chi.-Kent L. Rev. 101 (2008))

Spector, Horacio, Constitutional Transplants and the Mutation Effect, Vol. 83 Iss. 1 Chicago-Kent Law Review 129–145 (2008), (cited as: *Spector,* Constitutional Transplants and the Mutation Effect, 83 Chi.-Kent L. Rev. 129 (2008))

Stephenson, Stewart A.B., Role, Function and Development of Jamaica's Competition Law and Policy, paper presented at the UNCTAD/CARICOM/UWI Regional Workshop on Competition Law & Policy in Trinidad, 12–13 October 1999, Port-of-Spain, (cited as: *Stephenson,* Role, Function and Development of Jamaica's Competition Law and Policy, 12–13 October 1999, Port-of-Spain)

Stewart, Taimoon, An Empirical Examination of Competition Issues in Selected CARICOM Countries: Towards Policy Formulation, Sir Arthur Lewis Institute of Social and Economical Studies, St. Augustine February 2004, (cited as: *Stewart,* An Empirical Examination of Competition Issues in Selected Caricom Countries, 2004)

Stewart, Taimoon, Evaluación de la Relevancia de las Leyes de Competencia en Países Pequeños. El Caso del CARICOM, in: *Schatan, Claudia/Avalos, Marcos* (Eds.), Condiciones y Políticas de Competencia – Economías Pequeñas de Centroamérica y el Caribe, Fondo de Cultura Económica, Mexico 2006, pp. 331–389, (cited as: *Stewart,* in: *Schatan/Avalos,* Condiciones y Políticas de Competencia, 2006, p. 331)

Stewart, Taimoon, Regional integration in the Caribbean: the role of competition policy, in: *Drexl, Josef/Bakhoum, Mor/Fox, Eleanor/Gal, Michal/Gerber, David* (Eds.), Competition Policy and Regional Integration in Developing Countries, Edward Elgar, Cheltenham Northampton 2012, pp. 161–184, (cited as: *Stewart,* in: *Drexl/Bakhoum/Fox/Gal/Gerber,* Competition Policy and Regional Integration in Developing Countries, 2012, p. 161)

Stewart, Taimoon/Clarke, Julian/Joekes, Susan, Competition Law in Action: Experiences from Developing Countries, International Development Research Center, Moscow 29 May 2007, (cited as: *Stewart/Clarke/Joekes,* Competition Law in Action, 2007)

Stucchi López Raygada, Pierino, La Integración en la Comunidad Andina y su Sistema de Protección y Promoción de la Libre Competencia: Aspectos Institucionales y Procesales, No. 2 Revista de la Competencia y la Propiedad Intelectual 71–102 (2006), (cited as: *Stucchi López Raygada,* La Integración en la Comunidad Andina y su Sistema de Protección y Promoción de la Libre Competencia, 2 Rev. Comp. Propriedad Intelectual 71 (2006))

Superintendencia de Industria y Comercio (Colombia), Competition Bulletin – First Quarter 2012, Bogota 2012, (cited as: *SIC,* Competition Bulletin – First Quarter 2012, 2012)

Tangarife Torres, Marcel, Derecho de la Integración en la Comunidad Andina, 1st edition, Bogota 2002, (cited as: *Tangarife Torres,* Derecho de la Integración en la Comunidad Andina, 2002)

Tapia, Javier, Increasing Deterrence in Latin American Competition Law Enforcement, paper presented at the ASCOLA conference, 1–2 July 2011, London, (cited as: *Tapia,* Increasing Deterrence in Latin American Competition Law Enforcement, 1–2 July 2011, London)

Tchapga, Flavien, La politique de la concurrence dans la CEMAC et l'UEMOA: Entre urgences économiques et contraintes budgétaires, No. 1 Concurrences - Revue des droits de la concurrence 237–248 (2013), (cited as: *Tchapga,* La politique de la concurrence dans la CEMAC et l'UEMOA, 1 Conc. 237 (2013))

Teh, Robert, Competition provisions in regional trade agreements, in: *Estevadeordal, Antoni/ Suominen, Kati/Teh, Robert* (Eds.), Regional Rules in the Global Trading System, Cambridge University Press, Cambridge 2009, pp. 418–502, (cited as: *Teh,* in: *Estevadeordal/Suominen/ Teh,* Regional Rules in the Global Trading System, 2009, p. 418)

Temple Lang, John, EEC Competition Actions in Member States' Courts – Claims for Damages, Declarations and Injunctions for Breach of Community Antitrust Law, Vol. 7 Iss. 3 Fordham International Law Journal 389–466 (1983), (cited as: *Temple Lang,* EEC Competition Actions in Member States' Courts, 7 Fordham Int'l. L.J. 389 (1983))

Terhechte, Jörg Philipp, International Competition Enforcement Law: Between Cooperation and Convergence – Mapping a New Field for Global Administrative Law, Working Paper Center for Competition Law and Policy (L) 26, Oxford 2009, (cited as: *Terhechte,* International Competition Enforcement Law, 2009)

Thyri, Peter, Zusammenwirken von Kommission und nationalen Wettbewerbsbehörden im Kartellrecht, in: *Hummer, Waldemar* (Ed.), Neueste Entwicklungen im Zusammenspiel von Europarecht und nationalem Recht der Mitgliedstaaten, Springer, Vienna 2010, pp. 379–416, (cited as: *Thyri,* in: *Hummer,* Neueste Entwicklungen im Zusammenspiel von Europarecht und nationalem Recht der Mitgliedstaaten, 2010, p. 379)

Tokman, Victor E., Informality in Latin America: Facts and Opportunities, paper written as contribution to a WIEGO/OECD project under the OECD Regional Reviews on Informality, September 2008 <http://wiego.org/sites/wiego.org/files/publications/files/Tokman-Informality_in_Latin_America_2008.pdf>, (cited as: *Tokman,* Informality in Latin America, 2008 <http://wiego.org/sites/wiego.org/files/publications/files/Tokman-Informality_in_Latin_America_2008.pdf>)

Trebilcock, Michael J./Iacobucci, Edward M., Designing Competition Law Institutions: Values, Structure, and Mandate, Vol. 41 Iss. 3 Loyola University Chicago Law Journal 455–471 (2010), (cited as: *Trebilcock/Iacobucci,* Designing Competition Law Institutions, 41 Loy. U. Chi. L.J. 455 (2010))

Tridimas, Takis, The General Principles of EU Law, 2nd edition, Oxford University Press, New York 2006, (cited as: *Tridimas,* The General Principles of EU Law, 2006)

Trotignon, Jérôme, L'impact des accords de libre-commerce entre pays latino-américains – Les enseignements d'un modèlede gravité en données de panel -, Vol. LXI No. 2 Economie Appliquée 95–120 (2008), (cited as: *Trotignon,* L'impact des accords de libre-commerce entre pays latino-américains, LXI Economie Appliquée 95 (2008))

Tybout, James R., Manufacturing Firms in Developing Countries: How Well Do They Do, and Why?, Vol. 38 Iss. 1 Journal of Economic Literature 11–44 (2000), (cited as: *Tybout,* Manufacturing Firms in Developing Countries, 38 J. Econ. Lit. 11 (2000))

United Nations Conference on Trade and Development, Model, Model Law on Competition, UNCTAD Series on Issues in Competition Law and Policy, TD/B/RBP/CONF.5/7/Rev.2, United Nations, New York and Geneva 2004, (cited as: *UNCTAD,* Model Law on Competition, 2004)

United Nations Conference on Trade and Development, The relationship between Competition, Competitiveness and Development, Trade and Development Board, TD/B/COM.2/CLP/30, Geneva 3–5 July 2002, (cited as: *UNCTAD,* The relationship between competition, competitiveness and development, 2002)

United Nations Conference on Trade and Development, UNCTAD Guidebook on Competition Systems, UNCTAD/DITC/CLP/2007/2, United Nations, New York and Geneva 2007, (cited as: *UNCTAD,* UNCTAD Guidebook on Competition Systems, 2007)

United Nations Conference on Trade and Development, Voluntary Peer Review on Competition Policies of WAEMU, Benin and Senegal, UNCTAD/DITC/CLP/2007/1, United Nations, New York and Geneva 2008, (cited as: *UNCTAD,* Voluntary Peer Review on Competition Policies of WAEMU, Benin and Senegal, 2008)

United Nations Conference on Trade and Development, Voluntary Peer Review on Competition Policy: Jamaica, UNCTAD/DITC/CLP/2005/5, United Nations, New York and Geneva 2005, (cited as: *UNCTAD,* Voluntary Peer Review on Competition Policy: Jamaica, 2005)

Uribe Piedrahita, Carlos Andrés, Reforma al Régimen de Libre Competencia en Colombia - Perspectivas y Retos, Ibañez, Bogotá 2009, (cited as: *Uribe Pedrahita,* Reforma al Régimen de Libre Competencia en Colombia, 2009)

Urquieta Arias, Rodrigo, Bolivia, in: *CUTS International* (Ed.), Competition Regimes in the World – A Civil Society Report, CUTS Centre for Competition, Investment & Economic Regulation, Jaipur 2006, pp. 546–549, (cited as: *Urquieta Arias,* in: *CUTS International,* Competition Regimes in the World, 2006, p. 546)

Van den Boogaerde, Pierre/Tsangarides, Charalambos, Ten Years After the CFA Franc Devaluation: Progress Toward Regional Integration in the WAEMU, International Monetary Fund Working Paper, WP/05/145, July 2005, (cited as: *Van den Boogaerde/Tsangarides,* Ten Years After the CFA Franc Devaluation: Progress Toward Regional Integration in the WAEMU, 2005)

Venit, James S., Brave New World: The Modernization and Decentralization of Enforcement under Articles 81 and 82 of the EC Treaty, Vol. 40 Iss. 3 Common Market Law Review 545–580 (2003), (cited as: *Venit,* The Modernization and Decentralization of Enforcement under Articles 81 and 82 of the EC Treaty, 40 C. M. L. Rev. 545 (2003))

Vigil Toledo, Ricardo, La Estructura Jurídica y el Futuro de la Comunidad Andina, Thomson Reuters, Pamplona 2011, (cited as: *Vigil Toledo,* La Estructura Jurídica y el Futuro de la Comunidad Andina, 2011)

Waked, Dina I., Competition Law in the developing world: The why and how of adoption and its implications for international competition law, Iss. 1 Global Antitrust Review 69–96 (2008), (cited as: *Waked,* Competition Law in the developing world, GAR 69 (2008))

Weick, Daniel P., Competition Law and Policy in Senegal: A Cautionary Tale for Regional Integration?, Vol. 33 No. 3 World Competition 521–540 (2010), (cited as: *Weick,* Competition Law and Policy in Senegal, 33/3 W. Comp. 521 (2010))

Weiler, J. H. H., A Quiet Revolution: The European Court of Justice and its Interlocutors, Comparative Political Studies 510–534 (1994), (cited as: *Weiler,* The European Court of Justice and its Interlocutors, Comparative Political Studies 510 (1994))

Wesseling, Rein, The Modernisation of EC Antitrust Law, Hart Publishing, Portland 2000, (cited as: *Wesseling*, The Modernisation of EC Antitrust Law, 2000)

Wils, Wouter P.J., Should Private Antitrust Enforcement Be Encouraged in Europe?, Vol. 26 No. 3 World Competition 473–488 (2003), (cited as: *Wils,* Should Private Antitrust Enforcement Be Encouraged in Europe?, 26/3 W. Comp. 473 (2003))

Wils, Wouter P.J., Ten Years of Regulation 1/2003 – A Retrospective, Vol. 4 Iss. 4 Journal of European Competition Law & Practice 293–301 (2013) <http://ssrn.com/author=456087>, (cited as: *Wils,* Ten Years of Regulation 1/2003, 4 J. Eur. Comp. L. Practice 293 (2013))

Wils, Wouter P.J., The Relationship between Public Antitrust Enforcement and Private Actions for Damages, Vol. 32 No. 1 World Competition 3–26 (2009), (cited as: *Wils,* The Relationship between Public Antitrust Enforcement and Private Actions for Damages, 32/1 W. Comp. 3 (2009))

Wißmann, Tim, Decentralised Enforcement of EC Competition Law and the New Policy on Cartels – The Commission White Paper of 28th of April 1999, Vol. 23 No. 2 World Competition 123–154 (2000), (cited as: *Wißmann,* Decentralised Enforcement of EC Competition Law and the New Policy on Cartels, 23/2 W. Comp. 123 (2000))

World Trade Organization, Trade Policy Review of Suriname: Trade Policies and Practices by Measure, WT/TPR/S/135, Washington 12 and 14 July 2004, (cited as: *WTO,* Trade Policies and Practices by Measure, 2004)

Ziller, Jacques, The Challenge of Governance in Regional Integration Key Experiences from Europe, European University Institute Working Paper LAW No. 2005/11, Florence 2005, (cited as: *Ziller,* The Challenges of Governance in Regional Integration, 2005)

Zoghbi, Valentina, Strategic Priorities of Competition and Regulatory Agencies in Developing Countries, in: *Mehta, Pradeep S./Evenett, Simon J.* (Eds.), Politics Triumphs Economics? Political Economy and the Implementation of Competition Law and Economic Regulation in Developing Countries, Academic Found, New Delhi 2009, pp. 89–210, (cited as: *Zoghbi,* in: *Mehta/Evenett,* Politics Triumphs Economics?, 2009, p. 89)

Zúñiga-Fernández, Tania, Fusionskontrolle in einer "small market economy" in Lateinamerika – Wettbewerbspolitische Untersuchung am Beispiel Peru, Nomos, Berlin 2009, (cited as: *Zúñiga-Feranández,* Fusionskontrolle in einer "small market economy" in Lateinamerika, 2009)

Kolibri 360 GmbH
Ferdinand-Jühlke-Straße 7
99095 Erfurt, Deutschland
produktsicherheit@kolibri360.de